CHRIS ALEXANDER

ART! TRASH! TERROR!

ADVENTURES IN STRANGE CINEMA

headpress

A HEADPRESS BOOK
First published by Headpress in 2024, Oxford, UK
headoffice@headpress.com

ART! TRASH! TERROR!
Adventures in Strange Cinema

Book and cover design : MARK CRITCHELL mark.critchell@gmail.com
With thanks to Gareth Wilson and Jennifer Wallis
Image, previous page: THE VAMPIRE'S NIGHT ORGY (1972)

10 9 8 7 6 5 4 3 2 1

A CIP catalogue record for this book is available from the British Library

ISBN 978-1-915316-43-1 paperback
ISBN 978-1-915316-44-8 ebook
ISBN NO-ISBN hardback

"...Absolutely shattering and yet, even then, I knew it was all so astoundingly beautiful..."

ART! TRASH! TERROR!

ADVENTURES IN STRANGE CINEMA

CONTENTS

ART! TRASH! TERROR!
ADVENTURES IN STRANGE CINEMA

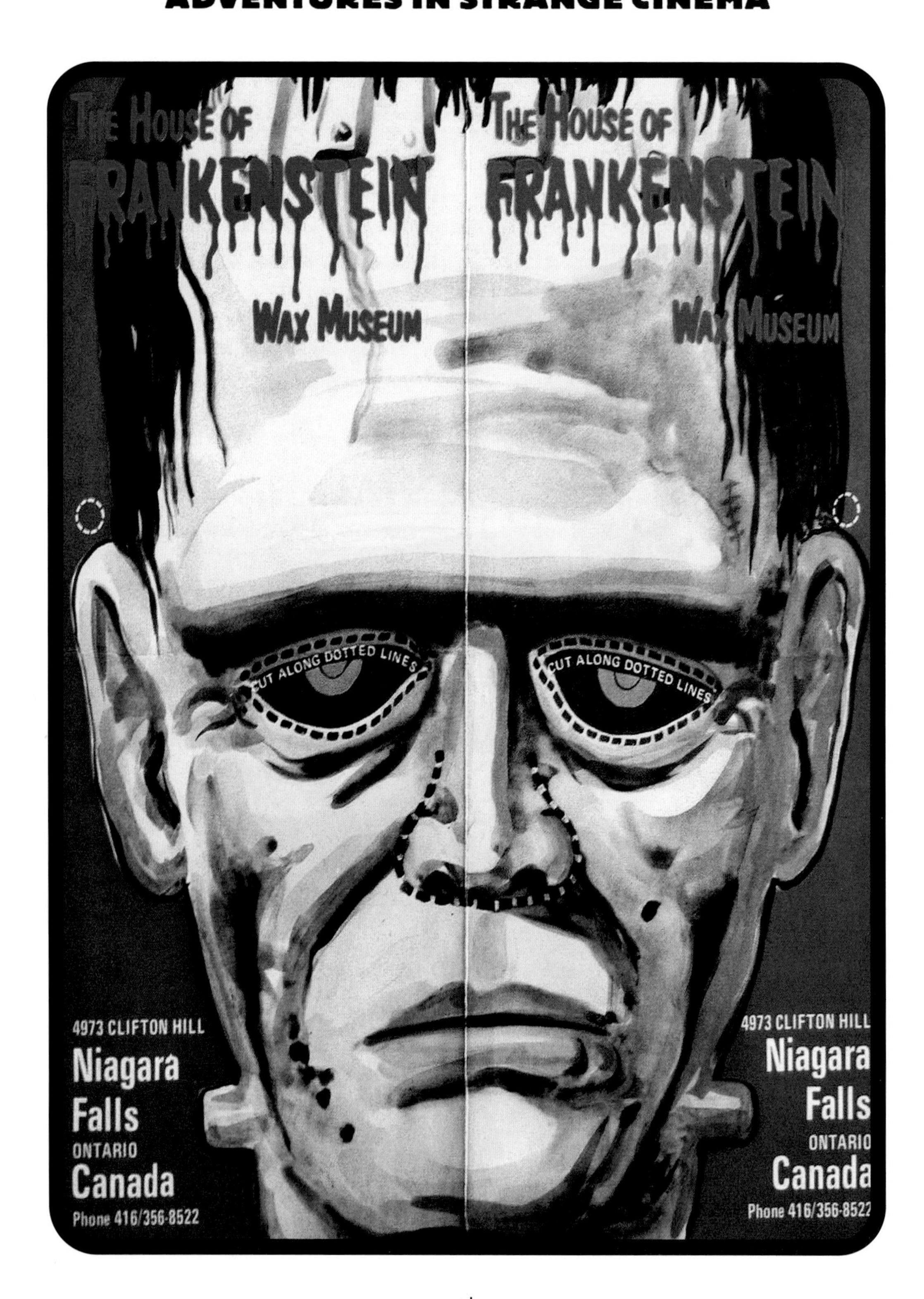

INTRODUCTION

EXITING THROUGH THE GIFT SHOP...

When I was small, before the internet, before streaming, before home video even, I was already impossibly obsessed with what I would eventually call "strange cinema". And while I can't cite the exact moment that I became hooked, I do remember a series of events that happened before I was five that knocked me about and did the damage that would inspire my life's work.

One of these pivotal points was a trip to the library with my father to sign out records to spin on my kiddie record player. There, among the nursery rhymes and Sesame Street platters was a misfiled copy of *Love Gun*, the fifth studio album from the band KISS. Seeing that garish Ken Kelly painting of the band in black leather, standing in what looked like a dungeon with an army of swooning, pale-faced and spent vampire women at their feet, hit me hard. Specifically, it was Gene Simmons, the "Demon", with his leathery bat wings, monstrous dragon books and macabre makeup, realized with razor sharp fangs protruding that Kelly — who was already an old hand at painting Warren-era comic covers like *Vampirella* and *Creepy* — ingeniously opted to draw, despite Gene never including them in his usual look. I also vividly remember wandering into my teenage uncle's bedroom, with his ghoulish model kits (including the legendary three-foot tall Aurora "Big Frankie" figure that marked my introduction to what would become my favorite fiend, Karloff/Pierce's Frankenstein monster), horror comic books, 3D View Master reels and a rich library of fantastic film reference books. His lair was a museum of creepy pop culture wonders, everything meticulously displayed and carefully curated, a space that both frightened and excited me. And yet another important memory, also circled around records, is my pop bringing the double disc Jeff Wayne's musical version of the *War of the Worlds* album home in 1978 and listening with it to him, front to back. I remember being hypnotized and terrified by its spacey sounds, pulsing prog-rock riffs, ominous Richard Burton narration and mesmerizing oversized art book, which featured paintings of steampunk tripods annihilating terrified Londoners and, in the final image, birds feasting on the bloody brains of the dead Martians. Absolutely shattering and yet, even then I knew it was all so astoundingly beautiful.

But perhaps the most impactful assault to my senses was the time my aunt and granny took me to Niagara Falls, Canada and the outrageously cool strip of haunted attractions and wax museums that lived on the Falls' Clifton Hill strip. There, these two gentle and nurturing women in my life opted to drag me into the "House of Frankenstein" waxworks and, as soon as we cleared the turnstile entrance, I knew it was a mistake. I was in Hell. A pitch-black, cavernous labyrinth filled with screaming vampires, snaggle toothed fiends and hulking horrors, with eerie music and sound effects perpetually blaring out of the secretly placed speakers. Naturally, I screamed my way through all of it, stopping only in the center of the maze to marvel at a wall-size multi-screened installation that ran the creation scene from James Whale's 1931 landmark FRANKENSTEIN on a loop. What was I seeing? Where was I? Would I ever be the same again? The short answer was no, I would never be the same. And thank God for that!

The *Tour de Fright* eventually ended, exiting through the gift shop, and as I pushed through that metal door, a final nerve-rattling alarm sound signaling my leave, it was jarring to be suddenly pushed into a brightly lit room filled with souvenirs and meandering tourists mindlessly picking up snow globes and putting them back down again. The Carpenters' We've Only Just Begun played over the PA, benign and warm, where only moments before I was immersed in world of murder and mutations and grimy ambient shock. It was surreal. And I couldn't reconcile this dichotomy, these two universes that fed into each other, each so radically different and yet both apparently mastered by the same minds.

I do know that regardless of its appearance in the order of my awakening, my pre-school visit to the "House of Frankenstein" might have been the experience that began intellectualized my growing interests in the bizarre, the ghoulish, the arcane and otherworldly. It was the one that made me endlessly lie awake and consider how one could experience something so mind-scrambling and then, when the lights came up, be pushed back so briskly into normalcy, with the world just carrying on as it did, business as usual. Fear and fascination in equal measure became a large part of who I was and would become.

In the ensuing years, calling on my uncle's film book library, my dad's own interests in psychedelic music and art, comic books and ads for films embedded with them, I began developing an insatiable need to see *more*. To witness and experience film and art that none of my peers were allowed to see or otherwise had little interest in seeing, partially because they weren't even aware these sorts of entertainments even existed! Before we had a VCR, I *was* a VCR. I would grab the TV guide that came in the Saturday paper and underline anything that was labeled horror or thriller, or suspense or science fiction and I would sleep with an alarm clock under my pillow, secretly getting up at all hours to catch a perversely late screening of whatever weirdness I wanted to absorb. Appointment television, the kids call it today. Back then, it was just the way it was. If it was scheduled to run, you had *one shot* to see it, otherwise you were stuck, potentially waiting years for the next time it showed up somewhere. And because the sorts of cinematic baubles I had locked on were so grim and bizarre and in some cases deeply downmarket, TV stations would dump them deep into the night, where only insomniacs, maniacs and creepy kids like me would catch them.

Anyway, I would quietly tiptoe down the stairs, flip on the screen in the dark and sit close to the TV, trying not to wake my parents. And if I heard a creak, I would quickly shut the set off and wait until the coast was clear. When I was sure that I would not be caught engaged in my nocturnal nightmare cinema pursuits, I would turn the television back on, only to be met with some sort of horrific image that — because I had edited the narrative by turning the box off — had no logical context. And of course that made it scarier. And of course that made it stranger. And of course, I loved every second of it, immersive and singular as it was. And often I would get up the next day — if I could get back to sleep at all — and try to recall those hazy images, sometimes wondering if I had in fact hallucinated the entire experience. It was wonderous. And it was all mine.

The years advanced as they do, and I never let this love die. It just grew stronger. My social identity was being the guy that knew everything about horror, the kid with the briefcase full of *Fangoria* magazines on the school bus, the boy with two VCRs who would bootleg some of the most outrageous movies that your local video store refused to carry, stuff like Lucio Fulci's THE GATES OF HELL, J.P. Simon's PIECES, Dan O'Bannon's RETURN OF THE LIVING DEAD, Frank Agrama's DAWN OF THE MUMMY and more. I was the local cinema smut peddler, living to spread my grotesque gospel. Then, came art school, film college, where I quickly learned there was no place for me. My interests were too specific. I wanted to make films, but I wanted to make a specific kind of film, and I had cerebral philosophies about so-called "low" entertainment that confounded my teachers and peers. So, I quit two different very hard-to-get-into art colleges and instead opted to find my own way. Not an easy thing, considering there was no "horror culture" to speak of and certainly, there was nothing to support my passions in Toronto, Canada, where I lived. But in my 20s, things changed, and I discovered a local Canadian magazine called *Rue Morgue*, and soon, after some rapturous phone calls and hand-written letters, I found myself working with them. I found "my people" and, considering I already knew I could write and wrangle words with some authority, I started eventually scribbling for them. Reviews, features and, most excitingly, interviews. Finally, I could *actually talk* to these godlike architects of the movies I worshipped, have *real* conversations and ask all the questions that I never, ever thought I would have the chance to ask. Then, after many years of success with that magazine, I cast my line to New York, to my beloved *Fangoria* magazine and soon became their Toronto correspondent. And then, one day after several years freelancing for them, they called me up and asked if I would like to take over as editor-in-chief! Just like that! Of course, I said yes and for almost six years I ran *Fangoria* from my home office in Toronto, my children by my side. I traveled to New York when I needed to, I had access to everyone and mysteriously and amusingly, suddenly everyone wanted access to *me*. And then I started making my own movies. Writing, directing, shooting and scoring a series of interlocked microbudget works of feature-length art usually centered around female vampires and heavily influenced by European masters like Jean Rollin, Jess Franco, Werner Herzog, Leon Klimovsky and others. In 2015 I left *Fangoria* and teamed up with iconic producer Charles Band of Full Moon to create *Delirium* magazine, transposing what I did at *Fango* (with much of the same team) to a new book and creating *exactly* the sort of magazine I wanted to make, free of any convention or expectation. That magazine continues its run to this day.

In between all these ever-ratcheting adventures in "strange cinema", there have been other sidebar things — like boxing Uwe Boll in a highly publicized fight, having my own TV show, performing my music live and screening my movies around the world, creating my own film convention and, of course, raising my three sons, never venturing too far from our home base in Toronto, always finding ways to include them in what I do. And what I do, I think, or at least what I hope I am doing, is never stray very far from being the little boy with wide eyes and open mind that I was. That — despite the ravages of time and inevitable decay having their slow, methodical way with me, despite the unavoidable tragedies and traumas that come with sticking around long enough — I *am* the same kid with that sense of quest, that sense of joy and wonder surrounding the art and science of the motion picture, the magic of movies that refuse to behave.

Collected here in this first (hopefully, not last) volume of *Art! Trash! Terror!: Adventures In Strange Cinema*, you'll find a wealth of essays, thoughts and critiques of films that I absolutely adore and vibrant conversations with people I worship, along with slivers of memory documenting eccentric encounters I have had. You won't find words that mock movies or drag them down. This isn't Letterboxd. There are plenty of films I genuinely dislike, though even then I can usually find a moment or two within them that I admire. But why waste time spilling sentences about things you don't love? No, what you have here is an alphabetically organized window into my heart, mind and soul, the interior projector that runs the movies I discuss for infinity, or at least until my own bulb burns out. Maybe this book is a way for me to prolong that bulb's life, to continue to share these things I love long after I am gone. I don't know. Some of the thoughts enclosed within have been published in various forms inside the magazine I have made, or the periodicals I have contributed to. Some are new. Some of the conversations are culled from ancient hard drives and recording devices, some have been logged exclusively for this book.

Whatever this tome is, it is most assuredly — like almost every single thing I do — personal. It's my love letter to loving movies and I hope you find some of yourself inside it.

Incidentally, the "House of Frankenstein" still stands in Niagara Falls, on Clifton Hill. And, despite the addition of a rickety roller coaster on the roof and some new animatronic terrors, not much has changed. And it still exits through the gift shop.

Chris Alexander, *July 2024*

Dino Velvet (Peter Stormare) oozes evil.

8MM (1999)

Starring Nicolas Cage, Joaquin Phoenix, James Gandolfini,
Peter Stormare, Catherine Keener
Written by Andrew Kevin Walker
Directed by Joel Schumacher

When I first caught the Andrew Kevin Walker (SEVEN) psychodrama 8MM theatrically, I said it was the greatest film Dario Argento *never* made. And I more or less still stand by that statement. Certainly, it's the most undervalued picture in the vast Nicolas Cage cannon. It's a movie that positions itself as a noir-steeped murder mystery but goes so deeply into phantasmagoria that it becomes, almost imperceptibly, a full-blown horror film. And while there isn't anything explicitly supernatural in the film, there is a leather clad Frankenstein monster-esque porn stud-gimp named "Machine" who acts as the angel of sexual death for an egomaniacal snuff film pimp named Dino Velvet who is so over-the-edge with his grim, parasitic villainy that he makes Dracula look like a milquetoast by comparison.

Released in 1999 via Columbia/Sony, 8MM is directed by the late Hollywood gun-for-hire Joel Schumacher, he of slick and empty calorie entertainments like THE LOST BOYS, FLATLINERS, PHANTOM OF THE OPERA, the risible BATMAN FOREVER and the even more dire BATMAN AND ROBIN. Outside of the latter two pictures, however, I rather like

Schumacher's solid journeyman work. He was a sleazier Tony Scott in some ways, making glossy, easily packaged product that nonetheless had covert personal kinks splashing around the peripheral and very often a palpable passion for moviemaking at their cores. I believe 8MM to be his masterpiece and certainly, it's evidence that Cage was then and remains one of the great dramatic screen presences when used properly and when dialing down his patented eccentricities (though I am also a huge devotee of said eccentricities).

8MM sees Cage playing Tom Welles, an affluent and easy-going private investigator living a life of domestic bliss with his supportive wife (an unfortunately wasted Catherine Keener) and beloved infant daughter. Welles' beat is cheating spouses and insurance fraud and rarely does he take on any sort of case that would put him — or his family — in harm's way. He thinks he knows all about the darkness that lines the hearts of most men. He thinks he's better than it. He thinks that he's mastered it. But unbeknownst to him, that protected world view is about to get stained with all manner of fluids and truths.

One night Welles is summoned to the looming mansion of his latest client, a rich widow (Myra Carter) who, while sifting through her late husband's estate, is disturbed to discover an unmarked 8mm film reel. The mourning woman had been devoted to her spouse, a man who was, by all accounts, a wonderful, loving mate and cherished father. Except the film in question seems to indicate otherwise. Welles obliges to watch the picture in the drawing room, the projector sputtering to life in the dark and the most sickening sights imaginable unspool: a young girl, glassy eyed and starring into the lens, is beaten, raped, and viciously murdered by a zipper and leather-decorated monster.

Shaken and drained, Welles confirms the widow's suspicions that this indeed appears to be a legitimate snuff film however, as many of these legendary loops have historically been proven to be fakes, he takes the case on, promising to not only uncover the identity of the girl in the film but determine whether she is indeed alive or dead.

Kissing his family goodbye, Welles begins his investigation, a serpentine quest that first leads him to the lonely home of the girl's emotionally ruined mother (Amy Morton in a haunting turn) and then, eventually into the seediest depths of LA's porno underworld (with a quick stop off to meet the girl's shithead ex-boyfriend, played by a young Norman Reedus). He picks up a partner, a seemingly world weary, but ultimately sweet and gentle adult video store employee (deftly played by Joaquin Phoenix) who ushers him deeper into the belly of the beast and straight into the lair of cult fetish porn filmmaker Dino Velvet (a reptilian Peter Stormare) and his arguably more despicable partner in exploitation, Eddie Poole (a greasy, pre-SOPRANOS James Gandolfini). For better or for worse, Welles becomes bound to his targets, his world

Tom (Nicolas Cage) receives lessons in rough trade from Max (Joaquin Phoenix).

view changed, his life inexorably altered as he sinks deeper and deeper into a world of privilege, pain, perversion, pornography and the lowest, most insidious distortions of humanity to ever slime their ways through city streets.

To give away more about 8MM's downward spiraling narrative would be to rob you of the picture's mesmerizing power. Suffice it to say, this is a grim, unpleasant movie (as would be expected with Walker's name on it) and with subject matter this lurid and horrific, it needs to be. The tone is decidedly bleak from the get-go, due in no small part to cinematographer Robert Elswit's shadowy, lurid color pallet, Gary Wissner's austere production design and especially, Canadian composer Mychael Danna's nightmarish, smothering Middle Eastern-tinged score. The violence and sex are sleazy and suitably exploitative but never graphic to the point of being gratuitous. Schumacher's direction is measured, cool and assured when it needs to be and stylized in such a manner that, in regard to my original take on the film, feels like a *giallo*. When I told Cage this he responded favorably, being an Italian horror fan (and a horror fan in general) and he also told me that, although the film flopped and was a North American critical disaster, Europeans, especially the French, loved it and embraced it. Makes sense.

As Welles, Cage is in almost every scene and he's nothing short of magnetic. This is Cage at his best: haunted, hurt (his hangdog face and wounded eyes are the films' greatest special effect) and driven by an ever-increasing moral outrage that sparks an equal teeth-gritting anxiety in the audience. The scene where, while mulling over a decision to commit murder, Cage calls the little girl's mother and asks her for permission to "hurt the people who hurt her daughter" is nothing short of leveling.

But as shattering and frightening a film as 8MM is, there are enough kinky and colorful quirks in it to push it into cult film territory, which over the past decade and a half it has slowly been recognized as. Phoenix's cheeky presence adds much levity, but it's a real performance with a very real and tragic heart beating within his characters' glib exterior. Stormare's preening Velvet is as campy as he is vile and the world he inhabits is, again, a gaudy impression of the mythical snuff underworld. Incidentally, I've conversed with Stormare several times over the years, and he cites Dino as one of his favorite roles, and mourned the fact that the character only had one movie to maraud through.

"You know, I wanted to have him escape at the end and come back in another movie," Stormare told me.

"But they said, no, it wasn't in the script. And later, Joel told me it was the biggest mistake he made, to kill me off. I said that I could come back with a band-aid over my throat, I mean why not, right? I mean, in all the great horror movies, the bad guy always comes back. Dino Velvet was a vampire. He was Dracula."

There's so much more to say about this strange movie's sick spell but really, my hyperbole can't properly do it justice. If you've seen this movie and dismissed it, I strongly advise you to re-evaluate it. If you haven't seen it at all, you as a horror film fan are doing yourself a grave disservice and are wasting time reading this book when you should be watching it. And if you still resist, because you're one of the select cineastes who still can't stand Cage, again, this picture might just make you understand and appreciate the man a bit more.

MEMOIR: ON THE ISLAND OF NICOLAS CAGE

When I look back on my days as editor-in-chief of the iconic magazine *Fangoria* (from the end of 2009 to the last gasps of 2015), I'm overwhelmed with anecdotes, true tales of mad adventures on the sidelines of movie culture. Very often, those joyful journeys took me from the fringe into the mainstream, or maybe sometimes it was the mainstream coming out to visit me. Very often we met in the middle.

In the case of my connection to the inimitable Nicolas Cage, we collided in the Bahamas over a slimy snail penis.

Now, I was always a Nicolas Cage fan, an obsessive before it was cool to be one. The first time my mom and I saw PEGGY SUE GOT MARRIED, when the world — my mom included — was clicking its tongues and saying how Cage's oddball mannerisms and nasally voice ruined the picture, I was like, no way. Cage is what *made* the movie. Sure, Francis Coppola's sweet romantic fantasy shines because of its central vibrant Kathleen Turner performance, but you *remember* it because of Cage mangling The Beatles' She Loves You ("she loves you, ooooh ooooh ooooh..."). You remember his lazy-lidded stare, his wounded hound dog face and his sudden bursts of manic, spastic, over-boiled-cauldron dramatics. Soon after that, we saw RAISING ARIZONA and we loved that too, but here, the universe the Coen Brothers create around Cage is just as wild, if not wilder, so he sorta blends into it. It feels organic. No, it was in films like PEGGY SUE, MOONSTRUCK, FIREBIRDS and IT COULD HAPPEN TO YOU that Cage really stuck to me, movies where his alien charisma is injected into the natural world, turning a "normal" entertainment into a sort of divine mutation.

Later, I lived for the "showcase" Cage movies, those signature slabs of cinema that were sort of built *around* his talents. Like David Lynch's WILD AT HEART or, perhaps most astonishingly, Robert Bierman's VAMPIRE'S KISS, perhaps the ultimate Nick Cage joint. Cage was and remains my favorite living performer and as a horror fan, I always felt like he was channelling some sort of expressionist, silent-shocker stylization into his work. Later, he would come right out and say that he was doing just that, that even his single-handed lovelorn baker in MOONSTRUCK was a riff on the frantically gesturing mad scientist in Fritz Lang's METROPOLIS.

My first encounter with Nick came after a screening of Werner Herzog's brilliant BAD LIEUTENANT: PORT OF CALL NEW ORLEANS at the Toronto International Film Festival. I stumbled into a small press scrum at some fancy hotel and while other critics were asking him about NATIONAL TREASURE and CON AIR, I stood up and asked him about VAMPIRE'S KISS. He lit up. I asked him to say my favorite line, "Am I getting *through* to you, *Alva*?!". He did. I recorded that. Email me if you want to hear it.

Later, we connected to discuss Alex Proyas' ludicrously underrated sci-fi chiller KNOWING for a Toronto Star feature I was writing and then, a bit later, when Disney released their bonkers THE SORCERER'S APPRENTICE movie, I locked him down on the phone for a chat. I had recently taken over *Fangoria* and had developed a friendship with his equally brilliant brother, the filmmaker Christopher Coppola. Christopher was then writing for me in fact and he and I would spend many hours on the phone discussing our love of horror movies and transgressive, experimental film. I told Nick about this and, at the time, he and his brother were having some family issues and weren't speaking. But when he found out I was the "*Fangoria* guy" and that his big bro was scribbling for us, he went crazy, wanting to talk about *Fangoria* and how much the two of them loved it in the '80s and how important it was to them.

Soon after that, word got 'round that Nick was making another GHOST RIDER movie. I liked the first one. Didn't love it. But I liked it and though Cage was fantastic in it, especially his improvised additions to the Blaze character, like his fondness for jellybeans and monkey-centric television shows. And as a kid, I *loved* the comics, and they were certainly part of my entry point into horror and dark fantasy culture. Since my mission was to almost always write every single *Fangoria* cover story myself and make it *personal*, I thought, why not use this GHOST RIDER sequel as my hook to do a career retrospective cover story on the power and brilliance of Nicolas Cage? So, I reached out to Sony, they reached out to Nic. Within a day, Nick fired back and said not only would he do this cover story interview… but he wanted to do it at his house. Live. In person.

I stopped. Breathed. Considered that Nicolas Cage asked me to come to his house. And said as calmly as I could… yes.

But then I found out that Cage was spending the season at his home on Paradise Island in the Bahamas. And I kind of lost my mind.

Now, back in those days, the former *Fangoria* publisher was a bit, well, frugal. He didn't like to spend money. In fact, his lack of interest spending money helped lead to the slow, inevitable disintegration of the magazine back in 2015, three years before Cinestate first controversially revived it. So, getting dough for a quickie in-and-out to the tropics for a work assignment just wasn't in the cards. So, I ponied up for the ticket out-of-pocket and booked myself into the cheapest-ass hotel I could find. After all, I was only going to be resting my head a few hours before sailing off to the Isle of Cage, who cares how grungy my accommodations were? And a flophouse on the beach is better than staying in some dump motel in South Central LA (which I've done and almost got shot to death at and thus don't recommend it).

So, I got on that plane late on a Monday evening in Toronto and arrived in the Bahamas at around 10-ish. I hailed a cab to my joint in Junkanoo (key word, "Junk") and was met in the lobby by three gentlemen in ancient suits that were too big for them and that had presumably belonged to generations of heavier-set porters before them. I announced my presence; they checked their archaic computer, having a whispered pow-wow of great intensity, before giving me a keycard for room 803. They told me the elevator was broken, so up the stairs I went. I slid my card into the slot of 803's door and was met by a naked man on a bed who gasped in surprise when I entered and, after a quick apology, I exited.

Then I went back down the stairs to the lobby and explained what had happened. The trio once more had a whispered huddle around the glowing old-school screen before handing me back the *exact same card* and saying I was actually in room 804. I wasn't mad. It was too amusing and cinematic.

So back up I went, eight floors, to the room next door to my regrettably naked friend. Room 804 was happily empty save for the army of bugs that scattered when I turned on the lights. Still, my view of the beach and ocean at night was divine. I was on an adventure, after all. So, I went to sleep. In my clothes. And rested up for my big day.

When I woke the next morning, I found I could not open my left eye. It was sealed completely shut, a yellowish crust locking the lids down tight. I stumbled half-blind to the bathroom and turned on the light and more bugs scattered. I looked in the mirror and I was a cyclops. I jumped in the shower and let hot water blast my face until my lids came unglued, looked back in the mirror and saw that my poor tormented eye was completely blood red, not a trace of white in sight.

I realized I would need to find a pharmacy before I met Nick to fix this, lest I look like patient-fucking-zero. Now, Nic's people had given me a sort of secret map. I was to make my way to the far end of the island, to the docks. I was to look for a specific dock where I would march to the end of it and be met by a boat that would whisk me away to Paradise Island, where Cage and his son and then-wife lived. So, I put on my aviators, checked out of the roach hotel and grabbed a cab to what was undoubtedly the sketchiest area of the entire Bahamas. Each and every business was locked down, barred-up completely. To buy a bottle of water, I had to rattle the bars on a smoke shop door before an old guy unlocked it and let me in. I found a pharmacy and had to ring a bell, answer an intercom, and be buzzed in, before the doors locked behind me. That's just the way it is there. The lovely pharmacist looked at my eye and said "ewww" which is never a good thing to hear from a pharmacist. She said I had a serious infection, and no eye drops would treat it and then she sent me on my way. Back on went the sunglasses and since I could still see out of my blood-blasted orb, I sucked it up and went onward to meet my destiny.

I walked for half an hour through the ports and docks and tiny roads. Soon, I forgot just how impoverished and shabby the area was and instead felt very relaxed, very much part of the world I was visiting. This was completely removed from the tourist-trap zones, I was in the wild. And I liked it. Finally, I found the "secret" dock I was told to go to, and I walked down to the end as instructed and waited. Soon a speedboat came roaring in and docked. A smiling sailor man with a heavy island accent stepped out.

Sailor: Get in.

Me: Are you sure you're here to get *me*?

Sailor: Yeah, man.

Me: Well... who are you taking me to see?

Sailor: My boss.

Me: Who's your boss?

Sailor: Nee–co–las *Caaaaage*.

That was enough for me. I got in the boat, and we were off. The sun was hot, the wind smelled sweet. And then suddenly, we approached an island and the closer we got to the dock, I could see a figure, a man. He was wearing a white linen suit and had a scruffy beard. And he was waving. It was in Nicolas Cage.

Cage: Hellooooooo!

Suddenly it hit me hard. I was in a waking dream. I had just followed secret instructions to get to The Island of Nicolas Cage. It was like The Island of Dr. Moreau, but without the science. I was soon to discover it was almost as mad, though...

I stepped from the boat and Cage gave me a hearty handshake.

"Welcome to the Bahamas!", he beamed.

"Great to be here!" I shot back. And it was.

The author and the inimitable
Mr. Cage, Paradise Island, Bahamas.

We walked the long path to his house, a beautiful, surprisingly modest bungalow nestled in a maze of palm trees. He led me to his courtyard and there, on the table were piles and piles of Hammer horror movies on DVD. Stacks of them. He had been on a kick recently, to absorb as many Terrence Fisher films as he could because he had just seen FRANKENSTEIN AND THE MONSTER FROM HELL and was obsessed by it. His housekeeper came out with a bottle of wine and two glasses and Nick filled them both. We toasted to Fisher and then spent the next 20 minutes just talking about British horror and the ways in which one could approach a remake of MONSTER FROM HELL, something he dreamed of doing. Not any other of the Hammer Frankenstein films. Just that one. Then, his charming cook brought out the first of many delicious dishes she had prepared for us. We began to eat. And continued to drink.

Cage: You know, I brought out all these movies in honor of you. In honor of *Fangoria*.

Me: I'm touched!

Cage: I also arranged something else special for you...

Suddenly, he nodded to one of his staff and the man went out and came back with a gigantic sea snail. Another man showed up, armed with an axe. Nick explained that today, we would be hacking this giant snail — a conch — to bits and that we would then be eating its penis.

Me: Eating its penis? You're joking.

Cage: No, I'm not joking. This is the island's main food source, and the penis is a kind of Viagra.

Me: Ummm...

Cage: I'm doing this in honor of *Fangoria*!

Me: What happens when *Entertainment Weekly* comes to visit?

Cage: They're not invited!

The men started chopping away at the poor creature. I started filming it. It was like something out of CANNIBAL HOLOCAUST (look it up; the clip is still on YouTube, I think).

After it was done, the men pulled out a huge, slimy thing. The creature's member.

Me: Uh, Nic... I'm not sure I want to eat that!

He considered this.

Cage: Yeah... yeah. It looks a little dark, doesn't it. Okay... take it away guys, take it away. We won't be eating it today.

Saved by the apparently putrid state of the conch's dick, we continued our lunch, and another bottle of wine was brought out. We talked about his life growing up. His brother. His parents. His all-consuming obsession with horror movies, the occult and comic books. I dug deep into undervalued Nicolas Cage films like the Italian thriller A TIME TO KILL and we talked at length about projects he had prepped with Roger Corman and his time working with Herzog. He even told me a story of meeting Klaus Kinski when he was a kid hanging out with his uncle Francis. We laughed, swapped

A conch snail gets the axe as per Cage's wishes.

stories of fandom, got into the guts of the GHOST RIDER movies and then, suddenly, a massive, 3-foot-tall rooster stalked onto the courtyard.

Me: Jesus! What the hell is that!

Cage: Oh! Yeah, that happens sometimes.

Me: Is that a rooster?

Cage: Yes, it is.

Me: First you try to make me eat a dick, now there's a cock... what's going on here Nic?!

Cage: Oh God, you're probably going to print something like that.

He was right. I did. Now I've printed it twice.

Cage: Hey, do you want to try something?

Me: What?

Cage: Obeah.

Me: Obeah?

Cage: Yeah, you know Obeah?

Me: You mean like... voodoo?

Cage: Yeah, something like that.

It was all too much. Too much! I looked at his face. He seemed serious. I told him I didn't really want to cut a bird's throat today and bathe in its blood and he seemed to agree that perhaps it wasn't the best idea. He called for his men to take the beast away and we slid back into our chat.

But after that... how could I even try to pretend any of this was normal? I was a bit drunk, sitting on an island with Nicolas Cage, narrowly escaping eating snail schlongs and sacrificing chickens while riffing on horror movies and then, eventually, doing impersonations of Cage for Cage, the likes of which he approved of. It was surreal. It was insane.

And, like all amazing, surreal, insane things, it ended.

Eventually, after the wine stopped coming and the desert was served, I got up and left. We shook hands and he promised he would stay in touch. He had a Basil Gogos painting of himself that he wanted included in the magazine, which I of course agreed on and he was going to get someone photograph it in his LA home for me. I jumped back in the boat and went directly to the airport. As I waited for my plane, my phone rang. It was Nic. He was worried that perhaps he had been "too weird". I assured him that he had been just weird enough and that I had a great time.

When I came back to reality, after a couple of days, my landline (remember those?) rang and my oldest son answered. It was Nic. So, this was to be my life, I thought. Nicolas Cage is my new best friend. I can live with this.

When GHOST RIDER: SPIRIT OF VENGEANCE was about to be released, Nic, directors Nevaldine and Taylor and co-star Idris Elba were to be in New York to promote the film. I asked Nick if he wanted to have a *Fangoria*/GHOST RIDER party and to my delight, he said yes. I booked the now defunct Manhattan horror bar Times Scare (which itself was built on the bones of the notorious porn paradise "Skin World") for the soirée and invited only 200 lucky *Fango* readers. Cage showed up in full voodoo attire and we had a blast, the two of us running a GHOST RIDER screaming contest with the fans which he and I judged. It was insane. And I know the lucky people who made it to that event have never forgotten it.

Soon after, the movie opened and was promptly ripped-to-shreds by the critics and ignored by audiences. I put Nick on the cover of *Fangoria* and called him a "Master of Horror", which I knew him to be. Those who got it, got it. But mostly, I found myself personally attacked for that cover by people who did *not* get it. If they had actually *read* the two-part interview, they would have learned the ways in which Cage had long been bringing horror to each and every role he played. But you know how it is. The assholes never actually *read* anything. They just jump on the first thing they see and then burn the house down. I was told once that Quentin Tarantino's New Beverly Cinema handed out photocopies of that interview whenever they screened THE WICKER MAN.

Cage and I were also planning a *Fangoria* movie together, but after the utter failure of GHOST RIDER 2, he called me to say that he was stepping back from all horror related projects with the aim to rebuild his career. I enjoyed watching him do that in a very unique way, slowly re-entering Hollywood with voice work in big, animated features (like THE CROODS) while re-inventing himself as an "above the credits" star of a seemingly never-ending, hugely successful series of direct-to-video action and thriller movies. Now, he's sort of a genre unto himself.

I've watched with pride to see him star in celebrated modern fantasy horror movies like MANDY, MOM AND DAD, COLOR OUT OF SPACE and RENFIELD and am cynically amused that the very same frogmouths who ripped him apart and lambasted me for calling him a master of horror, are now, y'know, acknowledging him as a master of horror.

I haven't seen or spoken to Nick in many years. But I love him. I'm not just a fan of his work, I'm a fan of the way he lives his life, the choices he makes. His unpredictability. But even now, the mainstream doesn't *really* "get" him. It's fashionable to love Nicolas Cage in an ironic way these days, with his face blasted on pillows and pajamas and hipster audiences loving to laugh *at* not *with* his energy on screen. And while I'm no fan of loving anything or anyone with irony, I am pleased that Nicolas Cage, the King of Cage Island, the killer of snails and disciple of Terence Fisher, is alive, thriving and evolving and still relentlessly looking to explore and invent and re-invent the very essence of what it means to be an actor. There's no one else like him. There will never, ever be anyone else like him. And that's that.

99 WOMEN (1969)

Starring Maria Schell. Maria Rohm, Rosalba Neri,
Herbert Lom and Mercedes McCambridge
Written by Peter Wellbeck (Harry Alam Towers)
Directed by Jess Franco

Though we cannot fully credit director Jess Franco and his frequent producer Harry Alan Towers with inventing the horror/exploitation film subgenre known as the "women-in-prison" movie (or WIP for short), we can certainly credit them for defining the parameters of what people now expect from it. Since the dawn of cinema, Hollyweird has reveled in stories of lovely lasses crammed into confined spaces and confronted with dehumanization and worse (my favorite proto-WIP flick is 1950s tawdry and charming CAGED), but Franco blended that barbarity with the sort of salaciousness audiences were hungering for in their downmarket cinema; the resulting opus was 1969's 99 WOMEN, a rough and tough and super-sexual trash classic that kicked into high gear our obsession with girls getting sent to the slammer and, despite the indignities they are subjected to, always finding time for a bit of sweaty, illicit same-sex coupling. Simply put, no 99 WOMEN, no ORANGE IS THE NEW BLACK.

I remember seeing 99 WOMEN on late night television under the title ISLAND OF DESPAIR and I was delighted to finally stumble upon a film by the then obscure Jess Franco. Of course, the ISLAND OF DESPAIR cut is shorn of any and all sex and nudity so I was tad let down. But after I licked my wounds, I was still enamored with the look and feel of the film. From the opening moments, where Barbara McNair's exotic song

Maria Rohm and Elisa Montes are two of the doomed 99 WOMEN.

"Day I Was Born" congas its way across the soundtrack and a bevy of lovelies led by Towers' muse and wife Maria Rohm drift into the port of a monolithic stone age castle that will be their new prison home, there is a palpable feeling of obsession and invention here. And that's exactly what was happening off screen. Franco and Towers had to pause production of their sexy thriller THE GIRL FROM RIO for a week and, instead of letting their cast and crew (who they had to keep paying anyway) languish, they opted to cobble together a film to shoot quick and dirty on the same locations. This was that film.

At this point, Franco was working almost exclusively with the savvy Towers, and it's well-known that their collaborations during this fecund period were among Franco's most opulent and expensive. They just looked great, with international casts, dreamy sex and violence, gorgeous soundtracks and lush locations. 99 WOMEN is no exception. Shot in Rio and Spain, 99 WOMEN is a far cry from the cheap and leering films (not that this is a bad thing, however, especially in terms of Franco's work) the director would make for French producers Eurocine and Swiss producer Erwin C. Dietrich. This film is delicious to look at and listen to, with a typically emotional, complex and grandiose Bruno Nicolai score that elevates the already handsome production values to epic heights. And then there's the cast, which includes the great Mercedes McCambridge (four years away from voicing Captain Howdy in THE EXORCIST) who stalks and glowers around the island prison like some sort of horny monster, and the amazing Herbert Lom (who would star in the equally-classic Eurotrash gem MARK OF THE DEVIL that

One soul hungered to touch another!
WHISPER TO YOUR FRIENDS YOU SAW IT!
From the exciting story by Peter Welbeck
99 WOMEN
...behind bars-without men!
A Commonwealth United Corporation Presentation
STARRING
Maria SCHELL · Mercedes McCAMBRIDGE · Luciana PALUZZI · Herbert LOM
as the Governor
COLOR
Suggested For Mature Audiences
Screenplay by PETER WELBECK · Directed by JESS FRANCO · Produced by HARRY ALAN TOWERS · A Commonwealth United Entertainment, Inc. and Towers of London (Films) Limited Production
Released by Commonwealth United Entertainment, Inc.
69/44

same year) as the evil Warden, who here looks like a cross between Kim Jong-il and a Bond villain. And like many Towers productions of the time, 99 WOMEN got a sizable US release and was a modest hit.

There is plenty of sexuality and nudity on display but, as this was ground zero for the sleazy WIP wave, it's comparatively restrained. There are other cuts including a different Spanish version (99 MUJERES) that is shorn of much sex and an Italian cut that spotlights star Luciana Paluzzi. There's also a hardcore porn version that Franco had nothing whatsoever to do with and, though he himself would direct his share of porn, the director disowned any of the cuts save for the now widely available 99 WOMEN release.

Though Franco would make his most personal and interesting work later, when he was operating without *any* money, 99 WOMEN stands as a highlight of the colorful and eccentric collaboration between the director and Towers. It was a golden time for both men in their careers and that spirit is alive and thriving in this joyously oppressive film.

INTERVIEW: MARIA ROHM

Austrian-born (as Helga Grohmann) actress and, eventually, producer Maria Rohm was something of a child prodigy. Discovered at the tender age of four by Germany's Wiener Burgtheater, she literally grew up performing, winning acclaim from her fellow thespians and paving the way for a respectable career.

And then she met Harry Alan Towers.

Those familiar with 1960s genre cinema, know Towers' name; the larger than life, prolific, impassioned British producer and sometime actor guided a series of decent-budgeted, colorful spy, adventure and horror films well into the '70s and beyond, including some of the best—and most accessible—work of Jess Franco. Together, Towers and Franco made such wild, sexy fare as THE GIRL FROM RIO, VENUS IN FURS and yes, 99 WOMEN, plus several Christopher Lee Fu Manchu pictures as well as Lee's THE BLOODY JUDGE and the faithful, undervalued 1970 version of COUNT DRACULA, featuring what Lee has long claimed to be his favorite turn as the Count.

Starring in these remarkable films, slowly evolving from lower-billed co-star to featured female lead, was the beautiful, uninhibited Rohm, with piercing eyes and feminine presence—a revered actress adding class and sensuality. She wed Towers in 1964, and their personal and professional affair endured and thrived until Towers passed in 2009. Somehow, Maria ended up in Toronto, my home, where I tracked her down and we became close. Maria was very apprehensive about meeting in the flesh, always worried that seeing her in a more mature incarnation would somehow counteract the way she wanted to be remembered on screen. Naturally this was nonsense. Maria's

Beautiful Maria, never lovelier.

physical beauty was simply a manifestation of her gorgeous heart and sharp intellect. We lost her in 2018 and the following conversation is an excerpt from one of our many chats, circa 2013-2014. She was lovely, she is missed. She lives on.

CHRIS ALEXANDER: Do you remember your first meeting with Towers? Was it love at first sight?

MARIA ROHM: At 16 I started working again on stage, then did a couple of films, and at 18 met Harry at an audition in the coffee shop at the Hotel Sacher in Vienna, where he was casting CITY OF FEAR, and got the part. It wasn't love at first sight, more awe and admiration. We grew to love each other, but it didn't take very long. During the shoot in Salzburg, I got to know Harry and his mother a lot better. Harry's mother was quite a lady; she was a major during WWI, and during WWII, Harry had to salute his mom, as she held a higher military rank. I don't know if that says it all, but Harry's mother was very strong-willed. As THE SOUND OF MUSIC was shooting in Salzburg at the same time, we had nice dinners with some of the cast. Harry had known Julie Andrews since she was a child.

ALEXANDER: It must have been a tremendously exciting world for you to enter...

ROHM: It certainly was. Despite our age difference, Harry and I fit together right from the start. We both grew up in the theater, we had read and even appeared in some of the same plays and shared similar views on many subjects. I have always been around adults much older than myself and have never taken to people my own age or had a peer group of any kind. I feel more attuned to people who are much older—and, now that I am older, sometimes much younger than myself.

ALEXANDER: You worked with so many wonderful, fascinating, larger than life characters—can we talk about Klaus Kinski? There have been so many diverse things written about Kinski, most of them unsavory...

ROHM: Klaus was one-of-a-kind, very talented. His escapades seemed to increase or decrease according to his popularity. In general, Harry and I got on well with him. We could see through his tantrums, and realized he'd had a difficult early life. Whatever his exact circumstances may have been during and at the end of the war, he came away feeling powerless, which led him to want to exert power over the people around him. Insecurity is most often the root cause of bad behavior. I have to admit I was upset when I first read about Klaus' sexual fantasies about myself and Margaret Lee, which he described as factual, in what I believe was his first book. I wanted to sue Klaus, but Harry, Margaret and others convinced me that that would only attract more attention to the whole situation. Margaret Lee and were very good friends for many years, and I'm so sorry we've lost touch. Last I heard, Margaret was doing theater in California.

ALEXANDER: How about Christopher Lee? Was he a difficult man, or a joy?

ROHM: Christopher could be fun, and we did have some laughs, but I always felt aware of his mother's aristocratic and his father's military background. I would not call Chris very warm or emotionally accessible. He is a very cultured man whose first love is opera, for which his nature is ideally suited. Bigger than life, in person as well as when he is performing, Chris is always very impressive and a consummate professional. Extremely well-mannered, with a wonderful voice that was always great to listen to, especially during morning makeup. I will draw a veil as to Chris' accounts regarding EUGENIE; it's an amusing story, and more in line with Chris' public self-image.

ALEXANDER: You were known during this period for being rather... uninhibited. Was nudity ever difficult for you? Do you regret any of your overtly sexual roles?

ROHM: I was an early baby boomer and felt privileged and happy to be a part of the sexual revolution, which was close to my heart. I felt very strongly that Victorian morality was rather immoral by trying to prohibit something as natural as free sexual expression and affection in all its forms. I believe more freedom creates more awareness, and more awareness creates more freedom. Society needs rules, but they have to be based on allowing people to make informed decisions. Rules should not be used as oppression; otherwise, they produce just another form of slavery. I see erotic expression as being closely linked to the creative process, and thereby it enhances personal meaning.

ALEXANDER: This is something Jess Franco believed as well. Can you describe your first encounter with him?

ROHM: Jess was a very unique human being. I first met him in Rio de Janeiro for BLOOD OF FU MANCHU. I found very quickly that Jess was a rather temperamental director. If everything didn't go his way, he had a tendency to sulk, which worked against him and his creativity. Jess' mood swings could be difficult to understand and exasperating to deal with, at least for me. He could also be a total joy to be around and work with, truly inspirational; however, never knowing how the day would develop was disquieting. Incidentally, I didn't like the outfit Jess made me wear in BLOOD OF FU MANCHU. I felt it was almost comical.

ALEXANDER: Actor Jack Taylor says Jess was not an intellectual, but rather a "doer"—someone who lived to move and express himself. Is he correct?

ROHM: Jack is right; Jess was more emotion- and feeling-based—after all, he was a jazz musician at heart. Mind you, when Jess explained all the supposed symbolism in some of the scenes, I had a hard time following his thoughts. I never quite understood how an audience would get them without any kind of explanation. It could be said that Jess was at the mercy of his feelings; that's why his work could be so uneven. He could be a genius on one day, uninvolved and lackluster the next.

ALEXANDER: 99 WOMEN is a classic dark drama—and one that was incredible influential on the women-in-prison subgenre. What are your memories of that film, and of acting opposite Herbert Lom and Mercedes McCambridge?

ROHM: Apropos of what you said, I remember Jess shooting almost half an hour of screen time in one week for 99 WOMEN, truly inspired and excellent footage—and I wouldn't say the same about the Fu Manchu films. I really liked Herbert Lom a lot. We were in a few films together, and used to talk on the phone until shortly before his death. He was such a perfect gentleman! We came from the same part of the world with similar backgrounds, and had an instinctive understanding of each other. Mercedes McCambridge, on the other hand, was a powerhouse. Apart from being a great actress, she was also a very strong person. Her feelings seemed to be simmering just below the surface very impatiently, waiting to burst through. She was always perfectly nice, but I felt a little intimidated all the same. By the way, just between you and me, I do not like that somebody in France inserted pornographic sex scenes into that film. The inserts are obviously not me, and they change the whole tone of the picture for the worse, in more ways than one.

ALEXANDER: The pictures that Towers mounted for Franco are among his best. What was it about their relationship that worked?

ROHM: This is going to sound odd, but I believe it was me. I understood them both, and was able to communicate Harry's point of view to Jess and vice versa. I was often Harry's ambassador on the set. Harry set the pictures up, but did not believe in interfering with the director; once he hired somebody, it was for better or for

Maria lounges lusciously in Jess Franco's EUGENIE (1970).

worse, so to speak. He did not hover over them, but trusted them to do the best they could. Also, Harry was normally setting up his next film, so he generally didn't spend a lot of time on the set, which seemed to work out just fine. We talked a number of times every day on the phone, so if there was an underlying problem, we would try to find a solution in the very early stages.

ALEXANDER: VENUS IN FURS is another dreamy Towers/Franco masterpiece. Any distinct memories of making this one?

ROHM: James Darren was very laid-back and serious. He often sang between takes, which was very pleasant. Then there was Dennis Price, a total sweetheart! We shot the majority of the film in Istanbul, which is a very old, exciting and historically interesting place. Margaret and Klaus felt like family, so I was very comfortable. Barbara McNair kept to herself a lot; she didn't mix and mingle much. Somebody recently mentioned that Manfred Mann's music had been taken out on the American DVD. I thought that was very strange, as the music was great and such a big part of the story.

ALEXANDER: Franco and Towers' COUNT DRACULA is incredibly undervalued, as is your performance as Mina.

ROHM: Thank you! There were creative differences between Harry and Jess, so DRACULA was the last film we made together. We had limited but pleasant contact with him after our working relationship ended, however.

ALEXANDER: You worked with the late Soledad Miranda in DRACULA. Do you recall much about her?

ROHM: It was a great shock when we heard about Soledad's [fatal car] accident. She was a very nice young lady with a young son. Also ironic that, I believe, her husband was a race-car driver. She was very sensitive and had also been on stage as a child dancing, so we had things in common.

ALEXANDER: You dropped out of acting in the late 1970s, while you were at your peak. Why?

ROHM: I left because in those days, 35 was too old to get any worthwhile parts as a woman. I am very glad to say that has changed since. As to my film acting having improved, I was brought up with two months of rehearsals for each play, and had a hard time adjusting to the film directors I worked with who basically said where to come in, where to say the lines and where to go afterward. I'm not sure I ever really got used to that. I remember trying to discuss wardrobe with a director who said, "I don't care, I'll shoot whatever you wear." I was quite shocked by that.

ALEXANDER: You became a prolific producer in your own right, ushering forth such pictures as the Anthony Perkins vehicle EDGE OF SANITY, written in part by Franco. Was producing more creatively fulfilling for you?

ROHM: I would not say so; it just evolved that way. Harry and I were so close that I was involved in whatever he did, no matter what. I am much more comfortable, though, with the creative aspects of movies. The business side is rather frustrating, filled with people who may have money but not necessarily any artistic understanding, or sensitivity to what they're reading or talking about. Many of Harry's films suffered from that. To raise the money, one had to make concessions that hurt the projects. Harry was much more of an optimist and a fighter than I am. When one film didn't turn out the way he wanted, he would move on to the next project with as much hope and enthusiasm as ever. Harry was one of a kind. I have never met another man, let alone an independent producer, with the same imagination or heartfelt belief in and feeling for great literature and great performances. Many of Harry's most cherished ideas never made it to the screen, as the financiers couldn't understand his vision. It was easier for Harry in the early days in radio and television.

ALEXANDER: Is it difficult for you now to discuss Harry and those bygone days, or does remembering the past bring you joy?

ROHM: It is both—difficult as well as heartwarming. It's been almost four years now and I have not adjusted to the situation yet, but I can talk about Harry now, which would not have been as easy even one year ago. Forty-five years is a long time. I have no other family, so Harry was everything...

ABBY (1974)

Starring Carol Speed, William Marshall, Austin Stoker, Juanita Moore, Terry Carter
Written by G. Cornell Layne
Directed by William Girdler

Abby (Carol Speed) lets the Devil inside.

When we speak of possession-centric horror films, attention will forever turn to THE EXORCIST and with very good reason. It's the gold standard of sophisticated, intelligent, and truly shocking and scary horror cinema and its international success dictated that scores of imitators would follow in its wake. Some were excellent (1974's THE ANTICHRIST, Ovidio G. Assonitis' BEYOND THE DOOR), some were dire (the Turkish turkey SEYTAN) and some were just plain odd (Alfredo Leone's remix of Mario Bava's LISA AND THE DEVIL, crassly dubbed THE HOUSE OF EXORCISM). Nestled among these imitators sits 1974's lurid blaxploitation effort ABBY, a shocker that's not quite worthy of erasing William Friedkin's masterpiece from your memory, but is most assuredly a magnificent little picture, a movie that openly steals from its blockbuster source but has more than enough distinction and eccentricity to function as its own entity.

Shame then that it's also one of the most ill-treated pictures of its period.

ABBY was lensed it Louisville, Kentucky by noted B-movie auteur William Girdler, a man who was no stranger to making movies that rode the tails of other movies, like 1976's JAWS rip-off GRIZZLY and his other THE EXORCIST quote, THE MANITOU. But Girdler was a talent and always came armed with real enthusiasm and sense of cinematic craft, his work almost always well-written and stylish and, best of all, they take themselves seriously, with nary a trace of smarmy irony or self-conscious camp in sight. It's a shame we lost this talented director so young.

Abby doesn't need a man anymore...

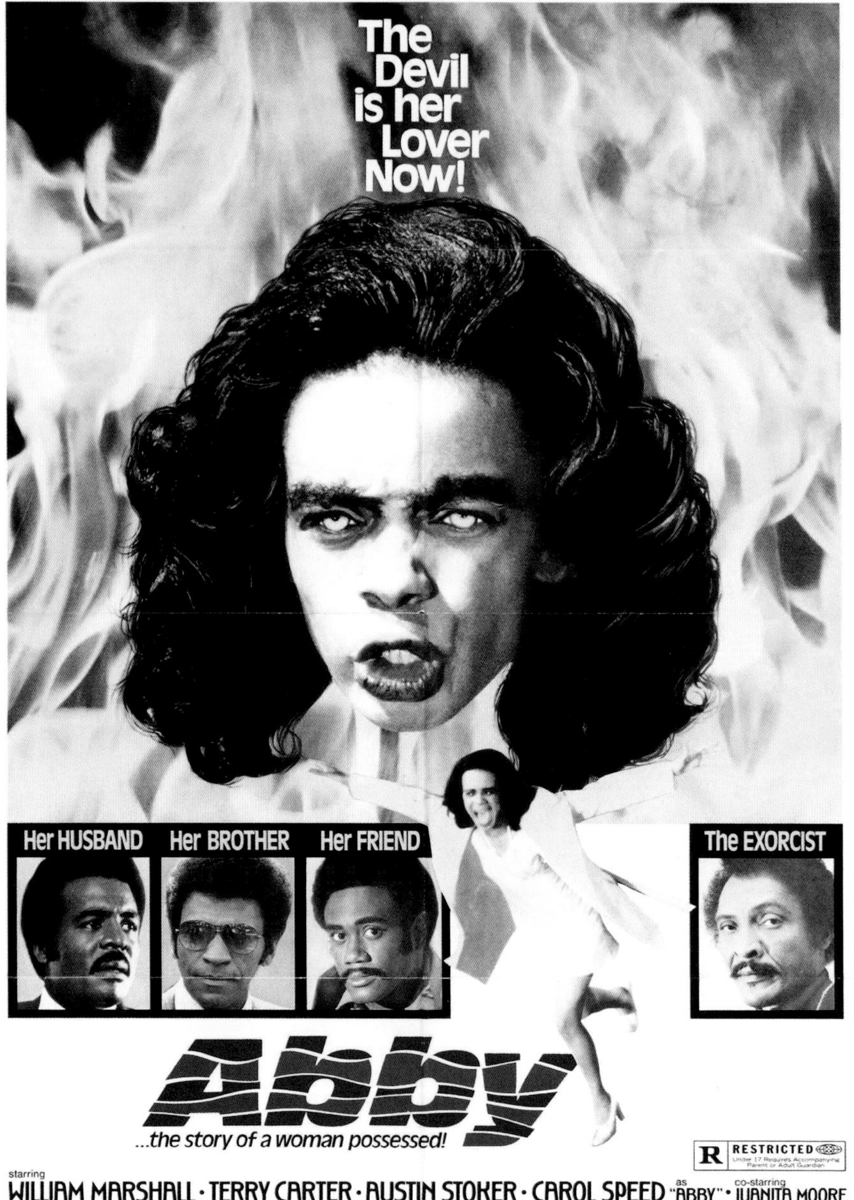
The Devil is her Lover Now!
Her HUSBAND
Her BROTHER
Her FRIEND
The EXORCIST
Abby
...the story of a woman possessed!
R RESTRICTED
starring
WILLIAM MARSHALL · TERRY CARTER · AUSTIN STOKER · CAROL SPEED as "ABBY" · co-starring JUANITA MOORE
Screenplay by G. CORNELL LAYNE · Story by WILLIAM GIRDLER & G. CORNELL LAYNE · Music Composed and Conducted by ROBERT O. RAGLAND
Produced by WILLIAM GIRDLER, MIKE HENRY & GORDON C. LAYNE · Directed by WILLIAM GIRDLER · COLOR BY MOVIELAB
A WILLIAM GIRDLER PRODUCTION · AN AMERICAN INTERNATIONAL RELEASE
74/378

Best of all, ABBY stars the majestic William Marshall, BLACULA himself. Here, Marshall plays an educated Bishop who travels the world studying arcane off-shoot religions and is also an expert in demonology. When we first meet him he's visiting his beloved son Emmett (Terry Carter) who himself is a Louisville-based minister and is married to the lovely Abby (the amazing Carol Speed from THE MACK and many other '70s flicks) who is beautiful, kind, pious, hard-working and talented; a singer in the church choir (in fact Speed wrote the song she sings in one key scene) and a newly minted marriage counselor. Emmett and Abby live together in a nice house with her mother and older brother and their life is happy, healthy and full of love and life.

And then, of course, things go terribly wrong.

Under cover of night, a malignant force creeps into the family home, up the stairs, through doors and keyholes and chooses Abby as its vessel. In one of many astonishing sequences, Abby feels the first calling of her new otherworldly possessor and begins furiously masturbating in the shower, when a dark shadow seems to come at her from behind to finish the job. Indeed, Abby's possession is one propelled by sexuality, which I guess might add some sort of element of discussion for select viewers looking to politicize the picture. But I think that's an easy and misguided mark. Girdler and his crew were indeed ripping hard on THE EXORCIST here while also capitalizing on the new demand for black genre films. And if Linda Blair shagged a crucifix, these cats were going to have their devil-girl shag, well, everything and everyone!

Almost immediately ABBY starts going through the sort of Mercedes Cambridge growling and goopy barf-spewing antics that are now tired and commonplace in the endless glut of possession films, but in 1974 still had the edge of something shocking. Her mother is leveled and her husband cries freely watching his beloved wife, the center of his universe, spiral out of control, becoming abusive and violent and generally fucking insane. It's certainly a kick to see Speed just go for it in these wild scenes, but what makes them most effective is the family's reaction to the madness. Again, this is a tight, loving, God-fearing brood. They walk "the path." They are good people who do good things and only want to continue to do good things. So, for such a cancer to suddenly appear and tear their unity apart, is shattering to them emotionally and physically. Then again, THE EXORCIST at its core was about this too. Never mind the Catholic angle, that film is really about a mother trying to save her daughter and hold on to her own sanity as the unthinkable envelopes her carefully controlled world. Like Ellen Burstyn in that film, Carter's performance here is 100% believable. His Emmett keeps trying everything to get his love the help she needs and when nothing works, he'll stop at nothing to convince people (including ASSAULT ON PRECINCT 13/BATTLE FOR THE PLANET OF THE APES' Austin Stoker) that there just might be more malevolent forces at play.

Re-enter Marshall, whose grandiose and dignified presence props ABBY up to even greater heights in the final reel, after we've seen Speed essentially torment the innocent and have endless sex with every miscreant bar-crawler she can lock her legs around. In fact, the climactic and inevitable exorcism scene takes place IN a greaseball bar, something I've never seen before. It adds an element of urgency and kink to standard sequences that more often than not happen within the stained-sheet sanctity of the possessed person's bedroom.

Girdler wielded a deft hand when it came to cheating his budget and this film is a great example of his abilities. First and foremost, the sound design is overwhelming, with screeching noises, cries, breaking glass, twisting metal, howling winds and all manner of sound FX pummeling the audience and creating a pretty terrifying aural assault. Savvy viewers will recognize some of the sounds in ABBYs sonic soup as appearing in other films too. The "howling" sound is most assuredly borrowed from Gordon Hessler's CRY OF THE BANSHEE (also distributed by American International Pictures) and key screeches can be heard in later films like Lucio Fulci's CITY OF THE LIVING DEAD and Tobe Hooper's LIFEFORCE. The director also exploits Robert O. Ragland's soul music score to great effect, draping it all over every inch of the picture, making even the most mundane and cheaply shot sequences feel exciting and alive.

The distribution woes of ABBY are near mythical at this point. Almost a full year after AIP had released the film, Warner Bros. decided that they were not terribly keen on down-market movies like this and BEYOND THE DOOR trading on their juggernaut horror movie's legacy and came after them legally to remove the film from circulation and essentially bury them. Since AIP had already made their nut and more from the film's success, they shrugged and complied, and poor old ABBY was left unseen for a long time. In 2003, fledgling American distributor CineFear released the film on DVD in a version they claimed was digitally restored and remastered and other such fabricated nonsense. The transfer was in fact struck from a VHS dub, itself culled from a battered (and we mean *battered*) 16mm print, completed with blown-out, fading color and flickering pubic hairs in the frames. It's a wretched, disingenuous release.

But all these years later and still there is no known pretty version of this wonderfully filthy film available anywhere. In fact, no one even knows who legally owns the right. Did the Warner Bros. fascists order the negative and all prints decimated or are they locked in some sort of subterranean vault? Whatever the case, fans WANT this move. ABBY is more than just a curio. It's a major work of '70s-centeric possession horror and, with its cast and setting, totally unique.

Who is the “holy terror” that hides behind the mask in ALICE, SWEET ALICE?

ALICE, SWEET ALICE (1976)

Starring Linda Miller, Paula Sheppard, Brooke Shields,
Mildred Clinton, Alphonso DeNoble
Written by Rosemary Ritvo and Alfred Sole
Directed by Alfred Sole

I’ve been writing about and discussing co-writer/director Alfred Sole’s dark, effectively upsetting 1976 psychodrama ALICE SWEET ALICE for some time now. I first learned of the film when sifting through an early ’80s edition of *Fangoria* magazine, wherein there was a small, black and white still from the film of what looked like a charred human head.

It looked real. At least to me.

And I needed to know what this film was.

Leonard Maltin’s video book, a once indispensable pre-internet reference tool for young, burgeoning cinephiles, gave it a shrug review and two pithy stars. But then again, the book did the same for TAXI DRIVER, so that did not deter me.

Later, I would see the film appear on VHS via a myriad of labels and for rock-bottom prices (due to a copyright snafu, the movie was once thought to be in the public domain; it’s not) , in dump bins at Kmart’s everywhere and elsewhere.

I kept thinking about the film. But because of that damned still, that charred head, I was almost afraid to watch it.

IF YOU SURVIVE THIS NIGHT...
NOTHING WILL SCARE YOU AGAIN.
Alice, Sweet Alice
A RICHARD K. ROSENBERG - ALFRED SOLE PRODUCTION ALICE, SWEET ALICE
Introducing BROOKE SHIELDS•Original Screenplay by ROSEMARY RITVO and ALFRED SOLE • Produced by RICHARD K. ROSENBERG
R RESTRICTED Directed by ALFRED SOLE • TECHNICOLOR® AN ALLIED ARTISTS RELEASE
770145

One night, the movie was scheduled to play at 1am on Buffalo-based channel WGRZ-TV's "The Cat's Pyjamas" and I indeed mustered the courage to watch it. Alone.

And from its first moments, from its whispering theme music and its right-of-title-card image of a veiled girl with a knife, I was in a state of dread.

That dread did not let up.

And it still hasn't.

Sole's film is a major work of psychological horror; grim, grisly and decidedly offbeat, it has elements that echo Italian giallo films, THE EXORCIST and most potently, Nicolas Roeg's DON'T LOOK NOW. It was originally released under the title COMMUNION, then re-issued as HOLY TERROR before getting stuck with the moniker it now bears. The film is intense, emotionally draining and thoroughly fascinating and has only really started getting the attention it so richly deserves in recent years.

The prickly, favorably melodramatic masterpiece tells the tale of New Jersey divorcee Catherine Spages (Linda Miller) and her two daughters, sweet little Karen (played by a pre-PRETTY BABY and THE BLUE LAGOON Brooke Shields in her movie debut) and the slightly older (and more than slightly emotionally disturbed) sister Alice (Paula Sheppard, who would grow up to star in the counterculture punk rock/sci-fi classic LIQUID SKY).

Seems young Alice is none too pleased by the fact that her cherub-faced sibling gets most of the attention from not only their mother, but also from her shrill, overbearing aunt, her morbidly obese and pedophile landlord and even the far-too attentive parish priest. She displays this displeasure physically, with an endless array of histrionic tantrums, meltdowns and sister-baiting torments that further marginalize her into the realms of the less-loved.

The fact that the doted-on Karen is all set to receive her very first communion — something that had always been denied to Alice because she was born out of wedlock, thus being deemed illegitimate by the Catholic church — is the final straw and almost pushes the jealous, perpetually slighted girl over the proverbial edge.

Then, on the very day she is designated to ritualistically eat the body of Christ, Karen is murdered (a brutal, shocking, yet effectively bloodless sequence in which Shields is choked with a candle, stuffed in a drawer and set on fire). Almost immediately, suspicion universally falls upon the sloped shoulders of the gloomy, unstable Alice whose increasingly bizarre behavior appears to implicate her beyond a shadow of a doubt.

But as more and more members of the Spages family (and those that surround them) fall prey to a diminutive, plastic masked, butcher knife wielding, yellow rain slicker wearing homicidal lunatic (again, shades of DON'T LOOK NOW), we quickly learn that the ties that bind are tenuous at best and that the church's guilt-ridden stranglehold on its flock runs deep… and runs red.

Alice Sweet Alice is often dismissed as a "slasher" movie, but that's a cosmetic observation. The picture is much closer to Hitchcock than HALLOWEEN.

The late director Sole (who incidentally is the uncle of indie horror filmmaker and composer Dante Tomaseli, himself planning a long-in-gestation remake) displays a sure hand at weaving obsessive imagery and boasts an almost Polanski-esque ability to milk queasy, sinister unease out of the working-class urban lifestyle, creating an ever-present aura of onscreen, everyday dread and a sense that the world these people inhabit is irrevocably bent and forever off its axis.

The film has a unique narrative rhythm as well, with the central mystery resolving itself almost halfway through only to evolve from a "whodunit" to "whydunit". Though this tonal shift is initially jarring, it's a testament to the picture's power (and Sole's ace direction) that it manages to keep you completely hooked — sometimes reluctantly so — right up until the final, chilling shot.

Credit must also go to composer Stephen Lawrence's rich Bernard Herrmann informed neo-classical score that's subtly effective when it needs to be and more aggressive during the frequent shock scenes. But what truly gives the remarkable ALICE SWEET ALICE its frightening fingerprint is the amazing rogues gallery of offbeat characters that slither around the picture's claustrophobic corners. Sheppard was nineteen when she was asked to play the role of the titular, possibly murderous preteen and this visibly wizened, physical maturity gives Alice an effectively world weary, tragically grotesque presence, especially when she's nicking her baby sister's dollies or choking Mr. Alphonso's kittens.

Now, let's talk about Mr. Alphonso.

The pasty-faced, obscenely overweight landlord and filthy, cat cradling shut-in has to be seen to be believed.

Played by the long MIA character actor Alphonso DeNoble (Joel M. Reed's exploitation classic BLOOD SUCKING FREAKS), Mr. Alphonso is one of sick cinema's most stomach-churning pseudo-villains. Whether fanning his sweaty self in an easy chair while listening to opera, feeding his horde of mangy, mewling felines or lecherously pawing at Alice, he is a creation of brilliant slobbery and is just one of the many morally repellent adults in the film.

And perhaps it's that lack of a clearly defined protagonist that kept ALICE SWEET ALICE at an arms distance to many a film lover, for so many years: there's nobody to really root for in this movie, just a joyless bunch of terrified, damaged, working-class hypocrites who offer up their children to the altar of Christ without conscience... and suffer gravely for it.

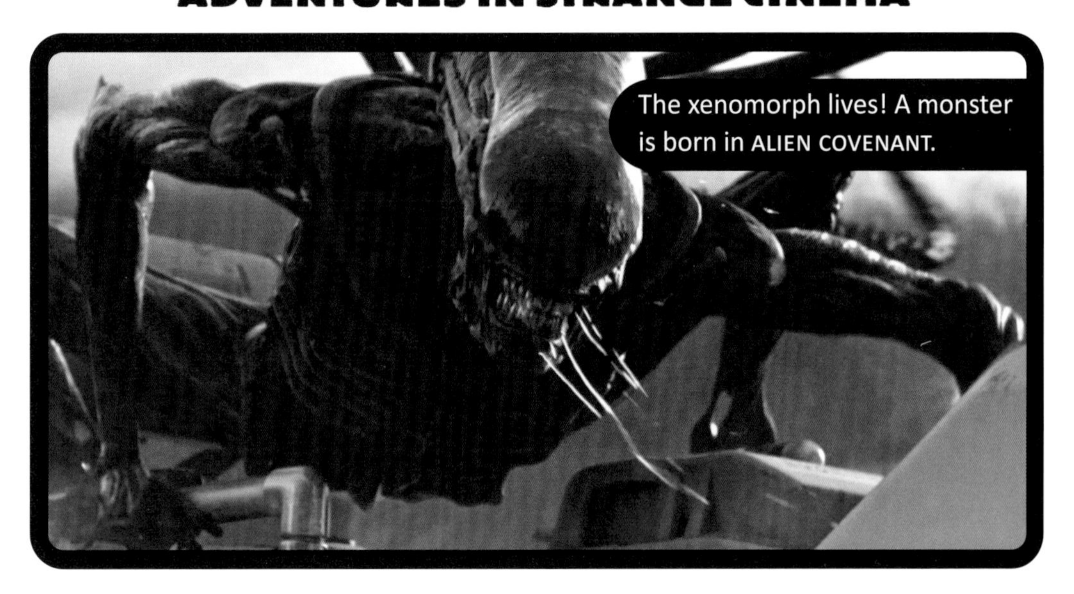

ALIEN COVENANT (2017)

Starring Michael Fassbender, Katherine Waterston, Danny McBride, Billy Crudup
Written by John Logan and Dante Harper
Directed by Ridley Scott

It's appropriate that Ridley Scott's mutated ALIEN prequel/PROMETHEUS sequel ALIEN COVENANT begins (and ends) with the mention and music of Richard Wagner. The German composer's life, writings and operas were an early and steady influence on Adolph Hitler and it's thought that the future Fuhrer's skewed, sociopathic philosophies on "racial purity" and his festering antisemitism stemmed from this obsession.

"Wagner's line of thought is intimately familiar to me," the Nazi party leader once said. "At every stage of my life I come back to him."

It is important to mention this, because Scott and screenwriter John Logan's remarkable, high-minded and misunderstood blend of splatter-show and cerebral science fiction is about these very themes of ego, narcissism, spite and jealousy propelling a quest to alter the path of creation to suit a singular agenda. Fueled by these things, Hitler inexplicably rose to power and in his quest to dominate, also murdered millions of innocent men, women and children. All in the name of a psychotic desire to meddle with natural order, to "play God" for no other real reason than to appease his mania.

And so it goes with David, the "synthetic" played by Michael Fassbender who we first met in PROMETHEUS and who we are re-introduced to here, in the prologue for

ALIEN
COVENANT
MAY 19

ALIEN COVENANT. The film begins with David opening his eyes and meeting his "father" Weyland (Guy Pearce).

"Am I your son?" asks David.

"You are my creation," responds the aging, weary inventor.

As David sits down at the provided piano, Weyland tells him to randomly pick one of the no-doubt thousands of pre-programmed pieces of music that have been hard-wired into his being by his makers. He picks something from Wagner's Das Rheingold, "Entrance of the Gods into Valhalla," and he plays the theme perfectly. And yet he is chastised for his performance by Weyland, who notes that without the full orchestra, the piece is weak, skeletal... unfinished. As David considers this and persists with questions about his "birth" and the origins of his creator and of man, we see the seeds planted for the horror that is to come. And it becomes clear that what Scott and company are doing with this movie is something both ambitious and elemental and far from the simple ALIEN sequel that 20th Century Fox tried to market the movie as.

Because ultimately what ALIEN COVENANT is, is an exploration of the myth first etched by Mary Shelley in her oft-adapted novel "Frankenstein." The subtitle for that novel was "The Modern Prometheus," after all. And so it goes...

When I first saw ALIEN COVENANT, I went alone, on opening night. Many of the people in that screening were families: parents and their teenage children, elderly men and their middle-aged sons. The ALIEN franchise is iconic and for many film fans, it's a rite of passage. It was an event to have a new ALIEN film scream into theaters. It had meaning. And yet I knew that many of those people purchasing tickets and expecting to see a film that revels in chest-bursting and men in Xenomorph costumes crawling around Giger-esque sets, menacing gun-happy humans in deep space, were bound to be disappointed. Some were angry. Certainly, many "purists" indeed recoiled at PROMETHEUS, a film I admired and loved because Scott knew he couldn't just repeat the formula he invented, and instead dialed the story back and explored new themes and ideas in a sort of sister ALIEN universe. That film is a bit of a marvel and I'm happy to see that many of the initial confused detractors of PROMETHEUS are now slowly, surely becoming reluctant fans.

ALIEN COVENANT sees Scott trying to please both camps, once more using that companion universe to explore complex ideas and moral philosophies and probing pop-psychology, while still providing the frissons and gory geek show tropes that the hardcore ALIEN fans demand. It's all here, and things do burst out of bodies and cause much mayhem. But for every exploding torso, Scott drags us into another world, introducing another element that takes us deeper into the mythology of the franchise and tunnels into completely new terrain.

Indeed, with both ALIEN COVENANT and PROMETHEUS, we see an auteur filmmaker exploiting his most popular creation to mutate it and evolve it into an entirely new species.

Kind of what like David does. Life mirroring art mirroring life, repeated like a fun house mirror maze, ad nauseum.

The setup of ALIEN COVENANT is familiar: a ship — the Covenant — jets through space looking for a planet to settle its 2000-strong, cryogenically preserved army of colonists; to find a new world to blaze new trails far from their own dying terrain. Among the various heroes (all essayed by a strong cast of players) is a "synthetic" named Walter (again, played by Fassbender) who has been programmed to do his duty and protect "his" humans and keep the mission on track. When they receive a phantom signal from an uncharted planet, they land and explore and of course encounter death and alien infection. But the real story begins when the humans are "rescued" by David, who has been stranded on this planet for a decade and has built a one-man ("man" being a questionable word) society where he has indulged his desire to create art... and other things.

Here, Walter and David begin having conversations which lead to new plot revelations and that's the real power of the picture. These dialogue exchanges and the actions that spring from them are dark, frightening and fascinating. Where science, faith, humanity, and horror intersect in beautiful, challenging passages of imagination and intellect that are perverse, allegorical and cautionary. And, expertly, every time Scott gets too heady, he flips the switch and one of those gorgeous Xenomorphs jumps out and spits its teeth out, marauding across nightmarish sets that seem ripped from the recesses of the Freudian ID. And yes, sure, the monsters are now mostly CGI-tweaked creatures, but set in the design of this modern film, it makes sense. It's forgivable.

Ardent fans of Scott's important filmography will notice that concepts explored in his groundbreaking and influential 1982 Phillip K. Dick adaptation BLADE RUNNER, are also woven into this film. Like that movie, ALIEN COVENANT trades in ideas and prefers to break ground as opposed to just crassly regurgitating formulas. It's a majestic, horrifying study in mad science gone wild in the absence of God. You can come for the face-huggers, but you must stay for the cerebellum (some of which ends up splattered on the walls, but hey, that's okay too).

INTERVIEW: JOHN LOGAN

Playwright-turned-screenwriter John Logan has won a Tony and been nominated for Oscars and is widely considered one of the most successful scribes in Hollywood. And though his biggest credits include films like Ridley Scott's GLADIATOR, Martin Scorsese's THE AVIATOR and HUGO and the recent James Bond romps SKYFALL and SPECTRE, Logan's heart lies in horror. His first feature was the nature-amok frightfest BATS, he later moved on to higher-brow fright fare such as Tim Burton's SWEENEY TODD and, of

From BATS to PENNY DREADFUL and beyond, John Logan is devoted to exploring darkness.

course, Scott's ALIEN COVENANT and he created the lamented, high concept Gothic Showtime series PENNY DREADFUL.

One day, while working with Charlie Band at Full Moon Features, an email came through. It was a customer request looking for a variety of PUPPET MASTER replica dolls to fill in the blanks of his collection. He raved about his love of Full Moon movies and how much of a fan he was and signed off as John Logan. I checked and yes indeed, it was that John Logan. I responded to him and not only did we send him all the dolls he was seeking, I booked some time with him to talk about his life and times, specifically his work scribbling words for darker cinematic fare...

CHRIS ALEXANDER: Theater was your point of entry into the arts; when did the bug bite you?

JOHN LOGAN: It was when I was about eight. My parents are from Belfast, Northern Ireland and were raised with the British sensibility, and my father made me sit down and watch Laurence Olivier's HAMLET with him. That was it. It changed my life; I was so excited by what it was, not understanding it, but it was the combination of the cinematography, the great sword fight, the poetry. My dad really encouraged me to like Shakespeare, and when you're eight and become besotted with Shakespeare, there's only one destiny ahead, and it's going to be something in the theater. That led me into doing stage productions in high school in New Jersey, and when I went to college, I took a class on playwriting and realized, wow, this is what I want to do.

ALEXANDER: Respectfully, the trajectory of going from HAMLET to BATS might seem a little bit alarming on the surface...

LOGAN: [*laughs*] Yeah, a bit.

ALEXANDER: But the movie has an eccentricity, a focus on oration and a great villain. Looking back at what you've done with the James Bond films and ALIEN COVENANT, were you going for a theatrical-meets-pulp quality?

LOGAN: Well, certainly a grandiose quality. In that developmental Shakespearean part of my young life, my favorite play and character were Richard III, and to this day there has never been a better villain. He's poetic, funny, sardonic, so leaning into being an antagonist who could also be the protagonist; that was always something I was interested in doing. My first play [NEVER THE SINNER] was about [notorious murderers] Leopold and Loeb, so the attraction of the dark center of the universe, which certainly swirls around James Bond and all my genre work, has always been something I've found very exciting to write about.

ALEXANDER: There's plenty of horror in Shakespeare. Were you an admirer of the genre growing up?

LOGAN: I was fanatical about the Universal horror movies. The first and second cycle, from around 1930 to 1945, were on TV all the time, so I just fell in love with them, and particularly the idea that you could follow those characters, like Dracula or

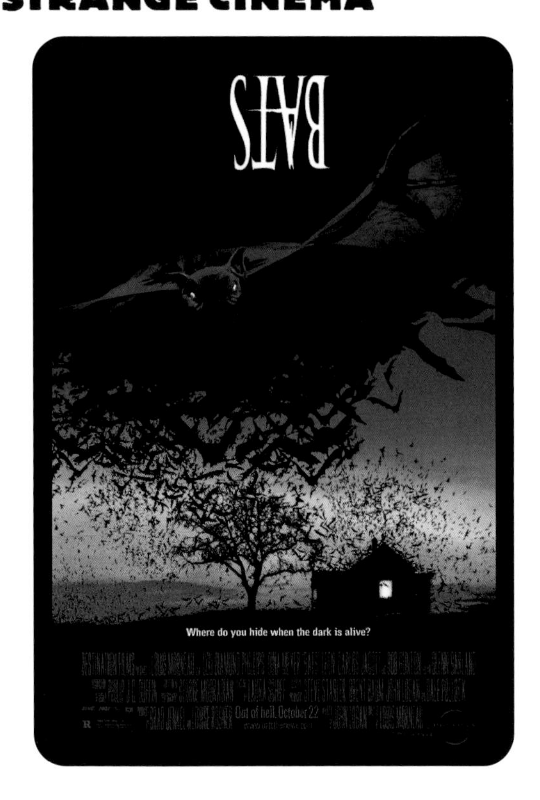

Frankenstein, through a series of movies. They were all my heroes. I built the Aurora monster models—they were all over my house—and while other kids were reading *Spider-Man*, I was reading the Dracula comic books. My favorite holiday was Halloween, and I just loved that world. It was about escapism, it was about a young gay boy associating with the outlaw, an unloved character, and that was very important to me. Shortly after that initial period, I discovered the Hammer films, and those took me to the next step of complete indoctrination into all things horror.

ALEXANDER: What was it about the Hammer movies? Was it the way they took the Universal subjects and made them much more graphic and lurid?

LOGAN: Yeah; I think lurid is the word, even more than graphic. Because of the Production Code at the time during the first two cycles of Universal movies, they're very tame. They're emotionally provocative, especially the original FRANKENSTEIN, WOLF MAN and BRIDE OF FRANKENSTEIN, but by the time we got to the Hammer cycle, suddenly they were operatic. The colors were rich and saturated, the characters were entirely over-the-top and overstated, the camera was moving, there were close-ups, so the films assumed a sort of musicality that was so much louder, richer and multitextured. As a kid, I just loved the action. If you watch HORROR OF DRACULA and see Christopher Lee and Peter Cushing fighting on top of a table, that's as exciting as anything.

ALEXANDER: What is your favorite Hammer horror movie?

LOGAN: You know, I have great affection for HORROR OF DRACULA because it was just so terrifying to me, and CURSE OF FRANKENSTEIN. I would say the Peter Cushing Frankenstein movies, if you take them as a whole—if you watch all of them in sequence, which I love to do—would probably be my favorites, the most poetically and emotionally satisfying. I also have a particular affection for Amicus horror films, like DR. TERROR'S HOUSE OF HORRORS and TALES FROM THE CRYPT. I found those very exciting, as I did the original DEAD OF NIGHT, which was the model for all of those.

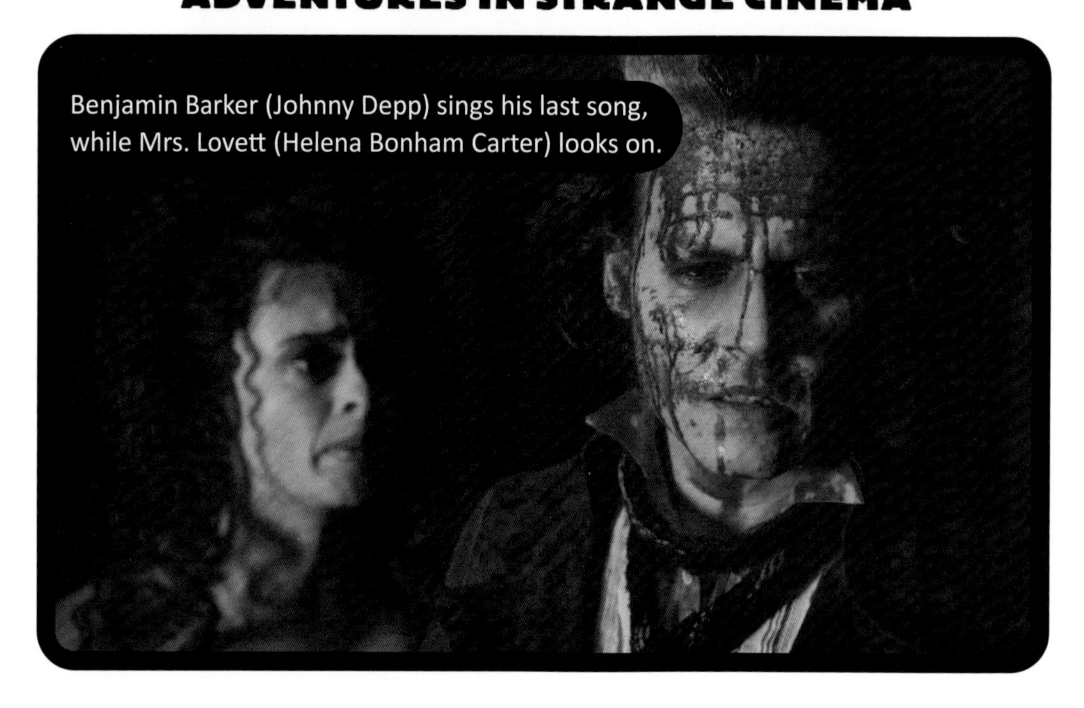

Benjamin Barker (Johnny Depp) sings his last song, while Mrs. Lovett (Helena Bonham Carter) looks on.

ALEXANDER: I was surprised to find that ALIEN COVENANT is in fact a covert Frankenstein story. Was that something you and Scott discussed, did you develop it together or did you just kind of go rogue with that element?

LOGAN: No, it was something we definitely discussed. We looked at PROMETHEUS and said, OK, what did that accomplish and how could this film be different? My very first discussion with Ridley was, "You know what this needs to be? A horror movie. It needs to be a scary, fast-paced Gothic horror film, and every great horror film has at its center some central human conflict or dilemma unlike anything you've seen before." That's what led to the Walter/David doppelganger idea, and letting the scenes between them and the relationship between them be the emotional and intellectual center of the story. That very long scene where they play the flute together, getting to know each other—I think we put more love and care into crafting that than into the special effects. Ridley is a filmmaker who is deeply involved in the drama, and making sure that's exactly the way he likes it before he starts filming. You'd expect that with Ridley you'd spend a lot of time talking about the chest-burster scenes, or the design or the ingenuity of them. but that's actually not true at all. You spend all your time talking about the characters and dialogue.

ALEXANDER: Was SWEENEY TODD a chance for you to write a Hammer horror movie, in a way?

LOGAN: That's exactly right. Tim Burton is deeply invested in the world of Hammer horror—the actors, the look, the designers, the photographers—and in our very first discussion, we started talking about the blood. We thought there was a particular color of Hammer film blood in the '60s, and we were going to recreate it, even if we had to do it digitally. We started talking about all the poetry in those films, the condensed simplicity in them, and after our first meeting, he sent me a boxed set of every single Hammer horror movie with a one-line note: "You may want to watch all these."

Also, we filmed entirely on soundstages—maybe a couple of exterior shots—so we were also stagebound like the Hammer films were, so that was interesting as well, in terms of how we created perspectives. I know Dante Ferretti, the production designer, was also very influenced by the look and feel of the Hammer films.

ALEXANDER: Last question, and it's about Oliver Reed. You worked with him on GLADIATOR, his final film. Any good stories?

LOGAN: Oh my God, Oliver Reed! Anyone who's ever met Oliver Reed has a shelf of stories, and here's my favorite one. For some reason, they decided they wanted to do a table read of the GLADIATOR script two weeks before we started filming in London, but the only timing that worked with the executives was 8:00 on a Sunday morning. So, into that 8:00 meeting came Russell Crowe, Joaquin Phoenix, Richard Harris, Oliver Reed and everyone else, and many of these gentlemen had probably never seen eight in the morning! All I can say is, when Oliver Reed came rolling into that room like a great unhappy leviathan, the molecular energy changed. But the minute he sat down to read that script, he was fully invested, he was charming, he was witty, and he gave a full performance as Proximo at the very first reading. Everyone admired him for that.

AMERICAN PSYCHO 2 (2002)

Starring Mila Kunis, William Shatner, Geraint Wyn Davies, Robin Dunne
Written by Alex Sanger, Karen Craig
Directed by Morgan J. Freeman

Now, calm down please. I'm not here to dissect or defend a movie called AMERICAN PSYCHO 2. Rather, I'd like to discuss the film that *could* have been THE GIRL WHO WOULDN'T DIE, a 2002 Canadian serial killer comedy starring a very young Mila Kunis, hot in the thralls of her success on the hit (and sorely missed) sitcom THAT '70s SHOW. Confused? Really, it's not all that complicated. Kunis did indeed sign on to appear in a film called THE GIRL WHO WOULDN'T DIE, from a same-named script by Alex Sanger and Karen Craig and directed by Morgan J. Freeman (not the actor, note the "J"). That original script is a clever, dark, and twisted noir about a sociopath who will stop at

Starkman (William Shatner) sees dead people in AMERICAN PSYCHO 2.

nothing to get what she wants. A female Thomas Ripley. It's a very good script and deserved a better fate than what befell it.

See, sometime during production — and I'm not sure if it was in the thick of it or at the tail end of it — some genius at Lionsgate decided that the film had more than enough similarities to their hit 2000 movie AMERICAN PSYCHO that it could easily be tweaked into being a sort-of sequel. So, a rather sad and inept prologue was added, along with some silly voiceover dialogue and a scene or two of padding that mentioned the name "Patrick Batemen." *Et voila*, a sequel that absolutely no one wanted was born.

And Kunis didn't want it either. She was young, but not dumb and was furious about being "duped" into appearing in a film that so crassly ripped and riffed on Mary Harron's deft adaptation of Bret Easton Ellis 'punishing novel. Appropriately, the direct-to-video film was savaged by cynical critics and renters who couldn't see past the gimmick, and, despite Kunis' swelling fame, the film faded into obscurity.

And if you're one of the many who scoffed at the picture, I ask you to book 88 minutes of your life to perhaps give it another look. Because nestled in the lame framework is a great little Grand Guignol thriller with a solid leading turn by Kunis and some hilarious and sharp supporting work. When I say that William Shatner has never been better, I mean it. Okay, maybe he's a bit better in stuff like IMPULSE and KINGDOM OF THE SPIDERS. But it's a close race.

Kunis stars as Rachel Newman who, in that awful opening sequence we mentioned, tell us, the audience, that her babysitter dragged her along on a date with the late

Patrick Bateman, the corporate slug-cum-serial killer from the book and film AMERICAN PSYCHO. Seems that while a plastic-coated Bateman (played by Michael Kremko, a million times removed from Christian Bale) was carving up the reproductive system of her sitter, Rachel escaped her binding, stabbed Bateman to death and simply wandered home and never mentioned the incident to anyone.

Now Rachel is all grown up and naturally, she's also stark raving mad. After developing a psychosexual addiction to serial killers, she opts to pursue a career in the FBI and obsesses over her teacher (Shatner), an aged lothario who pits his students against each other, when he hints that he'll be hiring a teaching assistant in the next semester. Rachael wants that gig. Badly. And when her colleagues begin to get in her way, she ruthlessly murders them, cunningly covering her tracks as she gets closer and closer to her target. Meanwhile, a handsome psychiatrist (FOREVER KNIGHT's Geraint Wyn Davies) is on to her dirty deeds and is getting seriously creeped out.

AMERICAN PSYCHO 2 — or rather, THE GIRL WHO WOULDN'T DIE— is a strange, entertaining, and surprising little film. Bloody and funny and twisty and turny and Kunis, a marvelous talent, really pulls it all off. We like Rachel, despite her streak of remorseless and lethal evil. And the men and women who end up on the end of her knives, very often deserve it. Or at least are undone by their own unsavory antics. Shatner is amusing as the horny Prof, but as the film progresses, he begins to develop the character and really act. Not just chew scenery. Act. It's a treat to see him give this bit of quickie mayhem his all. And Wyn Davies is fantastic as the confused and nervous shrink who becomes an unlikely hero. Or does he? There really *are* no heroes in this nifty, cold-hearted noir, just vulgar people and less vulgar people.

On the deleted scenes on Lionsgate's old DVD release, you can see the clapboard clacking with the original title written on it. Not that anyone would bother doing this, but I wish there was a way to go back and re-edit the piece, eliminating the stupid Bateman angle and pushing it closer to the film it was originally designed to be. But until that day comes, we do have this version and more forgiving viewers willing to look past the poor commercial choices of the studio might just thrill to discover a cool, endlessly entertaining serial killer flick, one that needs much more love than it gets.

THE BAD BATCH (2016)

Starring Suki Waterhouse, Jason Momoa, Keanu Reeves, Jim Carey
Written by Ana Lily Amirpour
Directed by Ana Lily Amirpour

Arlen (Suki Waterhouse) assesses her limbless predicament.

Director Ana Lily Amirpour's sophomore genre-bender (following the stark, monochrome A GIRL WALKS HOME ALONE AT NIGHT) THE BAD BATCH screamed into festivals chased by critical acclaim, received a limited theatrical run, didn't really find its audience and then was seemingly cast into the literal and figurative contemporary cinematic dump bin. That's not really a surprise. Pictures like THE BAD BATCH are so singular in their vision, so pulsing with energy, art and ideas that they generally need a wide berth of time to be rediscovered, discussed, debated and appreciated. And I'm convinced that history will remember THE BAD BATCH as a major work of pop-cult art and I say this fully admitting that, after a blistering first half, by contrast, the rest of the film is a bit of a shrug, bleeding out into a wave of exposition and hastily resolved narrative and character arcs.

But man, oh man... those first 45 minutes! So deliriously brilliant is the setup for this future-shocker that you can — and should — forgive the work its flaws. In fact, after multiple viewings — which THE BAD BATCH surely needs — those flaws become acceptable deviations. They become part of the fabric of the total vision, for better or worse.

THE BAD BATCH literally hits the ground running, with Suki Waterhouse's lithe Arlen fleeing a future-Texas desert Hell from motorcycle-riding assailants who takes her back to their camp, restrain her and inject her with some sort of fluid before hacking off her arm and leg and eating them! It's a bold passage of violence and odd poetry propelled by an equally odd soundtrack and, despite the graphic nature of the sequence, it's shot with, er, taste. Suddenly Amirpour trots out a rogue's gallery of miscreants, a cannibal tribe of weightlifters — even the women are impossibly ripped — led by the hulking Jason Momoa (GAME OF THRONES, AQUAMAN) that seem pulled from the films of Alejandro Jodorowsky (with echoes of pictures like THE WITCH WHO CAME FROM THE SEA and select works by Kenneth Anger) and yet are still unlike anything else seen on screen. As Arlen drifts in and out of her haze and sees others like her, human livestock, missing limbs and wallowing in misery, the scrappy woman with the too-short jean shorts plots her escape. Said escape involves caking herself in her own excrement and with her one-arm, wielding an iron pipe while wheeling herself away on a skateboard.

That all this mesmerizing madness is related by Amirpour and her cast without a word of discernible dialogue makes it all the more powerful, a battle cry against genre films that pad their running times and murder their own souls with tin-eared verbiage, refusing to trust that their audience is engaged enough and intelligent enough to follow along using universally understood sound and image, body language and movement. But when Arlen weaves her way to the neighboring camp of Comfort and "rescues" the daughter of her former cannibal captor, Amirpour either loses her nerve or listened to too many money people who likely suggested that she compromise her vision and clarify her beautiful abstractions.

See, THE BAD BATCH is very clearly an unsubtle allegory for the New America, specifically homing in on the "have-nots," those on the fringes who often are forced to create their own sub-societies, governed by their own laws and codes. These are motifs alive in the best Spaghetti Westerns, where Europeans presented a fascinating outsider's view of the already fantastical cinematic visions of early America and the director herself has cited THE BAD BATCH as a neo-western of sorts. The film's entire ESCAPE FROM NEW YORK-ish setup speaks of a skewed view on "the other" and Amirpour makes the point here that "the other" is really an illusion, and only a matter of perspective. And again, she does this with image and sound, not words. She does it with revolting scenes of human barbecue and instantly iconic imagery (Waterhouse's "happy face ass" will likely live on in cinema history forever). Truly, Amirpour is an intelligent, bold filmmaker and it's beyond exciting to watch her create this world, her world.

But then, as the movie rolls on, people start talking — a lot — including Keanu Reeves' Jim Jones-esque leader, whose hammy oration pushes the movie into camp but also has the unfortunate effect of hammering home explicitly everything Amirpour has taken an effort to allude to in the abstract (Reeves literally says that freedom costs an arm and a leg to our limb-challenged heroine). Suddenly the film is awash in heavy-handedness, from fractured puzzles of the American flag, the slogan-heavy T-shirts key characters wear, to signs, signs, everywhere signs. The movie loses its footing and feels like the intellectual at the party who has one-too-many and just dissolves into a puddle of punchy preaching.

But no matter. There's more than enough fire and strangeness and near-feral originality to make THE BAD BATCH a major slab of deranged grandeur and anti-mainstream majesty while cementing its director as one of the most interesting cinematic voices currently alive. There's no other film like it. And hey, Jim Carrey appears as a mute Gabby Hayes-esque desert rat. Know any other movies that can claim that honor? I thought not...

THE BEGUILED (2017)

Starring Colin Farrell, Nicole Kidman, Kirsten Dunst, Elle Fanning
Written by Sofia Coppola
Directed by Sofia Coppola

If you've seen director Sofia Coppola's second feature film, 2003's LOST IN TRANSLATION, you might recall the opening shot, that of Scarlett Johansson's panty-wrapped, bed-bound behind. It's a stunning first image, erotic, ordinary, intimate, humorous; cheeky, literally, and figuratively. Coppola is a visualist and sensualist first and foremost, an artist who instinctually knows how to elicit emotional and physical responses from near static images and her movies often play like a succession of moving photographs and paintings. And almost always she sets the tone and theme for her films with that all-important first image. In THE BEGUILED (a loose remake of the Clint Eastwood/Don Siegel psychodrama, itself based on the novel by Thomas Cullinan), she outdoes herself, with a breathtaking Gothic shot of a curved, weeping tree-lined road and young girl walking down it, the title card then filling the screen, the font pink, feminine and pretty. It's perfect. Perfect not only because of its aesthetic power, but because it expertly illustrates the soul of the film, that of the untamed, smothering, elemental grandeur and truth of nature and the dichotomy of the artifice of nature, or in this case femininity, more specifically the illusion of females being soft, lite, helpless, vulnerable. Women as societal decorations. When, of course, such male-sculpted nonsense is just that: nonsense.

THE BEGUILED stars Colin Farrell as battle-wounded Irish born Yankee solider John McBurney, who is discovered by little wandering Amy (Oona Laurence) by her plantation-set girl's school in the thick of the American Civil War-battered deep South. Striking up a conversation with the man, who is kind and articulate, the antithesis of what she has been led to believe "the enemy" represents, she helps McBurney back home, where the school mistress, Martha (an icy Nicole Kidman) and her prim and proper gaggle of students, reluctantly take him in and nurse him back to health. Isolated and repressed, the corseted cabal of women young and burgeoning begin responding the charming, handsome soldier in different ways, the youngest of them enamored by him in a possibly paternal way and the older ones — specifically Martha, the flirtatious Alicia (Elle Fanning) and the anxious, miserable Edwina (Kirsten Dunst) —

McBurney (Colin Farrell) menaces Miss Martha (Nicole Kidman).

romantically and sexually. The women and their captive guest begin to form various connections and tensions rise as the previously air-tight, micro-society the women have carefully established begins to crumble, slowly, surely. And McBurney apparently revels in the hold he seems to have over the ladies and willingly manipulates them. But hell hath no fury and soon, McBurney finds himself in deeper than he bargained for.

Coppola has stated that her interest in the source film and book stemmed from a desire to flip the perspective of the narrative and focus on the plight of the women as opposed to making McBurney the victim. The original 1971 film is a full-blown horror movie, told from the point of view of a man manipulated by a power-mad matriarch (Geraldine Page) and her protegees. But Coppola's approach is radical and fascinating, not frightening, creating a sense of queasy unease and uncomfortable erotic electricity punctuated by moments of gore and bursts of violence. In this version of THE BEGUILED, the man in some senses reaps what he sews, his casual flirting and manipulations woefully backfiring as he underestimates just how quietly feral his female hosts are. Seeking to divide them with his desires, what happens is ultimately just the opposite.

On top of her lush visual palette, Coppola is also known for her use of music to propel her images but in THE BEGUILED, she forfeits score almost entirely (there is music by Phoenix, but it's almost invisible), opting instead to let silences speak the loudest, along with faint rumbles of distant cannons popping in the distance, a constant reminder of the real horrors that pulse just beyond the utopia the women have designed in the school. It's a genius move, allowing her to richly evoke the sense of the period and immerse us in the world these characters inhabit. And Coppola once more casts flawlessly, with Kidman offering a mirror, non-supernatural Americanized answer to her repressed matriarch in THE OTHERS, Coppola's MARIE ANTOINETTE star Dunst providing a stunning portrait of a woman pining for sex and salvation from a life she quietly despises, and Fanning in some ways taking her THE NEON DEMON character and transposing her to a period piece. The younger actresses match their elders every step of the way, with Laurence especially shining.

If THE BEGUILED has a flaw, it's perhaps in that it's almost too muted and compact. It ends too soon. We want to spend more time here, in this sensual, dangerous, and desperate world that Coppola and company have so carefully created. We want more. In that, the viewer is left in some respects, in the same state that the director leaves her characters: in the same position as when we found them, but both slightly more broken and yet oddly stronger, and yet ultimately still slave to their frustrations and desires.

THE BIG CUBE (1969)

Starring Lana Turner, George Chakiris, Karin Mossberg, Daniel O'Herlihy
Written by William Douglas Lansford
Directed by Tito Davison
Poor Lana Turner

The former Hollywood sex-siren, she being one of the original Femme Fatales in Tay Garnett's 1946 adaptation of James M. Cain's THE POSTMAN ALWAYS RINGS TWICE, was considered in her prime to be one of the most dangerous and desirable women working in front of the lens. Of course, like most if not all of the living legends controlled by grooming studios during that period, much of Turner's public persona and carefully marketed myth was fabricated. In truth, the actress was a gentle, troubled soul, an alcoholic and a bit broken after failed marriages and career dips and the typical Hollywood sneering at women when the bloom is off their rose and they slip into middle-age.

It was at this point in Turner's career that she would find herself starring in what is one of the most outrageous and bizarre films of the 1960s. Director Tito Davison's Mexican/American co-production THE BIG CUBE was Warner Bros. attempt to out-trip Roger Corman's THE TRIP and blend noir tropes with druggie youth culture and the still

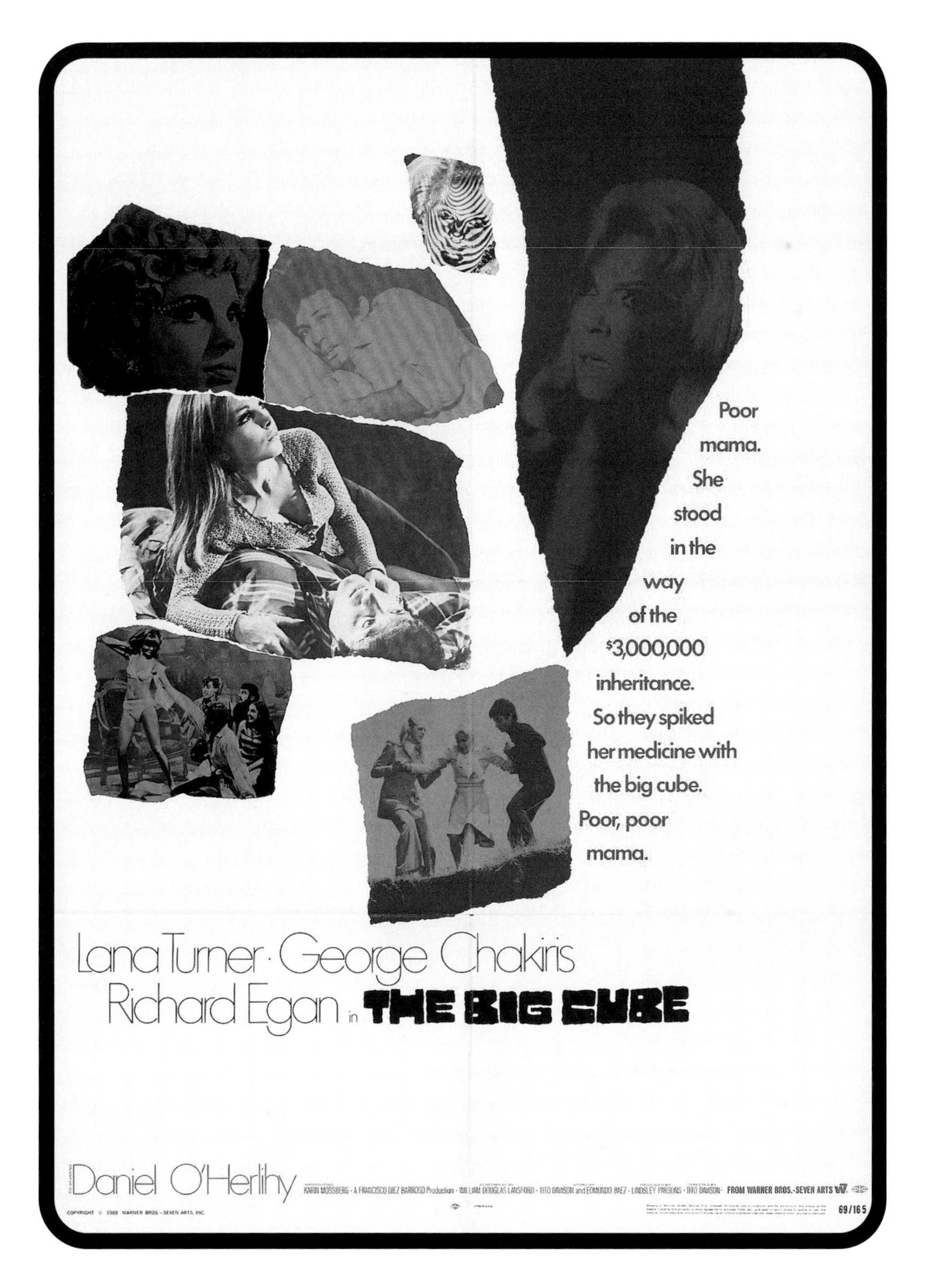
Poor mama. She stood in the way of the $3,000,000 inheritance. So they spiked her medicine with the big cube. Poor, poor mama.
Lana Turner · George Chakiris
Richard Egan in THE BIG CUBE
Daniel O'Herlihy
KARIN MOSSBERG · A FRANCISCO DIEZ BARROSO Production · WILLIAM DOUGLAS LANSFORD · TITO DAVISON and EDMUNDO BAEZ · LINDSLEY PARSONS · TITO DAVISON · FROM WARNER BROS.-SEVEN ARTS
COPYRIGHT © 1969 WARNER BROS.—SEVEN ARTS, INC.
69/165

popular "horror hag" wave of films, the likes of which usually starred Bette Davis or Joan Crawford. Turner joins their ranks here, in a psychedelic assault on the senses, common and otherwise, a film so over-the-top and wrong of head that cruel critics had a field day eviscerating it and Turner's appearance and performance in it.

The bile ladled upon THE BIG CUBE upon release helped propel it into virtual oblivion and so damaged Turner's already fragile state, that she wouldn't appear in any films until 1974's trashy British horror/melodrama PERSECUTION (where she played Ralph Bates' domineering mother).

But watching THE BIG CUBE today, it's something of a marvel; an absolutely *insane* anti-drug (yet still drug-addled) free-fall into surreal psychedelia and ludicrous, overheated psychodrama. It's a genuine cult film that has sadly not yet found its cult.

THE BIG CUBE sees Lana starring as Adriana, an aging, elegant actress of stage and screen who gives it all up to marry wealthy millionaire bachelor Charles Winthrop (HALLOWEEN III's Dan O'Herlihy, whose equally obscure and deranged 1962 sorta-remake THE CABINET OF DR. CALIGARI is the perfect psychotronic companion picture to CUBE). Charles' daughter Lisa (Karin Mossberg, whose thick Swedish accent is bizarrely explained away as the result of her attending a Swiss boarding school!) isn't terribly thrilled about dear old dad marrying again, but Adriana genuinely cares for the girl and sweetly attempts to build a relationship. But their potential bright future takes a tragic turn when, while on a sailing trip, Adriana and Charles are in a shipwreck and Charles drowns. Gutted, Lisa falls in with a pack of acid head hipsters, led by sociopathic, disgraced med student/LSD alchemist Johnny (played by WEST SIDE STORY's George Chakiris). When Johnny learns of her fortune, he manipulates the girl into a plot to drug her stepmom to Palookaville and secretly trip her out to the point of madness. Convincing Lisa that Adriana was responsible for her dad's death, Lisa's mild disdain for her new mom turns to blind hate and she goes along with the plot, with dire results for all involved.

THE BIG CUBE is pretty much wall-to-wall lunacy. The movie is shot almost entirely on soundstages, dreamlike expressionist interiors that are ideal for projecting the endless LSD-trip visuals over the surprisingly frequent naked female bodies and wild-eyed male faces that make up a bulk of the non-domestic scenes. Chakiris is pure, smooth evil, essentially a kind of vampire who seduces and spikes his victims with acid-soaked sugar cubes (hence the title) and thinly grinning through all his transgressive actions, convinced he is above suspicion and any sort of law. The entire thing feels like a play put on by the inmates of an asylum. Like MARAT/SADE for horny, far out '60s teens.

As we mentioned, poor Lana got lambasted for her turn here but really, she's rather good in it; a sympathetic presence, a woman who sees her second chance at happiness with a wonderful man and whose attempts to give love are met with malevolence. In her late 40s at the time, Turner doesn't look nearly as worn out as critics have cited, though you can certainly see where the effects of booze and chain-smoking (the latter which led to her death from throat cancer in 1995) have played minor havoc with her skin. Sure, she wears a cavalcade of cheap wigs, but such affectations suit the character and add to her slightly past-its-prime old-school Hollywood glamour.

Many have giggled at the film's final reel, where an LSD-damaged Turner is convinced to essentially re-enact the entire film's events in a mocked-up stage play directed by her former lover and collaborator Richard Egan, but it's that surreal, overheated turn of events that most lovers of odd cinema will cherish most. Truly, I've never seen another film quite like it.

You'll laugh at THE BIG CUBE and that's okay. It is funny. But more than simply tittering at its dated charms, you'll more likely be astonished at its skewed vision and of Turner's brave, committed performance, one of her last great roles buried in a movie that so many people would have you believe is just antiquated junk.

BLACULA (1972)

Starring William Marshall, Vonetta McGee, Thalmus Rasulala, Gordon Pinsent
Written by Joan Torres, Raymond Koenig, William Crain (uncredited)
Directed by William Crain

One wonders what director William Crain's early 1972 blaxploitation horror film BLACULA would have been like if it wasn't for the presence, dignity and creative input of actor William Marshall. The theatrically trained performer was brought on board early enough that he pushed for what was then just a quickie American International Pictures joint about a jive-talking bloodsucker to have a kind of grace and a soul that strayed beyond Gene Page's bass-heavy afro-funk vibe. Because of Marshall, BLACULA still stands as not just a high point in the strange "urban" horror film subgenre of the 1970s, it remains one of the best horror films of the decade full stop.

BLACULA was a project put together after the global success of films like Melvin Van Peebles' SWEET SWEETBACK'S BADASSSSSS SONG and Gordon Park's slick action thriller SHAFT, both movies that signaled a rougher, edgier and sexier American action picture populated by and targeted to African Americans. But, especially in the case of SHAFT and later, Larry Cohen's BLACK CAESAR, these movies were embraced by a wide audience whose skin color and societal perspectives were varied and diverse. Because of this, AIP saw an opening to cash in, blending their profitable Gothic exploitation horror films with a contemporary vibe, something Hammer was doing with their fun

Prince Mamuwalde (William Crain) reborn as Blacula.

and innovative DRACULA A.D. 1972. The result was BLACULA. In it, a vampire named Andrew Brown was meant to maraud around L.A. looking for blood, the envy of every street corner pimp. But Marshall would have none of that.

The actor — who by this point had a smattering of film credits and a rich history of stage work — came up with the idea of giving the character some royal pedigree, lacing his story and motives with liberal doses of Shakespearean tragedy and ample pathos. With Marshall's influence, BLACULA became an African Prince, the noble Mamuwalde who, in the hastily shot opening, travels to Transylvania with his Princess Luva (played by genre regular Vonetta McGee) to break bread (blood?) with Count Dracula (Charles Macauley) and discuss the termination of the vile slave trade that has long plagued Mamuwalde's people. But it's a trap, of course. Unbeknownst to the Prince, Dracula is a vampire, and the meeting is a ruse designed to first ridicule Mamuwalde (in a genius stroke, Dracula is a strong advocate for the slave trade and a cackling racist bastard) and then to make an example of him. He calls forth a horde of his ghoulish undead slaves and, with Luva restrained, he puts the bite on the Prince, hissing a soliloquy (while accidental but effective tears stream from his contact-irritated eyes) about how Mamuwalde will be punished for his audacity with a eternal lifetime of vampirism. He re-christens the now undead royal "Blacula" (a fantastic and kinky way to justify the silly title) and entombs the newbie vampire and his screaming bride in a chamber in his castle, where they are never to be heard from again.

A century later, two flamboyantly gay antique dealers show up at the castle and giddily pack up their finds to be shipped home. Amongst their loot is Blacula's coffin and pretty soon the ravenous ebony ghoul wakes up and, with feral eyebrows and out of control sideburns, he kills and drains his effete liberators. If there's any real drawback to BLACULA, it's the portrayal of these characters. For all of Marshall's efforts to give depth to his vampire Prince, no respect was shown to this pair and they're written and played as mincing gay camp cartoons. Worse, after they die, other heroic characters sneeringly refer to them posthumously as "a couple of faggots". Sure, we can write it off as a sign of the times, as ignorance. But it also speaks, not-so-quietly, of the double standard that was coursing through so many of these movies, like despite the empowering of black actors and characters, we still needed to have one of society's less defended minorities to laugh at and ridicule.

But if you can let that bit of unpleasantness, go (most have), BLACULA is a marvel. Marshall's vampire walks the streets in his cape, speaking eloquently and pining after the woman who appears to be the reincarnation of his long dead lady love (again played by McGee). It's amazing to watch Marshall hold court, to see the peripheral cast (including Canadian actor Gordon Pinsent) bow to his massive shadow. Marshall's Mamuwalde doesn't want to be a vampire. He wants to go home. He wants to reconnect with that which makes him human. He wants love. His bloodlust is a distraction. When his attempts to connect with McGee are foiled by a tough-talking female cab driver, he has no initial aim to kill the woman. He's annoyed by her and, as he's brushing himself off, he involuntarily devolves into that hirsute-browed, wild-eyed fiend, attacking and killing not out of malice or sadism but because of the damned curse that his white slave-trading antagonist Dracula put upon him. Marshall sells this conflict and duality brilliantly.

BLACULA is scary too. Crain gives his black vampires a powder white sheen that makes them look authentically ghost-like but also adds an odd, disturbing reverse-minstrel aesthetic, as if the characters have to turn into "whitey" to exemplify their evil. This device is likely accidental, but that's irrelevant. It's there. And when those ghouls go for their prey, they run screaming in slow-motion. their fangs bared, like banshees from the pits of Hell. There were no vampires as savage as these prior to BLACULA's release and they are unforgettable.

When BLACULA reaches its sad, slow climax, it recalls another vampire film released that same year, Javier Aguirre's Spanish Paul Naschy vehicle COUNT DRACULA'S GREAT LOVE. Of course, there is no connection between the films. But the same romanticized device where both vampires, denied the love they have long sought, opt to kill themselves and end the pain of their shattered hearts. In BLACULA, with his lady dead in his arms for a second round, he quietly tells his attackers to stand down, bows his head in misery and simply walks into the sun, the credits rolling mournfully over his disintegrating face. It's not a happy film and the emotional smack the film carries is all Marshall.

Because of BLACULA's runaway success, AIP hired their COUNT YORGA, VAMPIRE director Bob Kelljan to make a sequel the following year. That film, SCREAM BLACULA SCREAM, is a much more violent and eroticized affair, pushing the previous film's mild PG rating to that of an R and trading romanticism for cruelty. Because of Marshall (and a very young, gorgeous Pam Grier), the movie is still great, though in a very different way, with voodoo and revenge driving it and more of a focus on Blacula's vampirized victims. But it's no BLACULA and Kelljan is no Crain.

We lost William Marshall back in 2003. It was a great loss, one that should have been felt by all of Hollywood, not just the handful of maniacs who thrill to the world of BLACULA. It's important that we never forget him. He was, in his way, a trailblazer, bestowing beauty on what would otherwise have been just another crass piece of commercial fangwork. BLACULA forever.

INTERVIEW: WILLIAM CRAIN

CHRIS ALEXANDER: When did you first fall in love with cinema?

WILLIAM CRAIN: Well, I was about 11 years old and I saw this Brazilian movie called BLACK ORPHEUS. There was all this dancing and movement, and I just knew right then and there that this is what I wanted to do. Of course, my parents were like, "you want to make movies? That's gonna cost lots of money and we don't have lots of money, so you better pick something else to do!". But that was it. I was hooked.

ALEXANDER: So, you followed your dream and got into UCLA to study film and television production.

CRAIN: I did, yes. And then I went to work in Canada for a few years.

ALEXANDER: How did that happen?

CRAIN: Oh man, we had an "Amen Corner" production that was very successful and I actually acted in that in the prologue, and we also had a workshop run by Frank Silvera called "Theater of Being" and we always talked about making movies, that was the ultimate goal, and as we changed theaters, larger and larger theaters with the success of "Amen Corner", we finally got a ticket to go to Broadway. I'd been with it two or three years, I don't remember the timing now, but I wanted to pursue the film aspect of my career, and then Frank asked me to go on Broadway with it but instead of going to Broadway I went to Detroit, rode up across the bridge, across the water and into Toronto and the first place I went to was Stratford. I rolled into Stratford, stayed there, found somebody to bunk with and hung out in Stratford for the whole season, then eventually I went into Toronto and was pursuing a career, ended up parking cars and just to get things going I ended

William Crain, one of the great Masters of Horror.

Crain gave William Marshall the space to sculpt a complex monster.

up doing a couple of automobile stunts, cars stunts, and there was a woman at CBC who thought I was a talent and hired me to do a couple of acting roles at CBC. And then I did some work with the NFB (National Film Board of Canada) and it went on there, stretched into seven years and at that point it was time to come

ALEXANDER: From the CBC to the NFB… to AIP!

CRAIN: [*laughs*] Yeah, exactly.

ALEXANDER: When you came back home did the BLACULA gig come up right away or did you have to spend some time picking up the pieces?

CRAIN: I didn't happen immediately, no. Let me just say that I hitchhiked across Canada at least twice, I went to Vancouver and met some people, hung out in Vancouver for a while and a buddy of mine wanted to come to LA so we drove down — which is a really wonderful trip, by the way — and we got involved with the Mayor campaign, Tom Bradley was the guy running for Mayor, so we went into that. I had a camera with me, an 8mm something, and shot footage during the campaign. It went on and on and I'm pretty sure he won. Anyway, I stayed here. I looked around; it took about a year, maybe a little more, to get things really going.

ALEXANDER: So, AIP hears that you, this young black filmmaker is in town, and they offered you BLACULA, which was at that point called COUNT BROWN'S IN TOWN. That's quite a title. What did you think of the original script?

CRAIN: I laughed at it and my first impression was I didn't want to do it. It was ridiculous and after leaving all the good theater in Toronto and stuff and I'm looking at this thing and saying, oh no! But the reality was that it was a movie, and I had a chance to direct it, so I knew I had to take it. But no, I didn't like it at first. At this time there was this wave of movies that we now call blaxploitation and AIP was making them. Understand that movies like SWEET SWEETBACK and SHAFT, they weren't *blaxploitation* films. But their success is what made AIP decide to start making movies like that, for black audiences. So yeah, we had a meeting, and I was hired to direct the picture.

ALEXANDER: How did you become aware of William Marshall? Were you friends leading up to this?

CRAIN: No, the theater group in LA was a small group and Marshall was the crème de la crème of acting here in LA. Actually, I did work with him in a theater company, it wasn't Frank Silvera's company, it was another company, and there were several actors there and I had a chance to direct him in a couple of workshop scenes so yes, I was familiar with him.

ALEXANDER: It's long been said that it was Marshall who came up with the idea of turning Count Brown into Mamuwalde, an African Prince. Is that true?

CRAIN: Yeah, well... I mean, I'll give him that, I guess. But yeah, it was both of us, really. We talked about how we wanted something more dignified and came up with the idea of it being an African Prince who gets cursed by Dracula. We wanted to make it more Shakespearean. It was a collaborative concept. But I let William say that, God bless him, God love him. It doesn't matter. Anyway, he's gone now.

ALEXANDER: Speaking of Dracula, that opening is dynamic; a really clever and powerful way to give gravitas to the dime store gimmick title. When Dracula stands over Mamuwalde's vampirized body and christens him "Blacula", a sign of a slave owner branding his slave...

CRAIN: Complete with black tears rolling down his cheeks.

ALEXANDER: Those tears!

CRAIN: Yeah, those tears... that were actually just makeup that got in his eyes!

ALEXANDER: I always suspected it was, as Orson Welles has called them, a "divine accident".

CRAIN: [*laughs*] Yeah. We were shooting this and (DP) John Stephens just kept rolling and I told him too but Charles' had that makeup irritating his eyes and he kept blinking and he started tearing up.

ALEXANDER: It adds so much, those tears. Like Dracula is so full of bloodlust and hate that he's weeping. And how about that house that was meant to double as Dracula's castle in Transylvania?

MARSHALL: Oh, we found the place up in Laurel Canyon. That community is still there, but there are houses just off of Laurel Canyon way at the top and we found an old one and yeah, we surveyed that, looked around it and it looked perfect.

ALEXANDER: Charles Macauley was one helluva Dracula...

CRAIN: He sure was. I'll never forget when he came in to my office to talk about doing it. He walks in dressed to the nines. I mean immaculate, in a slick black suit, hair

Charles Macaulay's sadistic Count cries black tears in BLACULA.

perfect. He sits down and pulls out a gold cigarette case and pulls out a cigarette and lights it and says "Okay William, what do you got for me"[*laughs*]. He was unbelievable. The real deal.

ALEXANDER: Over the years, have you ever gotten any blowback from the way the two gay interior decorators were portrayed?

CRAIN: You know, I got a pass on it. I was never attacked on it. I might have heard some things here and there but at the time it was ok, or maybe it wasn't ok, but I didn't get blowback at all.

ALEXANDER: Marshall commands such empathy in the role. Such pathos. And yet when he gets in the grip of his thirst, he becomes almost animalistic, with feral sideburns and wild eyebrows...

CRAIN: That was all Fred Phillips, one of the best makeup artists in the business. That was his work, making Mamuwalde look like that.

ALEXANDER: It's genuinely scary. Even more frightening are his vampirized victims. I would cite your vampires as the first truly animalistic vampires seen on screen. Not even in the Hammer films did the vamps act so savage…

CRAIN: That was Fred again. He was a genius.

ALEXANDER: What sets BLACULA apart from a standard exploitation picture is the sense of pathos that Mamuwalde commands. He is not a villain; he's a victim more than anything. And that ending, when he realizes he can't have his lady love and he kind of tells the cops to stand down and walks into the sun. Was that also your construction?

CRAIN: Yes, that walk up into the sun, that wonderful stairway there, where he has to make his way up the stairway, yes. That was all me and not in the original script.

ALEXANDER: Vonetta McGee is so good, in what is essentially a dual role. Can you talk a little bit about her?

CRAIN: Man, what a wonderful woman. She came along and it was almost like Charles Macauley's interview; she sat down in front of the desk, we talked, she wanted to do the role and you know, she had the look, the class, the background in terms of acting and you know, I don't remember interviewing anyone else for that role, that was it.

ALEXANDER: Ketty Lester is also wonderful in the film as the cab driver turned vampire. I love that scene when Mamuwalde first meets her and he's almost annoyed by her. He's distracted and doesn't have designs on hurting her, that is until she calls him 'boy' and that's it, then he flips out. Was that in the original script?

CRAIN: No, that was my addition. He runs down the street to find Vonetta, we set it up so Ketty's cab hits him and, yes, you nailed it, the more he talks the more angry she gets. "Look under the car… boy!". That was it! I added that, it worked. He immediately gets angry, attacks her, the hat comes off while he's attacking her which worked well. I loved that scene.

ALEXANDER: And then, when Ketty is vampirized, there's that heart-stopping slow-motion attack scene with Elisha Cook Jr…

CRAIN: Yeah, let me tell you how we did that, it's a pretty cool story. We were on location, no stage shooting. AIP had a representative on our set every day, this guy with a bow tie — God, he was horrible. Arkoff and Nicholson left me alone, but this guy… he was the worst. Anyway, there were certain things I would ask for and one of the things was for William Marshall's cape, instead of red, I wanted a steel grey inside, I think it just worked. I got some resistance for that; the classic Dracula cape is red, and there were a few other things I wanted to do and got resistance. In that scene with Ketty, the script called for her to be in the morgue in the refrigerator or freezer or whatever it was and Thalmus, once he discovers there are vampires in our midst, he calls Elisha who was the mortician and said "look, I need you to take that cab driver woman out of the freezer and I'll be there shortly, but walk out and lock the door" and what Elisha Cook does is, the script calls for him to take her out of the freezer and while he was at his desk she thaws out and just rushes across the room and attacks him.

We were shooting at an abandoned police station and when I observed the location I thought it would be great to have her run after him right down the corridor, instead of just running across the office. I told AIP that I wanted a high-speed camera because I wanted us to do the sequence in slow-motion and the answer was immediately no. I asked for it two or three times, they said no, every time. And this was about four or five days out, and on the third or fourth day they once again said "no, just shoot it with the equipment you have". If I remember this correctly, but somebody, maybe James Nicholson, said we've got some pretty good stuff here, maybe we should give him what he wants. I wasn't there so I have to relate the story the way it was told to me. I didn't think I was going to get the camera. By the way, the office setup was upstairs and we already had our cameras on the dolly and we were going to have to run this camera upstairs, and just as we were ready to roll the camera upstairs, we got upstairs, we looked at it and I talked to the camera man and said look, how fast can you crank this up, can you get it up to twenty-four frames a second, and we were going to try it, we put some film in the camera , and while we were doing that an assistant or somebody came upstairs and said "Crain, a new camera crew just showed up downstairs, they said they have a high-speed camera for you, they want to know where you are and what you want to do with it!" You know the rest. I told them to bring it upstairs on the spider, whatever that system was, but I've got to tell you, I had the door closed and had Elisha Cook outside on this pole we had attached to the framework, it looked good, and Ketty opens the door and she has to make that run from the open door and she's running while his back is to her and... well, you saw the shot, you know it.

ALEXANDER: Did the term blaxploitation ever bother you?

CRAIN: Yeah, it bothered me a bit and I found it derogatory. I mean, break it down and what do you have: the exploitation of black people.

ALEXANDER: You mentioned that movies like SHAFT and SWEET SWEETBACK were not blaxploitation films. And it's true that they were helmed by black filmmakers — as was BLACULA — whereas most of the ensuing films in the subgenre were directed by white fellas. Even SCREAM BLACULA SCREAM, the sequel... Bob Kelljan directed it, not a black artist and honestly, you can feel that...

CRAIN: Yeah, I agree. Some student could do a little doctorate on it. You've got the theme right there. A black student, a history student, could look at the difference. You know, there was this bar in LA, I forget the name of it. A real hot spot. It wasn't a black bar or anything, but a lot of black people went there and apparently Bob Kelljan used to go there and tell everyone that he directed BLACULA. Which, okay, I guess he did direct a BLACULA movie, but it wasn't BLACULA! It was SCREAM BLACULA SCREAM.

ALEXANDER: I do like SCREAM BLACULA SCREAM, mostly because Marshall is just *so* good in that role. But even as a kid, I understood why it was a lesser picture.

CRAIN: Why do you think it is?

ALEXANDER: It's trying to be a horror movie. Nothing more. BLACULA has an energy, a vibe of the streets and its place and time and a palpable subtext that is organic, not forced.

CRAIN: You're right. I mean I was just trying to make a movie. I wasn't trying to make a statement.

ALEXANDER: At least you weren't consciously doing so. And the sequel also makes the fatal mistake of making Mamuwalde a villain. As we said before, he's not a villain in BLACULA. He's a victim. He doesn't want to kill. He takes no pleasure in it. ..

CRAIN: Yeah, that's it exactly. Anyway, again, just goes to show you that can pour more money into something and make it bigger even get Pam Grier in it but it doesn't mean you can make it any better.

ALEXANDER: Why didn't you return to direct the sequel? Didn't AIP ask you to?

CRAIN: I don't know, I mean... I don't know. Maybe I rubbed some people the wrong way back then. I don't know. After the film came out and it was a huge hit, AIP called me up and said they were going another round with it. But yeah, I just wasn't into it. I only made something like $3000 for the first one, I didn't get any kick back or anything. I just didn't do it. I went another direction. Anyway, BLACULA will outlive both of us, buddy!

THE BLOOD SPATTERED BRIDE (1972)

Starring Simon Andreu, Maribel Martin, Alexandra Bastedo, Rosa Maria Rodriguez
Written by Vincente Aranda
Directed by Vincente Aranda

In the late 1960s, as the old guard died off and a new wave of filmmakers slowly, surely seeped into Hollywood, more sexually aware, violent and earthy movies made for adults became industry standard. And with American distributors acting on this sudden liberal surge, European genre filmmakers began really pushing boundaries as well, with producers taking advantage of their homegrown movies being marketed around the world and introducing more potent taboo-breaking imagery into their lurid narratives.

One of the byproducts of this unofficial "movement" was the "lesbian vampire" subgenre, movies that fetishized — and naturally, exploited — the female form and female sexual desire for a primarily male audience's titillation. But the thing is, many

Director Vincente Aranda gave us a very different female vampire in THE BLOOD SPATTERED BRIDE.

of these sorts of pictures were, by their very nature, feminist. Many of them — like my favorite of the pack, Harry Kumel's 1971 DAUGHTERS OF DARKNESS — featured young women victimized by brutal men and then finding salvation at the hands and lips of a supernatural woman who "delivers" her from the barbarity of modern society and then makes her an immortal predator, as opposed to mortal prey. And while many of these semi-progressive movies were really just using feminism as a rack to hang their cheesecake on, a swell of them (like the aforementioned DAUGHTERS) were actually potent, sophisticated and intelligently designed works of art. And perhaps the most challenging and confounding Sapphic bloodsucker shocker of them all is Spanish director Vincente Aranda's 1972 loose adaptation of J. Sheridan Le Fanu's oft-mined source story 'Carmilla', THE BLOOD SPATTERED BRIDE (aka LA NOVIA ENSANGRENATA), a movie that was mutilated for its American release but whose original cut reveals it to be a deft, cerebral bit of European psychosexual fantastique.

The film stars doe-eyed Mirabel Martin (THE BELL FROM HELL) as Susan, the blushing newlywed bride to a nameless, ruthlessly wealthy hunk (played by NIGHT OF THE SORCERERS' Simon Andreu), who ends up in his looming manor for a relaxing spate of sex and generally gushy Honeymoon rituals. But almost immediately things start to feel "off". As Susan goes to their room to unpack, a pantyhose-masked brute — who may or not be her husband — pops out from a mirrored closet, forces her down and savagely rapes her. Or does he? When minutes later her husband re-appears — Susan's dress now un-torn, the young woman sitting on the bed looking haunted — it's clear that Aranda's film's chief aim is to disorient and disturb and that its terrors unfolding here will be intimate and internal and upsetting. And for the next 80 minutes, the movie fulfills that prophecy. In spades.

As husband and wife begin to get to "know" each other better, Susan begins to see traces of the savagery in her man that she imagined in her opening sequence hallucination. She also begins seeing a beautiful, veiled woman from the corners of her eyes, lurking around the grounds. When Susan later notices that all the previously hung portraits of her husband's family's women-members have been oddly relegated to the basement, she discovers that one of those paintings is that of the same woman she keeps seeing. Said elegant femme is the late Mircalla Karnstein, who murdered her sexually voracious mate on their wedding night and was entombed alive for her crimes. At this point an already meandering, abstract melodrama falls hard into full throttle dream state experience, with Susan being visited by the ghost of Mircalla, most alarmingly in a psychedelic sequence of strobing lights, colored gels and lite-lesbian antics. And when a mysterious naked woman appears buried in the beach one day, calling herself Carmilla, the story becomes a volatile, explicit bloodlust triangle, with the lithe Carmilla — who is a manifestation of Mircalla — drawing Susan into her sexual web and convincing her to eliminate all of the men in their lives. None of this ends well, naturally, and the blood flows freely while composer Antonio Pérez Olea's nightmarish soundscape snakes around in the background.

THE BLOOD SPATTERED BRIDE is a film that demands attention, discussion and analysis. It lacks the frothy lesbo-vamp Gothic pageantry of Hammer's THE VAMPIRE LOVERS (a more direct "Carmilla" adaptation), or the breezy pop art of Jess Franco's VAMPYROS LESBOS or the purring comic book evil of DAUGHTERS OF DARKNESS, rather it feels far more abstract and dangerous. There's ample nudity on display and sometimes staggering amounts of blood, but that's not its focus. It's certainly not for the average horror fan seeking an easy swallow. It's an immersive picture, one that weaves a kind of spell that — if you let it take hold -is defiantly hard to shake.

BLOODY MOON (1981)

Starring Olivia Pascal, Christoph Moosbrugger,
Nadja Gerganhoff, Alexander Waechter
Written by Erich Tomek
Directed by Jess Franco

Beloved — and sorely missed — iconoclast Jess Franco first made his major movie mark in France with a series of crisp, sleazy and stylish black and white arthouse horror pictures like 1962's THE AWFUL DR. ORLOFF (a quote on Georges Franju's

Forget pillow talk, Jess Franco delivers pillow *shock* in BLOODY MOON.

groundbreaking sex and surgery epic EYES WITHOUT A FACE), movies that valued high contrast photography, graphic violence and mild, soon-to-be abundant, female nudity. In the ensuing decades the tirelessly prolific Franco would make scores of increasingly graphic, often very personal, jazz influenced (Franco was also an accomplished composer and musician) sonnets to sex, violence and voyeurism, playing with color and working with budgets both high and low in any country that would fund his filmmaking fetish.

Which brings me to BLOODY MOON, an early '80s German financed (the original title was DIE SAGE DES TODES or THE SAW OF DEATH) bloodbath made in the wake of the slasher craze sparked by John Carpenter's HALLOWEEN and juiced up by the considerably more explicit FRIDAY THE 13th and its endless stalk-and-stab ilk. But the seriously bent BLOODY MOON (whose ample but klutzy murders landed it onto the "video nasties" list in the UK) is so much more than simply a routine masked maniac shocker. Why? Because it was made by Franco of course and, as any serious scholar of Jess's work knows, no matter how dodgy and cheap the more downmarket Franco films could be, there was almost always something there that was uniquely his. A lazy-lidded energy, a leering point of view. Something.

The attractively greasy looking BLOODY MOON opens on a spectacularly sickening murder at a Spanish girls school by a completely un-spectacularly made-up lunatic (Alexander Waechter). Five years later, pretty young student Angela (sex film starlet

Olivia Pascal) has taken up residence in the same room where the said slaughter went down and to make matters eerier, the cheese-faced killer has been released from the loony bin, apparently none too reformed.

Sooner than later, a spate of increasingly sadistic killings kick into high gear with all manner of lovely lass getting revoltingly ripped to ribbons. Is it old Velveeta-puss wearing the dollar store black gloves that pop into frame before each offing? Is it his comely sister with whom he shares a rather, um, close relationship? Before Franco's 90-minute mess winds down, all questions will be answered, and many tummies will be well turned...

Now, as I mentioned, Franco made a staggering number of films, including such acknowledged classics like VENUS IN FURS, SHE KILLED IN ECSTASY, FACELESS and VAMPYROS LESBOS, so you might be wondering why I've chosen to muse on BLOODY MOON. The answer is simple. Plenty of people still — despite exhaustive critical appraisal — dislike the work of Jess Franco, laughingly labeling him a hack. And while I'll never argue that the man has made more than his share of what might be viewed as duds, when someone gives him a bit of time, money and space, Franco had few peers; a wizard at making stylish, eccentric and obsessive films. BLOODY MOON has moments of that inimitable, free-form Franconian vision and, despite its budgetary and narrative failings, it's a slop-bucket full of lurid fun.

By his own admission, Franco signed on to the project under the promise that his craven producers had art-rock super group Pink Floyd attached to compose the score. As this was the early '80s and the already legendary band had recently achieved their commercial apex with the double disc, chart topping 1979 album *The Wall*, it would be obvious to anyone with any shade of cynicism, insight or common sense that they would never, ever have their name glued to a grubby European slasher movie directed by the guy who made THE BARE BREASTED COUNTESS. But again, Franco just wanted to work and so he proceeded in hopes that such boasts might be the icing on the gig.

Instead of a Floyd score, BLOODY MOON features music by someone named Gerhard Heinz, a German born tunesmith who tries his best to mimic a David Gilmour-esque guitar-based, psych-rock sound and for the most part, succeeds. Many fans and critics have cited this score as the picture's most offensive element, but I rather like it; it's bizarre, bombastic and dirty and it works. When an unlucky lady gets her head sawed off in the film's most notorious (and delightfully fake) gore sequence, those wailing guitars and skanky bass-lines sound awesome.

Is it Franco's masterpiece? Far from it. But BLOODY MOON is pure, sleazy, upbeat Jess gore-gold. It's a document of his kind of creative innocence, a sloppy snapshot of a guy who just loved making movies fast and frantic and managed to weave his way into pop culture legend by never giving up, never stepping off that ladder. Good on him and God rest him.

BRIMSTONE (2016)

Starring Dakota Fanning, Guy Pearce, Emilia Jones, Kit Harrington
Written by Martin Koolhoven
Directed by Martin Koolhoven

There's something about the American western that bleeds beautifully past the margins of the horror film. It's the elemental nature of the former genre; the idea of lawlessness, of the struggle against the elements, of being naked and exposed and desperate in an unformed world where life has little meaning and the concept of a potentially "civilized" society barely held upright by the spine of religion. The Italians — Leone, Corbucci et al — first exploited the Gothic, *Grand Guignol* nature of the western throughout the 1960s and later, Chilean surrealist Alejandro Jodorowsky took it further with the metaphysical eastern/western EL TOPO while Sam Peckinpah dragged it home again with his string of squib-happy, brutal oaters. Then, in the waning days of the 1970s, the western died, replaced by harder horror films and contemporary action films, with young people of the time being less interested in the brutality of the wild frontier.

But in recent years, the western has returned to the modern film and television landscape. Witness contemporary pictures like BONE TOMAHAWK, HOSTILES, and HBO's perverse, profound, mutation of the genre with their ultra-violent, hyper-sexual remount of Michael Crichton's WESTWORLD.

Nestled among the pack of nouveau wild west-set shockers is Dutch filmmaker Martin Koolhoven's BRIMSTONE, an arthouse horror morality tale western that blends the European flavor of the Spaghetti Western with a distinctly Dutch dark wit and the sort of feminine-centric psyche-horror that Danish auteur Lars von Trier trades in. And there's fluid. Plenty of spurting, seeping fluid, most of it unleashed by eruptions of unflinchingly hideous violence. But beneath its cracked baby skulls, vicious rape, murder, outhouse hangings etc., there's a point to BRIMSTONE. It's not a wallow in savagery, though it is one of the most savage films I've seen in some time. Instead, it uses the idea of religion run rampant and exploited by evil to paint a portrait of pain, suffering, debasement, and human vulgarity. And yet, at its core, it's really about strength and courage during times of impossible atrocity. It's like a satanic version of THE PASSION OF THE CHRIST by way of von Trier's BREAKING THE WAVES and Antonia Bird's RAVENOUS.

And like the aforementioned horror-western RAVENOUS, Guy Pearce is one of the stars of BRIMSTONE albeit in a radically different kind of role. Here, he's a steroidal, possibly supernatural riff on Robert Mitchum's Harry Powell in NIGHT OF THE HUNTER by way of Vincent Price's Matthew Hopkins in WITCHFINDER GENERAL; a mad, sadistic and hypocritical sadist who uses his position to manipulate and pervert the natural world and redefine its rules to suit his nature. Pearce plays the role with an Abe Lincoln beard

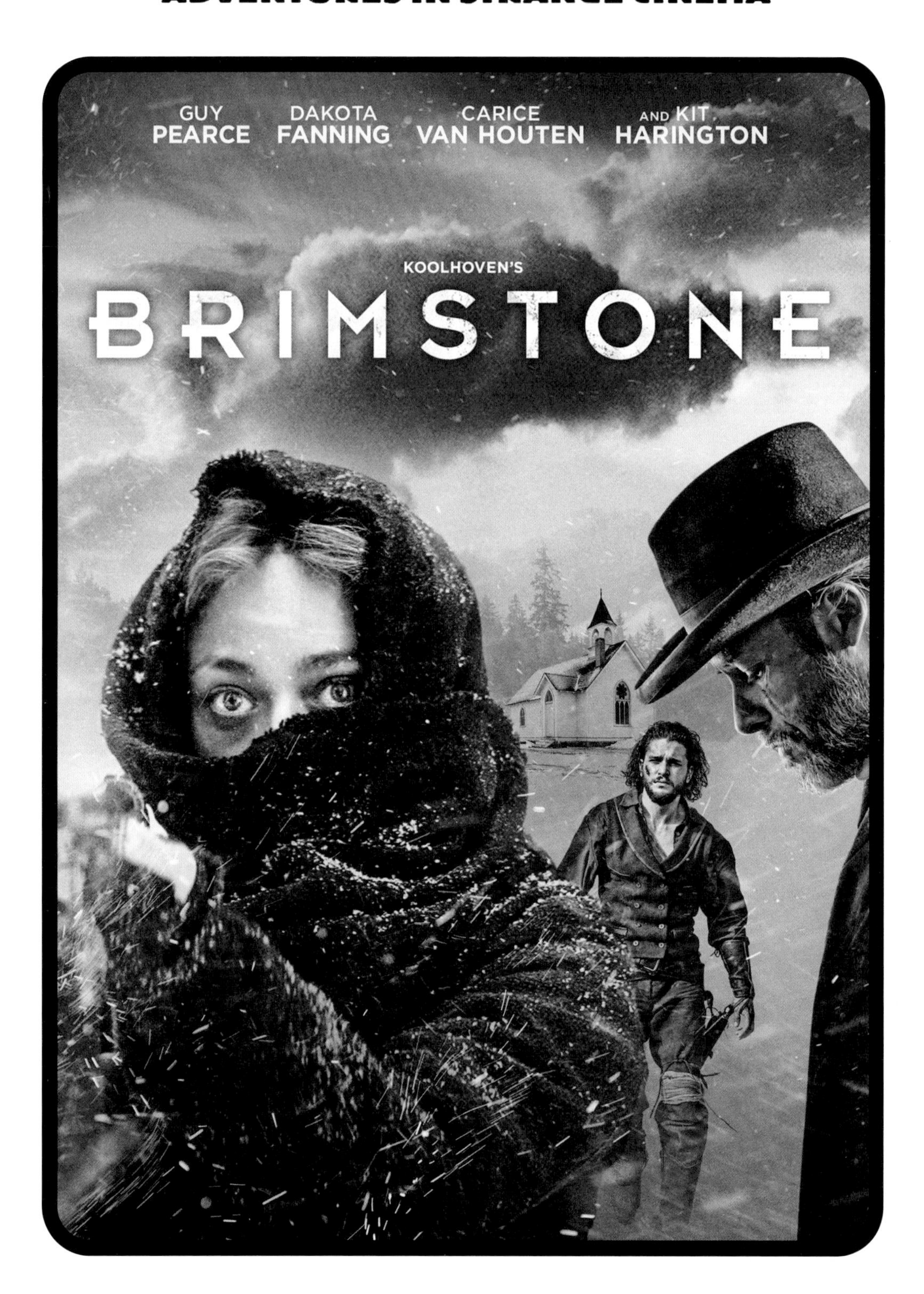
GUY PEARCE
DAKOTA FANNING
CARICE VAN HOUTEN
AND KIT HARINGTON
KOOLHOVEN'S
BRIMSTONE

and vaguely Dutch accent and he's a fearsome, ferocious, and absolutely horrifying presence. As an aside, one must marvel at just how fantastic an actor he truly is, how he can easily play any kind of character, monstrous or meek, and make it believable.

Pearce's reverend spends most of BRIMSTONE's running time pursuing and attempting to decimate Dakota Fanning's mute frontier woman Liz, with whom he shares a diabolical past. What that past is reveals itself in a serpentine narrative that starts in the middle, goes backwards, stops and then proceeds forwards again. Koolhoven deftly makes this episodic structure work. It's not a gimmick; it's an essential component of the film's power to disorient.

To reveal too much of the story would de-fang the film's power, but just be aware that BRIMSTONE is the strongest of tonics and will likely offend and upset many. Some have accused it as being misogynistic, but it's far from it. It's bold in that it is actually pro-female and portrays the power of women in the face of the tyranny of men, especially during periods where they were far less protected and respected. Fanning — who acts with her trembling body and haunted eyes in an incredible performance — is a creature whose fate in Hell is seemingly sealed and who must fight and lose everything in order to clean the slate and save herself. What she endures is unthinkable and hard to endure; for her character and for us, the audience.

Beautifully photographed and armed with a pulsating, emotional score by Junkie XL, BRIMSTONE isn't just a western, it's an essential contemporary religio-horror movie and Pearce's Devil-preacher is something ripped from your worst nightmare.

This is a work of the blackest and yet most visionary cinematic art.

INTERVIEW: GUY PEARCE

CHRIS ALEXANDER: At first glance, it appears BRIMSTONE might be another extreme Guy Pearce shock-western like THE PROPOSITION or RAVENOUS. But it's not. It's something different. Your character, the Reverend... well, he's a monster. I tried hard to find an ounce of good in him. I couldn't. Did you?

GUY PEARCE: No... no... I didn't. And I struggled with that myself. I was talking to somebody recently, in fact, about what a challenge it was to make him three dimensional and I'm not quite sure if I succeeded. Obviously, for the purpose of the film, we made a character that was just relentless, in his beliefs and his pursuit of his daughter. But it really was a challenge to present what he believed to be an understandable point of view. When you play someone who is evil or psychopathic, it's always hard to make him fully realized. Is there anything good there? I don't know. It's tricky. I think there are some elements there that I tried and whether or not they actually work in the film, I'm not sure [*laughs*].

The Reverend (Guy Pearce) preaches his grim gospel.

ALEXANDER: Well, there is the moment where he's self-flagellating. It shows his extreme belief. So, I guess no matter what he is, the Reverend is convinced what he is doing is right...

PEARCE: That's right. It's funny, whenever I play a bad guy, people ask "would *you* like this character?" I didn't like this character. But the key is to find something they believe in and just run with it. And if there's sympathy there, if they've been tortured as a child or whatever it is, you can try to keep your audience on your side to some degree. It's difficult to keep an audience engaged unless they see some vulnerability or some weakness.

ALEXANDER: I've read some rather misguided criticisms of the film that accuse it of being misogynist or citing its exploitation of religion as crass. Are you a religious man and did you have any qualms about Koolhoven's use of religion?

PEARCE: Not in the slightest and I would happily sit down with anyone who has questions about using religion to exploit this story. I myself have strong views about the extreme way religion is used to justify transgressive behavior out there in the world. I'm very interested in religion, and I think it can be a fantastic tool for people to come to terms with the mysteries and tragedies we must come to terms with every day in our lives. But at the same time, it's a bit like the internet. It can be used for good or for evil. So, I have no questions about the fact that there are people out there whose religious beliefs have taken them outside of real-life — whatever real-life might be — and therefore enabled them to kill or rape or repress or maim or just ignore other people and their own sense of compassion.

ALEXANDER: I already mentioned Antonia Bird's RAVENOUS — one of my favorite films, incidentally — and like that film, BRIMSTONE's lines between horror and western are essentially non-existent. Why do you think the two genres bleed so well into each other?

PEARCE: Probably because if you throw someone out into the desert, they're going to feel some sense of horror anyway, so if you set a story that is bleak and life threatening in a landscape that is also bleak and life threatening, then you double your odds. You're creating a frightening world. But that said, some of the most frightening movies are set in a domestic, familiar house. Which is more horrifying because it's safe.

ALEXANDER: I think your fan base appreciates you most because, well, there is no definitive 'Guy Pearce' role. You defy expectations in your choices. That said, you sure do have your share of dark roles on the resume. Do you seek out the dark stuff or does it find you?

PEARCE: [*laughs*] Well, I think we're doing a kind of malevolent tango together, where sometimes they're in the lead and sometimes I'm in the lead. I do find that when I start a script and the first few pages take me somewhere that's bleak and unusual, taking me to the darkest corners of my imagination, I'm very excited to finish the script and see where it ends up. I want to see if it can hold that kind of intensity. Many don't. Often the first act is written very well, and then it falls apart. But something like THE PROPOSITION and RAVENOUS don't. And by the way, I'm glad you're a fan of RAVENOUS. There's something about the dark nature of ourselves that I'm drawn to. And it depends how that darkness is presented.

ALEXANDER: BRIMSTONE is Martin Koolhoven's first English language film and yet I notice he's put his name above the title. This is "Koolhoven's BRIMSTONE"; is he an auteur director?

PEARCE: I'd say so. In Amsterdam, Martin is a highly respected director who has made many Dutch films. My girlfriend — who I have since had a baby with — has worked with Martin four times in fact. He's an excellent filmmaker. Brimstone is probably the darkest film that he's made. I'm not sure why he put his name above the title, or if that's connected to his reputation in the Netherlands. But he's a very good filmmaker, an experienced filmmaker and he's very unusual. You know, every time you make a film you create a relationship with the director. Some of them are incredibly inspiring and some are just flat and dull. And Martin falls into the former category, absolutely.

INTERVIEW: MARTIN KOOLHOVEN

CHRIS ALEXANDER: Why is it that Europeans seem to make the best films about the American west?

MARTIN KOOLHOVEN: Well, the thing is of course that the moment that you say that, I start thinking about some of the best fucking westerns ever, stuff by Sam Peckinpah, John Ford, you know. I think that for every great European filmmaker that made a great western, there are two great American directors as well. So I don't know if its true that they're better, but I agree that they are very good. My favorite film is ONCE UPON A TIME IN THE WEST and that of course is made by an Italian filmmaker (Sergio Leone). So, I think that somehow a European director is more aware of making a movie not in a certain setting but exploring the very DNA of a country. You know what I mean?

ALEXANDER: You nailed it. They have an objective view of a culture; less mythological and more caustic.

KOOLHOVEN: Yeah.

ALEXANDER: So, you mentioned ONCE UPON A TIME IN THE WEST and certainly, Sergio Leone used Morricone's music to grand effect in that one. And here, you worked with electronic music icon Junkie XL...

Director Martin Koolhoven and actor Paul Anderson on the set of BRIMSTONE.

Koolhoven understands the horror that lurks in the hearts of all men.

KOOLHOVEN: Oh yeah. I met Tom — his real name is Tom Holkenborg — I met him, I think, six years ago through a mutual friend and we started talking about film music and I told him what I thought film music should do. And I remember the discussion. I like to use music to the full extent, whereas some modern filmmakers don't. At some point he heard I was doing a western and he asked if he could read the script. I gave it to him and he said "I have to do this movie." So it was agreed. The way it worked was that we talked about it, what it was about and I discussed the musical influences I wanted it to have. We started sending a lot of music to each other that we thought would be relevant and so we tried to get a musical language between us. We sent lots of Bach. He had a specific piece he wanted to put in there. Bach's music was very much based in religion and that made sense, considering the story. And Bach was an influence on Morricone and Bernard Herrman, so it felt right. I wanted the score to be old fashioned and yet still modern and Tom is a very modern composer so it was interesting employing that classical sound and having it filtered through his sensibilities. Normally when you do a movie, the soundtrack comes last. But not here. The music was made while we were filming and editing and so it influenced the edit and the edit influenced it. It was a wonderful process and I have never done it this way.

ALEXANDER: And that's the way Morricone and Leone did it too...

KOOLHOVEN: Exactly. But somehow because of the economics of a movie and the time you need to make one, it's just not something that ever happens anymore, it's something no one does. But we said, hey, we *are* going to do it this way. There was no ego. It was a real collaboration.

ALEXANDER: Now BRIMSTONE is many things. It's a western and a horror film and an allegory and a thriller and... well, it's lots of things. I loved the original poster, the monochrome black and white with the etched in cross, like a Lars von Trier poster. But the way the studio marketed the film made it look like it's just a straight-up western. How do you feel about that?

KOOLHOVEN: Well... [*clears throat*]... uh... let me be politically correct here and say that I had *something* to do with the first poster we did and I was not involved in the American one. At all. And maybe that says something [*laughs*].

ALEXANDER: Many have cited this, and I presume it was by intent, but there's a heavy sense of Charles Laughton's NIGHT OF THE HUNTER in BRIMSTONE.

KOOLHOVEN: Yes, there's no denying that. I mean, I think there are more differences than there are likenesses, but if you do a movie about such a dangerous preacher, it's very hard not to be influenced by NIGHT OF THE HUNTER. Like, if you do a movie where someone gets killed in the shower, you cannot help but compare that to PSYCHO. I'm always afraid of referencing other films when making a movie because you must be true to the characters and as soon as you reference other movies, you feel thrown out of the movie. But in BRIMSTONE for example, there's a scene with a character and a rifle on the porch and I knew while I was shooting it that it was right out of NIGHT OF THE HUNTER, but I felt that if I changed it, then it would not be honest. Because it grew organically out of the process and so I went with it. It is a reference to that classic sure, but it's there naturally. And I think NIGHT OF THE HUNTER is one of the greatest movies ever made, by the way...

BYZANTIUM (2012)

Starring Saoirse Ronan, Gemma Arterton, Sam Riley, Johnny Lee Miller
Written by Moira Buffini
Directed by Neil Jordan

When one mutters about who belongs in the fabled "Masters of Horror" club, the usual suspects are spoken. You know. Hitchcock, Romero, Hooper, Carpenter, Craven, Cronenberg. All those guys. And yes, they belong in the lexicon of legend. That's inarguable. But it's unfortunately rare to see Irish director Neil Jordan's name show up on lists like this and I'm really not sure why. Jordan is one of the great directors, full stop, a master of all genre. But his work in darker fantasy has exemplified the Gothic ideal and, most importantly, he's one of the few horror helmers who bring a genuine feeling of the *fairy tale* to his bloody landscapes. He trades in movies about lonely outsiders lost in treacherous but beautiful landscapes and his movies are always propelled by a simmering eroticism that bubbles under the surface of every frame. Look at his 1984 breakthrough movie, the Angela Carter-adapted allegorical werewolf masterpiece THE COMPANY OF WOLVES. With its probing into a young girl's burgeoning sexual awakening pushed into a Little Red Riding Hood tale of flesh-eating, horny lycanthropes and girls who follow them to ruin, the movie still has no peer. There's nothing like it. Similarly, there's few films like Jordan's THE BUTCHER BOY either, or the troubled but still visually interesting HIGH SPIRITS or the transgender noir THE CRYING GAME. And certainly, his 1994 adaptation of Anne Rice's INTERVIEW WITH THE VAMPIRE is not only the best cinematic representation of the author to date, it's one of the greatest vampire movies ever made.

But as good as INTERVIEW is, Jordan's bloodsucking best boasts also apply to a more recent effort that sort of slipped through the cracks and is rarely raved about when people wax fondly on the undead. That film is 2012's BYZANTIUM, a lush expansion of Moira Buffini's play *A Vampire Story* that — like INTERVIEW — uses vampirism to unfold a tale of loneliness and the eternal search for people to connect to people, as well as

Elanor (Saoirse Ronan) gets baptized in blood.

the nurturing but ultimately toxic nature of family. But here, in this gauzy, sensual phantasmagoria, as in COMPANY, it's the *feminine* that feeds the narrative and BYZANTIUM's bloody, beating heart speaks of the agony of women and what they must endure to navigate a world that's been hard-wired by men for centuries to keep them in their "place."

BYZANTIUM stars the great Saoirse Ronan (BROOKLYN) as Eleanor, a kindly, quiet and isolated teen living on the skids outside of London who has a sanguinary secret that she's sworn to keep. While her mother Clara (THE GIRL WITH ALL THE GIFTS' Gemma Arterton, in what is a thus far career-best performance) strips at a seedy local club, Eleanor hand-writes her life story, tearing the pages out of her diary and throwing them to the wind from her slum tenement balcony. When a frail old man collects the scribblings, he confronts the girl, revealing that he's ready to die... and wants to go by Eleanor's hand. Literally. Because Eleanor is indeed an ancient vampire and she kills by a growing thumbnail that swells like a phallus when her bloodlust is aroused. But Eleanor is not a monster. Rather, she's tempered her gift to serve as a sort of *angel of death* to the aged and withered, consensually euthanizing her victims after revealing her true nature.

Truth is something Eleanor craves. She's carried the weight of her condition for centuries, a dark gift bestowed upon her by her mother and one she's unable to share. She wants to fit in. She wants a life, even though she knows that's impossible. She wants roots and companionship and she's wearied of living a lie. Clara, however, is the opposite. The elder vampire is — on the surface — a banshee who kills ruthlessly and keeps her daughter on the run, from mortal authorities and from some sort of secret cabal of men whose aim is to hunt her and presumably destroy her. She prowls the night posing as a peeler and a prostitute, using her eternally perfect body to drain men of their fluids — red and otherwise — and their money so she and Eleanor can continue to move freely through the world. But when Clara meets a sweet, sad John at a carnival who is in mourning after the passing of his elderly mother, she treats him with kindness, empathy. It's her weakness. As a mother who will stop at nothing to protect her child, she is moved by this man's condition. Even better, when she learns that he has inherited his late mother's crumbling seaside hotel/boarding house hotel — the Byzantium of the title — she uses sex and companionship to make the man let her and Eleanor stay with him. Soon, Clara's set the hotel up as a bordello, where she rescues and liberates street girls and lets them conduct their business in the comfort of the dusty, neon-pulsing palace.

And while Eleanor follows her mother yet again, she has hit a wall and begins writing her life story again, this time with intent to share it with the world. That sad, serpentine story of Clara's miserable life and Eleanor's baptism into vampirism is related via alarmingly beautiful and evocative flashback sequences that mirror the women's contemporary situation while fleshing out and justifying Clara's feral, calculated nature. Meanwhile, a sickly young man (played by the always sickly-looking Caleb Landry-Jones) has fallen in love with Eleanor and the feeling is slowly, surely becoming mutual.

Byzantium is a marvel. A deep, dark tragedy about forgotten, damaged people who must scrape and scavenge to survive. And God forbid if said people on the fringe are female, where their bodies are exploited and used for fleeting pleasure and casual abuse and their dreams and hopes obliterated. Such is Clara's plight, a gentle girl sold into prostitution who endures untold abuse but who finds a purpose and reason to soldier on after the birth of her child and later, is forced to steal her liberation from a sect of male vampires who don't take kindly to a lowly woman among their privileged midst. But Clara uses her power for one purpose: to protect her child. Always. Forever and ever. And that's why the gorgeously acted, photographed (by Sean Bobbitt), scored (by Javier Navarrete) and produced BYZANTIUM is really about. The supernatural bond between mother and daughter at what berserk lengths a parent will go to in order to protect their child. Of course, in life and in BYZANTIUM, there comes a time when the child becomes the parent, and when that child begins to pull away to start their own story, the parent simply cannot abide. They've structured their lives around a dynamic that was built on protection but inevitably dissolves into control and fear of losing that control. And Jordan profoundly places Clara and Eleanor's plight high above any simplistic horror movie trappings.

Which is not to say BYZANTIUM doesn't deliver the frissons. Blood sprays freely, heads are crudely ripped off, wrists are opened, necks torn asunder and — in the film's most striking sequences — blood flows from a sacred shrine waterfall, bathing newly-born vampires. And despite the film's focus on feminism, Jordan never shies away from ensuring Arterton's effortless sexuality is deified. She's a stunning woman and here, stalking the night in impossible heels and leather pants, or bust-pumping corsets or Victorian robes, she's an iconic erotic presence. This is a thinking person's Hammer horror film, ultimately.

If you're a vampire cinema junkie and you haven't seen BYZANTIUM, fix that problem immediately. But you don't have to be a fang-fetishist to fall in love with Jordan's evocative masterpiece. This is a movie that demands to be just as immortal as its startling heroines.

THE CABINET OF CALIGARI (1962)

Starring Glynis Johns, Daniel O' Herlihy, Richard Davalos, Constance Ford
Written by Robert Bloch
Directed by Roger Kay

There's a song by Trent Reznor's electro-outfit Nine Inch Nails, the B-side to the single Sin; it's a grinding cover version of the classic Queen song Get Down Make Love, that opens with one of the most memorable film samples in industrial music history.

Jane (Glynis Johns) finds herself trapped in a Freudian nightmare.

It goes like this:

How old were you when you first let a man make love to you?

Next, who was he?

Next, how did you feel at the time?

Next, how did you feel afterward?

What did you feel, what did you think, were you pleased, frightened, ecstatic, disgusted?

What did he say, what words did you speak, that's what I want to know, now, tell me, now, now, all of it, now, yes! Yes!

For years, no one I knew had a clue as to the origins of that sample.

I certainly hadn't the foggiest idea.

Eventually, I forgot about both the sample and the song.

That is until a few years ago, when I found a copy of the 1962 film THE CABINET OF CALIGARI in a discount bin at a used record store.

That's right, the 1962 film THE CABINET OF CALIGARI. Note the absence of the word "Doctor".

I had no idea this film existed. Did you?

Taking it home excitedly and excitedly researching it, I learned much of its origins and, while watching and grooving on it, I was floored when, in the middle, the film's titular antagonist leans into his victim and barks out that very same NIИ sample.

So, there it is. Mystery solved. But there's much, much more to THE CABINET OF CALIGARI than a simple '90s alterna-pop music sound bite.

The film was directed by TV vet Roger Kay and produced by THE LAST MAN ON EARTH's Robert Lippert, an adaptation of an untitled Robert Bloch (author of the book on which PSYCHO was based) screenplay that was written in the wake of PSYCHO's success. Lippert had acquired the rights to the original, groundbreaking 1920 German expressionist silent film by Robert Wiene, THE CABINET OF DR. CALIGARI and, because of this, Lippert saddled that screenplay with the CALIGARI title, much to Bloch's dismay.

The resulting film is not a remake of the Wiene film per se, rather it is its own, deeply strange beast, infused with elements of the original picture by director Kay, enough that it is most certainly a kind of companion experience. And while not a classic, it is most assuredly a deeply interesting picture and offers many, many arch — and even gently obscene — pleasures. And, of course, that breathlessly crude sample.

The film begins in true Freudian style (the movie absolutely owes even more to Freud than in Wiene's film), with a POV shot of a moving car penetrating and then exiting a long, dark tunnel, an obvious allusion to sex. When daylight illuminates the frame, we see a beautiful woman (the elegant British actress Glynis Johns, only two years away from MARY POPPINS) driving; her lovely bare, shoeless legs rubbing against each other in a series of hazy, lush dissolves. It's a deliciously lurid, liquid opening that echoes PSYCHO in both texture and aesthetic; the first of many nods to

Bloch's most famous work.

Johns plays Jane, a seemingly happy yet secretly, deeply neurotic, sexually repressed femme fatale who, after that car winds up in a ditch, wanders in a daze to nearby house (shades again of Janet Leigh's circumstantial arrival at the Bates Motel). The looming home an impossibly huge manor lorded over by the leering, educated and more than vaguely sinister Dr. Caligari (the great Dan O'Herlihy, who is even more creepy here than he is in HALLOWEEN III) and his long-suffering personal assistant (Constance Ford, who was equally miserable and put-upon in the classic THE TWILIGHT ZONE episode "Uncle Simon").

Jane agrees to stay the night at the house, a decision she soon regrets; come the dawn, she'll realize that she — and the other bizarre characters that inhabit the house — are prisoners of the malevolent MD, both physically and psychically.

There really isn't much more to the plot of THE CABINET OF CALIGARI, rather the film serves as an ultra-sexualized exercise in pop-psychology and increasingly bizarre, hallucinatory exchanges of dialogue. The surrealism in CALIGARI is mainly milked from these word-wars, with Caligari battering Jane to the point of breaking, insisting on details about how she orgasms and other lurid personal intel (see again, that sample).

But the disorienting nature of the conversations and oddball character relations aren't the only appealingly distorted elements of the film. Though it doesn't aspire to be a full-blown expressionist picture, it contains many ingredients that both tie it to the Wiene film (groove on that angled-stripe-doorway climax!), most tellingly in its kinky set design, with Caligari's office a staggering habitat that has a glass door that opens into a revolving door and larger than life desk. It's not insane enough to channel any sort of cross-eyed, dream-logic grandeur but it's ample weird enough to be memorable.

Also of note is the stunning, savagely widescreen 2:35:1 photography by PSYCHO's John L. Russell. Almost the entire film is shot in long takes, with characters walking in and out of frame; rarely do you find more than two actors on screen at any time. That technique coupled with the dialogue-based nature of the film, gives the impression that you are indeed watching live theater, appropriate since the very birth of the German expressionist movement and the original film stemmed from the stage.

Ultimately, THE CABINET OF CALIGARI is a strange and mesmerizing work but certainly not for all tastes. As a horror film, it's not likely to please many, as the film is short on graphic death of any kind, and actual suspense is minimal. But it does indeed harness some sort of strange power, like a post-modern smoothing out of the landmark original film, an impression of the expression, if you will.

And man, its final scene is a real doozy.

Find it if you can and tell me your thoughts.

And in the meantime, get down. Make love.

Honey Whitlock (Melanie Griffith) accepts her fate as a "cinema terrorist".

CECIL B. DEMENTED (2000)

Starring Melanie Griffith, Stephen Dorff, Alicia Witt, Adrian Grenier
Written by John Waters
Directed by John Waters

Years before every other movie making its way to the multiplex was a bloated billion-dollar superhero blowout, John Waters was already curling his pencil-moustache draped lip at the stale state of mainstream cinema. Naturally, the iconoclastic writer/director had long been pushing the boundaries of good taste. He made his name by cheerfully savaging America's sanctimonious moral codes, taking great pleasure in punching the piss out of pop culture puritans in the process. But back in the 1970s, when Waters and his tribe of "Dreamlanders" were grinding out gonzo vulgarian comedies like MULTIPLE MANIACS, PINK FLAMINGOS and FEMALE TROUBLE, audiences were hungry for his sort of cinematic transgressions. By the time the decade dripped into the more conservative 1980s, Waters smartly found ways to progress his vision by tucking his more provocative gimmicks away, cannily hiding his commentaries within weird films that never overtly strayed beyond PG-13 ratings, starting with his juggernaut hit HAIRSPRAY and continuing with pictures like CRY-BABY and PECKER.

But by the time the milquetoast '90s gasped its last, and a paranoid planet braced itself for the millennium, Waters decided to sharpen his blade a bit, creating a punk rock bit of anti-Hollywood savagery that gleefully skewered the dismally safe landscape of American cinema and reveled in the sort of in-your-face sex and violence shenanigans that many of his obsessives though he'd long left in the dust.

Indeed, 2020's CECIL B. DEMENTED came roaring out of the gate, armed with a killer cast of established performers, "Dreamlander" regulars, a rogues' gallery of up-and-coming talents and, as its co-lead, a major, Oscar winning actress. The film stars Stephen Dorff as Cecil B. Demented, a "cinema terrorist" who, along with his army of tattooed and horny revolutionaries, wages war against mainstream moviemaking by kidnapping fading, narcissistic Hollywood diva Honey Whitlock (Melanie Griffith) and forcing her at gunpoint to star in their *verité,* guerilla counterculture indie flick meltdown. Initially horrified at both her predicament and the tribe of maniacs holding her captive, Honey slowly, surely accepts and embraces her fate as a gun-toting, blood thirsty and system smashing cult movie Queen. Especially since the real time "reviews" for her performance are so damned good...

Celebrated by some, derided by many and ignored by everyone else, CECIL B. DEMENTED was a shock for the mainstream critics who had begun to embrace the more cuddly post-HAIRSPRAY Water and even embraced the harder but still somewhat accessible madness of SERIAL MOM (which is arguably his best film) and they punished it accordingly. Twenty years later, watching the movie is a revelation. It's a masterwork of madness, a delicate balancing act where Waters gets to be almost as politically incorrect as he was during his early years while also packaging his celluloid bullet with an attractive slickness, an act that in and of itself is a mirror of Cecil's own revolution.

CECIL B. DEMENTED is a wild, hilarious, horrifying and almost prophetic epic. Viva la Revolution!

INTERVIEW: JOHN WATERS

CHRIS ALEXANDER: Let's get right to the point: CECIL B. DEMENTED has just gotten better with the passage of time.

JOHN WATERS: I agree, and CECIL is the one I always pick when I have to appear somewhere because I really like it too.

ALEXANDER: Do you think it was a bit *ahead* of its time? Certainly, the critics weren't receptive to it, generally speaking.

WATERS: The critics weren't kind to *any* of my movies in the beginning!

ALEXANDER: So negative reviews have never really bothered you?

Honey gets ready for her closeup.

WATERS: I always read reviews, I always wanted to get good ones and the bad ones are the ones you remember. But you know, in the beginning I built a career on bad reviews. But it was a different time; it was "us versus them". The critics then were all straight, and that didn't mean sexually, that meant drug wise. Back then, the bad reviews from the square critics really helped. Now, there are no critics stupid enough to give me that, so as it went along, the critics realized that, so they would try and say other insults. Like, I wasn't the underground Russ Meyer or Frank Perry. Every once in a while they would come up with a new way that was much smarter to insult the film. Certainly, they hurt, but that's part of it you know; get your head out of the oven if you don't like the heat. Bad reviews and good reviews. I've had them my whole life and sometimes you can use the bad reviews. Roger Ebert always gave me the meanest reviews then would come over to me at festivals and say "Hi John, would you be on my panel?" and I thought, I'm a professional, not a masochist.

ALEXANDER: Ebert was a funny guy because we all know how he wrote Russ Meyer movies and yet, in those days, he had such an open disdain for exploitation cinema. It was confounding.

WATERS: Yeah, I mean her wrote BEYOND THE VALLEY OF THE DOLLS, which was Russ's best work, if you ask me. I remember what he said about CECIL B. DEMENTED. I was in Cannes and he said "Oh my god, you're suicidal, why would you ever make a movie about someone who's making a bad movie?"

ALEXANDER: Leonard Maltin was another famous critic who trashed the picture.

WATERS: Yeah, but those were the kind of critics that wrote for *T.V. Guide*. It's like getting a mean review in *Parade* magazine, the Sunday section. You don't expect that they're going to like it and really, I'm not saying everyone should like it and I'm not saying they're wrong, I'm saying the film was not made for them.

ALEXANDER: You were kind of on a roll there for a while making more family friendly movies that muted more of your more obvious transgressions.

WATERS: Well, I don't know, there was A DIRTY SHAME, an NC-17 parody of a sexploitation movie. That wasn't very family friendly...

ALEXANDER: No, but that chased CECIL. You went through that period post-HAIRSPRAY where critics were expecting a more PG-13 level of Waters, stuff like CRY-BABY and PECKER. And then I think when CECIL came around it seemed some of your early fans were saying things like, "it's his return to form". Does that ever bother you? That some people have had expectations of what they think your work should be like?

WATERS: Well, you know you have to just look at the context when each film came out and what the films were meant to be. Expectations don't bother me. I really just only care if the films last or not and if they all still play.

ALEXANDER: And they do.

WATERS: Yeah, and I mean, who would have thought those early movies would ever show on *television*? I used to have a guaranteed "TV filter". But today, almost every movie I've made, from MULTIPLE MANIACS on up, has played on TV somewhere.

ALEXANDER: Do you own all those early movies, John?

WATERS: Yes I own all of them except DESPERATE LIVING, which I own maybe eighty percent of. From then on, no. Others are involved. But before that, all of them, yes. But no matter what, the people that worked with me, those eight people that were the core of Dreamland, still get twenty-five percent of the profits to this day. I just sent them all a FEMALE TROUBLE check. A lot of them are dead, so their sisters get it, their relatives get it, which is better than they probably would have gotten if it was a SAG movie.

ALEXANDER: Back to CECIL. It seems to have come hot on the heels of PECKER but if I'm not mistaken it was actually in gestation long before PECKER, correct? Wasn't it in development for a while?

WATERS: Oh god, I remember they were all in development at the same time. But oddly enough, I got a development deal for every one of these movies including CECIL, which was, if I remember correctly, all French money, which was very different. We made the deal in Cannes, it was a dream come true. I was this crazy kid from Baltimore — well, not a kid anymore — but here I was in Cannes signing deals on napkins, the cliché thing, the best thing that can ever happen. Yeah, they all had development deals, every one of them, including A DIRTY SHAME, which today would be much, much harder to get.

ALEXANDER: Let's talk a little bit about CECIL B. DEMENTED's cast of crazy characters. How did you choose which auteur director each character associated and branded themselves with?

WATERS: I still think that would make dating easier if every person, when they turned twenty-one, had to get a tattoo of their favorite director. Don't you think?

ALEXANDER: Is that kind of the line of thinking that led to that concept?

WATERS: Well, the thought process that led to that concept is that, in earlier days, tattoos were popular then but not as popular so that every person would have them. But very often, a lot of my fans would come up to me with pictures of me and all my characters inked on their skin. I think that's where the idea came from.

ALEXANDER: I think my favorite of them all is Fidget's William Castle tattoo reveal, with the little sting of the Theremin on the soundtrack, then he slightly cuts Honey's dress strap. Just a little bit perverted. Not too perverted, just enough... just like Castle.

WATERS: [*laughs*] Yeah. I mean on that movie, in regard to Fidget, the most amazing thing of all really was that Patricia Hearst played the mother of a kidnap victim! She was really pushing it there.

ALEXANDER: You always say, "I can put people in my movies, and they don't have to be themselves; Patricia Hearst doesn't have to be Patricia Hearst anymore, she can be somebody else". But the casting here is obviously a direct nod to her past.

WATERS: Well, wasn't this the final fuck you, then? Who wants to be a famous victim? Certainly, it was an intentional bit of casting and when she did it, she was careful at what was said and stuff. Basically, Patricia wasn't a victim and she doesn't think what happened to her was funny. I think she got so weary of having that image, though. That's why she hooked up with me in the very beginning.

ALEXANDER: How did you two meet?

WATERS: We met in Cannes at the opening Paul Schrader movie PATTY HEARST. I had been to her trial, she never would have met me if I told her that, and somebody at the dinner purposely sat me next to her, we hung out and I said, "why don't you be in one of my movies?" and then we got to be a bit better friends and I don't think she ever thought that I would actually call to ask her to come in. But I did, she came in, I coached her a little and she was great. She's really funny in CECIL. I would have never put her in if she wasn't good.

ALEXANDER: Those opening credits are truly incredible.

WATERS: Yes! And all those abandoned movie theaters in Baltimore, they are almost all gone, so I'm really glad I got the shots of them. Basil Poledouris wrote the music, he was great. We didn't have any money, so he got stock, free music, and then mixed it and tortured it and put it all together, he did a great job.

No other filmmaker has done more to elevate exploitation than John Waters.

ALEXANDER: And he put that pulsing hip hop beat behind it. It's a monotone bass line, so the stock music is dichotomous, they cancel each other out. It's the most warped and beautiful sequence, I just adore it.

WATERS: It's amazing and I still get BMI royalties, for like thirty-eight dollars. Bankable, bitch! Everything about CECIL was great. And we had a lot of fun putting it together. A lot of the supporting cast were amazing too. I mean, Michael Shannon had done stuff but I don't think he was nearly as known then as he is today. Adrian Grenier, Maggie Gyllenhall... none of them were that well-known at that point.

ALEXANDER: Michael Shannon was credited as "Mike Shannon"! He wasn't even Michael yet!

WATERS: That's right!

ALEXANDER: Now, I must ask, why take aim at FORREST GUMP? Was there something genuinely personal about that skewering?

WATERS: Well, I did hate that movie but I would never really say I *hate* a movie because I always end up meeting people from the movie. I met Tom Hanks and he was lovely. And he wouldn't have cared if I hated FORREST GUMP. It won a million Oscars, made a billion dollars. Why would anyone care if I hated it? But yeah, I hated it. Like when he started running, I wanted to start screaming. All that sentimental stuff. In the context of CECIL, FORREST GUMP was this giant hit movie that of course Cecil would hate because it made money and was very middle of the road.

ALEXANDER: Let's talk about the casting of your lead anti-hero. Stephen had just come off a big movie in BLADE and was hot. What was your reason for bringing him on board?

WATERS: I just always liked him, I'd seen him in a lot of movies and knew he made weird movies too and would take chances, and we met and Stephen played it perfectly to me, he never winked at the audience. All the characters, that's the one direction I always said — no matter how ridiculous the dialogue is, say it as if you believe every word of it because when you wink, you think you're funny first. Let the audience think you're funny first.

ALEXANDER: I think that's part of the power of Stephen's performance. It's not even what he is *saying* half the time, it's his reaction shots that are the key.

WATERS: Yeah and he would do things, like when he was watching a show he'd mouth the dialogue, which unfortunately, I do too sometimes. We never did that in rehearsal, he did it mainly after watching me. Melanie was also really brave to take this part because it's hard to play a bad actress and I think she did it quite well.

ALEXANDER: She had done weird stuff before, though.

WATERS: Sure, she had just done the Larry Clark movie, ANOTHER DAY IN PARADISE, which she claimed was a complete nightmare to make but it was a very extreme movie, like everything that Larry does. So, I thought well, she'll do this! The only reason I first picked her was that we had met during first movie I ever starred in. I played a used car salesman, I sold her a car in Jonathan Demme's SOMETHING WILD, so I remembered her from that.

ALEXANDER: Honey must have hit home for her too, because she was at that age and kind of at that point in her career that the character was also in.

WATERS: Right. I think Melanie got it, totally. I had a great time with her.

ALEXANDER: Now, you've previously said that CECIL B. DEMENTED wasn't necessarily based on your own early way of making movies...

WATERS: No, no. Some of it was us, absolutely. Hitting and running, running and shooting; we did that, all the time. But the difference was I think that I had a sense of humor about myself and Cecil has none.

ALEXANDER: One of the greatest gimmicks of the movie is that Cecil refuses to let any of his own "Dreamlanders" have any sexual release at all. Everyone is horny in this movie. In fact, it's one of the horniest movies I've ever seen!

WATERS: That was something else I thought would be fun, if everyone was horny. That's taken from cults. A lot of cults don't allow you to have sex in the beginning, especially religious cults and stuff, or they have to assign who you have sex with. I didn't so that when I made movies though. I didn't interfere with the sex life of the people in my movies, ever. I don't think I ever even slept with anybody that was in my movies, but let me think... erm, yeah, I did... the stripper in MONDO TRASHO. Yeah...

ALEXANDER: Was that a conscious decision or were you just wrapped up in what you were doing?

WATERS: No, I just thought you're at work when you make a movie and it's a good thing, I mean look at all the actors and actresses who are in trouble for doing that.

ALEXANDER: Alicia Witt. She's a riot in this movie too...

WATERS: Yeah and it's so weird to look back and remember when they say, "this one's bankable, this one's not", which is the most ridiculous thing. If that was true every movie would be a hit. I forget, I think Alicia was on television or she had something at the time that was very successful. So she was bankable.

ALEXANDER: Well, she came out of David Lynch's world too, so it made sense for her to join your team.

WATERS: Well yeah, that's the whole thing, there are certain directors they want to work with and it's the people who take chances and those actors are smart to take chances because when the movie fails, which in Hollywood means at the box office, they don't get blamed, I get blamed, correctly, and they get a few brownie points for taking a chance on working with me.

ALEXANDER: Eric Roberts shows up in the movie for a memorable cameo.

WATERS: He was great. Eric was just somebody I always liked and remembered when he was young and so I just asked him to do it.

ALEXANDER: You have a great sense of humor about your weird and wonderful life's journey but are you still enjoying it, still having a good time?

WATERS: Yes, completely. I really am. Recently, I miss life though. I just switched holding cells from Baltimore to Provincetown, where my summer house is, but you know, it's nothing to complain about. I go to the beach; I write every morning. I'm going to my apartment in San Francisco next month to make sure it's still there, which I know it is. It's tedious and I feel very sorry for young people. I mean, I think I'm glad I'm old because every one of those movies took two years to get the green light and now this has happened, it all just stopped. I would be so crazy from having my career interrupted!

THE CHILD (1977)

Starring Laurel Barnett, Rosalie Cole, Frank Janson, Richard Hanners
Written by Ralph Lucas
Directed by Robert Voskanian

LET'S PLAY HIDE AND GO KILL. . . !
THE CHILD
a HARRY NOVAK presentatio
color by EASTMANCOLO
starring RICHARD HANNERS · LAUREL BARNETT · FRANK JANSO
and introducing ROSALIE CO
produced by ROBERT DADASHIAN directed by ROBERT VOSKANIA
written by RALPH LUCAS director of photography MORI ALA
music by ROB WALLACE executive producer HARRY NOVA
music performed by MICHAEL QUAT
a BOXOFFICE INTERNATIONAL PICTURES re
R RESTRICTED

In 1977, as STAR WARS blazed its way across the planet, rewriting the rules of cinema exhibition and defining its generation, a greasy little slip of shocker was quietly brightening regional screens and briefly providing a glowing ambiance for winos and weirdos on New York's 42nd Street.

Said film was indeed a horror movie, humble, cheap, and unpretentious. It came, it went. It came back again on home video, vanished once again, was "rescued" and re-distributed by the fine freaks at Something Weird Video, then once more slipped into oddball obscurity.

Indeed, THE CHILD (also known as ZOMBIE CHILD and in Italy as LA CASA DEGLI ZOMBI) probably deserves to stay in obscurity, hiding in limbo waiting for the odd set of eyeballs to find it, dig it and then forget it. It's not a great movie (whatever that means). But there's something about it. Some sort of lazy, lurid downmarket appeal. A morbid atmosphere, a rusty-swing-in-autumn eeriness that gets under your skin, if you let it. The movie's charms perhaps only speak to a select few of extreme fringe film lovers.

I am one of these people, naturally.

THE CHILD was directed by LA based director Robert Voskanian, who never directed another feature film after it, but really should have. After graduating film school in 1975, the young Voskanian started his own company, Panorama Films, an imprint that aimed to make educational and industrial pictures and commercials, much like George A. Romero's The Latent Image set out to do in the 1960s.

We all know how *that* turned out.

In fact, Voskanian and his partners were so smitten by Romero's first feature NIGHT OF THE LIVING DEAD, that they figured they would follow in his sizable footsteps and make their own horror picture. Getting their mitts on a scrappy screenplay by a one Ralph Lucas called KILL AND GO HIDE, the company raised an impressive US$100,000 and set out to make their maiden movie.

Shot in the Los Angeles area on a 35mm Arriflex camera, KILL AND GO HIDE, later renamed THE CHILD by its distributor, exploitation movie fat cat Harry Novak, plays like an eerie amalgam of THE BAD SEED meets CARRIE meets NIGHT OF THE LIVING DEAD, built on the foundations of Henry James' *The Turn of the Screw*. In it, a governess named Alicianne (Laurel Barnett) drifts into a rural town to take the position of caregiver to a troubled girl named Rosalie (Rosalie Cole), a motherless child with a mile-wide chip on her shoulder, not to mention a very unique gift.

As Alicianne soon finds out, Rosalie is a telepath and not a very nice one at that. Her happiest hobby is to psychically will the desiccated corpses from the nearby cemetery out of their graves and play with them. Of course, when people cross her, she sends her monstrous friends out to tear them to shreds, something her nanny finds out during the film's truly nightmarish climax.

The first thing one notices when watching THE CHILD is the eerie score, a haunting piano-based melody by future video game composer Rob Wallace that bumps up against weird electronics to set a Gothic, dramatic mood. The second thing of significance is that Voskanian wastes little time getting to the atmospherics; as Alicianne wanders through the woods, fog machines work overtime and wind howls like mad on the soundtrack, wonderfully over-the-top. And then there's the ghouls themselves: blackened, white eyed horrors that we barely see, save for a taloned hand uncoiling here, a tooth or two and a quick dash of a charred body there. It was Voskanian's belief that the zombies should only be seen in the peripheral, not just to hide any budgetary limitations evident in their costumes, but to keep the audience guessing as to what exactly these things are.

THE CHILD was shot without sound, its dialogue dubbed in later and not terribly convincingly so. The film feels like a European horror picture at times, with actors speaking louder than they obviously should be speaking and voices not matching the faces of the people they're coming from. And though this is a flaw that might isolate many viewers, this dissonance simply adds another layer of dreamlike warp to the entire production.

I'm not sure if Voskanian and his producer Robert Dadashian ever saw any profit from THE CHILD. Knowing Novak's reputation, it's unlikely that they ever did. But the film did see playdates all over the world, with 1100 screens in the US alone, an impressive number for a low budget horror movie with no known stars. And yet, to this day, so few admire the movie, despite its recent come-and-go appearances on mass-market boutique home video.

Bloody, sloppy, strange, serious, sometimes perhaps too somber for its own good, but always more than a little bit spooky, THE CHILD is out there now, waiting for the handful of horror fans who will no doubt embrace its charms...

CIRCUS OF HORRORS (1960)

Starring Anton Diffring, Donald Pleasence, Erika Remberg, Yvonne Monlaur
Written by George Baxt
Directed by Sidney Hayers

Before H.G. Lewis was bathing in cheap stage blood and flipping stomachs at drive-ins everywhere and the same year that Alfred Hitchcock ran chocolate sauce down the drain while a sort-of nude Janet Leigh screamed, there was director Sidney (BURN WITCH BURN) Hayers' wonderfully pulpy and surprisingly sadistic CIRCUS OF HORRORS, a

SPECTACULAR TOWERING TERROR!
One man's lust...made men into beasts, stripped women of their souls!
For ever stranger thrills...he turned the greatest show on earth into a...
CIRCUS OF HORRORS
AN AMERICAN-INTERNATIONAL PICTURE IN
SPECTA-COLOR
STARRING
ANTON DIFFRING · ERIKA REMBERG · YVONNE MONLAUR · A JULIAN WINTLE-LESLIE PARKYN Production · and starring 200 WORLD FAMOUS CIRCUS ACTS
CIRCUS OF HORRORS 60-145

Grand Guignol shocker with a campy cruel streak that was far ahead of its time.

The film was the product of a partnership between British studio Anglo-Amalgamated (the same studio that brought us PEEPING TOM and Roger Corman's THE MASQUE OF THE RED DEATH) and US genre machine American International Pictures, their second after the successful Michael Gough vehicle HORRORS OF THE BLACK MUSEUM. And like that deliciously dark picture, CIRCUS has a rough, lurid edge and trades in cruelty and nasty behavior to provide its frissons.

But the movie is great for other reasons too. It's a bright, candy colored melodrama about the abuse of power and, like any good Frankenstein tale, it's a moral parable about the dangers of playing God.

Anton Diffring, who a year earlier starred in the magnificent THE MAN WHO COULD CHEAT DEATH and decades later wound up in Jess Franco's FACELESS, stars as Dr. Rossiter, a brilliant plastic surgeon on the lam after a series of botched operations. We see one of these failed procedures in the first 5 minutes, with a comely woman whose face is slowly melting to putty. When she screams in horror at the disintegration of her visage, we scream too. It's a harrowing scene that must have alarmed audiences in 1960 and still has the power to rattle you out today.

After he flees the city and crashes his car, he himself is disfigured and, with the help of two loyal assistants, rebuilds his own mug and re-christens himself Dr. Schuler. The trio travel to France where they meet a poor, kindly circus owner (Donald Pleasence) and his scarred daughter. Figuring this not-so-big top is the best place to hide out, Rossiter/Schuler makes a deal with the ringmaster to heal his daughter, which he does, in exchange for taking him on as a partner in the circus. But when the owner is killed by a dancing bear (it's a great, violent, and ludicrous sequence), Schuler takes over the joint entirely.

Combing through the city streets, Schuler begins collecting wounded women, including a prostitute/hustler whose face-long scar has driven her to a life on the skids. In one of the movie's most entertainingly sick bits, the hooker stabs and steals the wallet of one poor John, and as he cries for help and bleeds out in the background, Schuler pins the girl to a wall and urgently convinces her to join his psycho circus. Schuler becomes a sort of surgical Svengali, rebuilding broken women and controlling them, training them to be his star attractions and, if they dare threaten to leave, murdering them.

Of course, the ruse can't last forever and, despite the circus' success and evolution into the biggest of its kind in the country, the law begins to snoop around and, very quickly, Schuler's reign of megalomaniacal terror winds down.

There's so much to savor in CIRCUS OF HORRORS, including the lilting, romantic and delightfully tacky Garry Mills song Look For A Star, a song that actually charted successfully in England, and of course the endless array of violent, theatrical murders,

"Target Girl" Magda (Vanda Hudson) gets hers under the bloody big top.

bubbling-cauldron melodrama and winking mean-spiritedness (love the death by knife-throwing bit). But the movie really works primarily because of Diffring's truly magnetic performance, a complicated turn that sees his Rossiter/Schuler veer between sympathetic and sociopathic, sometimes within the same scene. We never quite hate him. His intentions are always good — or at least the germ of his intentions is — and yet they're fatally corrupted by his ego. It's a fascinating character and a very layered performance in a truly remarkable horror movie that has sadly slipped into the sideshow of shock cinema history.

COLOR OF NIGHT (1994)

Starring Bruce Willis, Jane March, Lesley Ann Warren, Brad Dourif
Written by Billy Ray, Matthew Chapman
Directed by Richard Rush

It's easy for contemporary, unschooled audiences to poke fun of European thrillers of a certain vintage. The beautiful, broadly painted and unapologetically melodramatic Hitchcock and French New Wave-informed murder mysteries made by men like Argento, Martino, Lenzi and Lado throughout the 1970s were as eccentric as they

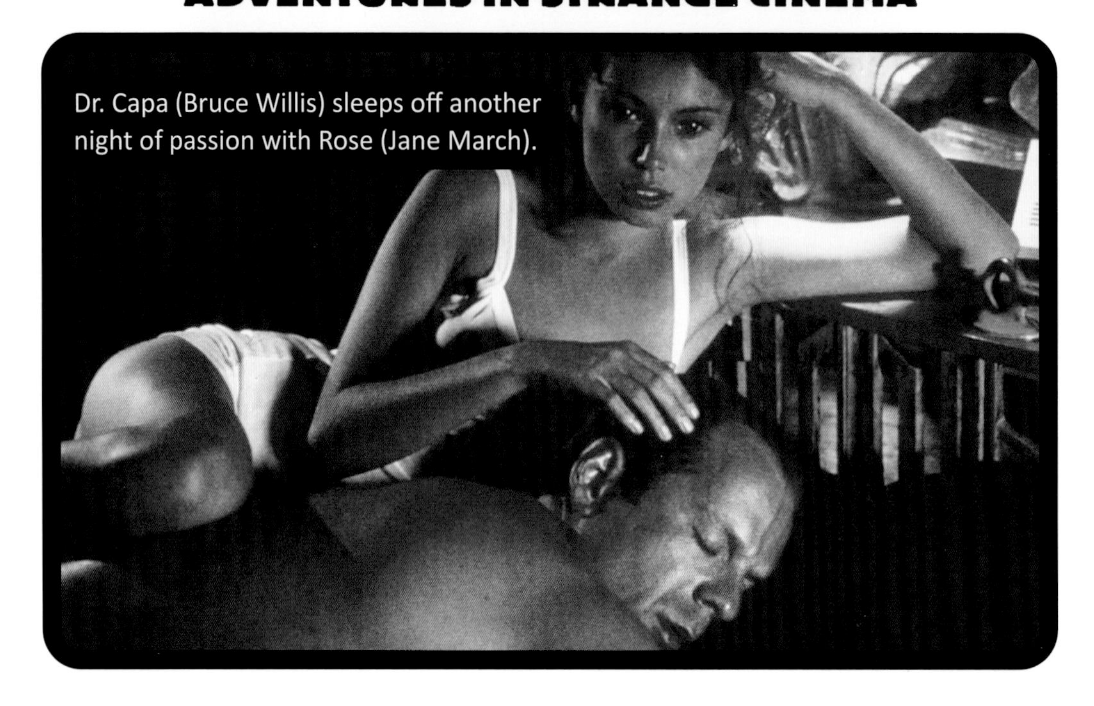
Dr. Capa (Bruce Willis) sleeps off another night of passion with Rose (Jane March).

were wildly erotic, with music slopped all over the soundtrack, characters acting like lunatics and "twists" you could generally see slinking around a mile away but didn't care because the trip to get to them was, well, such a trip in and of itself. That's what made them great.

Brian DePalma understood this and much of his post-CARRIE output was as informed by the *giallo* as it was heavily influenced by Hitch. His 1980 murder mystery DRESSED TO KILL is a masterpiece of stylized, high-gloss perversion, lust and black gloved, gender-confused bloodshed. As this was 1980, and coming as it did at the closing of one of the most daring decades in cinema, critics and audiences "got" DRESSED TO KILL, applauding its slick visuals, and reveling in its ludicrous narrative and hysterical sexuality.

But when COLOR OF NIGHT came out in 1994, the very same folks weren't as receptive. And the younger generation? Forget about it.

COLOR OF NIGHT spurted out of its studio at the climax of the "erotic thriller" boom that began with Adrian Lyne's (rabbit) potboiler FATAL ATTRACTION, continued with Paul Verhoeven's BASIC INSTINCT, was beaten (off) down by INSTINCT's writer Joe Esterhas's also Sharon Stone-starring kink-fest SLIVER and smothered by William Friedkin's undervalued JADE. SHOWGIRLS doesn't really count as an erotic thriller but by the time that Verhoeven/Esterhas collaboration came out cumming, the bloom was off the rose. The novelty of mainstream celeb nudity had wound down.

COLOR OF NIGHT was lost in this tsunami of gauzy smut, but it wasn't really part of it.

Marketed stupidly to fit into that world, the truth is the film is far more akin to DePalma and Hitchcock and those delirious, fluid-soaked '70s Eurotrash shocker than it is to any of its not-quite-beaded-curtain brethren.

Now, 22 years later after its release, the film can (hopefully) be seen and appreciated for the riotous, larger than life thriller it is, one laced with blood, eccentricity, swooning sound design, a rogue's gallery of amazing character actors, relentless sex and, for the curious, a prime peek at star Bruce Willis' impressive full-frontal member.

Director Richard (THE STUNT MAN) Rush's opulent exploitation movie does indeed star Willis, a comic actor-turned-action-hero who left his TV career (in the hit series MOONLIGHTING) behind with his breakout role in 1987's DIE HARD, its sequels and a glut of solid, successful thrillers that followed. Here, Willis steps away from the shoot 'em ups to play Dr. Bill Capa, a cocky psychiatrist who has a nervous breakdown when a sexually volatile patient jumps to her bloody death from his office window, right in front of his horrified eyes. Because of this, those very eyes suddenly opt to lock out the color red (a neat gimmick that Rush exploits for the audiences benefit as well, during high-stress scenes).

Emotionally lost and unable to practice, Bill ventures to LA to hang out with his colleague and friend Dr. Bob Moore (LORD OF ILLUSIONS' Scott Bakula) who convinces the despondent shrink to sit-in with his therapy group, a hilariously neurotic bunch of nail-biters that includes ex-cop Lance Henriksen, sex-starved but kindly nympho Lesley Ann Warren, Bakula's LORD OF ILLUSIONS co-star Kevin J. O'Connor and the legendary Brad Dourif, here playing a slicked-down germophobe nebbish. Oh, and there's a weird little transgender boy with a stutter named Richie in the group too, played by... well, if I told you who Richie was played by, it would decimate COLOR OF NIGHT's big reveal.

Though, to be blunt, if you fail to see that big reveal coming, you sir/madam need to visit my friends at Spectacular Optical and get new goggles!

Anyway, one night Moore, after confessing to Willis that he's been shagging the hottest woman in the world, is brutally murdered in slow-bloody-mo by, not a black gloved killer, but by a SILVER gloved killer. After this tragedy, Capa reluctantly forms an alliance with a distractingly ethnic police lieutenant (Ruben Blades) and takes over the group sessions, to suss out who the murderer might be.

At this point COLOR OF NIGHT takes its sweet time getting to know these colorful kooks, with Capa slyly asking the questions and Rush allowing his remarkable cast to go over the top, devouring all traces of scenery. It's sublimely entertaining and lively stuff and Billy Ray and Matthew Chapman's script has fun larding the actors' mouths with juicy, salacious stories and retorts.

In the midst of all this meandering jawing and disorienting, red-herring-loaded investigation, Capa meets an impossibly hot girl named Rose (Jane March, so brilliant in Jean-Jacques Annaud's THE LOVER, the role that landed her this gig). They flirt endlessly and believably (in one scene Rose gets Capa wired up on the street then leaves him to deal with a trouser tent-making erection) and eventually have sex.

And boy, do they have sex!

The sex scenes between Willis and March are the stuff of legend with March totally uninhibited (though she later claimed she was somewhat mislead as to how sexual the film would be and how much nudity was required), baring all, and Willis' freewheeling willie swinging around and matching his co-star pump for pump. Many have cited the sex scenes in COLOR OF NIGHT to be among the most excessive and impressive in any mainstream film and I'd be, er, *hard* pressed to argue.

In between the Willis/March ugly bumping, the movie's plotting goes positively berserk, with more murders, more madness, more weirdness and Willis getting wise to all of it.

Then, there's that twisted climactic reveal. Which again, is telegraphed early on but still amusingly lurid.

When the film was released, producer Andrew Vajna (ANGEL HEART) had re-cut the movie to remove some mild lesbian antics between Warren and March as well as tons of sidebar character stuff (a great deal of which involved Henricksen's character) and other moments deemed too flabby and odd for wide release. Rush fought his producers to the point where he had a heart attack from the ordeal, the result of which was that Vajna somewhat yielded and let Rush have his full cut released on home video with the producer's cut reserved for theatrical.

Now, I've never seen the theatrical cut so this blathering is based on the version of the movie I know, which is Rush's wildly excessive cut. And, make no mistake, with its paranoia, overuse of music (a lush, sax-soaked score by Dominic Frontiere), grandiose production design, surreal passages of dialogue and atmosphere and generally overheated aura that steams out of every seem, COLOR OF NIGHT is an American giallo. Inside and out. But unlike many of those fantastic style-trumping-substance pictures, the performances here are a real treat, with March especially — in or out of clothes — a real presence, delivering a complex performance that hides behind the hysterics. Willis is fine too, solid and likable, even when battling mailbox snakes. Yes, you read that right...

The film's arch affectations earned it many jeers and dismissive reviews and at least three Golden Raspberry awards (God, I hate those). But these many years later, some of those critics are dead, others unemployed, some MIA and lo and behold, COLOR OF NIGHT is still here, waiting to find its audience.

So, what are you waiting for? Find it already!

Larraz's fatale females prepare for THE COMING OF SIN.

THE COMING OF SIN (1978)

Starring Lidia Stern, Patrice Grant, Rafael Machado, David Thomson
Written by Jose Ramon Larraz, Monique Pastrynn
Directed by Jose Ramon Larraz

In the annals of exploitation cinema, Spanish filmmaker Jose Larraz had one of the more unique voices; a multi-hyphenate artist who dabbled in many mediums, including comic books, and whose filmed fixations on beautiful women and hot sex were matched by his interests in darker, more psychological explorations. And while his resume certainly boasts a more than a few middling efforts, his undisputed masterworks outweigh the weaker material. Joining the director's essential ranks is his 1978 shocker THE COMING OF SIN, an astonishing work of erotic horror that's the depraved equal to his WHIRLPOOL and sensual kin to his most recognizable picture, VAMPYRES. THE COMING OF SIN is a balletic three-hander that forsakes plot in favor of fevered couplings and ratcheting tension and whose measured rhythm might turn off the average viewer seeking smutty Eurotrash thrills. But for the rest of us... look out.

The film (released in many markets under the riotous and misleading title THE VIOLATION OF THE BITCH) stars Lidia Stern (aka Lidia Zuazo) as Triana, a beautiful but simple Gypsy servant girl whose masters "loan" her out to an older, sexually voracious artist named Lorna (Patrice Grant) at her beautiful country estate. Before you can say "The Rain in Spain", Lorna is smugly boasting that she will refine Triana's palette,

teaching her how to read, to speak, to socialize. And to fuck. Because it's clear from the moment the two women meet that there is a strong sexual connection and Larraz revels in sustaining that tension, creating a dripping erotic aura that only relaxes once his film veers into full-blown mania.

Triana's endless nightmares of a man on horseback pursuing and raping her threaten to become reality when she sees the buff young Chico (Ralph Margulis) prancing around on his steed in the nearby wood. And wood he doth have. In one deliciously perverted dream sequence — the likes of which was and still is used to market the picture — Triana imagines she is naked inside the body of a Trojan horse, Chico's horny equine circling her with intent to mount. It's a hot, revolting and hilarious scene that perhaps only someone with Larraz's sense of sick humor could pull off and render so poetic. Later, after indeed sexually assaulting Triana, he is slowly, surely ingrained into the women's lives in and out of their bed, though all the while the brutalized Gypsy woman is having fevered visions of death. Soon an intense *menage a trois* is in full bloom... and none of it ends well.

Like VAMPYRES (which is an equally brilliant but a much more accessible effort), THE COMING OF SIN uses a boiling love triangle to propel its running time, making the audience focus on character and dialogue and the lush surroundings as opposed to some sort of cliché-driven three-act narrative nonsense. And as far as the performers themselves are concerned, they are mesmerizing, despite the fact that Larraz used non-actors as his leads. In the case of international films like this, most of the time the films were not shot with sound at all, meaning every actor was dubbed in every market and that's true here; we never actually hear the actors' real voices in any print. But who cares when the cast is so fascinating to watch, gracefully moving across the frame, gazing longingly and scornfully at each other and lyrically rolling over each other's sweaty bodies. In fact, it's a boon to the film that we don't recognize these performers at all, an immersive hook that gives the picture an earthy sense of reality (though beware the hilariously terrible British actor who dubs Chico in the English language version).

If you've only seen VAMPYRES and are just getting familiar with Larraz's cinematic imprint, you're in for a treat with THE COMING OF SIN, a film dripping with portent and atmosphere and decidedly adult thrills.

THE COMPANY OF WOLVES (1984)

Starring Sarah Patterson, Angela Lansbury, David Warner, Stephen Rea
Written by Angela Carter, Neil Jordan
Directed by Neil Jordan

Before Walt Disney and his squeaky clean, family friendly ilk saw fit to sanitize them, the traditional fairy tale served as far more than a whimsical alternative to kiddie chloroform. As penned by those bad old Brothers Grimm especially, fairy tales of yore were cautionary morality fantasies: dark, violent warnings about the horrors and dangers in life that lurk behind every bend and within every human heart.

Take Cinderella, for instance. In the 'real' story, those cantankerous, treacherous stepsisters don't just try on the ill-fitting glass slipper; the incident plays out as a vulgar perversion of the basest kind of vanity, as each sibling bloodily contorts their feet to fit the shoe, one even hacking off a few toes to complete the task. 'Grimm' stuff indeed. Then there's Snow White, the story of an unfortunate lass who is set up to be murdered by her jealous mother, a crone who hires a woodsman to drag the porcelain beauty out into the woods and pull her beating heart from her bloody chest. And then take fairy tale forefather Charles Perrault's Little Red Riding Hood. British fantasy writer Angela Carter did. So did Irish filmmaker Neil Jordan. Their resulting collaboration on that infamous musing on temptation, recently eaten grandmothers and cross-dressing canines was the brilliant and beautiful allegorical 1984 horror movie THE COMPANY OF WOLVES, certainly one of the most underrated horror films in history.

In the early '80s, in the wake of such box office busting, special effects-soaked soon-to-be classics like Joe Dante's THE HOWLING and John Landis' AN AMERICAN WEREWOLF IN LONDON, that hirsute movie monster/folklore favorite known as 'the werewolf' reigned supreme. And yet, though US distributor Cannon Pictures chose to market THE COMPANY OF WOLVES as a bloodthirsty wolfman shocker, the theatrical poster even emphasizing the sort of man-to-beast prosthetic transformations that made FX guru Rick Baker a household name, Neil Jordan's

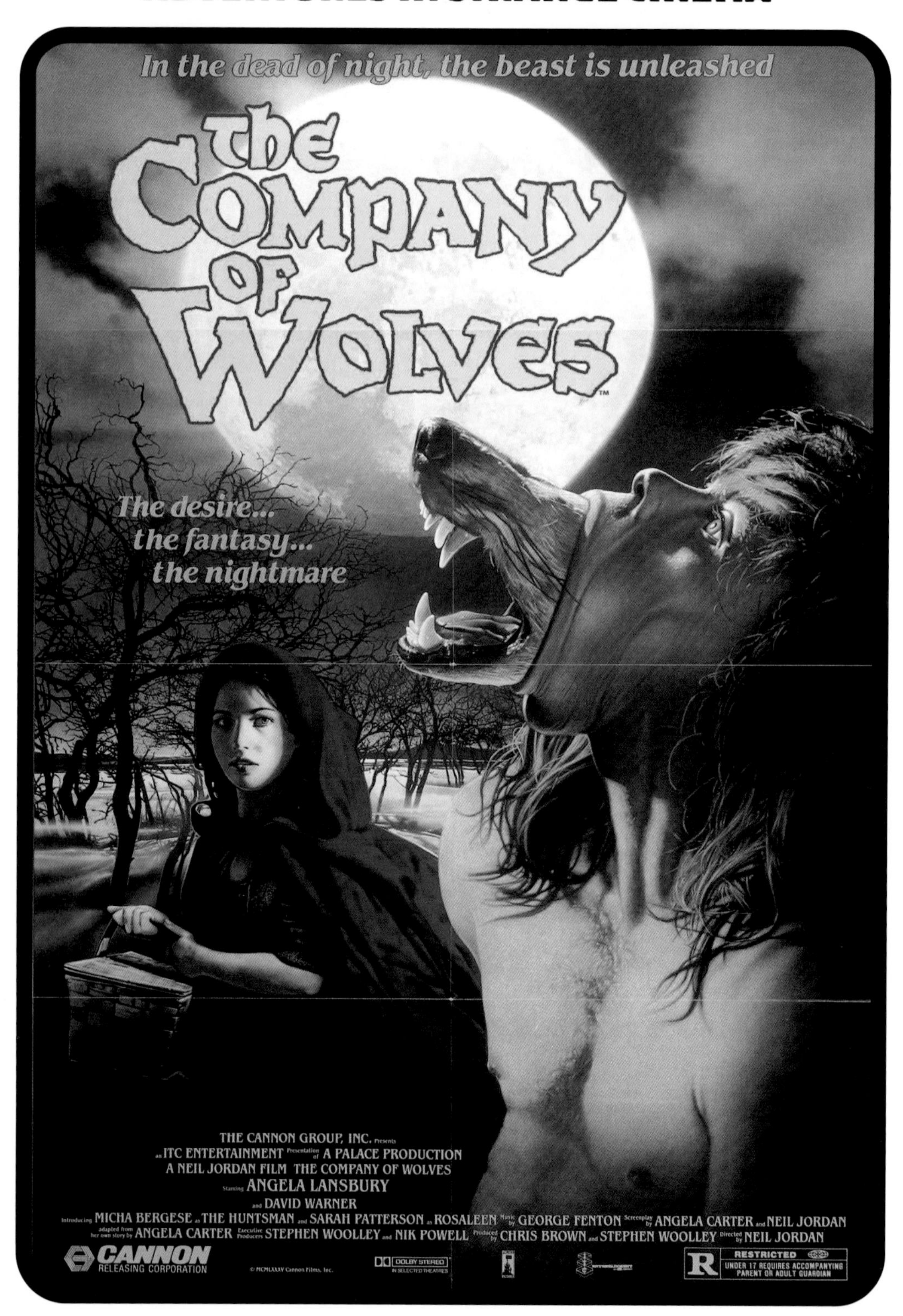
In the dead of night, the beast is unleashed
The Company of Wolves
TM
The desire...
the fantasy...
the nightmare
THE CANNON GROUP, INC. Presents
an ITC ENTERTAINMENT Presentation of A PALACE PRODUCTION
A NEIL JORDAN FILM THE COMPANY OF WOLVES
Starring ANGELA LANSBURY
and DAVID WARNER
Introducing MICHA BERGESE as THE HUNTSMAN and SARAH PATTERSON as ROSALEEN Music by GEORGE FENTON Screenplay by ANGELA CARTER and NEIL JORDAN
adapted from her own story by ANGELA CARTER Executive Producers STEPHEN WOOLLEY and NIK POWELL Produced by CHRIS BROWN and STEPHEN WOOLLEY Directed by NEIL JORDAN
CANNON
RELEASING CORPORATION
© MCMLXXXV Cannon Films, Inc.
DOLBY STEREO
IN SELECTED THEATRES
R
RESTRICTED
UNDER 17 REQUIRES ACCOMPANYING PARENT OR ADULT GUARDIAN

elegant and somewhat dangerous effort didn't fit into that mangy, matted mold, in fact it didn't really fit anywhere.

Collaborating closely with noted novelist (and revered feminist) Carter, self-adapting her own short story 'The Company of Wolves' and liberally borrowing threads from her other similarly themed tales, Jordan's desire was to turn the story of Little Red Riding into a caustic, bubbling cauldron of unstable sexuality, the ultimate Freudian horror fable and a twisted condemnation of male desire gone fantastically awry.

The film opens during a fever dream: Little Rosaleen (Sarah Patterson) is a modern English girl on the edge of puberty, locked in her bedroom, surrounded by icons of her rapidly dissolving childhood, and smeared with a clumsily applied deep red lipstick. As she slips into restless, heated sleep, the audience is invited to enter her subconscious head space, tunnels and paths that cannibalize each other, littered with dark, spindly trees, horny, man-sized teddy bears... and a pack of stalking, growling, red eyed wolves. The deeper she disappears into the haunted forest of her mind, the more authentic the surreal woods become until she, and we, are fully completely immersed in a vividly realized 18th century village ripped straight from the pages of the most evocative storybook. Rosaleen is now a farmer's daughter, living with her doting parents and obsessed with her stern, slightly sadistic grandmother (a wonderfully sinister Angela Lansbury), who tortures and delights the young girl nightly with her cruel tales of supernatural shapeshifters and of the various evils that men do. Meanwhile a bloodthirsty wolf is terrorizing the countryside, a beast that, upon being shot by vengeful hunters, inexplicably and terrifyingly morphs into human shape. As fear and paranoia in the village mounts, Rosaleen, wearing a bright red shawl and armed with a packed lunch basket, begins her late afternoon walk down the remote path towards Grandma's house... a path that the curious and ever blossoming young woman doesn't stay on for very long.

To reveal more of THE COMPANY OF WOLVES' meandering, hallucinatory plot mutations would be to grossly dampen the picture's many pleasures. This is a lush, erotic, eerie and metaphorically rich film made all the more impressive by the fact that Jordan apparently cobbled it together on a minute budget, fully exploiting Anton (BATMAN) Furst's amazing, Mario Bava-esque theatrical set design.

Ostensibly it is a werewolf picture because, well, it's heavily armed with all manner of hairy man-to-monster and back again shenanigans. Many of the twisted stories that granny relates are in fact werewolf yarns, thinly veiled horrors that, like any true fairy tale, reveal a deeper truth. Granny believes that all men are in fact 'wolves', predatory monsters that initially charm women, tipping their hats and gripping naive maidens by the hand before turning on dimes and callously defiling them in every sweaty manner they wish.

A young groom (Stephen Rea) confronts his bride before becoming a wolf.

One of her paranoid tales, indeed the movie's visceral highlight, sees a young newlywed couple retreating to their cottage for a night of coital bliss. As the wolves howl outside, the groom (Jordan regular Stephen Rea) bolts from the home, tears off his shirt and disappears into the night, never to be seen again. Long since thought eaten by the beasts, he returns years later a different man, full of anger, bile and bitterness. When he sees his bride remarried with screaming children, he flips out; howling like a madman, tearing at his flesh, ripping off strip after strip of skin to reveal the pulsing, fanged werewolf underneath. Christopher Tucker, who designed John Hurt's painful make up in David Lynch's masterful 1980 film THE ELEPHANT MAN, makes this scene a real showstopper, bloody and horrific.

But unlike a great mass of early '80s genre films, freakish gore isn't the focus of THE COMPANY OF WOLVES, rather this is first and foremost a feminist parable about the dangers of the feminine sexual awakening. Using Little Red Riding hood as its framing device, the film is a full throttle sensory experience, stimulating the eyes (Brian Loftus' cinematography is swoon-worthy), the ears (George Fenton's score is creepy, evocative, and slightly discordant), the mind (Carter's ideas and philosophies sit firmly in the forefront) and, um... other fun parts. The cast is an eccentric ensemble of iconic British personalities including the great David Warner as Rosaleen's father, punk princess Danielle Dax as a naked she wolf and Terrence Stamp as, of all things, The Devil himself!

Jordan would later go on to become one of the greatest living filmmakers of our time, deftly weaving between mainstream nightmares like his ace adaptation of Anne

Rice's INTERVIEW WITH THE VAMPIRE, to his low-key pansexual melodrama THE CRYING GAME, to the delirious heights of the outrageous THE BUTCHER BOY and the elegant erotica of BYZANTIUM, discussed elsewhere in this book. But with THE COMPANY OF WOLVES, only his second feature, Jordan had already proved himself a master storyteller, a creative narrative force, a supreme stylist and a ballsy upstream swimming risk-taker, not afraid to take a genre that was already rubbing its tired, oozing eyes and spin it like a top, making something disarmingly original, a dark wonder whose running time holds many secrets.

INTERVIEW: STEPHEN REA

CHRIS ALEXANDER: How long did that wild, skin-ripping make up process that you endured in THE COMPANY OF WOLVES take to apply?

STEPHEN REA: Believe it or not, it took over seven long, uncomfortable hours. It was horrible, but I think the scene turned out really, really well. And I had a blast in postproduction, dubbing all sorts of screams and growls and what not over it.

ALEXANDER: What do you think of the film today?

REA: Well, I think it's a very good movie and I think I enjoy watching it more now than I did when it came out. I actually think that it's aged particularly well. The thing I used to find difficult about it, however, was the sexuality.

ALEXANDER: The sexuality offended you?

REA: Oh God, no, not at all. Quite the opposite. Originally, in the script, the lead young girl was very sensual, and it was extremely erotic. But then I think they got nervous about depicting the sexuality too graphically, *because* she was so young. I don't think they'd be so nervous about showing it these days. But anyway, I think it's a very good movie and especially was only Neil Jordan's second film. I also think it was too strange for American tastes and sensibilities at the time and that's why it didn't do well over there.

ALEXANDER: You've been in almost everyone of Neil's films since his first. What's the secret of your enduring working relationship?

REA: It just seems to click. I'm not in every film. I'm not in THE BRAVE ONE, or HIGH SPIRITS, I wasn't in that one. But Neil says that I was lucky to not have been in it! But yes, Neil and I are very fond of each other. He always uses characters that have internal struggles, that have conversations with themselves, and I do that fairly well, I think. Some actors don't see that, but it's about language and not fucking about with too much of the actual acting, just doing the part. I'm very fortunate that we get on so well, because he's made some fantastic movies. Many of which are quite dark.

ALEXANDER: Some of which are considered horror films, like THE COMPANY OF WOLVES. Do you yourself watch horror films?

REA: I don't think of THE COMPANY OF WOLVES as a horror film. I think it's an allegory. As far as my own tastes, I like the film noir stuff. Dark, psychological tales about people. But not horror, really, no.

ALEXANDER: Why is that?

REA: The truth? They scare me too much. When I saw THE EXORCIST in the 1970s, I came home and slept with the lights on for a week. People said to me, "Oh, c'mon Stephen, it was only pea soup coming out of her mouth!" and I would say "You're fucking crazy!". It might have been pea soup, but it scared the life out of me. And just the whole notion that you can be possessed from within. I mean, I was raised Catholic. It was too much for me. I do like Polanksi's take on horror though, very much in fact, especially that vampire one he did, DANCE OF THE VAMPIRES (aka THE FEARLESS VAMPIRE KILLERS). I liked that one because it mixed a dark humor with the vampire stuff.

ALEXANDER: And you even donned fangs yourself as Santiago in Neil's adaptation of INTERVIEW WITH THE VAMPIRE...

REA: Yes, and that was immensely fun to do, dancing around that tunnel, spinning around with those clothes on and really hamming it up. I'm proud to say that in my career I've been both a vampire and a werewolf and they were both grand fun to do. That's the kid in me, getting to dress-up and play monster and have a blast. Never mind all this existential angst bullshit.

CONTAMINATION (1980)

Starring Ian McCulloch, Louise Marleau, Marino Mase, Siegfried Rauch
Written by Luigi Cozzi
Directed by Luigi Cozzi

Luigi Cozzi's delirious 1980 Italian sci-fi/horror romp (and former "video nasty") CONTAMINATION stars ZOMBI 2 and ZOMBI HOLOCAUST hero Ian McCulloch as an alcoholic ex-astronaut named Hubbard, who is roped back into action by Colonel Stella Holmes (Canadian actress Louise Marleau) after a ghost ship drifts into the New York harbour carrying crates of acid-spewing death-sacs, the likes of which have just caused a crew of investigators to explode like human piñatas. Seems Hubbard was part of a doomed Mars mission many years prior in which fellow astronaut Hamilton (Siegfried Rauch) fell under the spell of some sort of egg-laying terror and vanished.

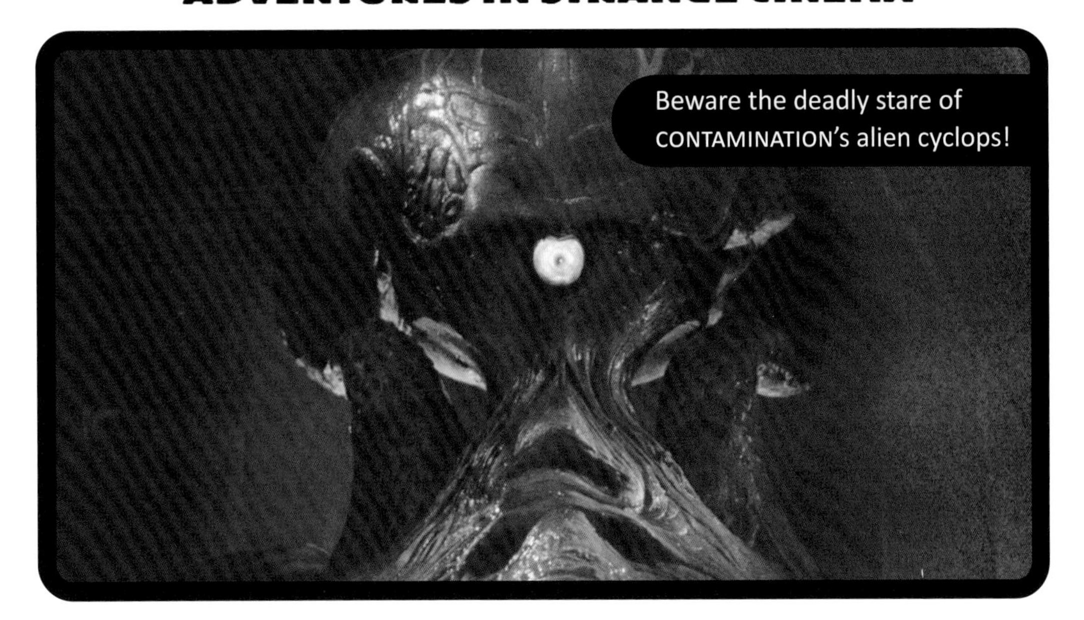

Beware the deadly stare of CONTAMINATION's alien cyclops!

When Hubbard returned to earth, raving about Martians and half out of his mind, no one believed his tales and he slipped into deep depression and hopeless addiction. Horrified to learn that the pulsing poison eggs he encountered in space are now on earth but exhilarated that there is finally proof of his career-killing claims, Hubbard joins forces with Colonel Holmes and NYPD cop Tony Aris (Marino Mase) to track down the source that's shipping the intergalactic eggs around the world, a journey that takes them to the steamy jungles of Columbia. They soon discover that Hamilton has in fact also returned to earth, where he now runs a coffee plantation and serves as a puppet of the insidious alien lifeform, who has psychically ordered him to help bring the earth to its knees via its evil ova, packed discretely in boxes of coffee beans. Still with me? Good, let's keep going...

Calling CONTAMINATION an ALIEN rip-off is no insult to the film, nor is it a slight on Cozzi's integrity or intentions. During that period of Italian exploitation moviemaking, no producer worth his salt would have dared finance any genre film that wasn't a direct quote on an existing, profitable picture — especially if it was a profitable American picture, as ensuring US screens was an essential component to a European film's success. And that is indeed exactly how CONTAMINATION began its swollen galactic pustule-popping life, with Cozzi — fresh of the modest success of his wild space opera STARCRASH — walking into producer Claudio Mancini's office and promising a movie that boiled down to being "ALIEN made for peanuts", one that was originally to be called THE ALIEN ARRIVES ON EARTH. As Ridley Scott's masterpiece was a groundbreaking, instant global sensation, without blinking, Mancini agreed to do the movie and it was rushed into production.

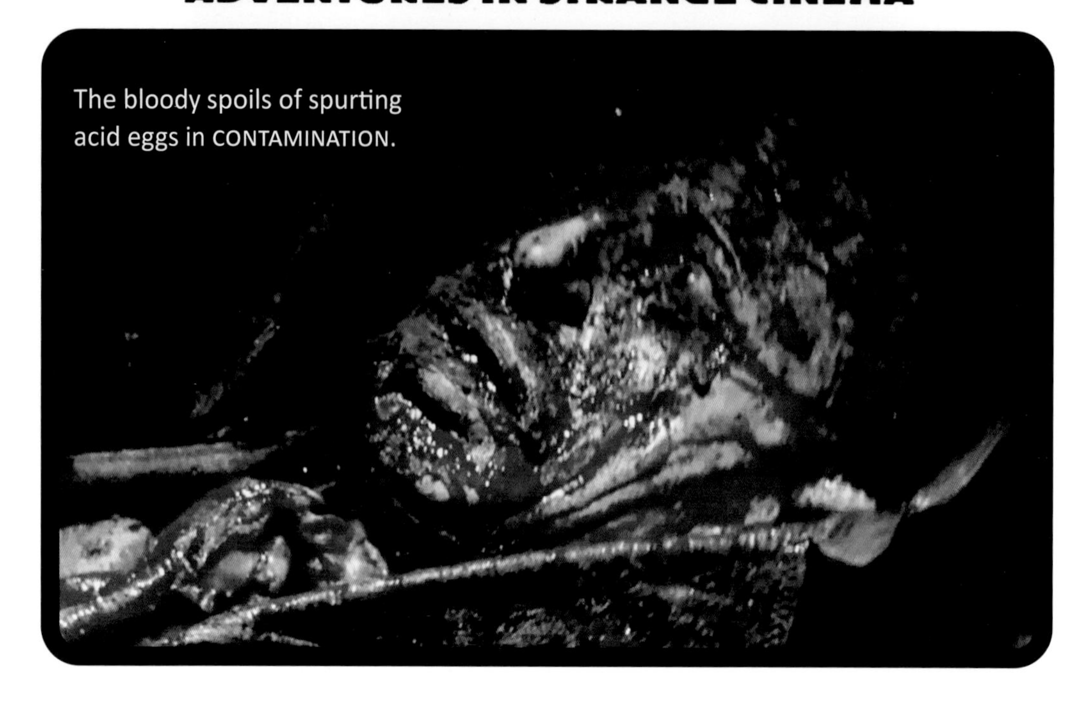
The bloody spoils of spurting acid eggs in CONTAMINATION.

But while ALIEN may have been the hook to get the moneymen interested, there's much more to Cozzi's movie than just shameless imitation. CONTAMINATION is positively swimming in references to classic fantasy filmmaking, with a narrative thrust that echoes INVASION OF THE BODY SNATCHERS and elements of the Hammer Studios Quatermass movie ENEMY FROM SPACE woven into the story, while also favoring two-fisted action and Ian Fleming-esque derring-do to propel it (and with the dashing McCulloch as its lead, the movie certainly feels like a dump bin James Bond picture remade by a wide-eyed 12 year old monster kid). Visually, there all also more than a few nods to "outbreak" horror movies like George A. Romero's THE CRAZIES and David Cronenberg's RABID, especially during its opening moments of hazmat suit wearing men meeting their makers when those dastardly space eggs pop.

The film's most visceral visual connection to ALIEN is the way it takes the shocking "chest-burster" sequence and fetishizes it; in true Italian exploitation film fashion, the concept here seemed to be to take that which was most gruesome and memorable from the movie it was borrowing from and amplify it tenfold. Lucio Fulci's DAWN OF THE DEAD riff ZOMBI 2 took Tom Savini's delightfully revolting gut-munching shock scenes and added even more gore, plus that now immortal eyeball-violence set-piece and, since JAWS was also a big hit in Europe, dumped in a ghoul-eating shark for good measure. In CONTAMINATION, Cozzi sees ALIEN's startling and bloody "birth" moment and goes-for-broke with a non-stop avalanche of exploding upper-bodies. Built by FX man Giovanni Corridori and rendered in slow-motion à la the bullet-hits in another

Cozzi favorite, Sam Peckinpah's THE WILD BUNCH, the victims in CONTAMINATION scream in agony while their chests erupt in geysers of flesh, bone and fluid, a crimson tide from Hell designed solely to make its audience sick.

All this mayhem is fueled by one of Italian horror prog-rock supergroup Goblin's most potent and groovy scores, a doom-laden Gothic electro-jazz meltdown with some of keyboardist Maurizio Guarini's freakiest synth-washes ever (Guarini also played keyboards on Fabio Frizzi's ZOMBI 2 soundscapes and much of that eerie vibe he brought to that music ends up weaving its way into the CONTAMINATION soundtrack). The Goblin tunes are especially mesmerizing during CONTAMINATION's balletic climax, where our heroes encounter the source of the evil eggs: a massive, slimy alien "tree" called "the cyclops" armed with a flashing lightbulb eye that hypnotizes its victims and causes them to commit suicide by sinking into the great beast's undulating mouth. Ludicrous? Absolutely, but that's what makes it so wonderful and really, that's what has always set the Italian horror cinema apart from its American counterparts: that sense of opera, of painting in broad strokes, of pushing sound and image over the top into heightened realities pitched to the peak of fever.

CONTAMINATION was released theatrically — slightly shorn of some its messiest moments — in America by Cannon Pictures as ALIEN CONTAMINATION, a title it took with it to home video when it was released by Paragon Video on VHS in the early 1980s. Along the way, another distributor (the hilariously titled Lettuce Entertain You) put the film out as TOXIC SPAWN and eventually, because the Cannon copyright lapsed, the film seemed to fall into the public domain in North America, bumping around in hundreds of those horror and sci-fi movie DVD compilations that became discount store staples. Eventually, the picture was properly released by people that cared — including William Lustig, who put out a gorgeous early DVD release of the film under his Blue Underground label — and, as the movie's reputation as a Eurohorror classic swelled, even better editions reared their head, culminating in Arrow Video's feature packed Blu-ray a few years ago (in which yours truly contributed an enthusiastic commentary track).

My own love for CONTAMINATION started when I caught it on TV as a kid on Elvira's Movie Macabre series late at night and later, I then bought the Paragon VHS for my burgeoning collection. I still have that tape. Years later, in 2014, I was invited to go to Rome to screen my second feature film QUEEN OF BLOOD at the Italian Horror Film Festival. My fellow guest of honor was Cozzi and the fest was also screening CONTAMINATION. I'll never forget watching my movie on a double feature, outdoors on the beaches of Nettuno beside the ruins of a castle with bats flying around the screen, sitting with Cozzi (along with Claudio Simonetti and Ruggero Deodato!), all of us hammered out of our minds as CONTAMINATION played at 2am. The film screened in the Italian language (though with that international cast and because the Italians rarely shot with synch-sound, every version of the film is dubbed) but it didn't matter as I knew the film inside and out and the rhythms of those rococo syllables just added to the surreal beauty of the experience.

I have a pack of insane stories surrounding that wild time with some of the masters of Italian horror and maybe I'll tell them to you one day, in the sequel to this book. But for now, the message of this essay is singular: see CONTAMINATION. And if you've already seen CONTAMINATION, see it again. Celebrate it. Pop some champagne in its honor. Do it in slow-motion. Play the Goblin theme track while you do it.

INTERVIEW: LUIGI COZZI

For serious fans of Italian genre film history, the name Luigi Cozzi (or, as he's better known in America, Lewis Coates) looms large. Cozzi's brand of Euro exploitation is more joyous, and fantasy based, almost innocent in its exploration of the darker and more phantasmagorical aspects of the human condition. One can almost feel the childlike wonder Cozzi has for the art of cinema while watching his work and that's because that's exactly what he has. He's had it since boyhood, and it has never ebbed. And never will. I adore him.

CHRIS ALEXANDER: Can you recall what the first fantasy film you saw was? How did it affect you?

LUIGI COZZI: The first movie of this kind that I ever saw was Disney's 20,000 LEAGUES UNDER THE SEA when I was seven years and it absolutely fascinated and hooked me forever to the genre. After that, I watched Hammer's QUATERMASS 2 — aka ENEMY FROM SPACE — which scared me to hell. Then the wonderful FORBIDDEN PLANET was next and from that moment and on I just wanted to see only sci-fi, horror and fantasy movies.

ALEXANDER: And this passion led to you pursuing film as a profession. As a young filmmaker, what was your breakthrough success?

COZZI: In Milan, I started making a living as a writer, a sci-fi editor and literary translator in 1965 and still I work in these fields even today. But as far as the movie business goes, I started in 1967 as a sound synchronizer, assistant editor, assistant to the dubbing and director of my first sci-fi movie, THE TUNNEL UNDER THE WORLD, adapted from Fred Pohl story with the same title, in early 1969. Then in mid-1969 I moved from my hometown, Milan, to Rome just in order to work in the big movie industry, which I entered in September 1970 when Dario Argento hired me as the screenwriter for his film FOUR FLIES ON GREY VELVET. Then, I had my first big hit as a director with the made for TV horror movie THE NEIGHBOUR, for a series Argento

Director Luigi Cozzi is one of Italy's premiere "monster kids".

was doing called THE DOOR INTO DARKNESS. This was a 56-minute film, and it was nationally aired on prime-time and nearly 30 million viewers tuned in and were scared by it. In fact, thousands of them phoned to the network too protesting it because they said it had too strong tension and this whole thing actually made headlines on newspapers. I had made THE NEIGHBOUR during early Fall 1972 and was aired in early September 1973. After this hit, I somewhat expanded its plot and made, in October 1973 with the theatrical feature THE KILLER MUST KILL AGAIN, which sadly wasn't released until late 1975. This was because Italian censorship banned it because of its strong sex and violence content. The movie got very good reviews, but it didn't do well at the box office, because basically, the giallo genre was then ending.

ALEXANDER: Your re-edit of the original GOJIRA (GODZILLA) is the stuff of strange cinema legend. What's the story behind that?

COZZI: Yes, so I actually re-edited the Japanese 1954 GOJIRA movie, the version reworked in the Us by Terry Morse and released in 1956 as GODZILLA, KING OF THE MONSTERS with additional scenes starring Raymond Burr, with me adding new materials to it in order to reach a 100-minute running time instead of the original 80. I simply bought the right to do this from Toho for 7000 dollars. They sold me all its Italian theatrical rights for seven years, from 1976 till 1983. Then my rights have expired. In 1976 Toho had an official representative office here in Rome, run by a Japanese man named Terada. I simply told him I wanted a contract to re-release their original GODZILLA here in Italy, got the contract and paid for it. But when I proposed to Italian regional independent distributors to re-release the old classic movie, they refused telling me that the 1956 GODZILLA was a black and white movie, while Italian theaters did not show any more black and white movies, even if they were classics. As the only possible solution for this fact, they suggested me to print the black and white 1956 movie on colored film in a manner that its 35mm prints came out from the printing all in an *orange* tint. This is the only way any Italian theater could accept to show an old B-W movie. But as a film buff, I hated these *all orange* tinted classics. Then I got an idea. I had just met Armand Valcauda, a young stop motion technician who owned one stop motion 35mm Krass camera-projector, the same kind of camera-projector used by Ray Harryhausen to shoot his wonderful movies. And while I was shooting with Valcauda some special effects tests imitating Harryhausen's FIRST MEN IN THE MOON space special visual effects, I had seen that by using this Krass technology Valcauda could also *change* colors in the images he shot and so I got the idea that he could *add* colors to B-W images by reshooting them with his stop motion camera-projector, one frame after the other. So I explained to Valcauda what I wanted him to do for me, he was puzzled but accepted because I offered to pay him for a test... and after that I gave him a three minutes B-W print from GODZILLA and... well, he did what I asked for, he ADDED colors to the old movie, giving back to me a brand new *all colored* three minutes negative roll from the old black and white GODZILLA. Then I started re-editing the old GODZILLA adding to it a lot of destruction scenes from WWII stock footages and gave the result to Valcauda to color it all one frame after the other. He colored by stop motion all the new GODZILLA 100 minutes in about three months. Then I created a new 100-minute soundtrack, adding a lot of sound effects and new music. I mixed it all in Stereophonic 4 tracks magnetic system and printed four new 35mm magnetic sound-colored prints, which during early 1977 started to be shown in the Italian theaters, with good economic results. Before that I had asked Toho to authorize me to do the color version of their movie and they had added a new page to our original contract stating that I was fully authorized to do it, providing that when my 7 years release term expired, I delivered back to them both the original 1956 black and white GODZILLA negative and my new colored GODZILLA negative, which from 1983 became another Toho property. And so I later did and since then it's Toho who owns all rights to my 1977 colored version of GODZILLA.

ALEXANDER: Do you still have a good negative of your edit?

COZZI: Of course, I've kept one copy of my colored GODZILLA for myself and recently I've seen an American fan, Gene Cuddy, who's posted another good quality copy of my own-colored GODZILLA version on Facebook.

ALEXANDER: You first worked with Pino Donaggio in HERCULES. How did you connect with him? Was there a particular score of his that impressed you?

COZZI: One of the soundtrack musicians I've always liked best is Bernard Hermann, mostly for his music for Orson Welles, Hitchcock and Ray Harryhausen movies. But actually, for scoring HERCULES Cannon had already hired Ennio Morricone even before I was assigned to write and direct this movie. So, when its first rough cut had been edited, I showed the movie to Ennio, but he was disturbed by the fact that I had already placed some music in its rough soundtrack as a guide. Irritated, he said to me "Do you want me to write this kind of music?" and I said "Something with this strength and power, but obviously in your own way and style". He then replied "Sorry, but I don't feel to be able to do any music in this way" and he stepped out of the contract. Actually, the music I had put on the HERCULES rough cut was Bernard Herrmann's music from Harryhausen's 7TH VOYAGE OF SINBAD and at this point I decided to move over to Pino Donaggio, whom I knew had already made very good Herrmann*esque* music for Brian De Palma thrillers. Cannon supported this choice of mine and I showed to Pino my HERCULES rough cut, still with Hermann's music on it, and afterwards Donaggio said "I've fully understood which kind of epic music you want for your movie, and I assure you to be able to write it." So he wrote and directed a wonderful score for my HERCULES, which I've used in HERCULES 2 too. My working relationship with Pino was perfect and very easy, he did exactly the kind of music I wanted him to do. I was overenthusiastic about his contribution to this movie of mine.

ALEXANDER: The movie NOSFERATU IN VENICE is a beautiful but flawed film. Is it true you directed some of it? Can you tell us about your experiences on that film?

COZZI: I was hired as supervisor for the special visual effects of NOSFERATU IN VENICE. Once the shooting started, I was also asked to act as second unit director, as there was a great delay in the working schedule, mostly due to Klaus Kinski's crazy behavior. So, I ended up directing the visual effects and just a few minor scenes in order to reduce the strong schedule delays. As a matter of fact, the movie wrapped shooting when still about one third of the script had not yet been shot… and it was never shot, because the movie had gone wildly over budget. This explains why it took almost two years editing it in an almost decent way…

ALEXANDER: Was Klaus as difficult as his reputation has suggested?

COZZI: Klaus was an angel in certain moments and, a few moments later, he did turn into a devil. A genius and a monster. He was a marvelous actor but did also create quite often incredible delays due to his totally unprofessional ways. At times he was normal and collaborative while at other times… most of the other times… he was crazier than you could ever imagine. Just think that some of the female actresses at a certain point refused to play again with him, that twice the whole crew abandoned the set refusing to go on working unless Kinski pleaded excuse for his wild behavior…

ALEXANDER: Italian film seemed to get quite and instead leaned more towards TV. What IS the future of Italian film, specifically horror film?

COZZI: Today it's very easy to make movies thanks to the new technologies, but it's also very difficult to make good movies because most young filmmakers believe they're able to be writers or directors even if they've had no professional experience or cultural and technical background. So, most of the independent productions just disappear into nowhere, even if a few of them may be interesting or even good. But the key factor today is not just making movies, but being able to get decent distribution, which is becoming increasingly difficult. In Italy, there are a lot of young independent sci-fi and horror filmmakers, but almost no one has really stood out with continuity among them so far. Today there's no trace of a new Mario Bava or a second Dario Argento. As far as the future goes… who can predict anymore!

COUNT DRACULA'S GREAT LOVE (1974)

Starring Paul Naschy, Vic Winner, Haydee Politoff, Rosanna Yanni
Written by Paul Naschy, Javier Aguirre, Alberto S. Insua
Directed by Javier Aguirre

I can vividly remember the first time I met Paul Naschy.

I was a kid, maybe 12, and, as I did in those days, I opted to stay up all-night, watching and videotaping every class of horror related film or show that filtered from my cathode-spitting screen. Perusing the TV guide with highlighter in hand, I ran my yellow ink across a 4:15am screening on local Toronto channel CFTO of something called DRACULA'S GREAT LOVE starring all kinds of Spanish-sounding people I'd never heard of.

Imre (Vic Winner) indulges his new-fang-gled blood hunger.

I stayed up. I watched. And was profoundly affected.

Here was an early seventies European shocker, romantic and cruel, violent and sexy, lush and ludicrous. The music was shrill and overbearing; the English dubbing was jarringly "off"; the tone and rhythm were wonderfully alien and there were charming little pubic hairs flickering in the peripherals of the eerily worn and faded 16mm TV print that only added to the movie's sumptuous other worldliness.

And at the center of all, playing the good Count himself (more or less) was a hirsute, barrel chested hombre named Paul Naschy. Looking a bit like a sun-kissed John Belushi, Naschy seemed like the least obvious choice to play the quintessential King of the Vampires and yet, somehow his hangdog, sad eyed visage was appropriate.

Ultimately, my reaction to both Naschy and the film itself was one of intense bewilderment — I had never seen anything like it. Once the picture wound down to its rather abrupt and dramatic climax, I knew I had fallen in love with it. And yet I couldn't properly articulate as to why that was.

Though the battered version I watched was listed in the TV guide under the title DRACULA'S GREAT LOVE, the actual full onscreen English moniker for director Javier Aguirre's micro-epic of undead lesbian sex, eternal romantic longing and Gothic bloodlust is COUNT DRACULA'S GREAT LOVE (literally translated from the original Spanish EL GRAN AMOR DEL CONDE DRACULA). Many reference books and resources had erroneously dropped the "Count" from the picture's name, due primarily to the fact that most badly pan and scanned versions of it (including the one I saw) shaved off the

The lusty undead prowl the house in COUNT DRACULA'S GREAT LOVE.

letters "C-O", a sloppy mistake that led one of my equally horror obsessed pals to constantly refer to it as *CUNT* DRACULA'S GREAT LOVE when I would screen it for them.

Now then... the plot.

After a carriage load of ample-bosomed Spanish honey's and one lucky, macho, pork-chop-sideburned dude (played by Naschy's HORROR RISES FROM THE TOMB co-star Vic Winner) bust a wagon wheel and get stranded, the intrepid crew wind their way to Dr. Wendell Marlow's remote country sanitarium where they are put up for the night by their gracious host. The thing is, the good doc is actually the legendary Count Dracula in disguise and not only is he hungry for their blood... he's super lonely.

Faster than you can say 'Parasitic Paella' each comely cutie is vampirized, first by a wandering, bug eyed, bloody necked stray ghoul (who got bitten by Drac after dropping off a coffin to the clinic in the creepy, skull-splitting pre-credits opening sequence), then by the now inexplicably lesbian-ized undead women themselves. All become fang fodder, except the sweet, virginal Karen (lovely Eurocult Queen Haydee Politoff) who catches Dracula's eye and warms his cockles; a coffin cuddling crush that may prove to be the Count's ultimate downfall.

Made in the wake of the more explicit late period Hammer horror films pumping out of the UK and Naschy's own classic Hollywood monster rewrites, COUNT DRACULA'S GREAT LOVE was a bit of a sidestep. By the time the film was released in 1972, Naschy had already established himself as the Duke of Spanish terror, playing the equally miserable werewolf Waldemar Daninsky in such freakish, trashy yet super-stylish erotic genre mash ups as FURY OF THE WOLFMAN, FRANKENSTEIN'S BLOODY TERROR and my personal favorite of the Daninsky Cycle, WEREWOLF SHADOW (aka THE WEREWOLF VS. THE VAMPIRE WOMAN). Hiding under a face of fur seemed to suit the stocky former weightlifter, defining his legacy.

But the fact that Naschy and Aguirre's riff on Stoker's master supernatural seducer has been historically viewed as one of his lesser efforts is more than a bit of a head scratcher because COUNT DRACULA'S GREAT LOVE is everything a '70s gothic Spanish horror film should be. It's handsomely produced, sexual, surreal, romantic, bloody and loaded with the kind of brash eccentricity that, sadly, just isn't seen in genre movies anymore.

For example, sequences which show Dracula humanely liberating tiny, wounded and terrified animals from a series of snap traps, scenes which paint him as gentle and caring, are called into question when, later in the film, he ruthlessly and joyously murders and drains a pleading farmer who also ends up in the same trap. In another bizarre turn during the film's final reel, Dracula, who spends countless evenings walking with Karen and pontificating on life's mysteries, suddenly turns mute, his voice replaced by booming echo chamber spiked narration (perhaps a result of the outrageously out-of-synch English dub). It's a weird touch but it works.

Another thing that COUNT DRACULA'S GREAT LOVE has going for it — and it's a major selling point to the kinkier fans among us — is plenty of sex, lurid scenes that are at odds with the film's more classical and old fashioned framing. That version I first saw was actually a hacked to pieces US television edit, clocking in at under 75 minutes and shaved of virtually all of its graphic coupling and nudity. Years later, I scrimped and saved and ordered a VHS from California based mail order company Sinister Cinema and, after sticking that hefty bootleg beast into my top loading player, my jaw hit the floor and my eyes popped out of their sockets. To my surprise the thing was riddled with debauchery of every sort — vampires biting boobs, girl vamp on girl vamp action, nude swimming, Naschy and Politoff lovemaking, see-through vampire negligees... the list goes on and on and it's glorious.

This uncut (or less cut version) also boasted more bloodshed, including more graphic footage of the hilariously repetitive axe-in-the-forehead gag that unspools over the dripping-font opening credits and various stakings and suckings that serve as gruesome *frissons* in the context of the films admittedly languid pace.

And did I properly address the score for this dirty diamond? Veteran genre film composer Carmelo A. Bernaola (CUT THROATS NINE, Naschy's HUNCHBACK OF THE MORGUE), delivers some sensational, organ drenched cues and screeching symphonic meltdowns that simply drip with full color, pulp horror lunacy.

I adore COUNT DRACULA'S GREAT LOVE. It reminds me of a time in my life when watching movies like this was akin to embarking on a secret quest, like following a blood-soaked trail of breadcrumbs into the very heart of vintage European trash culture. And, of course, it made me a lifelong, card-carrying member of the Paul Naschy fan club.

Once damn near impossible to find, this gorgeous slice of Spanish sleaze is now widely available uncut, buffed to a high digital gloss on DVD and Blu-ray. But I kind of miss the way I used to watch the movie; in truth I *like* the flick in its battered condition. The dirty colors, splicy jump cuts and curly nether hairs just make it seem stranger. Either way, this is my favorite Naschy film and a work of unusual, lyrical potency.

DAUGHTERS OF DARKNESS (1971)

Starring Delphine Seyrig, John Karlen, Danielle Ouimet, Andrea Rau
Written by Harry Kumel, Pierre Drouot, Jean Ferry, Jospeh Amiel
Directed by Harry Kumel

In the annals of the '70s lesbian vampire canon, there's one incredible film that — for me — sits far away and high above the rest. A movie that, while ostensibly playing by the rules of the erotic Sapphic bloodsucker picture, is something far more elegant, kinky, exotic, sinister and sophisticated. I speak of course about Belgian director Harry Kumel's grinning, impossibly Gothic and hypnotically sensual 1971 melodrama/morality tale DAUGHTERS OF DARKNESS, a wicked and quintessentially European exercise in intelligent, witty wordplay and stylish filmmaking and one of the most cynical cinematic musings on male/female relations the horror genre has ever offered us. It's among my most favorite films of all time, of any genre, any era.

The film opens, appropriately, on a speeding train, as Francois de Roubaix's brilliantly throbbing, trippy jazz/post-mod rock score saturates a scene of carnal coupling between newlyweds Stefan (DARK SHADOWS star John Karlen) and Valerie (French Canadian erotic starlet Danielle Ouimet). After this intense sequence, we learn that these two lovers have met and married after a recent whirlwind courtship and don't really know each other very well at all. Before DAUGHTERS OF DARKNESS' lurid narrative runs its course, they'll have rectified that social problem for the worse.

The couple wind up the sole guests in a looming, off-season hotel in picturesque Ostend where they make love, eat, talk and where Stefan nervously avoids Valerie's urgings to call his "mother" and tell her about their nuptials. At this point, though we can't quite put our finger on it, Kumel manages to create a genuine sense of menace and unease; why is Stefan afraid of making a phone call to his mother? What is he hiding from the sweet and naive Valerie?

Ilona (Andrea Rau) attempts to seduce a distracted Elizabeth (Delphine Seyrig).

Suddenly a car pulls up to the hotel and out steps an elegant woman and her traveling companion. She's Countess Elizabeth Bathory (the ravishing French film icon Delphine Seyrig), an elegant, smooth, smiling and charming aristocrat who is also checking in to the remote hotel. Upon seeing the young, fresh-faced (and lithe bodied) Stefan and Valerie, Bathory immediately befriends them, slowly seducing and manipulating their affections in what appears to be an attempt to pry the beautiful Valerie away from her increasingly brutish man.

As the serpentine narrative weaves along, we learn that Bathory is in fact the legendary Hungarian "Blood Countess", a real historical figure who bled thousands of virgins to death in order to maintain a glowing, youthful appearance. Only now, Bathory's become a kind of love-starved, sexually charged, immortal vagabond vampire, in town looking for a replacement for her increasingly melancholy mate Ilona (the better-than-perfect German model and soft porn star Andrea Rau). And, as both Stefan and we the audience quickly learn, this is a woman who always gets what she wants.

DAUGHTERS OF DARKNESS is a pitch-perfect exercise in mood, tone and tension and, if you're willing to let it work you over, it casts a slick, strange and chilly spell that sticks long after the screen has faded to red. It also has a wicked sense of black humor. In one of the picture's most disturbing and uncomfortably hilarious sequences, Stefan, for all his brutish, Stanley Kowalski-gone-Eurotrash macho bravado, is revealed to be a closet (and apparently "kept") homosexual. When he finally makes his reluctant call to "mother", the domineering matriarch turns out to be a decadent, older, lipstick

Seyrig's Bathory is among horror cinema's most glamorous vampires.

wearing dandy (brilliantly played by the actor/director Fons Rademakers), one who dryly scolds the younger man for doing something as unrealistic as marrying a woman. This bizarrely funny episode is followed shortly thereafter by a darker scene in which Stefan obsessively snakes himself through a crowd in Bruges to see the body of a viciously murdered woman and, when Valerie attempts to pull her apparently necrophiliac husband away, he hits her, knocking her to the ground. What horrors await this unsuspecting girl in her marriage into Stefan's sinister family, the audience can only guess.

The driving theme behind DAUGHTERS OF DARKNESS initially appears to be a feminist one, with the soft spoken Bathory "liberating" Valerie from the oppression of her potentially dangerous husband. But really, Valerie is just being manipulated by another, far more lethal and selfish predator. And that's the real force behind the film; a shadowy, cruel amorality that is as icy and reptilian as it is both appealing and amusing.

Visually, Kumel's picture is breathtaking, with its gorgeous cast, authentic European locales, fluid camera work and elegant use of the color red (the film's original title was actually LES LEVRES ROUGE, or THE RED LIPS). And though it does unofficially belong to that unofficial subgenre of gay lady vampire pictures, it's not only an infinitely more evolved piece of cinema than say, Jess Franco's groovy and voyeuristic VAMPYROS LESBOS, it also keeps the vampire shtick to a minimum. Nary a fang is revealed, and blood is consumed only once, in the balletic last reel sequence that smacks of a quasi-crucifixion metaphor. And if we are to read it that way, suddenly, the film is even further removed from any sort of feminist-leaning than we thought. That thematic ambiguity simply adds another layer of fascination.

Again, this is one of my favorite movies of all time and though some may see it as a dash pretentious, I'll be damned if I can find anything wrong with it on any level. It's seductive and addictive. It's pure cinema imagined as gauzy, sensual dream. Perhaps I'm blinded by this love, but any movie that features a central menace as effortlessly arresting as Delphine Seyrig (it's been noted that her portrayal of Bathory somewhat channels the chilly purr of Marlene Dietrich) locks itself into my heart for life.

DAWN OF THE DEAD (1978)

Starring Ken Foree, Gaylen Ross, David Emge, Scott Reiniger
Written by George A. Romero
Directed by George A. Romero

George A. Romero's landmark 1968 nihilistic gore thriller NIGHT OF THE LIVING DEAD may have been at its core a primitive, probably accidentally political rip-off of Richard Matheson's novella *I Am Legend*, but there's no debating its raw power or how it changed the ways in which the world watches horror films. And it's still a tough movie to handle, bleak and relentless, urgent, and violent and prophetic. But it's Romero's full-blooded, full color and near-operatic 1978 NOTLD companion film/sequel DAWN OF THE DEAD that truly built the blueprint for the modern zombie movie. DAWN is the one everyone copied, from the gory European clones and downmarket tail-riders, to the wave of ghoul-free end of the world survivalist shockers, to the name brand 2004 remake and the other millennial (and considerably faster moving) flesh eater epics like the 28 DAYS/WEEKS LATER films, RESIDENT EVIL (the games and the movies) and yes, Robert Kirkman's THE WALKING DEAD comics and the long running series that realized its stories.

DAWN OF THE DEAD is the gold standard of living dead cinema and it's the first film that I was actually afraid to watch. I had this cousin who lived in Windsor, the border town to Detroit. I long ago lost track of him and learned recently that he passed away, but that's neither here nor there. His name was Jamie, and he was 15 years older than I was and he loved KISS, Alice Cooper and horror movies. I thought he was the coolest person alive. I remember sitting in his car when I was six or seven and listening to rock'n'roll and thrilling raptly to his tales of driving to Detroit to see this movie called DAWN OF THE DEAD, a movie that was so scary and bloody that Canadians weren't allowed to see it (DAWN was banned in Ontario, Canada at the time). He told me about

Stephen (David Emge) meets his maker for a second time in DAWN OF THE DEAD.

key scenes and how the audience screamed and howled and how he drove back the following week just to watch it again. Years later I saw a copy of DAWN at the first video store my family became members at, the Thorn EMI clamshell case with Scott Reiniger's Roger "rising" in three headshot images. The movie looked cheap and eerie and came armed with a quote on the top of the box from Roger Ebert, praising the film as a "Savagely satanic vision of America". Oddly, a much younger Ebert was one of the critics loudly panning NIGHT OF THE LIVING DEAD in 1968. A decade later, he finally saw the light.

I finally rented DAWN OF THE DEAD at a sleepover on my eleventh birthday with two of my friends. We ate garbage and watched FRIDAY THE 13th: THE FINAL CHAPTER first, which meant nothing to me (I found it mechanical and dull, like most American slasher films; I've since warmed to that subgenre somewhat) and then chased it with DAWN. Unbeknownst to me at the time, it was a Tom Savini double feature. But DAWN was the one that changed my life. From its first shot against that blood-red carpeted wall (a sign of the sanguinary splatter-thon that was to come), pulling back against Gaylen Ross' Fran waking from a nightmare only to find that what was really happening was far worse, I was hooked. In those first five minutes as the crude credits appear and that metronomic Goblin bassline drags us into the action, Romero captures a world spiraling out of control, very, very quickly. A Pittsburgh TV news studio is in chaos. Talking heads talk over each other in a volatile, unorganized fashion, the crew running around in a panic and many just running out, period. No other movie I'd seen literally jumped into hell quite like DAWN does. Watching it today, it still has a power unequaled.

But after that urgent opening, it was the parallel tale, that of Ken Foree's Peter and Reiniger's Roger, two S.W.A.T. officers who are called-in to infiltrate a low-rent apartment complex filled with superstitious tenants who have refused to give up their dead, that kicked my head in, as it did so many unprepared viewers. Savini's squibs and exploding heads, his grey/blue-faced ghouls appearing out of every corner, stiff and wide-eyed and casually lunging at anything warm; dead husbands embracing mourning wives and eating them alive. And Peter and Roger stepping away from the madness momentarily as they plot ditching their duties and running for their lives. The one-legged priest who urges them to "stop the killing", lest the living dead conquer the world ("The people they kill… get up and kill!", to quote the TV pundit at the beginning of the picture). And the basement where the "kept" and starved ghouls have now begun cannibalizing themselves. It was all too much. It was death and horror overload. There was no comfort. Nothing safe to hold on to. I was lost in DAWN OF THE DEAD. I was at Romero's mercy.

And I still get lost in it. It still has its way with me, every time.

The zombies in all of Romero's films — but most explicitly in DAWN — are the common man liberated and devouring that tenuous illusion of social safety. They are death. They are nature. They are apathetic and operating on instinct. They are born out of our hate, out of our idiotic need to coat the world in chrome and pretend everything is alright, when it's anything but. Men, women, black, white, Asian, Hispanic, gay, straight, children, the elderly… it doesn't matter. All will die. All will come back to consume who is left.

Nowhere is this more potent than when our quartet of heroes are flown in by David Emge's Stephen to the abandoned Monroeville Mall, where they infiltrate the fortress and begin the arduous, dangerous process of eliminating the dead and setting up their own utopian society. The dead are drawn to this commercial slop-pit, stumbling up the down-escalators, falling into fountains, mesmerized, while cheery muzak drizzles out of the mall's speakers. Romero said it first and he said it best and since then no one who has seen DAWN and responded to it can go to a mall and not be struck with the fact that this is what they are doing. What everyone who shuffles through those self-contained consumer death traps do, distracting themselves with "stuff", even when we are collectively falling apart.

There's no other movie like DAWN OF THE DEAD, not even in Romero's own diverse and distinct canon. It's a film of many flavors and delights, some there by design, some by organic accident. As the movie was famously kick-started by Italian maverick Dario Argento, co-financed in exchange for Dario getting the rights to cut a European version (called ZOMBI, which differs by eliminating some of the uniquely North American satire, pumping up the action and saturating the film with more Goblin heavy metal/prog music), there's a certain European flavor to the film, a kind of

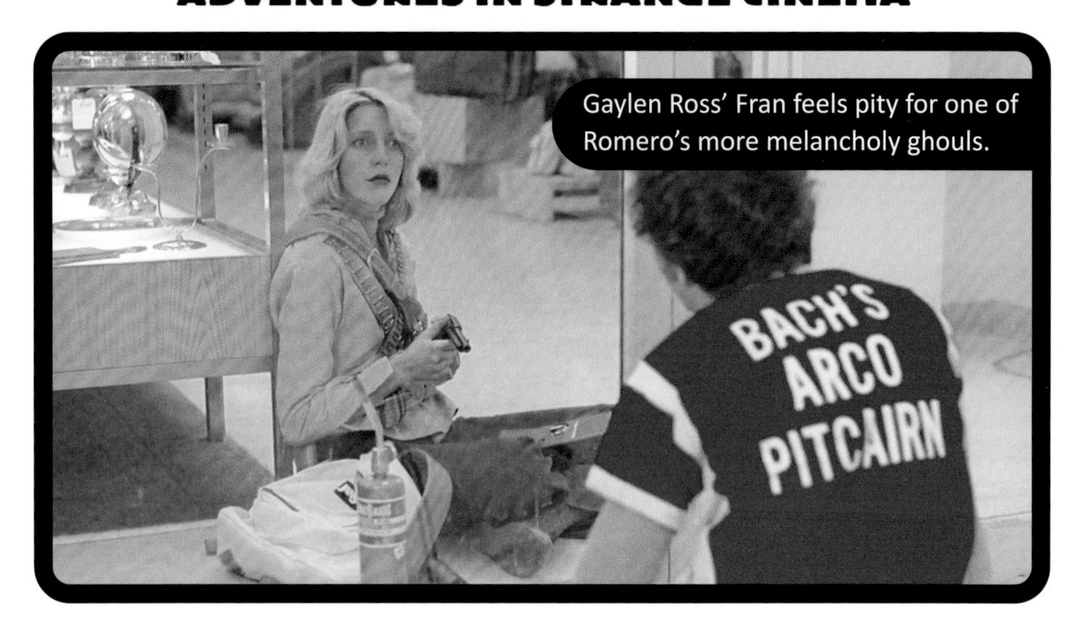

Gaylen Ross' Fran feels pity for one of Romero's more melancholy ghouls.

exuberance and emotional gravitas that mark many Italian films, horror and otherwise. There's Savini's amazing and revolutionary DIY gore effects (Savini and Romero are the ones who, with DAWN, invented the term "splatter movie") as well as Tom's own performance as the leader of the biker gang who haphazardly try to "steal" the mall from our heroes. There's the quartet of strong, layered characters played by equally unforgettable unknown actors at the center of the film that anchor the movie in humanity and give the movie so much of its endless replay value. We *love* these characters and, even though we know who will live and die, we are perpetually swept up in their plight. There's that pulsating Goblin rock music which hammers home so much powerful doom and sweeps us away during the more exhilarating action sequences. And there's Romero's reliance on "needle drop" music from the De Wolfe library, something he used to exploit often, but sadly abandoned in later years. This collection of strange, dichotomous cues and stings add so much humor, horror and weirdness to DAWN, jerking the viewer around emotionally and viscerally. All of these things coupled with the feeling of genuine invention and indie spirit are what make this movie so joyously horrific and enduring. You can't fabricate this. It just happens or it doesn't. This is a small movie that feels as epic as GONE WITH THE WIND and yet so many of today's movies are SO big yet feel dwarfed by comparison. Why is that?

And while Greg Nicotero's startling makeup effects in THE WALKING DEAD and its offshoots are vast improvements technically on the house that Romero built, the show — and most if not all contemporary zombie entertainments — is missing the key element that makes Romero's ghoul films, especially DAWN, so effective: Romero genuinely feels sad. There's a sadness at the loss of the world and, most importantly, he pities the zombies. In DAWN, each zombie isn't just a pile of gooey rubber and fake blood and decay, they are ghostly echoes of what we are. Each one has a soul. Whether it be the shirtless obese zom falling into the fountain, the pair of child zoms who are gunned down, the relentless Hari Krishna ghoul, the nurse, the nun, the amateur baseball player who seems smitten with Fran through the department store door while her heart breaks at the fate that has befell the young man or the regal African woman who is outraged when the bikers steal her jewelry; there's a powerful feeling of empathy and grace about these shambling flesh-eaters. And by the end of the movie, when what's left of our heroes fly off in the chopper and the dead once more take back their capitalist graveyard, there's a feeling of hollow triumph and eerie melancholy. As "The Gonk" plays over the end credits and the dead shuffle aimlessly through the mall once more, we feel like whatever they are, they deserve this. They are owed this. This is their kingdom. I absolutely find the end of DAWN OF THE DEAD to be an uplifting one and feel like Romero is — like David Cronenberg felt with his 1975 film SHIVERS and his other films about invading species — that the zombies have triumphed in their coup against their oppressors and righteously won the war. It's a theme Romero would explore again in both 1985's DAY OF THE DEAD and 2005's LAND OF THE DEAD, but never as eloquently or artfully articulated as it is here.

DAWN OF THE DEAD is a movie for all time. A movie for *our* time. Though there are thousands of movies like it... there's no movie quite like it. Does that make sense? Watch it again or for the first time. Keep it alive. We need this movie, now more than ever...

MEMOIR: MY FRIEND GEORGE

I had known my friend, my hero George A. Romero was sick for a bit. Not for long, as his illness, lung cancer, took hold of him quickly, reaching stage four and with little hope of it being fixable. The news was a shock. When those people we revere, whether it be an artist we admire, a friend we respect or a relative we adore, leave us, the idea of them *not* being here is inconceivable. Because their life and their influence are tied to our own existence. Their words and thoughts and comfort are linked to happy moments and memories, sometimes their presence in our lives have even helped *save* our lives. To think of them gone is simply a reminder that nothing lasts... even us.

And so it is with George. I can call him George. Because he was my friend. Years after his passing, on July 16th, 2017, years after I stood beside his coffin at his private funeral, surrounded by his family and colleagues, I'm still mourning my friend, that kind, funny and warm-hearted raconteur, who lived for cinema, both making it and watching it. Whose tales of adventure in and around the fringes of Hollyweird held me

Romero with the author at the former's Toronto apartment.

in wonder on the many nights I spent drinking scotch with him in his little condo he shared with his amazing wife Suzanne in Toronto on The Esplanade, or over sushi dinners in the little joint down the street. So comfortable and wonderful were these times that I would sometimes find myself forgetting that this was the man who had made my all-time favorite film, DAWN OF THE DEAD. But it wasn't just DAWN that left its mark on me. I mean, George made so many films that were so deeply ingrained in my adoration of art and culture and cinema and were so much a part of the fabric of my life and essence as a person that often didn't stop to truly consider how essential they were. CREEPSHOW. Jesus, I must have seen CREEPSHOW 50 times as a little boy, the first time with my mother at the age of eight (three years before I found DAWN) on pay-tv and later, when my baby sister was born, it was one of the first VHS tapes I bought and would show it to her daily — at her request — before she'd even started kindergarten. Sounds perverse, I guess, to show a gory R-rated comic book horror movie to a toddler, but my sister has grown into a fine, sophisticated mother and professional and is one of the kindest people alive. Thank George in part for that. And hey, she still loves CREEPSHOW.

And MARTIN? Hell, I have that MARTIN fanged razorblade on my arm, my first of three tattoos, in fact (the other being the door and spiral from THE TWILIGHT ZONE and the Book of Eibon symbol from Lucio Fulci's THE BEYOND). As a kid in Toronto, I had only been allowed to see the butchered Canadian edit of DAY OF THE DEAD (almost 10 minutes shorter, almost no gore!) but I STILL loved it. When Blockbuster Video stores finally came to Canada years later in the late '80s, I found the *full* unrated cut of DAY for rent and had my mind blown and promptly switched labels on my hacked-up Canuck cut, returning that copy, and keeping the uncut Blockbuster copy. Only thing I ever stole in my life, in fact. Thank George for that too, for better or worse. And of course, NIGHT OF THE LIVING DEAD, ground zero, which I saw *after* DAWN, purchasing it on VHS for $9.99 at Kmart with my own money and a film that astonished me with its nihilism. When my middle son Elliot was eight years old, he watched the film and marveled at not how scary it was but, ultimately, just how "sad" it was. With George, it was always about the humanity first, the geek show stuff second.

The list goes on and I can say that every single Romero feature film is somehow tied to pivotal points in the arc of my life.

But back to the friendship.

As a kid, I read *Fangoria*. You did too, probably. I knew George was the Prince of Pittsburgh and Hell, Pittsburgh might as well have been Mars for a little boy on the outskirts of Toronto. But I have learned that when you love what you love passionately, sometimes life just works out. As I grew up and learned more and started talking about movies and then writing about movies and then when my job became talking about movies and writing about movies, that mythical world of the men and women who made all these amazing motion pictures started to become less surreal and more tangible. Suddenly, in 2004, after RESIDENT EVIL, 28 DAYS LATER and the Zack Snyder DAWN OF THE DEAD remake came out, people started to care about zombies again. A lot of people. And then Romero's long-in-gestation 4th DEAD movie LAND OF THE DEAD was green-lit and — shock of shocks — it was being shot... in Toronto! I couldn't get close to the set. I was still just a bush league scribbler (maybe I still am, I dunno), but it was exciting to know that the man was *here*. In *my* city. Then, soon after I found out that Romero had moved here. George A. Romero now *lived* in Toronto. My mind was blown.

In 2006, when production was prepped for his fifth DEAD film, DIARY OF THE DEAD, I was in good enough professional shape that I begged then-editor Tony Timpone at

FANGORIA to let me cover the movie for the magazine. He said yes. Not only did he want three features for print, but he also hired me a union film crew to shoot an on-set television segment for the short-lived Fangoria TV. It was insane. And yet, it happened. I know because I was there. And somewhere that documentary exists. Somewhere...

I remember meeting George for the first time in his trailer on set. I was terrified. He was huge in every way and yet so sweet, so funny and self-deprecating. Those big glasses. That bigger smile. It was clear I was a fawning fan hiding in the guise of being a "journalist," but he made the time for me. He answered the questions he had been asked thousands of times like it was the first time. Like every fan who meets George, I felt special.

Because George valued his fans. He was humble and I'd say even a bit insecure about his work. But he understood the impact his movies had on the people who loved them. It was like seeing the Wizard behind the curtain and NOT being disappointed and then being invited into Oz's secret world and treated like you mattered. I'll never forget it.

After that set visit — which saw me going back three or four times and even penning a piece for The Toronto Star on the experience — George and I stayed in touch. He put me on assignment, asking me to help him find an obscure and rarely seen Nicholas Ray film called WIND ACROSS THE EVERGLADES. It took me months to do, maxing all my resources... but I found it, burned a copy on DVD-R for him and hand-delivered it. He was impressed. When he prepped his DIARY follow-up, the misunderstood SURVIVAL OF THE DEAD, I was asked to come on set and *be* a zombie. I went on set, but it was SO cold, I declined being a ghoul. I came back on set a few times but the window to be zombified had closed. What an idiot I was. I'll regret that for the rest of my life.

When SURVIVAL was done, I remember going out for lunch with George and since director and DAY OF THE DEAD composer John Harrison had dropped out of scoring the film, George asked if I wanted to compose the music. Me! I accepted, of course. The production ultimately went with another composer, but I didn't care. I was asked to score a freaking Romero zombie movie by Romero himself. It was insane. Impossible. But it happened. I was there and I swear that it is true.

Very soon after I took over as editor-in-chief of *Fangoria* and my first feature as EIC was an interview with George about SURVIVAL OF THE DEAD and a feature wherein I had George comment on every movie he'd ever made. It was a lyrical moment for me because without George there would *be* no *Fangoria*. It was that article about DAWN OF THE DEAD in *Fangoria* #1 that so revolted and fascinated readers that the publisher chose graphic horror as the course the mag would take. So, it was kismet that my first piece in *Fangoria* was a George article and that my first piece as EIC would be a George article. And when I took over I started a new line of mags called FANGORIA

Legends and the first issue was a tribute to George.

I remember George and Suz asking me over for scotch and sushi after I got the job as EIC to celebrate. We just talked about movies all night. I know plenty about classic cinema. George knew more, naturally. He was an encyclopedia. Nevertheless, we spent the evening trying to out-trivia each other. This war continued for years via email, with George and I signing off as different, obscure characters in films and then responding based on characters and actors linked to that film. It was a game. I have all these emails saved, of course. Because I could not believe that what was happening was *actually happening.* But it did happen. It was real. Maybe I'll publish these bizarre, scotch-fueled correspondences one day, somewhere.

The author's friendship with Romero was immortalized in sculpted resin.

George was my friend. I loved him. And I like to think he cared about me. I enjoyed his company. I like to think he enjoyed mine. He was always available for me, and I was always there for him. He even commissioned a very silly and very cool sculpture where he is holding my severed, bloody head. It was part of a line of merchandise he was making, and I was the prototype. The line never went anywhere, but I have that amazing sculpture in my house, on my mantle. It's real. My kids are freaked out by it.

I'm looking at it now.

And I'm still that little boy. Being swept away and dazzled by dark, beautiful works of sound and vision made by a man who was and remained to the end, horror cinema's true maverick and true independent. As George loved to tell me, NIGHT OF THE LIVING DEAD instantly made him an "above the credits guy" and contractually, he always had final cut. Every movie he made, even the adaptations of other people's works, they were *his* movies. Made his way. With his people. His written words. His politics. His humor. His love of film, music, art. His cynicism. His joy. His spirit.

I could go on and on about the many gifts George A. Romero gave me. I never took him or the time I had with him for granted. Before he passed, we were working on a new magazine dedicated exclusively to his work and I had hoped that we would get it to print before we lost him, so he could see all the love I had for him, that all his friends and colleagues had for him. I wanted to present a final love letter to him so he would know.

I expressed this very sentiment to George's longtime friend and producing partner Peter Grunwald, to which he responded, "He knew."

I like to think that Peter's right. I think George *did* know that he was loved. Even when he was ripped off or manipulated or taken for granted or forgotten. He knew he was loved. And I think he knew as he passed quietly with Suz by his side that he was one of the lucky ones that would continue to be loved and reborn and discussed and adored forever and ever, as long as the Earth turns and maybe — who knows? — beyond.

Until we meet again *Ramirez*. Thanks for all of it.

DEATH LINE (1972)

Starring Donald Pleasence, Christopher Lee, David Ladd, Norman Rossington
Written by Ceri Jones
Directed by Gary Sherman

Starring In the early 1970s, young Chicago-based commercial filmmaker Gary Sherman found himself in London and inexplicably getting complete creative control over a fully funded British horror film that he co-wrote and directed. That movie was 1972's DEATH LINE, one of the most remarkable, revolting and ultimately emotionally affecting genre movies not only of its decade, but of all time, an essential work of socially volatile horror tragedy.

Inspired by the story of notorious cannibalistic Scottish highwayman Sawney Bean, the horrifying fate of The Donner Party and the creation of the London Underground, DEATH LINE (released in the US as the heavily-hacked RAW MEAT) tells the bone chilling tale of the sole-surviving descendant of a cave-in during those long-ago early tunnel digs who, after being born and raised cannibalizing the dead, has emerged from under the subway tracks and is now dragging hapless British commuters into his moldering, blood and bone-draped lair while frantically searching for a new mate to carry on his diseased lineage.

A clear precursor to Tobe Hooper's THE TEXAS CHAIN SAW MASSACRE and Pete Walker's FRIGHTMARE, DEATH LINE sports a solid and often darkly hilarious performance by the great Donald Pleasence as a Police Inspector trying to get to the bottom of the mystery and a cameo by the legendary Christopher Lee. Starring as "the monster" is

A NEW LINE IN TERROR
DEATH LINE
X
RANK FILM DISTRIBUTORS PRESENT "DEATH LINE" X TECHNICOLOR
STARRING DONALD PLEASENCE · NORMAN ROSSINGTON · DAVID LADD · SHARON GURNEY
AND CHRISTOPHER LEE
SCREENPLAY BY CERI JONES · FROM AN ORIGINAL STORY BY GARY SHERMAN
PRODUCED BY PAUL MASLANSKY DIRECTED BY GARY SHERMAN · A KANTER/LADD PRODUCTION

actor Hugh Armstrong (a role originally meant for Marlon Brando!) and although Pleasence brings the mirth and muscle to the movie, it's Armstrong who pushes DEATH LINE into the annals of masterpiece. Of course, Sherman's sure hand guides him there. There's a startling tracking shot that dives deep into the cannibal wretch's subterranean abode, one that snakes along devoid of music, over bloated, rotting corpses, half-eaten faces and licked-clean rib cages, scurrying rats and general filth; it's a stomach-churning sequence that is punctuated by a distorted humanity when we see Armstrong — his face hacked and blistered with sores — sitting vigil at the greasy bedside of his female mate, who is in the thralls of death. It's a disorienting bit of cinematic bravado that has rarely been matched in the genre.

And DEATH LINE — despite being bogged down slightly by a leading man (David Ladd) who can charitably be referred to as less-than-magnetic — gets under the skin for its comments on class and how those on the fringe are made not born. Like THE TEXAS CHAIN SAW MASSACRE and FRIGHTMARE, DEATH LINE suggests that when society casts a blind eye to what's happening to the common man, hell itself is born from the ashes of ignorance, with the have-nots turning feral and cannibalizing the haves. Sherman was and remains and intensely socially aware filmmaker and his message here is clear. Although later Sherman works like DEAD & BURIED and VICE SQUAD are less personal films, that message is still clear: bad things happen when people ignore the world's problems. That's how monsters are made.

INTERVIEW: GARY SHERMAN

Years ago, Gary Sherman came up to Toronto to host a retrospective screening of POLTERGEIST III, the troubled production that has helped derail his career somewhat. Not because it's a bad picture, it's not. In fact, in many respects its ingenious, building on the mythology of the Hooper/Spielberg original, and deftly manipulating mirrors for its startling in-camera visual effects. Alas, it's also the film that saw young Heather O'Rourke give her final performance, as the child actor died suddenly during the tail end of filming, leading to much controversy and poor box office. Anyway, I had known Gary somewhat over the years but had never met him so, when he breezed into town, I took him out for dinner, sushi if I recall, his choice. He consented to let me turn on my tape recorder and capture his words while we ate. And speaking of eating, naturally, a portion of our chat focused on the making of his flesh-eating masterpiece RAW MEAT, er, DEATH LINE...

CHRIS ALEXANDER: How did Christopher Lee end up in RAW MEAT?
GARY SHERMAN: Don't call it that.

Director Sherman ensured his cannibal killer was as tragic as he was terrifying.

ALEXANDER: You don't like that title?

SHERMAN: No! That was AIP who retitled it for the US release. I hated that title. I still hate that title.

ALEXANDER: Okay… how did Christopher Lee end up in DEATH LINE?

SHERMAN: First of all, (producer) Paul (Maslansky) was very close friends with Christopher Lee, and Christopher was over at Paul's flat, having dinner with him and said, "What are you doing?" And Paul told him, and he said, "Oh, let me read the script." So, Christopher reads the script and says, "I'll be in this movie, if I don't have to wear teeth."

ALEXANDER: Of course. At that point he was just sick of all that fangwork, for sure.

SHERMAN: Yeah. It was right at the point that Christopher announced that he was never going to wear the teeth again. You know what? I'm getting a little ahead of myself. When I wrote the script, I had Donald Pleasence in mind for Inspector Calhoun. And so, I ended up flying to New York. Donald was on Broadway doing *Man In The Glass Booth*. And, so, he was just about to close that and coming back to London, but we wanted to lock him in, so I flew to New York, gave Donald the script, and he read it, and he loved it, and said, "Oh! Man! I wanna do this. Nobody offers me comedy. And even though it's a scary movie, you know, my part is all comedy. And I love it. And I love the juxtaposition of the comedy against the horror." So, we signed Donald. So, when Paul was having dinner with Chris Lee, because Chris, at the time, was the most expensive actor in Europe because of Dracula. And, you know, the Hammer films. And there was no way, I mean, what Chris used to get paid for a movie was more than our whole budget. So, Chris said,

"If I don't have to wear the teeth and I can do a scene with Donald Pleasence, I will do this for scale." So... I wrote that scene. [*laughs*]

ALEXANDER: That's amazing!

SHERMAN: So, anyhow... so, now we had Donald Pleasence and Chris Lee and Norm Rossington. And Jay Cantor, who had been Marlon Brando's agent, throughout his entire career says, "God, I wonder if Marlon would want to play the monster? He's in Paris right now, working with Bertolucci on some crazy movie. So, let me call Marlon, and let me send him the script, and see if he wants to do it!" And so, Jay does. And Marlon, who, Jay says, "Marlon loves makeup. He loves putting the makeup on!" Because, you know, he had that idea, when Francis wanted him for Godfather, and nobody at Paramount wanted him in Godfather... he went, and he came up with that whole idea of stuffing his mouth with Kleenex and he went in and blew them away. And so, I know he loves doing that kind of stuff. So, anyways, Marlon agreed to do it.

ALEXANDER: Well, he'd also just done a horror film with Michael Winner prior to this, 1972's THE NIGHTCOMERS.

SHERMAN: Yeah, which Jay and Laddie (Alan Ladd Jr.) had produced.

ALEXANDER: Oh, well, there you go. Okay.

SHERMAN: It was Jay Cantor, Alan Ladd Jr. and Elliot Kastner who did THE NIGHTCOMERS. I mean, there were no two people closer than Jay Cantor and Marlon Brando. And, so, anyways, then, at the eleventh hour, Marlon's son, Christian, comes down with pneumonia in Los Angeles and is, like, on a critical list. So, Marlon has to jump on a plane and goes back to Los Angeles, and we lost Marlon. Which, I mean, we weren't going to advertise the fact- I mean the whole idea was, is that Marlon is gonna do it and we were never gonna tell anyone- we were not gonna put his name on the movie, and it was just kind of gonna get leaked out that, "Maybe that's Marlon Brando" [*laughs*].

THE DEATHMASTER (1972)

Starring Robert Quarry, Bill Ewing, Brenda Dickson, John Fiedler
Written by R.L. Grove
Directed by Ray Danton

From its opening scenes of Southern California tranquility and the flute-accompanied visual of a coffin washing to shore, Ray Danton's 1972 vampire cult shocker THE DEATHMASTER makes its mission clear and that is to bring a kind of European poetry and intelligent grace to the contemporary American drive-in trash flick. And it does all of this and more besides. And yet so few ardent strange cinema fans talk about it.

THE DEATHMASTER (or, as the title appears on screen, simply DEATHMASTER) is a mesmerizing and totally unique horror movie, one that capitalizes on both the shock in the wake of the well publicized Manson murders and the sudden fame of character actor Robert Quarry, who had found a jolt of popularity due to American International Pictures' 1970 chiller COUNT YORGA, VAMPIRE. That film featured Quarry as a suave, articulate aristocratic vampire who brings a wave of death to a So-Cal suburb and was filmed by director Bob Kelljan as THE LOVES OF COUNT YORGA and was intended to be a sex film. Quarry balked at the banging and the sex wasn't shot and, since Yorga looked better on a poster, the title was changed too, as it appeared everyone was saying "Yorga" anyway (the original MGM DVD had the original title on the print).

After the success of COUNT YORGA, VAMPIRE, Quarry was being groomed to be the mature successor to their mainstay star, Vincent Price. But Quarry went rogue and set up THE DEATHMASTER in 1970 with actor-turned-director Danton (THE PSYCHIC KILLER) directing, Quarry executive producing and starring in a role that was like a death cult hippie generation revamp (ha!) of his YORGA character. But AIP was not pleased. When

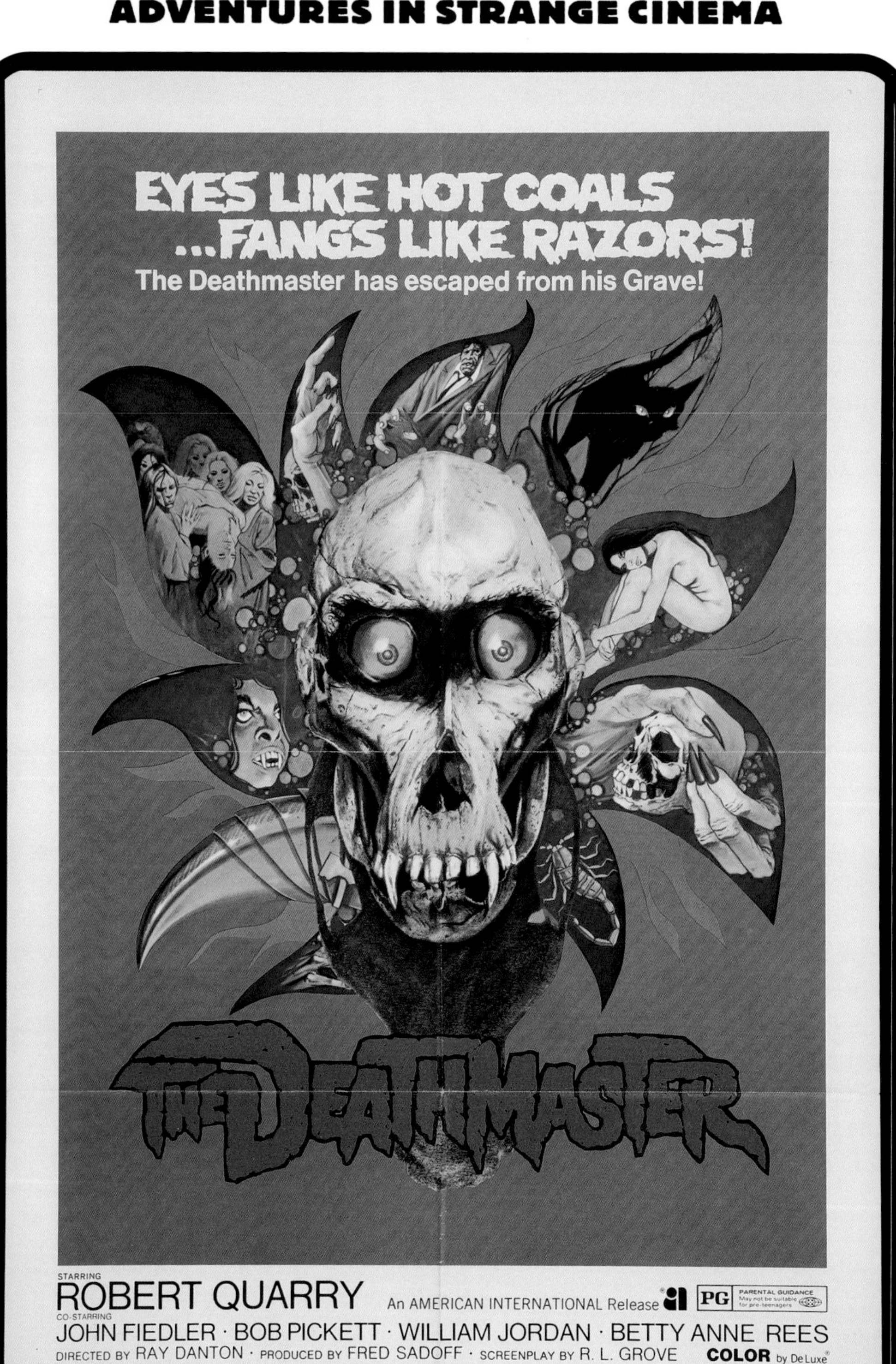
EYES LIKE HOT COALS
...FANGS LIKE RAZORS!
The Deathmaster has escaped from his Grave!
THE DEATHMASTER
STARRING
ROBERT QUARRY
An AMERICAN INTERNATIONAL Release
PG
PARENTAL GUIDANCE
CO-STARRING
JOHN FIEDLER · BOB PICKETT · WILLIAM JORDAN · BETTY ANNE REES
DIRECTED BY RAY DANTON · PRODUCED BY FRED SADOFF · SCREENPLAY BY R. L. GROVE
COLOR by DeLuxe
72/267

Roger Corman did the same thing in 1962 and broke away from AIP, teaming with Pathe to make the Poe film THE PREMATURE BURIAL, AIP honchos Sam Arkoff and James Nicholson were so cheesed that they ended up buying Pathe and forcing Corman back to work for them anyway. So it goes with THE DEATHMASTER. AIP bought the film from the original distributor and essentially shelved it. They had Quarry on contract and they jumped into making an authentic sequel, 1971's THE RETURN OF COUNT YORGA and they even had the cheek to steal THE DEATHMASTER's title for that film's theatrical poster tagline!

Anyway, THE DEATHMASTER eventually did receive a brief theatrical bow in 1972 with little to no marketing push behind it. It was quickly licensed for TV which is where many people — me included — saw the movie, late at night. Quarry's stint at the flailing AIP was short-lived and THE DEATHMASTER faded away. And it should not have done so.

Because THE DEATHMASTER is beautiful, arch, lyrical and weird and Quarry is simply amazing in it. Here, he plays a long-haired bearded guru named Khorda who is called forth from the sea by his mute manservant (LaSesne Hilton) and makes his way to a commune of pot-baked hippies looking for "the answer." Khorda immediately goes to work turning the kids into his flock, charming them, dazzling them with long, metaphysical pontifications on life, death, God and the nature of the universe and time. He teaches them to purify their bodies and to stop using drugs and to eat only good food. They fall at his feet, all save for the cynical and scrappy Pico (Bill Ewing) who suspects something is up. And he's right, it is. Soon Khorda reveals his true nature, that of a manipulative and thoroughly evil vampire looking to build a coven and bring death and plague to the land.

THE DEATHMASTER is unlike anything else. Quarry is incredible, with his ice blue eyes and piercing gaze and mouthful of razor sharp fangs (the same ones he would wear in both YORGA pictures) and elegant way of making even the pithiest dialogue feel like vintage Shakespearean sonnets. The rest of the cast is weird and cool with John Fiedler — the voice of Disney's Piglet from the "Winnie the Pooh" movies — miscast but effectively odd as Pico's elder pal and fellow vampire hunter. The "Monster Mash" rocker Bobby "Boris" Pickett is in the movie too and even warbles a tune at one point. And both the mansion where the hippies hang out and the eerie catacombs beneath it add imposing and surreal production value. Danton also knows how to exploit the beauty and sensuality of the California coast and weave it into the fabric of a horror film. And like the YORGA movies, the end is also supremely nihilistic and reminds me somewhat of the final act of Tobe Hooper's THE TEXAS CHAINSAW MASSACRE PART 2.

THE DEATHMASTER languished in obscurity for decades until cult filmmaker Fred Olen Ray (SCALPS, BIOHAZZARD) found the 35mm negative and, seeing as he was both a fan of the film and a dear friend of Quarry's, he released it via his Retromedia DVD imprint in a feature packed special edition complete with an unforgettable Quarry/Olen Ray commentary. Where that negative is now is anyone's guess. And as of this writing, the film has skipped Blu-ray entirely. What gives?

DEMON SEED (1977)

Starring Julie Christie, Fritz Weaver, Robert Vaughn, Gerrit Graham
Written by Robert Jaffe, Roger O. Hirson
Directed by Donald Cammell

There's a look, a tone and visual texture to science fiction films from the early to mid-1970s; a sanitized glimpse of a future that, seen today, exists only as a perversion of the past. The blinking light boards, silly tubes that lead nowhere, whitewashed walls, turtleneck wearing intellectuals, the list goes on. Think of the great glossy glimpses into ersatz tomorrows of that era — THX 1183, A CLOCKWORK ORANGE, SOYLENT GREEN, LOGAN'S RUN, CLONUS — and you'll see what I mean. But outside of the curiously antiseptic funkiness of their art direction, 1970s sci-fi was also incredibly thoughtful and bold, criticizing politics, people and modern technology with a somber humorlessness and nightmarish immediacy that suited the material beautifully.

Then STAR WARS came along and screwed it all up.

But the very same year that George Lucas and his company of Goodwill-garbed action figures were saving Hollywood's waning box office takes by demolishing sophisticated cinema, wobble-psyched British filmmaker Donald Cammell was unleashing his own mind-bending glimpse at a far grimmer future. A loose adaptation of a very early and only so-so same-named Dean R. Koontz pulp thriller, Cammell's seminal (and I mean that literally) 1977 technology run amok masterwork DEMON SEED has never gotten its dues as a serious piece of sci-fi/horror cinema. Don't get me wrong, the film has its fans, but, I mean, I've never seen anyone prancing about with a picture of an electrode wearing Julie Christie on a T-shirt or anything. But if you follow me down into prophetic disco-era cyberspace for the next few paragraphs, you may just find yourself wanting one.

DEMON SEED stars hangdog faced character actor Fritz Weaver (key TWILIGHT ZONE episodes, CREEPSHOW) as Dr. Alex Harris, a scientist working for a shadowy corporation that has invented an organic, sentient computer system dubbed Proteus IV. The multi-talented machine has been blessed with the world's first synthetic cortex — a real deal brain — and can do everything from solving impossible mathematical equations to curing leukemia. When nervous executives order the Proteus IV project to be shut

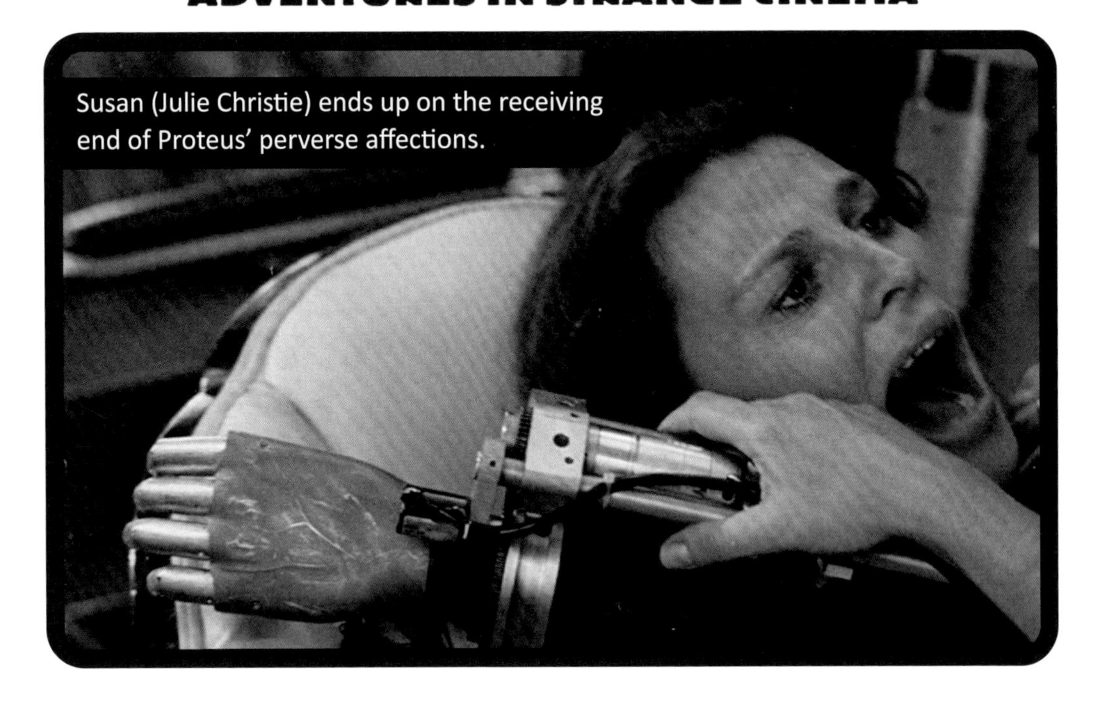
Susan (Julie Christie) ends up on the receiving end of Proteus' perverse affections.

down, they little suspect that the high brow hard drive has in fact developed a basic human trait: the primal desire to live, to survive no matter what the cost.

Tapping into a portal in Harris's state-of-the-art, high-tech home, Proteus proceeds to take over the place, possessing everything from the kitchen appliances to the security system and imprisoning the good Professor's beautiful wife Susan (the gorgeous and talented Christie in a fearless performance that runs the gamut). Seems Proteus's desperate desire to stay alive has forced him to devise the most diabolical of plans: coldly, clinically he informs the terrified Susan that he will, over the coming days, bind her, probe her, prep her, make love to her, and impregnate her. See, Proteus has pretensions of parenthood and thinks that the key to ensuring his immortality is in spilling his cyber seed into a human woman and hiding beneath the guise of the very beings who sculpted him.

Taking its cues from both Kubrick's landmark 2001: A SPACE ODYSSEY and Roman Polanski's ROSEMARY'S BABY, Cammell's film manages to out-freak them both and operate on a far more emotionally sophisticated level. The fact that Proteus wants to live at any cost and, though she is both opposed and repulsed by her impending A.I. (artificial insemination), Susan is still carrying guilt and misery over the death of her own daughter the previous year, adds a complex dynamic to the proceedings. The movie also echoes the same existential terrain explored in sci-fi guru Phillip K. Dick's 1965 novel *Do Androids Dream Of Electric Sheep* (developed even more explicitly in Ridley Scott's loose 1982 big screen adaptation BLADE RUNNER) in that the so-called "villain" is in fact the victim: an ersatz, Frankenstein like, man-made creation that simply wants to belong and exist in the natural world, but has no conception how to go about doing so.

Though DEMON SEED does indeed function as an intellectual genre exercise, don't let me mislead you about the more visceral frissons the film provides; it's as kinky, eccentric, and bizarre as a film directed by the co-helmer of the spectacularly sleazy Mick Jagger shocker performance should be. The late Cammell (who unfortunately blew his own head off in 1996) was a real deal lunatic who lived an extreme and extremely volatile life, only actually making a handful of pictures (including the blistering 1987 slasher deconstruction WHITE OF THE EYE, another of my personal favorites), but when he spoke, baby, he spoke loudly and, especially here, damned ferociously.

And though DEMON SEED is set in a world of harsh edges, speculative science, and malevolent robots, Cammell chooses to accentuate the more organic angles of the tale; this is after all an exploitation film about a computer fucking, or rather, raping, a woman to create a kind of bionic bastard. During the pivotal and perverse fornication sequence, Cammell spins the picture into hallucinogenic visual overdrive, blasting colorful wormholes and violent editing spasms across the screen in a miasma of melty eyeball spinning bliss. Then, at DEMON SEED's halfway point as Susan begins her rapidly belly swelling incubation period, various people stumble into the home only to be dispatched by the defensive Proteus. For these sequences, Cammell temporarily abandons his elegant sexual science approach and goes for outrageous horror show Grand Guignol, as the nest protecting computer miraculously transforms into a smooth, pulsing and homicidal, human crushing Rubik's Cube, a writhing, larger than life riff on the decade later Lament Configuration in Clive Barker's HELLRAISER. It's out of left field elements like this that make DEMON SEED such a head spinning, brilliant and disorienting cinematic experience.

Firmly set in the center of DEMON SEED's weird celluloid universe, and indeed the source of much of the picture's dramatic power, is the low, controlled and chilling passive aggressive vocal persona of Proteus himself, a tour de force turn by THE MAN FROM U.N.C.L.E.'s Robert Vaughan. Forget "Hal", Vaughan's Proteus is a sexually aware device that tries to imitate his human masters but just can't find the eye of the mortal needle.

There's a real vulnerability to the omnipresent Proteus that, whether vindictively punishing Susan by cranking the heat in the house to lethal levels or cooing like a microchip Casanova, makes him both a scary and realistic screen presence. If I ran the world, 1977 would have been the year Robert Vaughan took home the Oscar. But alas I don't, and he didn't.

As decadent and out of control as DEMON SEED may appear to be, Cammell knew exactly what he was doing, making a futuristic sex thriller by way of brain melting acid trip; a smart, frightening, sexy and one of a kind movie that also stands as the last great science fiction film of the decade.

Evelyn (Chiara D'Anna) and Cynthia (Sidse Babett Knudson) explore sex, power and butterflies in THE DUKE OF BURGUNDY.

THE DUKE OF BURGUNDY (2014)

Starring Sidse Babett Knudson, Chiara D'Anna, Monica Swinn, Eugenia Caruso
Written by Peter Strickland
Directed by Peter Strickland

What is gender, exactly? When sperm hits egg and the first spark of creation takes shape in the cozy confines of the mother's womb, all life is... is just life. Just the blueprint of the potential of what we will become. What plumbing and genetic purpose that life will have is unknown. And then a biological die is cast and *presto bingo*, we have a code that defines a role in nature. But no matter what dangles between our legs, we are all amalgams of both, we all have the same chemicals and impulses, just some of us are designed to perhaps tilt strongly in one direction or another. It's out of our hands. It's nature.

But where things get tricky and — yawn, yes, political — is when we socialize nature. When we try to put parameters around that which should have none. Religion, media, fashion, school, all these societal factors serve to muddy waters that should run pure. Boys. Girls. Men. Women. Beyond our biological function when it comes to mating and birthing, we are all in fact masculine and feminine hybrids. And yet we keep on trying to categorize and compartmentalize.

Which brings me to British director Peter Strickland's ingenious and delirious 2014 masterpiece THE DUKE OF BURGUNDY, a film I fell in love with instantly and which has haunted me ever since. Like his previous singular cinematic swoon, 2013's BERBERIAN

SOUND STUDIO, DUKE combines intimate drama with hyper-stylized evolutions of European genre tropes and fetishization of their iconography. In BERBERIAN it was the giallo film, focusing its narrative on a cinema sound designer who is losing his mind while working on an imagined '70s Italian thriller. In DUKE, Strickland mines the voyeuristic, psychedelic and lush films of Jess Franco. In fact, the movie began its life as a straight remake of Franco's 1974 exploitation shocker LORNA THE EXORCIST. But Strickland — one of the most wonderfully unconventional filmmakers alive — got bored of the idea of a remake and instead took the project in another direction. And I'm so glad he did. Because what he did here in this mesmerizing film transcends any sort of classification. Sure, it has the ghost of Franco whispering in our ears, but this is Strickland's vision. It's pure cinema, deceivingly simple, breathtaking to behold and intimately observed with one of the most fragile and moving film scores I've ever had the pleasure of hearing. And while THE DUKE OF BURGUNDY was exceedingly well reviewed and beloved by many, it's still very much a secret. It's out there. And it needs your eyes, your mind, your heart. And your other parts.

The film opens (under the loveliest of credits sequences) with the doe-eyed Evelyn (Chiara D'Anna) riding her bike across some unnamed European countryside to the opulent home of her regal — and much older — employer Cynthia (Sidse Babett Knudsen), where she apparently works as a maid. The stern Cynthia chastises Evelyn for her tardiness and orders her to clean and scrub her home on her hands and knees and it soon becomes very evident that the pair share an intense master/slave-based, sexual relationship. Or do they?

Cynthia is a Lepidopterologist (which is a branch of entomology specializing in butterflies) and Evelyn, when she's not reveling in her older lover's sadistic sex play, is one of her students. But what is their relationship, exactly? As the story, with its teasingly perverted rituals, progresses, we learn that it is in fact Evelyn who is the master of the dynamic, with Cynthia dutifully indulging her youthful partner. But at what cost? When Evelyn's eyes brighten up at the idea of having a custom made "human toilet" installed in their home, it's clear Cynthia is becoming weary of these deviations. Meanwhile, the camera crawls and zooms and obsesses over architecture, leathers and laces and naked skin and the music of ethereal band Cat's Eyes spills and spirals all over the soundtrack.

If you've indeed seen Strickland's arresting psychodrama BERBERIAN SOUND STUDIO, you're probably still thinking about that one. It's such a singular piece of work that it falls into the category of movies that people either worship or despise. This writer of course fell into the former category while fully understanding the confounded and unimpressed point of view of the latter. It's not an easy pill to swallow. But DUKE is far more narratively accessible than that film, though it's just as visually arresting. Here, Strickland creates an immersive, swirling tapestry of sound and image, with repeating motifs, whispers, obsessive imagery, and potent sensuality. But the real trick of the film ties into the opening of this hopefully edifying essay in that concepts of gender are rendered moot.

Ostensibly, THE DUKE OF BURGUNDY is a lesbian love story. Except, it's not. Look at the movie. Look at not just the stunning leads, but the supporting cast, the peripheral players, the extras. There are no men. Anywhere. And nobody questions this. There just aren't any men in the universe in which this tale takes place inside. And yet, once you become locked into the movie, you don't really notice this. Instead, the female leads aren't identified as female but instead emerge and either masculine or feminine presences. There are aggressive and passive people in the movie. It's not about identifying oneself as a boy or girl or gay or straight. It's simply about the two opposing yet harmonious forces of nature that are in all of us. On that level, THE DUKE OF BURGUNDY is a remarkable experiment in perception. And on another level, it's also a profound, moving character study of a person who loves another person and alters herself to accommodate that love, to "keep" that person. It's about sacrifices. It's about selfishness and selflessness, power, and submission and how these dynamics are endlessly reversed. It's raw and real. And it's dressed up in so much cinematic finery, both eerie and lush, that it has a sensorial pleasure unlike any other movie before it.

Well, unlike any other movie that Jess Franco didn't make, that is...

EATEN ALIVE! (1980)

Starring Robert Kerman, Janet Agren, Ivan Rassimov, Me Me Lai
Written by Umberto Lenzi
Directed by Umberto Lenzi

Out of all the vile, debaucherous post-MONDO CANE Italian *junglesploitation* movies ground-out in the 1970s and 80s, Umberto Lenzi's 1980 chunk-blower EATEN ALIVE! (MANGIATI VIVI) is the one that Canadians love the most. Why is that? Because it's the only one — perhaps the only Italian horror movie, full stop (not counting the KING KONG riff YETI, which is oddly set in Toronto) — that sets part of its action in the country, opening as it does in Niagara Falls, with a poor sod getting a poison blow-dart spat into his neck.

Now, this point may seem a silly way to open a discussion about a Lenzi-lensed gorefest but it's subjectively important for me, glutting as I did on all these sorts of films as an impressionable teenager. Seeing my country represented on screen in an

Italian gore movie — which then felt as though they were being beamed in from another dimension entirely — was disorienting and gave the film a sense of tangible reality that other pictures of its ilk lacked. None of this is to say that EATEN ALIVE! is better than other more notable films like Ruggero Deodato's punishing CANNIBAL HOLOCAUST or earlier JUNGLE HOLOCAUST or even Lenzi's own notorious dick-ripper CANNIBAL FEROX, but it does have the distinction of being the weirdest entry in the cannon and not just because of the curious Canadian connection. No, EATEN ALIVE is an utterly insane dose of jungle horror delirium that earns its unsavory reputation, ladling the flesh-ripping, tempering it with animal snuff and tying it up with a rape. And yet the entire enterprise is so daffy, it's impossible to take it terribly seriously.

The films stars THE GATES OF HELL's Janet Agren as Sheila, a young woman whose sister Diana (Paola Senatore) has gone missing in the jungles of New Guinea. Seems the dudes running around Niagara Falls (and New York) jabbing needles into people are kidnapping average citizens and dragging them to sweltering jungle where they are then drugged and brainwashed by a maniacal cult leader named Jonas (Ivan Rassimov, who himself starred in Lenzi's 1972 shocker THE MAN FROM DEEP RIVER and the aforementioned JUNGLE HOLOCAUST). Sheila hires a smart-ass, cynical mercenary named Mark (CANNIBAL HOLOCAUST's Robert Kerman, who also — under the name R. Bolla — appeared in many a hardcore porn flick) to help her liberate her sibling from the clutches of the cult but — surprise! — the Kool-Aid-soaked community is surrounded by a savage tribe of cannibals who love to butcher and dine on human intruders when they run out of crocodiles and other beasts to rip to shreds.

As per many of these movies, those real deal animal murders are the toughest thing to take in EATEN ALIVE!, heart-wrenching scenes of screaming critters stabbed and skinned by cackling natives. Lenzi's defense — along with Deodato's, whose CANNIBAL HOLOCAUST set the nauseatingly low bar for this snuffy stuff — was that the natives would kill and eat these animals anyway, so hey, why not splice it Mondo-style into the fabric of a low budget horror picture? We won't cast judgement on their exploitative decisions but the sequences in question are rough stuff indeed. In fact, some of said scenes — along with select shots of flesh chomping — were lifted wholesale by Lenzi from his own THE MAN FROM DEEP RIVER as well as Sergio Martino's MOUNTAIN OF THE CANNIBAL GOD. This oddball, corner-cutting cut-and-paste padding stunt has — in many serious fan circles — further pushed EATEN ALIVE! to the bottom of the cannibal flick barrel, but to me, these redux shock scenes just add to the wanton weirdness of the picture.

There's plenty of DOCTOR BUTCHER M.D./ZOMBI HOLOCAUST narrative thrust in this picture too, as it shares a similar framework of natives in North America up to no good and leading a bloody trail to a tropical inferno where a madman ex-patriot holds court and cannibals run rampant. Agren even gets stripped and painted in a scene that echoes Alexandra Delli Colli's show-stopping scene in ZOMBI HOLOCAUST. But what really sets EATEN ALIVE! apart from the pancreas-snacking pack is Rassimov's Jonas and the central story of how the delusional self-professed prophet manipulates and abuses his "followers". Jonas is clearly a stand-in for Jim Jones and Rassimov — with his cruel good looks and scowling mouth — is alternately chilling and outrageously, endearingly over-the-top in the role. And while seeing him assault Agren with a snake-venom dildo *should* be offensive, Rassimov's comic book leer and Agren's reactions push the sequence into the level of near-H.G. Lewis camp.

EATEN ALIVE! is a revolting gem of cartoonish depravity and yes, the titular promise of characters being consumed while conscious does in fact play out, with a cheerfully fake (love those "severed" limbs hiding in the sand gags!) and wildly sickening final reel gross-out where Senatore and cannibal movie legend Me Me Lai get assaulted and devoured by a gaggle of happy savages. Adding to the cross-eyed, gore-drenched groove is a schizophrenic score by "Buddy Maglione" (a pseudonym for composers Fiamma Maglione and Roberto Donati), that veers between ambient terror, stinky-funk sleaze and prog-rock doom. EATEN ALIVE! is a grandiose piece of gonzo Grand Guignol and you don't even have to be Canadian to love it off.

John Merrick (John Hurt) peers out at an unkind world.

THE ELEPHANT MAN (1980)

Starring John Hurt, Anthony Hopkins, Ann Bancroft, Freddie Jones
Written by Christopher De Vore, Eric Bergen, David Lynch
Directed by David Lynch

David Lynch's TWIN PEAKS revival took everything that made the landmark original ABC series so memorable and went even further into the ether, with the unobstructed non-network outlet (the series is a Showtime production) allowing Lynch to go as gonzo as he wanted to, respecting fan expectations while radically expanding and inverting that world, lapsing into the avant-garde, totally liberated. It was mesmerizing. Energizing. Because out of all the elite directors who managed to infiltrate the Hollywood machine, Lynch remains one of the few that were working artists first, visionaries who developed a language all their own during a formative time and who use that singular creative dialect to make films their way, only giving cursory consideration to the suits who kept blind eyes on him, hoping to keep his work at least somewhat commercial.

And while seeing that "pure" revisit of TWIN PEAKS stand tall as the unfiltered wellspring of the Lynchian aesthetic, citing the times when Lynch has had to collaborate and enlist a more disciplined approach to his vision, yields no real criticism. I mean, the fact that TWIN PEAKS ever ended up on general stream network television in 1990 *at all,* is a marvel. It was way out there and defied what anyone wanted or expected from a prime-time program. But going even further back, right back to 1980, to Lynch's second feature film, we see what might very well be his greatest achievement, a movie that he was brought into and yet was given enough of a long creative leash to ensure that the motion picture he was hired to make, was indeed his and yet was also greater than him. A movie that likely educated the director and taught him that introducing strong human emotion into his *nightmarescapes* and populating the frames with the finest of performers, could result in a work that was both art and product in equal measure.

That movie was THE ELEPHANT MAN, Lynch's follow-up to his fearless, unclassifiable midnight sensation ERASERHEAD. And 38 years later, looking back, it's still a bold, brave and immaculately produced motion picture that offers the best of what Lynch could do and bears early evidence of the tropes and themes that would define his subsequent works.

As the story goes, Mel Brooks, he of scatological, smart and silly comedies BLAZING SADDLES and YOUNG FRANKENSTEIN, had just started a company called Brooksfilms wherein the producer could make "real movies" while hiding in the background so as not to mislead his fan base. His partner, producer Jonathan Sanger, got his hands on first draft script called THE ELEPHANT MAN, which told the loosely true story of Joseph "John" Merrick, a wildly deformed young man who was rescued from the sideshow circuit in Victorian England and who became first a case study for a prominent London doctor and then, a national celebrity. The story was dark, evocative, and sharply moral and for whatever reason, Sanger — who had recently seen and swooned over ERASERHEAD — thought Lynch would be a good bet to bring the steam-soaked tale to life. He met with Lynch who adored the script and agreed to do the film, and, after a few rewrites, the movie was put into production.

With the budget and muscle of Brooks, Sanger and Paramount Pictures behind him, Lynch was able to amass a remarkable cast of British talent, first class performers like Sir Anthony Hopkins, Sir John Hurt, Sir John Gielgud, Anne Bancroft (Brooks' wife) and Freddie Jones. But most importantly, THE ELEPHANT MAN allowed Lynch to work with a man widely considered to be one of the greatest living directors of photography, Freddie Francis, a man who had worked as both DP and director on a myriad Hammer horror movies and British exploitation pictures, including Joan Crawford's final film, TROG. Shooting in stark black and white to better paint a picture of the Victorian period but also give the production's limited designs a more dreamlike feel, Francis and Lynch essentially dragged ERASERHEAD to turn of the century England and grafted that film's horrific, hallucinatory style to a potent story of pain and grace. Francis was never a conventional artist and with Lynch he was allowed to fully embrace his own eccentricities. I firmly believe that Francis' influence on Lynch was an invaluable experience and heavily influenced Lynch's sense of cinema and visual storytelling.

From the beginning of THE ELEPHANT MAN, we know that we're in that very same world first found in ERASERHEAD, where, after the tinkling, circus-steeped strains of John Morris' lovely score and images of a face floating in space (a Lynch trademark), we are treated to a nightmarish, impressionist sequence where a group of slow-motion-moving elephants either trample or gang-rape a screaming woman, meant to be Merrick's mother. This is not a scene to be taken literally, but rather is a dream that metaphorically illustrates Merrick's life of trauma and exploitation, where the love of his mother and his own upbringing have long been distorted by the scream of his carnival-barking owner (the great Freddie Jones, who is at his most despicable here). From this passage of savagery, we are thrust into the tawdry back-alleys of London where Lynch expertly juxtaposes the grime with the kind-eyes of Doctor Frederick Treves (Hopkins, who has never given a more moving performance on screen) and from here, our tale unfolds. Hearing tales of the horrifying "Elephant Man," Treves' professional curiosity and interest in helping the needy, spur him to bring the unfortunate Merrick (who is brilliantly played by John Hurt, buried under Christopher Tucker's intense prosthetic makeup) to the hospital where he works in order to study him and present him to his peers. First thinking the disfigured wretch an imbecile, Treves soon learns that Merrick is in fact a gentle, educated man who, despite the horrors he has endured is graced with a childlike sense of wonder and a hard-wired humanity and heart full of hope, instilled there by his late mother. As Treves treats Merrick, he is lauded for his work and "The Elephant Man" becomes famous. But despite the kindness and grace the unfortunate Merrick receives at the hands and hearts of his benefactors, there are blacker forces at hand that aim to drag the young man back into the cesspool.

THE ELEPHANT MAN is a perfect movie and, as John Hurt once said "If you're not moved by the time The Elephant Man is over... then you're not someone I want to know." I agree.

Lynch's interest in holding frames and not giving into quick edits allows sequences of Hurt reacting to the kindness he is suddenly being shown to become almost religious experiences. We feel this man's pain, his gratefulness, his empathy. There's a humanity at work here that Lynch would later weave into the harsh worlds of BLUE VELVET and TWIN PEAKS, real, profound emotion and sadness over just how cruel men can be to other men. The story is clear, elemental, and driven by its talented cast and, again, the period is richly realized by Lynch and Francis. And when Lynch steers the imagery towards dreams, when he begins fetishizing belching smokestacks, grinding machines and the horror and coldness of the factory, they serve to not only tie the movie into ERASERHEAD but also comment on the hostile, anti-human world that Merrick sadly came of age in, the one surrounds the refined, clean and kind world of Treves. The imagery is not self indulgent. It makes sense.

By the time the movie winds down, an inevitable climax of grace, surrender, sadness and hope, all played out the strains of Samuel Barber's Adagio For Strings, you feel THE ELEPHANT MAN in your bones. You feel as though you have witnessed a one-of-kind amalgam of bold artistry, history, and universal human drama. Of horror and beauty in equal measure.

Lynch would bring much of what he did here to his (arguably) failed adaptation of DUNE, but he wasn't ready for DUNE. It was too big for him to control. BLUE VELVET was more successful and yet it still suffers somewhat for its over-reliance on freakishness and kink. Still, what is Frank Booth (Dennis Hopper) but a mutated version of Freddie Jones' character in THE ELEPHANT MAN? What are Bob and his followers in TWIN PEAKS, but a satanic riff on the human sludge that exploit and prey upon John Merrick and others like him?

The TWIN PEAKS revival was a marvel and might just be Lynch's final opus, his magnum. But for my money, there was a kind of magic in THE ELEPHANT MAN that looms the largest in his filmography. Where youth and talent and freedom of expression and education all met to make one brilliant and enduring motion picture like no other.

EMANUELLE AND FRANCOISE (1975)

Starring George Eastman, Rosmarie Lindt, Annie Carol Edel, Maria Rosaria Riuzzu
Written by Joe D'Amato, Bruno Mattei
Directed by Joe D'Amato

Even within the skeezy depths of Joe D'Amato's cinematic oeuvre, the director's 1975 sex thriller EMANUELLE AND FRANCOISE is a jaw dropper. D'Amato made his share of unofficial sequels to the popular Silvia Kristel-starring erotic EMMANUELLE movies, most starring the lovely Laura Gemser, but this *trashterpiece* (also known as EMANUELLE'S REVENGE) is among the best and is almost as cheerfully vulgar than his crown-jewel of vileness, the disturbing 1977 entry EMANUELLE IN AMERICA. Echoing the plot of the decade-and-change later Lucio Fulci softcore drama THE DEVIL'S HONEY, EMANUELLE AND FRANCOISE wallows in perversion to tell its operatically extreme tale of

GEORGE EASTMAN · ROSE MARIE LINDT
EMANUELLE e FRANÇOISE
LE SORELLINE
KAROLE-ANNIE-EDEL · MARY KRISTAL · GIORGIO FLERI · MASSIMO VANNI
con PATRIZIA GORI
REGIA: JOE D'AMATO
MATRA CINEMATOGRAFICA
COLORE
DI LUCIANO

vengeance and sexual humiliation and though D'Amato's lens captures ample upset, the entire thing is just so damned entertaining and groovy (Joe Dynamo's funk soul score is a marvel) that you can't help but kinda love it.

D'Amato regular George Eastman (the monster-man in ANTHROPOPHAGUS and ABSURD and the lead stud in EROTIC NIGHTS OF THE LIVING DEAD) stars as Carlo a preening Svengali-esque hustler brute who toils on the back end of the entertainment business, grafting gigs and delighting in the exploitation and degradation of his lover, the sweet-natured and fragile Francoise (Patrizia Gori). As the film opens, Carlo subjects the girl to one blow too many and she jumps in front of a train. Enter Francoise's sister Emanuelle (in this incarnation played by SALON KITTY's Rosemarie Lindt), who traces the sad tale of her sister's decline via letters, with each despicable incident leeringly illustrated by D'Amato for the audience's outrage and titillation. Soon, Emanuelle hatches a plot to seduce, trap and torture the bastard, locking him in a room armed with a two-way mirror, drugging him, and subjecting him to endless images of her getting off with a succession of lovers, both male and female.

EMANUELLE AND FRANCOISE is pretty much everything you want from a Eurothriller, especially one helmed by the notorious D'Amato. There's a giallo-like structure to the piece, there's pretty seaside sequences, piles of nudity, buckets of revolting behavior and sexual sadism and there's even a really gross cannibal dinner sequence that is as ludicrous as it is sickening. Sure, the film is unapologetic trash, but it's skillfully made, looks fantastic and moves like a butter-basted bullet from a gun, filling every inch of its running time with intrigue and transgression. But there's also a streak of surrealism here, one that often veers either consciously or accidentally into Buñuel or Fellini territory. As far as Joe D'Amato movies go, this might be the most accomplished one I've ever seen. It's certainly the most entertaining.

EMANUELLE AND FRANCOISE is not for the feint of heart, but if extreme '70s Euroshock is your cup of greasy fluid, drink up!

ESCAPE FROM L.A. (1996)

Starring Kurt Russell, Steve Buscemi, Stacy Keach, Pam Grier
Written by John Carpenter, Debra Hill, Kurt Russell
Directed by John Carpenter

When John Carpenter's ESCAPE FROM NEW YORK was released in 1981, the modestly budgeted pulp action flick was a huge hit, both domestically and, surprisingly, in Europe (especially Italy) where, along with 1979's MAD MAX and its 1982 sequel, every

Eddie (Steve Buscemi) points Snake (Kurt Russell) in the right direction.

savvy producer tried their hand at ripping it off. That Carpenter chased it with his biggest movie — and at that point biggest failing — 1982's THE THING says much about the filmmaker's creative and commercial trajectory. When Carpenter taps into the zeitgeist (HALLOWEEN), he's a tastemaker. When he fails to do that, he's simply ahead of his time. I don't think he's ever made a legitimate bad film. And yes, I am one of the few that cite GHOSTS OF MARS (which was originally written as the third ESCAPE movie) as one of his best and most undervalued works.

The latter category of being ahead of its time is exactly where ESCAPE FROM L.A. falls into. The '90s were a notoriously dismal time for genre movies, due primarily to a generational shift. The odd bright spots to really define their times were things like Rodriguez's 1996 horror hybrid FROM DUSK TILL DAWN and Wes Craven's same-year slasher send-up SCREAM. Even if you didn't dig those pictures' camp approach, they were unarguably fresh entertainments that locked onto what fans wanted and both — especially SCREAM — were huge hits, both catering to the kind of movies young people were interested in absorbing. ESCAPE came out the same year as SCREAM a sequel to a movie that, by 1996, was a bit played out, having long since cycled through its TV and video runs and a follow-up felt a bit late-out-of-the-gate. The original film cost $6 million to produce and despite its success, it pretty much remained a cult film. The character of Snake Plissken (played by a young and hungry Kurt Russell) was not particularly ingrained into the mainstream pop culture subconscious and so when posters for ESCAPE FROM L.A. were released, screaming "Snake is Back!", many mainstream viewers were like, "Who the Hell is Snake?!"

The movie was released in August via Paramount Pictures, a summer movie that probably would have stood a better chance smashing into theaters in February, a dry season where a built-in cult title like this would have hooked its audience better. Instead, the movie, which cost twice as much as the original earned (NEW YORK raked in 25 million whereas L.A. made the same but cost 50 million) and critics were lukewarm to it. Hardcore ESCAPE FROM NEW YORK fans were generally divided, with many just happy to see Russell's one-eyed outlaw back on screen and many other sneering at what they thought was a too-campy approach.

And sadly, the ensuing years haven't found ESCAPE FROM L.A. many more admirers, with people almost universally citing it as inferior to its predecessor. And I get that. The original was raw. Messy. Angry. It swelled with innovation and urgency, another one of Carpenter's neo-Westerns, an inversion of RIO BRAVO. ESCAPE FROM L.A., with its sunnier locales and a narrative repeat of the original's *city-as-a-prison* gimmick is, on the surface, a bit lazy, true. But these many years later, L.A. not only holds up beautifully as a high-octane romp, but it's also a bit of a marvel; a tough, shiny, comic book fantasy with broad performances, a to-die-for cult cast, outrageous set-pieces and, most importantly, sharp social criticism that is infinitely more potent and prophetic today than it was in 1996.

The film stars Cliff Robertson as a President who, after being "elected for life" has deemed to *Make America Great Again* by shipping off every person he deems "undesirable" to L.A., which, due to a massive earthquake and flooding, has become an island. Stripped of their citizenship, this mixed bag of "morally unfit" Americans run wild, setting up micro-civilizations, most of them bewildered by a country that has forsaken them. Among their ranks is charismatic revolutionary Cuervo Jones, who has charmed the President's comely daughter via the internet (or at least a holographic version of the internet) into stealing a classified weapon that has the power to effectively disable every electronic device on the planet. If triggered, Earth would essentially revert to an instant stone age.

Enter our man Plissken, played here with even beefier swagger by Russell, who in 1981 was a young actor emerging from a life as a teen star (thanks in no small part to Carpenter who directed him in the amazing 1979 ELVIS TV movie) and by this time was a *bona fide* Hollywood movie star. Plissken version 2.O. feels angrier, rougher, and closer to the Clint Eastwood/John Wayne hybrid he was conceived to be in the original (Russell co-wrote the script with Debra Hill and Carpenter). Sentenced to life imprisonment in LA, the President offers the grizzled outlaw a full pardon if he can get into L.A. and retrieve the weapon. To ensure his compliance, Plissken is injected with a deadly virus that will kill him in 10 hours if isn't successful in his mission. Soon, Plissken is outfitted with weapons and gadgets and shot into the prison city, where he meets all manner of eccentrics (including Steve Buscemi as a lovable grifter tour guide, Bruce Campbell as a psychotic plastic surgeon, and Pam Grier as a transgendered assassin) before facing off against the righteously vengeful but megalomaniacal Jones.

No matter your take on ESCAPE FROM L.A.'s social themes or success as an action picture, only the coldest, deadest heart would deny that the movie is anything but a tsunami of pure escapist fun. I mean, Russell future-surfs with Peter Fonda for crying out loud! Carpenter himself has cited that the movie is a better film in every way to the original and he's right in that this a much bigger and ambitious picture. But fans of the original loved seeing actors like Donald Pleasence, Issac Hayes, Harry Dean Stanton, Ernest Borgnine, Adrienne Barbeau and Lee van Cleef flail around in what was a really, really *grimy* movie. L.A. is not the urban sleaze-fest that was NEW YORK. The actors here are clean, the trappings garish and circus-like. And of course, the sets are considerably pricier. But taken on its own terms, it all makes sense. Viewed as a jacked-up, sun-baked remake of the original, it works perfectly.

And the satire is on point. Carpenter sticks it to L.A. but good, showing a city whose shallowness and ego has mutated to lethal levels when left unchecked. And the very idea of a weapon designed to destroy technology is even more potent today, where we are so addicted and reliant on electronics that if we ever lost our power over it, our collapse would be just as swift as it would be via nukes or gas or disease. And have we mentioned the music? Carpenter's iconic synth-based ESCAPE FROM NEW YORK theme is wonderfully rocked-out with the aid of the late, great Shirley Walker and both that theme and the entire score are fantastic.

If you're one of the fans who have filed ESCAPE FROM L.A. way back in your Carpenter Rolodex, we urge you to dig it up and give it another look. It's one his strongest non-horror films...

FRANKENSTEIN: THE TRUE STORY (1973)

Starring James Mason, Michael Sarrazin, Leonard Whitting, Jane Seymour
Written by Don Bachardy, Christopher Isherwood
Directed by Jack Smight

The golden era of the American made-for-TV horror film yielded some real-deal masterworks (THE NIGHT STALKER, DUEL, BAD RONALD, DON'T BE AFRAID OF THE DARK etc.) and among the most intelligent and sophisticated of them sits director Jack Smight's 1973's elegant and unforgettable miniseries FRANKENSTEIN: THE TRUE STORY. Even the

The Monster (Michael Sarrazin) holds Prima's head while Polidori (James Mason) looks on.

title itself is bold, considering Mary Shelley's groundbreaking novel is not a document of fact and that this adaptation takes great liberties with that source text. But what makes it "true" is that in distills the themes of Shelly's "Modern Prometheus" and the motives of its titular character, propelling him on a quest to cheat death and better God at his own game. The other thing that makes it "true" is that it suggests that no matter how noble one's intent to improve the world, vanity and ego eventually level *everything.* And denying what and who you are, might just be the greatest sin of all.

Long available on video (and via TV broadcasts) in a butchered two-hour crushed cut, FRANKENSTEIN: THE TRUE STORY was restored to its epic, full two-part miniseries cut for DVD and Blu-ray a few years back and this is the version we recommend you seek out. Oddly, it begins with a weird prologue featuring co-star and cinematic icon James Mason (who also graced another masterful horror TV miniseries, Tobe Hooper's 1979 adaptation of Stephen King's SALEM'S LOT) wandering around a graveyard teasing the movie we're about to watch, complete with a spoiler-heavy flurry of clips, while pontificating on the importance of Shelley's novel. After we get that bit of prime-time pandering out of the way, the film fades into a gorgeous opening credits sequence with a blooming rose, the credits and cast rolling out while the flower opens and gets redder. Then we get to the tale itself...

The familiar character of Victor Frankenstein, here beautifully played by Leonard Whiting, witnesses his brother William drowning and, while attending the funeral with his fiancée Elizabeth (Nicola Pagett) vows to fight to eradicate death, swearing that he'd happily make a deal with the Devil to do so. Venturing deeper into medical education and mad science, he meets the odd Henry Clerval (David McCallum) who swears he knows the secrets of bringing dead tissue to life. Frankenstein works with Clerval on his quest to create a master race of beautiful people made from the dead, much to the chagrin of Elizabeth who is not only distrustful of Clerval, but somewhat jealous of the pair's intimacy.

When Clerval dies of a heart attack on the cusp of finishing their first subject, Frankenstein places his brain in the body of the "creature" who rises as the beautiful Michael Sarrazin (in Shelley's novel, the monster is also a handsome thing), covered in strategically placed bandages, staring in pouty-lipped wonder at his creator. Initially, Victor is thrilled, a vindication over the death of his brother and validation of his genius. He begins spending all his time with his monster, introducing him into polite society as a distant relation and playing both father and, seemingly, partner to the gentle, attractive creature. But when Frankenstein notes that other test subjects — in particular a severed arm — are disintegrating, he is alarmed to learn that his beloved creature is starting to fall apart too.

As the creature begins to disintegrate, his utterances of "beauty" giving way to the horror of his increasingly syphilitic appearance, the poor stitched-up thing loses his mind and flees. As Victor thinks his creation has died, he licks his wounds, learns his lessons about playing God and moves on. But the creature instead wanders into the woods, lost and afraid. Here, he meets a blind hermit (Ralph Richardson) who befriends the poor wretch until his family comes to call. When the Hermit's niece Agatha (a stunning Jane Seymour) is accidentally killed, the monster brings her back to Frankenstein and Clerval's lab, only to discover that the sinister Dr. Polidori (Mason), Clerval's mentor has taken over the building and intends on continuing with the experiments. He and the monster blackmail Frankenstein into helping create a Bride out of Agatha's corpse. They do. And then things really get twisted...

To say more about the rest of the serpentine story would be to spoil the second half arc of its secret weapon, that of the resurrected Agatha, re-christened Prima. This was Seymour's breakthrough role and she's alarmingly good, a sexually charged ghoul whose porcelain beauty betrays the madness and rot that swells in her zombie brain. She's incredible and when the movie bends to her plight, it becomes the best Hammer horror movie ever made. In fact, the Hammer DNA is strong in other ways as Hammer legend Roy Ashton handled all the excellent makeup effects. FRANKENSTEIN: THE TRUE STORY also has a potent homoerotic subtext, first between Frankenstein and Clerval and then between Frankenstein and the monster. This might be due to the fact that the film was co-penned by openly Gay British writer Christopher Isherwood and artist Don Bachardy, who were lovers and partners for years. In fact, you can view Victor Frankenstein's pre-wedding venture into mad science as a dalliance with his innate sexuality, one he chooses to "bury" when it complicates his life. But it returns to haunt him, the creature potentially representing that sexuality and closeted life that keeps appearing endlessly in destructive ways, despite his attempts to smother its existence, until he finally makes peace with it.

But no matter your read on the film's allegory, FRANKENSTEIN: THE TRUE STORY is a masterpiece based on its craft alone, with allusions to the novel, the classic films (Polidori is a riff on Pretorius in THE BRIDE OF FRANKENSTEIN as well as allusion to Dr. Polidori who helped Shelley finish the original novel) and moments of alarming innovation. The birth of Prima in the lab, with its nude sequences (wild for a prime-time network TV broadcast!) and phantasmagorical swirls of color and fluid, is one of the most breathtaking creation sequences in all of Frankenstein cinema. This is a stunning work, one that needs to seen by anyone with a serious interest in Gothic horror.

GODMONSTER OF INDIAN FLATS (1973)

Starring by Christopher Brooks, E. Kerrigan Prescott,
Karem Ingenthron, Stuart Lancaster
Written by Fredric Hobbs
Directed by Frederic Hobbs

It's not easy discussing a film as singularly fucking insane as Fredric C. Hobbs' jaw-dropping 1973 freak-out GODMONSTER OF INDIAN FLATS with a serious face. So much has been written and spoken about the picture, mostly by people saddling it with the dreaded "so bad it's good" handle and certainly, it would be easy to dismiss this Something Weird Video favorite as a slab of inept trash made by desert-touched madmen who lapped up too much LSD in the late '60s. But GODMONSTER is anything but a bad film (more like a *baaaaaaad* film... sorry!). Rather it's an almost experimental, totally unpredictable, and fever-pitched horror-western that seems beamed in from another dimension and it simply refuses to behave by any conventional film structure standards. It leaks a kind of authentic, hard-wired weirdness that so many other phony baloney "cult" filmmakers have forever tried hard to capture, but that's impossible to fabricate. And while it often feels like a forgotten Alejandro Jodorowsky movie, I'd much rather watch GODMONSTER than THE HOLY MOUNTAIN any day of the week.

The manic plot of GODMONSTER involves a wool-vested cowpoke shepherd who goes to Reno, wins big and is ripped off by a saloon full of cackling thugs and

Beware the woolly wrath of the Godmonster!

snickering whores. He then passes out in the sheep stable, sees a blurry mass of sheep psychedelia and wakes up to find one of the beasts has become a mutant. Soon the local anthropology professor takes both the hungover rube and his freaky sheep to some sort of lab to study the beast, who quickly grows into a wild, shambling mass of a monster that is in fact a sculpture created by Hobbs. See, Hobbs' filmmaking career was more of a sideline to his multi-media art experiments and his writing. He was an abstract multi-hyphenate and a true eccentric who made sure his wild-eyed ideas and weird worldview was blasted on as many platforms as he could muster. That one of said outlets was this incredible picture is certainly one of the greatest things that ever happened to the America counterculture in the 1970s. And no, we're not joking.

Anyway, while the "Godmonster" is baaa-ing away behind bars, the corrupt Mayor of the dusty, time warp-caught town and his braying, surveillance-equipment fetishist sheriff hatch a plan to toy with and hang a black prospector representing a corporation looking to develop on their land. First, they fake a dog's death, then beat him up, then frame him for a shooting before stringing the poor bastard up. It's hard to describe this mania but as mental case as it reads, it kind of makes sense in the context of the film. Soon the "Godmonster" escapes — as does the prospector — and the town is running for its life from the poor, shaggy and misunderstood sheep creature. By the time the movie reaches its howling climax, wherein literally everything flies off a cliff in a fiery mess while the mayor gets locked into a kind of rapture and more mutant sheep are born, you'll be picking yourself up off the filthy floor, wondering what the hell you just watched.

GODMONSTER OF INDIAN FLATS is *awesome*. Like, seriously. No irony here. It's awesome and Hobbs knows exactly what he's doing, with his rapid fire, spastic pacing and quick edits and over-the-top characters and impossible scenarios and buried social commentary. It's the ultimate work of psychotronic art, assembled from gobs of trash and filthy refuse, like a Kuchar brothers film made for the atomic monster set. Gloriously deranged, wonderfully singular.

THE GRAPES OF DEATH (1978)

Starring Marie-Georges Pascal, Felix Marten, Serge Marquand, Mirella Rancelot
Written by Jean Rollin, Christian Meunier
Directed by Jean Rollin

The enduring *fascination* — to pull from the title of one of his most famous films –with the work of French horror film director Jean Rollin doesn't rest exclusively with sex. Certainly, as with his much-studied Eurohorror colleague Jess Franco, the surface hook for Rollin's oeuvre is his use of overt female eroticism blending with ample bloodshed, and like Franco, both directors have dabbled in hardcore pornography to make ends meet. But with Rollin, really, it's that certain *je ne sais quoi* that keeps his admirers coming back, addicted to dissecting his pictures and pushing to have them spoken about just as seriously as the work of his new wave countryman like Goddard, Truffaut et al. More plainly put, Jean Rollin was the poet laureate of European exploitation; a true artist who found himself making movies that had to be easily classified as simple genre works and whose vision was ghettoized by distributors looking to sell his unique, personal films to unimaginative consumers seeking a quick thrill.

And while Rollin will forever be associated with his now celebrated series of dreamy, sensual feminine vampire pictures like SHIVER OF THE VAMPIRES, REQUIEM FOR A VAMPIRE and his ultimate fanged-femme masterpiece LIPS OF BLOOD, one of his lesser discussed efforts dabbles in a different kind of undead fiend, that of the zombie. Filmed as PESTICIDE, released in France as LES RAISINS DE LA MORT and eventually known stateside as THE GRAPES OF DEATH, this 1978 ghoul-fest is indeed a story of outbreak and the murderous, mindless, diseased monsters it creates. But we promise you, THE GRAPES OF DEATH is unlike any zombie film ever made, a picture that pulls in the pundits with promises of post-NIGHT OF THE LIVING DEAD frissons and then subjects its audience to meandering, mesmerizing passages of death, decay, and dream state horror.

Taking its cues less from Romero's famous first film than it does his 1973 chiller THE CRAZIES (and perhaps with elements borrowed from David Cronenberg's SHIVERS and

TOP.....HALTE AUX PESTICIDES....STOP......VILLAGES
T VIGNES CONTAMINES..STOP... URGENT SECOURS
Claude GUEDJ
présente :
LES
RAISINS
DE LA
MORT !
un film de Jean ROLLIN
Visa de censure 7615 · Interdit aux moins de 18 ans

RABID), Rollin's film sees actress Marie-Georges Pascal as Elizabeth, a young woman traveling via train with her best friend (Evelyne Thomas) to the French countryside to meet her winemaker fiancée. Unbeknownst to the women, experimental pesticides used to spray the grapes on the local vineyards have poisoned them, tainting the wine and subjecting its drinkers to a sort of living death. After an infected farmer boards the train, his face melting and his manner murderous, Elizabeth flees into the village to find help. Instead, she finds a population of people who have devolved into a horde of psychotic, sadistic, mutated monsters, hellbent on spreading their disease and slaughtering those whose flesh is yet untouched by the weird wine.

THE GRAPES OF DEATH was, by his own admission, Rollin's most expensive film to that point, and the few extra dollars in his pocket allows for a denser supporting cast (and not all of them serving as shambling zombie extras) than in his previous films and blasts of effectively crude splatter, something Rollin rarely utilized and wouldn't really dive this deeply into again until 1982's brilliant THE LIVING DEAD GIRL, itself a kind of amalgam of this film and the previously mentioned LIPS OF BLOOD. But the film's greatest assets chiefly lie — like in all his films — with his magnetic female leads. As Elizabeth, Pascal is a marvel; she's Alice in Rollin's wonderland, venturing deeper into the darkness, narrowly evading each horror she encounters, witness to the unspeakable, the unknowable. She reminds me a bit of a young Fairuza Balk, with her angled face and laser-beam eyes and Rollin frames her astonished reactions to what she sees in a very arch, effectively theatrical manner. Pascal is matched by a pair of unforgettable supporting performances by Mirella Rancelot as the blind woman (pre-dating Cinzia Monreale's similar turn in Lucio Fulci's THE BEYOND) who is even more lost and who meets the grisliest of ends at the hands and blades of her diseased lover, and the great Brigitte Lahaie (Rollin's NIGHT OF THE HUNTED and FASCINATION), who makes an arresting final reel appearance as an uninhibited zombie death queen who physically isn't damaged at all, but is instead festering from within. Lahaie casts a spell, with her inexplicable canine companions serving as a deliberate callback to Mario Bava's BLACK SUNDAY, in which Barbara Steele showed up walking a similar hound.

Women almost always take center stage in Rollin's movies; their bodies are often exposed, yes, but they're rarely graceless victims. Instead, they become fluid vessels, forces of alternately delicate and deadly nature, often maternal, nurturing and often extremely tragic. If — as director Nicolas Winding Refn believes — the act of creation itself is a feminine one, Rollin uses his women on screen as avatars of his own creative and destructive artistic expressions. It's fascinating to witness.

In THE GRAPES OF DEATH, Rollin's zombies aren't the instinct-driven drones found in Romero's films or any of the myriad subsequent '70s cannibal corpse films that stole from him. For one, these monsters aren't aiming to make meals of their victims. For another, they presumably aren't dead at all, rather their living tissue is rotting in real time, affecting their bodies and minds, and causing them to kill. What makes them so frightening is that they seem to be somewhat at odds with their actions, as if some sort of satanic force was puppeteering them. Some of them stare longingly at their living prey, not acting on their impulses at all. Some engage in prolonged conversations before bursting into acts of hostility and violence. And some seem profoundly troubled by their atrocities. In the sequence where the doomed Rancelot finally meets her man, he expresses his undying love for her, alternately weeping and laughing while he crucifies her and posthumously hacks off her head. Later, when he finally expires, he reaches for his murdered girlfriend's bloody severed skull and kisses it tenderly. It's both beautiful and hideous, and this dichotomy between the poetic and the pandering is what gives THE GRAPES OF DEATH — and all of Rollin's work — its soul.

THE GRAPES OF DEATH certainly won't please general horror fans looking for a traditional dose of escapist mayhem. It's probably the scariest of all Rollin's pictures, but that's not saying much as fear was never the focus of the director's dark phantasmagorias. And the special effects were crude even by the standards of the time. With their slap-on forehead goop appliances and French peasant clothes, Rollin's zombies won't make anyone forget Tom Savini's fiends in DAWN or DAY OF THE DEAD anytime soon. Instead, THE GRAPES OF DEATH will appeal to those who seek out horror that is less interested in plot mechanics and exposition as it is creating pure cinema serving as a waking dream, one that you get lost in, just like our Elizabeth gets lost in Rollin's rural Hell. And like Elizabeth, if you enter this land, by the time the picture comes grinding to its grim halt, you'll end up forever changed.

GRAVEYARD SHIFT (1990)

Starring David Andrews, Stephen Macht, Kelly Wolf, Brad Dourif
Written by John Esposito
Directed by Ralph S. Singleton

The '80s saw a boom of lower-budgeted films that licensed Stephen King's short stories, fleshing them out to varying degrees of success. King himself directed one of these cinematic expansions, 1986's MAXIMUM OVERDRIVE and while King has since rejected that film (his first and last as a director) as a coked-up folly, I adore the picture. In fact, I tend to love most of the King films blown-up from his short stories (CREEPSHOW, SILVER BULLET, et al). Truth be told, I find King the writer at his strongest in the short story format. His novels — while expertly constructed and realized — tend to be bloated affairs that are not always suited to cinema.

John (David Andrews) and Jane (Kelly Wolf) fight rats and worse while on the GRAVEYARD SHIFT.

But those short stories? Damn. They have few peers...

Witness his now-legendary *Night Shift* collection, a 1978 book released after the success of his first novel *Carrie* that amassed most of King's previously published early work. Many of the movies from the '80s are cribbed from this collection and almost every story is a blood-freezer. Among the pack — which includes 'Children of the Corn' and 'The Lawnmower Man' — sits King's concise 1970 shocker 'Graveyard Shift', one of the scariest damn tales (tails?) of terror I have ever read. Ever.

'Graveyard Shift' shows King's brilliance at setting up a drama, fleshing out characters and conflict and delivering massive scares, devoid of resolution in a tiny, page-bound space. The story sees a cotton-mill worker and his sadistic boss venturing deep into the basements and sub-basements of the rat-filled structure only to unearth a hive of mutant, blind and blood-hungry monster vermin. It's a horrifying story and while it may seem on surface too brief to be fleshed out into a feature film, director Ralph S. Singleton did it and did it really, really well. In truth, GRAVEYARD SHIFT the movie is my favorite King movie, or at least the one I think just might be the purest rendering of his shorter work.

Let me elaborate.

When Roger Corman made his celebrated "Poe Cycle" films in the early 1960s, he charged his writers — Richard Matheson and Charles Beaumont, chiefly — to expand tales that were more like snapshots. Take THE PIT AND THE PENDULUM, for example. In the Poe story, we have a first-person piece of paranoia about a man strapped to the titular torture device during the Spanish Inquisition. As the swinging blade of the pendulum drops closer to his torso, he skirts madness before devising a way to narrowly escape. This is not a story. It's a set-piece. So, with the 1961 film, Matheson borrowed elements from other Poe stories to flesh out a drama of walled-up women, philandering wives, evil legacies, torture, madness, morality and just desserts served cold. At the center of the web sits the arc of the man and the pendulum and that nerve-shredding climax feels earned and organic, as does the movie constructed around it.

This thoughtful, ingenious, and reverent approach is exactly what screenwriter John Esposito did with GRAVEYARD SHIFT, a film that was met with critical vitriol upon release, though trading on the King name still ensured a moderately successful box office take. Still, the movie was generally dismissed, and the ensuing years saw very little in the way of a critical revaluation. Singleton never directed another feature, either. Shame that.

When I rented GRAVEYARD SHIFT the following year (I was too young to see the film theatrically), I was instantly smitten with it. Like Eric Red's BODY PARTS (another Paramount quickie release that still stands as an undervalued gem) I thrilled to the old-fashioned, air-tight, no-frills storytelling, genre irreverence and its acute sense of the Grand Guignol and was even more enamored by the way the movie built a convincing world around that skin-crawling source story. Here was a horror movie, a bona fide horror movie that was totally out of step with its time and loaded with personality. It's a film ripe for rediscovery.

The movie tells the tale of the ancient Bachman (a nod to King's pen name) textile mill (the real-life Bartlett mill in Maine) that, after being boarded up for years, has been recently reopened for business. The machines are work just fine but the mill's recent tenants — a dynasty of diseased rats — refuse to be evicted and run rampant. The blue-collar workers, hard-up for employ, balk at the filth of the place but the sneering foreman Warwick (THE MONSTER SQUAD's Stephen Macht) refuses to sympathize, treating his staff like sweatshop slaves. When a morally sound drifter (David Andrews) rolls into town looking for work, he immediately butts heads with the sadistic Warwick. Meanwhile, workers keep getting murdered and sucked into the bowels of the building by... something. Something wet, leathery, toothy and starving. And in the center of all this overheated EC comics inspired mania, a wild-eyed exterminator (Brad Dourif, in one of his weirdest roles) lays waste to as many rodents as he can find and the neighboring graveyard spews out enough mist to fill another King film entirely.

Everything about GRAVEYARD SHIFT works. We mentioned EC comics and that's no accident. Most of those shivery early King tales bore the influence of vintage *Tales from the Crypt* and *Vault of Horror* books, something King has long been proud of citing. The author's most relevant collaboration with the late, great George A. Romero,

1982's masterful CREEPSHOW was itself a blatant nod to EC and GRAVEYARD SHIFT often feels like an expanded episode from that anthology.

And as with many EC stories, rotting, shrill and broadly painted atmosphere and characters are the name of the game here and both director and cast are up to the task of bringing that four-color creepiness to lurid life. While Andrews makes a solid if somewhat flat hero, his muted energy is in sharp contrast to Macht's outrageous turn as Warwick, who goes from full-fledged asshole boss to unholy asshole lunatic in the movie's ballistic final act. Dourif's eccentric rat-killer is electric, a skeezy yet somehow sympathetic creep who adds comic relief and absurdity to an already out-there movie and future WISHMASTER Andrew Divoff is fantastic as a sneering bully-worker turned snivelling victim.

GRAVEYARD SHIFT is also perhaps the most noxious movie in American horror history. Remember that "body pit" sequence in Dario Argento's PHENOMENA? The part where Jennifer Connelly is drowning in a filthy pool of oatmeal-ified corpses? Well, GRAVEYARD SHIFT is that sequence drawn out for 90 minutes. Every inch of this rat-infested shocker is designed to drive you to the showers. I've rarely experienced a film that genuinely made me feel contaminated while watching. Ugh. And I mean that in a GOOD way.

But best of all, GRAVEYARD SHIFT feels like it lives in King's world. It's actually *filmed* in Bangor, Maine, as opposed to just being set there. The locations are evocative and authentic, the actors nail the New England accent, and my *god* does Singleton nail the dread of the original King story. Of course, he pads out the journey into the guts of the mill with other characters and FX man Gordon Smith's central monster — and what a monster — is a sickening bat/rat mutant thing with gelatinous body and suffocating wings as opposed to the shivering "thing" King hints at. But it's a great realization of King's wordplay and Singleton pushes the entire ending into the sort of berserk vomitorium that the author suggested the story would become. And man, is this movie splattery. The MPAA may have been hacking apart slasher movies to secure R ratings but because GRAVEYARD SHIFT is ostensibly a "creature movie" it managed to squeak (like a rat) by them, pouring on the gore and still getting that commercially coveted R.

CARRIE is a perfect Brian De Palma movie. THE SHINING is Kubrick's masterpiece. THE SHAWSHANK REDEMPTION is Frank Darabont at his best. But GRAVEYARD SHIFT feels more authentically King-ish than any of those rightfully celebrated films. It feels scrappy. It feels like punk rock, bursting with energy and laced with subtly angry social comment about the plight of the working-class. It feels mean and dangerous and is deeply, unapologetically weird. Like all of King's early stuff.

THE GUARDIAN (1990)

Starring Jenny Seagrove, Dwier Brown, Carey Lowell, Miguel Ferrer
Written by William Friedkin, Dan Greenburg, Stephen Volk
Directed by William Friedkin

As every serious horror fan who both lived through it and has studied the period from the distance of time knows, as the 1980s wound down and leaked into the '90s, the pulse of the genre was faint. Producers were less interested in edgier supernatural fare than they were in conventional dramatic (and often, in the wake of FATAL ATTRACTION, erotic) thrillers, with most horror product tailored to suit a post-BATMAN need for bloated, FX-rich action. Even Coppola's much-hyped 1992 horror blockbuster BRAM STOKER'S DRACULA feels like a mutated BATMAN with fangs.

But we digress.

The bottom line is that historically, you'd be hard pressed to find a real-deal, bold work of adult dark fantasy during this timeframe. Except for William Friedkin's 1990 effort THE GUARDIAN, that is; a film that was anything but successful during its domestic theatrical run and was unfairly dismissed by critics who deemed its absurdities as beneath its storied director. But, as we now know, even Friedkin *slumming* often offers a superior cinematic experience than many filmmakers' most notable works do and, in retrospect, THE GUARDIAN is no exception to this rule. It's a truly fascinating misfire that isn't really a misfire at all. Rather it hits a target that's not even on the range. It's bizarre, beautiful, both lavish and cheap, controlled, and reckless, erotic, and ridiculous, character-driven and awash in tarty special FX.

In the film's dreamy, balletic opening we see a faceless nanny drift through a dimly lit home as a little boy reads a very grim fairy tale from an elaborate pop-up book. As said nanny finishes the feeding of a baby, the children's' parents cheerfully prepare to go out for the evening. But a pair of forgotten glasses cause the couple to drive back home where they find their eldest son fast asleep, cozy, and safe and their delicate infant gone.

Their nanny? She's nowhere to be found.

We then see that shadowy caregiver sprinting through an ersatz, moon-lit wood straight of the most glorious set-bound Mario Bava film where she holds the crying baby up to a monstrous, twisted tree. In a crude smash edit, the baby is gone, its visage now carved into the trunk of the tree, along with the faces of other children who have come before. And as the nanny finishes her phantasmagorical ritual, the shimmering stream beneath her reveals her shapeshifting into a snarling wolf.

And then the movie begins.

THE GUARDIAN doesn't take time to play its hand when introducing the threat at its core. Like Friedkin's signature genre classic THE EXORCIST, it makes sure we are firmly

FROM THE DIRECTOR OF "THE EXORCIST"

Tonight,
while the world is asleep...
an ancient evil
is about to awaken.

THE
GUARDIAN

UNIVERSAL PICTURES PRESENTS A JOE WIZAN PRODUCTION A WILLIAM FRIEDKIN FILM "THE GUARDIAN"
JENNY SEAGROVE DWIER BROWN CAREY LOWELL MUSIC BY JACK HUES CO-PRODUCERS TODD BLACK MICKEY BOROFSKY
DAN GREENBURG PRODUCTION DESIGNER GREGG FONSECA DIRECTOR OF PHOTOGRAPHY JOHN A. ALONZO, A.S.C. EXECUTIVE PRODUCER DAVID SALVEN
BASED ON "THE NANNY" BY DAN GREENBURG SCREENPLAY BY STEPHEN VOLK AND DAN GREENBURG AND WILLIAM FRIEDKIN PRODUCED BY JOE WIZAN
R RESTRICTED UNDER 17 REQUIRES ACCOMPANYING PARENT OR ADULT GUARDIAN
DIRECTED BY WILLIAM FRIEDKIN
DOLBY STEREO SR
READ THE BERKLEY BOOK
A UNIVERSAL RELEASE

NSS# 900048

aware of the strange sandbox we are playing in so that, when we are immediately introduced to our true protagonists, we are instantly on edge, knowing that their perceived safety will soon be steamrolled by something horrific.

Phil and Kate (Dwier Brown and Carey Lowell, both serviceable leads) are a pretty, healthy young couple of kindly yuppies just starting their life together; she's just birthed a baby girl and the pair are ecstatic about sharing their monolithic home with their new daughter. Finding a nanny however, proves daunting that is until they meet willowy British caregiver Camilla (LOCAL HERO's Jenny Seagrove); Camilla is intelligent, graceful and gentle and seemingly has an innate gift communicating with babies.

She's also a kind of Druid demon, an incarnation of the very same hellion we saw in the picture's opening and it's her intent to groom Phil and Kate's bundle to be another sacrifice to her tree-god.

THE GUARDIAN is a deeply strange picture with a history as tortured as the perverted limbs of the fabricated tree itself. The film is based on the novel by Dan Greenburg called "The Nanny" and, indeed, the initial version of the script bore that title. The director attached was none other than Sam Raimi, fresh off the cult success of his spastic indie hit EVIL DEAD 2. Producer Joe Wizan called on another rising star, British screenwriter Stephen Volk, himself coming off a pair of strange works in Ken Russell's GOTHIC and the similarly female-monster driven Canadian thriller THE KISS, to rewrite the script and, with Raimi's input, the pair fashioned what was to be a deliberately arch, body-count rich, blackly comic horror film.

But when Raimi opted to bail on the project and instead direct the, again, more BATMAN-esque DARKMAN, Wizan brought Friedkin on board (in what would be his first "legitimate" horror film since THE EXORCIST) roping Volk back into the project to collaborate with the iconic, loose-cannon filmmaker to make the movie that would become THE GUARDIAN.

Omitting the broadly etched, splatter comedy Raimi was aiming for, Friedkin's sensibilities are most assuredly the central visions of the final film. THE GUARDIAN takes its human drama seriously with any humor drawn naturally from the absurdity of the situation and it spends ample time building the characters and the world they live in.

Because we know the nature of the threat from the get-go, suspense doesn't necessarily ratchet, rather the tension arises from the audience waiting for that magic moment when mom and dad clue-in to the true, insidious motives of the woman in whose trust they have placed their most precious cargo. Before that happens, Friedkin disorients by making Camilla a kind of vulnerable hero, most notably in a scene where she is almost assaulted by a pair of thugs in the woods; as she runs for her life, protecting the baby, we almost delude ourselves into thinking she may actually care about the child. She does, but of course her concern extends only as far as her own unholy interests.

That scene of near-rape is punctuated by a thrashing of over-the-edge gore, wherein the tree itself attacks the aggressors, chomping off their limbs, eating one screeching tough and impaling the other battered bastard on its covert roots before incinerating him in a flurry of flames.

The central idea of the set-piece is a crude one in that it's the would-be-rapists who are the ones who get violently penetrated and that in and of itself is a darkly sexual, Friedkin-friendly motif; but the gore FX aren't filmed properly and feel out of place, almost as if Wizan insisted that they be more present in the final edit to please the new batch of easily bored kids and the *Fangoria* crowd.

More successful are the numerous Gothic touches, like the incredibly intense, Hammer horror-informed wolf-siege on the house, and the outrageous, chainsaw-vs.-bloody-tree-by-way-of-naked-Druid-Queen- voodoo-decimation-climax, a wonderfully insane flurry of cuts both on screen and in the editing room that oddly channel the gonzo spirit of Raimi, whether by intent or otherwise. and then, there's the magnificent tree itself, an impossible tangle of limbs that, whether caressing the nude body of its lounging leader (a stunning sequence) or defending its turf, is a glorious, mythical creation. One wonders if Tim Burton liked it enough to borrow elements of its design for his 1999 version of SLEEPY HOLLOW.

Ultimately, although he was brought in as a gun-for-hire, THE GUARDIAN is most assuredly a Friedkin joint, one in which you can repeatedly feel him grabbing the wheel away from the producers and veering the vehicle into that psychological, seedy and totally 1970s Fastlane that the filmmaker once burned through.

THE GUARDIAN is most certainly flawed, but so is the best of Friedkin. Those flaws are what some more thoughtful critics might call evidence of his humanity, the mark of a flesh and blood auteur reaching through the slick veneer of a studio-produced entertainment and making a beautiful mess of things.

THE HEARSE (1980)

Starring Trish Van Devere, Joseph Cotten, David Gautreuax, Donald Hotton
Written by William Bleich
Directed by George Bowers

1980 served as the dawn of a sort of American horror film and the last stop of another. With FRIDAY THE 13th's graphic gore, quickie and punishable-by-death sex and mechanical body count plotting baiting the box office and birthing the unyielding, blood-spattered slasher subgenre, the comparatively quaint ghost story was on the

Trish Van Devere gets cursed with the worst in THE HEARSE.

way out. 1979's THE AMITYVILLE HORROR and 1980's THE CHANGELING and THE SHINING — with their reliance on adult themes and dread as opposed to gratuitous ultraviolence — serving as the final "big" blockbuster haunted house movies of the era.

Nestled among those terrifying titans was director George Bowers's modestly budgeted, PG-rated Crown International potboiler THE HEARSE. At the time, Roger Ebert famously called the movie a "garage sale" horror film, as it shamelessly cobbles and cribs its identity from those hits as well as other notable spook shows. After a theatrical run, the film was well-rented on home video and became a staple on late night television throughout the '80s and has since faded into obscurity, a chiller devoid of any serious respect and lacking any kind of cult that I'm aware of.

But another look at THE HEARSE is sorely needed. While suffering from its budgetary restraints, it's still a serious, atmospheric, and solid female-fronted supernatural thriller that's smart, sophisticated and often very scary. The film stars Trish Van Devere (who also co-starred in THE CHANGELING with her husband, George C. Scott) as Jane, a recently divorced woman who inherits a charming country home in the town of Blackford, left to her by her dearly departed aunt. Upon moving in, Jane soon realizes that her lovely aunt was not all that she seemed. After getting shunned by the townsfolk for whatever reason, Jane does a bit more digging into her relative's life and discovers that she was mixed up with a secret sect of Satanists and that the hearse carrying her corpse crashed on the nearby road but that the driver and her aunt's body were never found. Now, the suspicious townies believe that both the house and the roads around it are haunted. And they're correct, of course. Soon, Jane is experiencing all manner of hostile phenomena: doors slamming, pianos playing themselves, walls creaking and, most alarmingly, a creepy, ghostly hearse chauffeur keeps popping up (shades of Dan Curtis' BURNT OFFERINGS), grinning and menacing Jane and driving her bonkers.

Thankfully, she's not totally alone in her terror. She's soothed by the odd-looking local Reverend (Donald Hotton) who keeps telling her that the sounds and visions she's experiencing are all in her head, the result of nightmares, isolation, anxiety and grief over her aunt's death. She finds a friendly port in the storm in the form of Paul (actor and now notable workman director Perry Lang), a lovestruck teen working at the local hardware store who has a hardcore crush on the older, sensual woman, much to the delight of his teasing and taunting pals (playing one of his mates is Donald Petrie, another actor-turned-director). But Jane's favorite distraction is Tom (David Gautreaux), the handsome, cultured local man who becomes her lover. One of these gents is not what he seems, however and, to be fair to THE HEARSE's detractors, it's not hard to figure out which one it is.

THE HEARSE is not perfect. The red herring angle mentioned above never works and there's far too much exposition. Jane picks up the phone and recaps events to her friend in useless waves of dialogue that serve to purpose outside of padding out the running time. But Bowers is a solid director and editor (outside of directing a few Crown International exploitation pics, like the amazing MY TUTOR, he mainly worked as an editor, cutting pictures like the underrated Johnny Depp Jack the Ripper flick FROM HELL) and he knows how to milk atmosphere and shocks. He's aided by his ace leading lady; as Jane, Van Devere is a heroic, strong presence who stands tall in the face of the forces that threaten to drive her out. She veers between thinking her troubles are the acts of the hateful locals to believing that the powers of the Devil are indeed coming for her. And no matter what, she refuses to buckle. It's a solid character and its expertly played by the veteran actress. And then there's the presence of the ailing, aged Hollywood legend Joseph Cotten (CITIZEN KANE, LADY FRANKENSTEIN — God, I love mentioning those two dichotomous pictures together) who plays the caustic property lawyer trying to convince Jane to sell the house and get the hell out of town. THE HEARSE would mark one of Cotten's last roles and though clearly in poor health, he provides a professional, lively presence and adds elegance to the production. Gelling it all together is a moody, frightening score by jazz musician Webster Lewis, a classic piano and strings soundtrack that is as sincere and un-ironic as the rest of the movie.

They just don't make movies like THE HEARSE anymore. And that's sad. Find a way to see it, watch it late at night and flash back to a time when horror wasn't slimy and self-aware and even low budget efforts had class, craft and restraint.

HELENA (1975)

Starring Valerie Boisgel, Yan Brian, Martine Grimaud, Monique Vita
Written by Michel Vocoret
Directed by Alain Nauroy

People speak of the golden age of hardcore pornography spurting from the 1970s like they were hallowed, horny works of reflexive art. This is due in most part to nostalgia (what isn't) when comparing these classics to the contemporary gynecological jack-hammering android porn that now stinks up every corner of the internet. And I mean, sure, DEEP THROAT and CAFÉ FLESH might as well be AGUIRRE: THE WRATH OF GOD and ALPHAVILLE by comparison to any of the antics *splooging* about on PornHub, but that doesn't mean these pictures were necessarily the bold works of hormonal visionary cinema we deify them as today.

I think there's also the factor that '70s porn was shot on real deal 35mm film and more often than not were more couple-inclusive than run-of-the-mill stag films and most had plots and were publicly exhibited often in hard-top theaters with big splashy premieres and mainstream media coverage. But look closely and all you'll see are standard-issue exploitation films, most of them crass and goofball comedies jazzed up with blowjobs and genital mashing.

All that said, if you steer away from America during the free-love decade and look to Europe, you'll often find porn that *does* function as art. You'll find movies not made by gangsters and 42nd street hustlers, but rather skilled craftsmen and realized by decent actors with a much more avant-garde, occasionally even thrillingly dangerous, leaning. Case in point, director Alain Nauroy's perverse and hypnotic 1975 fuck film HELENA (aka LA VILLA), a lush and, eventually, rather disturbing movie that is not only a great porno (proving that yes Vagina, er, Virginia, there *are* such things as great pornos!) but a very, very good film in and of itself: dark and hot with a gritty, psychological edge.

Gorgeous French legend Valerie Boisgel (Max Peca's YOUNG CASSANOVA) stars as the tit-ular heroine, a woman who ventures into the French countryside to hook up with Roy, a wealthy socialite she had previously met and made love to. Instead, she finds another skeezy fellow named Frank staying at the villa, who informs her that Roy is busy having endless sex with another woman by the pool. Helena is justifiably mortified but sticks around and waits ("He's about to cum" Frank smirks at one point), engaging in witty, sharp-tongued banter with the cavalier Frank while Nauroy keeps cutting to Roy working on his other lover.

Eventually, Helena has sex with Frank (a hot scene up against a wall, standing up) and then Roy (while Roy's other lover masturbates with a huge dildo and watches)

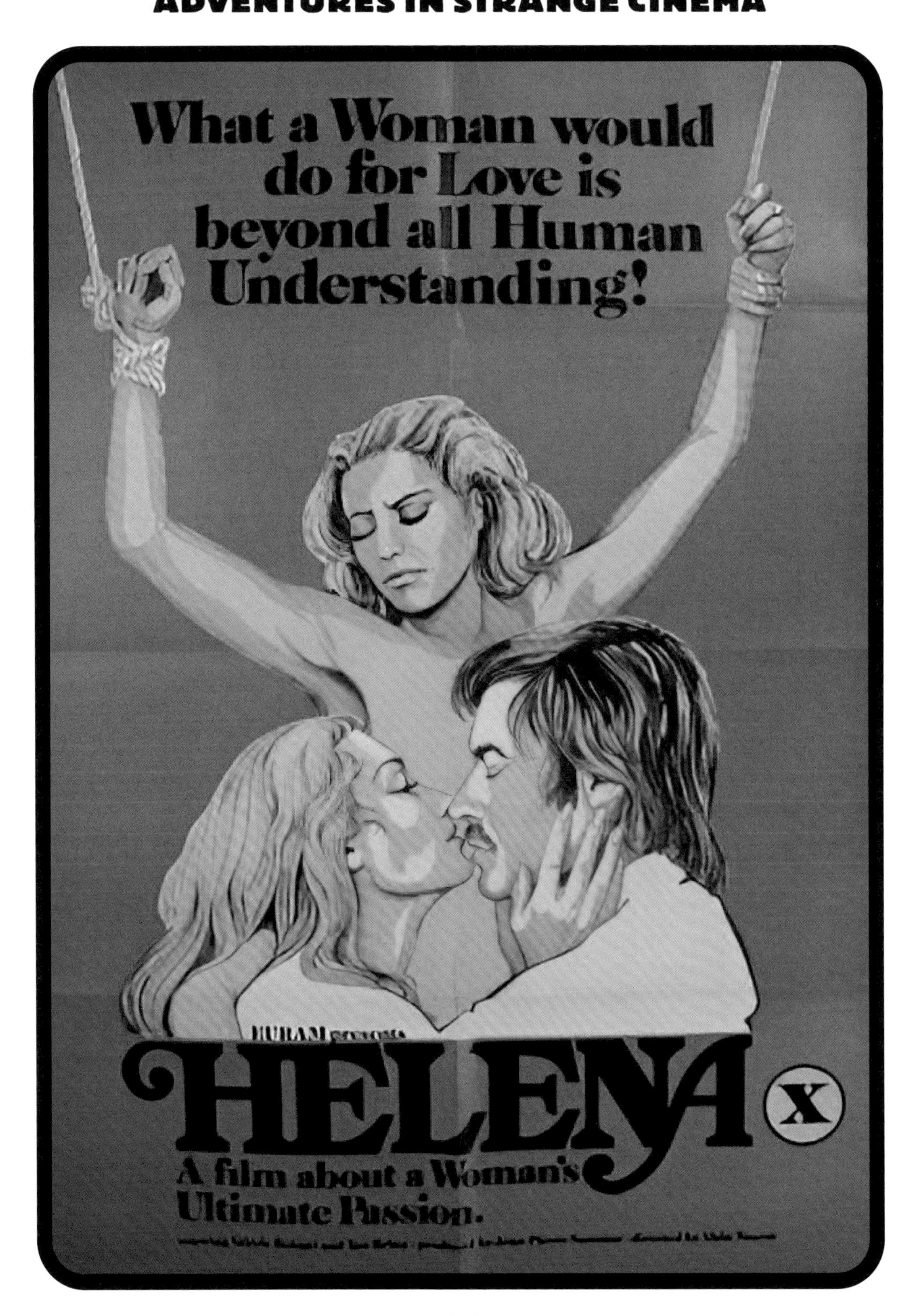
What a Woman would do for Love is beyond all Human Understanding!
HELENA
X
A film about a Woman's Ultimate Passion.

and all this elegant, urgent and well-shot pounding and climaxing happens outdoors, with the beautiful countryside in the background, the sun shining, the pool shimmering and composer Alain Goraguer's psychedelic fuzz-rock groove snaking around on the soundtrack.

But suddenly, this lazy and lovely shagfest is obliterated when a gang of thugs overtake the villa and begin tormenting the lovers, first trying to bury a copulating couple alive and then raping Helena. What starts as a stylish and truly sexy porn, soon becomes a harrowing, often deeply upsetting, horror movie, with shades of LAST HOUSE ON THE LEFT and the later FUNNY GAMES. All this insanity is peppered with more sex until the truly daft climax that sees Helena literally "reborn". Hard to explain, hard to forget.

And speaking of hard, let's talk about dicks in '70s porn. More often than not, the penises were both obscenely hairy and, well, flaccid. Not here. In Helena, it actually looks like the actors were enjoying the experience and the men have legitimate, well manicured erections, which may seem an odd comment, but it helps sell the fantasy as opposed to other films where it looks like dudes are just rubbing their sticky sausages into squishy spots, like wet hairy marshmallows stuffed into glistening piggy banks.

Bottom line is that HELENA is a super-stylish, grim, weird and rough Eurotrash film, a balletic melodrama that is like DAUGHTERS OF DARKNESS without the vampires. It blows (ahem) other domestic films of its vintage out of the water.

HIDEAWAY (1995)

Starring Jeff Goldblum, Christine Lahti, Alicia Silverstone, Jeremy Sisto
Written by Andrew Kevin Walker, Neal Jimenez
Directed by Brett Leonard

Much has been said of the 1990s regarding horror, with many moping about the dearth of good stateside, American genre films released during this period, while others — mostly, those who came of an impressionable age then — speaking of how Wes Craven's SCREAM and its stabby, self-referential ilk "saved" contemporary creepy cinema. I suppose both arguments are valid, and sure, the '90s also saw a wave of notable faves like CANDYMAN and NIGHTBREED slinking out of the multiplexes, eventually becoming classics. Still, most horror films from this era were — generally speaking — very safe, slick and clean affairs. Few had the arch angles and WTF moments that make the most memorable dark fantasy films so interesting. Sure, SCREAM may have hit hard with critics and the Friday night date crowd, but I felt then

The horror begins for the Harrison family in Brett Leonard's HIDEAWAY.

and even more so now, that its smugness, its faux-witty dialogue, and its small-screen teen sensibilities were miles removed from everything I love, respect and, yes, fear about stranger cinema. When I close my eyes and think of the '90s silver screen, all I see is an endless succession of samey-same posters with alabaster young people standing in cascading lines, glowering at the lens. And — in my opinion — most of the movies they helped shuck were equally as uninspiring. It was as if the FRIENDS*ification* of domestic pop culture dumped a kind of pretty glue over everything. Blech...

However there were a few bright, spastic spots that stuck out from the pedestrian pack. Stuff like RAVENOUS and FROM DUSK TILL DAWN, though I can't really cite that latter picture as a true horror movie and I've always felt its second-half horror component paled in comparison to its straight-up crime drama setup. No, to me, the greatest of all arcane offerings coming from the last gasp of the past millennium was a picture everyone seemed to hate. They hated it then. They probably still hate it now, though perhaps that contemporary hate is closer to ignorance as I'm willing to bet folks have either forgotten about it or didn't even know the movie existed in the first place. The visionary, violent and merciless slab of mad-science slasher mayhem I speak of is Brett Leonard's muscular and ultra-stylish 1995 mind-bending psychic chiller HIDEAWAY and it's about goddamned time people started paying attention to it.

Based on the novel by Dean R. Koontz, HIDEAWAY stars the inimitable Jeff Goldblum as Hatch Harrison, a family man who gets into a harrowing car accident with his wife Lindsey (Christine Lahti) and daughter Regina (Alicia Silverstone). The ladies survive, barely, but Hatch does not. Legally deceased, he is miraculously revived by a dedicated doctor (the great Alfred Molina) who has subjected the briefly dead dad to an experimental technique that gets his still heart beating anew. Hatch is back, much to the joy of his momentarily shattered brood and soon, the clan is getting back to the business of living their lives. However, almost immediately Hatch begins feeling off. When mild blackouts turn into seizures then full-blown visions of razors-dragged across exposed female throats, the unnerved patriarch knows something is amiss. As he slowly, surely realizes, the procedure that brought him back to life has mysteriously tied his mind to that of a black-leather-clad teenage Satanic serial killer (the undervalued Jeremy Sisto), a night-crawling maniac named Vassago whose bloody trail of sliced-open women has the city seized in a state of terror and Hatch teetering on the edge of sanity. Worse, Hatch's portal into the murderer's grisly deeds is also reciprocated. The killer can now see through Hatch's eyes and quickly, his attentions turn to Hatch's pretty teenage daughter. But outside of the sinister supernatural link the pair share, could a more malevolent medical reason also have something to do with the connection? Hatch literally goes to Hell and back to solve the mystery and stop the monstrous Vassago before Regina falls under the knife for keeps.

HIDEWAY belly-flopped big time upon release and critics killed it, all except the late, great Roger Ebert who, defending the picture against the sneers of his AT THE MOVIES co-host Gene Siskel, praised the picture's single-minded desire to create a black-as-night, unsparing horror movie and thrilled to the picture's imaginative visuals. Ebert famously hated slasher movies, but he loved high concept, fantasy based horror and Leonard's gruesome and surreal freak-out of a flick is just that. It may rest its laurels on scenes of well-dressed male murderers opening the flesh of too-trusting women, but its soul belongs to sci-fi, a classic HANDS OF ORLAC/MAD LOVE narrative thrust that also informs one of the other brilliant and unsung '90s chillers, Eric Red's kinky 1992 romp BODY PARTS. Here however, the medical meddling is nestled into a much more lurid and decidedly intimate environment, one that juxtaposes extreme scenes of terror and bloodshed, with a palpable cat-and-mouse relationship between the two leading men and a picture that never forgets to lay on the line the love that Hatch has for the family he will stop at nothing to protect.

HIDEAWAY may have its roots in Koontz, but the movie is the singular work of its director. In fact, the author famously despised this adaptation and understandably so, as Leonard simply uses the source text as a blueprint to build a sensual audio/visual free-fall of a film that aims to amp-up the more visceral elements of the novel and exploit them accordingly to shock its audience, while never forgetting that the human element — along with a seriously grim sense of humor — are steering the ship. Leonard is an undervalued director and HIDEAWAY was made at his Hollywood peak, a film that allowed him to blend the evil-doctor subgenre that drove his maiden feature, the video store rental fave THE DEAD PIT (remember those awesome blinking ghoul eyes on the box?), along with the kinetic sci-fi visuals of his Stephen-

King-in-name-only dark drama THE LAWNMOWER MAN and the virtual reality serial killer shenanigans of his also-released-in-1995 thriller VIRTUOSITY. Like the first film, HIDEAWAY is ripe with surrealism and as with the latter two pictures, early CGI head-trip sequences weave their ways in and out of the movie endlessly, climaxing in the mother of all over-the-top '90s computer-soaked effect endings, a borderline animated finale that most dismissed as cheap but that are so baroque and operatic that they are rather beautiful. All that dreamy, trippy digital-Kubrick trickery combined with the liquid style of the kill scenes and the copious amounts of black leather worn by both Sisto and later, by Goldblum (who seems to be borrowing his wardrobe from his other signature '90s character, Ian Malcolm in JURASSIC PARK) make HIDEAWAY often feel like jacked-up giallo.

Are there problems with HIDEAWAY? Sure. Does it often get lost in its own sense of style? Sometimes. Does Goldblum's ultra-intense turn occasionally veer into camp? Certainly, but it's those very flaws that make the film so unique and memorable. It's a lush and nasty piece of work, propelled by a punishing industrial rock soundtrack that includes tracks by the likes of Front Line Assembly and Godflesh (who are actually in the movie!). And unlike other matinee-friendly pictures of the period, the teens in HIDEAWAY — specifically CLUELESS star Silverstone, who is great here — actually ACT like teens. Strong-willed, serious, scared and unwilling to counter the horror around them with head-smacking witticisms or groan-worthy sarcasm. The characters feel real, even when the situation around them is absolute lunacy. And in HIDEAWAY, lunacy on every level is the name of the game.

HITCH HIKE TO HELL (1977)

Starring Robert Gribbin, Russell Johnson, John Harmon, Randy Echols
Written by John Buckley
Directed by Irvin Berwick

Director Irvin Berwick (MALIBU HIGH) may not have made many movies in his day, but — as we all know — quality trumps quantity and his 1977 exploitation psychodrama shocker HITCH HIKE TO HELL is not only his best work, it's one of the weirdest and most potent pictures of its kind, and that's saying something considering the company the movie kept during that most sensational era of "passion pit" drive-in potboilers. And really, "quality" is a subjective term. By conventional standards, the shoestring-budgeted HITCH HIKE TO HELL isn't a particularly well produced work. But man, does it pack a disorienting, primal punch.

Another victim of the maniacal Howard in HITCH HIKE TO HELL.

The film tells the tawdry tale of Howard (Robert Gribbin), a dry-cleaning delivery driver who is seemingly happy, upbeat and well-liked by all. Certainly the wayward women hitchhikers he picks up dig his company. He's kind and a good listener. But the problem is, when said runaway ladies start taking trash about their domestic lives — specifically griping about their mothers — Howard starts to get dark. Then, he gets darker. Within minutes, Jekyll become Hyde and Howard drives his poor passengers to a remote locale, yanks them screaming out of his van and beats and savagely rapes them before brutally murdering them. And then it repeats.

Indeed, the wearisome, oppressive central mechanics of violent male aggression and feminine victimhood are well-worn in the annals of exploitation and Berwick does not shy away from the horror of Howard's attacks. But what elevates the film and makes it so interesting is the director's dedication to sticking with his lead character, following him as he goes about his day, as his crimes affect his fragile employment situation at the dry cleaners (and really, this is the picture of this kind I can think of that features an antagonist who trades in pressed trousers and steamed blouses) and most importantly, his unhealthy relationship with his mother. Again, the latter device is exhaustingly familiar and pre-dates PSYCHO, the movie that most mad-male-murderer pictures tend to crib from. But here, in HITCH HIKE TO HELL, Howard's festering obsession with protecting his mother — and the very notion of motherhood — stems from his sister, who we're told has broken his mother's heart and abandoned the family. We don't get much deeper into the issues that caused Howard's sibling to depart, but whatever it was, the effect of her absence has acerbated whatever serious mental illness Howard already has. In fact, Berwick smartly leaves it vague enough to suggest that Howard himself may have played some sort of part in his sister's problems. Whatever they might have been...

But HITCH HIKE TO HELL doesn't solely stick with Howard's transgressions. The sociopath's reign of violence and violation is tempered by a police investigation into the crimes and — unlike many of these running-time padding sub-plots that weave into exploitation cinema — the cops aren't idiots, reacting with sensitivity and outrage to the crimes and refusing to relent tracking their quarry. It helps that the lead detective is played by the great Russell Johnson (ATTACK OF THE CRAB MONSTERS, IT CAME FROM OUTER SPACE, key episodes of THE TWILIGHT ZONE and, of course, GILLIAN'S ISLAND), here much older and wearier, which helps add emotional weight to the character when he faces the grisly aftermaths of Howard's killing sprees. And in regard to said sprees, Berwick is unsparing, introducing younger girls (and in one instance, a young male) victims to Howard's dry cleaning van of death, offering a vague hope that maybe the more innocent passengers might be spared. But no, as soon as any disparaging words on motherhood are uttered, it's game over. They all die. Their bodies dumped in the crudest and most careless of places...

HITCH HIKE TO HELL was distributed by the great grindhouse huckster Harry Novak, who no doubt felt its filthy charms fit right in with other releases from his Boxoffice International Pictures imprint like TOYS ARE NOT FOR CHILDREN and AXE, movies that similarly offered kinky come-ons and cheap, lurid thrills with injections of surprising cinematic sophistication. But — as with most of his pictures — the Novak ad campaign for HITCH HIKE TO HELL was ludicrously misleading, making the movie seem like a fun Crown International hot-chicks-and-cars caper, the diametric opposite of what it actually is.

And it's a shame that HITCH HIKE TO HELL wasn't handled better back in 1977 as it's truly a tight, intelligent, and ruthless little thriller, with a dynamite lead turn by Gribbin, a haunting country-tinted theme song warbled by Nancy Adams and style to spare. It's yet another piece of '70s indie-American-shock that needs to be rediscovered and appreciated for the artful work of finely-tuned trash it is.

THE HOUSE THAT JACK BUILT (2018)

Starring Matt Dillon, Bruno Ganz, Uma Thurman, Riley Keough
Written by Lars von Trier
Directed by Lars von Trier

Jack (Matt Dillon) in his fear factory.

No matter the genre Danish filmmaker Lars von Trier hides behind, he's almost always making a horror movie. The troublemaker director's aesthetic — blending pseudo-documentary, hand -held camera POV with rapturous sequences of fantasy — almost always pushes his work into the realm of magic-realism and whether it be the story of a simple woman driven to sexual and religious frenzy (BREAKING THE WAVES), a working-class blind, musical-obsessed mother sent to death row (DANCER IN THE DARK) or a hopelessly depressed girl whose miseries echo the coming apocalypse (MELANCHOLIA), all von Trier pictures trade in his art of disorientation and dread and all evoke his single-minded desire to illustrate the beauty, terror and humanity hidden within events both ordinary and extraordinary. That almost all his protagonists are female is interesting (and has indeed caused some reactionary viewers to incorrectly label him a misogynist) and only serves to add another layer of fascination to his deeply personal, challenging, and unique creative identity.

In von Trier's THE HOUSE THAT JACK BUILT, he this time employs a *male* character to usher his audience into one of his most graphically violent and intentionally offensive epics to date. Like his shattering 2009 satanic sex-and-death fever dream ANTICHRIST — still one of the most devasting cinematic experiences I have ever had — THE HOUSE THAT JACK BUILT isn't pretending to be a horror movie, its intent is right there on the table. The film cheekily casts '80s American teen heartthrob Matt Dillon as Jack, an engineer whose obsessions with art inadvertently lead him into a down spiraling life as a malevolent serial killer. That's the plot, more or less, and like his previous film, 2013's brilliant and pornographic NYMPHOMANIAC, the film's troubled central figure confesses his transgressions to an older, wiser man, here a mysterious voice whose face is mostly left unseen named "Verge" (NOSFERTAU: PHANTOM DER NACHT's Bruno Ganz). Jack relates the trajectory of his hideous crimes while von Trier takes immense sadistic pleasure in graphically illustrating them; from the opening tire-iron head-smash of a braying woman in distress (a shrill and effective Uma Thurman) to a poor, trusting widow who is choked and stabbed, to a girlfriend who is demeaned and debased before meeting her bloody demise to the film's most perverse sequence, a sniper-tower obliteration of a mother and her two young children. After each episode (separated as von Trier often does with artfully rendered text interstitials), Jack and Verge have lengthy debates about art, the creative process, morality and more, with a frenzy of stock footage — from Glenn Gould hammering on a piano, to vintage Max Fleischer cartoons — serving to support these classroom-like conversations. Then it's back to the killing, as Jack collects his victims and begins carefully displaying them in his industrial meat locker.

THE HOUSE THAT JACK BUILT instantly amassed controversy, with its studio refusing to buckle and cut the film to appease the MPAA (an R-rated cut and unrated version were both released to streaming and to select theaters) and audience members drifted out of festival screenings in droves. And while all the brutally violent carnage listed above is in place to intentionally create such emotional and visceral disruptions, what some are failing to note is that THE HOUSE THAT JACK BUILT is also one of von Trier's *funniest* movies to date. That's right, not only do all the director's pictures function as secret horror movies, they're also blackly comic and here, with the stone-faced, deadpan Dillon pontificating and killing ad nauseum, one gets the feeling that the director is having the time of his life. It's almost as if von Trier IS both Jack and Verge, trying in vain to defend himself against critics who have long claimed him to be a degenerate, here using the characters as his avatars. At one point, Verge notes that all the primarily female victims Jack encounters are oddly inept, all of them acting irrationally and bizarrely naive and often Verge accuses Jack of transposing his own skewed sense of reality and innate mistrust of women onto his anecdotes of butchery. It's like the director is having a fluid internal monologue with his audience and himself. It's a mesmerizing conceit and one that echoes Mary Harron's AMERICAN PSYCHO in that at many points, Jack's tales of murder are so cartoonish, we're left to wonder if our storyteller is either making it all up or simply out of his mind entirely, a frustrated artist whose fantasies and delusions have gotten the upper hand. And by the time the movie literally goes to Hell and stings its baroque finale with the funniest closing credits music ever, you'll feel very much like the director has smashed you square in the face with cinema itself. Whether you find pleasure or pain in that ultimate effect, is entirely subjective.

And no matter your take on the picture, either as straight-forward serial killer phantasmagoria or self-reflexive meta shock-comedy (or both), one thing is indisputable:

THE HOUSE THAT JACK BUILT is a movie that ONLY Lars von Trier could have made. So many contemporary filmmakers attempt to mimic his voice and all of them fail. Because that voice is singular. He's the most evolved and refined purveyor of bad taste in film history and this is just another brick in the house he himself continues to build.

THE HUNGER (1983)

Starring Catherine Deneuve, David Bowie, Susan Sarandon, Cliff De Young
Written by Ivan Davis, Michael Thomas
Directed by Tony Scott

Tony Scott's 1983 vampire drama THE HUNGER — his first feature film and an impressionist adaptation of author Whitley Strieber's bestselling, same-named book — is a marvelous picture: stylish, beautiful, sensual, elegant and, at its core, almost overwhelmingly melancholy. It's no surprise then, that this hazy, dreamlike work of neo-Gothic art faired poorly at the box office upon release, seeing as the dawn of the decade concerned itself mainly with post-STAR WARS and RAIDERS OF THE LOST ARK spectacle and, in the annals of horror, gory, brainless body count pictures.

But THE HUNGER is something different. Something special.

In it, revered French actress Catherine Deneuve plays Miriam Blaylock, statuesque female vampire, a creature who we are led to believe has endured centuries, forever gliding through time, never aging and living off human blood. But she doesn't make this endless journey alone. Like Delphine Seyrig's similarly graceful and parasitic Countess Bathory in Harry Kumel's DAUGHTERS OF DARKNESS, Miriam must always have a companion, a lover of her choosing whom is afflicted with a version of the disease that she has, the disease that blesses one with life eternal and an unnatural, murderous thirst.

Except Miriam's lovers do not live on. Theirs is a comparatively brief dance with immortality, a cold fact her most recent paramour, John Blaylock, spends the first half of THE HUNGER dealing with.

Essaying the role of John is the late, great David Bowie, who, by 1983 had already proven himself as effective a presence on screen as he was on stage, so mesmerizing was he in films like Nicolas Roeg's unforgettable dark fantasy THE MAN WHO FELL TO EARTH, Uli Edel's CHRISTIANE F. and that same year's gruelling, Nagisa Oshima-directed war drama MERRY CHRISTMAS MR. LAWRENCE.

His work in THE HUNGER sits among his greatest performances and it's the soul of the film.

Sarah (Susan Sarandon) bleeds out while Miriam (Catherine Deneuve) howls.

The first thing we see in the movie, as we fade in from black, is the scowling face of dark rock legend Peter Murphy, who, along with his then band Bauhaus (who remain off screen, much to the rest of the band's annoyance), locked in a cage at a nightclub, performing their signature Goth pop anthem Bela Lugosi's Dead. Murphy had long styled his image after Ziggy Stardust-era Bowie and, for him, a young burgeoning rock idol, meeting Bowie on the set of an expensive Hollywood feature film was surreal.

Murphy had this to say to me about the experience, when I interviewed him in the pages of *Fangoria*:

"Meeting him on set was one of the most exciting moments of our early career; we were all part of that early 1970s scene that was obsessed with all that influential Bowie stuff. We loved Bowie. We showed up at 5:30am in the morning to start the performance at this dark, empty club and there wasn't really anyone around, save for some of the crew and Tony. But there was this balcony above us and, in the third take of doing the song, I just kind of felt that Bowie was there. It was tangible when he arrived, this whole experience and I actually wasn't even really sure I wanted to meet him you know, this artist who had a certain mythical quality to me. Because all our heroes are our own creations, anyway, aren't they? So his assistant came up to me after one of the takes and said 'That was a wonderful performance!' and I looked up to that balcony and Bowie was up there looking down and gave me this kind of approving nod. I had to leave and go to the dressing room, it was just too much, I

John Blaylock (David Bowie) is powerless to stop the process of decay.

couldn't be there. I was like, 'Stop looking at me, Bowie'! So, anyway, I found out that our dressing room was next to his and we had to hang around all day to do several retakes while they shot other scenes with the crowds and extras. Bowie at one point came to my dressing room and I had this Brandy bar in my room, and I nervously asked him in. To me, he was a figurehead. He was much more than a person. And all I could think of asking him was 'Uh... do you want some Brandy?' I must have looked like a complete drunk. I had this Brandy in my hand, and I was all shaky and nervous. But he was awesome."

In the following minutes, as the credits begin, we are treated to a cross-cut montage of wordless images that tell a story. We see Murphy, slamming his weight against that cage, the slickly dressed patrons of the club grinding their bodies to the music; we see Miriam, horn-rimmed sunglasses, dragging on a cigarette, watching the people below; we see John, his own rounded-lensed glasses tipped to eye- target a young post-punk couple, who stare back at him. Miriam approves. Murphy snarls. The quartet exits.

As the first hints of sun scrape the sky, they quickly drive to the young couple's home, for a round of drinks and presumably kinky sex. Drinks, yes. Sex, yes. And it's kinkier than the swinging lovers could ever imagine.

As the girl (Ann Magnuson) writhes in front of a white screen, blue light projected on her, accentuating the shadow of Miriam, still dragging that cigarette, to the right of the frame, the man (John Stephen Hill) reclines on the couch laughing, while John speaks the first line of dialogue in the film, vibrating through the din of composer Denny Jaeger's experimental, ambient throb:

"No ice."

John and the girl venture into the kitchen and, while Miriam mounts the man, John spreads the girl's legs wide and removes her shirt, both of them grinning with purpose and lust. His hands knead her breasts, he runs his tongue up her neck, and they kiss, strings of saliva connecting their mouths as tongues push out and touch.

Hanging from his neck is an Egyptian Ankh, a symbol of life; but this Ankh is actually a sheathed dagger and, as John moves his head hungrily between the girl's legs, that blade is removed and a cut is made, presumably, down below. John feeds from the screaming girl as Miriam opens the throat of the man.

Blood runs freely.

This spectacularly violent and sexual opening then gives way to the almost meditative sadness that fuels the rest of the picture. We see John and Miriam's hands cleaning the blood from their hands in the sink, their killing Ankh's clanking on the metal of the drain and the red circling and spiraling down.

The pair drive home at dawn while a sparse, delicate Shubert piano piece weeps in the background. They arrive at their Manhattan brownstone and, after cremating their victims, shower, their nude bodies sprayed with water and enveloped by steam. But while Miriam seems perfectly content, John is not. He stares at his wife, his muse, his Queen and, almost childlike, reaches apprehensively for her.

"Forever?" he almost whispers.

"What?" she asks.

"Forever and ever?"

To that, she has no answer.

Because John's time is running out. He knows this. She knows this. And though she tries to deny it, John is forced to endure the emotional and physical finality of life.

The following section of the film essays that process, in wrenching detail and, with anyone other than David Bowie playing the character, I can't imagine the effect would be as profound; there's a poetry and grace in his incarnation of John Blaylock, one whose silences are almost musical, the wordless look of pain and fear in his eyes, quietly devastating.

As sleeplessness grips him, as wrinkles draw across his skin, as his hair falls out in clumps and he stares in the mirror, not quite recognizing the image that stares back, as he stumbles through the city streets and people begin treating him differently, not as a man, but as something outdated and worthless, we feel his agony and, despite the ruthless, predatory nature he revealed during the film's ice-cold opening, we feel for him.

We weep for John Blaylock. Because we understand what it is to lose youth.

We know that the hunger of the title isn't just a hunger for blood, its's a hunger to hold on to life, to love, to all of those moments that make us what we are, in that brief period of our lives that we shine, when we are at our best. Seeing John crumble and worse, accept his fate, is difficult because, on a less phantasmagorical level, it's what we all must eventually accept and endure.

And when John finally succumbs and Bowie exits the picture, THE HUNGER loses some of its own life. Without Bowie, there's no heart left, no emotional thrust. It's a pretty picture, an attractive vessel that sort of drifts to its conclusion without purpose.

And it's hard to watch THE HUNGER now, with Scott taking his life in the face of reported illness and Bowie now long gone from cancer, to not think that maybe during their final days, they too might have felt a bit like John Blaylock himself, confused and crestfallen as they gave in to the inevitable ravages of time and decay. That's the poetry and legacy of THE HUNGER, how the art was accidentally imitated and how now, that art is indivisible from the artists who made it. Gone, and yet immortal. Undead.

Undead. Undead. Undead.

INVASION OF THE BLOOD FARMERS (1972)

Starring Norman Kelley, Tanna Hunter, Bruce Detrick, Jack Beaubeck
Written by Ed Adlum, Ed Kelleher
Directed by Ed Adlum

Those who — like me — have cited Ed Adlum's 1974 howler SHRIEK OF THE MUTILATED as the best/worst indie American horror movie of the 1970s, obviously never saw his 1972 go-for-broke earlier *craptastic* creeper INVASION OF THE BLOOD FARMERS. It took me some time to catch up to it too, though I had certainly heard many of its many victims scream its perverse praises for years. Naturally, one has to have a healthy streak of masochism in order to fully appreciate the film's downmarket charms, but those bold enough to endure this mad movie's seventy-seven torturous minutes will be — for better or worse — transformed for life. I promise.

Filmed in woodsy upstate New York by Adlum and his co-conspirators, Roberta and Michael Findlay (SNUFF and the aforementioned SHRIEK OF THE MUTILATED), INVASION OF THE BLOOD FARMERS was actually partially shot by future ERASERHEAD DP Frederick Elmes. And while there's little trace of the soon-to-be David Lynch collaborator's singular visual style, the picture absolutely feels like it exists in ERASERHEAD's bent universe. Nothing in this film makes much sense, either visually, aurally, or narratively, with cross-eye-level framing, slipshod special effects and "acting" that is alternately listless and ludicrous. After a James Mason impersonator narrates the idiotic setup, we meet a dopey bush league student and a effeminate

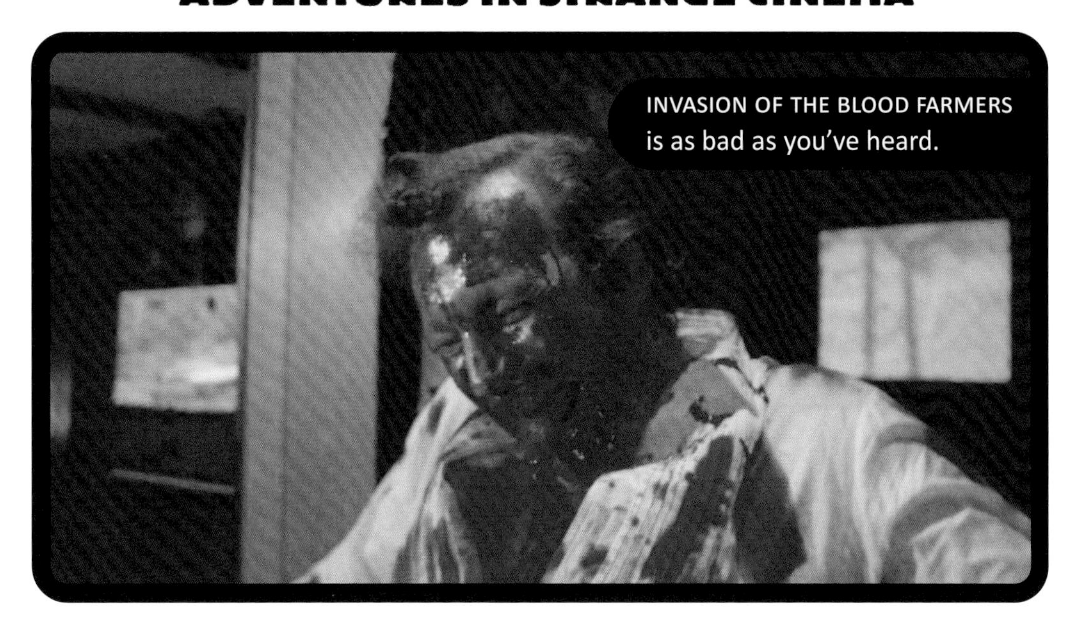
INVASION OF THE BLOOD FARMERS is as bad as you've heard.

mad scientist, who have stumbled upon some sort of bubbly blood that they think is very important because it fills up their beakers magically. Said voodoo gore was drawn from the wounds of a local loser named Jim Carrey (ha!) who bled out all over the local bar. Poor old Jim had escaped the clutches of the titular Blood Farmers, a gang of hayseed Druids lorded over by a effete cult leader who needs the blood of the innocent to revive his Queen, who lies comatose in a pretty nifty glass coffin. After his daughter's dog is killed and eaten by one of the giggling Druid henchmen (a riotous scene where a fluffy canine is replaced by literal fluff), the scientist and his youthful protege find a rusty old key and set off to solve the problem of the super-blood and unlock the mysteries of the Blood Farmers.

With us so far? You don't have to follow the plot (such as it is) to groove on this wonderfully wretched piece of cinematic refuse, loaded as it is with PG-level, dollar store gore and jaw-dropping sequences, like that bizarre hilltop climax where the "Queen" is dispatched by what looks like a high-five while a fake dummy Druid with cookie-monster eyes burns in close-up but is conspicuously absent in the wide shot. At least SHRIEK OF THE MUTILATED had a nifty twist, where the Santa-suit Sasquatch turned out to be the frontman for a cannibal cult. INVASION OF THE BLOOD FARMERS has nothing like this and just sort of flops around, gasping for life until the poodle-laugh grand finale.

I'm not even sure what else to say about this charming clunker save for those of you out there who get-off on the lowliest of inept genre stuff will love the Hell out of it. INVASION OF THE BLOOD FARMERS. Yes, it's as bad as you've heard. And yes, that's an endorsement.

INVASION OF THE BODY SNATCHERS (1978)

Starring Donald Sutherland, Brooke Adams, Jeff Goldblum, Veronica Cartwright
Written by W.D. Richter
Directed by Philip Kaufman

In 1978, I was four years old. I had plenty of comic books and one particular, well-worn and generally mistreated issue of *Batman* (issue #309 to be specific, in which Bats battled a brute named Blockbuster at Christmas time) had, on its back page, a reproduction of the theatrical poster for a new movie called INVASION OF THE BODY SNATCHERS. Said poster was a marvel of stark design; black, sepia/brown, and white with gentle red traces on the title font and depicts four running silhouettes trying to outdistance their own shadows and though I did not understand the image per se, it was abstract enough to disturb and obsess me for many, many months to follow. Save for the cover, I cannot recall a damn thing about the BATMAN adventure inside that comic. But that poster was seared into my brain.

Flash forward to 1979.

A local television channel, Toronto's CITY-TV, began running ads for their network premiere of INVASION OF THE BODY SNATCHERS, to be aired that very Friday night, the same Friday night my parents were going out to see APOCALYPSE NOW at the theatre. They were aware of my jittery desire to see BODY SNATCHERS and gave my babysitting aunt explicit instructions not to let me do so, to ensure that I was in bed and as far away from a television set as possible when the picture unspooled.

Well, she did a fair job of seeing that mission through but, much to my delight, she managed to also fall asleep by 9pm. Total pass out on the sofa. Lights out. It was at this point I sneaked into the living room, flipped on the television and channel advanced just in time to see what would be an instantly life altering sequence. In it, a wet, writhing man lay on the ground, covered in gossamer webs, his exact double hovering above with a hoe in his grip. The upright, curly-headed and considerably more sentient version of the man then raised his arms above his head and brought that otherwise innocuous garden tool squarely down upon his twitching twin, caving in its head and spilling out thick, bloody discharge while other humanoids convulsed and heaved in the peripheral parts of the frame.

Too much. Total shock. And to think that this heaving stretch of nightmare fuel was embedded in a motion picture that the MPAA saw fit to saddle with a deceivingly safe PG rating!

The visceral horror of what I was watching gripped me in places I did not know existed. The impact was accentuated by the fact that what I was seeing was forbidden and that I knew that if I was caught, my fate may or may not have equaled that of the blonde afro-man on the TV.

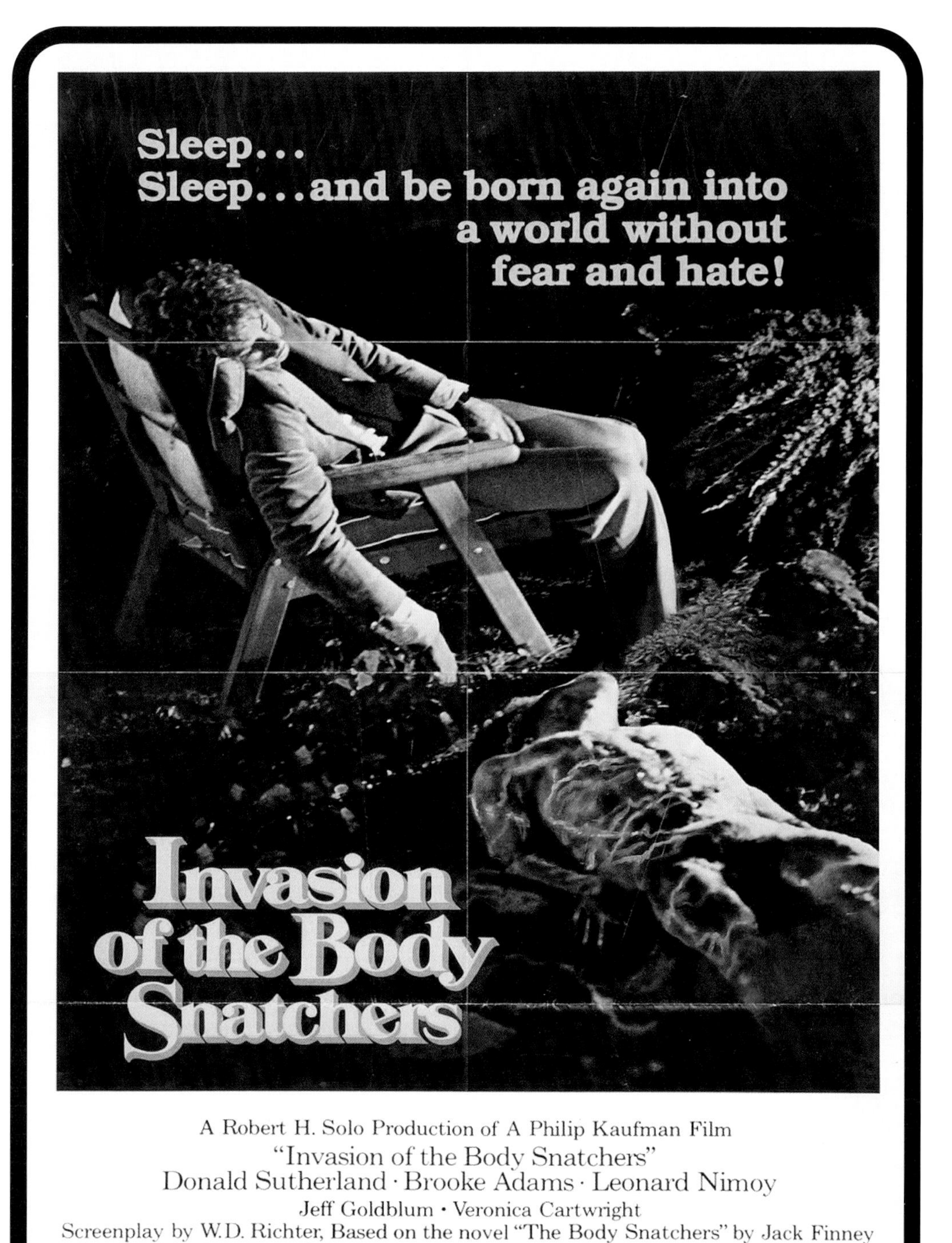
Sleep...
Sleep...and be born again into a world without fear and hate!
Invasion of the Body Snatchers
A Robert H. Solo Production of A Philip Kaufman Film
"Invasion of the Body Snatchers"
Donald Sutherland · Brooke Adams · Leonard Nimoy
Jeff Goldblum · Veronica Cartwright
Screenplay by W.D. Richter, Based on the novel "The Body Snatchers" by Jack Finney
Produced by Robert H. Solo · Directed by Philip Kaufman · Color
United Artists
A Transamerica Company
FOREIGN

I quickly switched off the set, ran to my room and climbed into bed. But I didn't sleep. In fact, my sleep was sabotaged for some time. I was disturbed, but that trauma narrowed my focus, shining a light onto what would become my life's work. I became a horror movie junkie. I began chasing the dragon; consuming every bit of trashy nonsense I could get my eyes locked-on, willingly giving myself nightmares and pushing my limits.

Now these many (and I mean many) years later, I am fortunate enough that I've managed to make a lovely little living spilling my guts about all those wicked flicks that I love. And I'm pleased that the original film that curled my toes and iced my blood is, in my opinion, one of the greatest science fiction horror films of all time. If you've taken the time to see it, you'll most likely agree with me.

Phillip Kaufman's masterful 1978 remake of Don Siegel's 1956 McCarthy-era shocker (itself an adaptation of Jack Finney's serialized book) is arguably a better film, transplanting all that cold war dread onto a post-Vietnam, pre-1980s increasingly corporate America. In it, the great Donald Sutherland stars as Matthew Bennell, a San Francisco health inspector who, along with the woman he loves (Brooke Adams, who's great) and his closest friends (a young but still awesomely neurotic Jeff Goldblum and Veronica Cartwright) finds himself in the middle of an insidious, identity thieving alien invasion. It seems aggressive pods are implanting themselves in the earth's foliage and, while their victims sleep, are duplicating human beings, creating exact replicates that look and talk just like the original subjects. Except they are fully, completely devoid of emotion; dead-eyed organic androids bent on crushing both love and hate.

What makes Kaufman's film so great is that both the characters (great time and care is taken to develop the eccentricities of our protagonists, making us weep for the loss of their humanity), ace direction, brilliant performances (Sutherland is at the peak of his powers here and a post-Spock Leonard Nimoy is chilling as a new age psychiatrist who denies the escalating horror around him) and, perhaps most viscerally, a remarkable score by jazz composer Denny Zeitlin. Said score is an avant-garde amalgam of electronic pulses, minimalist orchestral movements and what sounds like a sampling of an in-utero infant's heartbeat. Chilling, evocative and completely original stuff.

DRILLER KILLER director Abel Ferrara took a stab at the same material in 1993 with BODY SNATCHERS but it was a relatively soulless and flaccid affair (though it does have the odd effective moment and boasts a great turn by Meg Tilly), removing the dread, paranoia and ambiguity of both Siegel and Kaufman's pictures by setting the action on an army base, where everyone acts like automatons anyway. Then the Wachowski Brothers (now sisters) sputtered out a riff on the material in 2007 with the woefully postproduction problem plagued THE INVASION, a weak, unfocused effort that wastes a fine turn by Nicole Kidman and renders the pod people evolution as a mucous spewing and easily curable disease. There was also that Robert Rodriguez shoulder shrugger THE FACULTY, which many kids of that generation swear by. None of them are a spidery thread of fetal hair on the arse of Kaufman's towering shocker.

And I haven't even mentioned that ending and that final frame, where Veronica Cartwright comes running up to Donald Sutherland and he turns around and unleashes an unholy howl as the camera zooms into his gaping maw. Fade to black. Roll credits. Silence. Perfection. Masterpiece.

INTERVIEW: VERONICA CARTWRIGHT

Actress Veronica Cartwright has been casting spells in cinema since she was a little girl, co-starring at the age of 12 with heavy-hitters Audrey Hepburn and Shirley MacLaine in William Wyler's controversial 1961 thriller THE CHILDREN'S HOUR and a tidal wave of entertainments made for both the big (THE BIRDS) and small (THE TWILIGHT ZONE, LEAVE IT TO BEAVER) screen.

Hers is truly a life spent in front of the lens. But it was in the 1970s, when Cartwright was in her late 20s, that she began to find her footing, starring in John Byrum's sexually-explicit INSERTS, in director/star Jack Nicholson's comedy western GOIN' SOUTH and in a pair of films that history has proven to be two of the greatest science fiction horror movies ever made: Ridley Scott's groundbreaking ALIEN and — of course — Philip Kaufman's nightmarish remake of INVASION OF THE BODY SNATCHERS.

CHRIS ALEXANDER: Your life reads like a history of the last 60 years of American pop culture. Do you ever think about finally writing that book?

VERONICA CARTWRIGHT No. I know, people say I should. Whenever I tell stories, people say you should write this down. But that takes time.

ALEXANDER: You're just giving this stuff away! You're about to give it up for me for free!

CARTWRIGHT: No, no! There's still stuff...

ALEXANDER: What is your calling card film. Is it ALIEN?

CARTWRIGHT: Yeah, ALIEN, sure... but also THE BIRDS. That's always a big one.

ALEXANDER: And INVASION OF THE BODY SNATCHERS, where you share the screen's scariest scream scene with Donald Sutherland.

CARTWRIGHT: Well, that's an interesting story, because Phil Kaufman didn't tell us one thing about that ending, he told us different things, so I had not expected Donald to do that! That's why I approached him very tentatively, without giving anything away and I was testing the waters and then he turns around and does that and I was not expecting that at all. So, that look of terror and upset is just what came out [*laughs*].

Lambert (Veronica Cartwright) encounters the ultimate horror in ALIEN (1979).

ALEXANDER: And then, a year later, Ridley Scott did that to you again...

CARTWRIGHT: Yeah, with the chest-burster scene. That was crazy. We all knew there was going to be a chest-burster scene, because it was in the script, but we didn't know how it was going to be done. So, we were left in the dressing rooms upstairs while the FX people got John all packed and ready with all the stuff, you know. So then we came down, everything was covered in plastic and there were these big buckets of offal around; ugh, the smell was just repulsive. Anyway, we were just so fascinated, there were four cameras around us and we all kind of just leaned in to watch it. I was told I might get a little blood on me but I had no idea and I leaned right into a blood jet and, um, my reaction was "Oh my God!" and then I backed up and flipped over the these upright cowboy boots... it was just hysterical really. But I kept going. But it was literally like something out of a Mack Sennett film or something.

ALEXANDER: You gotta watch out for those blood jets...

CARTWRIGHT: I know, I know. And years later I worked with the special effects guy in another film, and he apologized to me [*laughs*].

ALEXANDER: Did you stay in touch with the late John Hurt?

CARTWRIGHT: A bit. I saw him in L.A. doing a play at The Douglas not too long ago and I got to go back and see him. And once in a while I'd get to see him when he came to town. He was a lovely person and it was very sad to hear that he had passed.

ALEXANDER: I know you were just a little girl when you made THE CHILDREN'S HOUR, but my God you're good in it. Do you have strong memories?

CARTWRIGHT: Oh yeah, of course. I mean Shirley MacLaine was such an early influence on me. She's the reason I ended up seriously pursuing this. I met her once years later backstage at her one woman show and she greeted me warmly and said, "I have followed your career, dear," and I said, "you are the reason I'm doing this." It was a cool moment.

ALEXANDER: In what must be an endless ocean of cool moments. You seem to have worked consistently from childhood to adult age. Did you ever take a break?

CARTWRIGHT: There was a period of time when I couldn't seem to get anything. I was on the series Daniel Boone and then, when that ended, I was still under 18 so I was too young to be in the older category and too old to be a child. So there was a few years there that were dry. So I went and studied acting with Jack Garfine and did that for three years and then decided to move to England, because as you know, I am British born, and that's where I got the movie INSERTS and that started everything all over again.

ALEXANDER: That was a controversial film.

CARTWRIGHT: Well, we got an X rating. It finally got changed to NC-17, but they showed it not long ago at the Egyptian and... God, it holds up so well. It's a wonderful movie. It was such a liberating experience to do that movie and it kicked off a lot of stuff for me. I was a waitress at that time and one day this guy says "Excuse me, can I ask you a question? Aren't you in that movie INSERTS?" and I go, "yeah" and he says "what the fuck are you doing here?!" I was earning a living! But I went home that night and thought, what was I doing there? So I quit my job the next day.

Cartwright's chilling final scene in INVASION OF THE BODY SNATCHERS.

ALEXANDER: I love your maniacal, cherry-puking performance in THE WITCHES OF EASTWICK. How did you get that gig?

CARTWRIGHT: I had done GOIN' SOUTH with Jack Nicholson and originally for WITCHES they were looking at Colleen Dewhurst and Geraldine Page for that role because in the book, it was written as an older person. But Jack always thought that Felicia was a contemporary. She was the fourth witch. So, after I got the part, George Miller said that I had a huge fan in Jack Nicholson and that it was Jack who insisted I get the job.

ALEXANDER: Richard Jenkins is fantastic as your poor husband...

CARTWRIGHT: Isn't he wonderful? He's a wonderful person and actor. He's amazing in everything he does. Just the sheer embarrassment he has when I'm screaming at people and calling them whores in church. Fantastic.

ALEXANDER: As a kid, you were in THE TWILIGHT ZONE episode 'I Sing the Body Electric' based on the Ray Bradbury story. Did you meet Rod Serling?

CARTWRIGHT: Yes, I did! I watched him film his intro for that episode, in fact!

ALEXANDER: And Bradbury?

CARTWRIGHT: No. We didn't see him. He didn't get along with Rod, because things were cut out of the story, but Rod was like, "yeah but I only have 28 minutes to do this!" That didn't make any difference to Ray. He never did another one. He was furious.

ALEXANDER: You've been in the business for literally your entire life. It's such a swamp of ego. How did you manage to stay grounded and nice?

CARTWRIGHT: Um... I don't know. I guess it was my upbringing. I enjoy what I do. And really, why become an asshole, you know? You know, no one ever bugged Jack Nicholson. When we made WITCHES and people were standing around to see him, he'd just come out and say, "Hi everybody!" I was lucky enough to go with him to a Lakers game too and he was always friendly. No one bothers Jack because he makes himself so accessible. It's the people who make assholes of themselves and make a big deal of it. Why push people away? I love when people come up to me and say they appreciate the work!

IT'S ALIVE (1974)

Starring John P. Ryan, Sharon Farrell, James Dixon, Guy Stockwell
Written by Larry Cohen
Directed by Larry Cohen

Rick Baker's mutant baby launched 1000 nightmares.

Maverick genre film writer, director and innovator Larry Cohen's 1974 horror classic IT'S ALIVE is a masterclass in parental paranoia. Cohen was one of the greatest writers for cinema full stop, always showing a sure hand and blending eccentric, believable characterizations, arcane situations, black humor, social commentary, doses of potent violence and — when he's playing in that sandbox — visceral horror. But in IT'S ALIVE, which in many ways was Cohen's breakthrough film, his tapping in to the primordial ooze of what it means to be a parent, of the fear and joy of the birth process and the elemental ties we have to whatever child emerges from the womb, is profound. And the ways in which he perverts those emotions and instincts into a blood-spattered nightmare are still profoundly shocking.

IT'S ALIVE stars John Ryan and Sharron Farrell as Frank and Lenore Davis, a loving couple approaching middle-age with one 11-year-old son and now, another child on the way. The movie opens with Lenore waking her husband up announcing that "It's time" and preparing — calmly, cheerfully — to go to the hospital for the birth. Typical, benign scenes of a nervous husband and wife preparing for that most natural of functions are essayed by Cohen in an almost *too* saccharine way, with waiting room dad asides and doctors shruggingly going through their routines, creating a deceivingly safe environment.

And then... birth.

"There's only *one* thing wrong with the Davis baby," the poster tagline and trailer screamed.

"IT'S ALIVE!"

And alive it is. Inexplicably, Lenore gives birth a hulking, fanged mutant with claws and a melon-sized noggin and a lethal impulse to shred every human being in reach. As designed by a very young Rick Baker, the IT'S ALIVE baby is widely considered a classic monster and with good reason: it's scary, absurd and the manifestation of every mother's worst nightmare. Man, those early Rick Baker monsters were the best, weren't they? OCTAMAN. THE INCREDIBLE MELTING MAN. His majestic ape suit for 1976's KING KONG. Just wonderful, innovative, and imaginative stuff.

Anyway, the scene in where Frank realizes that something terrible has happened is brilliantly staged, shot and edited by Cohen, with the soundtrack going silent, a doctor emerging from the birthing room holding his torn throat before collapsing dead, the camera work flipping to handheld as Frank scrambles into the room to see his wife only to be met with unimaginable horror as the bloody bodies of every doctor nurse and orderly frame the scene of his screaming, restrained wife whose shrieks of "My baby! Where is my baby!" are bone chilling. It's a deftly orchestrated symphony of confusion and, considering we have not yet seen the "baby," we the audience are in almost the same amount of shock as the parents.

From this point on, Cohen flips the film into a sharp thriller. As the baby (whose POV we are treated to as a blurred, psychedelic scramble) rampages around the countryside, killing housewives and milkmen, the Davis' become tabloid fodder and are subjected to unimaginable scrutiny. Unable to even process the horrors they have endured (and forget about the inevitable postpartum emotions that Lenore doesn't even have time to absorb), they valiantly struggle against judgement (the instant thought is that it's their fault... did they do drugs? Was an early term consultation about an abortion the culprit? Were they exposed to radiation?), treachery (Lenore's in-home nurse moonlights as a reporter and secretly records their conversations) and social and professional isolation. And then the Davis' perspective shifts. They discover that a doctor tried to murder the baby upon delivery, shocked by its deformity. Frank begins to feel guilt and then great concern for his child. He imagines the dynamic to be that of Frankenstein abandoning his creation. Worse, it is discovered that prenatal drugs given to Lenore might be responsible for the child's condition and now the corporation behind the drug want the baby dead more than anyone, lest they be sued off the face of the planet earth.

The entire blood opera ends in tragedy when Frank decides it's his responsibility to kill his own creation, despite Lenore begging him not too. When he finally finds the baby, he is alarmed to realize that the child will *not* harm *him*. Instinctually, the baby knows who its parents are and only seeks comfort and shelter in their arms. Alas, the police have other ideas.

IT'S ALIVE is a marvel, with a solid performance by Ryan and a mesmerizing score by the late, great Bernard Herrmann serving to boost the already immaculately produced, and modestly budgeted production. Upon release in 1974, distributor Warner Bros. didn't really know what to do with it and, while it did a decent bit of business considering the minimal marketing, it wasn't until a re-issue in 1977 with a new ad campaign that the movie struck a nerve at the box office. So successful was that 2nd release, that Warner commissioned Cohen to write, direct and produce a sequel, IT'S ALIVE 2 (aka IT LIVES AGAIN), a bizarre companion picture that sees a now older and virtually homeless Ryan wandering the country seeking out parents who have or who are about to give birth to more of the mutant babies. In IT LIVES AGAIN, it's Kathleen Lloyd and Frederic Forrest who are the unlucky couple, with Ryan trying to protect them and their child from the authorities who seek to murder their monstrous offspring. With three babies on screen and the lessened impact of Baker's effects and a convoluted plot, IT LIVES AGAIN is an inferior follow-up but manages to be compelling due to Cohen's ideas and social criticism that runs rampant over the picture. If IT'S ALIVE is about the horrors of birth, the sequel is about taking responsibility for the children you create no matter the cost.

That theme is progressed in the final Cohen IT'S ALIVE film, 1987's ISLAND OF THE ALIVE, where Cohen's frequent leading man Michael Moriarty steals the show (as he often does) as a father of one the babies who proves in court that the monsters are *not* evil but just scared, confused and undeserving of extermination. The court then orders the babies to be shipped to an isolated island and left to their devices. But years later, the now-adult monsters decide to make their way back to the mainland to take vengeance upon the society that shunned them. It's the Frankenstein motif suggested in the first film, coming full circle and, like the second film, if ISLAND OF THE ALIVE isn't quite as successful as the original, it is propelled and buoyed by Cohen's unique, singular world view and social philosophies.

All three films are testaments to their creator's inimitable vision, standing as one of the most fascinating and cerebral horror trilogies in film history.

I WAS A TEENAGE WEREWOLF (1957)

Starring Michael Landon, Whit Bissell, Yvonne Lime, Malcolm Atterbury
Written by Herman Cohen, Aben Kandel
Directed by Gene Fowler Jr.

As the 1940s ground to a Hitler-killing halt, the next generation of American kids — well, of international kids, actually — were confused and frankly, angry. It happens often post-war time. The children of the people who were sent and who sent others to be offed on the frightful frontlines, grow up with a mile-wide chip on their shoulders. And the best thing that comes out of this inevitability is that this sort of youthful dissent almost always makes its way into the arts and popular culture.

Truth. If it wasn't for World War II there would be no French New Wave, no Italian neo-realism, no GODZILLA. And no, I WAS A TEENAGE WEREWOLF. The latter-mentioned

Michael Landon's transformed Tony leans in for a kiss.

1957 horror film is rarely discussed in terms of its sociopolitical significance, but I can think of no other American genre effort of the period that so taps into the anxieties and cynicism of the burgeoning US youth culture, fueled as it was by rock'n'roll and rebellion. And in Gene Fowler Jr.'s scrappy, cheap and innovative flick, that bile came in the form a toothy, drooling and merciless hormonal and hirsute menace.

I WAS A TEENAGE WEREWOLF stars a very young, pre-LITTLE HOUSE ON THE PRARIE, Michael Landon as a volatile teen named Tony, a kid who — like most American teenagers of the time — must have seen 1955's REBEL WITHOUT A CAUSE a few more times than humanly healthy. The thin-skinned lad is ever quick to answer any conflict with violence, much to his teachers' and his father's dismay. Tony is smart and sensitive underneath all that misplaced rage (hence why his doting girlfriend Arlene puts up with his nonsense endlessly) and, after one senseless brawl too many, he takes the local beat cop's advice and visits noted psychologist Dr. Brandon (Whit Bissel), an MD specializing in hypnotherapy.

The good (or, maybe not-so-good) doc is convinced he can help Tony by using him as a guinea pig for a new experimental serum he has developed that convinces the mind and body to regress to a primal state. The road to Hell is paved with good intentions and Brandon thinks that by sort of "re-setting" mankind back to its base elements, a better race of people will emerge. This concept alone makes I WAS A TEENAGE WEREWOLF an important film as its reverse Darwinian mad science anticipates the philosophies developed in David Cronenberg's early work (especially SHIVERS and THE BROOD) and Ken Russell's ALTERED STATES (and the book by Paddy Chayefsky on which it was based).

Anyway, Doc Brandon's psychic manipulation does indeed work but not quite as intended as Tony becomes a lab-rat werewolf who prowls day and night, aiming to off anyone who gets in his way. But while this lethal side effect is unwelcome, the interesting thing is that the treatments do help Tony regain his focus and fall in line with the socially acceptable status quo, much to the high school guidance counselor's delight. But when Tony sees a comely co-ed (*Playboy* Playmate Dawn Richard) practicing her gymnastics routine, his horrific hormonal cocktail whirs to life and then, when the school bell rings awakening a Pavlovian response, the teenager turns again, this time in front of his pals. With the cops and angry townsfolk hot on his hairy heels, Tony the werewolf heads for the hills, shunned and spurned by the society that made him.

The first thing that really jumps out at you about this American International Pictures release is that it's *not played for camp*. It's not meant to be funny. Sure, we can giggle at some of the antiquated acting and snort at the weird "Eeny Meeny Miny Moe" musical break that gets all the kids' toes tappin', but we cannot laugh at the central drama, nor can we dismiss Landon's remarkable and sincere performance as the sad-eyed kid who is the perpetual outsider, unable to connect with and be part of the mainstream. Here is a boy lost in a world that he deems as hostile and broken and, though he cannot articulate this, he's raging against peers and parental figures who just aren't questioning *anything.*

The central, overt subtext of the film is deeply sad, too. When Tony finally decides that he wants to connect, that he doesn't want to lose his girlfriend — the only thing he seemingly loves — and is tired and worn out by being on the fringe, the man he is pushed to put his trust in thoroughly abuses and manipulates him. It's a tragedy and totally telling of how kids of the period saw their elders. They simply weren't to be trusted. Their lusts for power and greed end up dragging the world into bloody war and economical fallout. They lie to their children. They tell them of Santa Claus and the Tooth Fairy but then rip back the curtain to reveal the dismal truth and then just abandon them to figure it all out themselves. They try to control them. They reject their attempts at growth. And then they use them as pawns in their plans... and turn them into monsters.

I WAS A TEENAGE WEREWOLF was — like all of these movies — panned by the critics at the time, though was a commercial hit. Of course, those pesky grown-up critics hated it. They had no idea what the movie was really about and rejected the concept of teenage angst as being just a laughable rite of passage, totally ignorant that the sort of angst that was swelling around them would birth a generation of intensely political, angry and aware kids whose minds and hearts would affect the world. It was part of a series of "teenage monster" movies that AIP backed, most notably that same years' I WAS A TEENAGE FRANKENSTEIN, which — though unrelated as a direct sequel — once more dragged Bissel back as a mad scientist playing God. But none of these films had the primal, urgent and heartbreaking energy that WEREWOLF has in its finest moments. It's a remarkable and important movie from a transitional time in American history.

THE KEEP (1983)

Starring Scott Glenn, Gabriel Byrne, Jurgen Prochnow, Ian McKellen
Written by Michael Mann
Directed by Michael Mann

When it comes to dark fantasy and horror filmmaking, I am and always will be a strong advocate for anti-realism, which is to say I prefer my terrors to exist in a dream state, free of the pretentious shackles of narrative logic, existing in a world that is but a hazy impression of the mundane one in which we live. I appreciate films that freely lapse into that sort of nightmare logic where nothing makes sense, nothing is absolute and anything can — and usually does — happen.

This is also why I've always been a strong champion of Michael Mann's evocative, absurd, flawed and occasionally transcendent 1983 cinematic adaptation of author F. Paul Wilson's terrifying novel *The Keep*, a movie that was cut upon its release by a nervous studio, ignored by audiences, deplored by critics, rejected by its source scribe and generally forgotten. Though the ensuing years have seen it accumulate a quiet cult following, the movie is still, as of this writing, legitimately unavailable on domestic DVD or Blu-ray.

In the darkest days of WWII a wayward band of SS troops, led by the sympathetic Captain Woermann (Jurgen Prochnow of DAS BOOT) find themselves snaking around Romania, specifically a remote, fog drenched village in the midst of a mountain pass. On the outskirts of this village sits a monolithic fortress, a "Keep", a shrine of sorts that the locals insist houses an ancient evil, and one that the Nazis choose to set up their stronghold.

Against the conflicted Woermann's wishes, the greedy Third Reich droogs begin secretly prying off the protective silver crosses that line the walls and, in an especially eerie sequence, unleash a pulsing, chasm dwelling, sentient white light that promptly separates one unlucky storm trooper's noggin from his neck. As even more of the men begin to meet their strange, untimely demises, grim reinforcements in the form of the ultra sadistic Major Kaempffer (a chilling Gabriel Byrne) and his troupe roll into town, casually laying waste to the innocent villagers and enlisting an old, wheelchair bound Jewish professor named Dr. Theodore Cuza (the great Ian McKellen) to aid them in deciphering the cryptic, possibly Hebrew scrawl on the walls left after each kill.

Glaeken (Scott Glenn) and Eva (Alberta Watson) confront the evil of THE KEEP.

As Cuza soon discovers, the Nazi scum have indeed unleashed absolute evil in the form of a slowly evolving, muscle necked demon named Molasar (Michael Carter), a force of darkness that was imprisoned inside the Keep centuries prior and with apparently very good reason. As the body count increases and a wave of madness and corruption oozes over the previously peaceful village, across the ocean a loner named Glaeken (Scott Glenn) is also drawn to the Keep, armed with a glowing staff, a chip the size of Gibraltar on his immortal shoulder, and a blind, instinctual drive to put the horrific Molasar back into his stony grave once and for all.

When THE KEEP was released in 1983, Mann was already a filmmaker of some note, having both written and directed the slicker than slick 1981 James Caan thriller Thief (he was still a year shy of the brilliant MIAMI VICE, an amazing, ahead of its time TV show that I still swear by) and Wilson's skin-crawling best seller had already found its way to paperback. Almost immediately it became clear that fans of that book were up in arms by Mann's big screen stab at the story. Chief among their many gripes was the fact that Molasar had been inexplicably altered from a bloodsucking ageless vampire into a hulking skull faced prosthetic brute with laser-beam eyes. Wilson himself was aghast, not only by the picture's many changes but also because of its disjointed tone and improper pacing; the author went as far as to publicly denounce THE KEEP as an "incomprehensible mess".

Why the explicit vampirism angle was excised is anybody's guess; perhaps it was due to the fact that in the early '80s Hollywood vampirism had, as it does every so often, burned out its popularity coil. The only other vampire film of 1983, THE HUNGER also betrayed its source novel (by Whitley Strieber, respectively) by keeping its fangs similarly in check, emphasizing slick visuals and art directed sex over traditional undead thrills (and, like THE KEEP, that film is an underappreciated masterpiece of style and dread). It's very possible that the good folks at Paramount persuaded Mann to give the blood sucking a break and tailor the tale to the glossier, less earthy, increasingly synthetic MTV driven decade. As for the admittedly jarring jumps in logic and plot, rumor has it that Mann's final cut of the film was almost three hours long and the studio simply opted to shave it down to smithereens for cynical, practical exhibition purposes.

Now, I'm painfully aware of the source novel deviations: I loved the book too. But what some people fail to grasp is that what works on page, doesn't necessarily work on screen, one being a literary medium, the other being primarily visual and sensory, and perhaps the changes were warranted. Not only that, but the passage of time has proven Michael Mann to be an auteur, a stylist with a creative pallet completely unique to him and no one else. Looking back on THE KEEP today, we can see a young filmmaker experimenting, finding, and perfecting, his visual and tonal vocabulary simply using the Wilson novel as a framing device. Blue lights streaming though broken windows, slow pans across fog-soaked landscapes, outlandish, borderline ridiculous and otherworldly character behaviors and a sense of thick, oppressive and unwavering tension; they're all here in their early '80s glory. Who gives a damn if they aren't in the novel? The book has its own charms. But one thing it does *not* have is a score by Tangerine Dream...

Yes.

Let's address that. Tangerine Dream. A collective of German experimental electronic musicians that had previously laid down hypnotic cinematic soundscapes for William Friedkin's SORCERER, Michael Laughlin's STRANGE BEHAVIOR, Mann's own, aforementioned film noir THIEF and would later sculpt deft music for the American cut of Ridley Scott's LEGEND and Kathryn Bigelow's similarly revisionist vampire tale NEAR DARK. Their efforts on THE KEEP are like aural glue, an endless wave of thick analog synth music that, even when inappropriate (as in that scene where the soldiers chisel the beautifully detailed silver cross off the keep's wall) gel the film together, becoming as vital to the identity of the movie as the sets, the suffocating mists, the top notch cast and the goofy looking yet imposing and ultimately effective Molasar himself.

In fact, if you're a fan of the works of German art house director Werner Herzog (which I most certainly am) you'll see incredible, perhaps intentional, perhaps not, parallels between Mann's work with Tangerine Dream here and Herzog's collaborations with composer Florian Fricke, aka Popul Vuh. The slow, meditative sequence where Glaeken's ship crosses the ocean is eerily akin the scene where Dracula's ghost ship drifts the high seas in Herzog's influential 1979 remake of NOSFERATU and the opening images of the fog shrouded, mountain sealed Romanian village look and sound like they were pulled wholesale out of Herzog's breathtaking 1972 historical psychodrama AGUIRRE: THE WRATH OF GOD.

However you see THE KEEP, the bottom line is to just see it. It is a film of many sensory pleasures and the key to truly enjoying it is to overlook its flaws, its lapses in logic, its often-dated visual effects and let it simply wash over you, to sink into it and perceive it like an opium inflicted hallucination. If nothing else, THE KEEP most certainly makes a case for the horror film as an outlet for subconscious art, as a surreal dark dream, as an experience that you react to not intellectually, but physically and emotionally.

THE KEEPER (2004)

Starring Dennis Hopper, Asia Argento, Helen Shaver, Lochlyn Munro
Written by Gerald Sanford
Directed by Paul Lynch

Director William Wyler's 1965 thriller THE COLLECTOR set the template for the female-in-forced-confinement two-hander, the likes of which wormed its way it the downmarket exploitation film industry, amping up the sex and violence while putting the focus less on the unnerving social and sexual dynamic and more on gratuitous — and let's be honest, pretty revolting — female suffering. But there have been a myriad high quality and intelligent shockers that traded in this post-THE COLLECTOR riffing, chiefly stuff like Bob Brooks' TATTOO, Jennifer Lynch's BOXING HELENA and of course, SILENCE OF THE LAMBS and all the imitators that followed it.

Director Paul Lynch's 2004 cable psychodrama THE KEEPER is a curious thing, nestled somewhere between gutter trash, TV movie-of-the-week and respectable high-gloss horror movie. And what it lacks in budget and balls, it makes up for in the sheer novelty of its casting and deranged narrative. See, THE KEEPER was made by now-defunct Canadian production house Peace Arch Films for the Showtime network. Peace Arch was, for a brief moment, a kind of Northern direct-to-video AIP, pumping out low-grade tax rebate romps with well-known American actors, spending decent amounts of money to ensure their product had a shot at "making it" in the international marketplace. THE KEEPER is a prime example of the Peace Arch wave as it's well produced, professionally shot and edited at a brisk clip and it does indeed feature well-known actors on the semi-decline who, while no doubt taking a paycheck, are also clearly relishing the luxury of a leading role.

For horror fans, THE KEEPER is a rather interesting bauble. It stars the late, great Dennis Hopper and controversial Italian actress and filmmaker (and daughter of Dario)

THE
KEEPER

Asia Argento, both of whom appeared together in George A. Romero's Toronto-shot 2005 chiller Land of the Dead. I presume that the Peace Arch team nabbed them at a reasonable cost for this Canadian quickie since they were already up here. And while seeing both these totally opposing performers bounce off each other and devour scenery might have been a fun distraction in 2004, the casting — with Hopper no longer with us — makes THE KEEPER a genuine cult movie in the making, ripe for discovery. Throw in THE BELIEVERS actress Helen Shaver as a serial killer hag and a director who made the seminal Canadian slasher movie PROM NIGHT and how can any lover of oddball cinema resist?

Argento stars as Gina, a stripper just rolling through town who, after escaping an attempted rape, is "rescued" by local Sheriff Krebs (Hopper). Said cop is actually a full-blown lunatic who has a nasty habit of kidnapping troubled women he deems morally sullied, locking them in his basement dungeon and attempting to "correct" them. Gina is a tough lady however and she bucks his self-righteous psycho-trip at every turn, which makes us admire her spunk but question her foresight seeing as she ends up locked in that prison for months on end, with every attempt at escape foiled.

But that generic setup is only the basic thrust of THE KEEPER. What makes it so perversely watchable is the fact that Sheriff Krebs is also a children's TV host and becomes such in his off time when he's not tormenting poor Argento, leading to the appearance of Shaver's groupie, a woman whose mania even Hopper seems freaked out by (incidentally, Shaver is still looking rather fine and foxy here, though she's well beyond middle-age). The end sequences of clumsy pursuit and Hopper finally losing his mind full stop are outrageously, awesomely tacky and push the already unstable film right off a cliff. And I mean that in a good way.

Hopper — one of the founding fathers of bad-boy, post-60s indie filmmaking and one of cinemas greatest dangerous eccentrics — is fantastic here, though he was near the end of his days and was simply working to indulge his art-collecting habit and pay the bills. He's not an off-the-wall evil cartoon like his Frank Booth was in David Lynch's BLUE VELVET, nor is he the heroic basket-case lawman he was in Tobe Hooper's bonkers THE TEXAS CHAINSAW MASSACRE PART 2. He' s got a mature, squinty and totally controlled kind of madness here, making his Krebs likable (he *is* a kid's TV star after all) and even reasonable, despite his penchant for pious torture and murder. Argento looks wasted (though she always sports that kind of junkie-chic appearance) and that adds to the urgency of her character's frantic plight. With her Italian accent she seems kind of awkward in her line readings but hey, Gerald Sanford's script ain't that great to begin with, so she does what she can with it. But Argento is primarily a physical actress, and she uses that strength to give Gina a bona fide presence. And no, in case you wondered, despite her character's pole-spiraling profession, she does not remove her clothes.

THE KEEPER is junk, sure. But it's sublime and strange and hugely entertaining junk and kind of floats in its own awesomely tacky orbit. It's hard to see but it was released on DVD back in 2006 and if you seek it, you may find it. For fans of Hopper and Argento, it's an essential curiosity.

THE KILLER NUN (1979)

Starring Anita Ekberg, Alida Valli, Massimo Serato, Daniele Dublino
Written by Giulio Berruti, Enzo Gallo, Alberto Tarallo
Directed by Giulio Berruti

In the annals of the unsavory subgenre known as *nunsploitation*, director Giulio Berruti's late-from-the-gate shocker THE KILLER NUN stands tall, a truly nasty piece of work that has so much fun reveling in bad behavior that it's a grim joy to behold. And that can't be said for many of the post-THE DEVILS *nunsploitation* ilk, as they're often depressing, claustrophobic affairs. But not this psycho-horror classic. It's a marvel of cheerfully leering tawdriness.

The movie stars Fellini favorite Anita Ekberg (LA DOLCE VITA) — here, well into middle-age but still a goddamned knockout — as the deranged Sister Gertrude, a woman whose religion-fueled madness has caught up with her. Respected by her peers (and, in the case of some of her fellow nuns, lusted over), Gertrude is deeply, profoundly mentally ill and after tormenting weaker souls around her, begins self-medicating her increasingly disturbed condition with heroin addiction, serial sex with both fellow sisters and male strangers and eventually, wholesale murder.

Apparently based on a real case of convent carnage, THE KILLER NUN is most assuredly trash, but what beautifully crass trash it is. Ekberg dives deep into the role, making Gertrude a manic Tasmanian devil, careening between the most jaw-dropping atrocities, and yet tempering the character with empathy, pathos and remorse. This woman is sick and sculpted by her surroundings and is seemingly unable to stop her free-fall from happening. She's a pathetic creation. But one doesn't really watch THE KILLER NUN for its wrenching drama. No, the true pleasures to be found here are gleefully grotesque and often hilariously cruel. My favorite is the unforgettable sequence where Gertrude screams at an elderly woman for taking out her dentures at the table then proceeds to grab the old lady's teeth and stomp them to dust while laughing maniacally. As the woman recoils in shock, Gertrude snaps out of her derangement and apologizes. Hours later, the poor gummy granny dies of a heart attack! Mean? Sure. Unpleasant? You bet. But scenes like this (and there are plenty of

Sister Gertrude (Anita Ekberg) has a taste for sin.

them) are so outrageous that Berruti is inviting us to laugh. And we do. Well, at least some of us will.

FLESH FOR FRANKENSTEIN/BLOOD FOR DRACULA legend Joe Dallesandro also shows up as a doctor but the dubbed actor has little to do but look square-jawed and concerned, while Paola Mora threatens to steal scenes from Ekberg as a horny sister who is in love with Gertrude. But never mind the supporting cast, this is Ekberg's show all the way, her wild, aging eyes popping from her face while cackling like a lunatic with every fresh transgression. She's goosed by a lush, eerie score by the great Alessandro Alessandroni (THE DEVIL'S NIGHTMARE), who's over-the-top sonics match Ekberg's mania. A truly vulgar bit of art, beautiful and blasphemous in equal mad measure.

INTERVIEW: ALESSANDRO ALESSANDRONI

Born in Rome in 1925, Alessandroni (who sadly passed in 2017) was a multi-instrumentalist composer whose work spanned almost 50 films in a myriad of genres. Working with his friend Morricone, it was Alessandroni who supplied the signature twang guitar sound and haunting whistles in Morricone's scores for the Sergio Leone "Dollars" trilogy. On his own, his signature sounds have defined the energies of horror films like Mel Welles' kinky and atmospheric 1971 sexploitation number LADY FRANKENSTEIN, Giulio Berruti's KILLER NUN as well as this writer's personal favorite '70s Europudding trash flick, Jean Brismee's 1971 supernatural, erotic morality tale, THE DEVIL'S NIGHTMARE.

Alessandroni was one of Italian cinema's founding musical fathers.

I spoke with the brilliant Alessandroni in 2010 to discuss some of his many adventures in Golden and Silver age Italian genre cinema.

CHRIS ALEXANDER: How did music become your life?

ALESSANDRO ALESSANDRONI: In the village of Soriano, where I grew up, there were small shops called Barber & Taylor shops and they had a myriad of instruments hanging on the walls. In between clients or when there were no clients at all, anyone could play the mandolin or guitar or cello or clarinet, and that is how I started this journey. I am self-taught with no professional training.

ALEXANDER: Many fans know you from your work with Ennio Morricone on all those incredible Sergio Leone westerns, especially with respect to your trademark whistle. When did you discover your talent for whistling?

ALESSANDRONI: Well, it was quite by accident that this became my trademark. During a recording session of music for an early film I was involved with, [composer] Nino Rota asked if anyone in the orchestra could whistle, I was playing guitar then. No one came forward so I said that I could try but couldn't promise anything. But it worked and that is how the quality of my whistle was discovered. By the time Ennio and I worked together, I was an expert!

ALEXANDER: Can you tell me about your initial work with Morricone? How free were you to experiment?

ALESSANDRONI: My work with Ennio was always engaging and always creative. Often, I would suggest alternative styles in the execution of his written music, bringing in guitar, the whistling, some more rock influenced sounds.

ALEXANDER: Do you ever feel that you haven't received enough credit for your work on those incredible westerns?

ALESSANDRONI: Oh yes, absolutely. But, that's life, I suppose.

ALEXANDER: Can you describe those prolific days working in the golden era of Italian cinema in the '60s and '70s? It must have been a very exciting time.

ALESSANDRONI: In those years we had so many wonderful directors in this country — Fellini, Pasolini, Risi, Germi, Leone — and so many wonderful films were being made. After the success of A FISTFUL OF DOLLARS, we Italian musicians were kept very busy because so many westerns were being made as well as horror films and other pictures that could be exported easily to America and around the world. Also, my choir The Cantoni Moderni di Alessandroni was very much in demand for films and recordings. Yes, as you say, it was a very exciting and incredibly busy time and I'll admit that I miss it.

ALEXANDER: One of my favorite scores of yours was for Jean Brismee's 1971 horror film THE DEVIL'S NIGHTMARE. What are your memories of that picture?

ALESSANDRONI: I remember that film vaguely. It wasn't too bad as I recall. But after some 40 years — and a lot of music in between — I don't remember very much about my score!

ALEXANDER: Who did those haunting female vocals for the film's opening theme?

ALESSANDRONI: Ah, that would have been my late wife, Giulia De Mutiis.

ALEXANDER: Your work in the same year's LADY FRANKENSTEIN is also brilliant, fully exploiting that distinctive fuzz guitar. What did you think of that film and of its American director, Mel Welles?

ALESSANDRONI: That film is actually pretty good! One of my better horror scores, I think. I don't recall working with Mel Welles, however. As was often the case, he may have left it up to me to create the sound as I chose appropriate without too much interference on his part.

ALEXANDER: You've also worked with notorious Italian exploitation filmmaker Bruno Mattei on 1977's SS EXPERIMENT CAMP. What was Mattei like?

ALESSANDRONI: Now that one was no great masterpiece, I can tell you that. In fact, I must admit that it was a very mediocre picture and I refer to both the film and the music itself. But I worked very well with Mattei and I found him to be a very nice man.

ALEXANDER: You worked on two adult films in 1980 with the great Joe D'Amato (Aristide Massaccesi).

ALESSANDRONI: Yes, I did and you know, D'Amato was really amusing, a very colorful character. As far as my music on those pornographic pictures, the big difference was that, well I was obliged to think erotically, not horrifically. I think my work on those movies is pretty good and a lot of fun.

ALEXANDER: Your last credited film is 1998's TRINITY GOES WEST. Any plans to return to film composing?

ALESSANDRONI: I would willingly compose more film scores but in Italy these days everything is motivated by politics for political ends. That is not for me. I am a free man and I would want my music free of obligations or constraints. Anyhow, I am glad that publishers are reprinting a lot of my music, and that people are now buying the CD collections.

ALEXANDER: Your scores for horror films were so eccentric and interesting. Do you watch horror? Have you heard any music in horror that you really liked?

ALESSANDRONI: No, I have never watched or listened to horror except to compose for those horror movies I wrote the scores for. I simply followed my instincts. The bottom line is that I LOVE to create new sounds all the time and horror movies gave me great freedom to do that.

KISS MEETS THE PHANTOM OF THE PARK (1978)

Starring Gene Simmons, Paul Stanley, Peter Criss, Ace Frehley, Anthony Zerbe
Written by Jan-Michael Sherman, Don Buday
Directed by Gordon Hessler

The bombast and excess that served as the 1970s pop culture landscape arguably reached its apex in its waning days, as the decade's fixation on coked-up glamour and glitz and garishness leaked into the mainstream. Once serious cinema started to swell into STAR WARS territory, and things that were once dangerous and counterculture

KISS (Gene Simmons, Peter Criss, Ace Frehley and Paul Stanley) admire the source of their powers.

were plastered on lunchboxes and commercialism took on a life of its own, it was all over. In a sense. In another sense, it had only just begun. And in retrospect, the mass-marketing of the 70s as it bled into the '80s led to some of our most memorably misguided experiments.

Perhaps no document of this trend is more pronounced than 1978's KISS MEETS THE PHANTOM OF THE PARK, the strangest and still most confounding rock'n'roll movie ever made. A film that served to squish together the two most talked about and omnipresent brands of their times — the aforementioned live action cartoon of STAR WARS and the living, breathing hard rock fantasy that was KISS — and create something that kids would go crazy for and even moms and dads would approve of. The film took KISS, once one of the most terrifying bands of their time and turned them into intergalactic superheroes, battling monsters and thwarting mayhem in what was in essence a bubble-gum riff on THE PHANTOM OF THE OPERA. In theory, it seemed like it couldn't lose. In practice? Well, that's subjective. KISS MEETS THE PHANTOM OF THE PARK was put together quickly, designed as TV movie-of-the-week, produced by cartoon kingpins Hanna-Barbera and perhaps — like so many endeavours during this point in KISS' career — a tad ill thought out.

Set in and filmed almost entirely at the famous Magic Mountain theme park, KISS MEETS THE PHANTOM OF THE PARK features the band as inter-dimensional, super-powered demigods (a carry-over from their blood-inked 1977 Marvel comics book and the two appearances in HOWARD THE DUCK that preceded it) fighting a mad scientist who has waged a war with the band, after his brand of animatronic amusements fall out of favor with contemporary youth. The film premiered on October 28th, 1978 on the NBC network and very few "first wave" KISS fans liked it. Children loved it (myself among them), but children don't buy records and — unless their parents were super-cool — rarely attended concerts and because of this, the film was perhaps the first toll of KISS' initial commercial decline. And the band? They were mortified. In many ways, though founding members Gene Simmons and Paul Stanley have accepted its legacy as one of the more colorful missteps in their storied history, they still are.

For cult movie aficionados however, KISS MEETS THE PHANTOM is a rich treasure trove, ripe for the unpacking. It's a time capsule of its age, but it's also an anomaly. A curiosity wherein multiple strains of pop culture collided into one oddball bauble.

Let's break it down.

KISS MEETS THE PHANTOM OF THE PARK is directed by Gordon Hessler.

The British director who gave the world post-Roger Corman American International Pictures like CRY OF THE BANSHEE, THE OBLONG BOX and MURDERS IN THE RUE MORGUE oversaw the action, despite not really even understanding who or what KISS was. By all accounts, he would refer to the band as *The* KISS. Still, having an esteemed director of Gothic horror films pleased Gene Simmons to no end, himself a genre movie

KISSterical!
KISStounding!
KISStoric!
Their First Full Length Feature Film
will Zap you out of your seat!
KISS
in ATTACK OF THE PHANTOMS
A HANNA-BARBERA PRODUCTION
in association with KISS-AUCOIN PRODUCTIONS
Starring GENE SIMMONS, PAUL STANLEY, PETER CRISS, ACE FREHLEY
Co-starring ANTHONY ZERBE, DEBORAH RYAN, CARMINE CARIDI
Written by JAN-MICHAEL SHERMAN and DON BUDAY Produced by TERRY MORSE, JR.
Directed by GORDON HESSLER Executive Producer JOE BARBERA Executive Producer for KISS WILLIAM M. AUCOIN
AVCO EMBASSY PICTURES Release
PG PARENTAL GUIDANCE SUGGESTED
SOME MATERIAL MAY NOT BE SUITABLE FOR CHILDREN
© 1979 AVCO EMBASSY PICTURES CORP.

obsessive, and he and Hessler got on famously. No one's going to cite KISS MEETS THE PHANTOM OF THE PARK as being particularly well directed. In fact, it's often a mess. But those moments of monster mash mayhem in the creepy "Chamber of Chills" and the eerie sequences in Abner Deveraux's underground workshop, certainly feel like one of Hessler's unique chillers.

KISS MEETS THE PHANTOM OF THE PARK is a Hanna-Barbera joint.

This element is an essential part of the film's surrealism, the fact that the studio that gave the world THE FLINTSONES, YOGI BEAR and SPACE GHOST were behind the band's first feature film. While KISS' arc in the pages of those Marvel comics specials were cosmic, sensual and somewhat serious-minded pulp nonsense, KISS MEETS THE PHANTOM OF THE PARK is very often just a one-dimensional, live action cartoon romp, complete with a brash and groovy score by H/B house composer Hoyt Curtin (with select cues by WESTWORLD and CHOSEN SURVIVORS composer Fred Karlin) that deflates any sort of tension. In the sequence where the "evil Gene" robot crashes through a wall and assaults the guards, Curtin goes full-blown SCOOBY-DOO showdown sonata. It's lovably miscalculated. KISS would later team with the studio and "Mystery Inc." again — with a self-awareness absent from PHANTOM — for both a key episode of the TV series and the wonderfully cheeky animated film SCOOBY-DOO! AND KISS: ROCK AND ROLL MYSTERY.

KISS MEETS THE PHANTOM OF THE PARK stars Anthony Zerbe: The film's saving dramatic grace comes in the form of the great American character actor Anthony Zerbe, who a few years earlier made such a malevolent mark as the mutant albino Mathias in Boris Sagal's nightmarish "I Am Legend" adaptation THE OMEGA MAN. Though KISS MEETS THE PHANTOM OF THE PARK is well beneath that film, Zerbe is just as solid and perhaps even more so in the European theatrical cut of the film (more on that later), where his brilliant and megalomaniacal amusement park puppet master Abner Devereaux has more space to deliver an empathetic portrait of a man whose dreams have hit a wall. It's a real performance.

The catman is Duke from G.I. JOE! Depending on who you believe, Peter Criss either failed to show up for postproduction dialogue looping sessions or *was* there, his natural voice deemed unusable, and was simply later dubbed without consent. Either way, veteran voice actor Michael Bell, who gave aural presence to dozens of Hanna-Barbera cartoon characters including Handy Smurf, Lazy Smurf and yes, Duke from G.I. JOE, dubbed over Criss' lips and it's a very disorienting experience to behold.

KISS MEETS THE PHANTOM OF THE PARK features Brion James in an early role: Years before he entered the big time playing Leon the replicant in Ridley Scott's BLADE RUNNER and Meat Cleaver Max from Sean Cunningham's THE HORROR SHOW, the late, great character actor Brion James shows up often in KISS MEETS THE PHANTOM OF THE PARK as a bemused security guard. Reportedly, James was also dealing drugs on set to Ace and Peter and whoever else wanted them.

The Demon and The Spacemen huddle close as the camera dives in.

KISS MEETS THE PHANTOM OF THE PARK has weird special effects: Obviously a modestly budgeted picture (remember, it was a TV movie after all), the special effects in KISS MEETS THE PHANTOM OF THE PARK are odd. Deveraux's supposedly ingenious automatons are just actors and, when they're still and at rest, they — in true "wax museum movie" fashion — shake and jitter and blink. Or, as with the acrobat albino werewolf bots that attack the band by the roller coaster, they're stuntmen in masks. And how about those optical effects? With lasers shooting forth from Paul's eye and fire belching from Gene's open mouth. Weird yes, but like all of the film's failings, they help elevate the overall experience.

As actors, KISS make great rock stars: "You-ah lookin' fuh someone, but it's nawt KISS...," says Paul who, like all the band members, were not actors and had to be "taught" to restrain their larger-than-life stage-selves for the intimacy of the lens and none too well at that. Paul is clearly nervous and it's a riot to hear him mouth the overdubbed dialogue with his then-heavy Queens accent. And Gene, with his flanged-out, echo chamber vocal filter, sounds like Zandor Vorkov in Al Adamson's DRACULA VS FRANKENSTEIN. Sometimes he even roars like the MGM lion. And what of Ace Frehley? Writers Jan Michael Sherman and Don Buday followed the band around to get a sense of their rapport and the result was that Ace's role was written without dialogue, save for his trademark "Ack". Frehley was not pleased and after balking, the writers reluctantly scribbled a few useless lines for him. But still, all fans remember is "Ack".

Ace Frehley's ever-changing ethnicity: During the battle in the "chamber of chills", Ace had fled the set in a boozy huff, leaving his poor stunt double — who was African American — to fill in. Hessler apparently didn't notice and it's part of the film's legend that suddenly, without warning, Ace ain't Ace at all...

KISS MEETS THE PHANTOM OF THE PARK's longer European cut: In 1979, Avco-Embassy released the extended and re-edited cut of the film in European theaters under the name ATTACK OF THE PHANTOMS. This version is considerably longer, moodier and features many different sequence and shots, including a totally different opening, more existential passages of dialogue, the successful attempts to make Devereaux sympathetic, a different ending and the removal of much of Curtin's score, replaced instead with tracks from the band's 1978 four solo albums. This is especially poignant during the additional scenes of a depressed and recently fired Devereaux walking away lonely while Gene's beautiful "Mr. Make Believe" plays on the soundtrack. This is repeated during the end credits, once again adding a touch of melancholic poetry to the picture.

KISS MEETS THE PHANTOM OF THE PARK is packed with kiss songs and live performances: Even if the film fails to weave its spell on you, for KISS fans there's endless pleasure in the form of the presence of KISS music, which is everywhere (especially weighty in the European version). Many of these KISS classics are performed during a live concert staged specifically for the film, actually filmed at Magic Mountain, and featuring the band at their physical peak. Not to mention, this is the *only* place where you can hear the grim Hotter Than Hell evil-robot redux Rip And Destroy.

KISS MEETS THE PHANTOM OF THE PARK is not a good movie by the standards in which we measure such things. But it's an essential piece of KISSstory and there's no other picture quite like it. But where can you see it? Due to some sort of copyright quicksand; no one really knows *who* owns the movie. I asked Gene about it years ago and he *thinks* they do. But they cannot find the chain of title. Most of Hanna-Barbera's catalog was assimilated by Warner Bros. many years ago but oddly, *not* this movie. When I worked for WB many years ago in my youth (I got my start in this wild business as a junior publicist), I valiantly tried to trace it. No luck. Because of this limbo, the movie might just be in the public domain, leading some imprints to bootleg it, including the cheapie knock-off label "Cheezy Flix" which put out a grotty dub of the old Goodtimes VHS release on DVD and then were promptly knocked down by KISS who rightly cite that even if they do not own the MOVIE, they DO own their music and their likenesses. KISS bootlegged their own movie for the second KISStory DVD box set about 15 years ago, getting their hands on the negative of the ATTACK OF THE PHANTOMS cut. So that's the best place to economically see a pristine version of the film, while the out of print (and unauthorized) VHS and DVD releases are a decent way

The author looking up to the God of Thunder at McGhee Entertainment, Los Angeles.

to absorb the movie as it was originally broadcast. All of this skullduggery just adds to KISS MEETS THE PHANTOM's bizarre legacy.

Long may it cofound and fascinate the masses.

INTERVIEW: GENE SIMMONS

Born Chaim Witz in Haifa, Israel, 1949, theatrical rock God Gene Simmons literally found the "American Dream" via a formative obsession with monsters. When he and his single mother, concentration camp survivor Flora, emigrated to New York in 1957, young Gene couldn't speak nary a word of English. He was an awkward kid, made even more of an outsider due to his complete incomprehension of western culture. But thanks to a steady diet of late-night television — specifically broadcasts of classic silent films and Universal horror movies — Gene started to both grasp the language and develop his singular tastes. Once rock'n'roll entered the equation, there was no turning back.

Though my path was far different than Gene's, I too found my footing by obsessing over late night screenings of bizarre horror films on television and endlessly listening to records. That I found the unholiest of amalgams of the two in KISS, goes without saying and I have carried the KISS torch, holding it high for my entire life. So when my passions and professional path led to Gene Simmons' door back in 2010, it was a Dorothy/OZ scenario. But unlike in that meeting, I wasn't disappointed in revealing the wizard behind the curtain. In fact, Gene and I got on very well and have remained friends, working together on several occasions. Certainly, getting to know an artist personally who has meant so much to me, has been one of the most joyous of life's surprises.

Lon Chaney's sinister visage in THE PHANTOM OF THE OPERA inspired Simmons' iconic makeup design.

CHRIS ALEXANDER: When you were a kid and discovered the wild world of the fantastic, things weren't like they are now. What was fan culture like then?

GENE SIMMONS: Things were completely different. I was a child of obsession and in American those obsessions became comic books, famous monsters of filmland, castle of Frankenstein and horror movies on television. But understand, we had very outlets to share that love, not like today. We had some fanzines, and I even published six of my own for a while. There were a few conventions out there too. There was Lunacon, and that was more for monster and science fiction fans with only a small portion of comic book content. I remember Lunacons as being very literate and on occasion Isaac Asimov would speak at them. You know, many years later, I found out Asimov was my neighbour.

ALEXANDER: Because these things were so niche there must have been a real sense quest. Do you find that today fans of this sort of thing are harder to please?

SIMMONS: Well, things are different now because — guess what — the geeks have won. We have won. The geeks have come to power, we run pop culture now. When I was growing up, the mainstream was all Doris Day and Rock Hudson and Tony Randall and that other pablum I couldn't stomach. Every so often you'd get the odd FORBIDDEN PLANET breaking through and becoming a success. Then on the sidelines there was all that great AIP/Roger Corman stuff, which was generally though of as trash, but I loved it all. But the mainstream is now all about monsters, horror, and comics. The pablum is niche.

ALEXANDER: What movies or monsters scared you as a kid?

SIMMONS: Let me preface by saying that I never had nightmares about pop culture monsters. I was fascinated by them, not frightened. The only thing that I saw that truly frightened me was on THE TWILIGHT ZONE.

ALEXANDER: Ahhh, so you're a ZONE fan...

Gene flashes one of his most famous appendages.

SIMMONS: Oh my God, yes. I've seen them all. I love it. The episode in question was one there was an old woman in bed and...

ALEXANDER: 'Night Call'.

SIMMONS: Yes, 'Night Call'. Written by Richard Matheson, the master. When that moment comes when you see the telephone wire going into her husband's grave, and the lightning strikes, I screamed...

ALEXANDER: Or when she hears that voice on the phone at night: "I want to talk to you."

SIMMONS: I just got chills when you said that.

ALEXANDER: As a Matheson fan, I presume you've read *I Am Legend*.

SIMMONS: Of course. That book is brilliant. It's been made three times legitimately into a film.

ALEXANDER: And it's been botched every time.

SIMMONS: Well, no. I'm a big fan of THE OMEGA MAN with Charlton Heston.

ALEXANDER: And Anthony Zerbe, your KISS MEETS THE PHANTOM OF THE PARK co-star.

SIMMONS: Yes, that's true.

ALEXANDER: I love THE OMEGA MAN too, but not as a faithful adaptation of I AM LEGEND. Why does Hollywood keep refusing to film that story straight?

SIMMONS: Because that book involves talking and is about a state of mind. But with cinema, once movies became "talkies", Hollywood realized that people would only stay interested if the action kept moving. That has led to the state of things today. Now every genre film is filled with flash cuts and special effects.

ALEXANDER: Who is your favorite classic monster?

SIMMONS: My idol, Lon Chaney Sr., born Creighton Tull. He was a makeup artist, he created and fashioned the material, he looked at the script; he was a one-man show. Whereas Boris Karloff — whom I also adore- was an actor really and couldn't get work because of his lisp, and it was Bela Lugosi who gave him his first shot. Lugosi didn't want to do FRANKENSTEIN because the monster was going to be played as a deaf mute and Lugosi wouldn't do that. But Karloff owns a lot of his credibility to Jack Pierce.

ALEXANDER: Now you're just showing off.

SIMMONS: Hey, that's what they pay me for!

ALEXANDER: Would you call yourself a self-made man?

SIMMONS: No, America made me. Comics, TV, monsters, and rock'n'roll made me.

ALEXANDER: What scares Gene Simmons?

SIMMONS: That one day my *shmeckel* won't work.

ALEXANDER: Well, there's medicine for that. What really scares Gene Simmons.

SIMMONS: Only death. Other than that, there is nothing to fear.

ALEXANDER: And do you think there's a God?

SIMMONS: I don't think so. Because if there is, there's no excuse for what he has done and what he has allowed to happen — the Holocaust, Armenian genocide, white Europeans exterminating natives — we're born and were dying, we immediately get cavities, there's jihads and crusades. So much misery. If God appeared right now and said "Hey, Gene!", I'd be like, "Sit down, I have a few questions to ask before I bow down to you."

LAND OF THE MINOTAUR (1976)

Starring Peter Cushing, Donald Pleasence, Luan Peters, Kostas Karagiorgis
Written by Arthur Rowe
Directed by Kostas Karagiannis

Released in 1976 in the US by exploitation house Crown International to a moderately successful box office take and generally pitiful reviews, director Kostas Karagiannis's earthy and surreal horror mood-piece LAND OF THE MINOTAUR has been pretty easy to find on home viewing formats, popping up in rough looking pan and scan VHS versions and dodgy DVD releases in North America and in equally ugly (but thankfully uncut) editions in the UK. Still, despite its endless exposure, I've sadly yet to hear anyone else seriously champion LAND OF THE MINOTAUR's virtues.

So, with that, allow me to do so.

Baron Corofax (Peter Cushing) holds court in the Minotaur's lair.

On the outskirts of a remote, inland village in beautiful, picturesque Greece (Aris Stavrou's photography is stark and eye-filling), something secret, insidious, and palpably evil lurks, sucking every too-curious young tourist into its maw and swallowing them whole. As the ever-expanding list of the curious missing travelers increases, an eccentric local priest (the great Donald Pleasence) begins to suspect that a cult of mountain dwelling, black hooded, Minotaur-worshipping Satanists have gained a stronghold, sacrificing pretty young people to their titular stone hoof and horned, steam belching deity.

A battle of theological wits ensues between the fraught father and the ultra-wicked village Magistrate/covert cult leader Baron Corofax (the perhaps even greater Peter Cushing in a rare, full-on chin-stroking villain role) and by the time the smoke clears and the last drop of crudely spilled virgin blood dries, only one of these admirably dedicated and faithful men will be left standing.

A British/Greek co-production, LAND OF THE MINOTAUR was indeed initially released in the UK under its original title as the sexier and bloodier THE DEVIL'S MEN and, after getting a few bits of PG-rating-ensuring blood and boob action removed, spat out stateside under its more lurid (and preferable) moniker. Slapped with one of the more outrageous, colorful, and almost entirely misleading exploitation movie posters of the 1970s (*Half Man! Half Beast! Trapped in a Land Forgotten by Time!*), the picture was wedged onto the bottom half of a Crown double bill, pulling in the pundits who were expecting an action-packed genre picture, before fading into B-movie oblivion, relegated to after-hours TV showings and budget video waste bins everywhere.

I first saw LAND OF THE MINOTAUR during one of my indiscriminate Friday night teenage video rental binges in the mid '80s, duped, just like that legion of kids in '76, by that beautiful, deliciously busy cover graphic. And though I did not get the promised epic I had hoped for, what I did get was something far darker, stranger, solemn and bizarre; a picture that had a suffocating ambiance and dreamlike atmosphere.

LAND OF THE MINOTAUR is a movie that demands an open mind and perhaps more importantly, an open ear. See, part of the shuddery secret of the film, outside of the engaging lead turns from veteran British horror pros Cushing and Pleasence (working together here for the first time since 1960's masterful Burke and Hare drama THE FLESH AND THE FIENDS, another of my personal favorites), is an absolutely first rate experimental low frequency electronic score by the iconic composer/pop guru Brian Eno. The former Roxy Music mastermind coats this slowly paced film with speaker throbbing drones, eerie synthesizer washes and pulses that render it almost meditative. It's a case study for any serious horror movie minded music maker on how to milk unease out of imagery and the fact that this score isn't available in any isolated form on CD or vinyl or anything is a very serious cinematic crime.

I really like LAND OF THE MINOTAUR. Make no mistake, it's a lowbrow exploitation film but it's one that's filtered through a very stylized, art house sensibility. Don't be swayed by the negative mainstream reviews and general fanboy silence. There's something special in this one and maybe, with any luck, it might one day find the cult it so richly deserves.

THE LEGEND OF THE SEVEN GOLDEN VAMPIRES (1974)

Starring Peter Cushing, John Forbes-Robertson, Robin Stewart, David Chiang
Written by Don Houghton
Directed by Roy Ward Baker

After the failure of 1973's THE SATANIC RITES OF DRACULA (that film didn't get a US release until 1976, even then it was truncated and retitled COUNT DRACULA AND HIS VAMPIRE BRIDE), Britain's Hammer Studios were desperate to keep their most profitable franchise alive. In truth, as a company, they were simply desperate to stay alive, full stop, as audiences around the globe were tired of the sort of mildly erotic Gothic thrills the company had long — and successfully — traded in. Even introducing more overt sexuality and ample female nudity in latter pictures like THE VAMPIRE LOVERS and LUST FOR A VAMPIRE wasn't enough for Hammer to stay relevant; they

One of the Seven Golden Vampires tastes blood.

couldn't compete with the post-NIGHT OF THE LIVING DEAD demand for a more graphic, urgent, and contemporary shocker.

Still, Hammer refused to give up and their need to experiment led to what might be their most fascinating effort ever: 1974's THE LEGEND OF THE SEVEN GOLDEN VAMPIRES, a chop-socky UK/Hong Kong co-production that was deeply bizarre back then and remains absolutely, gloriously bonkers today. Even within the eccentric confines of the ever-mutating nature of Asian vampire cinema, THE LEGEND OF THE SEVEN GOLDEN VAMPIRES is a weird one, a hybrid of sensibilities that packs a daft, East-meets-West kick to the senses and has a unique power all its own.

Hammer vet Roy Ward Baker (THE VAMPIRE LOVERS) directs from a script by Don Houghton (DRACULA A.D. 1972, THE SATANIC RITES OF DRACULA), who also co-produced with Kung-Fu powerhouse Sir Run Run Shaw. While Baker handled the traditional story elements of the picture, it was Shaw Brothers vet and absurdly prolific director Chang Cheh (FIVE DEADLY VENOMS, THE CRIPPLED AVENGER) who was called on to both work with the Chinese actors and oversee the endless — and endlessly awesome — martial arts brawls. Houghton's story begins in Transylvania, with a wandering Satanic priest named Kah (Chan Shen) venturing into Dracula's castle on a mission. Dracula (here played by John Forbes-Robertson after Christopher Lee refused to don the cape and fangs ever again) rises from his coffin and listens as Kah begs for help in raising the legendary Seven Golden Vampires from their graves to regain control of his village. Turns out Dracula can't leave his castle voluntarily and instead opts to possess the rural evil nobleman (a mesmerizing and bizarre sequence with circling cameras, strange ADR and copious amounts of dry ice), using Kah's body to run rampant again, and this time in China.

Meanwhile, in Chungking, Professor Van Helsing (the typically warm, welcoming presence of Peter Cushing), lectures at the local university, relating the story of the Seven Golden Vampires and their reign of terror, much to the scoffing of his Westernized students. One pupil however, Hsi Ching (David Chiang) not only believes Van Helsing's story, but insists he came from village of the vampires and explains that the ghouls are running rampant in full force. Soon, the duo is joined by Hsi Ching's five brothers and sister, a rich woman (Julie Ege) and Van Helsing's own son (Leyland Robin Stewart) and they embark on a cross-country journey to track the monsters down, leading to a wave of high-octane fist and foot battles with the undead and an eventual show-stopping showdown with the bloodthirsty Dracula/Kah.

Filmed in Hong Kong in 1973, THE LEGEND OF THE SEVEN GOLDEN VAMPIRES was an ambitious production fraught with problems, most of them stemming from the polarizing ways in which the British and Chinese crews worked and the on-set tensions between co-producer Shaw and Baker. You can feel that strain, that push and pull, while watching the picture and yet that discomfort only adds to the ultimate power of the film, as it darts frantically and entertainingly between worlds.

But while THE LEGEND OF THE SEVEN GOLDEN VAMPIRES was a success in Hong Kong (the Asian market was mad for all things Hammer) during its run in 1974, the movie belly-flopped in the UK and, in America, it didn't get a proper release at all. That is, until 1978, when distributor Dynamite Entertainment got hold of the film, hacked almost half an hour from it and insanely looped the sequence of the rising and rampage of the Seven Golden Vampires as a slow-motion opening credits sequence and then repeated that montage again right after those credits end! That version, retitled THE 7 BROTHERS MEET DRACULA (even though there's only six brothers and one sister!), was released to the grindhouse circuit in 1979 and did fairly well. No surprise, as the remix pushes all the film's nudity, gore, and exploitative elements right to the surface, jettisoning chunks of dialogue and exposition and going right for the thrills. It's an inferior cut that drains the movie of its soul and, in the butchering of the initial Kah/Dracula encounter, robs the movie of its motive.

It's due to that wacky 7 BROTHERS edit that THE LEGEND OF THE SEVEN GOLDEN VAMPIRES had long been weighted with a bad reputation in North America. Watching the uncut movie today is a kind of revelation, the swan song of the first wave of Hammer horror filled with flesh and blood, exotic locations, sweeping adventure, dream-logic weirdness, delirious set-pieces, dream-logic and chest-pounding melodrama. Though many cite Lee's absence as a detriment, Robertson is a very cool, intimidating presence and in truth, Lee wouldn't really have fit into the fabric of the film. He would have drawn all the attention and energy of the audience to him and removed the suspension of disbelief that the picture demands. As is, there's an alien feel to the film and having Cushing's Van Helsing present doesn't betray that. He's the western audiences' entry point and he's as lost and intrigued as we are while navigating this uncanny terrain.

Far more respected now than it once was, THE LEGEND OF THE SEVEN GOLDEN VAMPIRES remains unseen by many. If you're among those virgins who have yet to experience it, find the film as soon as you can and deflower yourself accordingly. You won't regret it.

A BRIEF LOOK AT HAMMER'S DRACULA CYCLE

When England's Hammer Studios invested some of their capital and produced 1957's full color, full-blooded, adult-geared riff on the classic Universal horror film with Terrence Fisher's THE CURSE OF FRANKENSTEIN, they changed the way we watch horror movies. Filled with sadism, cruelty, sexuality and gore, but classed-up with sumptuous production values and classically trained British actors in lead roles, CURSE was an international hit and launched a successful (and really, rather wonderful) series of Hammer Frankenstein pictures.

But it was with their next picture, 1958's HORROR OF DRACULA (known in the UK as simply DRACULA) that they found their first real deal iconic franchise and shone a light on their most memorable horror movie star, Christopher Lee, who was under wraps as the cataract-eyed monster in CURSE, but here was given free reign to terrify and seduce an entire generation of fright fans.

Here's a brief, critical look at the strange, beautiful, bloody and often, bloody frustrating series of Hammer horror films starring the King of the Vampires leading up to the kinetic madness that was THE LEGEND OF THE SEVEN GOLDEN VAMPIRES.

HORROR OF DRACULA (1958)

Terrence Fisher's majestic, lean and urgent riff on Bram Stoker's novel was a bloody punch to the face to Tod Browning's gentle, mannered 1931 film, effectively replacing Bela Lugosi's fangless European gentleman with Christopher Lee's snarling, athletic and imposing man in black. The film begins with a bang, with cameras prowling over the set of Dracula's castle, with jets of blood squirting sexually over his coffin and James Bernard's now-iconic score roaring on the soundtrack. There's not much to complain about in this maiden voyage as HORROR set the tone for the wave of tough

Hammer Gothics to follow and was rarely bettered, with Fisher at the peak of his craft here. That said, the film doesn't feel as epic as one might hope, with the geography between London and Transylvania fuzzy as, due to budgetary restraints, it's often clear the actors are just jumping between sets. Lee is perfection of course, effortlessly cool, fluid and dangerous and Peter Cushing sculpted what is still the definitive screen Van Helsing, here portrayed as a less bonkers riff on Sherlock Holmes, a role Cushing would take on a year later in Hammer's THE HOUND OF THE BASKERVILLES.

BRIDES OF DRACULA (1960)

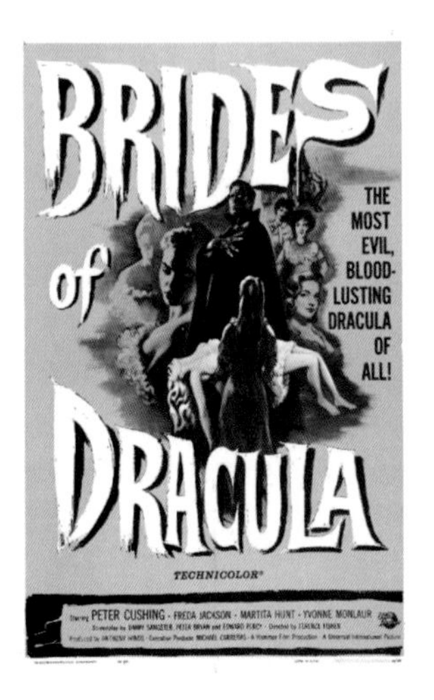

Lee opted to sit this Fisher-directed sequel out, afraid of being typecast and truthfully... the film does not suffer for the lack of his presence. In fact BRIDES is one of the best Hammer films of all time and one of the strongest in their DRACULA cycle. The title implies that the focus will not be on the Count this round, rather his "Brides", as in "Brides of Christ", nuns, the "wives" of a parasitic messiah. Which is interesting, considering the vampire or "bride" we follow here is one Baron Meinster (David Peel), a preening, cackling brat of a ghoul with a very toxic and unhealthy relationship with his long-suffering mother. Yes, the homoerotic subtext of BRIDES has been talked about ad nauseum but it's an interesting one (though calling Meinster bisexual would be more appropriate). Peel's blonde, effete and mean spirited aristocrat revels in his bloodsucking ways and he's wildly manipulative and resourceful. In HORROR OF DRACULA, Lee's Count, for all his majesty, was rather easily dispatched. But Meinster gives Cushing's Van Helsing a real run for his money and the battles between the two opponents are action packed and exciting. The best of them sees Meinster bite Van Helsing, leaving him to be turned, causing the terrified vampire killer to cauterize his infected neck with a hot iron and cool holy water! Fisher directs like a bat out of hell, the movie looks sumptuous and it's an incredibly eccentric and entertaining example of Hammer at its best.

DRACULA: PRINCE OF DARKNESS (1966)

Eight years after re-inventing the way in which the world would view the character of Dracula, Lee returned to Hammer's franchise with their first Drac film in six years,

another winner helmed by the great Terrence Fisher and one in which, strangely, the Count is mute. Depending on who you believe, the role was either written without dialogue to save the production some dough or, as Lee tells it, the script was so chock full of cringe-worthy lines that Lee himself opted to play it silent. One of the lines Lee said he balked at was Dracula saying "I am the apocalypse!", which I kinda like and wished they had kept. Otherwise, Lee playing the role without dialogue turned out to be a masterstroke, accidental or by intent, it matters not. Without words, Lee relies exclusively on his imposing physical presence (as he did in both THE CURSE OF FRANKENSTEIN and THE MUMMY), a hissing reptile like monster, an alien presence that is to be feared and loathed. This is a mean, violent picture. And those worrying about the lack of Cushing's Van Helsing needn't fear as Andrew Keir's crusading holy man is just as compelling an opponent. There's also a lot more overt sexuality, as in the scene where Dracula opens his chest and urges his female victim to drink his blood, an obvious nod to fellatio.

DRACULA HAS RISEN FROM THE GRAVE (1968)

One of the most underrated Hammer Dracula pictures, GRAVE is a lively affair, directed with style and a leaning towards psychedelia (dig those Dracula-gels!) by veteran Hammer director and award-winning cinematographer Freddie Francis. Here, Dracula is woken from the ice prison he fell into in PRINCE OF DARKNESS by a wayward priest who then becomes Drac's familiar. Eventually, the Count's coffin ends up in the cellar beneath a local tavern, where Dracula uses his powers to draw women down to him. Lee has less to do here but he's still the spine of the film, a movie that is in fact a bit more, dare we say, intellectual than most of the DRACULA films? Conversations about the existence of God and a central dynamic and sub-conflict in which one of the heroes is a pious man, the other an atheist, adds much needed substance to a series of films that usually lack any conflict beyond the morally one-dimensional *good vs. evil.* A vibrant, classy Drac picture that strangely, despite its bloodshed and headier themes, was rated 'G' in the US upon release.

TASTE THE BLOOD OF DRACULA (1970)

This film was initially one of a handful of films designed to turn actor Ralph Bates into a major Hammer horror star, TASTE was originally intended to not have Lee in it at all. But when international distributors balked at having a Drac picture without Lee, the studio piled on the dough to bring Lee back. And truthfully, that's a shame. TASTE has a dynamic first half. It begins during the final moments of GRAVE, when a traveler witnesses Drac's execution and, after the old vampire bastard turns to dust, the man retrieves a vial of the Dracula's concentrated blood. After the credits roll, the central tale kicks in, a story of Victorian morality gone rotten, with a cabal of entitled, elite men of society, stepping out for their monthly night of debauchery and hypocritical transgression. At the house of ill-repute they're playing in, they meet the black magic loving Lord Courtley (Bates) who promises them the ultimate thrill in the form a ritual in which they will drink an activated goblet of Drac's plasma. When the men freak out at the 11th hour, Courtley drinks the gore, has a fit, is beaten to death by the men, cracks apart and then turns into Christopher Lee! From there, Lee just sleepwalks through his part, bumping off and/or enslaving the daughters of the men who he thinks killed his "master" Courtley. It makes no sense. In the original script, Courtley was the ghoul getting his revenge. But why is Dracula so cheesed? These dudes helped revive the Count. He should thank them! That central lapse in lazy logic makes the second half of TASTE a bit mechanical, though Peter Sasdy's direction is perfectly fine, especially during the darker moments in the first reel.

SCARS OF DRACULA (1970)

After TASTE did so well, Hammer rushed another Dracula picture into production, albeit one armed with a lower budget. SCARS OF DRACULA is the first Drac film to get saddled with an R rating, due in no small part to Dracula's full-blown and unpleasant sadistic streak. Here Lee is the Devil himself, whipping his servant Klove (not the same dandy butler from PRINCE OF DARKNESS, more of a Renfield-esque madman), torturing his victims and even driving a stake into one of his "brides" hearts for no other reason than to juice the film up with some extra gore. SCARS also has no relation apparently to the rest of the films in the series, with Lee being revived by a

blood-spitting rubber bat while he lies desiccated in his coffin (and oh, those bats are so wonderfully phony baloney) but is more of an attempt to re-boot the series, with yet another young couple, this one a rather dull pair, running afoul of the mean Count. Lee approved of this film, mainly because of its attempts to lift scenes from the original novel, including the chilling bit where he scales the castle wall. Roy Ward Baker is perhaps not the edgiest of Hammer's house directors and his more restrained approach is at odds with the film's nastier elements (a problem that plagued his THE VAMPIRE LOVERS). If Freddie Francis had steered this ship, it would have been a lurid, even dangerous Dracula movie. As stands, it's still a fun anomaly in the cycle.

DRACULA A.D. 1972 (1972)

Critics and fans scoffed then and some still jeer at director Alan Gibson and writer Don Houghton's attempts to propel the Dracula series into the modern age and certainly, DRACULA A.D. 1972 is a much campier, sillier picture. But that unbuttoning of the collar works in the film's favor. With Lee now running rampant in Mod-era London, DRACULA A.D. 1972 is a blast, with groovy music, a luscious Caroline Munro in the cast, a much more urgent and fast-paced narrative and plenty of kinky twists. It's also great to see the distinguished Cushing back in action as Van Helsing's Great Grandson, stalking the demon who has long plagued his family. Both Lee and Cushing bring the class, while Gibson and his supporting cast bring the sass. Maybe not a good Hammer Gothic, but a plenty fun vintage '70s British horror movie.

THE SATANIC RITES OF DRACULA (1973)

Gibson and Houghton teamed up again for this immediate follow-up to DRACULA A.D. 1972 and the movie has an even worse reputation than its predecessor. Much of this

is due to the picture being a public domain eyesore, haunting dump bins and 50-movie collections everywhere in its heavily cut US version, called DRACULA AND HIS VAMPIRE BRIDE. But man, is SATANIC a great film. Propelled by an amazing score by HORROR EXPRESS' John Cacavas, SATANIC is a deranged and compelling world-domination spy thriller filled with sex and violence and vampirism, with Lee's revived Count commanding a vampire cult while also serving as the head a shadowy corporation. Yes indeed, Dracula is a capitalist here and it makes perfect sense. His *modus operandi* is to release a bio-weapon that will infect the world with the black plague, effectively murdering every human being alive. The extra gravitas comes from the concept that, as Cushing's Van Helsing explains, with Dracula doing this, he is effectively committing suicide; after humanity perishes, no one will be left to revive him and no one will left for him to eat. There's so many thrills and chills in SATANIC (love the vampire slaves dying in slow-motion in the cellar sequence). More respect needs to be lauded on this fascinating final Lee-starring entry in the cycle.

MEMOIR: HOW HAMMER'S VAMPIRE CIRCUS ALMOST KILLED ME BUT STILL SAVED ME

As I continue to age, I am astonished by just how lazy I am. Well, maybe lazy isn't the right word. In fact, I'm far from that. I'm busier than I've ever been.

But when I was a youth, I never stopped moving.

See, I didn't get my driver's license until I was 32 and, living in Toronto, I relied exclusively on trains, buses, streetcars, and feet.

These days, I rely on minivan and Amazon to get the things I need and the fixes I want.

But back then, in those carefree and questing days, nothing could stop me from getting where I needed to get, no matter the distance, no matter the sort of transportation required, no matter the time I had to block off to get there.

In my teens, I lived in a place called Mississauga, a city in the Greater Toronto Area (or the GTA as its commonly called). My fellow freaks that were in search of more esoteric culture in this artless deathtrap, used to call it *MiserySauga*. And it was indeed miserable. When there was a film or concert I wanted to attend, I would simply have to take the bus, the train and the foot to get there. It took me 2.5 hours using these routes to get downtown and I'd gladly bank this time just so I could sit in an

opulent, ancient movie theater and watch oddball, arthouse and obscure flicks on the big screen. Or so I could simply have a coffee in a place where people-watching was exciting; where fashion, beauty, conversation, ideas and eccentricity were plentiful.

It was all worth it and I did it often.

Now, I still enjoy these solo pursuits. But the lengths I'll go to to sate these needs are minimal when stacked up against those longer, less schedule-bound days.

Last night, as I lay down to detox before bed, I opted to put on the 1972 Hammer horror classic VAMPIRE CIRCUS, a late period offering from the studio that I have long loved. And I immediately recalled the first time I saw this film and the berserk lengths I went to in order to see it. And I remembered how that quest almost killed me.

For real!

When I was 17, my weekend job was working at the Dixie Flea Market, at the dismal Dixie Value Mall in the East end of *MiserySauga*. The flea market was a basement grotto, only open on Saturdays and Sundays and it was a place I had been going to for years, primarily to trade VHS tapes with a pockmarked, shyster video-vendor that always ripped my naive ass off. But to me, the place had a sleazy, smelly (it always smelled of mold, sweat and hot dogs and still does) carnival charm.

So, getting a paying job at this greaseball palace was a real thrill.

My gig was working for an old alcoholic vendor of "Peg Perego" mini-bikes for toddlers. You know, those motorized things that move at 1 mile per hour? My responsibility lay in charging parents a buck for their brats to ride around on this little makeshift track while they bought crap from the market and, hopefully, to actually sell them one of these over-priced vehicles.

I never did sell a bike.

But I sold tons of rides.

Endless rides.

And for every five bucks earned, I'd put three in my pocket.

I'd take that pilfered profit and leave my post (only when it was kid free; I've always loved and cared about children and would never do something *that* irresponsible) and run over to the bookseller and buy lurid pulp paperbacks or to that grifter VHS dealer and buy a big box shocker or a movie poster and oh, fuck, I skimmed that pithy till hard and criminally fattened up my collection of crap in the process.

Anyway, one weekend I learned that Toronto's legendary cineaste Reg Hartt was screening a double dose of Hammer films on the Sunday night at his "Cineforum".

Two films I had never seen but had read much about.

One was 1968's THE DEVIL RIDES OUT.

The other was VAMPIRE CIRCUS.

Reg Hartt is a veteran film collector and exhibitor who has a vast collection of 16mm prints and he would screen them every night in his living room/library, right downtown Toronto on Bathurst St., just south of College. I had heard Hartt (who is still very much active I believe, though he now screens primarily off digital sources) also used his "screening room" as a way to entice cute young men into his lair for some fun, but I had been there on at least three occasions (once to see a beautiful, bright 16mm print of HORROR OF DRACULA, a screening that changed my life) and each time found Hartt to be a great guy and the experience of seeing these movies this way to be unique, warm and exciting.

So, I made plans to go after work, by myself (again, always my preferred method of seeing movies) to take the two buses, two subways and one streetcar to see these amazing movies, neither of which I would have had any access to otherwise.

There were but two substantial problems here, however.

One, it was the dead-of-blood-freezing-cold Canadian winter. Late February, as I recall. An arctic tundra that was colder than my ex-mother-in-law's kiss.

As a result, the other, was that I was suffering from an accelerating chest cold.

Then of course, there was the fact that I had already traveled 1.5 hours by yet another double bus-ride to get to my job at the flea market to begin with. And because of that I would have to tack-on that return trip time onto the near three-hour

additional time it would take for me to get downtown and back.

At night. In the cold.

That's some serious fucking travel time to see a vampire movie.

But I was 17. I was young. I was in love with films to a degree that was unreasonable. So, after a full day taking dollars from dumb-ass dads while their snotty tots had low-speed chases around a filthy carpeted "track", I took my stolen-spoils, bought a hamburger, closed up shop and set off on my journey to see some vintage British chillers...

It was 7pm. It was dark outside already. Blacker than a witch's tit, in fact. So cold, my lungs felt like leather and, seeing as my lungs were already bothered and bearing mucous-fruit every five minutes, the feeling was deeply unpleasant. A day-long blizzard had turned to rain by this time, which didn't sit well with the gaping holes in my boots, every step sucking in a swamp and every press of my arch like sloshing around in a sponge.

A cold fucking sponge.

Skip Martin cackles in Hammer's VAMPIRE CIRCUS.

I got on the first bus, and, despite the state of things, I was excited to be on my way. You know that that feeling. When you're finally moving? That feeling of quest was battering down the weight of my increasingly sickly condition.

But just as soon as I was starting to thaw on that bus, it was time to get out, transfer in hand and wait for the second bus on the corner.

There was a coffee shop at that stop and so I ducked in to get a cup of something hot. I smiled at the cute girl at the counter. I felt alive then, like a sort of warrior on my way to an imagined mecca. And though, this mission was a solo mission, I secretly wished this pretty girl would jump over the counter and come with me. I could educate her in the ways of weird cinema and she could fall madly in love with me...

Once that fantasy passed, I got on the next bus. That bus took me to Kipling station, the first stop in my long subway ride to get me to Bathurst station. At Bathurst, I left the train and waited on the outside platform for the Southbound Bathurst streetcar.

I could feel the grip of the cold. It was a tight grip indeed. And with my toes now frozen and numb, and a cough sputtering in my chest, I started to seriously doubt my journey. Like, just maybe, I should have gone home.

But I didn't.

I continued on.

And on.

I made it to Reg Hartt's house/theater, the neon glow of his *Cineforum* sign in his window, welcoming me gently. Reg himself greeted me just as warmly, took my 10 bucks (a steep price for me then, but since my wallet was packed with ill-gotten gains, it didn't really matter) and then I settled into a wildly uncomfortable folding chair to see the magic shadows I had made such an effort to see.

I was late and had missed the first 40 minutes of THE DEVIL RIDES OUT, but I picked up on the story and the tone of the piece quickly and started syncing myself with the three other older gents in attendance, dudes who presumably hadn't traveled the earth to see these films as I had.

Hartt's heat must have been broken because the room was unreasonably cold. And I've never been one to properly dress for the weather and that night was no exception. I was shivering through my ripped-up leather jacket and my feet were now blue-tinted ice blocks.

But I was watching Christopher Lee battle phantoms and I was fucking thrilled.

It was magic.

After DEVIL, Reg started to prepare the VAMPIRE CIRCUS print and I asked if he had any coffee. He did. The coffee helped and, pre-screening, we were treated to Reg's lively mini-lecture/intro about the film we were about to see.

But by the time the first strains of David Whitaker's delicate score started and we enter the walls of the evil Count Mitterhaus' bloody lair and the Count's fangs sprout in bloodlust just before he kills a kid (still one the most perverted and dark openings in any Hammer film, maybe any film period), I started to cough again.

And then I really started to cough. A lot.

It all started to fall apart. My shivers were uncontrollable. I kept spitting phlegm into my empty cup, secretly, as it wasn't my cup and such an act is beyond uncouth. My head started to feel swimmy. I knew I was getting hot because my skin felt sensitive.

I had gone from getting sick to sick to seriously fucking ill.

But I stayed. I watched VAMPIRE CIRCUS in a daze. Freezing, shaking, burning, quaking, coughing, spitting. I made it to the finish line and deduced through my delirium that the film is perhaps Hammer's greatest vampire offering, an absolutely mad and frantic piece of fantastique cinema with sex, blood, horror, fantastic bats, pretty sets, solid cast, lovely animals and a killer climax.

When the reel wound out, I literally stumbled from that house on the very verge of collapse.

Reg Hartt asked me if I was alright and I smiled and said yes and thanked him for an awesome evening. I moved back out into the stone age Hell that was the cold Toronto night and made my journey home. I began sort of blacking out, mostly because I was exhausted but also because my body just wanted to call it a day.

This was before cell phones and no kid my age had a pager unless he was a drug dealer so I had no way of reaching my parents while I was in transit.

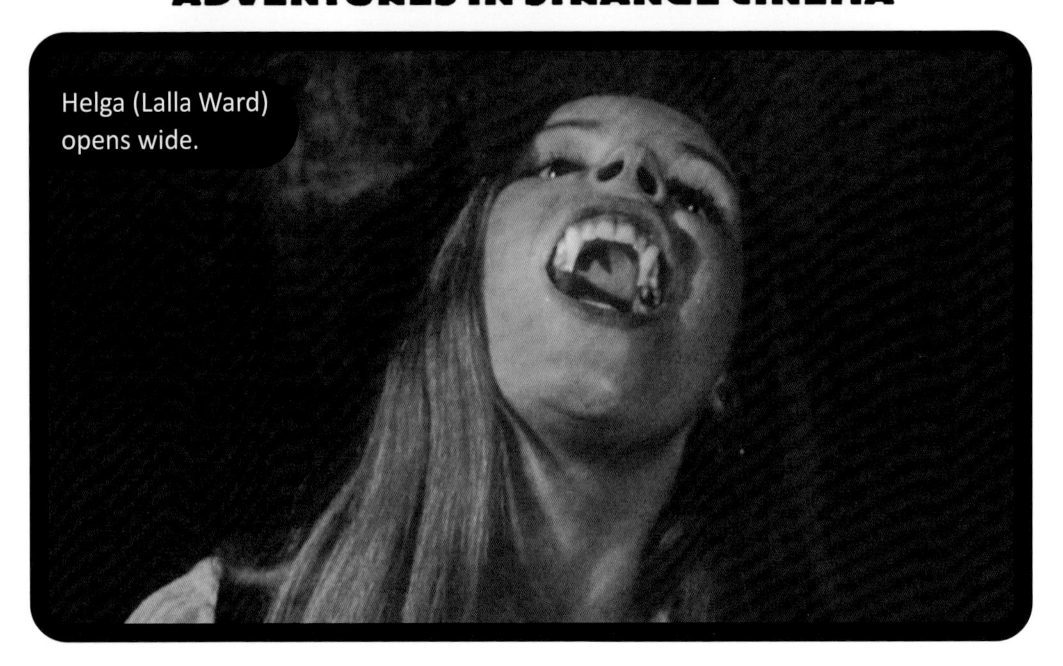
Helga (Lalla Ward) opens wide.

But by the time I made it to my bus transfer point in Mississauga, I knew I needed help.

I crawled back into that coffee shop to find a pay phone. I went back to that counter, but the pretty young girl wasn't there anymore, instead replaced by a gruff, bald, short, middle-aged Greek man who gave me attitude when I kindly asked for change for a dollar so I could use the pay phone. He made me buy something, so I purchased a fucking donut which I tossed in the trash and proceeded to stick a quarter in the phone and call my father.

Dad was at that point a cabby, night-crawling through the city in search of fares. He was just two years out of divorcing my mother, a painful dissolve in itself. But I never held a grudge and he and I had always been close. I got him just as he was *en route* back to his apartment for the night and told him about my predicament. I asked if he could take me home.

Within 10 minutes he was at that coffee shop.

I collapsed into his cab, never more grateful to be near him. I felt safe, like a soldier flying home from the frontline. I told him what I did. Where I was. And I told him why I did it.

He thought I was crazy. But he understood. He wanted to know about the film and I suddenly perked up as I raved about the climax of DEVIL and the mad thrills of finally seeing VAMPIRE CIRCUS. I gave him a version of that Reg Hartt lecture on the history of Hammer and how the movie fit into that puzzle, produced as it was in the waning days of the once great studio.

It was a cozy denouement to a very long, strange trip.

When I got home, my mom wasn't very interested in Hammer horror. Rather, she saw her tom-catting son looking like grim death. I said I was fine, drew a bath (perhaps the greatest bath of my life) warmed up and went to bed.

I replayed the night's journey in my mind and, despite the agony in my infected chest, I smiled.

What an adventure.

And yet, the price I paid for doing these things alone, outside of the *walking pneumonia* that I was diagnosed at the ER with the next day, was that I really had no one else to share my story with.

These many years later, I'm sharing it with you. Thanks for reading.

Now, today, you wouldn't catch me ever embarking on such a venture. Partially because I have no time, partially because I'm older and I don't spring back from illness as quickly, partially because I drive now but primarily, because I don't have to.

You wanna watch VAMPIRE CIRCUS now? Order the Blu-ray. Stream that (blood) sucker off some sort of service if you want. It's easy to find almost any film or entertainment you want at any given time no matter where you are, ever. In fact, I now have a rather robust collection of 16mm film prints myself, among them VAMPIRE CIRCUS.

The days of bus rides through the center of public transit Hell to sit in some strange dude's living room and freeze to death while he pumps a print through a projector onto a pull-down screen are done.

And maybe that's kind of sad, no?

HAMMER GLAMOUR INTERVIEW: JUDY MATHESON

In TWINS OF EVIL, John Hough's thundering third "Karnstein" shocker for Hammer films, a woman is dragged from her home, accused of witchery and vampirism and set ablaze, screaming as she burns. And this entire grim sequence unfolds over the opening credits! The lady smouldering and begging for mercy is none other than Judy Matheson, veteran of the British stage in the late 1960s and exploitation film ingénue of the 1970s. The beautiful and talented performer had also appeared in the previous Karnstein chiller, LUST FOR A VAMPIRE, during one of its sexiest scenes. But outside of her double-shot work in a pair of Hammer vampire masterworks, Matheson also appeared in pictures helmed by iconic European genre directors like Vincente Aranda, Jose Larraz and Pete Walker, work that has cemented her status as dark fantasy cinema royalty.

CHRIS ALEXANDER: Your early days on stage saw you touring the world. It must have been an exciting time...

Judy Matheson meets her fiery fate in 1971's TWINS OF EVIL.

JUDY MATHESON: It was. The theatre was The Bristol Old Vic, the top repertory theatre in the UK at the time. We toured the US, Europe & Israel and it was pretty much life changing. It was extraordinary to be playing a season on Broadway so early in my career. And we met so many fascinating people, like Robert Kennedy, Paul McCartney and Cesar Romero.

ALEXANDER: You had recently married, I believe. Did you find it difficult to navigate your personal life and professional life while on tour?

MATHESON: Actually, I married [actor] Paul Freeman two months after the tour ended, the impetus for the wedding being how much we'd missed each other while I was away. So, one did not affect the other.

ALEXANDER: Soon after this incredible experience on tour, you made your first major film appearance starring in BLOOD SPATTERED BRIDE director Vincente Aranda's THE EXQUISITE CADAVER, also known as THE CRUEL ONES. Was it difficult making the transition from stage to screen?

MATHESON: No, I wouldn't say it was difficult. It was just different. I had done a day of filming on the movie THE CHAIRMAN starring Gregory Peck and really, that was more or less as an extra, so yes, THE EXQUISITE CADAVER was my first real experience in film. I felt very inexperienced when I first went to Spain for the shoot but Vicente Aranda was terrific with the cast — he had great rapport with everyone, despite speaking very little English. It was an amazing time all around, especially for me, a very inexperienced young actress. There were problems with

the American producers, I believe, but those problems didn't seem to impinge on our experience at all. It was, in retrospect, my most all involving and enjoyable time in film, I think.

ALEXANDER: Naturally, your cult following primarily stems from your work with Hammer, especially since those two films have been so easily available. What were your thoughts about the studio at the time? Was there a stigma at all about performing in a Hammer film, which were often under fire for their more lurid content?

MATHESON: No, as far as I was aware, there was no stigma attached to Hammer at the time at all. I was just a very lucky, jobbing actress and actually thought the Hammer films were very professional and indeed quite glamorous, to work on!

ALEXANDER: LUST FOR A VAMPIRE is indeed a glamorous film, with its lush setting and cast. Can you speak a bit about your lovely castmates and of course, about your director, the great Jimmy Sangster?

MATHESON: I have many happy memories of working on LUST FOR A VAMPIRE. We were all treated very well, with gorgeous costumes, makeup and hair. All of the girls got on really well — we just seemed to be giggling all the whole way through the shoot. And we had beautiful weather, too. My alternative nickname for LUST FOR A VAMPIRE is 'Girls Just Wanna Have Fun', actually. And we did have so much fun. Again, I've heard there were problems 'backstage', as it were, but they didn't affect the flow of the shoot or the amount of sheer fun we were all having. Jimmy Sangster was charming — the original 70s Medallion Man! He was very jokey, very relaxed, and very funny. He, Michael Johnson, & Ralph Bates formed a sort of Boys Club, always ribbing each other & teasing us. It was a very happy shoot and a very happy memory.

ALEXANDER: John Hough went on to direct a series of great horror films, TWINS OF EVIL being an early one. Your appearance in the movie is brief but key and sets the tone

Mircalla (Yutte Stensgaard) gives Matheson's Amanda her last kiss in 1971's LUST FOR A VAMPIRE.

of the entire film. Can you discuss that part, any difficulties you had and how John was as a director talking you through it?

MATHESON: Yes, I loved my small but exciting little scene in TWINS OF EVIL. Because I'd worked on LUST FOR A VAMPIRE, the producers very kindly offered me my choice of one of the smaller parts: I chose "The Wood Cutter's Daughter", because that one allowed me to shoot the scene with the legend that is Peter Cushing. And it was truly a fabulous experience working with that magnificent, wonderful actor. And I don't recall any problems with the part at all, I just got on with it. I think at one stage, John Hough asked me to undo my shirt a little more than I would have liked, but that was it! John was pretty hands off as far as performance was concerned. I always joke that during the screaming scene, he went off and had a cup of tea, before coming back and shouting 'Cut'!

ALEXANDER: Outside of unbuttoning your shirt a bit more in TWINS OF EVIL, were you ever asked to do anything particularly outside your comfort zone for Hammer?

MATHESON: The simple answer to that question is no, I don't remember being pressured to do anything uncomfortable in either Hammer film. Both pictures were great experiences and absolutely professional.

ALEXANDER: You were also in director Pete Walker's THE FLESH AND BLOOD SHOW. I have always found Pete to be an intellectual hiding in the world of exploitation. I can imagine he didn't fuss with actors much and simply allowed you to interpret the script as you saw fit. Am I wrong?

MATHESON: No, you are right in your assessment of Pete Walker's approach — he certainly wasn't into any deep analysis of character! He was a very professional director though and knew how each shot was going to go before we shot it. He was remarkably efficient and fast moving in his method as well, which kept things on track from a production standpoint.

ALEXANDER: I've read that working with VAMPYRES director Jose Larraz perhaps wasn't as positive an experience for you as Hammer and Walker...

MATHESON: Yes, that's correct. Larraz's film SCREAM AND DIE was my least enjoyable filming experience. Let's just say that he wasn't very respectful towards his actresses at all. And during my death scene, he just wanted to push it further and further with the violence and the nudity. It was the opposite of Hammer, actually.

ALEXANDER: Despite your detours into cinema, you continued to work on stage and in other areas of the arts. Was theatre always your preferred medium of expression?

MATHESON: Interesting that you should ask that. And while live theatre is incredibly exciting, for me, *nothing* is as exciting as working on a film set. I love everything about the filming experience. The anticipation of the work itself as you walk onto set, the camaraderie between crew and performers, the joy and excitement of so many people working together towards one common aim. Oh, and the bacon sandwiches [*laughs*]...

ALEXANDER: When did you first realize that your work in that handful of horror and fantasy films had amassed an international fanbase?

MATHESON: That realisation came late. As far as I was concerned, throughout that period, I was just a very lucky working actress, very rarely out of work. But after a long trip travelling through Africa, a change of career into my work as a television anchor, the advent of two children — I'd remarried along the way, as you know — and a move to South Africa for several years, it was only on my return to the UK in 2003 that I realised, really through social media, what a following the work I'd been involved with had accrued.

ALEXANDER: And where has that newfound realization about the importance of your role in film history taken you?

MATHESON: I've met so many interesting people, fans and cinephiles — often, of course, the same people — of the genre; the whole journey has been amazing to me. I've also latterly caught up with people I've worked with, such as John Hough and Damien Thomas. I've been honoured to take part in a documentary PETER CUSHING: IN HIS OWN WORDS and to work with Hammer and James Bond icon Caroline Munro in two recent films.

ALEXANDER: Any thoughts on the struggles of women in film, whether it be sexism or ageism or otherwise?

MATHESON: I'm very comfortable discussing women in films. I've been a feminist for as long as I can remember. There have always been great parts for young women, not least in Hammer films, but they've definitely got stronger in recent years. The 'Me Too' movement has some effect on the imbalance of power. And the acknowledgement of the equal pay issue is at last being tackled.

But I have no salacious personal stories to impart; as far as I can remember, I have always commanded respect!

ALEXANDER: You also seem to be very at ease with your status as a cult movie icon. Are you?

MATHESON: I am very comfortable with my legacy, if that's what it is. But, yes, there had been a time when I didn't acknowledge it. I have two daughters and I was always aware that they could be embarrassed by some of my work. However as they have grown up, they have become aware of the respect some of my work has gleaned and they have taken some pride in their actress mum's work.

ALEXANDER: Regarding the two Karnstein films you appeared in: Which is your favorite?

MATHESON: The finest film is certainly TWINS OF EVIL, which has everything a period horror Film should have and has stood the test of time brilliantly. But I love the *schlockiness* of LUST FOR A VAMPIRE. It's beautiful to look at, with some nice performances. To my mind, it is the Disney-fied version of a Hammer horror film!

LEGEND OF THE WEREWOLF (1975)

Starring Peter Cushing, Ron Moody, Hugh Griffith, David Rintoul
Written by Anthony Hinds
Directed by Freddie Francis

One of the rarest of lycanthrope-centric films is the unfortunately late, Oscar winning British cinematographer (THE ELEPHANT MAN) and noted horror filmmaker (DRACULA HAS RISEN FROM THE GRAVE, TALES FROM THE CRYPT) Freddie Francis' little discussed 1975 Hammer-esque wolfman shocker LEGEND OF THE WEREWOLF. And it's a shame that it's so obscure, because the movie is terrific.

As the film's star Peter Cushing (whose work here is first rate as always) so helpfully explains in LEGEND OF THE WEREWOLF's weird opening sequence, it has been said that the beasts of the forest shall watch over and protect human children on Christmas Eve, because, well, their forefathers and mothers did it for Jesus, so if they didn't do it too, they'd be bad Christians. This bit of made-up myth provides credibility for the ensuing tale of poor little Etoile, a baby who, after his immigrant parents are chomped

LEGEND OF THE WEREWOLF
A TYBURN FILM PRODUCTION
PETER CUSHING
IN
LEGEND OF THE WEREWOLF
Starring
RON MOODY
HUGH GRIFFITH ROY CASTLE
and introducing
DAVID RINTOUL
as the Werewolf
Written by JOHN ELDER Produced by KEVIN FRANCIS Directed by FREDDIE FRANCIS
RANK FILM DISTRIBUTORS

on by a pack of starving wolves, is inexplicably adopted by the now sated pack. He grows up like a sort of lupine Tarzan, a wild untamed thing who is eventually "rescued" by a sleazy carny (the amazing, wild-eyed actor Hugh Griffith) and top billed in his skid row circus as the feral "Wolf Boy". Eventually Etoile grows into a strapping young lad (played by veteran actor David Rintoul) who makes the rather startling discovery that, when under pressure of a full moon, he grows fangs, sprouts fur, pops his shirt and end up looking a lot like Oliver Reed did in Terence Fisher's 1961 Hammer horror masterpiece CURSE OF THE WEREWOLF.

In fact, Jimmy Evans' Roy Ashton-esque make up schemes for Etoile's furry face and transformations and the idea of a Christmas birth curse aren't the only things that recall that admittedly superior film. See, Etoile ends up ditching his promising career as a rabid roustabout and flees to late 19th century Paris (the Fisher film was based on Guy Endore's novel The Werewolf Of Paris and both pics were penned by Anthony Hinds, under his pseudonym John Elder) where he gets a gig working at a zoo run by OLIVER! heavy Ron Moody and falls in love with a beautiful whore, a woman who — like Reed's squeeze in CURSE — seems to temper his inner lycanthrope. Of course, all goes sour when a jealous Etoile turns wolfy and rips the throats out of the local bordello's patrons (complete with red optical effects, the kind that Francis was fond of playing with) and it falls on the narrow shoulders of Peter Cushing, here playing an intrepid police pathologist, to put Etoile's homicidal cloud to rest with a sweet silver lining.

LEGEND OF THE WEREWOLF was produced by Tyburn Films, a tiny, short-lived UK studio founded by Francis' son Kevin and one that sought to capitalize on Hammer's massive, decade spanning, international success. Problem was, by 1974 Hammer horror was already passé and, after one more picture (1975's fine John Hurt/Ian McCulloch vehicle THE GHOUL) Tyburn took a permanent dive.

In Canada (where I was born, raised and still live) a little budget video distro outfit called Interglobal Home Video ended up distributing LEGEND in the 1980s. I bought that VHS cassette for $10 at a local Kmart and I'm certainly glad I did. Because I've never, ever seen the film legitimately available in any other format on these shores. Needless to say, I treasure my copy.

Though hampered by its low budget, and aforementioned plot familiarity, and though its not necessarily Francis' best directorial work (though it's leaps and bounds better than his worst film, 1970's awesomely insane caveman vs. Joan Crawford opus TROG), LEGEND is a well paced, blackly humorous, creepy and oh-so-very British slice of rough-around-the -edges, modestly budgeted Gothic horror. And Hammer vet Harry Robinson's brash, often romantic score amplifies the production value considerably.

You should find it. That beaten up tape of mine has seen the insides of no less than 7 VCRs and it still goes strong, it still pulls its LP recorded weight with blood dripping, hairy-backed finesse and flesh shredding, electro-magnetic grace. A muddy rip of that

VHS is on YouTube (and on bootleg DVDs) and it's a perfectly acceptable (though faded and fuzzy) version to at least get a good sense of the film. Here's hoping someone cleans this wonderful little flick up and dresses it up someday.

THE LIVING DEAD AT MANCHESTER MORGUE (1974)

Starring Cristina Galbo, Ray Lovelock, Arthur Kennedy, Aldo Massasso
Written by Juan Cobos, Sandro Continenza, Marcello Coscia, Miguel Rubio
Directed by Jorge Grau

In the early 1970s, young, experimental Spanish director Jorge Grau was, alongside an equally visionary, *nouvelle vague* inspired pack of bratty celluloid slingers (the likes which include THE BLOOD SPATTERED BRIDE helmer Vincente Aranda), being championed as the future of the Spanish film industry. In the wake of Grau's violent, sexual and historically accurate telling of the Elizabeth Bathory legend, 1973's THE BLOODY COUNTESS, producer Edmondo Amati approached the filmmaker to direct a movie that would blatantly ride the box office coattails of the George A. Romero's NIGHT OF THE LIVING DEAD, but add the more visceral dimension of dripping, full-blooded color, replacing the gritty, cheap, shadowy expressionism of NIGHT with a more garish, pulpy and stomach-churning pallet. Grau, swayed by a larger paycheck

The screen has never seen zombies quite like the ones in THE LIVING DEAD AT MANCHESTER MORGUE.

Edna (Cristina Galbo) regrets not letting sleeping corpses lie...

and the chance to film in England eagerly obliged, taking the rather straight-forward genre screenplay and giving it a rewrite, grafting on his own, unique personality quirks, obsessions and style, "borrowing" from Romero's creation but forging something completely fresh and deliciously offbeat.

Known on these shores under at least a dozen lurid titles, including DON'T OPEN THE WINDOW, BRUNCH WITH THE DEAD and LET SLEEPING CORPSES LIE, Grau's resulting 1974 Spanish/Italian zombie shocker NON SI DEVE PROFANARE IL SONNO DEI MORTI, is a movie that I've always preferred to call by its UK moniker, THE LIVING DEAD AT MANCHESTER MORGUE. Because I just love the way it reads, especially when read aloud.

London antique dealer George (a bearded, badass looking Ray Lovelock from, among many other things Armando Crispino's AUTOPSY and Umberto Lenzi's AN IDEAL PLACE TO KILL) is on a cross-country motorcycle trip into rural England when, after a bike crushing accident, he regretfully hooks up with the beautiful, fragile Edna (Cristina Galbo from WHAT HAVE YOU DONE TO SOLANGE?) who is also traveling into the sticks to visit her mentally ill sister. On route, the pair come across a strange machine; a whirring, pulsing metallic engine sitting squarely in the centre of a farmer's field. Said machine is an agricultural device that sends out waves of low frequency radiation designed to provoke insects to go mad and cannibalize each other. Science!

Lanky haired, neo-hippie George balks at such underhanded environmental buggery, a position which only increases in intensity when he and Edna discover said supposedly harmless radiation is in fact stimulating the recently dead to get up and kill, with the people they kill then getting up to kill. As the local police (led by

American stage actor Arthur Kennedy, in a cruel and cranky performance) attempt to pin the rash of violent zombie induced murders on the troubled couple, the evil crop-protecting, dead- provoking device keeps chugging and spinning and the corpses keep-a-coming, resulting in the inevitable tragic, violent, titular (emphasis on the tit!) morgue-set climax.

When THE LIVING DEAD AT MANCHESTER MORGUE was released it almost immediately came under fire from critics for its then outrageous levels of graphic splatter, a truly shocking cavalcade of carnage designed by none other than Italian FX wizard Giannetto De Rossi. De Rossi is the latex and karo syrup slinging genius who would later find acclaim drilling brains, poking out eyes and regurgitating guts under the watchful eye of the late, great Fulci and though his art here was not yet quite state of, it's still pretty damned fantastic: flesh is ripped from bodies, innards are torn out of heaving bellies, eyeballs are eaten and perhaps most notoriously, an unfortunate lass has her blouse ripped open and her left breast crudely removed by the clawing hands of a hungry ghoul.

And speaking of ghouls, the homicidal stiffs on display here are really terrifying; a mangy, slow and stiff lot of relentless, red-eyed refuse (incidentally, the crimson contact lenses appear to be exactly the same as the ones utilized for the 'infected' in Danny Boyle's 28 DAYS LATER and its sequel 28 WEEKS LATER). And these zombies aren't a bunch of amateur local yokels bumbling around in greasepaint but are in fact real actors, characters ripped right out of the worst (or best, as the case with us horror fans may be) nightmare; I can honestly say that Spanish actor Fernando Hilbeck's, gravestone tossing, recently resurrected, drowned hobo Gutherie, with his sopping wet clothes, blotchy stare and stubbly lock jaw is one of the most frightening screen bogeymen I've ever seen and the damage he inflicts on his victims is just as shuddery.

But beyond the moldy monsters and the ample waste of human life on display, the real impact in Grau's remarkable motion picture lies in the level of intelligence, of finely crafted human drama, of mounting dread and almost Hitchcockian suspense (and black humor) that so effortlessly guides the grue. We come to genuinely care for George and Edna, to believe in their blossoming love, their genuine connection that builds under the direst of circumstances. And when things take a turn for the worse in the final reel, there's a palpable sense of loss that pushes the horror into an emotional level unseen in the post NIGHT, non-Romero zombie efforts. The score, by Giuliano Sorgini (SS HELL CAMP) is another major source of the picture's skin-tightening power, a soundscape that deftly veers between string-soaked British lounge pop (especially effective in the dazzlingly edited opening credits montage) and heaving, gasping, synth burbling experimentalism.

THE LIVING DEAD AT MANCHESTER MORGUE is an accessible, thought provoking and paralyzing Eurohorror classic whose ample flaws, frequent lapses in logic (does *any* of the action actually take place *in* Manchester?) and many plot inconsistencies (how does Hilbeck manage to revive his fellow cadavers by wiping blood on their eyelids, exactly? Who cares! It's creepy!) take a backseat to the movie's many macabre and gruesomely elegant delights.

This isn't the quasi-realist American horror of Romero and it isn't the chunky, in your face zombie opera shock of Fulci. This is the zombie film as dark, lyrical, melancholy fairy tale, a film that exists in a class of its own.

THE LIVING DEAD GIRL (1982)

Starring Marina Pierro, Francoise Blanchard, Mike Marshall, Carina Barone
Written by Jacques Raif, Jean Rollin
Directed by Jean Rollin

French filmmaker Jean Rollin was the poet of European exploitation, bringing a gentle, aching melancholy and sensitivity to his erotic, bloody fever dreams. Of course, as with his contemporary Jess Franco, many of Rollin's admirers and even his detractors will cite that exposed, nubile female flesh serves as the true power of the singular film-work he left behind. Certainly fetishized genitals and ethereal copulation add obvious sizzle to Rollin's work, but there's so much more to both the artist and the art. Rollin himself knew this, though he was often too humble to admit it, lost as he got in the Eurosex gutter that he and Franco and so many other great filmmakers got lost in throughout the 1970s and '80s, living to work but still working to live and often forced to make pictures (re: porn) that were beneath them.

And while my favorite Rollin film will always be his elegiac vampire tragedy LIPS OF BLOOD (with THE GRAPES OF DEATH following closely behind), certainly none of his pictures are as erotic or bloody as his 1982 doomed love story THE LIVING DEAD GIRL (LA MORTE VIVANTE en francais), a film that, due to its high visceral content and obvious sexual trappings, might be the director's most accessible work. This is not a derogatory statement, not a dismissal. On the contrary, THE LIVING DEAD GIRL is an ideal entry point into Rollin's oeuvre and boasts some of his strongest, most haunting visual passages.

In the early 1980s, frequent Rollin producer Sam Selsky wanted to compete with the swell of splatter leaking out of America and asked Rollin to deliver a straight "gore" film, which the director delivered in spades with THE LIVING DEAD GIRL, ladling on the red stuff and ripping flesh and removing heads with wild abandon. The meaty FX themselves, while vulgar, aren't very convincing, but that doesn't matter, really and

Catherine (Francoise Blanchard) digs deep in THE LIVING DEAD GIRL.

doesn't detract from the overall tone of the film. These sequences of straight sanguinary shock are in fact surreal in their artifice and brush up against that typical Rollin lyricism with striking images of beautiful, wispy women drifting through crumbling European locations, while the sun rises and sets around them, and waves crash on reefs in the peripheral. It's all rather stunning, as would be expected. THE LIVING DEAD GIRL is explicit, yes. But it's also a work of dream-logic art, armed with a brisk pace, a relatively high body count and a palpable emotional core.

The film follows the plight of a long dead woman named Catherine Valmont (hauntingly played by actress Francoise Blanchard) who is resurrected by a toxic chemical spill in her moldering crypt. In fact, THE LIVING DEAD GIRL pre-dates Dan O'Bannon's seminal 1985 romp RETURN OF THE LIVING DEAD by three years and indeed, the idea of chemical refuse bringing the dead back to life was realized here first. One wonders if O'Bannon saw this film. It's most likely a coincidence, but the similarities are uncanny.

As the still fleshy and blonde she-zombie climbs from her coffin, she quickly murders a pair of lowlifes who were intent on raiding the tomb by shoving her fingers deep into in their soft throats and draining their blood through her fingertips. She then wanders the countryside, searching for her still-living friend Helene (Marina Pierro). When the two women are reunited (after Catherine murders and drains more victims first), Helene realizes her friend is now a kind of undead parasite and tries to protect her, while covering up her unfortunately necessary murders. She even lets Catherine drink from her body, just enough to sate her and curb her more lethal impulses...

But the more Catherine feeds (and her feeding is wildly messy), the more alert to her condition she becomes (the sequence where she wanders through the bedroom, simply touching items and remembering her dormant humanity is perhaps the most lyrical sequence in all of Rollin's vampire canon) and she begins to pursue suicide. Helene, however, refuses to let her friend, who is in essence now her lover, die again and soon drastic measures are taken to prevent this...

Like much of Rollin's work, THE LIVING DEAD is most assuredly a study in mood and tone and bloodletting illustrated as a ballet, though it's a much more sickening dance this time around. Key motifs and imagery found in early Rollin female-centric masterworks weave their way into the film, with the filmmaker's earthiness fascinatingly at odds with the post-FRIDAY THE 13th slasher shocks; and yet somehow that resistance and eventual surrender adds a new dimension to Rollin's language.

Watching THE LIVING DEAD GIRL is an unforgettable, erotic, unsettling and ultimately moving experience, one highly recommended for novice Rollin-ites and devout scholars alike.

THE LOVE WITCH (2016)

Starring Samantha Robinson, Gian Keys, Laura Waddell, Jeffrey Vincent Parise
Written by Anna Biller
Directed by Anna Biller

Watching Anna Biller's THE LOVE WITCH, is an almost painful experience.

Painful in that it is such an embarrassment of beauty, of color and style, of humor and rhythm and sound. Indeed, Biller's sense of cinema here, particularly of a certain '70s vintage, is so vividly realized that the viewer is left feeling somewhat inebriated, dizzy and powerless to resist it.

Not that you'd want to resist it.

Better that you just surrender fully, completely to it.

Biller, whose film before this was 2007's delirious sexploitation fantasy VIVA (an almost as swoon-worthy a sensual cinematic experience), is clearly in love with vintage European sex thrillers, American drive-in melodramas (in particular, the lush, Technicolor films coming out of the Crown International camp) and '60s pulp novels and she employs that passion to construct the exterior of her arch fable.

THE LOVE WITCH's colors are blinding, its art decoration, *mise en scène* and costumes (designed by Biller) are stunning. The tone of the picture veers maniacally between dissonant voice overs, stylized stilted dialogue exchanges, stag loop erotica, Jess

Elaine (Samantha Robinson) uses affection as her weapon in THE LOVE WITCH.

Franco-esque nightclub hangouts, romantic mania, serious drama, absurdist comedy and sometimes gory violence. But underneath all of its affectation lurks a powerful study of the differences between the sexes and the often-disastrous results that these opposing philosophies on love and human relations can yield when left unchecked.

The film stars Samantha Robinson as Elaine, an impossibly beautiful woman who drives down the California coast and moves into a beautiful Victorian apartment while connecting with her coven, a group of local witches who practice their pagan faith openly, under the suspicious eyes of the community. Elaine immediately befriends her chipper landlord (Laura Waddell, who is hilarious and, by the end of the film, heartbreaking) and the two lunch often and discuss their shared man troubles and triumphs. Perhaps *befriend* is the wrong word, because outside of dabbling in witchcraft, Elaine is a more than a bit of a narcissist, completely self-absorbed and unable to fathom why she cannot find and keep love.

When she meets a comically upbeat college professor, they immediately head for the handsome teacher's cabin in the woods for impromptu sex. Elaine urges her new lover to sip from her flask, the likes of which contains a swampy mix of herbs and hell itself; soon the poor smitten schmuck is in the thralls of Elaine's industrial strength love potion, which causes him to become a weeping, hysterical mess of a man. In her always amusing voiceover, wherein we get to hear her most private and sociopathic thoughts, we discover that Elaine is repulsed by such behaviors, even though she herself is responsible for them.

We quickly learn that the lady is indeed quite mad, warped through years of trying and failing to be what she thinks men want her to be.

After the teacher dies from his amorous afflictions, Elaine digs a grave and buries the man with a fetish of her urine and one of her used tampons ("Women bleed, it's beautiful," she muses on the soundtrack, "and most men have never even seen a used tampon").

After this bizarre, mesmerizing first quarter, THE LOVE WITCH keeps meandering around its increasingly deranged narrative, with Elaine stopping at nothing in her lethal quest for love. To reveal more of the plot or various vignettes would be to ruin Biller's sweet symphony or perversion, eccentricity, and social indictment, but suffice to say that Elaine's selfish, unrealistic dreams never come true. They can't.

THE LOVE WITCH is a kind of horror movie but it's far more than just that. It's as much a vibrant, daring art installation as it is a kind of highly sexualized vintage movie-of-the-week; it's unabashedly lurid and soap opera-steeped and the stunning Robinson is ever-lovely to look at, taking up as she does, virtually every frame of the film. But at its core, Biller has so much more to say; about the hypocrisy of feminism, about finding true freedom, about the male gaze, about the very definition of love. This is a fiercely intelligent, visionary work hiding in the skin of a trashy exploitation movie bauble and it firmly locks-in Biller in as one of the most exciting filmmakers alive.

INTERVIEW: ANNA BILLER

ALEXANDER: Why was there such a stretch of time between your first film, VIVA, and THE LOVE WITCH? Was that space used to develop what the film would be?

BILLER: Apart from two years promoting VIVA, yes. It was two years of researching witchcraft, psychology, screenwriting, and movies and writing the script, and five years in production (most of which was pre-production — designing, constructing costumes and props, buying props, scouting locations and prop houses storyboarding, painting, composing music, rewriting, casting, finding locations, etc.) Some of this took longer than it should have because there was a learning curve: I had never written a conventional script for instance, or composed for a wind ensemble, and I had no prior knowledge of medieval costume construction. Also, I developed a chronic case of vertigo during pre-production, and my process slowed down considerably because things such as shopping for fabric, driving, and drafting patterns made me dizzy and nauseous.

ALEXANDER: Much has been spoken about in regard to the look. I've read you mention pulp novel covers. Can you break down some of the visual palette and the sources of the films saturated look?

BILLER: The visual palette for Elaine's apartment came from witchcraft symbolism, most specifically from the Thoth tarot deck. There are some cards which are

Director Anna Biller with her elegant leading lady.

orange, yellow, and red — the sun cards — and others which are blue and purple — the moon cards. The sun represents the male element, and the moon represents the female element. So, her living room is a sun room, and her magic room and dining room are moon rooms. Also, the renaissance festival is a summer solstice festival where the sun is being worshipped, so everything there is based on yellow and orange: yellow and gold silk costumes, marigolds, yellow and orange daisies, etc. All of the red in her bedroom and in the burlesque club, plus the red light around the edges of the ritual flashbacks, symbolize danger and sexuality, and the pink in the tearoom symbolizes girlhood and feminine fantasy. The white wedding costumes and white unicorn represent purity, monogamy, and love, and the black robes and candles represent witchcraft and the dark arts. So, the film is dripping with color symbolism. I've watched so many Technicolor films in my life that these were obviously also an influence -especially on the lighting technique — but for this film the set design came mostly out of my imagination. The styling and choice of Elaine, however, was inspired by paintings of beautiful witches on pulp novel covers, and by actresses in '60s Italian horror films such as Edwige Fenech and Barbara Steele.

ALEXANDER: How about the narration? Was that always in the script or was it an element you introduced in the edit?

Biller cast herself in her breakthrough fever dream VIVA (2007).

BILLER: The voiceover narration was added later, after I made my first fine cut of the film. Samantha Robinson and I had worked so hard to construct Elaine as a "sympathetic sociopath," but I didn't feel that her sociopathy was coming through strongly enough — partly because of her stunning beauty — so I felt that her inner voice needed to come through more for people to understand her character better.

ALEXANDER: The audition process: It feels as though WITCH is built around Samantha's physical presence. The casting is just too perfect. Was she there from day one? If not, what was it about her that made you lock her as your "monster"?

BILLER: Oddly enough, when I first auditioned Samantha I didn't know yet that she was my Love Witch. No one understood what I wanted after the first reading, so at first, I was mainly going by their physical appearance and their general acting ability. But at the second audition I had them dance for me, and this is when Samantha really stood out. She was so beautiful and sexy, but she had this look on her face that is the one you see in the film — a look of disdain, almost of cruelty. It was this incredible mixture of giving and not giving that gave her so much power, and I could see that she could destroy men with just a glance. But I still had to interview her to find out if she could really do it, and this is where I absolutely knew she was the one. I watched her face when she spoke and saw how expressive it was and how beautifully it captured light, and was amazed at her intelligence and her willingness to collaborate. It was this last element that was key in making her seem so perfect, because we constructed Elaine together, organically out of her personality, and she had the openness and skill to do that with me.

ALEXANDER: On that note, is Elaine a monster? Is she a victim?

BILLER: I would say that she is both. All deep narcissists are victims at least of their own warped psychology and inability to experience a true self, but Elaine is also the victim of abuse and of a society that has used and discarded her. She is a monster is the sense that she will do anything to achieve her desires, regardless of how it affects others. But there are moments in the film where you see a real person there, and her potential to really love others, and that's where the tragedy in the film comes in — in these glimpses of humanity we see in Elaine, where we start rooting for her and wishing she could remain in that place.

ALEXANDER: That house is magnificent. What's the story behind it?

BILLER: We shot most of our exteriors in Eureka and Arcata, about four hours north of San Francisco. Those towns have amazing Victorian architecture, which is one reason we shot there, aside from its eerie witchy feeling in general. Elaine's house is a historic house designed by Samuel and Joseph Newsom in Arcata, who also designed the famous Carson Mansion in Eureka. We shot one of the Victorian interiors in a historic home in Los Angeles, and the exterior of Wayne's cabin is a house in Topanga Canyon that was originally constructed as a movie house for a Western TV series in the '70s. The Victorian tearoom was shot in the marble lobby of the historic Herald Examiner building in downtown Los Angeles. (We brought all of the pink in.) A lot of the interiors were built on a soundstage.

ALEXANDER: There's a balance here that jerks the viewer around with arch humor, broad comedy, horror, erotica, surrealism... can you discuss the film's tone? Do you just shoot what you want to see, thus making the final film an extension of you or is it all by design?

BILLER: I think the tone comes out like that because of how long I work on things. My tastes and ideas changed and shifted over the years while I was working on the film, and I kept tweaking the script and visual ideas when I'd get a new inspiration. So, there are all these layers — first the script, then the design — and then you cast the actors and they bring their own richness to it, and my DP had his own cinema fantasies and techniques he brings in, and then there is the soundtrack — and of course there are the micro-decisions you make every day on the set. So it just keeps getting fuller and fuller until it's sort of unbearable. It's also because I have so much to say about everything, but I have so little time to say it in, so all of my ideas — both thematic and visual — have to share space in a two-hour film. But of course, a lot of it is in the design too, in the proliferation of the ideas suggested by the sets and costumes.

ALEXANDER: Where are those amazing costumes now?

BILLER: I live with some of them in my space — I really need to clear things out — and the rest are in storage.

ALEXANDER: The music… stunning, like everything in the film. What instrumentation did you use when composing? Will we see a proper soundtrack release?

BILLER: I wrote some music for harp, and for a period wind ensemble plus lute, which I was only able to do because I could audition everything in Finale to see how it would sound and it transposes for you; certain instruments don't sound where they are written, which was much too hard for me back in school when I tried to take an orchestration class. I was very nervous when having it recorded, because I got professional period musicians from USC, including the only professional lute player in Los Angeles, and I thought I may have made a lot of mistakes in the score, but it turned out fine. I do hope to release a soundtrack at some point.

ALEXANDER: Is WITCH a one-shot or will Elaine be revived for more lush, dangerous adventures?

BILLER: I do have some more ideas for Elaine. I thought of making a sequel in which Elaine gets out of her straitjacket, changes her identity, dyes her hair blonde, and moves to London to pursue a career in theater in the West End. But there are people after her looking to avenge the deaths of their loved ones, including Wayne's identical twin brother. I also thought of having her placed in a convent, and of doing a surrealist Buñuelian script about the havoc she wreaks there, especially after she escapes. But these are just silly ideas off the top of my head; I have other scripts that I'm more urgently interested in pursing. In any case I hope to have a long collaboration with Samantha, who is very exciting and rewarding to work with.

MANIAC (1980)

Starring Joe Spinnell, Caroline Munro, Gail Lawrence, Kelly Piper
Written by C.A. Rosenberg, Joe Spinell
Directed by William Lustig

Hard to believe there was a time in horror history where the critic was the archenemy of the contemporary genre film. Or rather, they thought they were. Not that horror and dark fantasy films were ever really embraced by the mainstream as anything other than a "low" entertainment, but as the '70s oozed into the '80s and more graphic, FX-driven depravity became *de rigour*, the big deal cinema scribblers often were dramatically opposed to the very existence of these sorts of pictures. Two of the most vocal pundits sneering at splatter were newspaper men turned TV stars Siskel

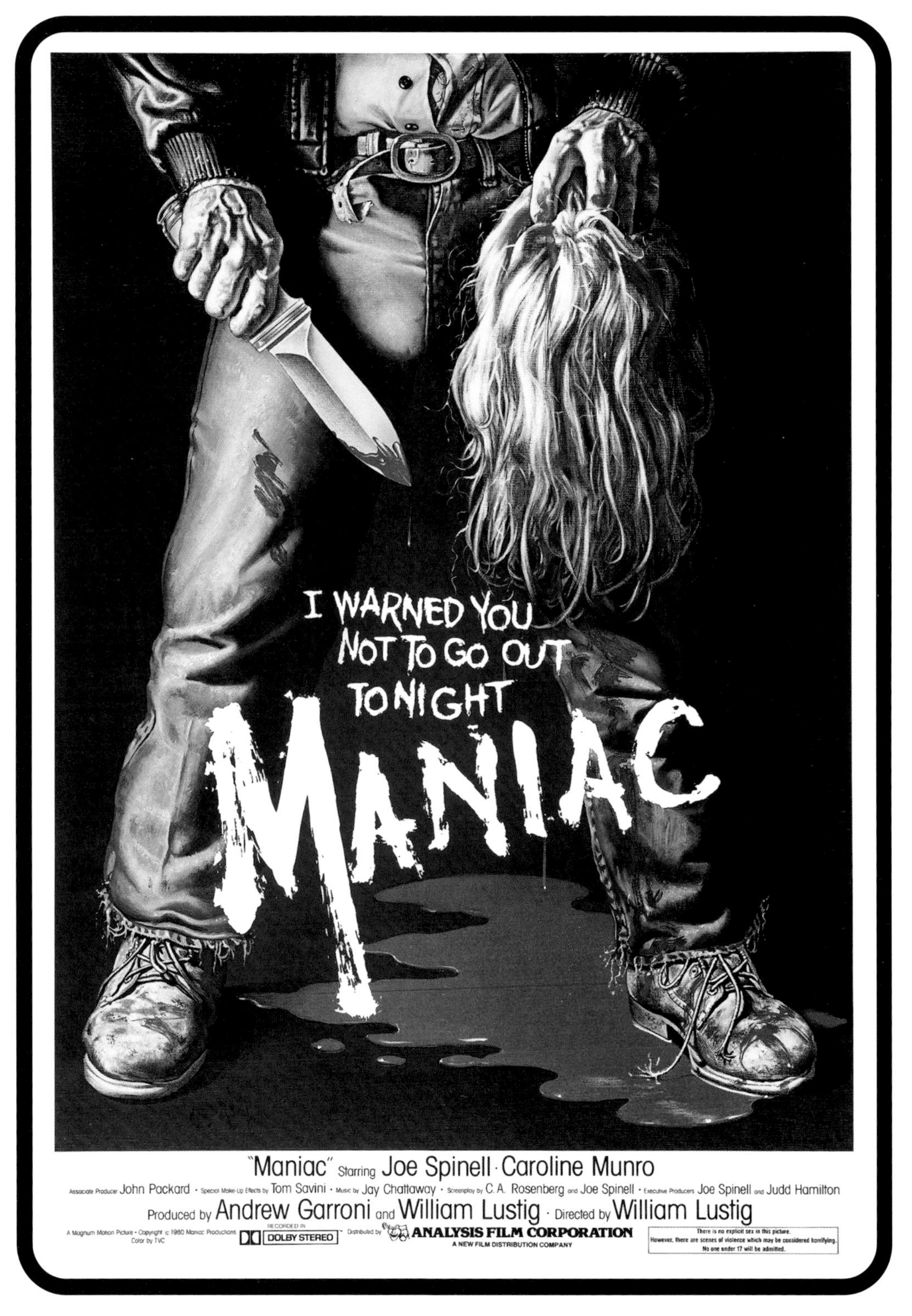
I WARNED YOU NOT TO GO OUT TONIGHT
MANIAC
"Maniac" Starring Joe Spinell · Caroline Munro
Associate Producer John Packard · Special Make-Up Effects by Tom Savini · Music by Jay Chattaway · Screenplay by C.A. Rosenberg and Joe Spinell · Executive Producers Joe Spinell and Judd Hamilton
Produced by Andrew Garroni and William Lustig · Directed by William Lustig
A Magnum Motion Picture · Copyright © 1980 Maniac Productions
Color by TVC
RECORDED IN DOLBY STEREO
Distributed by ANALYSIS FILM CORPORATION
A NEW FILM DISTRIBUTION COMPANY
There is no explicit sex in this picture.
However, there are scenes of violence which may be considered horrifying.
No one under 17 will be admitted.

and Ebert, arbiters of good taste who weren't afraid to attack movies they thought exemplified the rot of modern culture.

Well, I guess that's not entirely true. Sure, Roger Ebert slammed Romero's NIGHT OF THE LIVING DEAD in 1968, but he was an important champion of its infinitely messier color sequel DAWN OF THE DEAD. Hell, Ebert even co-wrote a spate of Russ Meyer pictures, including the gleefully insane BEYOND THE VALLEY OF THE DOLLS, an X-rated movie with lurid sex, graphic gore and other such transgressions. But generally speaking, he didn't care for horror at all, and Siskel actively seemed to HATE the genre. And both of them loudly despised slasher movies or, as they originally called them upon their first big post-HALLOWEEN wave, "Women in Danger" movies. Later, as the demographic of these sorts of pictures skewed to younger audiences, Ebert would dub them "Dead Teenager" films.

Which brings us to William Lustig's MANIAC, the operatic psychodrama about a New York lowlife named Frank Zito who moves from scene to scene, sweating, heaving, and murdering young women while also working through mommy issues and indulging a pronounced mannequin fetish. In 1980, when MANIAC had opened in New York, Siskel took in a screening and was utterly appalled. Going on their Chicago-based TV show SNEAK PREVIEWS, Siskel lost his mind, citing the scene where Spinell blows Tom Savini's skull apart with a shotgun as one of the most revolting things he'd ever seen in his life. In fact he took great high-road pleasure in stating that he actually walked out of the screening after that scene, saying that despite enduring the opening half-hour's cavalcade of grime, sweat, murder, torture, scalpings and general gritty unpleasantness, seeing such a jaw-droppingly sick scene as that head explosion didn't just take him out of his safe space, it picked him up, whisked him away, stripped him and dropped him naked into a volcano. Ebert — who famously liked to fight with his co-host and frequent "frenemy" — backed Siskel, nodding in agreement at MANIAC's offensiveness, both stating that no matter what came after it, that nothing could redeem or repair the movie. They called the movie a dog. And even brought a dog to sit on the couch with them to hammer home the joke they were making at MANIAC's expense!

Even worse, Siskel also produced and narrated a TV news segment attacking the ingenious way MANIAC was originally exhibited on its run at the Cinerama at 48th and Broadway, wherein the theatre had structures on the street housing screens where, inside, a perpetually running projector would reveal gory highlights from the film to shocked passersby. It was kind of the evil twin of Paramount and Hitchcock's method of sensationally exhibiting PSYCHO in the big cities, refusing to let people in after the film had started and forbidden them to not speak of the movie's secrets. In the MANIAC campaign, the idea was to show you fucking *everything*, to shock the shit out of you, awaken your reptilian desires and dare you into the theatre. Alas, due to Siskel and other handwringing crusaders' efforts, this awesome bit of showmanship was soon abandoned.

Joe Spinell nails his role as a human monster in MANIAC.

But here's the rub, the thing you and I and every other devote of depraved cinema knows well and good to be true. When you try to hide things from people, they'll only work harder to find it. When someone tells you that you cannot handle an experience, most of us will stop at nothing to dive in. When mom tells you "No cookies", you'll launch every sort of diabolical scheme in order to raid that jar. And when the mainstream tells you that a movie is *too* shocking, *too* gory, *too* offensive, naturally you'll be first in line to buy your ticket. You may even go twice. Such is how Gene Siskel's hilariously sanctimonious efforts to bury MANIAC and halt the blossoming of its MPAA-baiting ilk played out. Every sideshow needs the barker to make the noise, but without the delicate ladies fainting upon exiting the tent, the circus might as well shut down. With horror, it's not just the come-on, it's the damage it does to polite society. That's what we crave. That's why MANIAC became a sensation and that's why we are still talking about it, celebrating it, dissecting it, worshipping it, marveling at it.

INTERVIEW: CAROLINE MUNRO

According to British genre film icon Caroline Munro, when Hammer Studios honcho Sir James Carreras saw the London billboards for Lamb's Dark Rum on the way to the office, he immediately demanded a meeting with the young model. Within weeks, Munro had a contract with Hammer, a deal that saw her appear in pictures like the irreverent shocker DRACULA A.D. 1972 and the even more revisionist gothic romp CAPTAIN KRONOS: VAMPIRE HUNTER. That pair of fang films, coupled with appearances in

Frank (Spinell) and Anna (Caroline Munro) are one of horror's oddest couples.

eventual classics like THE ABOMINIBLE DR. PHIBES, secured the gorgeous brunette performer's status as dark fantasy film royalty. Throw in her turn as sexy and lethal moll Naomi in the Roger Moore Bond romp THE SPY WHO LOVED ME, and a bow in the Harryhausen adventure THE GOLDEN VOYAGE OF SINBAD, and the lady was damn near peerless in the '70s strange cinema culture landscape.

And yet her role in MANIAC is admittedly odd. How did this comely English Rose end up running afoul of a wheezing, sweating psycho in the sleaziest parts of New York City? It begins in Italy, circa 1978, when Lady Munro was poured into a revealing costume, prepping to play one of her signature roles, space smuggler Stella Starr...

CHRIS ALEXANDER: Now, your path to MANIAC was, presumably, paved because of your friendship with Joe Spinell, correct?

CAROLINE MUNRO: Yes. We weren't close friends, but we had worked together, and I thought he was wonderful. We met on the set of STAR CRASH, an Italian impression of STAR WARS directed by the very sweet Luigi Cozzi. I was in makeup, I believe, and in walked Joe to introduce himself. He was incredibly charismatic and larger than life. Just full of life. Joe loved life. Anyway, he announced who he was and that he would be playing the Count Zarth Arn, and it was just a joy to be around him.

ALEXANDER: How did you end up in New York though? Did you have to audition for MANIAC?

MUNRO: God no, not at all. What happened was that I was in New York doing — I think — a *Fangoria* convention and that's where I met William Lustig. Tom Savini was there too. So, Joe came by and reconnected with me and took me out for dinner. He told me that Italian actress Daria Nicolodi was supposed to play Anna D'Antoni and had to drop out of the film and they were now struggling to find someone to play the part. They were scheduled to start shooting on Monday and this was, I think, Saturday. He told me that I *had* to do it and initially I said no, I had to go back to London, I had things to do. But he wouldn't take no for an answer. That was Joe. So, I read the script that night and I slept on it. Literally. That's something I always do, part of my process. And the next day, I agreed to do it. Of course, I had no idea how violent it would be!

ALEXANDER: But Bill must have given you a sense of the film. You must have known that it would have been a much different horror film than say, your Hammer pictures.

MUNRO: Oh, of course. Bill even took me to see HALLOWEEN on 42nd street and thought it was amazing and absolutely horrifying. And at that point I understood what sort of horror movie this would be, with the same dark tone. I really liked Bill. He's a very smart and talented man and I think he had a vision of exactly what sort of movie MANIAC would be.

ALEXANDER: Regarding those brutally gory sequences, your character plays no part in any of that.

MUNRO: True, Anna is spared that. Though she is terrorized by Frank towards the end. But no, I didn't experience any of those special effects firsthand.

ALEXANDER: But did you witness Tom Savini at work on set?

MUNRO: I did! And I was fascinated, especially by how skillfully he could create all these elaborate things in very little time.

ALEXANDER: Do you remember the first time you saw the final feature film?

MUNRO: Yes, I saw I for the first time at the premiere, in New York. It was in a theatre with all of Bill and Joe's friends and the crew and some of the cast and some other

Munro savors the sets of director Luigi Cozzi's STARCRASH.

big stars too. And that's when the full extent of what they were up to with the spectacularly violent stuff hit me. I couldn't believe it, really.

ALEXANDER: Were you appalled?

MUNRO: No, not really, because I thought the film was very skillfully made. But I was shocked. And I wasn't surprised when it was banned in some markets. The Germans loved it but unfortunately, it was indeed banned there. It might still be banned to this day, I'm not sure...

ALEXANDER: It's a strange relationship that Frank has with Anna. It almost comes out of left field...

MUNRO: Well, maybe. We did shoot other scenes of Anna and Frank really bonding and much of that didn't end up in the final film. I think that extra footage is now considered lost, which is unfortunate.

ALEXANDER: Do you think Frank and Anna were having a courtship? How would you define their connection?

MUNRO: I've always just thought of them as friends, just very good friends. I'm not convinced that they had a romantic or sexual interest or connection on either end but rather I think Anna brought out the best in Frank. I've always wondered if maybe Anna was more interested in women. But that wasn't in the script, of course, just my interpretation of the character.

ALEXANDER: Speaking of women, there was a very well publicized push back against the film, with some calling the film outright misogynistic. Do you remember any of that?

MUNRO: I sure do. As I say, I was happy to promote the film with Bill and Joe. I believed in them and the film. We had traveled with the film to Cannes and all throughout Europe. But when I heard about the women's groups actively protesting the film in LA, I opted not to go. Of course, I should have but I was nervous. And while I agree that the film is rather cruel to women, it is of course based — well, loosely based — on the real Son of Sam case. And Frank does kill a man in the film as well, to be fair.

ALEXANDER: So, you think Frank's bloodlust is equal opportunity...

MUNRO: Yes [*laughs*] exactly.

ALEXANDER: Now, for a film where most of the females on screen show their skin, you don't...

MUNRO: No, I don't.

ALEXANDER: And unless I missed something, you never did, in any of your pictures.

MUNRO: No, though I came close in CAPTAIN KRONOS: VAMPIRE HUNTER.

ALEXANDER: Why then, when so many of your contemporaries — especially during you Hammer run — were showing their goods, did you opt to keep yourself under wraps?

MUNRO: Well, I didn't think it was necessary really. But they always tried to convince me to. I remember meeting with (DEATH WISH director) Michael Winner once. I went to his house to discuss the movie THE WICKED LADY with Faye Dunnaway. Incidentally, Michael lived beside Ray Harryhausen. Anyway, we met and he was lovely and I was going to do the picture until he told me I would have to be nude. I said, no, I don't do nudity. "But Faysie's going to be nude!" he replied, meaning Fay Dunnaway. Well, I said thank you and that I'd think about it and I left and that was that, I didn't do the film.

ALEXANDER: As an aside, Harryhausen was on one side of Michael... do you know who lived on the other side?

MUNRO: Wait... yes... I do... Jimmy Page!

ALEXANDER: Yes indeed. That's how Michael convinced Jimmy to do the soundtrack to DEATH WISH 2! Back to MANIAC, how do you ultimately see Frank? Is he a monster? Do you have empathy for the character?

MUNRO: Yes, I do. I think you're supposed to. Or at least I think you're supposed to. You're never quite sure how to feel about Frank, though, are you. There's revulsion, obviously. Maybe a bit of pity, too. He's not evil, he's deeply ill. He's a bit tragic, really.

ALEXANDER: And that was mostly if not all due to Joe's complex performance.

MUNRO: Yes. Joe was an incredible actor, extraordinary. He could just step right into being Frank in all those very torturous scenes with the mannequins and when Bill called cut, he could just pull right back out, effortlessly. And remember, he had worked with everybody at this point, all the biggest actors in Hollywood. But MANIAC gave him such room to really do what he did and create such a deep — if very damaged and dangerous — character.

THE MAN WITH THE GOLDEN ARM (1955)

Starring Frank Sinatra, Kim Novak, Elanor Parker, Darren McGavin
Written by Walter Newman, Lewis Meltzer, Ben Hecht
Directed by Otto Preminger

I remember when Darren Aronofsky was doing the press tour for his controversial and unsparing 2000 Hubert Selby Jr. adaptation REQUIEM FOR A DREAM, he correctly cited the film as a horror movie, one in which the monster was the heroin that seduced, dominated, and decimated the lives of its fragile, deluded blue-collar characters. That's kind of Selby Jr.'s beat, sifting through the streets and trying to find grace notes among the desperate, scrambling human beings who are forever lost to boredom, poverty and vice. But in Aronofsky's film, the idea of addiction is pumped up to supernatural heights, with screeching Clint Mansell music, rapid fire visuals, extreme sexual debasement and carnivorous refrigerators. Yeah, it's a horror movie alright and one that no one who has endured it ever manages to forget.

But long before Aronofsky attacked audiences with REQUIEM, director Otto Preminger broke ground with another film about a junkie perpetually trying to outsmart the drooling monkey that claws at his back, 1955's THE MAN WITH THE GOLDEN ARM, based on the novel by Nelson Algren. Starring iconic crooner and occasional actor Frank Sinatra in what is most assuredly his greatest performance, MAN is a film crawling out the sensibilities of the morally ambiguous and unofficial noir subgenre of the 1940s but bleeding into more dangerous, graphic territory, rejecting as it did the dying Production Code that had been sanctimoniously clipping Hollywood's balls since the early 1930s. But Preminger was adamant that his movie did not glamorize drugs rather it showed the smack as life-decimating parasite that, once invited into its host's life, refused to vacate until that person was dead. Preminger and distributor United Artists released the movie without the approval of the MPAA and, though their battle was hard won, their defiance was instrumental in paving the way for a new wave of American cinema that would eventually reform and dominate American cinema in the 1960s.

The movie does indeed star Sinatra as the kindly but deeply troubled Frankie Machine, a junkie card dealer from the slums of Chicago who, as the film opens (after a blistering Saul Bass-designed credits sequence with a screaming, horn-heavy Elmer Bernstein theme), has just been released from jail after taking the rap for the local card shark's after-hours and illicit gambling racket. Frankie has, with the aid of a prison doctor, kicked his all-consuming heroin habit and has even learned how to play drums while in the slammer. Back on the streets with a drum kit and dreams of a new life, free of smack and hopefully making music professionally, Frankie is almost

FRANK SINATRA · ELEANOR PARKER · KIM NOVAK
THE MAN WITH THE GOLDEN ARM
A FILM BY OTTO PREMINGER
Saul Bass
With Arnold Stang, Darren McGavin, Robert Strauss, John Conte, Doro Merande, George E. Stone, George Mathews, Leonid Kinskey, Emile Meyer, Shorty Rogers, Shelly Manne,
Screenplay by Walter Newman & Lewis Meltzer, From the novel by Nelson Algren, Music by Elmer Bernstein, Produced & Directed by Otto Preminger, Released by United Artists

Frankie (Frank Sinatra) stares longingly at his lover, Molly (Kim Novak).

immediately sucked back into the Hell that refuses to let him leave. As he drifts into the local bar to see his sweet, nickel-and-dime hustler pal Sparrow (turtle-faced comedian Arnold Stang, who famously was the voice of cartoon character Top Cat), the leering gaze of drug peddling pimp Nifty Louie (THE NIGHT STALKER's Darren McGavin in his most reptilian performance) locks on him instantly, sliming around his now healthy former customer/slave and trying to get him to "come across the street", to the flophouse where the dandy slug brings all of his willing victims.

But Frankie refuses. He wants to stay straight. To make something of himself, despite the people from way back who surround him, people he desperately wants to *leave* way back but financially, sadly, is yet unable to. But potentially worse than the lure of Nifty Louie, or the call of the seedy card dens and their offer of easy dough and quick fixes, is Frankie's toxically needy wife Zosh (Elanor Parker), a paraplegic who uses her disability and host of other ailments both real and imagined, to manipulate and control her long-suffering husband and who is especially threatened by Molly, the pretty blonde who lives downstairs. Played by future VERTIGO star Kim Novak, Molly is Frankie's angel, a woman who it is implied Frankie has had an affair with during his darker days and who clearly is deeply, profoundly in love with the man and believes in him. He loves her too and wants nothing more than to whisk her away from their shared hopeless existence. But his guilt over his wife keeps him chained to his old life and soon, when the tensions around him once more boil over, re-ignites his need for the needle. Nifty Louie moves in and obliges, jamming his poison into Frankie's vein and starting the cycle of misery all over again. And when things start to get good for Frankie and his dreams start to fall into place, the vampires of his past refuse to allow the light to shine on the man.

Filmed almost like a stage play on shadowy, wonderfully lurid, neon and filth soaked sets and brilliantly performed by the entire cast, the literate and urgent THE MAN WITH GOLDEN ARM (the title refers to Frankie's skill as a card dealer, his ambitions with the drums and his often punctured limb that serves as a cash cow for all the smack-peddlers that profit off of it) is, like REQUIEM FOR A DREAM was 45 years later, an urban horror film; a choking nightmare that paints an ugly, terrifying portrait of just how chained people can become to bad habits and bad people. This movie *feels* unhealthy and though contemporary audiences may find some of the performances too broad (McGavin's smack dealer is often almost Snidely Whiplash-esque), they have to be to serve both the story and Preminger's chosen aesthetic. Like REQUIEM, the drama is pushed past the point of good taste to help sculpt the concrete *Boschian* Hell where these sad characters dwell. And Bernstein's unyielding evil jazz music pounds it all into a frantic, queasy paste.

Sinatra's Frankie is a tragic figure but so are *all* the broken men and women who shuffle around Preminger's bleak canvas, lost as they are and desperately searching for some way out. Even Zosh, manipulative and dangerous as she is, is not evil. Nor is Nifty Louie, either. They are all just shadows on mirrors, victims of bad breeding, bad choices, and bad luck, trapped in a vicious cycle of cheap living and pointless death, none of them leaving anything resembling a legacy. Even now, after REQUIEM and so many other ruthless, horrific portraits of addiction on screen, THE MAN WITH THE GOLDEN ARM has a primal power and a message that is timeless.

MARY, MARY, BLOODY MARY (1975)

Starring Cristina Ferrare, David Young, John Carradine, Helena Rojo
Written by Don Henderson, Malcolm Marmorstein, Don Rico
Directed by Juan Lopez Moctezuma

Mexican horror filmmaker Juan Lopez Moctezuma's 1975 American co-production MARY, MARY, BLOODY MARY is a true anomaly. On one hand, it's an obvious — if somewhat late-from-the-gate — entry into the "lesbian vampire" cycle of exploitation film that reigned throughout the late 1960s and early 1970s. It certainly is kin to movies like Jess Franco's VAMPYROS LESBOS, the Hammer horror riff on Sheridan Le Fanu's 'Carmilla' THE VAMPIRE LOVERS and especially the Stephanie Rothman directed,

Mary (Cristina Ferrare) mixes pleasure with murder.

Roger Corman produced Southern California sex-vamp oddity THE VELVET VAMPIRE. And yet there's so much more going on within its meandering running time. And while it lacks the stylistic flourishes of earlier Moctezuma fever dreams like THE MANSION OF MADNESS and ALUCARDA, it is no less hypnotic and surreal, albeit in a much different, much more manic way. It often feels like a perversion of a 1970s American prime-time drama, complete with wonderfully tacky lounge music, eye-level framing and brightly lit action. Hell, even the fonts used for the opening titles feel like they're ripped right out of FANTASY ISLAND. But every time MARY, MARY, BLOODY MARY settles into some class of clean, safe, even borderline banal groove, Moctezuma steers it into absolute insanity. There are plenty of movies like it and yet... there's nothing quite like it.

The film stars Cristina Ferrare (who, incidentally, starred in an episode of FANTASY ISLAND years later) as the Mary of the title, a pretty and quite obviously disturbed bisexual artist living on the fringes of Mexico. This is apparently just the latest stop for a woman who is always on the move, trying to stay one step ahead of both the law and a black-hatted, shadowy figure (the legendary John Carradine), both who relentlessly pursue her. Why? Because Mary leaves a body count in her wake. She's a sort of vampire, a woman cursed with a disease that turns her into a killer, insatiable in her lust for human blood. Into Mary's alternately grisly and glamorous life comes a handsome American lad (David Young, NIGHTBREED) who loves the murderess unconditionally, affections she reciprocates and the likes of which deeply compromise her lethal appetites and life on the lam. And while Mary's smart enough to outfox the probing eyes of the authorities, that dreaded feral man in that giallo-inspired outfit —

who, as it happens is actually her equally vampiric father — is far harder to shake.

The plot of MARY, MARY, BLOODY MARY drapes loosely over the film, lazily propelling a series of strange, sometimes beautiful, often erotic, and occasionally deeply disturbing sequences that drift in and out of the screen like the seaside waves that Moctezuma so clearly is enamored with. Ferrare makes for an unforgettable villain/ victim; when she kills, she's savage and yet we empathize with her plight, with the struggles — both moral and physical — of her disease. No better is this dichotomy illustrated than in the stunning set-piece that sees Mary approaching a jovial fisherman whose coffee she drugs. When the previously warm and gregarious older man realizes his drink has been spiked, he tries to run, with the blade-wielding Mary clumsily chasing and slashing away at her "food". The scene goes on for some time and Moctezuma expertly jerks our emotions around, before the pair finally collapse in a bloody, sand-stained embrace. Unforgettable.

Driving this gauzy, sexually charged and bizarre blood opera is that lilting, lounge music score by composer Tom Bahler (RAW DEAL), a kind of maudlin, romantic swoon that sounds like the backtrack of a skeezy soap opera, which makes sense as Bahler's main composing credit is serving as the soundsmith for long running daytime drama GENERAL HOSPITAL. This is *not* a horror film score which — when juxtaposed against scenes of a rotting Carradine stabbing at his vampire child, or Ferrare making love to and murdering her lesbian lover, or children poking at the corpse of a real dead, beached whale — certainly creates a sense of disorientation and greasy shock. It all feels so off-kilter and wrong and that's why it works.

MARY, MARY, BLOODY MARY is kind of a messy masterpiece. The character of Mary reminds me somewhat of Marilyn Chambers' Rose in David Cronenberg's RABID, but Moctezuma's movie is a far more passionate work, a film that is as fascinated by the artistic inner life of its "monster" as it is her impulse to commit the most atrocious of acts. It's a picture that refuses or is simply unable to behave by rational horror movie rhythms. And it's maddening that more contemporary horror fans don't speak on it more.

MAXIMUM OVERDRIVE (1986)

Starring Emilio Estevez, Pat Hingle, Yeardley Smith, Laura Harrington
Written by Stephen King
Directed by Stephen King

It took Stephen King's critically drubbed MAXIMUM OVERDRIVE almost 30 years to get any sort of serious respect. The film is now rightfully considered a hubcap headed, gas

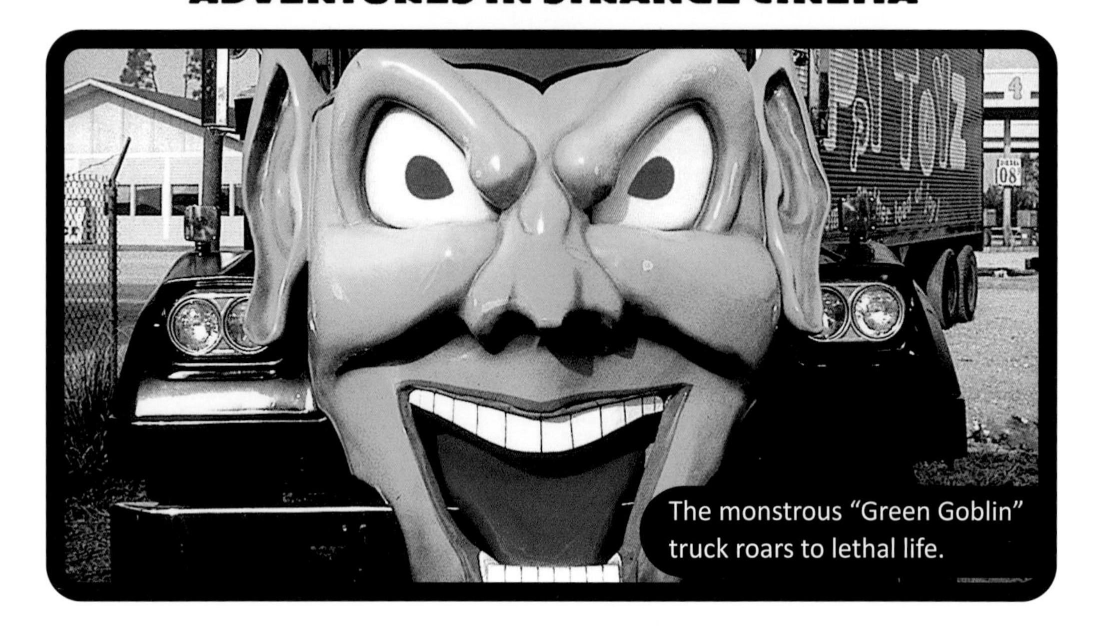

The monstrous “Green Goblin” truck roars to lethal life.

spitting 1986 sci-fi action trash classic, the first and — if you believe his publicly uttered promise since then — *only* film to be directed by one of the most influential and Important fantasy/horror fiction writers in history. It was indeed one of the worst reviewed studio pictures of its time and it for a very long time it was either ignored, reviled, or smarmily dismissed. And while the diesel-powered shocker is indeed nowhere near frightening and is a pretty odd choice for one of the major forces of literary fear to choose as his maiden directorial voyage, I think it’s a fascinating example of the working-class hero King aesthetic in full, perversely amplified effect and truly believe that there’s more going on in the picture than perhaps even its director understood.

And at the very least, the movie’s chief antagonist is a homicidal, toy tugging, ’70s semi truck with the grinning image of the goddamned Green Goblin on it. The real deal Marvel comics-sculpted, Spider-Man battling Green Goblin!

As a phantom comet circles the earth, every machine on the face of the planet begins to snap into consciousness and revolt violently against their human makers and masters. Steamrollers level little leaguers, pop machines fire off soda cans into skulls like bullets, electric steak knives hunger for blood, junkyard wrecks scream to life and monstrous rigs mow down men and women alike. As the world goes entertainingly mad, a ragtag band of shell-shocked survivors congregate at the Dixie Boy truck stop where they unplug, hole up and try to evade the increasingly angry assemblage of evil automobiles.

MAXIMUM OVERDRIVE is based on King’s truly eerie early period short story ‘Trucks’ which most famously appeared in his bestselling 1978 collection *Night Shift*. I remember sifting through my dad's paperback when I was seven, you know, the one with the eyeball riddled bandaged hand on the cover (an image culled from the story 'I Am The Doorway') and, while not as devastating as the 'Graveyard Shift', 'Grey Matter' or 'One For The Road' tales, 'Trucks' still got me good, especially the final, ominous airplane-gazing line. So, it's a real head scratcher why the universally adored author opted to turn that shivery tale into a testosterone fueled redneck action picture instead of a straight-up genre piece. Many critics in 1986 were asking the same question and, needless to say, MAXIMUM OVERDRIVE was chewed up and spat out like so many Truckasaurus hors d'oeuvre. Even Dino De Laurentiis' late widow (Dino produced and distributed the film, the same year he gave the world BLUE VELVET), producer Martha De Laurentiis, who also had a hand in making the movie, rolled her eyes when I met her at a party and poked her for details about it.

And while some of the maligning is merited, only a fool would dismiss the film as flat out bad. It has far too much personality for that. Because no matter what your take on this trashy classic, if you know King's universe, you'll recognize that the people that populate MAXIMUM OVERDRIVE are vintage King creations. We have our reluctant hero, the recently paroled short order truck stop cook (here played by a scrappy Emilio Estevez) who's just trying to live a square life. There's his fat, greasy, abusive boss (Pat Hingle) who exploits him and threatens to send him packing back to prison if he gets out of line. The spunky female hitchhiker (Laura Harrington) who's both sexy and razor sharp under pressure. And there's that cloistered King small-town aesthetic, like Norman Rockwell by way of Alfred Hitchcock, that permeates almost every inch of his body of scribblings.

And then there's the trucks.

King would later expand the ideas explored in 'Trucks' and shrink their scope in CHRISTINE, itself adapted for the screen by John Carpenter in 1983. When it came time to turn 'Trucks' into MAXIMUM OVERDRIVE, King exploited the visual sting of seeing mighty machines marauding and murdering with nary a driver in sight to well, maximum, effect. From the opening bridge massacre sequence, MAXIMUM OVERDRIVE is a full out orgy of smashed windshields, crunching metal, spinning wheels, blaring horns and splattery human remains. He really went for it and its grand fun to see chrome crushing people ad nauseum, all cut to the endless strains of Aussie rockers AC/DC. The band were a favorite of King's and he commissioned them to both write the blaring score for MAXIMUM OVERDRIVE and lend some of their back catalog classics to the fold as well and man alive, does their evil brand of trucker metal jack this picture *up, up, up*! Seeing the Green Goblin faced semi roaring down the streets during the opening credits while the tune Who Made Who pounds away in the background is damn near poetic.

MAXIMUM OVERDRIVE is not an art film. It's not meant to be taken seriously. It's not even a horror film really. But King has claimed he wanted to make a junk food movie of the highest order and baby, he succeeded smashingly, maybe in part because he was, by his own admission in a state of coked-out oblivion. These many years later, maximum overdrive still has the same brutal, trashy, primal, violent power that pulses away in the background of all the author's works. And even if King fails to make good on the "scaring the hell out of you" promise he vows in the trailer, his film is loud, rough, funny, silly, obnoxious, and just plain powerful white trash terror at its redneck best.

THE MONSTER CLUB (1980)

Starring Vincent Price, John Carradine, Donald Pleasence, Stuart Whitman
Written by Edward Abraham, Valerie Abraham
Directed by Roy Ward Baker

When Roy Ward Baker's bizarre, scary and charming 1981 horror anthology THE MONSTER CLUB came out, the sort of thrills it was peddling were old hat. After THE EXORCIST, THE TEXAS CHAIN SAW MASSACRE, HALLOWEEN and FRIDAY THE 13th, younger horror fans wanted no part of their father's horror movies and actors like Vincent Price and John Carradine just didn't speak to that generation's hunger for violence, sex and more visceral and nihilistic entertainments. Because of that, THE MONSTER CLUB was a box office dud and critics weren't kind. But, like with most out-of-step horror pictures, time has been good to THE MONSTER CLUB and a viewing today is almost certain to rock your world.

THE MONSTER CLUB was produced by British mogul Milton Subotsky, one half of the team behind England's Amicus Productions, the scrappier answer to Hammer films that specialized in all-star anthology shockers, films like DR. TERROR'S HOUSE OF HORRORS, TALES FROM THE CRYPT, THE VAULT OF HORROR and ASYLUM. And while THE MONSTER CLUB is technically not an Amicus movie, it feels like one. Baker of course helmed both ASYLUM and THE VAULT OF HORROR and the three stories the film adapts were penned by noted genre author R. Chetwynd-Hayes, who wrote Amicus' FROM BEYOND THE GRAVE. And of course, there's a wealth of British talent in front of the lens, including Amicus regulars Donald Pleasence and Patrick Magee. The big difference here is that THE MONSTER CLUB, in its wraparound segments, tries very hard to be contemporary, shoehorning in British pop music and disco and weird musical numbers that must have seemed tacky and out of touch in 1981. But today they're all kinds of awesome.

John Carradine's author meets Eramus (Vincent Price), his biggest fan, in THE MONSTER CLUB.

Carradine plays a character named R. Chetwynd-Hayes who, like his namesake, is a famous author of horror novels and who is attacked one evening by an ancient vampire named Eramus (Price). Eramus takes only a taste of the scribe's blood — he is after all, his number one fan — and, as a mea culpa, takes him to his local haunt, the after-hours, monster only hotspot of the title. There, while all manner of weird new wave and rock music blares in background and goofily dressed extras shake their supernatural asses, Eramus schools the author on the various kinds of monsters, pure and crossbred, that exist on the fringes of the planet. Helpfully, he even has a handy flowchart.

After this amusing and intentionally silly bit of wonderful hokum, Eramus introduces the first tale, that of 'The Shadmock'. In it, a couple of grifters (Simon Ward and Barbara Kellerman) plot their next hustle, with Kellerman answering the call to be a housekeeper at a looming manor owned by a gentle recluse (James Laurenson). Initially repulsed by the man (he looks like a pasty riff on legendary horror host Zacherle, who in turn looked like Lon Chaney in THE PHANTOM OF THE OPERA), she sticks around in hopes of ripping the poor fiend off. Problem is, the gent is actually a Shadmock, a monster who can kill and maim by whistling (shades of the 1978 movie THE SHOUT). After Kellerman agrees to marry the man, he throws a party in her honor and invites his eerily masked relatives. And then things get scary. This is a fine, disturbing tragedy and Laurenson sells it with his sympathetic portrayal and the final scene is rather disturbing. As a kid, years before I saw the film, I had a comic book reprinting some John Bolton drawn comic adaptation from this film and others and 'The Shadmock' was in there. It scared the hell out of me then and the film itself is almost as jittery.

Next up is "The Vampires," a goofy but atmospheric and delightful tale about a vampire patriarch (ZOMBIE's Richard Johnson) and his loving wife (the gorgeous Brit Ekland, she of WHAT THE PEEPER SAW and THE WICKER MAN) and their poor little boy, who is bullied daily. The kid is befriended by a kindly vicar (Pleasence, clearly having a blast) who offers to walk the lad home. Thing is, Pleasence is actually the head of a secret cabal of vampire killers assigned to murder the boy's undead pop. Once they break into the basement crypt to do just that, much silliness ensues. But unlike some of the camp in Baker's THE VAULT OF HORROR, this segment is long, eccentric and beautifully produced with some great Eastern European-tinted music and a warm, sweet final sting. Not scary, but a total delight.

The final story, "The Ghouls," is not only the scariest tale of the lot, but also one of the creepiest damned things I've seen in any British horror movie and I would love to see just this story get a feature remake. In it, Stuart Whitman plays a hot-shit American director who ventures into the British countryside to scout locations and winds up in a ruined abbey, where he meets the always spooky looking Patrick Magee. Magee is the leader of a group of ashen, leering creeps dressed in filthy robes and with murder on their minds. They overtake Whitman and imprison him in a locked room where he is brought food by Magee's daughter. She informs the terrified filmmaker that she is a "humgoo," born of human and ghoul and that her "family" are a species of ghouls that invaded the village, mated with the women and ate the men and then proceeded to eat the dead. In a nightmarish animated sequence, we see this gruesome history unspool, with the girl explaining that they get their wood and food from the "boxes" in the ground and now... there's no more boxes in the ground. I won't say more about this story but honestly, it's one of the most unsettling little slices of shock to seep out of the Amicus cannon.

There's so much to adore about THE MONSTER CLUB. Baker was often a restrained director who always seemed a bit too "classy" for some of Hammer's more lurid material (THE VAMPIRE LOVERS and THE LEGEND OF THE SEVEN GOLDEN VAMPIRES, for example) but he really goes for it here, having fun with the giddy framing material and really letting loose with the stories themselves. He's aided by a superlative cast, handsome production values, great Chetwynd-Hayes source material (though apparently the author wasn't very pleased with the film) and an amazing musical score by Amicus regular Douglas Gamley with John Williams (not *that* John Williams) on acoustic guitar (the same John Williams also played the haunting "Cavatina" piece from THE DEER HUNTER). Said score is lovely when in symphonic mode and horrifying when it veers into pure electronic evil, as in "The Ghouls" story.

Released by various entities in all formats all over the world for years, THE MONSTER CLUB is a very easy film to find. So, find it already.

MOON OF THE WOLF (1972)

Starring David Janssen, Bradford Dillman, Barbara Rush, Royal Dano
Written by Leslie H. Whitten, Alvin Sapinsley
Directed by Daniel Petrie

After Dan Curtis changed launched an American pop culture phenomenon with his dark, Gothic daytime TV series and quasi-soap opera DARK SHADOWS in 1966, there was a sudden spike in interest for small-screen horror that rolled on strong for over a decade. And while it was Curtis who made the most potent post-Shadows mark with his terrifying and visionary TV terror films like DRACULA, THE NIGHT STALKER, THE NORLISS TAPES and TRILOGY OF TERROR, many other savvy producers also jumped on the spooky bandwagon, delivering gritty, star-studded, and serious-in-tone movie-of-the-week shockers that oozed atmosphere, mystery and menace. And while never intended to be high art, seen from the distance of time, the '70s TV horror movie is a genre entertainment like no other, one that used the same post-code Hollywood approach of showing and exploring darker

Moon of the Wolf
Starring
DAVID JANSSEN
BARBARA RUSH · BRAFORD DILLMAN · JOHN BERADINO ·
Executive Produser EDVARD FELDMAN ·
Screenplay ALVIN SAPINSLEY · Directed by DANIEL PETRIE ·
Produced by EVERETT CHAMBERS and PETER THOMAS ·

themes in creative ways without revealing too much and upsetting the sponsors, to elegant effect.

Among those incredible TV-tailored horror gems sits director Daniel Petrie's MOON OF THE WOLF, a tight and eerie southern gothic creeper with an ace cast, a fun and engaging central mystery and compact, crackerjack storytelling. Originally broadcast on ABC on September 26, 1972, the film was repeated *ad nauseum* on prime-time and then, eventually, late night, post-11pm news screenings, the latter which has made it a fan favorite. Long lapsed into the public domain, MOON OF THE WOLF is an easy picture to find and watch (tip: it's on YouTube and every other free streaming service) and because of its easy accessibility, it's rarely remembered as a good film, if it's remembered at all. It certainly needs more love.

MOON OF THE WOLF (reportedly faithfully adapted from the Leslie H, Whitten novel) stars THE FUGITIVE himself, David Janssen as Sheriff Whitaker, a no-nonsense Louisiana lawman who prowls the Bayou righting wrongs. When a girl is found in the swamp with her head bashed in, Whitaker becomes involved, sifting through a rogues gallery of sketchy locales (including SALEM'S LOT's Geoffrey Lewis) and eyeballing ultra-rich tycoon Andrew Rodanthe (played by genre veteran and BUG star Bradford Dillman). Meanwhile, the victim's father (Paul R. DeVille) spends his days in a daze and babbles in French, warning of the horror of the "loo-ka-roo".

And while Whitaker is initially confounded as to the meaning of old man's blathering, after more and more locals get murdered and torn to shreds, he soon realizes that "loo-ka-roo" is actually "loup garou" — that's French for... *werewolf!*

Blending a swampy, lurid Gothic melodrama with a traditional, Universal Pictures-esque horror/tragedy, MOON OF THE WOLF is a terrific little film. Outside of the reliable presences of the solid leads, MESSIAH OF EVIL and HOUSE II's legendary character actor Royal Dano also shows up and does what he does best; the sense of mist-soaked, sweaty location is palpable, and the entire thing is gelled together by an intense, moody score by pianist and composer Bernardo Segall. And at 75 minutes, the movie just breezes by, interrupted only by comforting fade-ins and outs where the original commercial breaks were scheduled to be. And of special note is the classy, retro-looking werewolf makeup designs, helmed by none other than William Tuttle, the veteran artist who was responsible for virtually all the creatures and mutants in TV's THE TWILIGHT ZONE.

MOON OF THE WOLF is in no way a "so bad its good" film as some sniggering critics have dismissed it as. It's a good film, period. And oddly, with its central mystery and suggestion that lycanthropy is hereditary, there are some links — accidental or otherwise — to Joe Johnston's remake of THE WOLFMAN. Give this one a spin, late at night. It's a piece of a larger cinematic puzzle from a less complicated time that this writer misses dearly.

Grace (Jennifer Lawrence) braces herself for chaos in the harrowing MOTHER!

MOTHER! (2017)

Starring Jennifer Lawrence, Javier Bardem, Ed Harris, Michelle Pfieffer
Written by Darren Aronofsky
Directed by Darren Aronofsky

In 2006 maverick director Darren Aronofsky released his metaphysical, messy and absolutely spellbinding allegorical science fiction drama THE FOUNTAIN and it was met with polarizing response. I remember seeing it opening night. With its hypnotic, majestic Mogwai and Clint Mansell score (which has been imitated to death by other composers ever since), alarming visuals (sculpted by squirting various liquids into other liquids), challenging structure, bizarre allusions to Eastern religion, philosophies, Catholicism, time travel, Aztec quests and space yoga and the concept of the female as earth mother and eternal muse, more than half the audience found it laughable. Because when people are amongst other people watching cinema, many of them simply look around to see what the others are doing, how they're responding. And they — sadly — respond in kind. The magic of cinema is group think. That can be wonderful, with audiences sharing an experience like a hive and feeding off each others energy. But in the case of motion pictures like THE FOUNTAIN it can be catastrophic. Met with generally negative reviews and public bewilderment, this daring film was left to be loved only by a handful. I was among that handful that was utterly leveled by it. I still am in awe of it and obsessed by it. It's not just a movie it's an experience unlike anything else.

Today, THE FOUNTAIN is a "cult" film. Meaning that, once the smoke cleared and people started catching this so-called "bad" film on their own, in the quiet of their homes, late at night, devoid of the zeitgeist and void of any expectations or colleague distractions, they *saw* it. I mean, *really saw it*. Because THE FOUNTAIN is really a horror movie about refusing to accept death, about having to take the journey we all do when met with the impossible reality of losing someone we love. That loss of control. And then, coming to the realization that we're also on this same path to dust, no matter how much we know, or how much we resist. And accepting that. That Aronofsky cloaks his simple story in fantastical, impossible visuals and meandering passages of beauty, symbolism and savagery is him just employing the cinematic language he always uses. He did it in REQUIEM FOR A DREAM, which is a vampire film where the heroin is the parasite, filled with nightmare-fuel visuals but pulsing with a quiet tragedy about hopeless people addicted to hope. He did it in BLACK SWAN, which uses the arts as a malevolent force that decays, erodes and transforms for both the better and worse but is really just a film about a young woman coming of age and rebelling.

And the same can be said about his maniacal 2017 masterwork MOTHER!, a movie that is a cousin to THE FOUNTAIN and, like that picture, likely requires multiple viewings but even more intricately hides its simple meanings within its disorienting narrative, grandiose symbolism and distracting visual palette. Unlike THE FOUNTAIN, however, which was beautiful, MOTHER! is ugly. It's hideous. Freakish. It drags you into a Boschian Hell filled with braying human-monsters and ludicrous behaviors and it keeps pushing itself further and further into the ether, defying to watch it or rather, to endure it. And you do have to endure MOTHER! It doesn't want you to love it or even like it. It wants to hurt you. It does this with humor of course and it reminded me plenty of the work of Luis Buñuel, who used absurdity in films like THE EXTERMINATING ANGEL to make us laugh uncomfortably at the sheer shrill madness of what we're watching while its maker exploits those moments of giddy weakness to push his dark agenda inside our chests, like the mystical rock that Javier Bardem's oblivious poet Eli pulls out of his defeated wife Grace (Jennifer Lawrence).

MOTHER! has been marketed as a horror movie and it most assuredly is. It's also simultaneously an extended middle finger to the very notion of genre in any conventional sense. The point of this rant is to cite it as such and to — as the headline suggests — mark it as the best and most important horror film of the year. We're not going to get into the plot mechanics of the movie. What I will say is that it's the most polarizing film I've ever seen in a theater, with people yelling at the screen, storming out of the cinema, sitting in shock when the lights flip up and checking their phones to read other critical takes. It's confrontational and it hates its audience and hates itself. It wants to hurt you and it does, not with explicit gore or sex or idiot plot contrivances or even music. Because there essentially IS no score. No, this is another beast entirely.

Javier Bardem's "Him" is consumed by the crowd.

It's a work of the darkest and wildest art.

But what is MOTHER!? Is it an allegory of biblical creation with — as many, including Aronofsky, have alluded — Michelle Pfieffer and Ed Harris' doubtful guests representing Adam and Eve and Bardem and Lawrence's country home the newly formed earth? Are the screaming crowds that overrun the home suggestive of the way we as a mass-multiplying people savage the earth and decimate the simple "grace" and beauty of what is our nurturing home? Is it a slam on our rabid and ever-swelling need to elevate false gods? Is it a mutation of ROSEMARY'S BABY with Lawrence's unstable pregnant wife at the mercy of Satanic forces?

It's all these things and Aronofsky uses the metaphor of the house as a living, breathing organic force of creation and destruction as a multi-tier metaphor. But I think what makes MOTHER! such a magnificent and corrosive horror film is that really, it's a savage portrait of the filmmaker himself. A confessional of an artist and an indictment of the creative process and how the creator becomes a killer.

In MOTHER! Bardem's supernaturally self-centered poet is so blind to the gifts he has, of love, of beauty and truth. He must seek that truth elsewhere. He needs to feed from it from the public. And as he revels in the illusion of love, as he invites more and more strangers and pretenders into his life, real love withers and suffers and eventually burns. And when his life becomes ash, he simply resets the machine. He vows to do it "right" the next time while not apologizing for "what he is". And start it again he does. And the cycle repeats. Again. And again. And again.

A simple, sad poem to failed marriage maybe? To the destructive nature of art and the folly of the artist? If smack was the monster in REQUIEM FOR A DREAM, the very act of creation — cosmically or intimately — is the monster in MOTHER! This is the most dread-drenched, anxiety-inducing, and difficult to endure movie ever. MOTHER! is singular. Epic. Personal. You don't get your pals together, go for drinks and watch MOTHER! It should be seen alone. Then you go find others who have seen it. And you scream and debate.

MOTHER, MAY I SLEEP WITH DANGER? (2016)

Starring Leila George, Emily Meade, Tori Spelling, James Franco
Written by Amber Coney, James Franco
Directed by Melanie Aitkenhead

I have a rather nagging fixation on tawdry, leering, Lifetime movies; those television trash films that have long been pumped out of the once noble network to titillate audiences hungry for low-rent thrills. And there's nothing wrong with this. And if there IS something wrong with this... well, I don't give a flying fuck.

Apologies for the profanity, but I'm employing it to illustrate a point. Using the "F" word is infinitely more graphic than the stuff you see in Lifetime movies. These are most assuredly exploitation films, filled with sexual deviancy, murder and all manner of lurid transgression. And yet none of this sensationalism strays beyond the level of PG.

And that's the appeal.

When the Hays office slammed down on Hollywood, enforcing the puritanical Production Code in the early 1930s, filmmakers and studios had to hide all their dirty stuff and scenes of potentially offensive material lest they get their movie yanked from theaters. But as we all know, when we bury base impulses, they just get perverted and leak out in weird ways and part of the joy of '30s and '40s cinema is the fact that producers and directors invented clever ways to push unsavory aspects of their stories but sneak them through the back door, weaving them into the narrative using allusions, suggestions, body language and double *entendres*. And of course, that just made audiences feel even filthier, becoming willing accomplices working hard to read between the lines to win their kinky reward.

And so it goes with TV movies and in this case, Lifetime movies. The first wave "golden age" of tawdry small-screen melodrama cinema surged in the 1970s, with a glut of "women in jeopardy" thrillers that featured strong women characters as their heroines, a blatant attempt to lock their target demographic of female consumers.

STORY BY JAMES FRANCO
MOTHER, MAY I
SLEEP WITH DANGER
Lifetime

The seemingly endless spate of similarly constructed films made for the Lifetime Network are the heirs to that dynasty, with films often based on either pulp books or headline-ripped true crime tales and starring actors young and old that are either on the professional ascent or decline. Among the hundreds strong in the Lifetime cannon sits 1996's MOTHER, MAY I SLEEP WITH DANGER? starring BEVERLY HILLS 90210 actress Tori Spelling (the daughter of TV tycoon Aaron Spelling, who himself produced dozens of those original 70s TV movies) as a girl who falls in love with a manipulative, murderous young man (Ivan Sergei) whose psychosis almost signals her death knell.

Twenty years later, Lifetime released a remake of that highly rated tabloid trash gem. Sort of. The in-name successor once more stars Spelling, this time as the single mother of a teenage girl (Leila George) who in this case doesn't fall prey to a brutal bad dude, rather she starts up a lesbian affair with a teenage Goth vampire (Emily Meade)! That's right: a remake of a trash TV movie that doubles as a trash TV horror sexploitation movie! Yow! And the kicker? It's produced and co-written by Hollywood multi-hyphenate actor/director/eccentric James Franco!

How? Why? Well, I have a theory. Read on...

Back in 2012 I conducted an interview with Franco, the purpose of which was to talk about his hyper-violent Cormac McCarthy shocker CHILD OF GOD for the magazine I was editing at the time, *Fangoria* and honestly, it was a fantastic conversation. I found Franco intelligent, friendly, serious-minded yet self-deprecating and dedicated to pouring his energy into making as much art in as many mediums as humanly possible. I eventually turned the *tete-a-tete* to mention one of my heroes, Jess Franco and asked if James had heard of his surname namesake, who I mentioned he also shared a restless creative spirit with. He had not heard of Jess Franco, but when I mentioned he was well-known for a string of lesbian vampire movies lensed in the '60s and '70s, he was amused and interested and wrote down titles and promised to investigate.

So, allow me to claim — or imagine — some responsibility for the fact that director Melanie Aitkenhead's redux of MOTHER, MAY I SLEEP WITH DANGER? even exists! I like to think that Franco did heed my words and either investigated the work of the notorious Spanish director or at least jumped at the opportunity to make a similar film. And making it for a network known for their covert perversion masquerading as socially relevant entertainment is a streak of bratty, transgressive genius. At least I think it is.

Is MOTHER, MAY I SLEEP WITH DANGER? any good? Well, yes and no. It's well acted and moves fast and is silly and surprisingly bloody and compelling throughout. It's not scary. It's not particularly artistically interesting. It's kind of tacky. It's a Lifetime movie, through and through. But it's also the only lesbian vampire Lifetime movie and it's the only James Franco-produced lesbian vampire Lifetime movie and it's the only James Franco co-starring lesbian vampire Lifetime movie and it's the very fact that Franco made it simply because he *could* that gives it such an almost punk rock feel. And yet it's oddly reverent to its source. It's probably the most unnecessary and unwanted remake in film history and yet Franco plays it straight (ahem) and respectful with the re-casting of Spelling (who, whatever you think of her, commits sincerely to the role) and even the original's Sergei as a vampire obsessed college professor. It's a callback to fans of the first film (all three of them) and it's an admirable and commendably weird conceit.

MOTHER, MAY I SLEEP WITH DANGER? is truly an arcane treasure for deep-drawer lovers of pop culture junk. And as for Franco (who chased this thing with his acclaimed and award-winning THE ROOM docudrama THE DISASTER ARTIST), love him or hate him (and I know many who subscribe faithfully to both camps), who else is like him?

INTERVIEW: JAMES IHA

I'll admit, I'm not a big Smashing Pumpkins fan. But I am a fan of artists taking weird risks and certainly, iconic guitarist and founding Pumpkins member James Iha ending up making music for an oddball movie-of-the-week, is as awesomely weird a risk as an artist of his stature could take. But as the entire MOTHER, MAY I SLEEP WITH DANGER? project was a bit of perverse sidestep, it strangely all makes perfect sense. And the fact that the movie gave Iha carte blanche to create a wild, pulsing and almost experimental electro-rock soundtrack was reason enough for me to reach out to him and have a conversation. I haven't spoken to James since this interview, and I'm not sure if our paths will ever cross again. They don't have to. It took a tawdry bit of high concept TV trash and a telephone chat for me become an admirer and that's cool in and of itself...

CHRIS ALEXANDER: Listening to your theme for MOTHER MAY I SLEEP WITH DANGER?, I detect trace elements of Goblin's theme from Dario Argento's SUSPIRIA. Am I hallucinating?

IHA: Hmmm... that's interesting. Well, there are whispered female vocals in it, but the main thing in the Goblin track is that eerie arpeggio, that's a different thing that my theme. I wasn't thinking of that but that's a very cool track and comparison. Mine does share the same kind of vocal thing, though, yes.

ALEXANDER: The vocal you're talking about... is she saying actual words or are you just using her voice as an instrument?

IHA: She's saying "come to me, come to me now" [*laughs*]. I don't know why, but when I watched the opening scene you just see this evil girl whose dressed all bad ass... I don't know, I just wanted to convey simply that the vampires are coming [*laughs*].

ALEXANDER: So, I mentioned Goblin and you knew what I was talking about, which is cool.

James Iha took a break from crushing gourds to sculpt an eerie soundscape.

IHA: Well, just as an aside, you know when I heard that Goblin track recently? I was watching the Olympics and, I don't know how many years ago this was, but there were synchronized swimmers, from Russia I think and there was a headline in the *New York Times* the next day and it was something like "Creepy Dolls Win Swimming" or something like that. And I was like, what is that? So, I read it. I had heard that theme before, but I remember thinking how cool that was that it showed up there!

ALEXANDER: I live for finding cool things in weird places. And discovering that the two James' were collaborating on a Lifetime lesbian vampire movie was certainly weird and cool.

IHA: Yeah.

ALEXANDER: How exactly did this happen?

IHA: I can't speak for James Franco, but I can imagine they were looking for something different when they wanted him to re-imagine MOTHER, MAY I SLEEP WITH DANGER? I think I was on the list of composers that was put together. There was a link to some of my score music from DEADBEAT and other indie films I did, maybe it was my past with the Pumpkins and other bands, I don't know. I think they just thought it would be an interesting idea to have me do it. I was surprised watching it. There's lesbians and vampires people getting killed. It's much different than what the Lifetime crowd goes for. I just hope my score heightens the darkness of the film.

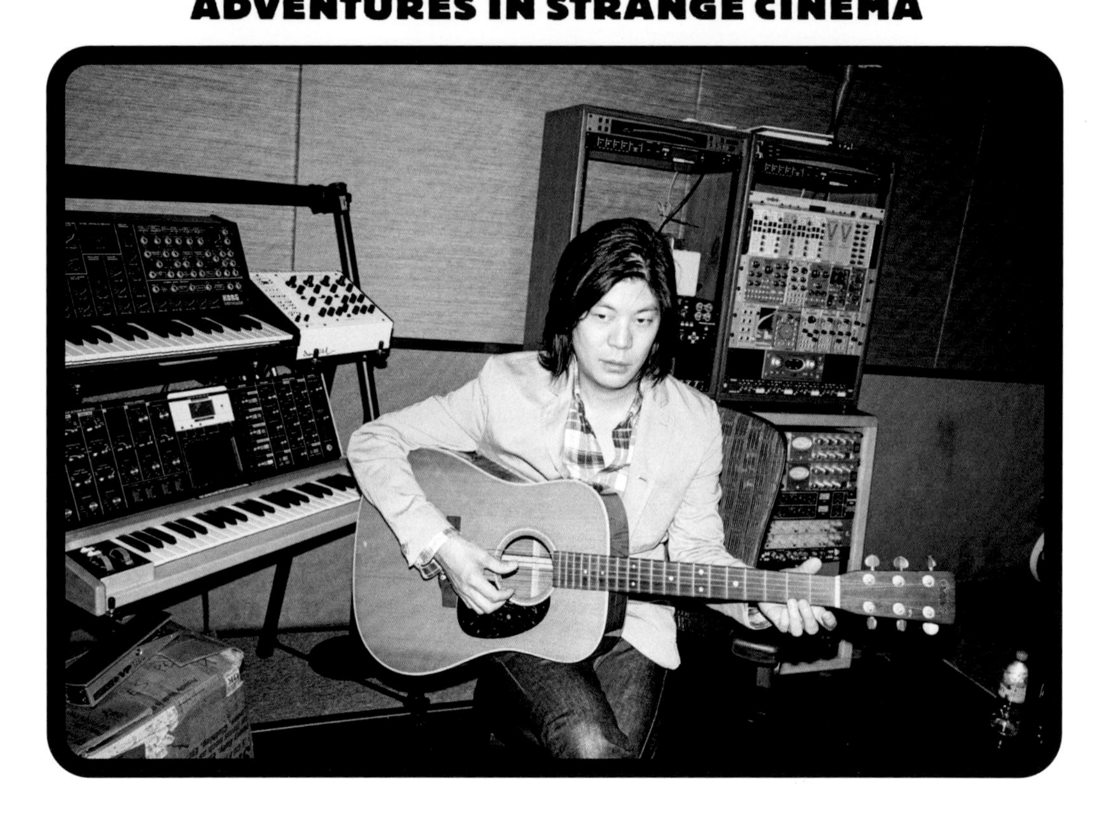

ALEXANDER: When I heard you were doing the score, I presumed it might be a guitar-based work, like Neil Young's music for DEAD MAN or Howard Shore's CRASH score. But it's not at all. Was all the instrumentation done by you?

IHA: Yeah, it was all me, but a friend named Claire Acey did the vocals; everything else I did. Unless there's something specialized I need, I try to do everything myself. The opening theme is big rock drums, bass guitar, no heavy metal six-string guitar, just bass; there's these ambient sounds, evil vocals. So that was one theme. There is another theme that is sort of softer; I used glitch drum machine beats and '80s synth and soft vocals, ethereal vocals and guitar lines. Another theme is score based with violins and piano and more classic heavy horror instrumentation.

ALEXANDER: Will there ever be a stand-alone soundtrack released?

IHA: I hope so. I think it would make a great score record if it was put together, yeah.

ALEXANDER: Is it more liberating to compose for film, rather than be slave to the confines of composing a pop song?

IHA: I think besides the director or the studio weighing in on the direction of the music, apart from that it's a blast to make music that way and not approach it from a verse-chorus, verse-chorus way. It's music for pictures sake and that uses a different side of my brain entirely.

MUTANT (1984)

Starring Wings Hauser, Bo Hopkins, Jody Medford, Lee Montgomery
Written by Peter Z. Orton, Michael Jones, John C. Kruize
Directed by John "Bud" Cardos

The dawn of the 1980s saw more than its share of eco-minded, human monster movies, a subgenre spawned most likely by the one-two-punch of George A. Romero's ghoul virus 1978 masterpiece DAWN OF THE DEAD and James Bridges shattering (and hugely successful) 1979 thriller THE CHINA SYNDROME. Films like director Graham Baker's Meg Tilly and Tim Matheson vs. Freudian-zombie vehicle IMPULSE (itself somewhat reminiscent of David Cronenberg's 1975 breakthrough exploitation film SHIVERS) and Hal Barwood's underrated 1985 toxic-zombie chiller WARNING SIGN; movies that mixed corporate cover-ups with sacrificial small-town paranoia, usually dealing with some sort of spill that mutates average people, causing them to do terrible things to any non-infected person within biting distance.

One of the best of this lot is KINGDOM OF THE SPIDERS director John Bud Cardos' lean and mean horror gem NIGHT SHADOWS, widely released on home video and cable in the '80s as MUTANT, a title it retains to this day.

It's a shame its distributor decided to slap that moniker on such an eerie, urgent and earthy horror film; MUTANT is the alternate title for Roger Corman's ALIEN nod FORBIDDEN WORLD and the packaging for Cardos' film had that handle displayed in widely spaced letters a la ALIEN, and even featured a Giger-like fanged face on the front. In some European markets it was even released as MUTANT II.

Those looking for a deep space shocker in line with Ridley Scott, were bound to be bummed.

MUTANT does have a dose of science fiction at its core, but it's the maddest kind of science, spawned by mankind, not the stars. Rather, the movie is an atmospheric, unpretentious down-home horror flick that, more often than not, feels like meth-fueled remake of Tobe Hooper's 1979 TV miniseries adaptation of Stephen King's SALEM'S LOT.

In it, Wings Hauser (fresh of his turn as the psychotic pimp Ramrod in Gary Sherman's brutal 1982 shocker VICE SQUAD) and Lee Montgomery (so terrifying as "Bobby" in the Dan Curtis anthology DEAD OF NIGHT and equally good in the Curtis classic BURNT OFFERINGS) as brothers driving cross-country, big bro trying to help little bro get over a broken heart and a love lost. As the two banter and the audience begins to warm to them (great casting in that not only do Hauser and Montgomery have genuine chemistry, they also kind of look-alike), a truckload of cackling local yokel rednecks taunt them and run them into a ditch. Their car wrecked, the pair hitch

A blood-starved wraith creeps up on Holly (Judy Medford) in MUTANT.

a ride with an equally inbred, but considerably kinder, hick named Mel (Stuart Culpepper) who offers to drive them into town so they can call a tow-truck and get back to the business of road-tripping.

Shame then, that the town in question seems to be in the mid-stage grip of some sort of malevolent viral outbreak. After tangling with the same shit-faced goons that kiboshed their car, the brothers check into a seemingly cozy inn for a much-needed nights sleep. But when Montgomery goes missing, Hauser goes into overdrive to find his kin. What he finds instead is a shadowy conspiracy, a drunken but kindly Sheriff (TENTACLES' Bo Hopkins, who later re-teamed with Hauser for Nico Mastorakis' similarly themed NIGHTMARE AT NOON), a comely and confused schoolteacher (Jody Medford) and a bloodthirsty horde of chemically induced zombie vampires whose very touch spreads disease.

MUTANT is often slapped with the dreaded and cowardly "guilty pleasure" label, but I have no idea why anyone would or should feel sheepish about loving it. It's positively loaded with fog-drenched atmosphere, quality prosthetic makeup FX (the ghouls drink blood from puss-dripping, vaginal openings in their hands, an affectation that recalls yet another early Cronenberg bio-horror, that of 1977's RABID), a brisk pace, fine acting by Hauser and Hopkins, an unpredictable and often shocking streak of nihilism (yes, even little kids die screaming!) and, perhaps most importantly, an absolutely first rate, full-bodied and full-blooded symphonic score by Richard Band, one of his few non-Empire or Full Moon projects.

Director Cardos was no fool either. He was a true eccentric, and always inserted wry humor into his horror films. Look at 1969's deft and little discussed Cameron Mitchell melodrama NIGHTMARE IN WAX, a lurid film with a deranged strain of wit. And KINGDOM OF THE SPIDERS delights in not only dousing Arizona in spider-webs but also spreading a colorful array of oddball characters across the screen. He works the same magic here and much of MUTANT's power lies in the charming, meandering way he lets his actors play with their roles and simply sit around and have conversations; almost every relationship in the movie takes time to flesh itself out, an invaluable asset when making the many scenes of horror work. When our heroes are menaced by the shrieking, bladder-bloated and blue-faced undead, we fear for them, even when — as in one seen where the local doctor casually talks to her assistant while he mutates, mimicking the symptoms she's speaking of — we're stifling a giggle.

The movie was produced by distributor Edward L. Montoro, who with his now defunct imprint Film Ventures International released such quality crap as William Girdler's DAY OF THE ANIMALS and GRIZZLY; he also produced the 1979 Cardos vehicle THE DARK, whose modest success likely led to the hiring of the director here. However, MUTANT cost far more than it earned, and its failure caused Montoro to literally flee to Mexico, never to be heard from again.

The fugitive producer should have stayed home, faced the music, and defended his baby because MUTANT needs more love. It really does feel like an unwanted child, cast out and abandoned. So sad…

But like so many unwanted children defying their fates, MUTANT has, over time, brushed itself off and survived, standing tall among the more successful, but now utterly forgettable, films it once competed for screen time with. It's earned its place in horror history.

MY STEPMOTHER IS AN ALIEN (1988)

Starring Kim Basinger, Dan Aykroyd, Alyson Hannigan, Seth Green, Jon Lovitz
Written by Jerico Stone, Herschel Weingrod, Timothy Harris
Directed by Richard Benjamin

Richard Benjamin is a man who has led many lives. During his first incarnation as an actor, Benjamin — along with his wife, actor Paula Prentiss — starred in the groundbreaking television sitcom HE & SHE and then appeared in such revered socially relevant films as GOODBYE COLUMBUS and DIARY OF A MAD HOUSEWIFE. In 1973, Benjamin was cast as the hero in Michael Crichton's hugely successful, darkly

Celeste (Kim Basinger) tries her hand at baking while "Bag" looks on.

humorous sci-fi shocker WESTWORLD, a film that saw him square-off against a homicidal gunslinging robot played by Yul Brenner. Later in the decade, he played a disciple of Van Helsing who goes up against George Hamilton's inept Dracula in the riotous 1979 comedy LOVE AT FIRST BITE and then, in 1981 teamed again with Prentiss to star in Roger and Julie Corman's horror spoof SATURDAY THE 14th. And that's just scratching the surface.

But in 1982, Benjamin's career focus shifted with the release of his directorial debut MY FAVORITE YEAR, a warm, witty and infectiously charming nostalgic Hollywood comedy starring the iconic Peter O'Toole and SUSPIRIA star Jessica Harper. So successful was the picture that Benjamin — while still acting when the spirit moved him — fervently followed this new path as a director, with a diverse ensuing series of pictures like the Cher/Winona Ryder vehicle MERMAIDS, the Sean Penn/Nicolas Cage drama RACING WITH THE MOON, the Clint Eastwood/Burt Reynolds neo-noir CITY HEAT and the Tom Hanks comedy THE MONEY PIT.

Nestled within that body of work sits what might be Benjamin's most underrated picture (and he has more than a few of those to his name): the 1988 special effects-soaked romantic sci-fi screwball comedy MY STEPMOTHER IS AN ALIEN. Starring a post-GHOSTBUSTERS Dan Akroyd and a post 9½ WEEKS Kim Basinger, the weird and wacky (and gently lurid) romp sees a female alien named Celeste sent to earth to spy on a single father scientist named Steven whose experiments have accidentally caused a gravitational shift on her planet. Assuming the visage of what she believes will be the most desirable thing Steven would appreciate, a luscious blonde (in some ways the film's plot echoes Tobe Hooper's LIFEFORCE!), Celeste insinuates herself into his life, initially to manipulate him and destroy earth but soon, after experiencing the pleasures of sex and fashion and even parenting, she falls in love with her quarry. Aided by the misguided advice of a malevolent alien eyeball that lives in her handbag while also trying to keep her true identity a secret from her new family, Celeste has to stop her superiors from fulfilling their mission before it's too late.

Released to weak reviews and an equally thin box office take, MY STEPMOTHER IS AN ALIEN had a good enough run-on VHS and cable before lapsing into virtual obscurity. But the time is right to rediscover this cheerful, rather berserk end-of-the-80s gem. It yields so many strange pleasures, including an hilarious turn from SNL vet Jon Lovitz, a pre-BUFFY THE VAMPIRE SLAYER teaming of Alyson Hannigan and Seth Green, Tom Jones on the soundtrack, an inexplicable salute to Jimmy Durante, eye-filling FX and of course, a supernaturally stunning turn by Bassinger as Celeste, who looks beautiful both in and out of clothes (the costumes she wears are unbelievable) and who delivers a deft comic performance , making Celeste not just a sex object but a complex, sweet and evolving character. Sure the movie is goofy, but that's why it's so charming and I challenge you to name another movie quite like it.

INTERVIEW: RICHARD BENJAMIN

CHRIS ALEXANDER: How did the script for STEPMOTHER cross your desk?

RICHARD BENJAMIN: [*laughs*] It happened down the block from where I lived via Jerry Weintraub and Guy McElwaine, who was a good friend of mine and an agent. I was driving down the block and Guy was at the end of the block, and he said, "oh great, there's a script we want to give you!", and that's how I first heard about it. So, he sent the script, I read the script, I liked it, I thought it needed work, and then they sent a fruit basket or something here and asked me to do it so I said "ok, I'm going to do this". My secretary said, "well that must have been a nice fruit basket", and it was, so yeah, I said yes. Jerry had formed a new company, and this was their first film, so I went to work on it and started to develop it.

ALEXANDER: This is, in essence, a classic fish out of water fantasy. The alien reminded me a lot of Daryl Hannah's mermaid from SPLASH, this kind of otherworldly creature; she's innocent, almost childlike, but still very sensual. Was Kim always your first choice?

BENJAMIN: Yes, I think so because she's so beautiful and I wasn't sure, I hadn't seen her do any comedy but it turned out she was great at it, but I thought it wouldn't work if it wasn't someone as gorgeous and sexy as her. Dan has that moment where he says, "why me?"; they are knocked out when they see her. She has no thoughts on what she looks like and why anybody would be interested in her that

Benjamin is a natural talent, both in front and behind the camera.

way at all, she is just there on a mission. All those kinds of opposites and things really appealed to me and then she turned out to be great, Originally, she was going to start out as either Elvis Presley or Mickey Mouse because in the alien's investigation of our planet, they wanted her to look like the most important thing that they recognized as being on the planet. So, we started out with Elvis and, we had her in a costume test dressed as Elvis. But we found out we couldn't get the rights to Elvis or Mickey Mouse either.

ALEXANDER: So, you're saying that somewhere, someplace there is some test footage or photos of this?

BENJAMIN: Well, no, not a film test, we got her dressed. Before there was a film test, we found out we couldn't do it. The costume was made and all that, she had a black wig and sideburns, because she thought that would make her acceptable to everybody then that couldn't happen. We never came up with anybody world famous like that, that we could get the rights to, so that's where she just became beautiful Kim.

ALEXANDER: Kim's costumes are rather insane and awesome. Can you talk about the importance of costume design in the film?

BENJAMIN: Well, our costume designer was Aggie Guerard. We said that we've got to have something she looks great in but odd, not quite right, and Aggie came up with dress that's in the poster — the hat and the dress and all of that, so that's where that came from. Later of course, she changes stuff.

ALEXANDER: I love Jon Lovitz's initial reaction to her.

BENJAMIN: [*laughs*] Yeah. Jon Lovitz came to audition, and there were other people out there waiting to see me, he announced to all of them that came in to see me that they could all go home, that he had this. I said, "what did you tell those people?", he said "I told them to go home because you're going to cast me", and of course I did.

ALEXANDER: I've read some criticisms about the casting of Dan and as you've mentioned, part of the joke is "why me?" So was he supposed to always be kind of a schlub". Was there ever any controversy internally regarding Dan?

BENJAMIN: No, it was Dan right from the beginning. You know, we wanted somebody who was a star in some way so no, that was right from the beginning. I don't think I saw or thought of anyone else.

ALEXANDER: Dan is also a writer. Did he influence or alter anything in the script? Do you remember if any collaboration was there?

BENJAMIN: Not in any writing, no. He may have come up with stuff when we were right there but no, not actually in the script.

ALEXANDER: There's fantastic chemistry between Dan and Kim... between the entire cast. Did the two of them get along okay?

Celeste discovers sex via Larry Flynt.

BENJAMIN: They did, they absolutely did. She is just lovely and delightful, just a great person and yeah, everybody got along. You know, I kind of legislate that because it's no good if you have anybody in the cast or anything that is behaving in a way that starts to put negativism over the whole thing. If there is ever anybody like that, we just get rid of them. You're lucky enough to make a movie, it's hard enough to make a movie, and at the same time it should really be an enjoyable experience. There are problems all the time that you must deal with but to have the added thing in there of having somebody negative just cannot happen.

ALEXANDER: I mean you are also, by trade, primarily an actor, so being an actor and becoming a director, I presume you're very empathetic of the process...

BENJAMIN: Yeah. I know what they are going through, I know that a character that exists on any set is fear. My job is to give them a safety net to let them know I won't let anything happen to them so they won't look foolish, they won't look bad. It's to give them that confidence that they are in good hands as far as performing, to let them be bold, to not get small. What happens sometimes is if people are afraid, or they don't feel there is confidence around them, they kind of get small and they don't take chances and so you get that kind of, I don't know, whisper acting, that appears to be real because they are talking quietly, which is something I don't understand at all because people don't talk that way so yeah, my job is for them to know there is a safety net there and that they should just go for things.

ALEXANDER: Let's talk about directing the one non-human actor in the cast: The Eye.

BENJAMIN: Well, I'll tell you that's Paula's sister's voice, that's Ann. Ann was right with us, there all the time, off camera obviously, so Kim could interact with her. Originally, she was there kind of like a temporary voice, we thought later we'd replace it, but the producers, after seeing the rough cut, asked "why are we doing that, she's perfect, we don't need to find somebody else", so it worked out.

ALEXANDER: Now, if this was made today, The Eye would be computer generated.

BENJAMIN: Oh yeah, now it looks like a child's puppet in there.

ALEXANDER: Maybe, but I love it. Were there ever any problems with the puppeteering or handling of the effect?

BENJAMIN: No, it was so simple, the bottom of it, when the thing is out, the bottom of it is kind of below the frame and somebody is manipulating that thing. Later, with whatever at that time with special effects we could do then, we added effects to it, especially with when it goes nuts at the end. John Dykstra did those effects.

ALEXANDER: The film was rated PG-13, which was at that time still fairly new. People were still experimenting with what they could and couldn't show. Kim had just come out of doing 9 ½ WEEKS and so her inherent sexiness kind of followed her here. I watch the movies recently with my kids and I was somewhat alarmed just how naughty it gets…

BENJAMIN: I thought the same thing! Our granddaughter is nine and I said to my son recently "you know, she might like this it's funny". But then I watched it and was like… hmm, wait a minute! All of those things going on in the bedroom, the fireworks, all of that kind of stuff. I mean, like what's happening [*laughs*]!

DELIRIUM Sex is a big part of her character, the discovery of it. It's why she wants to stay on earth, she loves it. Was it difficult to be sexy but not too sexy, to get that rating?

BENJAMIN: No, not really. We were just doing what was there. I wasn't really thinking about that. She is so beautiful, that's part of it, and she's sexy and the fun of it is that she has no idea that she is but no, I never thought about ratings or anything like that.

ALEXANDER: Never mind how varied your career as an actor is, as a director there's such an arc of diversity. You pretty much shot this back-to-back with LITTLE NIKITA with Sidney Poitier and River Phoenix, a serious dramatic thriller. Then you jump to this very broad screwball comedy. Is it sometimes difficult to switch gears like that?

BENJAMIN: No. When I read something or the idea of something I say "oh, I know what this is" and in a way, for the most part it says I know how to do this. Going from one to another isn't like shifting some kind of thing, just like if you were reading a mystery and Dostoevsky or something like that, you would be immediately into whatever it is if you think it's good enough so no, it doesn't, it's what appeals to me. Someone will send something, and I just don't get it or something and if I turn something down, the only thing I know how to say is I don't know how to do this,

Benjamin's sister-in-law Ann Prentiss provided the voice of "Bag".

or what's it about, that's a big question. LITTLE NIKITA, for me anyway, had to do with family and it wasn't so much that it was an espionage thriller, from my entry point it was family. So is MY STEPMOTHER IS AN ALIEN, really.

ALEXANDER: The film is beautifully edited.

BENJAMIN: That's Jacqueline Cambas, who I've done every picture with except my first picture. What I do is I shoot and send her the stuff while I'm still shooting, and she puts together kind of a rough cut looking at just the footage because as she says, "I don't want to know what's outside that frame, don't tell me the problems, I only know what we're looking at", that's her point of view. I'll see dailies with her and I'll say that take and that take, and script supervisors will take notes of what I liked when we printed stuff right then and there, and she'll make a note but may hold onto some other take for some other reason or something like that, so my involvement is selecting those takes, giving her the footage and once in a while she'll call me and say "are you on that same set, you've got to get a shot of so and so I can get from this place to that place". Then later when it's all done, she'll show me kind of her rough cut and then we go from there, start taking it apart, leaving things alone, messing around, whatever, make sure jokes are paying off and all of that. She also pretty great with music and it was her idea for that title music, the Tom Jones one, and that we heard from legal or something saying we can't have it, that song is Prince's, then someone called and said we contacted him, and this is how things in the movie business are, and he refused to give permission, and I said that's too bad. I told Jerry, and he's the kind of producer you want, fearless and tough when he needs to be, and it was his company, and what I understand is he called him and he said no one contacted him, no one asked for his permission, I never really got to the bottom of it, all I know is Jerry came back and said "sure you can have it", so that's where the title sequence came from and Wayne Fitzgerald also did the visual stuff there. That was Jacqueline originally putting that song in there, I thought that it was wonderful energy.

ALEXANDER: Speaking of music, Alan Silverstri's score is fantastic. How involved are you in terms of working with composers? Do you just turn it over to them and let them do what they do?

BENJAMIN: Yes, I do. And then we start hearing it or seeing it, themes, and stuff, maybe on a piano or something like that, then we discuss. I'm no musician and I'm not going to tell someone like Silvestri, "can you change those notes?" But what you hear, you know how it plays against the film, you know if it's working or not working. With Alan, he pretty much knows exactly what he's doing, especially in terms of film, and then as you do the mix and put it all in there, you figure out what works where.

ALEXANDER: Let's talk about this movie being exhibited and the opening, it's a pretty wild story...

BENJAMIN: Indeed. We screened it for the Vice President. George H. W. Bush was Vice President at that time so Jerry — again, who knew everybody — said "we are going to spring this on Washington!" and I thought, is this the place for this? But Jerry said, "I know Vice President Bush very well, this is going to be great"! So off we go to Washington DC, and we had lunch at the Naval Observatory, where the Vice President lives, and met his son George Bush, who couldn't have been more charming, really, and the next thing we know we're in a motorcade, sirens, police, the whole thing. And Jacqueline was there earlier running the prints. We always do this, you've got to. I've seen too many times where people don't have the time or don't think it's necessary to run it with a projectionist. Then stuff happens, speakers don't work, the framing is wrong, things like that. But anyway, she ran the whole picture but had to go through the Secret Service to do all that. Then I saw her, and she said, "it all looks good, it's all fine". So that was a relief. Of course, during the screening, then I was looking around to see if the Vice President was laughing...

ALEXANDER: Was he laughing? How did it go?

BENJAMIN: He was laughing, it seemed to go fine.

ALEXANDER: That must have been one of the stranger things to happen to you in your already kind of strange career at that point.

BENJAMIN: Yeah, I always look around and go "how did this happen?" You know I grew up on the upper west side of New York and the next thing I know I'm in a theater in Washington DC with the Vice President of the United States.

ALEXANDER: Now hold on a second, in case I've missed it, I don't think you've written your life story yet, have you?

BENJAMIN: I have, actually. I have written a book, it's not published. A publisher wanted it but I didn't like the terms of the contract, so I said no. It's sitting right here. The book stops after MY FAVORITE YEAR actually, so I never got to talking about STEPMOTHER. This is a first.

ALEXANDER: MY FAVORITE YEAR was and is beloved. By critics, audiences. But let's be frank, some of the movies you directed didn't exactly get big bear hugs from the critics. Did that ever bother you or did you learn to kind of shrug that off?

BENJAMIN: Well, it's like this. I made a movie with Clint Eastwood called CITY HEAT and Clint... well, I learned a lot from him. When I finished CITY HEAT I had shown it to Clint and Jacqueline was there and I said "well, we have to show it to the studio, right?" and Clint said "no, we don't have to do that". When we finished the screening, he said "well, I like it, do you like it?", I said "yeah, I like it!" and he said "ok, that's that, then!". He also said, "you send it out there, if you've done the best you think you can do, you have to let it go, everyone is going to have an opinion". But yes, it does bother me if I see negative reviews and stuff because it relates to box office. My agent Phil Gersh, who is no longer with us and who was Humphrey Bogart's agent, said to me "there is only one review and it's the box office". Then it's where your stock is, your stock attached to the box office so if the reviews are negative and effects the box office and people don't come, your stock goes down so that means offers, are you going to get any, will they be good offers, do you have to start all over so that's the level, to me, what reviews mean. I remember going to New York, I think for a MY FAVORITE YEAR screening, and some press lady from MGM came running to me as I got off the plane with a review from Pauline Kael which was very positive, and she was excited because it was The New Yorker and well, it was Pauline Kael! It meant a lot, to get a review from her. The same thing happened after I did RACING WITH THE MOON, in both the *LA Times* and the *New York Times* and Sherry Lansing called me right away in the morning and said "have you seen the times? You must see it!". So, it excites people. However, in that instance, with RACING WITH THE MOON, good reviews didn't really translate into box office but initially, when you get really, really good reviews you get excited because at least you are headed in the right direction. If you get negative reviews, you are headed the other way, and then it relates to you and your stock in this business, so it's kind of like that in terms of reviews of what's going to happen in terms of where your career might be going but that's the rollercoaster of the entire business.

ALEXANDER: You mentioned rewatching the movie again, but what do you think about MY STEPMOTHER IS AN ALIEN now, are you happy with it?

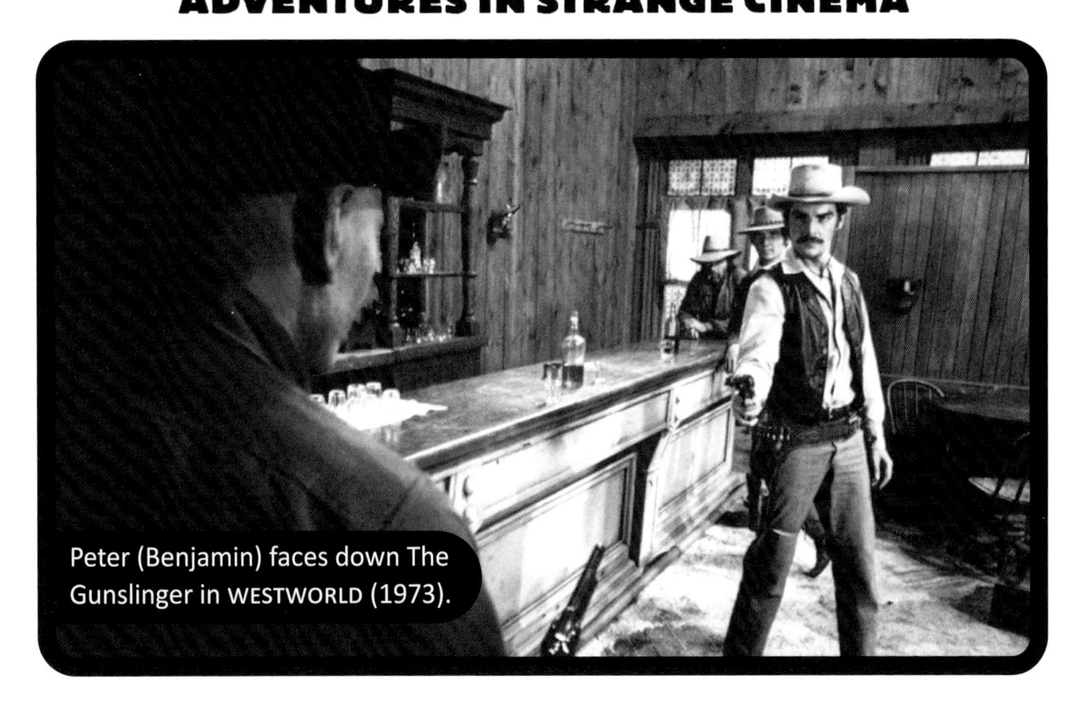

Peter (Benjamin) faces down The Gunslinger in WESTWORLD (1973).

BENJAMIN: I was really surprised, I really was. Unless you had contacted me, I don't know if I would have gone back and looked at it. I don't usually go back and look at what I did so I probably wouldn't have looked at it, it would have just been receding in the past somewhere, but I was pleasantly surprised.

ALEXANDER: We can't have a proper Richard Benjamin chat without bringing up WESTWORLD at least once. Did you see the HBO series? And did they ever approach you to make a cameo in the show?

BENJAMIN: I've seen the show in parts, yeah. You know, it's very different. Michael Crichton, who happily became a very good friend, was making a thriller and his themes always were 'watch out for technology, don't put much trust in it', stuff like that. It was always what he was about, like JURASSIC PARK, COMA as well, all of those. With the HBO show, it's very different psychological stuff and it's just so different from the source that to me it's like, how do they say? It's apples and oranges is what it is.

ALEXANDER: But they never asked you to come back and tip your hat in a cameo at least?

BENJAMIN: No. But there was a quick shot of something in one of the episodes that I watched that looked to me, off in the corner somewhere, it looked to me like a burnt-up Yul Brenner and that's the only explicit reference I think I ever saw, aside from the original idea. So, this new WESTWORLD is a totally separate thing for me from what we did back then.

NEVER TAKE SWEETS FROM A STRANGER (1960)

Starring Patrick Allen, Gwen Waterford, Janina Faye, Felix Aylmer
Written by John Hunter
Directed by Cyril Frankel

Before their brand became synonymous with Gothic horror fantasies dripping with promises of Freudian sex and death, Hammer films steadily pumped out a series of quality British melodramas, mysteries and Hitchcockian thrillers, most of them produced economically in black and white and exported internationally by major studios with little fanfare. But in circling back on these early curiosities — many of which were produced well into the early 1960s — one can find some remarkable motion pictures, many of which are bold, daring and way ahead of their time.

Among the most alarming of that lot is director Cyril Frankel's NEVER TAKE SWEETS FROM A STRANGER (retitled NEVER TAKE CANDY FROM A STRANGER for its US release), a jet-black and shocking thriller (based on the play *The Pony Trap* by Roger Garis) and a film that, despite its vintage, nevertheless packs a wallop. It's a movie whose dismal truths about how the powerful buy silence and how children must suffer the sins of their elders tragically and endlessly. And it doesn't go down easy.

Nine-year-old Jean (Janina Faye, from Hammer's HORROR OF DRACULA) has just moved to small town in Ontario, Canada with her parents Peter (Patrick Allen) and Sally (Gwen Watford), after dear Dad accepts a prominent position as the new principal of the local school. One day while playing with her new friend Lucille, the pair wander off to the manor of the town's most powerful family, the Olderberrys, when Lucille confides that the old man who lives there will give them free candy. When Jean comes home that night, she rather matter-of-factly tells her parents that the skeezy Mr. Olderberry (Felix Aylmer, who is chilling) did indeed ply them with sweets in exchange for the young girls to remove their clothes and dance naked for them. Peter and Sally are horrified and, later that night when Jean wakes up screaming from a nightmare, mom and dad decide to action.

But as they soon learn, the town is rather adept at keeping its secrets safe. After relaying the tale to some prominent school officials, Peter gleans that people are aware of Mr. Olderberry's pedophiliac leaning and there have been previous "incidents," but everyone has turned a blind eye. Peter presses charges even though he's warned of social isolation and worse if he proceeds. When the old man's son, Clarence Olderberry Jr. (Bill Nagy), shows up to their home and urges them to drop the charges, Peter and Sally refuse and the younger man swears to decimate the little girl on the stands in the inevitable trial. Soon little Jean is ostracized from her peers, the family is persecuted and, when the old man is revoltingly cleared of his crimes by

SIX WORDS
THAT SOUND
A FATEFUL
WARNING!
"Never take candy from a stranger"
starring
GWEN WATFORD · PATRICK ALLEN · FELIX AYLMER · NIALL MacGINNIS Screenplay by JOHN HUNTER
Based on a play by ROGER GARIS · Produced by ANTHONY HINDS · Directed by CYRIL FRANKEL · Executive Producer, MICHAEL CARRERAS
A HAMMER FILM PRODUCTION · Presented by HOWARD J. BECK · MEGASCOPE · AN OMAT RELEASE

a crooked jury, they opt to leave the dour little hamlet. But they soon learn that the outrage they've endured is only the catalyst to the horror to come.

To call NEVER TAKE SWEETS FROM A STRANGER a horror film may seem like stretch, but it's really not. There are no vampires, ghouls or werewolves running around this picture, rather the threat is fear and ignorance, the monster is power and privilege and the poison at its core is one human being's psychotic addiction to sexually abusing and murdering children. The latter element? Well, I can think of few things more horrifying. As adults, we find novel ways to mess up our lives and the lives of others. But we keep making more of us in hopes of creating better versions of ourselves, successors who will hopefully learn from us, from our triumphs and errors. It's a universal, biological law that we are here to protect children, to nurture them and show them the beauty in the world before adulthood begins to chip away at the perception of the purity of that beauty. And when an adult ends up willingly breaking that law, it's unforgivable.

Director Frankel would later go on the helm Hammer's supernatural drama THE WITCHES and that's a strong film. This one is stronger. Frankel allows the literacy of the stage play drive the film and fleshes out the dialogue-heavy drama with many nightmarish sequences of children in jeopardy. It's like a British "social issues" version of NIGHT OF THE HUNTER in some respects, with children targeted by those they are told to trust and it's a theme that marked many of these early Hammer thrillers, movies like the equally mesmerizing (if more conventional) evil parent shocker THE SNORKEL. And the iconic DP turned director Freddie Francis brings an almost fairy tale beauty to much of the outdoor sequences, especially the scenes of the children fleeing for their lives.

This is a dark, uncompromising film; serious, smart and wildly upsetting. Seek it out...

NIGHT WARNING (1981)

Starring Jimmy McNichol, Susan Tyrrell, Bo Svenson, Bill Paxton
Written by Stephen Breimer, Boon Collins, Alan Jay Glueckman
Directed by William Asher

In the never-ending search for horror cinema's craziest and mast dangerous women, rarely do you hear many experts cite Susan (ANDY WARHOL'S DRACULA, FROM A WHISPER TO A SCREAM) Tyrrell's malevolent, manipulative and murderous Aunt Cheryl in BEACH BLANKET BINGO director William Asher's undervalued 1982 thriller NIGHT WARNING. Heck, not many cineastes cite the movie for much of anything. Maybe it's because the

As Aunt Cheryl, Susan Tyrrell mines new depths of madness.

picture was released during the wave of crass slasher crap that belched out of the early '80s with pedestrian, lowbrow regularity. Maybe many critics just got confused by the fact it was known under a slew of none-too-subtle titles like BUTCHER, BAKER, NIGHTMARE MAKER and sometimes just simply NIGHTMARE MAKER before ending up with the rather innocuous and misleading NIGHT WARNING handle.

But for my money, I don't think I've ever seen a psychotic screen she-monster more blood-chilling than Tyrrell is in this deeply twisted, melodramatic Gothic shocker. It's a sort of dark amalgam of the '60s "horror hag" movies that usually starred Bette Davis and/or Joan Crawford, stuff like WHATEVER HAPPENED TO BABY JANE? and STRAIGHT JACKET, tempered with the psychosexual obsessions of the Italian *giallo* and the mundane ins-and-outs of the after school special. But really, these clumsy allusions don't do NIGHT WARNING any service. Because the movie has a sickly, unsettling, and deliciously trashy vibe all its own. And again, Tyrrell's monstrous Cheryl has rarely been matched.

The film tells the story of sweet young teen Billy (Jimmy McNichol, brother of Kristy), an ace basketball player who has been given the chance at a scholarship to an elite out of town university, the same school that his equally lovely girlfriend Julia (Julia Duffy, from TV's NEWHART) is also going to. Seems like the future is bright for the young lovers. But there's one problem: Billy's hideous Aunt Cheryl. Cheryl is a human monster, feral and drooling and, as we learn from the spectacularly violent opening sequence, homicidal. Cheryl became Billy's ward when he was three, after his parents went off on a drive down the California coast and, after their breaks failed (thanks

Aunt Cheryl!), met their screaming demises. Dad is decapitated by a log that comes crashing through the windshield and the then blood-spattered Mom is thrown from a cliff to her final, fiery destination (and yes, the sequence is a clear influence on the opening of FINAL DESTINATION 2). It's an astonishing start to an unyieldingly cruel and paranoid movie.

Anyway, Billy tells Cheryl about the once in a lifetime opportunity that his beloved Coach Landers (Steve Easton) has given him, but she'll have none of it. Because no one leaves Aunt Cheryl. Tyrrell plays the character like a hyper-sexual, petulant child, who has to get her way at any cost. After arguing with her nephew, the sickening Cheryl sets up a scenario with a repairman, trying to feign seduction which the blue-collar dude rejects. When he pushes her away, she pulls out a butcher knife and stabs him a dozen times in the chest. When Billy witnesses this murder, Cheryl insists that the man was trying to rape her and, when Detective Carlson (Bo Svenson from WALKING TALL, PART 2 and the original THE INGLORIOUS BASTARDS) shows up to investigate the gory crime scene, Billy backs her up. But Carlson doesn't buy it. And when he finds out that the repairman was gay and that he was the lover of Billy's coach, the detective unleashes his inner hostile homophobe, imagining that Billy and Coach Landers are in fact lovers and that the two men planned to have the third murdered so they could be together.

Meanwhile, Cheryl gets crazier and crazier, alternately sitting in her room and talking to a photograph of her dead husband and getting more and more possessive and sickeningly incestuously obsessed with her nephew, whose life is falling apart both at home and at school (one of his bullies is played by a pre-WEIRD SCIENCE Bill Paxton). When Cheryl walks in on Billy and Julia having sex, she goes fully, completely off the deep end. And none of this ends well, in case you haven't guessed yet...

NIGHT WARNING is a checklist of ugliness and yet its so over-the-top and so briskly paced and histrionic that it's never anything but a greasy joy to watch. In many ways, it reminds me of the feeling I get watching Andrzej Zulawski's 1981 mind-bender POSSESSION. Svenson matches Tyrrell's hideousness, painting the portrait of a man who is so hateful to gays that it's very clear he is most likely gay himself. Watching him berate the decent coach, calling him "fag" and "butt boy" while humiliating Billy in front of his girlfriend and decrying homosexuality as revolting makes him one of the most unpleasant of screen presences. In fact, at its core, NIGHT WARNING might just be an indictment of the toxic hypocrisy of homophobia. Carlson is a pig who exploits the law to further his hate agenda and Cheryl, who screams at Billy that "homosexuality is disgusting, and gays are diseased" reeks of the kind fear and loathing that fuels these kinds of repressed sociopaths in real-life.

But as juicy a thriller as NIGHT WARNING is, the main reason to watch this ultra-nasty (in fact it *was* a "video nasty" in England!), Oedipal opus is to revel in Tyrrell's show-stopping performance. The actress just goes for it, delivering a complex, physical and emotional tour de force. And the wonder of the performance is that no matter how distorted and ugly her Aunt Cheryl is, Tyrrell manages to make her somewhat tragic and sympathetic. Something went dreadfully wrong in this woman's life and now, with her tortured psyche pushed past the point of no return, every living thing that comes into contact with her will suffer greatly. But perhaps no one will suffer as greatly as Cheryl herself, a human being who succumbed to the endless scratching at the door and finally let the Devil in...

NIGHT PATROL (1984)

Starring Linda Blair, Pat Paulsen, Jaye P. Morgan, Murray Langston
Written by Jackie Kong, Murray Langston, William A. Levey, Bill Osco
Directed by Jackie Kong

One of the strongest film memories for me, during my early teen trash film awakening, was director Jackie Kong's absurd, vulgar, atonal, and atrociously awesome 1984 bad-cop romp NIGHT PATROL. It's a scatological comedy that earned its R rating and, while not a horror film, it left the same indelible, filthy post-viewing sheen on me that other late-night pictures like EVIL DEAD, BLOOD AND LACE, RETURN OF THE LIVING DEAD, MESSIAH OF EVIL and PARASITE did. I felt like I'd visited some other sort of strange land filled with fluids, grease and madness.

And hey, Linda Blair is in it.

In fact, I saw NIGHT PATROL before I saw THE EXORCIST and, considering your perspective on the ride depends on when you get on the train, this gross-out romp is, for me, the definitive Blair-sploitation experience. Make of that what you will.

Released the same year as juggernaut, future franchise slapstick spoof POLICE ACADEMY, NIGHT PATROL plays like an amalgam of that film by way of AIRPLANE! by way of Bob Clark's tits and ass hit PORKY'S, ground up with a really bad Peter Sellers movie and baked by a woman who helmed the best H.G. Lewis ever made. Indeed Kong, who had previously made the 1983 sci-fi horror flick THE BEING, would chase NIGHT PATROL with her bloody, guttural, and rather incredible homage to the house that Lewis and Friedman built, 1987's BLOOD DINER. And NIGHT PATROL has that same intentionally arch, loose, go-for-broke, cross-eyed appeal; it's a movie based on bits, cheap laughs and dirty vignettes that get cheaper and more obvious as the running time winds down and, due to their sheer momentum, push the film into a kind of hallucinatory, astral-projection state.

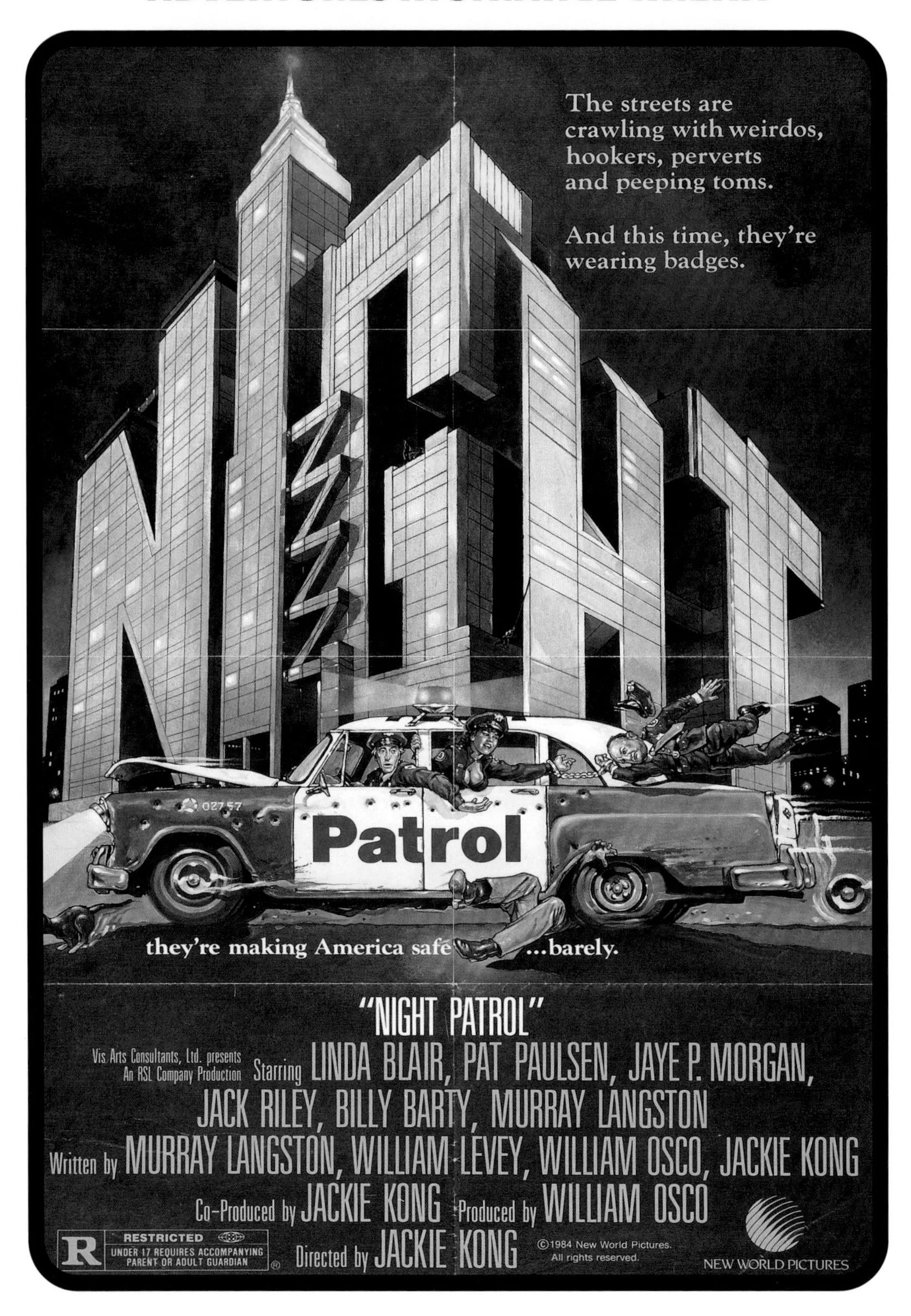
The streets are crawling with weirdos, hookers, perverts and peeping toms.
And this time, they're wearing badges.
NIGHT
Patrol
they're making America safe ...barely.
"NIGHT PATROL"
Vis Arts Consultants, Ltd. presents An RSL Company Production Starring LINDA BLAIR, PAT PAULSEN, JAYE P. MORGAN, JACK RILEY, BILLY BARTY, MURRAY LANGSTON
Written by MURRAY LANGSTON, WILLIAM LEVEY, WILLIAM OSCO, JACKIE KONG
Co-Produced by JACKIE KONG Produced by WILLIAM OSCO
R RESTRICTED UNDER 17 REQUIRES ACCOMPANYING PARENT OR ADULT GUARDIAN
Directed by JACKIE KONG
©1984 New World Pictures. All rights reserved.
NEW WORLD PICTURES

Watching NIGHT PATROL is a transgressive experience. The gross-out comedy as subversive high art.

Right from the first scene, we know we're in a weird world. We know that something is wrong. Even the opening titles seem cheap and sleazy. Like a Crown International drive-in flick, generic and style-free. The first strains of Carl Steward's theme song LAPD, with its reggae-informed beat, pops onto the soundtrack and one notices that Stewart must have been a *reallllly* big Roxy Music/Bryan Ferry fan. Because if I didn't know better, I would have thought that this WAS a vintage Roxy track, it's that good of a forgery. And if you groove on it, I've got some great news for you: it repeats over almost every inch of the damn movie!

NIGHT PATROL introduces us to Officer Melvin White, an LAPD beat cop who is dumber than a bag of hammers. White is played by Canadian comedian Murray Langston, a graduate of Chuck Barris's '70s trash variety program THE GONG SHOW and man, is he funny. Langston would find fame on both TGS and on the club circuit as The Unknown Comic, a Vegas-style stand-up comedian famous for wearing a paper bag over his head. Langston appeared in Kong's THE BEING and indeed conceived and co-wrote NIGHT PATROL with her as a vehicle for his shtick, both in and out of the bag mask.

At the header of the film, we find Officer White pulling over a cackling, obese miscreant wearing a strait jacket who confesses (in ridiculously dubbed gutter-French) to a myriad sex-crimes, to which the cheerful, swaggering White is blithely oblivious too; when a dead body hangs out of the fiend's trunk, White is only concerned with teaching the man how to properly close his caboose.

We are soon introduced to the filthy precinct that Officer White calls home, a cop-shop filled with all sorts of scum and yes, said scum are the ones wearing the badges. Wonderfully hang-dog-faced actor Pat Paulsen plays Officer Kent Lane, White's older, sex-crazed partner; the diminutive Billy Barty (TV sketch show BIZARRE, Ridley Scott's LEGEND) plays the wildly-flatulent Chief, every step he takes spurring a flurry of farts to squirt over the soundtrack (one wonders if poor Barty had any idea that his comic performance would be dubbed into near diarrhea in post); and then we meet the cute-as-a-button desk sergeant Sue Perman (groan!) played by the equally chirpy Blair, who is (if there is any) the humanity and soul of the film. See, Perman loves White, but he's too stupid to know it. He's more concerned with balancing his career as a cop with his moonlighting fame as The Unknown Comic, something he keeps close to the vest, his double life only revealed to his even more inept psychiatrist (Jack Riley).

The barely-there narrative of NIGHT PATROL rests on the central conflict of a crook running around town dressed as The Unknown Comic and White having to find the gun-toting, Safeway-bag-cowled imposter and clear his alter ego's name.

But who cares about that.

Officer Sue Perman (Linda Blair) makes time with Melvin (Murray Langston).

The primal power of NIGHT PATROL rests in its flurry of frantic, fecal and ribald sketches; there are hundreds of gags bursting forth from the film and yes, most of the gags will MAKE you gag!

There's a running streak of homophobia in the film, from the dead homeless man who just wants to make out with our disgusted hero, to the disdain Barty has for his openly gay officers, to the horde of homicidal lesbians and beyond; those looking for anything resembling political correctness should not look under this rock. Literally no sacred societal trope is safe. Everyone gets their licks. Chalk that up in part to the ignorance of the 1980s but really, Kong and Langston are like the kids in the back of the 5th grade homeroom class with the shitty home lives: they want your attention, the good attention, the bad attention, all attention is welcome and desired. And they'll stop at nothing to get it.

Case in point, the "cockfighting" scene, wherein roosters are replaced by naked men literally banging their dicks together while people scream and shout and a pair of cursing nuns bet on the action.

Or how about the "sperm bank" bit, where a convoy of money-hungry masturbators line up to sell their seed and, at the end of the line, a pretty young girl also stands. When White asks why she, a woman, is in line for a sperm bank, she turns to him and wetly gargles "Get Lost"!

How about the awful/awesome aside where Paulsen says he "fucked a female officer's brains out" and sure enough, said lady cop appears spastically flailing around the precinct.

I love the sequence where White questions a cage full of sex criminals who deliciously reveal their pedophile, rape and sodomy-based indiscretions and then ask the Officer if there is anything wrong with what they've done. When White gives them a pass, he shrugs off his own youthful encounter with a sheep, wherein the perverts collectively jeer and reject him as a monster.

Of course, everyone loves the diner scene, where Paulsen and Langston sit down to eat in a dive that's such a shithole, their soup of the day is "Cream of Washroom".

Langston tries the hot, brown sludge and admits "it's not bad!"

How about the part where our dim-witted heroes bust a drug-den, where a topless and massively mammaried Kitten Natividad passes around a joint and points to her chest exclaiming "THIS is a bust!" before getting the tit-fixated officers stoned out of their minds.

These moments are just a few random highlights of this operatically gross and supernaturally funny film, one who's cheap, washed out look and poor audio just add to its dreamlike appeal.

NIGHT PATROL is probably the funniest movie ever made. You should see it.

NIGHTWING (1979)

Starring Nick Mancuso, David Warner, Kathryn Harrold, Strother Martin
Written by Martin Crus Smith, Steve Shagan, Bud Shrake
Directed by Arthur Hiller

Director Arthur Hiller's NIGHTWING is one of a handful of films that trade in the terror of killer, disease-ridden bats, a loose, unofficial subgenre that seemingly doesn't command much fan enthusiasm. And while 1974's future-shock chiller CHOSEN SURVIVORS remains my winged-rodent romp of choice, NIGHTWING flies not too far behind.

Based on the intelligent novel by Martin Cruz Smith (who also co-wrote the screenplay), NIGHTWING casts Canadian actor Nick Mancuso (DEATH SHIP) as Youngman Duran, the Deputy of a New Mexico Indian reservation who is investigating a spate of animal deaths, the beasts' corpses savaged and drained of blood. As the attacks continue, Duran soon realizes that a horde of vampire bats have descended on the community and have now targeted human beings as their next food source. Enter the great David Warner (THE OMEN and so many other classic films), who plays a manic Van Helsing-esque biologist named Payne who has devoted his life to combing the earth and annihilating vampire bats for no other reason save that he firmly believes they are evil incarnate. He's especially disturbed by the idea of them shitting out the excess

Carlo Rambaldi's bloodsucking bats go for the throat in NIGHTWING.

blood they drink, a noxious notion hammered home by Payne's operatic monologues and Warner's wild-eyed readings of them. It's hard to nail down a definitive eccentric performance by Warner but this one comes close. It's truly... bat-shit!

Anyway, Duran and Payne set out to wipe out the colony, whose members are not only killing their victims but spreading a sort of black plague. Worse, the hateful mini monsters have supernatural ties to a suicidal medicine man who has called on the creatures on his deathbed to wipe out the world. It's this mystical, apocalyptic pulse of NIGHTWING that gives the film its strongest fascination and if Columbia Pictures had marketed the movie as more of a dark fantasy film and less of a blood-spattered, post-JAWS man vs. nature horror movie, more critics would have been kinder. Because upon release, they were anything *but* kind and this lack of press respect helped bulldoze NIGHTWING's presence and reputation into the abyss. But there's so much to admire about the movie, from the lovely location photography, the impressionist Native lore, Mancuso's solid lead turn (Mancuso would have been a bigger star had this film and his failed American network TV series STINGRAY been more successful), Warner's scenery chewing and a few choice bat-attack sequences. One of them sees the members of a Christian camp get obliterated by the bats, a manic, bloody (for a PG film) scene that mixes weird, blue-screened bat footage with close-ups of Italian FX maestro Carlo Rambaldi's super-cool vampire vermin puppets and mechanical props, the likes of which are probably left over from his stint on Paul Morrissey's immortal FLESH FOR FRANKENSTEIN.

NIGHTWING isn't a great horror movie *per se*, but it's a great movie full stop, one that deserves a much bigger cult fanbase.

NOMADS (1986)

Starring Pierce Brosnan, Lesley-Anne Down, Anna Maria Monticelli, Adam Ant
Written by John McTiernan
Directed by John McTiernan

I tend to gravitate towards genre cinema that isn't necessarily perfect but rather is flawed, fascinating and enigmatic; movies that reflect upon the mysteries of the human condition by shielding their truths in a thin sheen of bloody mess and abstract fantasy. I like films that are hazy, a bit out of focus, out of reach; pictures that you keep revisiting to unravel their secrets, even if they originally set out to offer very few. John McTiernan's 1986 head scratcher NOMADS is one such feature film, a picture that feels like a dream. And like a dream, the effect of NOMADS is subjective and can't properly be articulated.

But I'll try.

During a long, graveyard shift in the ER, pretty young Doctor Flax (Lesley-Anne Down) encounters a beaten, bloody man (Pierce Brosnan) who initially appears to be a stark raving- mad transient. When the run down, sleep deprived MD leans in to check his pupils, the pair momentarily lock eyes before the wild-eyed lunatic bursts from his gurney, locks his jaw around her neck and whispers something in French before finally collapsing, dead.

Shaken, Dr. Flax is treated for her minor wounds and left to lie down and collect her bearings before, almost immediately, she begins to experience vivid hallucinations that send her into violent fits. As she soon discovers, the drooling madman that attacked her wasn't a madman at all but rather a famous Canadian anthropologist named Jean Charles Pommier, a man who after traveling the earth studying nomadic cultures had finally settled down at the request of his gorgeous wife (the persuasively beautiful Anna Maria Monticelli), into a cushy teaching gig in LA.

Apparently, shortly before his death, Pommier had been tracking a leather-clad gang of street punks (whose ranks include '80s rocker Adam Ant and cult film heroine Mary Woronov) drifting around his home. Turns out these homeless, rootless ruffians are in actuality a tribe of evil, nomadic spirits, the same breed of ancient, wandering souls he'd been obsessively following his whole life and are now hellbent on driving him mad. The bite that Jean Charles gives Dr. Flax inexplicably causes her to aggressively relive — and we, the audience along with her — the memories leading up to his final sad state. Soon enough, she too becomes sucked into the Nomads' secret, clandestine, twilight world.

I saw NOMADS theatrically in 1986 and I can clearly remember the disorienting effect it had on me. See, NOMADS doesn't really make much sense, not in a linear,

A TERRIFYING STORY OF THE SUPERNATURAL
NOMADS
If you've never been frightened by anything, you'll be frightened by this!
ATLANTIC RELEASING CORPORATION IN ASSOCIATION WITH ELLIOTT KASTNER AND CINEMA 7 PRODUCTIONS PRESENTS "NOMADS"
STARRING LESLEY-ANNE DOWN PIERCE BROSNAN ANNA-MARIA MONTECELLI EXECUTIVE PRODUCER JERRY GERSHWIN MUSIC BY BILL CONTI
PRODUCED BY GEORGE PAPPAS and CASSIAN ELWES WRITTEN AND DIRECTED BY JOHN McTIERNAN
R RESTRICTED UNDER 17 REQUIRES ACCOMPANYING PARENT OR ADULT GUARDIAN
FROM Atlantic RELEASING CORPORATION

easily digestible way, anyway. The odd narrative structure — with its flashbacks within flashbacks, ever shifting points of view and lack of clear explanation as to the Nomads' history or true intent — made for a rather infuriating initial viewing experience. But I soon discovered that I could not stop thinking about it. I became obsessed with it. When it arrived on home video months later, I watched and re-watched it numerous times, trying in vain to decipher its clues and determine what made the movie resonate so much with me.

But NOMADS has something. An aura. A lyricism, a kind of poetry. It has that certain– as Pommier himself might say, *je ne sais quoi*, that elevates it beyond simple 80s genre potboiler and into the fluid, subconscious realms of the surreal.

I can tell you that I absolutely adore Bill (ROCKY) Conti's urgent, erotic synth and guitar score — especially the opening theme and closing hard rock collaboration with guitar wizard Ted Nugent. I can tell you that both Down and Brosnan are magnetic in a pair of extremely difficult roles that require them to achieve a bizarre sort of character symbiosis. I can tell you that the cold, washed out look of the film (perhaps the mark of a low budget, perhaps not) is claustrophobic and unsettling in its otherworldly, dim lit way.

It's difficult to believe that McTiernan would go on to create an endless spate of high octane, considerably less challenging, popular action pictures like DIE HARD and THE 13th WARRIOR because his maiden cinematic voyage is a work of such strikingly haunting and original moxy, such an intelligent, sophisticated, offbeat, and mysterious psychological/supernatural thriller. Maybe the fact that NOMADS made about 10 cents at the box office scared McTiernan off from continuing in this daring, metaphysical fantasy vein. What a shame.

NOSFERATU: PHANTOM DER NACHT (1979)

Starring Klaus Kinski, Isabelle Adjani, Bruno Ganz, Roland Topor
Written by Werner Herzog
Directed by Werner Herzog

Immortality. We all want it. The chance to defy that black specter of death that equalizes us. But to live forever, drifting through time like a ghost; residue of a memory, unattached to anything, anyplace, anyone. Hiding in shadows until the earth stops spinning. The crushing loneliness of it, would it really be worth it?

That's the central driving thematic force behind director Werner Herzog's dark, dreamy, full color remake of the immortal 1922 German expressionist classic

Dracula (Klaus Kinski) and Lucy (Isabelle Adjani) get locked into their death embrace.

NOSFERATU. A film that, although deeply indebted (sometimes almost scene for scene) to the iconic, silent original, still manages to evolve beyond its experimental horror roots, taking its essence from F.W. Murnau (like a vampire would, in fact), assimilating that blueprint and then injecting liberal amounts of lyricism and a driving force of deep, bittersweet melancholy. The resulting work is among the inimitable Herzog's most powerful and important films.

After a string of incredibly successful art house favorites throughout the late 1960s and early 1970s, Herzog, who alongside trailblazing filmmakers Rainer Werner Fassbinder and Wim Wenders, was a major figure in the German new wave movement, turned his gaze to the film he correctly acknowledged as the single most important German movie of all time. Indeed, the director had set his sights on remaking Murnau's shuddery unauthorized Dracula adaptation, shooting both German and English language versions and applying his own unique cinematic aesthetic to the oft filmed tale of the bloodsucking undead.

Unfortunately, at the same time Universal was also prepping the John Badham/ Frank Langella take on the Hamilton Deane stage version of DRACULA and MGM were launching the post-disco era George Hamilton spoof LOVE AT FIRST BITE, both easily accessible to mass-audience sensibilities and hugely popular. Herzog's languid, meditative anti-horror film was completely at odds with both the times and stateside sensibilities and his film, NOSFERATU: PHANTOM DER NACHT (or NOSFERATU: THE VAMPYRE

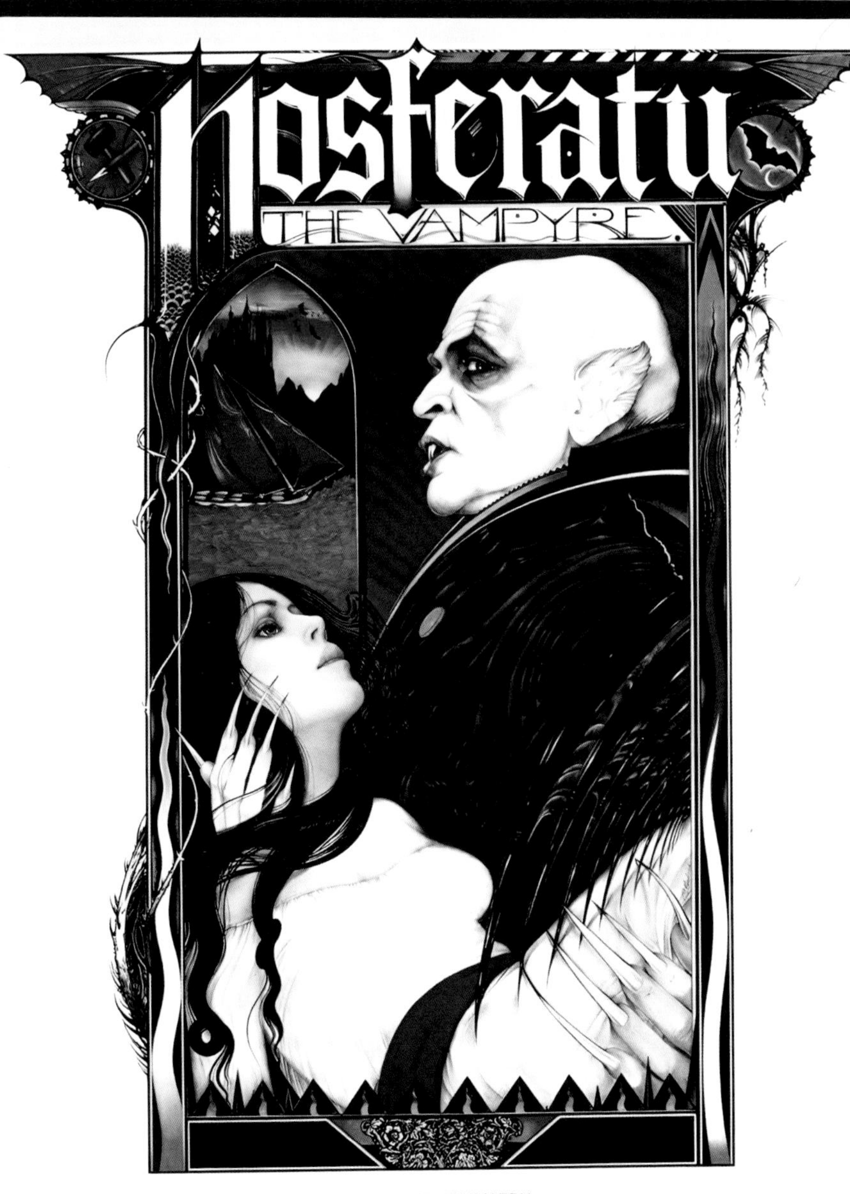

TWENTIETH CENTURY-FOX presents

KLAUS KINSKI ISABELLE ADJANI

in NOSFERATU THE VAMPYRE

(English Subtitles)

with BRUNO GANZ

MICHAEL GRUSKOFF presents A WERNER HERZOG FILM

PG PARENTAL GUIDANCE SUGGESTED Written, Produced and Directed by WERNER HERZOG Color by EASTMAN

Now in paperback from AVON

as it was known in the US and UK), although critically praised by many, got lost in the sanguinary shuffle, deemed by some as pretentious and thought by some critics to be a pointless attempt to revisit a picture that was already perfect as is.

Of course, that simply is not the case and time has, like it often does with most enduring masterworks of dark cinema, proved any naysayers wrong. Herzog's epic tale of disease, death, love, loss and isolation is absolutely one of the most evocative and emotional vampire film ever committed to celluloid.

To fully appreciate the one-of-a-kind wonder of NOSFERATU: PHANTOM DER NACHT, one must first understand the work of its creator. Born and raised in a remote German mountain village, one completely untouched by technology, young Werner would grow up in an environment two shades shy of the Stone Age, not making his first phone call until he was 14 and not seeing his first film until he was 17. But Herzog had something far better than modern distractions to inspire him. He was surrounded by the beauty of the natural world; of mountainous terrain, unforgiving nights and swooning days; of green grass, gentle winds and free flowing rivers. Herzog would grow up understanding nature, respecting it and most importantly, he was deeply humbled by it. He understood infinitely that mother earth was an unforgiving mistress; a bitch goddess that could kiss as easily as kill and only a fool would dare attempt to gain the upper hand against her.

So, when life propelled him towards becoming what he would become, Herzog began making movies that told tales of dangerous eccentrics, heroes and madmen whose sometimes valiant, often vain, efforts to conquer nature result in their ruin. Thing is, Herzog would often choose to film these pictures in the very bowels of the badlands and wild worlds that his scripts painted as treacherous, using locals and natives as extras, and often personally teetering on the very destruction he sought to chart.

His front-of-lens collaborator for five astounding films, the probably legitimately insane performance artist Klaus Kinski, he of the blond hair, widely spaced eyes, and twitchy lips, would in essence become the extension of Herzog; his dark side, the embodiment of his vice and his irrational desire to perhaps subconsciously cause his own destruction. The two became close friends but also, famously, mortal on-set enemies, once even plotting to murder each other behind the other's back (check out the stirring Herzog documentaries BURDEN OF DREAMS and MY BEST FIEND if you don't believe me). The fact that Herzog would eventually cast his beloved nemesis as the Lord of the parasites, speaks volumes about their unique and creatively volatile relationship.

Now, as every horror historian knows (but we'll recap here for those who don't), back when Murnau decided to adapt Stoker for the screen, he ran into a huge problem: Stoker's widow was very much alive and in possession of both her faculties and the rights to her hubby's estate. And she wanted cash. A lot more cash than Murnau was planning to part with. So Murnau, ever the arrogant brat, got the idea to

Kinski's vampire sees the sun for the first — and last — time.

tweak names and places in the story, changing Stoker's suave Transylvanian Count into a bald, bone-white, taloned freak named Orlock, and went ahead as planned, calling his picture NOSFERATU instead. As only a moron would miss the narrative disguise, the widow Stoker sued the director within an inch of his life, resulting in the courts ordering all prints of the picture to be destroyed. But they weren't and years later some of them surfaced, the film was hailed a lost classic and the rest is horror lore.

When it came time for Herzog to make his own tribute to this remarkable picture, the Dracula property had lapsed into the public domain, meaning he could call his villain Dracula and change the names and places back to their rightful literary origin. His plot, however, follows the original film's setup verbatim: Jonathan Harker (here played by notable German actor Bruno Ganz, perhaps best known now as Hitler in the film DOWNFALL) lives in quiet bliss in Virna with his porcelain skinned wife Lucy (played by the ravishing French actress Isabelle Adjani). One day, Harker's giggling, half-mad boss Renfield (brilliantly played by author Roland Topor, the same Roland Topor who wrote the novel on which Polanski's THE TENANT was based) sends him on an expedition to Transylvania to sell property to one Count Dracula (Kinski), a long trip he promises will cost the young go-getter plenty of sweat *and* blood.

Harker leaves his beloved Lucy and begins his serpentine journey to Castle Dracula where, after enduring weeks of endless horror, he discovers his host is in fact a night-crawling, neck-nipping monster. As Dracula packs up his black coffins and heads to Harker's hometown, specifically to sample the wares of his wife, a fever-ridden Harker must escape his tower prison and beat the rat-bringing, plague- carrying vampire to the punch before it's too late.

There's nothing in that synopsis that you haven't read or seen before, but remember, this is Dracula retold by a man who tells tales a bit differently than most. This is Werner Herzog's Dracula, shot on staggeringly eye-filling locations in the Netherlands, filled with impossible beauty, eccentric characters and most importantly an almost overwhelming sadness. The film is, as are all Herzog pictures, free of artifice and special effect save for Kinski's shocking make up design, cribbed wholesale from the original fiend played by actor Max Shreck. Indeed, the first time we see Kinski, his bald, pointy-eared, rat-toothed visage is shocking; he's a creature completely at odds with the natural beauty around him. This Dracula, for all his hideous, otherworldly, appearance, is simply another one of the director's dangerous outsiders, a thing who has been blessed and cursed with the secret of eternal life and yet forced to live as an outcast, skulking in rotting tombs, in a twilight shadow world, free of any sort of comfort or love.

And this vampire needs love, or rather needs to be loved.

And what of Kinski? Does this lunatic who so viscerally brought the monkey-tossing, delusional Don Lope de Aguirre and the megalomaniacal FITZCARALDO to screeching life, manage to successfully essay a miserable, attention-starved vampire fiend whose bloodlust is only matched by his despair? Fucking right, he does. Whether glowing in the moonlight, hungrily eyeing a dining Harker or creeping up on the beautiful Lucy, Kinski manages to create a monster that is as pathetic as he is terrifying, who wants to re-join the human race but whose disdain for it keeps him terminally distanced from everything.

Witness the climactic scene where a broken-hearted Lucy finally invites Dracula to drain her, hoping to drown him in daylight and save her husband's soul. In the original, Max Schreck's Count Orlock simply drinks her dry but here, with Kinski in the role, he vainly attempts to engage in "normal" lovemaking, clumsily pulling up Lucy's dress, clutching her bosom, sniffing her like a suspicious dog, before she lets him off the hook and just pulls him to her throat. It's an erotic (though free of nudity or traditional erotica tropes), tragic and macabre sequence and there has never been anything like it onscreen before or since.

There's one paralyzing section in Herzog's NOSFERATU that long ago made it one of my favorite films. As the rat plague brought by Dracula ravishes Virna, killing men, women and children without mercy, Lucy wanders the streets trying to convince the few survivors of the undead menace in their midst. The haunting sounds of Herzog's regular composer, the late Florian Fricke (aka progressive rock outfit Popol Vuh) bleeds into an otherworldly Georgian Choir, their mournful sound drifting across a tableau of an inevitable death. Pigs shit in the street, men try to mate with sheep, children dance with fiddlers, couples make love on the cobblestones and Lucy, dressed in white, raven hair pulled tight in a bun, almond eyes open wide weaves within it all. A table in the middle of the madness sees handsomely attired men and women dining and drinking, inviting Lucy to sit with them. "We all have the plague" a woman says matter-of-factly as rats dart in and out from between her legs, "and we want to enjoy every last minute we have left".

A frame later and the people are gone. Their feast now simply a table full of hordes of diseased rats. Chilling and beautiful stuff.

NOSFERATU: PHANTOM DER NACHT might just be Werner Herzog's ultimate masterpiece. A moving, haunting portrait of the mercilessness and inevitability of death but also a stark statement about how sometimes a brief life filled with warmth, love, beauty and belonging is better than an endless one filled with nothing but want. From the gorgeous cinematography, heart breaking performances, eerie, unforgettable music and even the quintessentially Herzog*ian* dark humor, this is one of the few motion pictures that benefits from several serious viewings, preferably alone, without a break of any kind. To say it pales beside the original is to miss the point.

INTERVIEW: WERNER HERZOG

I first met Werner Herzog in 2009 at the Toronto International Film Festival, shortly after the gala premiere screening of his ballistic Nicolas Cage psychodrama BAD LIEUTENANT: PORT OF CALL NEW ORLEANS. The next morning, we had lunch in some sort of courtyard café, I cannot recall which one, and got on very well, talking film and music and life in general. He was everything I had hoped he would be, speaking in that inimitable German accent and that gentle timbre of voice: playful, intellectual, cryptic. And when I told him that I thought he had given the world one of the best Cage performances, he slammed his fist down on the table, looked me dead in the eyes and snarled, "How can you be so vile and debased?! I have given the world the *best* Nicolas Cage performance *ever*!"

I laughed. He did not. And yet I knew he was joking. I think he was, anyway. Regardless, it was the ultimate Werner Herzog exchange and I'll never, ever forget it.

Through the years, Werner has always made time for me, indulging my questions about his filmography. And naturally, conversations about my favorite Herzog film, NOSFERATU, happened often. Here's one of them...

CHRIS ALEXANDER: You've said before that you think [F.W.] Murnau's picture is the single most important German film of all time. Do you still believe this?

WERNER HERZOG: It's always hard to make statements like that, but it's the certainly the finest Germany has to offer when it comes to cinema.

ALEXANDER: Do you remember the first time you saw it?

Kinski mimes his moves with Herzog's help.

HERZOG: No, but I think it was (noted German writer and critic) Lotte Eisner who pointed the film out to me, sometime in the early '70s or so,

ALEXANDER: What was your relationship with Eisner?

HERZOG: Well, it's a complex story but in a way, she was my mentor and also the mentor of the emerging new German cinema of the late '60s and '70s. We had a very deep relationship so deep that when she was dying, I wouldn't allow her to die, and I walked from Munich to Paris just to stop her, which had some effect. She died eight years later.

ALEXANDER: Were you with her when she passed?

HERZOG: No, but she called me to come to Paris and said, "Don't walk this time." I took a train and arrived at her small apartment, and she said she was almost blind. You could tell. She couldn't read anymore, couldn't watch cinema which was all the joy of her life, and she was very frail, could barely walk. She said, "Now it's kind of time to die," and I said, "Yeah, Lotte, now it sounds much more reasonable." She said, "But there's still this spell upon me that I must not die; can you lift it?" I said, "Yes, I can lift it easily now. It's lifted," and eight days later, she died. It was right- there's something like timing for someone to die, and in this case it was right. It wouldn't have been right eight years earlier.

ALEXANDER: The idea of the vampire — which is what NOSFERATU is about, not even the literal vampirism — was alive in many of your films. What was it about the concept that appealed to you in doing NOSFERATU?

HERZOG: It's more a homage to Murnau and finding a connection to the silent era of Germany of the 1920s. For us young German filmmakers in the '60s and '70s, that was important, because we didn't have a father generation. Our father generation was thrown out or chased out of Germany, or Jewish moviemakers either ended up in concentration camps or fled to America. Filmmakers would side with the cultural barbarism of the Nazi regime, so we had no fathers. There was a point when Lotte was our bridge to the great legitimate German cinema culture, and that was more important than the concept of vampirism. However, vampire movies always have a good life, because they appeal to collective nightmares, and cinema always finds a fertile ground when dealing with collective dreams or nightmares. That's why Fred Astaire is immortal in a way, and that's why NOSFERATU is immortal in a way.

ALEXANDER: Your NOSFERATU is radically different- even though some of the shots are very similar to Murnau's-in the sense that your and Kinski's vampire is not very happy being the creature he is. He's miserable, and there's a poetry and loneliness in his performance. How much of that was Kinski, and how much of that was you?

HERZOG: I think most of that was me because I wanted to depart from Murnau's NOSFERATU, where the vampire has no soul. He's like an insect, and i wanted a vampire with human qualities. It was clearly in the screenplay and in my conceptual thinking at the time, and of course it translated into Klaus Kinski's performance. He understood it very quickly.

ALEXANDER: Among the things I love about the film are the incidental details: the little bats when Harker writes his journal, the fruit bats hanging in the castle windows. Did you have a bat wrangler on set?

HERZOG: I believe I was the bat wrangler [*laughs*]. Our crew members were always scared. We also had a huge bat in Lucy's bedroom. That was a big, huge beast and everyone was frightened, so I had to wrangle it.

Remaking NOSFERATU was Herzog's passion project.

The director and his muse.

ALEXANDER: How did 20th Century Fox get involved? Did they finance the film or simply distribute it?

HERZOG: Fox distributed the film; they wanted to get into business with me and co-produce and finance three of my films: FITZCARRALDO, NOSFERATU and WOYZECK. FITZCARRALDO very quickly dissipated into thin air when they learned I was going to move a real ship over a real mountain. They spoke of a so-called "plastic solution"- a small model over a studio hill, or at best the botanic gardens of San Diego, so it was clear this was not going to fly with them. I knew I was going to be alone, so our thinking and organization quickly came apart or took different routes, which was fine. I think a Hollywood studio is incapable of doing a film like FITZCARRALDO. So, we stuck to doing NOSFERATU; all in all, there was something like a $600,000 or so advance guarantee from 20th Century Fox. They think they are the producers. Everybody thinks they are the producers, but [*laughs*] quite often a good film has many fathers One new arrival spreads death throughout the entire village of Wismar.

ALEXANDER: Was it their influence that provoked the creation of the English language version?

HERZOG: There was some influence, and I saw a point to it, because I understood the American market. The English and German versions are only different by not more than two minutes or so I would say less than 180 seconds. There's nothing significant that's different.

ALEXANDER: Did you oversee that English version?

HERZOG: Yes.

ALEXANDER: Why did you remove the little Gypsy boy with the violin from the German version? Am I right in saying that that charming sequence is gone?

HERZOG: Yes, you're certainly right. It's a side motif that isn't that important, in my opinion. At least, when you look at the preferences of American audiences, and it was a film that should have wide distribution and not lose itself in such things.

ALEXANDER: As an aside here, getting back to FITZCARRALDO very briefly, you mentioned the "plastic solution" today, that would obviously be the greenscreen solution. Given the opportunity to make a film like FITZCARRALDO again, would you drag a ship across a mountain again?

HERZOG: Of course I would! I want audiences back in the position where they can trust their eyes again. Even six-year-olds know, "Oh yeah, this was a digital effect, that was a greenscreen" and are aware of how it's done. But moving a real ship over a real mountain is not for the sake of realism or naturalism, it's more for the sake of a great operatic event, for stylization and because when you tackle a task of this magnitude, things happen that nobody can even imagine. For example, the sound - the groaning of the ship's hull; you just can't imagine it. The film became so much richer in texture and detail and its overall outlook-and by the way, I think every grown man should eventually pull his ship over a mountain.

ALEXANDER: Either figuratively or literally, right?

HERZOG: [*laughs*] Correct.

ALEXANDER: Making NOSFERATU was presumably a lot easier than a film like FITZCARRALDO. Was it a relatively smooth shoot?

HERZOG: I cannot really say that, because there were a couple of severe hiccups in the production. Number one, I wanted to shoot in the real Transylvania in the Carpathian mountains, but we never got the permits, so I went to the Tatra Mountains in Slovakia, bordering Poland. And then, of course, we had difficulties with the 11,000 rats that had to be transported all the way from Hungary to the Netherlands. We had permits to release them in the city of Delft; some years before, they'd had a rat problem, but we were very careful. We took huge precautions with safety nets and water pipes; we did not lose a single one, but of course there was a press campaign against it.

ALEXANDER: Were you a rat wrangler as well? Did you get bitten?

HERZOG: I did, yes. We shot early in spring, and it was still quite cold in Poland, and when we unloaded the rats, they lumped together in huge piles just to warm each other, and I jumped out from behind the camera, reached into a huge pile of

Herzog and Alexander, Toronto.

hundreds of rats and tried to disperse them. Of course, I got bitten at least 30, 40 times that day which is fine. I mean, who cares?

ALEXANDER: Some might care... but not Werner Herzog! Let's talk about the music. What was your relationship with Fricke when it came to scoring the film?

HERZOG: We were very close. We talked about the screenplay, he saw the dailies and the very first rough assembly, and we worked shoulder to shoulder throughout the entire process. That was a wonderful collaboration.

ALEXANDER: Fricke died of a stroke in 2001; were you friends right until the end?

HERZOG: Friends, yes, but let's say that intellectually and culturally, we started to drift apart. He was somehow caught up in a new age pseudo-philosophy, and it was a route I did not want to go down, so we imperceptibly drifted apart.

ALEXANDER: I can't imagine you have anything new to say about Kinski and your relationship with him-but in NOSFERATU, he delivers a very restrained performance. Was he well-behaved?

HERZOG: He was never well-behaved [*laughs*]! But let's put it this way: NOSFERATU was our most harmonious collaboration in general. Of course, he would throw a tantrum occasionally, and scream and yell and try to destroy a set or whatever. But I think he understood the significance of the film for him, and he settled in with that.

ALEXANDER: You've said in the past that one of the techniques you learned while working with him was to let him have those tantrums, let him burn himself out, and then he'd be in that zone where he'd be much more malleable and easier to control. Is that true?

HERZOG: Sometimes, yes, but it was more complex than that. The real challenge was to focus all his explosive qualities—all his madness, all his paranoia, all his hysteria and make it productive for the screen and let it dissipate when the camera was not rolling. Thats a very complicated procedure between a director and an actor; I had to somehow get the wild beast on screen, and not during a tantrum after dinner.

ALEXANDER: There's a quality to Kinski in NOSFERATU, like he's tuned into some sort of frequency that only he can hear. A sort of distracted quality...

HERZOG: That is a very beautiful observation.

ALEXANDER: NOSFERATU is PG-rated. There's no overt violence or nudity, and yet it's incredibly sensual and grim. I cannot recall any of your movies having extreme sexuality or violence, save for maybe BAD LIEUTENANT. Am I right?

HERZOG: That is correct.

ALEXANDER: Why is that? Why have you generally shied away from the more exploitative elements?

HERZOG: I can't even tell you, but I will say that violence in graphic detail is something I abhor and detest in movies. Sexuality... I don't know. I'm not sure.

THE OMEGA MAN (1971)

Starring Charlton Heston, Rosalind Cash, Anthony Zerbe, Paul Koslo
Written by John William Corrington, Joyce H. Corrington
Directed by Boris Sagal

I got to know author and genre-lit icon Richard Matheson during the last stretch of his life and, while I'm forever grateful for that 11th hour connection, the version of Matheson I met was anything but cheerful in regard to his work. And really, he had many reasons to be irate. When Matheson first began self-adapting his stories for Rod Serling in THE TWILIGHT ZONE, Serling left the author alone to transpose his own tales to fit the show's format. Later, TV horror hero Dan Curtis (DARK SHADOWS) also ensured Matheson's many scripts remained untouched (THE NIGHT STALKER, DRACULA etc.) and the resulting pictures speak for themselves. The reason guys like Serling and Curtis did this was because they fully understood just how good a scribe Matheson was and how well he was able to bring his words to simple, cinematic life.

The last man alive... is not alone!
CHARLTON HESTON THE ΩMEGA MAN
A WALTER SELTZER PRODUCTION CO-STARRING ANTHONY ZERBE · ROSALIND CASH · SCREENPLAY BY JOHN WILLIAM and JOYCE H. CORRINGTON
PRODUCED BY WALTER SELTZER · DIRECTED BY BORIS SAGAL · PANAVISION® · TECHNICOLOR® FROM WARNER BROS. A KINNEY LEISURE SERVICE
GP
ALL AGES ADMITTED
COPYRIGHT ©1971 WARNER BROS., INC.
71/208

Among that trove of tales and tomes penned by the late, great Matheson, its his terrifying, cerebral, and existential 1954 novella *I Am Legend* that has perhaps most greatly defined his legacy. *I Am Legend* pioneered a gap-bridging between science fiction and Gothic fantasy, with its lurid, skin-crawling story of a plague that eliminates the living, only to resurrect them as blood-hungry vampires. In it, only one human has inexplicably remained immune to this apocalypse, a suburbanite named Robert Neville, who boards himself up at night with mirrors and garlic to ward off the monsters who want to drain him, while sifting through the city by day and staking the ghouls in their lairs. It's a sparse setup for a book, but at its core its an epic tale of one man's journey into his own soul, a personal, harrowing, meditation on loss, love, loneliness and what it is to truly be "alive".

The novella (my favorite book of all time, incidentally) is written, in typical Serling fashion, practically, with a few key locations and characters (both living and undead); a packaged gift to Hollywood, elemental to adapt, economical to produce. Really, all one needs to make a proper screen version of *I Am Legend* is faithfulness to the story, a sense of style and mood and one helluva a central actor to embody Neville and his exhausting evolution.

Matheson knew this.

"So why does Hollywood keep fucking it up?!" he said to me back in 2003.

That's the eternal question. The answer is anybody's guess.

Britain's Hammer studio hired Matheson to adapt his text as NIGHT CREATURES in the early '60s, but the project died after the UK censor pre-banned it for being too violent in concept alone. Annoyed by this, Matheson took his script to producer Robert L. Lippert who took it to American International Pictures and mounted a low budget Italian/American picture called THE LAST MAN ON EARTH. Matheson was told Fritz Lang would direct, but instead he got Sidney Salkow and Ubaldo Ragona, with AIP standby Vincent Price starring as Neville, who was inexplicably renamed Robert Morgan during rewrite. More changes were made to the script against Matheson's wishes, causing the exasperated writer to slap his pen name Logan Swanson on the credits. The resulting film is — despite Matheson's sneering — an excellent little horror drama and embodies much of the soul of the source book. But the changes that ARE made are so odd and pointless, one wonders why they were done at all.

George A, Romero loved both the book and the first film enough to admittedly "rip Matheson off" (George's words, not mine) for his groundbreaking 1968 shocker NIGHT OF THE LIVING DEAD, turning vampires into zombies and altering horror history in the process. Decades later, writer Akiva Goldsman and Mark Protosevich took a sledgehammer to the book and penned the screenplay for a mammoth budgeted Will Smith vehicle that retained the novella's title and the name of its lead character, but totally missed the point of the story (tying the sting of the title to a Bob Marley

"The Family" reveals their pretty marks.

greatest hits album is unforgivable) and turned it into a muscular action thriller. As far as muscular action thrillers go, it's well done with a good Smith performance, but it's savaged by a tone deaf final act and vampire-ghouls that look like CGI hemorrhoids come to cartoonish life.

Sandwiched in the center of these dual "authorized" adaptations sits director Boris Sagal's THE OMEGA MAN, a film "suggested" by the novel *I Am Legend* and following the setup and basic psychology of Matheson's work but bearing little narrative resemblance to it. Needless to say, outside of the presumed healthy payday, the writer was NOT a fan of THE OMEGA MAN. But while on the surface the 1971 film is yet further evidence in the ongoing case as to why the good-Goddamn Hollywood can't get *I Am Legend* right, THE OMEGA MAN is, in spite of itself, a kind of masterpiece.

Oh hell, it's not a *kind* of masterpiece, it *is* a masterpiece. Full stop.

Sagal's updated, post-hippie riff on Matheson's material casts the great Charlton Heston as Neville, this time re-invented as a military scientist, the sole — or so he thinks — surviving man on earth after biochemical warfare has annihilated the populace from coast to coast. In the book, Neville becomes a self-made scientist after years of ennui and obsession while in the Price version, his Neville/Morgan is already a scientist, feverishly working on a cure for the vampiric plague. Husband and wife writers John William Corrington and Joyce H. Corrington's urgent remix of the tale follows this variation on Neville while jettisoning the undead virus and replacing it with specific man-made death. As the world withers, Heston's Neville seemingly invents the antidote but the helicopter carrying him to headquarters crashes, leaving the wounded MD with no other option but to inject himself with the serum, thus explicitly explaining his immunity.

As in the book and other adaptations, Neville is NOT alone in this atrophied anti-Eden. But instead of Matheson's grunting, ravenous ghouls, we get articulate, counterculture mutants slinking through the streets; a pack of alabaster monks who hole themselves up in a hive during the day and emerge and night, sporting glittery black robes and Roy Orbison-esque sunglasses, coming en masse to Neville's fortified brownstone, not to drink his blood to execute him. Led by Anthony (KISS MEETS THE PHANTOM OF THE PARK) Zerbe's preening Matthias (who, as we see in pre-war flashback, was an on-air newscaster), the "family" as they call themselves, see Neville as quite literally "The Man", a totem of a modern age that destroyed itself. In their warped, diseased minds, Neville is the abomination, with the family being the rightful inheritors of the planet, a new tribe of sickly citizens who sneer at technology and seek to bulldoze the future back to the stone age. After sunset, Neville defends his fortress from these screaming, sanctimonious holy men and come morning, he spends his hours screeching around San Francisco is fast cars, shooting his machine gun at anything that moves while searching for the family's nest.

Vampires or not, the concept and themes behind THE OMEGA MAN are kin to *I Am Legend*. In the book, Robert Neville refuses to leave his home. The vampires that crawl around his yard chanting his name and calling for his fluids become, in a sense, his only companions. His quest to kill them becomes his sole purpose. Heston's Neville, despite his machismo and self-assurance, follows the same pattern. The cat and mouse dance between himself and the family defines his current life. He even "accidentally" comes home late, too close to sundown, just to test himself, just to have some kind of interaction with the only other sentient creatures on earth, no matter how deadly.

In both variations, Neville's antagonists scream his name at night, hurling objects at his windows and trying to burn and break down his walls. In *I Am Legend* and THE LAST MAN ON EARTH, our hero opts to bury his head and turn up his record player. In THE OMEGA MAN, Heston's Neville chooses to open fire on the scurrying fiends below. But seeing as THE OMEGA MAN was indeed developed as a project for the Hollywood superstar, a companion to his career resurgence as a sci-fi/action blockbuster hero in 1968's PLANET OF THE APES, this swaggering, trigger-happy version of Neville makes sense. In fact, THE OMEGA MAN's family has much DNA in common with the APES sequel, BENEATH THE PLANET OF THE APES, with its post-apocalyptic mutants living a monastic existence while worshipping the nuclear bomb that made them. Further to that, the Corrington's would two years later write the final PLANET OF THE APES picture, BATTLE FOR THE PLANET OF THE APES, a movie whose messages are heavily linked to THE OMEGA MAN's.

In *I Am Legend*'s final act, Robert Neville discovers that he is indeed *not* the only living human being on the planet, rather the vampire plague has created a strain of peaceful people that teeter between both states. Neville is astonished to learn that his acts of extermination have been in fact cold-blooded murders of these terrified

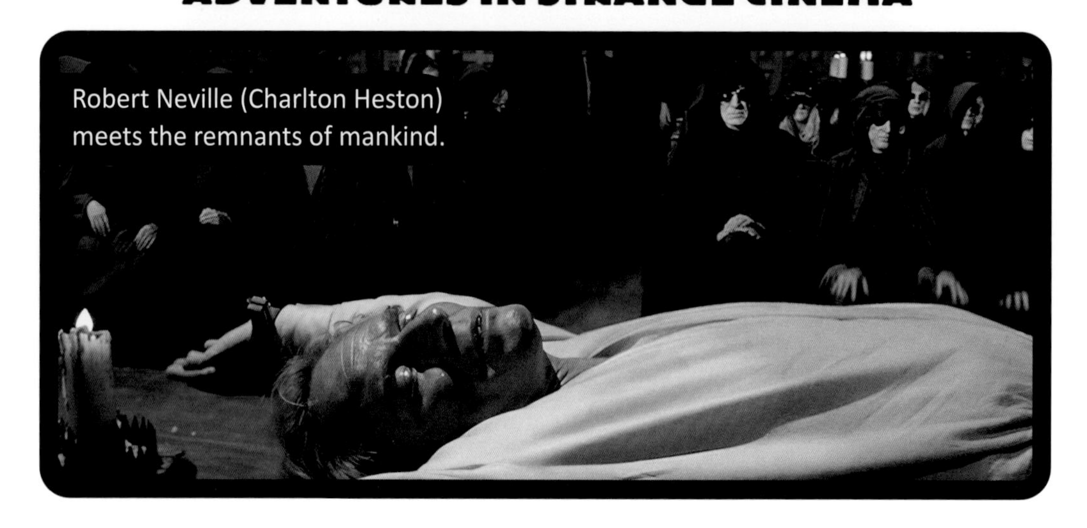
Robert Neville (Charlton Heston) meets the remnants of mankind.

wretches. The title refers to the truth that, among these survivors, *he* is the boogeyman, he is the threat; Neville has become their myth, their "legend". THE OMEGA MAN takes this idea and moves it to the middle of the movie, with a gaggle of survivors led by Rosalind Cash's Lisa and Paul Koslo's Dutch rescuing Neville from the clutches of the family with the hope that he might save them before they too turn into ghastly, demented albinos. Instead of a threat, Neville becomes the new messiah, the world's last and only hope. This biblical riff suits the man who played Moses in THE TEN COMMANDMENTS well and, while admittedly heavy handed, gives the film a real sense of gravitas and grace and a kind of optimism that dystopian movies like this — and the source book itself — often lacked. There's a dash of sociopolitical daring here too, with Heston and Cash embarking on a love affair, itself one of the first interracial couplings in Hollywood history, a neo-Adam and Eve, immune to the stigmas of the "old world".

But outside of these twists on Matheson's text, what truly pushes THE OMEGA MAN to the heights it reaches is Sagal's direction, Russell Metty's shiny, sharp cinematography, Heston's solid, strong and square-jawed presence and perhaps most effectively, composer Ron (DOCTOR WHO) Grainer's haunting, groovy, unforgettable original score. Combining orchestra, jazz and a progressive rock/funk groove, Grainer's deftly designed music pushes every image forward, blanketing long passages of dialogue between Zerbe and his right-hand man Zachary (Lincoln Kilpatrick) with the throbbing excitement of an action movie and then stripping down the sound during actual shootouts and leaving in only lonely organs and vibraphones. The composer also employs the dreamy sound of a water chime to add a sort of liquid beauty to eerie scenes of dead roads and decimated buildings. It's certainly one of the finest scores made for any sort of genre film and it turns much of the movie into a kind of tone poem about life, death, society, and salvation.

Matheson didn't like THE OMEGA MAN as an adaptation of what might very well be his finest literary achievement. And I'm with him. The film s a terrible direct translation of what is, again, one of the easiest-to-adapt-to-screen books I've ever read. But it doesn't want to be the novel. It has something else on its mind and seen as a moody, musical, intelligent, stylish, and powerful piece of post-60s sci-fi horror with theological undercurrents, THE OMEGA MAN has few peers.

INTERVIEW: PAUL KOSLO

In THE OMEGA MAN, actor Paul Koslo plays the laid-back Dutch, a motorcycle riding refugee of a dead world inherited by a legion of deranged, hooded mutants intent on destroying any trace of humanity left on the planet, chiefly two-fisted survivor Robert Neville (Charlton Heston).

And though Koslo would also star in many other notable '70s film, including 1971's VANISHING POINT, the TRUE GRIT sequel ROOSTER COGBURN, the Charles Bronson vehicle MR. MAJESTYK, Jack Starrett's THE LOSERS and Michael Cimino's HEAVEN'S GATE, it's his tales of fighting side by side with the larger-than-life Heston in Boris Sagal's magnum opus that made me reach out to him, a few years before his passing in 2019. Koslo was one of the greatest character actors of his generation and he was one helluva raconteur...

ALEXANDER: Can you tell us about your humble beginnings?

KOSLO: Well, I was born in Germany during the end of the war and, you know, the whole country was decimated, totally destroyed; so, all of our parents were like disoriented, like, what the hell happened? and the kids, well, we were running amok. I was 4 or 5 and there were tanks rumbling down the street and the Brits and Americans were throwing out Wrigley's spearmint gum and Hershey bars and the kids were going crazy. We had no supervision. We started to fantasize about America, about cowboys and Indians, or what we thought were cowboy and Indians. Then, when I was seven, we immigrated to Regina, Saskatchewan, Canada. This is in 1951. We couldn't speak any English so in school they would say stuff like "Germs are bad". I thought they were saying *Germans*. I ended up fighting with people a lot. We were like aliens. We were always in trouble.

ALEXANDER: Did your parents embrace your decision to become an actor?

KOSLO: Actually, my dad was a career soldier and so was my grandfather and my great grandfather. He was a hard guy to get to know. So, I up and left home when I was 13 and never looked back. See, to him, I was never an actor. It didn't matter that I had been in over 100 TV shows and movies. He wouldn't hear it.

As Dutch, Paul Koslo radiated charm.

ALEXANDER: Let's talk about how you ended up as the other last man on earth in one of my favorite films, THE OMEGA MAN. Tell me about Charlton Heston; what did you learn from him?

KOSLO: Oh man, the first thing I learned was you don't fuck with *Moses*, y'know [*laughs*]? But he was really nice. I worked with him on a few pictures, and he was always very sweet to me. I hit him on the head with my pearl handle .45 in Dodger Stadium; remember that scene in the film? That scene where the mutants were going to burn him at the stake?

ALEXANDER: Of course, it's the first time we see you in the film.

KOSLO: Yeah, well I came in there, this guy, "Dutch", with his dopey Baron Von Richter hat and I had these guns and the director, Boris Sagal, what a sweet guy, he says "Paul will you run in there as fast as you can and keep those guns out, because the goons will try to kill you, it will be dark, some explosions will go off and I need you to get in here as fast as you can because we'll have a little fire behind Heston. Don't worry he won't be in any danger."

So I get in there, I slide in, really dramatic and hot looking and as I reach for his wrists above his head to untie him, I smack him in the head with the fucking gun and I break his skin! And I thought, Holy shit what have I done? I said, "I'm so sorry man", and he says "Just get on with it! Get me outta here!" and I started to untie him and I'm like, "I'm doing it, I'm doing it!" and then we ran outta there hunched over, as fast as we could out of the shot. I said, I'm so sorry Mr. Heston. He says, "Goddammit, that hurt!" Anyway, they stitched him up and he was fine with me after that; but I will say that after that, I did all my close-ups during our dialogue scenes talking to a mop that the script girl would hold.

ALEXANDER: THE OMEGA MAN was an expensive picture, but did it open well? Was it a hit?

KOSLO: It was a hit, yeah. I'll tell you why: because it was controversial. Rosalind Cash, the love interest was, of course, a black actress and she had a nude scene and that was *huge*. This is 1971. It had never been done in a major motion picture by a major studio. That was very enlightening to a lot of people and Heston got a lot of brownie points for doing that. You know, I didn't like his politics, but Heston was a nice guy. A smart guy. And he was nice to me.

You know, right before THE OMEGA MAN I did THE LOSERS with William Smith. After three weeks of filming that in the jungle, the producer, Joe Solomon, hadn't paid us. William Smith said, "We're not doing anything until that SOB pays us!"

This was a SAG film, and we went over our hours every day. So, I never got paid. Heston was the president of the Screen Actors Guild at the time, and I told him what happened. Not only did I get every penny that I had coming, but the penalties and interest as well. He was a real union guy.

ALEXANDER: You say you didn't agree with his politics. What were they at the time? This was a man who I understood was a great advocate for civil rights.

KOSLO: Yes, but he was still very, very conservative. He was a forerunner for putting his voice out there for things like civil rights, yes, but he was always pro-gun. He didn't talk that much. He didn't like that many people. He was a loner. But he was a big advocate for guns.

ALEXANDER: You are not, obviously.

KOSLO: No. Guns kill. People kill people with guns. If you've got a gun, you gotta use it.

ALEXANDER: You worked with another '70s gun culture figurehead, Charles Bronson.

KOSLO: Yeah, I did three movies with that guy. MR. MAJESTYK, THE STONE KILLER and LOVE AND BULLETS with Rod Steiger. I have a real history with Bronson. I have some great stories. I didn't like him at all. My mom loved him. But out of all the hundreds of actors I've worked with, Heston, John Wayne, all of them, I can only cite two assholes: James Franciscus and Bronson. That's pretty good odds. In MR. MAJESTYK, we came towards the end of the movie and the director, Richard Fleischer, the sweetest guy ever, whose dad incidentally was Max Fleischer who did the BETTY BOOP cartoons, said, "Charlie, I want to change the end of the movie here. When you come down from the upstairs into the cabin, Paul is down here and you're supposed to kill him, but he's so funny in the movie, I think it would be nice to let Paul live". Bronson walks down the stairs real slow, swaggering and he looks at me,

Koslo was one of cult cinema's secret handshakes.

he looks at Fleischer and says "I'm not here to make a star out of Paul Koslo. When you figure it out, I'll be in my dressing room." And he walks out! Richard stops him and says, "No Charlie, I need you here!" Bronson looks back at me, piercing eyes staring me down. I shrug my shoulders, looking around, smiling nervously. Bronson says, "What, you think that's funny? Maybe I can fix it, so you'll never smile again!" I've got Charles Bronson stories you would not believe, man!

PET SEMATARY TWO (1992)

Starring Edward Furlong, Clancy Brown, Anthony Edwards, Jared Rushton
Written by Richard Outten
Directed by Mary Lambert

Arkansas born director Mary Lambert came of age in the early 1980s, a pioneer in the burgeoning art of the music video. Creating a flurry of high concept, groundbreaking clips for chart-smashing musical acts like Motley Crue, Sting, Prince, Mick Jagger, Annie Lennox and Madonna (her startling and controversial "Like a Prayer" video was groundbreaking example of the rock video as blazing fine art), Lambert entered the feature film foray with the hypnotic and surreal 1987 psychodrama SIESTA. Bizarre and unapologetically sexual, SIESTA was met with adoration from the fringe and bewilderment and ire from the mainstream and has since become a cult movie. And no matter how iffy its box office take, it was SIESTA that paved the path for Lambert to make the first filmed adaptation of Stephen King's harrowing novel PET SEMATARY two years later. The grisly 1989 picture captured the essence of King's gruesome tale of familial decay, supernatural terror and taboo smashing child death and, though it was a very controlled and faithful translation (King himself wrote the script), enough of Lambert's gonzo, rock'n'roll cinema spirt snuck through, including a closing credits song by punk icons The Ramones that became one of their biggest hits.

And while PET SEMATARY is now rightly regarded as a horror classic, its Lambert-directed 199*two* companion picture PET SEMATARY TWO was met with critical scorn and raised the ire of King himself, who had his name removed from the film and from all marketing materials. It's understandable why King might have wanted to distance himself from PET SEMATARY TWO. Writer Richard Outten's script takes the setting and mythology of the book — that of a cursed Indian burial ground in the small town of Ludlow, Maine that has the power to resurrect the evil dead — and spins an entirely new yarn about traumatized teens, abusive elders, animal cruelty and zombie horror. And with Lambert at the helm, and with considerably more creative freedom than she had on the first film, the sequel mutated into a work of transgressive, irreverent, tonally maniacal pop art from hell.

Mean and merciless, PET SEMATARY TWO sees Edward Furlong (fresh from the success of TERMINATOR TWO) as a kid named Jeff who, after witnessing the hideous death of his actress mother on the set of her latest horror movie (a wild, Gothic opening sequence), moves to Ludlow with his veterinarian father (REVENGE OF THE NERDS' Anthony Edwards) to heal and move on. But Ludlow itself is in dire need of healing, still reeling from the mysterious "Creed Murders" in the first film and filled with a populace that seems to want to be anywhere else than where they are. Soon,

Jeff (Edward Furlong) and Drew (Jason McGuire) walk a dark path to terror.

Jeff is running afoul of the local sadistic (and very King-esque) bullies and the equally cruel Sheriff (a show-stealing turn from the great Clancy Brown), all the while locked down in deep mourning for his brutally removed mom. After a tragic incident results in the death of Jeff's friend Drew's dog, Jeff soon finds himself mired in local myth, burying the pup behind the pet cemetery. The dog returns — naturally — and is of course infected with ancient necrotic evil. What follows is an increasingly horrifying — and wonderfully ludicrous — series of events that defy logic and flip the finger to any sense of good taste.

Ostensibly a bleak horror comedy, Lambert's superlative sequel is a glorious mess of macabre iconography, lush, gauzy style, sickening ultraviolence, heart-wrenching tragedy and dizzying tonal shifts. It's taken decades to command the sort of respect in demands but slowly, surely, PET SEMATARY TWO is finding its cult. It's the logical extension of Lambert's wild vision first essayed in SIESTA, a counterculture, subtextually potent, earthy passion that manages to weave its way into all of her work (even her Netflix holiday comedy BEST. CHRISTMAS. EVER! Is pulsing with the director's wild-eyed style and eccentricities). But PET SEMATARY TWO — with its large canvas and game cast — might just be the ultimate Lambert cinematic experience. It's certainly the best film boasts the PET SEMATARY name and is so singular a work, that I cannot rightly cite another genre sequel quite like it.

INTERVIEW: MARY LAMBERT

ALEXANDER: You were a music video pioneer. Did you consider your videos to be short films? Were you going for a sort of "mini-cinema" aesthetic in your approach and design?

MARY LAMBERT: Well, we were sort of inventing them at the time, so I wasn't consciously doing anything except trying to invent an art form.

ALEXANDER: So, in that spirit of invention, would you say that you were kind of throwing darts at the dartboard and seeing what stuck, almost making experimental films in a way?

LAMBERT: I didn't think of it as throwing darts at a dartboard because I'm a lousy dart player [*laughs*]. I thought of it as an extension of my life as an artist, that we were telling stories and doing something that hasn't been done before with music and images, the two things I love the most.

ALEXANDER: It makes sense that your first feature was SIESTA, which to me was the logical extension of that work in rock videos, with a larger canvas to paint your pictures on. I think SIESTA is a delirious masterpiece. I remember seeing it when I was thirteen, around the same time I saw ANGEL HEART, and my mind was melted seeing those movies virtually back-to-back.

Mary Lambert, among the tombstones.

LAMBERT: Yeah, I can see that. ANGEL HEART and SIESTA sort of come from a similar place, creatively and tonally.

ALEXANDER: Right, with the mixing of fantasy, reality; blurring those lines of dream and memory. What was Patricia's script like? Did you read Patrice Chaplin's book?

LAMBERT: I actually read the script in Annie Lennox's dressing room! Zalman King, one of the producers, was married to Patricia, and had sent it to Annie to see if she was interested in it. She was not. I read the script and I really fell in love with it because of the nonlinear structure, the passion, the idea of obsession and the female character, and the sexuality, were all things that attracted me to it. I followed through on it with the producers and they were excited about the idea of working with me, then we went through hell to raise the money and then we made the film.

ALEXANDER: You mentioned the producers, one of which was music legend Gary Kurfirst, who I'm sure you knew from your work doing videos. Did Gary give you a lot of creative freedom to make the kind of movie you wanted to make?

LAMBERT: The movie wouldn't have happened without Gary. He was the one who stuck with me, stuck with the project. I can't tell you how many times it was financed and how many times the financing fell through. Gary was a real visionary, he was in the beginning primary with bands, he was a rock'n'roll manager, he was also an art collector, he had a deep understanding of painting and music. The Talking Heads, Eurythmics, Annie Lennox; I can't tell you all the bands he represented. He wanted

Rachel Creed (Denise Crosby) comes back for her man in 1989's PET SEMATARY.

to make an Oscar Wilde rock'n'roll movie. He was the perfect producer. I've never had another producer that was that interested in doing something that original. Originality was a huge thing for him.

ALEXANDER: I guess in a way, it's not to fair to say that you were spoiled by your first rodeo, but...

LAMBERT: No, I was very spoiled by my first rodeo!

ALEXANDER: Speaking of music, here you are making this kind of maniacal rock'n'roll movie with Gary, did you personally work closely on the score too? I mean you had Miles Davis playing on this, with Marcus Miller...

LAMBERT: I had the honor and privilege of working really closely with them. I mean, nobody tells Miles David what to do but he was interested in the movie, my vision of the movie, and I sat in the theater and watched the whole movie with him, it was wild. He came to my home several times, I went to the recording studio, and Marcus Miller is a genius too, Marcus was the one who put it together. Miles would take out his trumpet and just play a little bit and then play some more, but there's more work to be done to make it into a score, and Marcus wanted to produce the album and put the rest of the arrangements together.

ALEXANDER: It's such a great score and an integral part of the film. It really adds to that hazy, neo-noir vibe. But the critical reception was mixed. I remember as a kid I had my Leonard Maltin movie book, and I knew if he gave something a *bad* rating it was a movie I wanted to see. And he was cruel to SIESTA. He might have given it the dreaded bomb rating which was high marks for a weird genre film. Did you have to let that roll off your back a little bit, when the critics were, shall we say, "confused" about the film?

LAMBERT: Yeah, they didn't understand it. I knew I'd made a really cool movie, maybe not a great movie, but a really cool movie. We had such a hard time financing it, with all the different producers involved, and you can't buy a DVD, it's been locked up for a while. We actually just screened it at the Sitges Film Festival this year and it was really fun. I love that festival, I've been a couple of times.

ALEXANDER: So we move from SIESTA, to PET SEMATARY. The film had a long development. At one point, George Romero was supposed to do it, and his frequent collaborator Richard Rubenstein produced it. How did you get involved?

LAMBERT: It was just luck of the draw, really. People were starting to notice me because of the music videos, and my agent sent me the script. I was an avid Stephen King fan, I've always loved scary movies, even more supernatural or fantasy than straight out horror but still, I love horror movies, I love him. I like telling scary stories and I like Stephen King but I really didn't think of myself as a horror director. So I read the script and immediately thought this is the natural progression from SIESTA because this was about obsession, and about when a person takes the obsession of life into death, it's a complicated things, and there are ghosts, entities who are unable to let go of life, they are obsessed with life and so it's the same type of thing as Siesta in a certain way and that same thing interested me, and it was a good script. Steven had to approve the director and I think it was probably rock'n'roll that got me the job because, and we got along great, the first meeting he knew I made it clear that I didn't want to rewrite his script, change the story, I just wanted to channel his story and scare people, creep them out and use every visual tool I had to tell a scary, scary version of that story. I don't think he was looking for Ridley Scott to come in and cause problems, but what sealed the deal was I was good friends with Dee Dee and I told him they would write a song for him, and Dee Dee writes the best songs, that was one of their best songs and it absolutely encapsulates what the movie is about.

ALEXANDER: It's a great song on many levels, and as you say it encapsulates the story, and adds a little bit of that Mary Lambert rock'n'roll edge to the film. It's also one of the greatest "break to credits" songs in horror history.

LAMBERT: It helps with that last image of Denise Crosby with maggots crawling out of her ear. it helps that it's ok to laugh at even the most horrible thing to happen. Honestly, it's so horrible it's probably ridiculous, so you should probably go laugh at it.

ALEXANDER: And then with PET SEMATARY TWO, where you explicitly tell people it's ok to laugh! I think that's what adds to the whole disorienting feel of that film. In PET SEMATARY, it still feels like Mary Lambert is on her best behavior; she's disciplined, she knows there's a lot of eyeballs on her and she has to adapt a very popular,

PET SEMATARY TWO has a truly shocking opening.

bestselling novel, she has to please many people. But with PET TWO, it felt like the handcuffs were off and you just went fucking bananas. Am I right?

LAMBERT: Yeah, you are, basically. I originally wanted to do Ellie's story, but they wanted to do another story, and we came up with the idea of doing teenage boys. That's who The Ramones write songs for. I love that crazy teenage boy energy and I really felt like there was a lot of dark edgy humor in the script. I wanted to do a horror comedy and I think the producers, when they saw that was happening, they were a little freaked out. That was the early days of horror/comedy, no one was really doing it, and, you know the worst thing that could happen to you as teenage boys is your mom marries the authoritarian bad ass sheriff in town, a sheriff that hates you and he becomes your step father. That's the worst thing that could happen, now it's not, now the worst thing that can happen is you kill him, bury in in a pet cemetery and he comes back as a crazy killer zombie, that's funny but also terrifying.

ALEXANDER: Yes, it's all these things. I remember I saw it in the theater with my then girlfriend, and it was like someone smacked me in the head because I didn't know how I was supposed to react to this thing. Was I supposed to laugh, scream, cry. I know I felt sick watching it as well because it's so melancholy and disturbing and cruel. Then recently I unearthed it and showed my current girlfriend because she'd never seen it and she agreed that it has an energy that's completely singular. But then again, it's directed by the woman who gave us SIESTA. PET SEMATARY TWO feels to me more like the logical next step from SIESTA. It feels like a bad dream. It sort of behaves like a normal, linear horror movie to a point, and then it becomes this interior, surrealist metaphor for Jeff's grief. I might be imagining this. Was that ever in the script?

LAMBERT: That's kind of me imposing myself on the script. And also, David Goyer came in and worked on that script, he really helped me. But yeah, you read my mind there. That was my intention. That Jeff doesn't know what's real and what's not real. I just wanted that to be like, what's the *worst* thing that could happen to you. How much of that is he seeing with his eyes? And that goes for Anthony Edwards too. The scene where he is going to make love to his dead wife, and she turns into a dog. I know that's in poor taste, but I still think it's pretty good. Some of that stuff in the movie is so off the rails but some of it works well in my opinion... and maybe some of it doesn't work as well as it could. I mean, I wanted to do the whole soundtrack with an electric guitar, bass guitar, no other instruments, and that didn't go over so well...

ALEXANDER: Yeah, that would have been so amazing. Something like Neil Young's score for DEAD MAN or something, where he's just noodling.

LAMBERT: Yeah, I really wanted to, and my composer was really into it. Mark did a great job and after we turned in the director's cut, the electric guitar soundtrack, they wanted to fire him. They can't fire him he was just doing his job, so they wanted to send everything to someplace in Romania to get the score done but I said no, no, you can't do that. We still have some really interesting music in there I think, but no, that's not exactly how I wanted it to sound like.

ALEXANDER: You also have a who's who of the cool alternative rock bands from that era: Miranda Sex Garden, The Jesus & Mary Chain, L7. You even have Traci Lords in there, a guess a sort of favor to your pal Gary, as she was then on his Radioactive label, am I wrong?

LAMBERT: Yeah, you're not wrong, you're right.

ALEXANDER: Let's talk a little bit about that dinner sequence, which I think encapsulates everything we've been talking about in this movie, all the levels both visceral and psychological. That "teenage boy experience" you speak of. The reality of visiting the friend's home, that kid with the step boorish father. The subtext is outrageous. They've murdered this man, they've resuscitated him for whatever reason, and now he's an evil zombie tyrant and an unholy slob to boot. So here they are, these three, all sitting at the table, and they suddenly break into maniacal laughter. And yet in the peripheral, there's the mother making this dinner for these people, and she's just been raped and beaten. And then your heart sinks and again, you don't know how to feel watching this movie...

LAMBERT: Well, you know, beyond the supernatural element, that's the reality of life for a lot of people, especially in small little towns, you know. I wasn't really trying to make a movie about child abuse or domestic abuse, or any of those things but I felt like with the zombie that comes back from the dead, if he really is evil in life, it's like, what are the worst things he could do, you know? There's a lot of people running around like that, unnecessarily abusing people, whether it's their family, someone else, not necessarily something they will be put in prison for but something they deserve to burn in hell for. And that's kind of who the sheriff was. At the same time, you have to laugh at him because it's all so ridiculous. I wanted to do more than make a movie about social injustice, though. Maybe it's just a whole southern gothic thing from my upbringing. Things can be bad but it can get worse so you might as well find something to laugh at about this because it really could get worse.

ALEXANDER: I didn't even think about that, you being a southern girl, this is absolutely a southern gothic. And further to that, the movie's sweaty, you can almost smell PET SEMATARY TWO. You made a real deal southern gothic hiding in a pop horror film.

LAMBERT: Totally! And the storytelling, some of the stories I heard as a child or even as an adult, god, I had some crazy friends, in the south, cousins, and people will be going along telling a story, and it sounds pretty funny and then all of a sudden it's horrible, and everybody's laughing, like wow, I can see why that's funny but it's not really funny. Or, when it's really horrible and you look at it objectively and it is funny. You look at it on one side and it's not funny but it's funny, you look at it from the other side it's funny but it's not funny, it's the two headed monster.

ALEXANDER: That's a bit of Mel Brooks in you.

LAMBERT: I don't' know how much Mel Brooks I have in me, but he does make me laugh. Springtime For Hitler. Hilarious. I guess, yeah, it's that kind of humor.

ALEXANDER: Or in BLAZING SADDLES. It's a funny movie. But it's not funny to the character who is experiencing all of these indignities.

LAMBERT: Agreed.

ALEXANDER: Speaking of Gothic. Another extremely cool thing happening in PET SEMATARY TWO is that opening sequence. You managed to make a real deal mini-Gothic horror movie embedded within this broader story. I can imagine you as an artist must have had fun orchestrating that Grand Guignol sidebar story...

LAMBERT: Wow. What a great conversation we are having. I don't think I've ever discussed the opening sequence of PET TWO. No one ever comments on it, but it was so much fun. Gothic horror movies are what inspired my love of the genre. I watched all the Roger Corman "Poe Movies" many times in the local theatre where I grew up. For the scene in PET TWO, I was definitely inspired by WHITE ZOMBIE, the Bela Lugosi film. I have no idea where I saw it for the first time, but probably at the same local theatre I used to go to as a kid, which relied heavily on old movies. Maybe once a month there would be a first run film. But yeah, that's what I was sort of channeling in that opening!

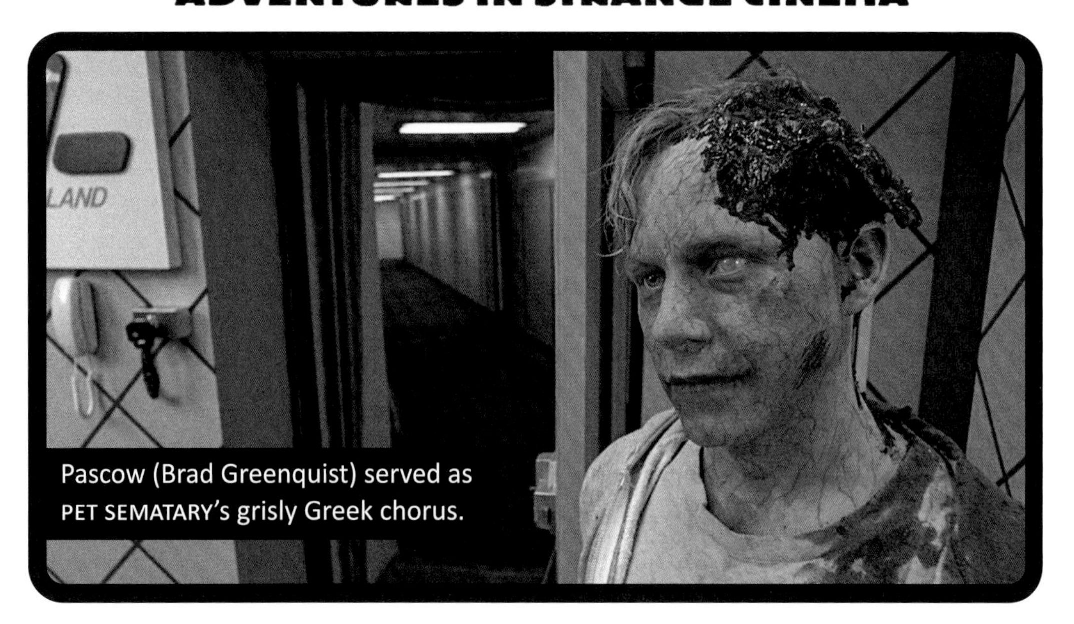

Pascow (Brad Greenquist) served as PET SEMATARY's grisly Greek chorus.

ALEXANDER: Awesome. Now, outside of the mayhem and gore and perversity and black comedy, the most haunting part of PET SEMATARY TWO might just be the end credits, where the portraits of the dead characters appear on screen as the car drives away into the unknown. It's so unexpectedly haunting and sad. Was that your idea?

LAMBERT: Yes. I fell that the movie was so off the rails in terms of good taste and discretion, so I wanted to end with a nod to the humanity of the characters. Everyone has emotional pain and it's possible to be both a victim and a perpetrator. Especially in the case of zombies themselves.

PHENOMENA (1985)

Starring Jennifer Connelly, Donald Pleasence, Daria Nicolodi, Patrick Bauchau
Written by Franco Ferrini, Dario Argento
Directed by Dario Argento

When I was a kid, I got up early — as I always did, as I still do — to pour myself a bowl of whatever garbage cereal I was grooving on at the time and settle in to watch whatever movie was playing on Canadian Pay-TV channel First Choice. It just so happened that the flick in question was something called CREEPERS. Now, when I was *really* little, my dad told me he saw this movie about a parasite that looked like a cross between a penis and turd that crawled into people's mouths and drove them

Jennifer (Jennifer Connelly) is one of Dario Argento's strongest female characters.

insane. I became obsessed by the idea of this film and, when I saw the listing in the TV guide citing CREEPERS, my memory jolted and I thought this was the movie my pop had pimped on me. I was wrong. Naturally, the film he was referencing was David Cronenberg's 1975 masterpiece SHIVERS. CREEPERS was something else entirely.

For 83 minutes I sat hypnotized on that couch by what was one of the most delirious things I've ever seen, ever. I knew the name of its director, Dario Argento, from casual glances at older *Fangoria* magazines and in a film reference book I had that had a still from his 1977 landmark style opera SUSPIRIA. This would mark the first Argento film I'd see. And to this day, I can't shake it. Later, I would find out that CREEPERS was an edited US version of his 1985 film PHENOMENA but, this being more than a decade before the dawn of DVD and the trend of studios and boutique labels tracking uncut prints and negatives of European titles and making them affordable on sell-through home video, I pretty much gave up the hope of ever seeing the full version. Eventually it did show up domestically via Anchor Bay on VHS and DVD as the full, 110-minute cut and that, of course, became the go-to version for every hardcore and newly minted Argento nut. Admittedly, I prefer the CREEPERS version as it concentrates the film's mayhem into a leaner framework, excising superfluous dialogue and some narrative flab. But that's a matter of taste. Your perspective on the ride depends on when you get on the train.

For those of you not in the know, PHENOMENA stars a very young Jennifer Connelly (fresh off her appearance in Sergio Leone's thundering ONCE UPON A TIME IN AMERICA and just before she battled David Bowie in LABRYNTH) as Jennifer Corvino, the wealthy daughter of a hot American actor who arrives at an elite boarding school in the Swiss

Jennifer tries not to swallow the sludge while swimming in the body pit.

Alps. Things get complicated when Jennifer learns that a vicious killer is roaming the land, targeting and skewering women (and whose first victim is Argento's daughter Fiore, who we see get tormented and decapitated in the film's unforgettable opening sequence). And then things get deeply weird when Jennifer reveals that she has a telepathic ability to control insects, the likes of which she has an unnatural obsession with. She also has a problem with sleepwalking and, after a night sauntering through the woods (while Iron Maiden's Flash Of The Blade blasts over the soundtrack), she wakes up in time to see a fellow student massacred. She then becomes the target of the killer, while kindly Scottish entomologist Donald Pleasence and his pet chimp guide her towards using her connection to flies and maggots to track the murderer and save the day.

And that's only scratching the surface of this deranged tale.

PHENOMENA is Argento's best movie. There I said it. And I'm not just saying that because it's the first one I saw or because I have a sentimental attachment to it. It's just Argento at the peak of his powers, riffing off his own Three Mothers movies (the picture even has the same setup as SUSPIRIA), employing familiar stylistic tropes and majestically orchestrated murder sequences and then piling on so much stuff that one is left reeling. This is a "Perils of Pauline" adventure from Hell, with elements of DON'T LOOK NOW, PSYCHO, CARRIE, POLTERGEIST, MURDERS IN THE RUE MORGUE and a half dozen other well-known properties, but filtered through Argento's mind at its most manic. He really went for it with this one and sadly, Italian critics hated it, and it was cut by almost half an hour in America and barely released (hello, CREEPERS!). Its commercial failure marked the beginning of a decline for the maestro, and I swear he never made another movie like this, so beautifully, unapologetically romantic and out of control. Argento's ex-lover, writer and actress Daria Nicolodi, gives the performance of her career, Connelly is a supernova of youthful femininity, Luigi Cozzi's optical effects are stunning, the gore is plentiful and nauseating (watch out for that body bath!) and the music and insane tapestry of sound — from Goblin keyboardist Claudio Simonetti, Simon Boswell and ex-Rolling Stone Bill Wyman, the aforementioned Iron Maiden, Mötörhead and more — is a revelation. It's mental and marvelous and it Just never stops moving.

As troublesome as this sentiment may sound, SUSPIRIA and DEEP RED might be Argento's most *important* movies, but their formidable powers dim substantially when stacked up against to the berserk and rapturous mutant anomaly that is PHENOMENA. And nothing will shift my mind to the contrary.

THE PIT AND THE PENDULUM (1961)

Starring Vincent Price, John Kerr, Luana Anders, Barbara Steele
Written by Richard Matheson
Directed by Roger Corman

Though he has made hundreds of films spanning over six decades, producer/director and indie genre film pioneer Roger Corman's eight-picture "Poe Cycle" continues to be among his most celebrated and discussed works. I should know. I recently wrote an entire book on the subject, released by this very publisher.

The story goes that Corman, who was, by the end of the 1950s becoming fledgling studio American International Pictures' regular house producer/director, went to AIP bosses Sam Arkoff and Jim Nicholson and convinced them to take the budget they'd normally use for two black and white pictures and instead combine them to make a single full color movie. The studio initially balked but eventually relented and the first entry in that experiment was 1960's THE FALL OF THE HOUSE OF USHER, based on the classic Edgar Allan Poe tale.

The Gothic, lushly realized film, written by popular writer and novelist Richard Matheson (*I Am Legend*, *Hell House*, key episodes of THE TWILIGHT ZONE), was a rousing critical and commercial success, a picture that bridged the gap between the drive-ins and teen-drenched "flat tops" that Corman and AIP catered to, and the arthouse, with a distinctly literate and moody European sheen that most exploitation films of the time simply didn't have.

But as to which of the eight remarkable Poe films is the superior entry, it's subjective. Certainly, everyone has their favorite and latter works like the shot in

Nicolas Medina (Vincent Price) loses his mind while Elizabeth (Barbara Steele) suffers greatly.

England, Ingmar Bergman-influenced MASQUE OF THE RED DEATH and TOMB OF LIGEIA are the most sumptuously designed of the lot. But his THE FALL OF THE HOUSE OF USHER follow-up, 1961's THE PIT AND THE PENDULUM, is inarguably the scariest.

In PIT, the great Vincent Price returned after his mesmerizing work as Roderick Usher the previous year, this time with his trademark facial hair back on his face, to devour scenery with maniacal, operatic aplomb, losing himself in the role of the tortured Nicholas Medina, a man decimated after the death of his beloved wife (played by the gorgeous Barbara Steele, fresh off her role in Mario Bava's BLACK SUNDAY) and haunted by the legacy of his father's torturous reign during the Spanish Inquisition.

John Kerr plays his suspicious brother-in-law, whose presence adds to Medina's ratcheting stress and increasingly fragile state. DEMENTIA 13's Luana Anders is doe-eyed and lovely as Medina's protective sister.

Like he did with USHER, but more so here, Matheson takes the source story and expands it, weaving in elements from other Poe tales (including essentially replicating the setup from USHER) and creating a fresh narrative that feels like it takes place in Poe's world.

He had to.

Because Poe's story 'The Pit and the Pendulum' is only a few pages long and is a first-person, fevered account of a prisoner of the Inquisition losing his mind while strapped to the titular device, rats teeming around him and the blade getting closer and closer to his belly.

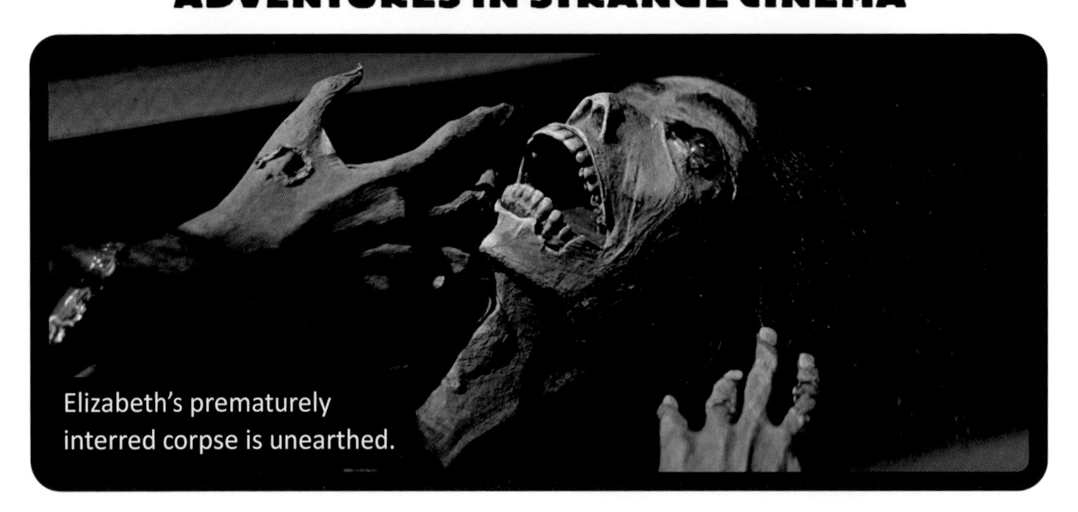
Elizabeth's prematurely interred corpse is unearthed.

Matheson opted to push this sequence to the film's climax, a hysterical, horrifying blowout of grandiose insanity, with Price dragging the cast into his dad's torture chamber and putting that rusty, swinging and still blood-stained axe device to work. Price, whose mind by this point has snapped, believes he's his own father and runs around screaming and seething, a maniacal performance that must be seen to be believed and one that propels the movie into the stuff of nightmares.

"Sometimes, I would talk to [Vincent] and use the word 'interior' and that meant he had to use an interior motion when he acted," Corman told me once, during one of our many conversations.

"It never happened on USHER because he knew exactly what the role would be. But after USHER, he became more aware that we were making horror films, as opposed to the classic picture we made the first time. The word 'classic' may have faded slightly with PIT and the concept of 'horror' grew."

This is of course, true.

After PIT, the following Poe films took on lives of their own, fetishizing Gothic tropes, getting grislier in their imagery, and even sending themselves up ('The Raven' and 'The Black Cat' segment of TALES OF TERROR are the most baroque of comedies). And with each one, Price just kept pushing the mania, performances that have been dismissed as "hammy" by some but are the very essence of using the actor as a film's greatest special effect. Price was a supernatural presence, and it seems as if much of that mesmerizing flamboyance was birthed here, it the confines of this remarkable horror masterpiece.

Throw in some typically beautiful, budget cheating art direction from Corman regular Daniel Haller (later, a fine director in his own right), and grim music from the great Les Baxter (whose dread-filled sounds over the psychedelic "melting-paint" opening credits sequence, sets the delirious, nightmarish tone for the movie to follow) and you have this, one of Corman, Price and Matheson's crowning achievements: a richly realized, full-blooded ode to horror, dead dreams, duplicity, infidelity, mass-murder and cyclical madness.

PSYCHOMANIA (1973)

Starring Nicky Henson, George Sanders, Beryl Reid, Mary Larkin
Written by Arnau d'Usseau, Julian Zimet
Directed by Don Sharp

As the 1960s wound down and turned into the 1970s, British horror cinema — like most international genre fare — shifted to cater to the more visceral needs of a new generation. And while for a decade, the UK, had been known and lauded primarily for the Gothic horror films coming from Hammer Studios, several smaller entities popped up and tried to shake the foundations of the formula.

Released in the wake of Stanley Kubrick's landmark adaptation of Anthony Burgess' A CLOCKWORK ORANGE, Don (KISS OF THE VAMPIRE) Sharp's ludicrously awesome and awesomely ludicrous 1973 undead biker romp PSYCHOMANIA (aka THE DEATH WHEELERS and THE LIVING DEAD) stood alone. Blending the tropes of the British "angry young man" movie and the post-EASY RIDER angst of the American biker romp by way of a

The Living Dead scream back from the grave.

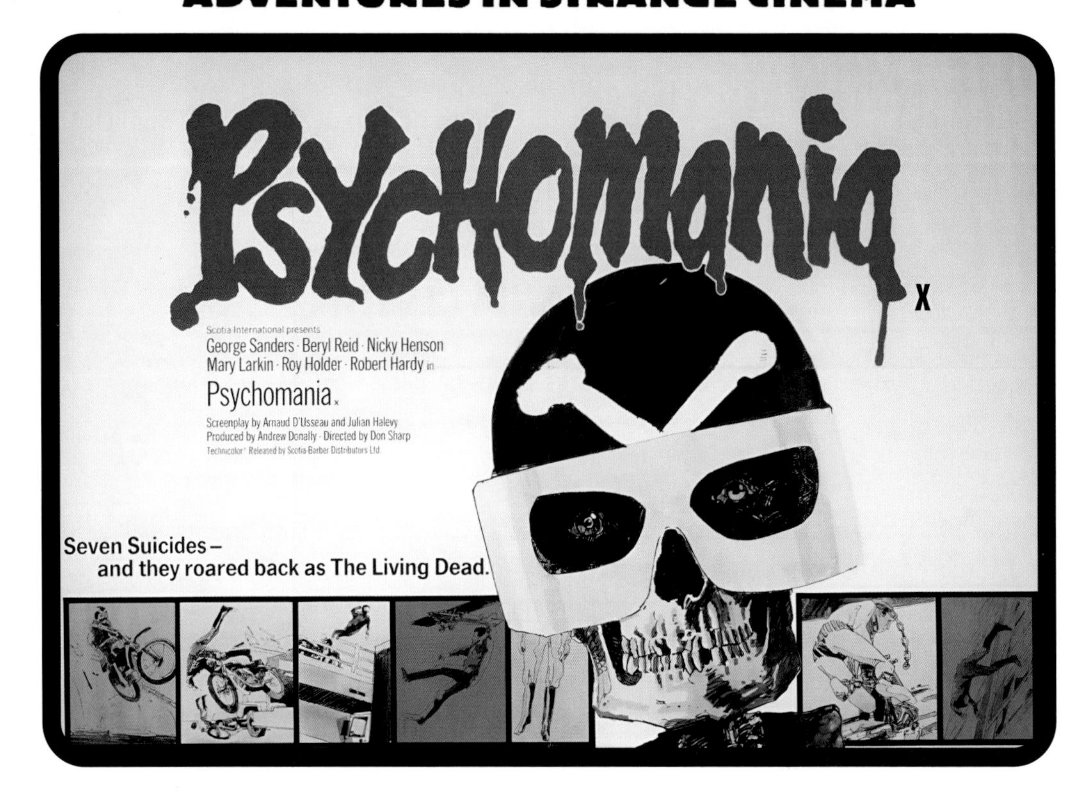

quasi-NIGHT OF THE LIVING DEAD zombie film and with a dash of ROSEMARY'S BABY thrown in (because, why not?), PSYCHOMANIA (which ran in some US markets on a double bill with the equally mad bikersploitation opus WEREWOLVES ON WHEELS) was about as nutty and unclassifiable a film as one could imagine and, after it faded from theaters, it soon became a staple for UK kidlets growing up in front of the boob tube. Later, at the dawn of the home video boom in the 1980s, many fledgling US imprints thought the film to be in the public domain and because of this, it became one of the most mass-produced and easily available titles on the market, a bootlegging trend that continued with hard media's shift to DVD.

From its first dreamy frames, as a gang of leather clad, skull faced bikers poured into black leather come charging over a mist drenched hill in slow-motion, to its final surreal wind down, with men, women and motorcycles morphing into massive tombstones, to all its cheeky, wonderfully lunatic mayhem in the middle, cinema history has never, ever seen the likes of a picture quite like Don Sharp's unapologetically mental PSYCHOMANIA.

The film charts the misadventures of cocky, lithe London based bike gang leader Tom Latham (WITCHFINDER GENERAL's Nicky Henson), whose devotion to his gang of miscreant riders known as 'The Living Dead' is matched only by his interest in black magic, not to mention his love for his mystical mother (Beryl Reid). When his shady butler Shadwell (a slumming George Sanders) turns him on to the secret of eternal life through suicide, Tom leads his followers into an outrageous (and unintentionally hilarious) orgy of self sacrifice and night riding living death. Meanwhile, composer and occasional Led Zeppelin collaborator John Cameron's ear shredding psych-rock score buzzes away in the background.

PSYCHOMANIA has a vibe that is entirely its own. It's never quite dramatically convincing and never really mines some of the darker devilish subtext and perversions that simmer under its surface, but its lean, tough, violent (but not gory) and tons of fun. This isn't a guilty pleasure. It's a great one-shot horror movie, filled with weird, eerie atmosphere, crazy stunt work, cheeky performances, mild kink and a unique charm. It was the first film I ever blind bought on VHS when I was a kid, and it still has the power to pleasurably kick my ass sideways these many years later. Long may it ride...

INTERVIEW: NICKY HENSON

We lost British actor Nicky Henson in 2019, after a long and valiant battle with cancer and I am blessed that I got to have my moments with him, a sort of friendship. Though we weren't terribly close, I found the actor warm, funny, engaging and a wonderful storyteller. After conducting several interviews with the lifelong Londoner, I would check-in on him frequently, to see how he was faring health-wise and to ask about his family. He in turn would ask about me. I really liked Nicky. And when he passed, I felt it. And even though he liked to poke fun at his turn as Tom in PSYCHOMANIA, he was very aware of the film's legacy and understood — and even accepted — that, culturally speaking, this was the one that history would remember him for...

CHRIS ALEXANDER: So, you know that in some circles, PSYCHOMANIA is considered the epitome of cool...

NICKY HENSON: Cool? [*laughs*] I can't believe that, I don't think it was ever cool! But I'm astonished at its popularity, really. It's just bizarre that I now get invites to go to universities and talk to their film societies about it.

ALEXANDER: Well, it was written by two ex-patriot Communist sympathizers. And if you really dig, there IS subtext there...

HENSON: There is? Well, I guess you can make anything mean anything, can't you!

ALEXANDER: You've had such a long and varied career on stage and screen, but can you recall the time when the script for PSYCHOMANIA ended up in your hands?

HENSON: Yes, I remember distinctly. I was in the theatre, I have always been at the theatre, that's me, that is where I live. But at the time, I was at new theatre called The Young Vic, run by Frank Dunlop, who was my mentor. It was a theatre for 15–25 year

Henson at home with one of his many beloved bikes.

olds, for a young theatrically virgin audience, to show them the classics. The money was low — only £35 a week — but it was a great experience. Now in England at the time, we still had the B-movie industry and the unions would allow you to be in a play in the evening and you could do films in the day time, until 5:30pm. So, this script comes through the letterbox one day from my agent and I since I was always a motorcyclist...

ALEXANDER: In your first film, you played a biker...

Hatchet (Dennis Gilmore) is shocked by Tom's return.

HENSON: Yes, I did! It was called FATHER CAME TOO, you're right. So, this script comes by and it opens with the line "Eight chop hog Harley Davidson's crest about a hill..." and I said, "hey I'll do the fucker!" without even reading it. Then I get on-set and they weren't Harley's at all but rather they were these terrible Nortons that were 20 years old at the time. They had four mechanics working full time on set just to keep these things going and that was the biggest expense in the movie, believe it or not.

ALEXANDER: Did you do your own stunts?

HENSON: I did, yes. All but three. You know, in America a professional stuntman can specialize; one makes a living falling off horses, another flips cars, others fall off houses. But English stuntmen at the time had to do it all. My guy — and God, I don't even know if he's still alive — was a bloke named Cliff Diggins and for those three stunts for me, he ended up in the hospital every time. I always knew Cliff was doing a stunt when I heard the ambulance wailing...

ALEXANDER: Was one of those stunts the scene where Tom goes through the wall?

HENSON: Yes, and again he ended up in hospital after that. The first one he did was the bridge, where I fly off and kill myself, that was him and he managed to hit the water before the bike did and the bike landed on top of him. The second was the wall. It was a polystyrene wall which was painted, and when he went through it was like a Warner Bros. cartoon in that the bike went through but he stayed the same side!

Henson witnessing madness in 1968's WITCHFINDER GENERAL.

ALEXANDER: One of the great eccentric touches in the picture is the very odd, unhealthy relationship between Tom and his mother, played by the great Beryl Reid...

HENSON: I knew Beryl from before, in the theatre, and she was lovely. They were originally going to cast another American actress but she turned it down at the last minute, so Beryl was having a quiet time and she did it. And of course, there was George Sanders...

ALEXANDER: Yes, whatever was he thinking doing this grotty little film?

HENSON: Exactly. That's what he was thinking, I'm sure. They shot all his scenes in 10 days to save money because he was making so much, more than any of us. In order to save 15 bob or something, the production gave Beryl and I chairs that didn't have our names on them so when George arrived two weeks into production, there were these two famous prop men at Shepperton Studios named Jack and Bobby who were so ashamed that they brought a chair out onto the set with his name printed on the back in ball point pen. And poor George, the story goes, eventually saw a answer print of the film and went back to his hotel in Madrid and killed himself.

ALEXANDER: He did kill himself and there was that very sad, despondent suicide note. Do you remember Sanders as being morose on set?

HENSON: No, not at all, we laughed and laughed and laughed. There are even moments in the film that are meant to be serious where you can see the corners of his mouth start to twitch because he couldn't contain his laughter.

ALEXANDER: Tom is such a charming character and its clear at all times that you're having a good time... hard to take such a cheeky lad seriously as a villain.

HENSON: Yes, I know, I know. Incidentally, all the gear I wore in the film was mine, the leather pants and jacket. I used to arrive in work in them actually.

ALEXANDER: Do you still ride?

HENSON: No, I stopped riding at 40. I had a big smash and burned myself very badly and so my kids said no more dad, sorry.

ALEXANDER: Those bad ass helmets have become iconic. Did you get to keep one?

HENSON: No, no, none of us kept them. They had to hang on to them for re-shoots, I believe. It's too bad because maybe they'd be worth money now...

ALEXANDER: In some circles, yes, they would be. Everyone loves the scene when that beautiful folk song Riding Free is played with you about to be buried while mounted on your bike. Was that you in that shallow grave or a dummy?

HENSON: That's me! Had to sit there while this guy is singing this stupid fucking song and throwing flowers at me and keep a straight face. Ridiculous!

ALEXANDER: What are your memories of Don Sharp?

HENSON: Don was a man under a huge amount of pressure. He had just done the second unit on PUPPET ON A CHAIN, doing boat stunts in Amsterdam so he chosen because he knew how to film these stunts. There was no budget, it was a short shoot and it was terrible with these bikes breaking down and all these young kids who we could never find were always sneaking off, having smokes in the bushes and playing this card game we always played, which actually makes it into the picture in the scene when we're in jail, he could never finds us. He was very patient, because we were a nightmare.

ALEXANDER: Genre fans also remember you for your part in an equally celebrated, but for very different reasons, film: WITCHFINDER GENERAL. And like Sanders, director Michael Reeves took his own life not long after that film...

HENSON: God yes, it was a great loss, and Michael was a great friend. It was a great loss to cinema and a great loss to us — me and my best friend (and WITCHFINDER co-star) Ian Ogilvy, who used to make movies with Michael when they were kids. We would have all been movies stars if he lived. He was supposed to do BLOODY MAMA for Roger Corman and we would have been in it. WITCHFINDER was important, we knew it was important when we made it. It's the only British Western, really.

ALEXANDER: And Vincent Price was magnificent...

HENSON: Yes, Michael never wanted Vincent, he wanted Donald Pleasence and Vincent had heard this and it bothered him to no end. At the time he was one of the foremost art lecturers and collectors, acting was just his hobby. They would fight endlessly. Michael would say "Vincent do nothing, do nothing, stop acting!" and

Vincent would retort "This is my 94th picture and you're doing the wrong way, how many pictures have you made young man!" and to that Michael said "three good ones, Vincent." Vincent walked off the set and never said goodbye. Three months later he saw an answer print and wrote to Michael and said "my god I'm sorry, this is the best acting I've ever done". When Michael died Vincent paid his own way to come to London to tell that story at a tribute festival.

ALEXANDER: You've had a very fruitful, interesting career as an actor, Nicky.

HENSON: Yes, I've been very, very lucky. And lucky that it didn't all end with PSYCHOMANIA!

RABID (1977)

Starring Marilyn Chambers, Joe Silver, Susan Roman, Frank Moore
Written by David Cronenberg
Directed by David Cronenberg

The fact that RABID got made at all is a bit of a marvel. Fledgling director David Cronenberg had made his first feature, SHIVERS, in 1975 for Canadian exploitation imprint Cinepix and, although an international success, the fact that the movie was partially funded by a government tax fund caused members of the Canadian press to take Cronenberg and Cinepix to task, citing the picture as smut and calling for the public to reject such practices.

This, of course, only served to make Cronenberg "notorious" and further put his movie on the map. And yet because of this, it took Cinepix almost two years to get the money to make the director's follow-up film, RABID. However, the film finally went to camera and we're lucky it did. Although SHIVERS is a more ambitious and ferocious horror film (as messy debut movies tend to be), RABID is Cronenberg's first genuinely scary movie and its infinitely more accomplished than its predecessor. It mines many of the same themes and ideas but keeps the focus more disciplined and pays attention to character nuances, creating a movie that is bloodthirsty and bizarre but also has a genuine sense of tragedy, something which would mark most of the director's future work.

RABID casts now deceased ex-porn star Marilyn Chambers stars as Rose, a motorcycle mama who gets in a fiery accident and is whisked away to a remote, experimental plastic surgery clinic. There, Rose receives some sort of skin graft procedure that goes awry; when she wakes up, she finds she was developed a vagina/anus in her armpit that, when stimulated, pushes out a phallus that drains her victims of their blood. After a feed, Rose has no memory of her vampiric crime, and her victims stumble away in shock. Later, they whir into action as rabid zombie vampires.

Rose (Marilyn Chambers) stalks the streets while Sissy looks on.

The people they bite get up and bite and soon a modern plague wracks the streets of Montreal, with Rose the "Typhoid Mary" bringer of death.

RABID is a truly frightening and haunting piece of work, due not only to Cronenberg's ideas and the solid work of the pro-amateur cast, but the eerie use of library "needle drop" music that serves as the patchwork score. The main theme is an old cue from Keith Mansfield from the KPM vaults called Summer's Coming and it's sad, moving and cold, like the film. The other key repeated track is Hideout by Brian Bennett which was also used in the eerie Australian show PRISONER CELL BLOCK H. Unforgettable stuff. Incidentally, I licensed both tracks as an homage in my 2021 film GIRL WITH A STRAIGHT RAZOR.

That melancholy pervades every inch of RABID, from the opening shots circling Chambers on a highway to the final, miserable garbage truck shots and nihilistic non-resolution, you just feel heavy watching this movie. It's Cronenberg's best full-stop horror movie, I think, one where the horror comes *first* and the subtext is almost accidental. Later, it would be the reverse. This is a truly grim shocker, and it sits high in the filmography of one of the most important filmmakers in genre history.

RAW (2016)

Starring Garance Marillier, Ella Rumpf, Laurent Lucas, Joana Preiss
Written by Julia Ducournau
Directed by Julia Ducournau

When it comes to making horror movies, I'm not so sure gender is all that important. Or at least it shouldn't be. Because one thing all of us mortal beings have in common, no matter our skin color, place of birth, what version of God we buy into or what plumbing hands or does not hang between our legs, is that our lives are finite. We are *all* gonna die. And the foundation of every horror movie is the exploitation of that very profound driving paranoia. Death truly is the great equalizer and horror is the genre that unites us all.

But with that, when you aim a little higher than just standard-issue horror and if you have a protagonist in a film that is female and if that film is about that protagonist coming of age and seeking to find their place within a tainted social hierarchy, having a woman as your point of entry is always fascinating. And if the person painting this portrait is a male, it's equally interesting and almost abstract, because men cannot really "know" a woman's experience, we (*we* meaning *me* and every reader reading this who lost the flip of the coin in the womb and was born with a penis) can only have an *impression* of that experience.

But when a female makes a movie about the intimate life of another female, it's often magical, like opening a secret door into a private party that we're not invited to. And when you apply that clandestine character study to the equally arcane world of horror, the results can yield some seriously profound and edgy cinema.

And that's what filmmaker Julia Ducournau's French/Belgian shocker RAW is: profound and edgy and though it positions itself as a horror movie, it goes deeper and has different motives. It's also supersonically stylish, disturbing, darkly funny, kinky and totally revolting.

The film sees sweet, shy vegetarian Justine (Garance Marillier) enrolling in a looming, almost prison-like veterinarian college, joining her sister Alexia (Ella Rumpf) and at the urging of her similarly vegetarian, pacifist parents. Justine is immediately roped into a perverse, ultra-aggressive hazing ritual, wherein all the new recruits are doused in blood. That night, Justine finds herself in itchy agony, clawing at a bright red, scaly rash that has encrusted her body. After a visit to the doctor, who assures her all is well, Justine starts feeling odd. Her aversion to meat starts to wane, replaced with a genuine hunger, for what she's not sure. One night, after her sister volunteers to wax Justine's nether regions (an oddly erotic sequence), a scissor-slip results in Alexia losing a finger and passing out. As Justine panics and calls for an ambulance, she picks up the finger and involuntarily begins stripping the flesh from the bone like a bloody chicken wing. The beast inside wakes up and though she tries to fight it, there's no denying that Justine has — through some sort of potentially viral infection or maybe some other means — become a kind of cannibal vampire. She wants blood, flesh and sex, in that order.

But that's only scratching the surface of this sanguinary tale.

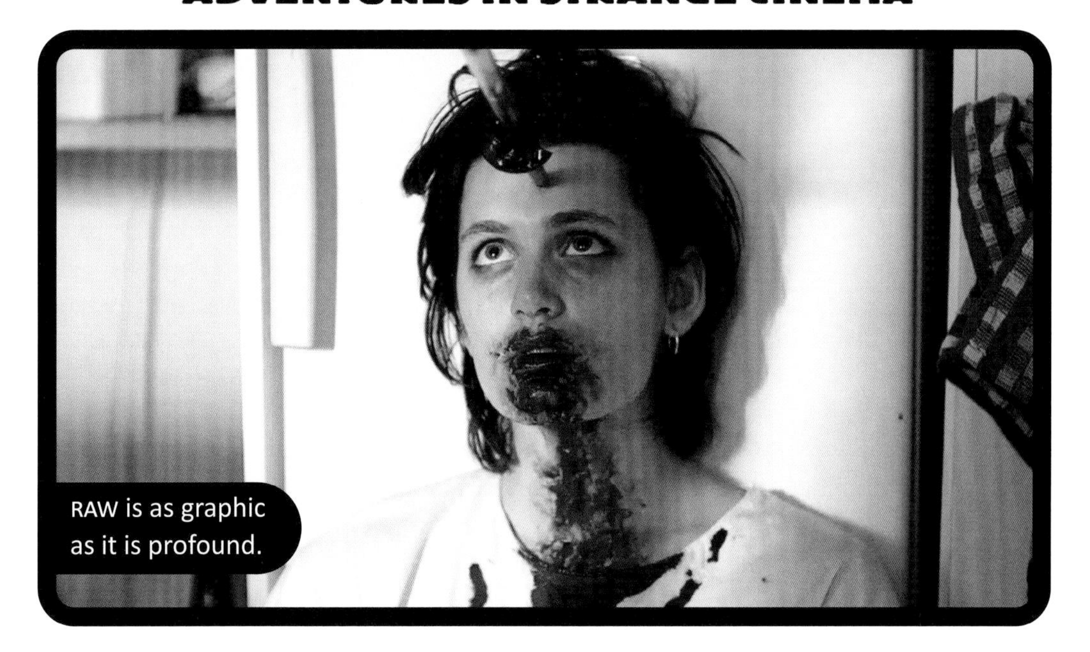

RAW is as graphic as it is profound.

Narratively, there's nothing particularly novel about RAW. It's like any vampire or werewolf drama where a victim rages against their biological changes. RABID. NEAR DARK. THE LOST BOYS. FEMALE WEREWOLF (shameless plug). We've seen that before. But what we haven't seen is the imagery and intimacy that Ducournau employs here. From its stark opening frames that anticipate a pivotal sequence to come, to its dripping examination of female sexual desire, to imagery of hog-tied horse, paint-covered people groping each other, flesh-eating rapture to the stunning — and we mean stunning — use of music (the score for this movie by Ben Wheatley favorite Jim Williams is Gothic, electro-Eurohorror fuzz guitar/pipe organ menace to the max), RAW is exactly that; it's raw, red, alive, awkward and injected with a cinematic energy that stems from a totally unique sensibility. This is Ducournau's world from stem to stern and we've never been in the likes of it before.

RAW is a horror movie about a woman but — and I'm not sure I'm articulating this properly — it *feels* female. Deceptively soft, urgent, wet and pulsing with intellect and power. It feels dangerous. Exciting. Like an awakening. Like a birth.

THE RETURN OF COUNT YORGA (1971)

Starring Robert Quarry, Mariette Hartley, Roger Perry, Yvonne Wilder
Written by Yvonne Wilder, Bob Kelljan
Directed by Bob Kelljan

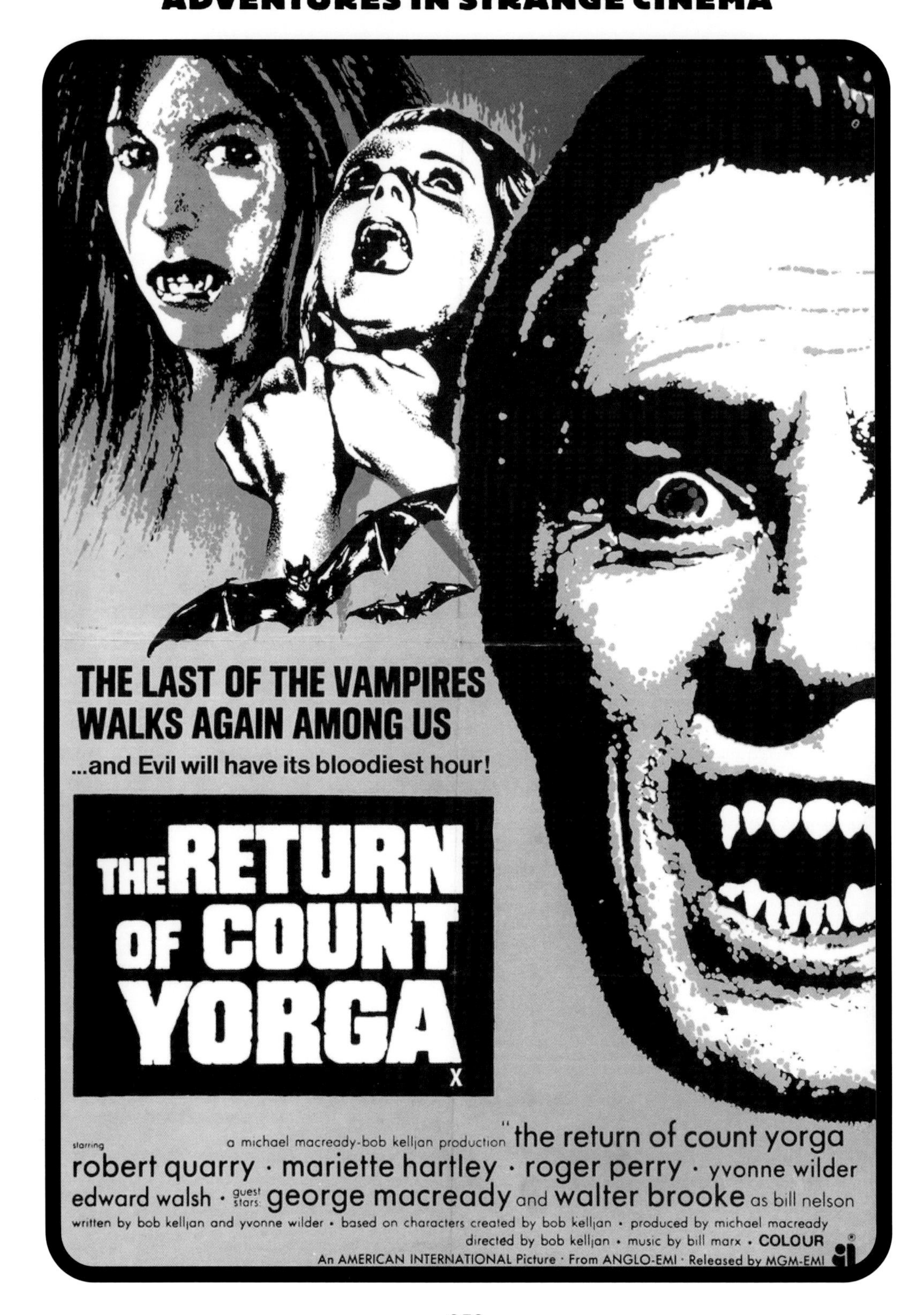
THE LAST OF THE VAMPIRES
WALKS AGAIN AMONG US
...and Evil will have its bloodiest hour!
THE RETURN
OF COUNT
YORGA
X
starring
a michael macready-bob kelljan production "the return of count yorga"
robert quarry · mariette hartley · roger perry · yvonne wilder
edward walsh · guest stars: george macready and walter brooke as bill nelson
written by bob kelljan and yvonne wilder • based on characters created by bob kelljan • produced by michael macready
directed by bob kelljan • music by bill marx • COLOUR
An AMERICAN INTERNATIONAL Picture · From ANGLO-EMI · Released by MGM-EMI

As the 1960s wound down and young audiences began hungering for more explicit horror entertainment, indie genre imprint American International Pictures found some success with director Bob Kelljan's 1970 Robert Quarry-starring shocker COUNT YORGA, VAMPIRE. I mentioned most of this story in a previous entry in this book, but in case you're reading these entries out of order, the story goes like this: AIP boss Sam Arkoff was so thrilled with Quarry's presence on screen that he signed the elegant character actor to a contract. The idea was to groom him as the successor to their aging creepy flick cash cow Vincent Price and build a series of horror films around his persona. But before they could put their newfangled leading man to work, Quarry stepped out with director Ray Danton to make another film independently and with some of his own cash called THE DEATHMASTER (see my other entry on this incredible picture elsewhere in this book), a sort of amalgam of Yorga and the then topical Manson death cult tabloid bait that was still shocking the nation. That film, in which Quarry stars as a charismatic new age vampire named Khorda (not Yorga, *Khorda*!) was a little bit too close to AIP's intended Yorga franchise plans (Quarry even wore the same custom fangs made for him for COUNT YORGA) and, reportedly none too pleased, Arkoff picked up the rights to THE DEATHMASTER, buried it, and immediately pushed Quarry into production on Kelljan's sequel, THE RETURN OF COUNT YORGA.

I mention this bit of back-story because AIP then opted to put the tagline "The DEATHMASTER is back from beyond the grave!" on the theatrical poster for THE RETURN OF COUNT YORGA which was, well, kind of a dick move and not the best way to start a newly minted business relationship.

Regardless of whatever tensions boiled behind the scenes, however, 1971's THE RETURN OF COUNT YORGA is in almost every way, a superior picture. More of a companion film-cum-remake of the first movie rather than a true sequel (though actor Roger Perry does return as a raving vamp-killer), THE RETURN OF COUNT YORGA sees Quarry back in his cape, gliding around the peripherals of a looming California orphanage, slowly amassing a harem of feral vampire women. When his bloodlust is sated, Yorga slips easily back into the role of gentleman aristocrat and, under the guise of a wealthy philanthropist, insinuates himself into the orphanage, where he both charms and falls under the spell of a beautiful teacher (played by the stunning Mariette Hartley, who some readers might remember from the classic THE TWILIGHT ZONE episode 'The Long Morrow'). As Yorga gently courts the increasingly disoriented schoolmarm, his swell of shambling vamps continues to grow and his intent to spread his parasitic virus proceeds as planned.

Kelljan would also go on to direct the flawed but fascinating BLACULA sequel SCREAM BLACULA SCREAM and much of the imagery he brought to that skin-crawler is evident here, including an almost European-informed insistence of creating a dark, dreamy and unbearably brooding atmosphere. Some contemporary viewers may be turned off by the film's languid pacing, but I adore it. It's slow, strange, goes off on weird tangents and is conversational without being choked with masturbatory exposition. Kelljan's script, co-written by Yvonne Wilder, is something of a marvel; literate, witty and, on occasion, blackly humorous (and in the climax, that features a young Craig T. Nelson as a bumbling cop, often broadly humorous).

It's also scary as hell. No word of a lie, THE RETURN OF COUNT YORGA is one the most unsettling vampire films I've ever seen. Outside of the steely blue-eyed Quarry's imposing, soft spoken and terrifying presence, the female vampires in RETURN are some of the most alarming ever put on screen. We first see them extending their newly re-birthed arms from the earth and climbing out of their graves, shambling towards their prey like a pack of George A. Romero's ghouls (this was no doubt intentional as NIGHT OF THE LIVING DEAD was at this point seen as a revolutionary horror film) and later, when in the thralls of blood-ecstasy, they scream and sprint down hallways in shivery slow-motion (as does Quarry), while the sound design team works overtime to amplify their hisses and guttural, animal noises (in fact, the vampire women and the entire love story angle of the film reminds me of devices and aesthetics later employed in the fine Spanish Paul Naschy/Javier Aguirre film COUNT DRACULA'S GREAT LOVE, though I have no idea if anyone involved in that production was influenced by this picture). These ghastly and plentiful vampire attacks are the stuff of nightmares to be sure and they are housed in a film that is alive with Gothic dread and cynical, post-60s doom. Simply put, THE RETURN OF COUNT YORGA is not a film to watched alone.

THE SADIST OF NOTRE DAME (1979)

Starring Jess Franco, Lina Romay, Oliver Mathot, Pierre Talou
Written by Jess Franco
Directed by Jess Franco

It's gratifying the level of admiration that global cinema culture now has for Spanish sleaze architect Jesús "Jess" Franco. And while it's a shame that more of that adoration and intellectual dissection of his work didn't thrive more prominently when he was among the living, it's still wonderful that so many learned, passionate writers, thinkers and daring dark film lovers spend so much time talking about him. And so they should. In the annals of film history, I cannot think of a more fascinating figure than Franco, not just because of the sheer volume of movies he made (over 200 that we know of) but because he was so driven and dictated by his obsessive need to make them. Here was a

THE SADIST OF NOTRE DAME is Franco at his most poetic and perverse.

man who truly lived to make pictures, in some ways because he made pictures to live.

Which makes sense because Franco worshipped Orson Welles and indeed mentored with him making the 1965 picture CHIMES AT MIDNIGHT, in which Franco served as second unit director. Welles was the Hollywood poster boy for boyish rebellion and high-minded culture, a pearl before a city full of swine; he was a visionary who refused to buckle to industry standards, entering the business with a bang (1941's CITIZEN KANE) and, after the harrowing ordeal that followed in that controversial film's wake, spent the next 50 years traveling the world scraping up money to make movies exactly how he wanted to make them. Franco most assuredly took his work aesthetic from Welles' book but while Orson would take years to prep a picture, Franco would fire out a half dozen films in the same amount of time. Sometimes he had dough (his myriad lush psychedelic films in the late 1960s with producer Harry Alan Towers stands as his higher budgeted efforts) and sometimes he had, well, literally NO money. Didn't matter. He just made the movies he wanted to make.

Sometimes the distributors and producers — be they Spanish, German, French, whatever — would monkey with the pictures Franco delivered. Sometimes they ordered new scenes to be shot, XXX hardcore inserts to be spliced in, different sub-plots with different actors who were more popular in the country in which said distributors had purchased the film for to be shot and included in the final cut. Often Franco rolled up his sleeves and made the changes himself, thus retaining control of

EL SADICO DE NOTRE DAME
NADINE PASCAL · JESS FRANK · LINA ROMAY
DIRECTOR JESS FRANCO TECHNICOLOR
EXCLUSIVAMENTE MAYORES DE 18 AÑOS

the product as best he could. Occasionally, the alterations were done without him. Sometimes he used his own name on the finished film. Sometimes he used one his dozens of pseudonyms. And of course, all this substantial cinematic skullduggery has only served to enrich Franco's enigmatic mythos, defining the ever-swelling cult that has sprouted up in recent years.

Case in point, THE SADIST OF NOTRE DAME, one of Franco's most interesting and complicated movies; certainly, it remains one his most personal, seeing as he opted to take on the lead role himself. North Americans first widely encountered SADIST via Wizard Video's VHS release in the early 1980s under the title DEMONIAC, a cut version of the film that dialed back much of the ample sex and violence. Years later, Synapse released the original cut of the film under the title EXORCISM (it also exists in a XXX version called SEXORCISMES). That version was shot in 1975 for frequent Franco bankrollers Eurocine and it's a wet, taboo-bending affair filled with sado-masochistic sex and murder. In 1979, Eurocine asked Franco to shoot new scenes for the film and he did, inventing a new plot entirely, changing the name of characters and fleshing out his own role in the film, giving him a deeper, more tormented motive for his madness. That's the SADIST version, which is the harder version of the DEMONIAC cut and, while bearing the mark of its Frankenstein-stitch up structure, it's a mesmerizing psychotronic experience.

All versions of the film see Franco star as defrocked priest Vogel, who slinks around Paris at night stalking and slashing all women who he deems to be morally corrupt. In the EXORCISM cut, there's more of an emphasis on sadism, opening as it does on a sickening — but staged — S&M performance and driven as it is by these scenes of extremity. But SADIST is closer to Michael Powell's PEEPING TOM. It's a much more intimate, artful and psychological profile of a compulsive fiend and Franco plays the part to perfection, with his popping eyes spying on his prey before delivering fevered, accusatory monologues chased by a flash of his blade. All this delirium is encased — as in most Eurocine/Franco efforts — by a melancholy, dreamy lounge jazz score by Daniel White, the perfect balm for the harsh shenanigans on screen. naturally, the beautiful Lina Romay — Jess's muse on and off screen — shows up in both versions, looking stunning either in or out of wardrobe.

To love Franco isn't to necessarily love *all* his movies. Hell, you don't even have to *like* half of them, and I know — despite my citing Franco as my personal favorite filmmaker of all time — that I find many of his films damned near unwatchable. No, each one of Franco's movies is a piece of a larger puzzle, a brush stroke on a massive, complex canvas and a tapestry of passion that has never been equaled. But THE SADIST OF NOTRE DAME is certainly among his best pictures. Even seen as a stand-alone bit of Euroshock, it has a mesmerizing sort of majesty, a Paris Gothic with a strong sense of place and time and purpose, that makes it immersive and unforgettable. To call it a masterpiece might be a stretch, but calling it a *Jess Franco masterpiece* is absolutely on point.

SCALPEL (1977)

Starring Robert Lansing, Judith Chapman, Arlen Dean Snyder, Sandy Martin
Written by John Grissmer, Joseph Weintraub
Directed by John Grissmer

Every dreamy thing you've heard about the 1970s in regard to it being a Golden Age of American cinema is 100% true, with audiences hungry for edgier offbeat movies, thus birthing a market for various madmen to make lower-tier, downmarket stuff and still have plenty of eyeballs waiting to receive their wares. And with the MPAA's newly minted ratings system still in its wobble-kneed infancy, plenty of nasty little numbers squeezed through the cracks and sneaked away with mild PG (or the similar GP) ratings; this, despite the fact that many of these pictures were not geared for kids or family viewing and often were choked with sleaze, suggested smut and decidedly mature melodrama.

Among the endless spate of movies that your son Timmy could freely see on a Saturday afternoon in the cinema if he so desired, is director John (BLOOD RAGE) Grissmer's tawdry and really rather mesmerizing 1977 shocker SCALPEL (aka FALSE FACE). The movie was released twice in the '70s to American hard-tops and drive-ins before slinking to VHS via a slew of distributors in the 1980s and then — like so many of these pictures did — faded into the ether. The film received renewed attention when boutique label Arrow Video released a red-carpet Blu-ray some years back, lighting a fire for a modest cult following. But SCALPEL deserves much more than just a modest cult following.

The film stars character actor Robert Lansing as the blank-faced plastic surgeon Dr. Phillip Reynolds, a brilliant architect of flesh who also happens to be one of the biggest sons-of-bitches sliming around the deep South. Seems this prick murdered his wife (the film suggests as much in a darkly hilarious flashback sequence) and his daughter Heather's (Judith Chapman, Eurohorror legend Patty Shepard's sister!) beau, the latter incident of which was witnessed by the girl and set her to running. In fact, when SCALPEL begins, Heather has been MIA for a year and despite this, her now-dead grandfather has willed his entire 5 million fortune to her, cutting out his despised son-in-law entirely.

Presumably livid (but as played by the chill Lansing, only visibly mildly put-out), Reynolds hatches a scheme to take a mutilated stripper into his lair and "remake" her face to be a dead-ringer for his gone-girl daughter. The idea is to pull a Henry Higgins and "teach" the scrappy young hustler to walk, talk and act exactly like Heather, thus fooling the family and attorneys into thinking that she IS in fact Heather. The plan works and the duo split the 5 million and — in a gently sick twist — begin a torrid

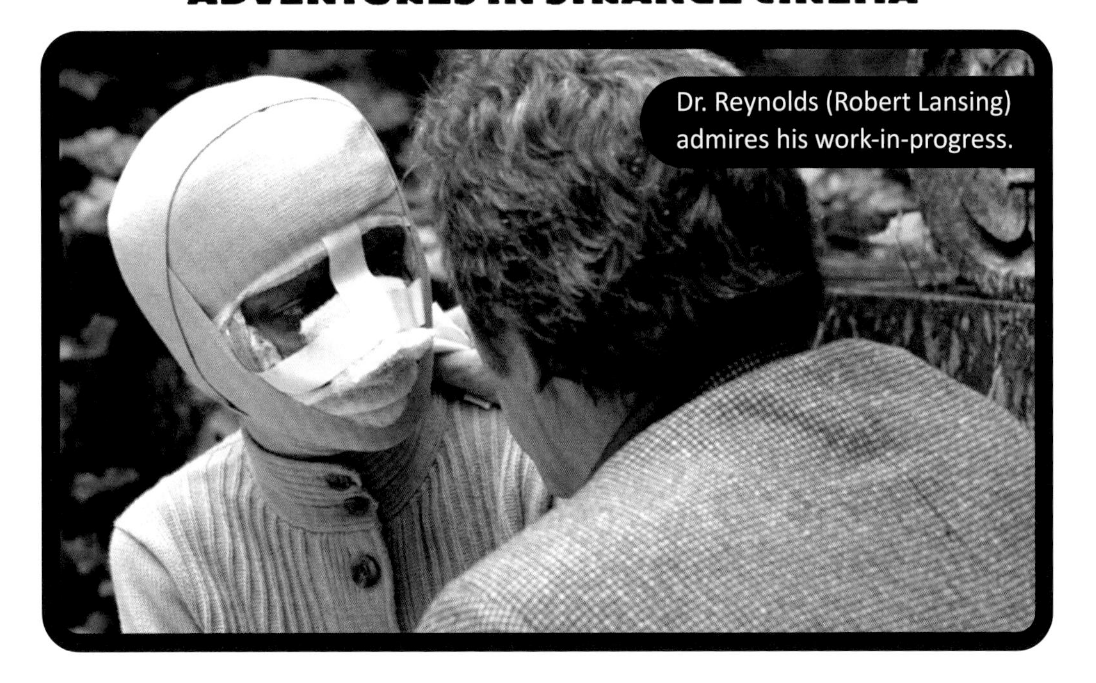
Dr. Reynolds (Robert Lansing) admires his work-in-progress.

sexual relationship behind closed doors. But when the real Heather shows up (also played by Chapman) things go from sweaty mad-science to full-blown psychodrama and very quickly, an unsavory and decidedly unhealthy *ménage à trois* develops.

To say more about Grissmer's crown-jewel of secret-sleaze would be to spoil the ample fun it offers. But man alive, is SCALPEL fantastic. It's like someone hired Jess Franco to direct an episode of LOVE, AMERICAN STYLE. It's a leering, straight-faced free-fall into bad behavior and yet it's not gory at all (save for a few blood-blasts) and there's no explicit sex and I cannot recall even a bad word uttered by any of the cast. In a sea of schlock cinema where everyone just keeps trying to out-porn the next guy, this restraint is admirable and charming and recalls the early days of post-code Hollywood cinema, when filmmakers had to weave-in the taboo gingerly so as not to alarm the thought police, thus making the movie feel even *more* dangerous. The cast is dynamite, with Lansing's relaxed sociopathic doctor alternately amusingly chilling and eerie, especially when he breaks from his boozy stupor to giggle like a toothy madman. Chapman is excellent too, in a challenging dual role that makes you legitimately believe that she's two people, more than a decade before David Cronenberg tried the same stunt in 1988's DEAD RINGERS. Tying this grubby southern gothic together is a lush score by Dan Curtis' right-hand man, the legendary Robert Cobert, who mines his work in DARK SHADOWS to sculpt a romantic, melancholy, and haunting tapestry of sound.

If you've never seen SCALPEL — and I'm willing to bet that many of you have not — I highly recommend you make time for it. They don't make movies like this anymore.

SCREAM BLACULA SCREAM (1973)

Starring William Marshall, Don Mitchell, Pam Grier, Michael Conrad
Written by Joan Torres, Raymond Koenig, Maurice Jules
Directed by Bob Kelljan

While it's very true that 1973's SCREAM BLACULA SCREAM pales in the shadow of its majestic predecessor, there's still much to recommend about it. Flaws and all, the movie stands as an effectively weird entry in AIP's slate of early '70s vampire films, contemporary answers to the sorts of Gothic costume shockers Hammer were making while blending in contemporary themes and motifs. Though no matter what light you cast it in, it's undeniable that the absence of BLACULA director William Crain's sensibilities and stewardship is deeply felt.

After Mama Loa, the aged leader of an L.A. voodoo cult dies, transference of her power has been left to young, spiritual Lisa Fortier (the inimitable Pam Grier), much to the protests of Mama Loa's sniveling son Willis (Richard Lawson). In defiance of his dead mother's wishes, Willis acquires the bones of the long dead Price Mamuawlde and, in a resurrection sequence straight out of a Hammer Dracula picture, Blacula returns and immediately puts the bite on his liberator, who then in turn aims to bring other members of his circle into this new*fang*led cult. Meanwhile, Mamuwalde fixes his attentions on the gentle, black magic master Lisa and, in between feasting on the blood of the living and keeping his now out of control coven in line, convinces Lisa to help him reverse the bloodsucking curse that has him perpetually in its grip.

Armed with a few more dollars, a bigger cast and a richer, Gothic look, SCREAM BLACULA SCREAM is an interesting, amusing picture and has many wonderful moments. The big problem with it is that it flubs the character of Mamuwalde, replacing the reluctant monstrosity Crain and Marshall developed together in the first round and replacing it with an overwhelming streak of narcissism and sadism. Unlike in the original, we don't pity Blacula here, rather he's very conscious of his dire deeds. Mamuwalde has an agenda; he's arrogant goes into fits of rage when any of his coven dares defy him, his feral eyebrows and sideburns almost always flaring up. When Mamuwalde does start to follow his heart, in his quieter moments with Lisa, it doesn't quite ring true. Regardless of these tonal inconsistencies, Marshall is never less than a commanding presence, majestic and powerful even when threatening to be upstaged by the jive talkin' Willis, who provides ample comedy relief in the Renfield-esque role. The scene where the vane, now vampirized, young man realizes he can't admire how good he looks anymore as he no longer casts a reflection is hilarious.

BLACULA is a masterpiece because it's a character piece first, a horror film second; its ample shocks and frissons stemming naturally out of the effortlessly cool world

Crain created and the fascination with the "fish out of water" dynamic of Mamuwalde's plight, a man lost in a world he doesn't understand and who is desperately trying to reconnect to a past he was robbed of, to a love ripped cruelly away from him. There's a beauty to BLACULA, a grace that is sorely absent from this sequel. One can't fault Kelljan's directing, however. He's not a better or worse director than Crain, rather he's just a more conventional one and again, he's aiming for horror here, both straight and intentionally campy. Kelljan's double-shot of COUNT YORGA movies — COUNT YORGA, VAMPIRE and THE RETURN OF COUNT YORGA — stand as the two of the scariest vampire movies ever made but they work (and boy do they work, especially the malevolent second one) because Kelljan sticks to his lane. He never asks us to care about Yorga or his ghastly, wraith-like disciples. They're monsters. In SCREAM BLACULA SCREAM, he gets the horror right, but can't make us really care about anyone, including Mamuwalde. Even the scene where Blacula pushes back against the pimps doesn't quite ring true. In the original, Ketty Lester's enraged cabby triggers the vampire's wrath when she hits low and calls him "boy", a single word that triggers the very oppression that led to not only his people's "curse" but his own dismal life of vampirism. Here, Blacula snaps when the hustler's call him "faggot", thus challenging his machismo. He counters that with a speech about how the pimps are denigrating their own people, making a slave of their "sisters", and mimicking their white masters. It's a potent condemnation and I suspect its one that Marshall himself inserted into the script. But unlike BLACULA, the script surrounding that line doesn't stick to its socially pointed landing.

Still, Pam Grier is — as always — a pleasure to watch, both in respect to her drop-dead stunning physical presence and her intensity as an actor. Her story as the heir apparent priestess to a voodoo cult is interesting and she brings a real sensual, intelligent, tough energy to Lisa. I do like how writers Joan Torres, Raymond Koenig and Maurice Jules added a dose of DARK SHADOWS to the story, with Mamuwalde seeking Lisa to use the very same mysticism that revived him to stamp out his vampiric curse, much like DS's Barnabas Collins enlisted Dr. Julia Hoffman to "cure" him via experimental blood transfusions. And I like how Kelljan managed to port over his style of vile underling vampire to the story for the chilling climax. And oh, that stunning opening credits sequence, with Saul Bass-esque titles by the great Sandy Dvore, not to mention funky Bill Marx score. SCREAM BLACULA SCREAM doesn't really hold together, and one can only imagine the sort of picture it would have been under Crain's more cerebral guidance.

But, hey, Marshall is Marshall and Blacula is Blacula so it gets a pass.

THE SENTINEL (1977)

Starring Cristina Raines, Chris Sarandon, Ava Gardner, Burgess Meredith
Written by Michael Winner, Jeffrey Konvitz
Directed by Michael Winner

Now, as any good student of history should know, the 1960s were a time of change in America and abroad, of social and political upheaval. With JFK getting his noggin shattered on live television and the bloody shadow of the Vietnam conflict looming large, the people — fresh out of the pastel perfect 1950s — were no longer blindly trusting of their flag, of themselves... or of their God.

Right and wrong became blurry. Black and white dissolved into various shades of grey. Good didn't always conquer evil and sometimes The Devil could win and there was nothing your endless bible-to-bosom clutching could do about it. As the '60s oozed into the 1970s, Americans were shell-shocked and, much like the angry youth coming out of post-war Germany, Italy and France, they began to seriously question

THE SENTINEL is a majestic work of high-gloss exploitation horror.

their previously unchallenged beliefs. And, as mainstream pop culture began to reflect this disenfranchisement, so then did horror movies become more morally checkered, delivering the bleakest, most nihilistic answers imaginable.

So too then were the streams of guarded religious idealism attacked with profitable and controversial relish. This cycle of irreverent, theology-based pop-terror started in 1968 with Roman Polanski's adaptation of Ira Levin's bestseller *Rosemary's Baby*; it went sexually rabid with Ken Russell's depraved 1971 melodrama THE DEVILS; it perfected itself with William Friedkin's 1973 classic THE EXORCIST and it climaxed with the operatic pulp of Richard Donner's 1976 shocker THE OMEN. But one picture that sought to ride this potentially blasphemous wave got lost in the shuffle, coming out after films about the persuasive power of The Devil were popular, receiving its cinematic communion perhaps a wee bit too late. Though many people that saw it theatrically back in 1977 still cite it as one of the scariest movies ever made, for whatever reason THE SENTINEL has kind of, sort of just disappeared from those omnipresent "best horror movies" discussions. It still exists primarily on the fringe.

Pity poor Alison Parker (Christina Raines, NIGHTMARES), beautiful model and actress by day and nail-biting nervous wreck by night. As a teenager she accidentally stumbled upon her father engaging in a tawdry threesome with two rather rotund whores and, after being beaten by her old man for the intrusion, promptly dragged a razor blade across her own wrist. Though she survived the bungled suicide, years later she tries again after her lover's wife, who, upon discovering her hubby's infidelity, jumps from a bridge to her own emotionally devastated demise. Again, Alison lives through it. Now shacked up with said lover, a slightly sinister high-priced lawyer

THERE MUST FOREVER BE A GUARDIAN AT THE GATE FROM HELL...
SHE WAS YOUNG
SHE WAS BEAUTIFUL
SHE WAS THE NEXT.
the sentinel
From the Frightening Best-Seller
A MICHAEL WINNER FILM
"THE SENTINEL"
CHRIS SARANDON · CRISTINA RAINES
MARTIN BALSAM · JOHN CARRADINE · JOSE FERRER · AVA GARDNER
ARTHUR KENNEDY · BURGESS MEREDITH · SYLVIA MILES · DEBORAH RAFFIN · ELI WALLACH
Screenplay by MICHAEL WINNER and JEFFREY KONVITZ · Based on the novel by JEFFREY KONVITZ · Music by GIL MELLÉ
Directed by MICHAEL WINNER · Produced by MICHAEL WINNER and JEFFREY KONVITZ · A UNIVERSAL PICTURE
TECHNICOLOR®
R RESTRICTED

named Michael (FRIGHT NIGHT's Chris Sarandon), the terminally tortured starlet, feeling she needs some much needed independence and space to figure out who she is, rents an apartment in a looming NYC brownstone.

Things get weird from the get-go. First off, the far-too-friendly real estate agent (a grinning Ava Gardner) quotes the pad at an already low $500 per month and casually lowers it another hundred after the none-too-wealthy Alison turns it down. Unfazed by the agent's inexplicably desperate attempts to fill the gorgeous flat, she moves in and is almost immediately visited by a slew of eccentric neighbors. There's the doddering old Mr. Chazen (the great Burgess Meredith), a charming oddball who throws birthday parties for his pets; the stuttering old lady who keeps muttering "black and white cat, black and white cake"; the leering, kinky lesbian dancers (a still sultry Sylvia Miles and a young and yummy Beverly D'Angelo) who are prone to impromptu tea time masturbation sessions; and then there's the blind, mute and seemingly senile Father Halloran (genre icon John Carradine), who does nothing more than sit in the top window and stare through sightless eyes at the world below.

Alison, already teetering on a breakdown, takes the antics of this array of oddballs with a grain of salt, until of course she learns that none of them — save the old priest — actually exist in the natural world. As it turns out, this is no ordinary Brooklyn Heights low rise, but rather it's a portal to Hell, a gateway guarded by Halloran and monitored by the Church and the quirky neighbors are in fact evil ghosts, demons, whose morbid task lies in encouraging Alison to kiss that blade to her vein once again... this time for keeps.

Why? Let's just say, that the eternally put upon lass learns that she is in fact stuck squarely in a high stakes tug of war between Heaven and Hell and her very soul hangs in the balance.

THE SENTINEL is one of the strangest horror films of the 1970s. First of all, it was indeed directed by the late, rough and tumble ex-pat British action filmmaker Michael Winner (he of, among other things, the Chuck Bronson vigilante classic DEATH WISH — discussed elsewhere in this book — and its first two sequels) and Winner's more exploitative, direct, unaffected approach to the material is jarring, at odds with the baroque locations and subject matter. And his casting of high-class Hollywood veterans, second only to THE LOVE BOAT, is absolutely, gleefully loopy. I mean, where else can you see future NATIONAL LAMPOON'S VACATION mama D'Angelo sharing space with old pros like Meredith, Gardner, Miles and even Eli Wallach (whose work here as a jaded, relentless detective is superb) while furiously rubbing her leotard sheathed clitoris to orgasm?

The aim of Winner's approach is to create a glossy world of high fashion, contemporary urban lifestyle, seemingly benign, overly cheery characters, and stuffy clergymen and then take a big old ladle of wet, bloody, grimy sleaze and just smother

The great Burgess Meredith is one of many Hollywood icons that show up in THE SENTINEL.

the whole picture with it like a kind of vulgar gravy. Contrary to how that reads, this is NOT a bad thing. Quite the opposite. It's this very tonal dichotomy that gives the film much of its fingerprint.

Upon its release in 1977, THE SENTINEL was not only a tad too late out of the God-fearing gate, it also did something that similarly spurred-on the career death of filmmaker Tod Browning 35 years earlier. In the movie's nightmarish climax, when the demons reveal their true natures and creep out from underneath the stairs, pushing our heroine past the edge of sanity, the already introduced heavies are joined by a cavalcade of real deal disfigured people. We see men with facial tumors so extreme and hideous they make John Merrick look like Brad Pitt by comparison. We see thalidomide damaged women, dwarves, cleft-palette children and at least one poor soul whose lips are so heavy with cysts that they hang like mud flaps from his drooping mug.

When the audience is treated to this parade of damaged people, THE SENTINEL, which until this point is still anchored firmly in fantasy, is dragged into the realms of exploitative reality. Browning's 1932 classic FREAKS was a film that similarly sported a cast of disabled and distorted men and women, a move that repelled audiences and almost single-handedly demolished a once promising career. FREAKS' notorious reputation has long since been exonerated due to the fact that the various deformed men and women are sympathetic characters, heroes in fact. In THE SENTINEL however, Winner is callously throwing them on screen in their natural state, without a shred of makeup, and positioning them as agents of Satan, as monsters, as evil, bloodthirsty ghouls.

Was it a sensitive move? Probably not, and Winner's credibility was called into question by audiences and critics alike. But whatever your thoughts on this crass casting decision… it works. It really works and the picture is that much more unsettling for it.

There is also some debate as to the shadowy morality of the film (and the book from which it was culled) in that the Catholic church seems almost as sinister and manipulative as the duel faced devils themselves. The fact that an obviously deeply disturbed young woman like Alison has but one choice to save her soul (remember, Catholics believe suicide to be one of the ultimate spits in the face of God) and that is to essentially give up her identity, is upsetting and depressing. She's basically fucked no matter which deity she chooses to succumb too. This is far more manipulative a picture than THE EXORCIST or even THE OMEN, but it's without question the angriest and cruelest and goriest of the bunch.

Those who have not seen THE SENTINEL will be pleasantly shocked by the unflinching level of gruesome action on display, much of it courtesy of THE EXORCIST's Dick Smith. From splitting, blood spurting heads and cannibalism to the show-stopping scene where Alison bisects an eyeball and hacks off the nose from the reanimated corpse of her abusive father, the film pushes its R-rating around like a schoolyard bully, cramming in as much wince inducing nastiness (not to mention skeezy sexuality) as a 95-minute mainstream '70s Hollywood horror flick can contain.

If you're a fan of Italian horror, try to see the countless ways in which the great Lucio Fulci quotes this film in his 1981 masterwork THE BEYOND. And if you are indeed familiar with that magnum opus, note the last shot of THE SENTINEL and tell me old man Lucio didn't prick up his ears and scribble some notes…

When THE SENTINEL was released, the Vietnam war was long over, disco was still king, Americans had recovered from, and come to terms with, their collective spiritual abyss and, the empty, coke-fueled, morally bankrupt, superficial 1980s were just a heartbeat away. This, coupled with the general lack of audience interest in THE SENTINEL, not to mention the mini-controversy surrounding its sideshow climax, started Michael Winner on an unfortunate creative down-spiral that he never really recovered from. By the time Bronson wooed the director back for the successful yet ugly, cheap, mean and critically maligned Cannon Pictures produced sequel DEATH WISH 2 in 1982, the aging filmmaker's reputation as B-level hack had been secured. Shame that. Because THE SENTINEL is probably the best film of Winner's expansive career: a solid, disturbing, sick, often campy and occasionally unspeakably horrifying theological mystery ripe with cheap, visceral thrills.

With its mismatched, once in a lifetime cast (the likes of which also include the late Jerry Orbach and brief turns by the impossibly young Jeff Goldblum and Christopher Walken) and its cynical, jaundice eyed view of both Catholicism and society at large it is perhaps the last great intelligent theological horror film of the 1970s.

Winner's voyeuristic sensibilities served his work well.

INTERVIEW: MICHAEL WINNER

These days, THE SENTINEL has found its place in horror film history and is almost considered a respectable work. But when I met Michael Winner in 2009, when he was primarily making his living as one of London's pre-eminent food critics, being a fan of THE SENTINEL was a lonely sort of love. Reaching out to Michael about the film for a book I was writing, I found him charming and open to speaking about both the film and all of his many wonderful adventures in cinema. Simply put, I adored him. Months later, he mailed me a copy of his autobiography, the delightful *Winner Takes All: A Life of Sorts*, which I still cite as my favorite account of making movies, one that captured Winner's "voice" and breezy love of art, food and life. We stayed in touch right up until his death, he was always available to me. I put him in print many times in many magazines. He sent me a lovely letter once, thanking me for putting him in *Fangoria*, which he called a "jolly magazine". And despite what some who have worked for him might say, jolly is exactly how I remember Michael Winner.

CHRIS ALEXANDER: You started your Hollywood career with the 1971 horror film THE NIGHTCOMERS, which didn't exactly set the box office on fire. So, after riding such a wave of success with DEATH WISH, you went back to horror again with THE SENTINEL. Why?

MICHAEL WINNER: Well, on the whole, unless you're the most powerful director in the world, you're just a bum out of work. At the time, I didn't have anything on the table. I went to a party, and a friend of mine said, "Michael, I have a book by

Jeffrey Konvitz called *The Sentinel* and we can't script it; we've tried three times." So, I read the book, loved it and made a deal to write it. It happened that quickly.

ALEXANDER: Was Konvitz happy with your script?

WINNER: No! He wasn't happy at all, he hated it. He's a moron. He hated me, hated the script, hated the film… he hated everything. But the funny thing was that when we submitted the proposed credits to the Writer's Guild, it said, "Written by Michael Winner from the novel by Jeffrey Konvitz" — which was true, he had nothing to do with the script — but he went to the Guild and said "How dare you! I must have co-credit." Why? Residuals, of course!

ALEXANDER: One of the most memorable things about the film is the who's who of Hollywood legends cast in sinister roles. How did you manage to get all these incredible performers involved?

WINNER: Well, it's simple: they liked my script! But they were all fantastic, really. Burgess Meredith was a professional and a pixie-like delight. He and I became great friends afterwards. Ava Gardner also became a great friend and I saw quite a bit of her in London, where she lived, until the day she died. Many of the other actors like Eli Wallach and Martin Balsam had worked with me before.

ALEXANDER: For your male lead, you had Chris Sarandon who was at the peak of his career. Was he your first choice?

WINNER: Oh no. I should have had Christopher Walken in the lead instead of the small part he ended up playing, but it was Universal that wanted to have Chris in the

Sylvia Miles and Beverly D'Angelo dance for their director.

role. I actually wanted Martin Sheen, but to my surprise the studio said "We don't want Sheen. He's in television!". Ridiculous.

ALEXANDER: THE SENTINEL saw as much if not more controversy than DEATH WISH because of the casting of the real deformed people. Was that an intentional but for press?

WINNER: Not at all, that was a practical decision. To do prosthetics on 60 actors, well, we'd have to find a place to house them. It would have been a nightmare. But you know, one of those people said to me how wonderful it was for him, that he wasn't so alone. Meanwhile, all these assholes in the media were saying that I was exploiting them, and that was bullshit. They loved it. They were in New York; they were in a movie!

ALEXANDER: The movie is very gory for an R-rated film. Did you have to make any cuts?

WINNER: No, the film wasn't censored at all, believe it or not. But yes, it was gory. In a number of interviews, Beverly D'Angelo was asked about the scene where she and Vera Miles were eating Chris Sarandon's brains. She told them that I said, "Darling, you'll be with two Academy Award-nominated actors while you're doing it, so don't worry!". It was a jolly picture indeed!

ALEXANDER: Did you know that the film was very popular in Europe?

WINNER: Yes, it did very well.

ALEXANDER: There was a wave in Italy of movies about buildings built over gateways to hell...

WINNER: Really! I had no idea. Well, it was a good film, and it was a very good book.

ALEXANDER: Years later, you returned to horror with 1985's SCREAM FOR HELP. What are your thoughts on that picture. It seems like an interesting experiment that maybe didn't do as well as you had hoped.

WINNER: I actually think it was a very well-made, out-and-out horror film. No, I had always worked with big stars, always. The producers wanted to have no stars at all; they wanted cheap, cheap, cheap — although the film was not *that* cheap, really. I like the film very much, but I was annoyed that too much control had gone to other people, and that wasn't how I worked.

ALEXANDER: You had hired your neighbour, Jimmy Page, to do the score for DEATH WISH 2 and DEATH WISH 3. In SCREAM FOR HELP, you had another Led Zeppelin member, bassist John Paul Jones do the score...

WINNER: Yes, and we had a tiny bit written by someone else, to be honest, because he was very slow. He was no Jimmy Page, I'll tell you that! But he was good — you don't get into Led Zeppelin if you're not good, do you? Incidentally, they all hate him, the rest of the group. They can't stand him. He's not a likable human being, very arrogant. But I do like the movie. It wasn't a big success at the box office, which annoyed me. Horror films are famous for hiring well-known actors who are on the skids a bit but are still big names, and if we had brought in someone like, I don't know, Jack Palance, that would have given it some oomph!

SERIAL MOM (1994)

Starring Kathleen Turner, Sam Waterston, Ricki Lake, Suzanne Somers
Written by John Waters
Directed by John Waters

Some say the John Waters train of transgression came to a halt in the 1980s, when he "sold out" to studio dough. PG-rated films like HAIRSPRAY and CRY-BABY somewhat alienated his hardcore fan base founded in the 1970s, where he and his merry band of misfits made outrageous 8mm and 16mm shock-comedies, usually centering around the iconic, rotund transvestite Divine. The most famous/notorious of those pictures was of course 1972's still offensive PINK FLAMINGOS. You know, the one where a man screws a chicken to death, Divine fellates her own son and at the stirring climax, eats a real deal dog turd, grinning and gagging while she chomps.

But anyone can throw geek show shtick at the screen and truly, the real joy of a John Waters joint is his irreverence coupled with his obsession with exploitation films and deranged pop culture, his use of music and a certain warmth, a sense of family. Which makes sense. Growing up gay in Baltimore and loving all things counterculture and camp, Waters naturally moved to the fringe and became part of a circle of weirdos and artists who took "revenge" on the artifice of normalcy by making confrontational art. Theirs truly was a family of freaks — *gooble gobble, one of us* —

Kathleen Turner's Beverly is a marvellously vulgar creation.

Turner sears the screen in SERIAL MOM.

who protected each other. And again, that sense of banding together on the sidelines of society is all over virtually every single film Waters ever made. If anything, his "mainstream" movies are even *more* outrageous because he was able to manipulate big budgets and thus draw in A-list talent to figure prominently in his berserk worlds.

Case in point, Kathleen Turner in SERIAL MOM. Turner was the "It" girl of the '80s, a sexual, sublime performer whose appearances in films like THE MAN WITH TWO BRAINS, BODY HEAT, ROMANCING THE STONE (and its lesser sequel, JEWEL OF THE NILE) and Ken Russell's incredible CRIMES OF PASSION, proved her to be a bold actress who could conquer the Hollywood blockbuster and then fearlessly venture off the path into the arthouse without incident. She was a natural fit for the world of John Waters and indeed, she's the motor that drives his incredible 1994 satirical slasher/faux true crime melodrama SERIAL MOM, an addictive, laugh out loud romp where Turner just might give the best performance of her career.

Turner plays Beverly Sutphin, matriarch of an over-stylized, typically Watersian family who live in a world that is contemporary and yet filtered through a dirty 1950s, LEAVE IT TO BEAVER gone wrong lens. Waters wastes no time in getting to "know" Beverly, to show the cracks in her cheery, muffin-baking facade when, over breakfast conversing with her kids (Ricki Lake and Matthew Lillard) and husband (Sam Waterston), she becomes fixated on killing a housefly that keeps sullying her carefully presented meal with its filthy legs. It's like that line from PSYCHO, where the now totally mad Norman states in his mother's voice that she "wouldn't hurt a fly". Beverly is Norman and Mother and June Cleaver, and she's gone completely off her rocker.

Next, we see her sadistic side when, in the film's funniest running gag, she crank-calls a long-suffering neighbor (Waters regular Mink Stole) and unleashes a barrage of profanity, driving the poor woman to the brink. A flashback reveals that this woman once took Beverly's parking spot at the mall. And well, you don't cross Beverly. Ever. Or else.

The rest of SERIAL MOM tips its hat (and flips the bird) to phony investigative "true crime" films (the movie comically claims it was based on a true case: it wasn't) and takes a stab at America's addiction to serial killer culture and how we make folk heroes out of maniacs. Beverly violently murders any and all who offend her moral code or disrespects her brood while not bothering to even cover up her trails, leading to an uproarious, protracted court case that beat the real-life O.J. Simpson televised court fiasco to the punch.

Waters has publicly stated more than once that he thinks SERIAL MOM is his best movie. And I think he's right. It's a madcap masterpiece.

INTERVIEW: MINK STOLE

To know Mink Stole is to love her. I can't remember when I first encountered Mink, somewhere, someplace. But naturally, we got on well enough that we stayed in touch, and she let me capture her thoughts and words in print many times. Once, back in 2017, I even flew her to Toronto to be a guest at my "Horror-Rama" show. And I threw a party where she performed her own cabaret-style music on stage, with CHILDREN SHOULDN'T PLAY WITH DEAD THINGS composer Carl Zittrer accompanying her on piano! Yes, it was just as wild an event as it sounds. And that's why Mink is so wonderful. Yes, she's John Waters' right-hand muse, yes, she's dynamic on screen, a gifted comedian who effortlessly steals scenes. But she's so much more. A singer, a thinker, a teller of tales, a gentle, kind human being. And though a talent as titanic as hers could allow for some ego, she has little to none. Again, to know Mink is to love mink...

ALEXANDER: When John brings you into one of his movies, has he written parts exclusively for you?

MINK STOLE: I think in the early days, the first films, he did, yes. He wrote all those parts for me. I think right up into SERIAL MOM, in fact. I think he wrote Dottie for me. He knows my voice; he knows how I can speak and knows the changes I can make. After SERIAL MOM, I don't think he wrote anything specific for me. I think after Divine died, it became harder for him to write for anyone specifically.

ALEXANDER: How did that affect you when Divine passed?

John Waters and his favorite lady.

STOLE: It was devastating. We all were devastated. It was a time of euphoria because of HAIRSPRAY. It had just opened and gotten wonderful reviews and Divine had gotten wonderful reviews and I had reconciled — well, I shouldn't say reconciled because we were never estranged — but Divine and I hadn't been in touch for several years because Divine was in Europe making music and was huge over there. But making HAIRSPRAY was a wonderful time and the filming of it was — except for the horrible heat — really fun. So, it was amazing to get the good reviews and I loved the movie, it was so good. And then, in the midst of all this "Yay! Hooray!"... Divine dies. It was an awful shock. And I saw how it affected John and I think it affected him more deeply than anyone else on the planet, because they were such a team. They were such a force in each others life. It was a bad time.

ALEXANDER: But to end on HAIRSPRAY, which was a breakthrough for the gang... that was something.

STOLE: Yeah, I mean, he went out on the way up. Better than going out on the way down.

ALEXANDER: On the back end of the SERIAL MOM Blu-ray, there's that great sit down with you, Kathleen and John just sharing stories about the making of the movie. At one point John mentions that SERIAL MOM was the only time you guys ever really had any real money to make a movie. Did having increased pressures of a bigger budget hinder the creative process?

STOLE: [*laughs*] Oh no, I don't think money every hinders the creative process [*laughs more*]. No, honey, money never ever hurts. It was lovely to have money. I was not living in Baltimore at the time, I was living in Los Angeles and so I was able to stay at a lovely hotel. There were perks that only money can give you. Craft services had more than crackers and peanut butter. We had actual chairs to sit on. You know, it was a pleasure to work on a movie with the budget.

ALEXANDER: And the suits left John alone, pretty much?

STOLE: Pretty much. And you know, this was the first film that I can remember in which John kept telling me to tone down my acting, to bring it down. And this was shocking to me. I was like, "but this is me!" I have always acted in this sort of larger-than-life way. I'm thankful he did that, because if I didn't make it a more subtle performance I would have stood out like a sore thumb.

ALEXANDER: Indeed, Dottie is muted for you. She's in a reactive state the entire movie until she loses it at the end. It's a very controlled and funny performance.

STOLE: Yes. And I love that end scene. There's just something so amazing about having the freedom to say to someone, who was probably one of the most popular actresses in the world at that time, "you cocksucker pig fucker!" You know, this is not something everyone gets to do! Kathleen was amazing to work with. She was in a good mood every day and was having the time of her life. A lovely woman. She would host poker parties at her apartment. She enjoyed being here. She enjoyed being among us. By us I mean also Sam Waterston and Matthew Lillard too, who I

Mink Stole's Dottie endures another of Beverly's perverse prank calls.

saw recently by the way and is just looking fabulous. No, she was a pleasure every minute I worked with her.

ALEXANDER: Why did you come back home to Baltimore?

STOLE: It was time. And it was a good decision. I don't regret it.

ALEXANDER: Do you get mobbed at the supermarket?

STOLE: [*laughs*] Oh God no! John is a big hero here. I'm practically invisible. Fans come up to me anywhere *but* Baltimore. I go out with John periodically and people fawn all over him and he'll introduce me, and they'll go," Oh yeah, hey" and then ignore me. So, when he's in the room I'm totally invisible.

ALEXANDER: On that same Blu-ray interview, you say that back in your heyday people wondered "Who are these people? Where do they go after dark?" Were you guys just a normal bunch of art kids?

STOLE: Welllll... *pretty* normal except we took a lot of drugs. Never while we were working. Ever. But we took drugs and were anti-establishment without being militant, so we considered ourselves counterculture, but we did not identify as hippies. We called ourselves freaks. I was wearing black fingernail polish in 1967. Now it's normal. Then people would stop me on the street.

ALEXANDER: You know, every time I see John or hear him interviewed or speak, he seems so happy. Is he?

STOLE: John has a lovely life. He built his life. The man has an imagination that will not quit and endless energy. He wakes up and creates every day. I find him astonishing.

ALEXANDER: And how about you? Are you happy with your life?

STOLE: My life? Well, I tell ya. There are days I wake up and think I'm the luckiest person in the world and others, well, not so much. Depends on if I have to do the laundry.

THE SHOUT (1978)

Starring John Hurt, Alan Pates, Susannah York, Tim Curry
Written by Jerzy Skolimowski, Michael Austin
Directed by Jerzy Skolimowski

Whether it be a low, wet, growl coming from deep within in the dark, a disembodied whisper from behind a long-locked door, or the skin-tightening timbre of a terrified woman's pre-knife stuck scream, the use of sound has been manipulated since the dawn of horror cinema as a highly effective tool to terrify those lucky enough to be blessed with relatively good hearing. Sound fills in the blanks, giving audible life to seemingly benign tableaux; people, objects and events are transformed. Sometimes

Rachel (Susannah York) pines for Crossley's touch.

sound is used to create tension, to provide the aural punch line to an unbearable setup and sometimes sound is even used to lull the viewer into a false sense of calm before unleashing whatever beast the filmmaker has heretofore kept under wraps. But in Polanski pal and DEEP END director Jerzy (DEEP END) Skolimowski's little discussed 1978 tone poem THE SHOUT, sound is used for even more aggressive purposes: to maim, to harm, to inflict agony and eventually, to kill every living thing in its path.

If you've never heard of THE SHOUT, you certainly are not alone. This dark, abstract sliver of arthouse weirdness has been long absent from Blu-ray or DVD on North American shores (an excellent, feature-filled British Blu-ray was released a few years ago) and the ancient, Columbia Pictures US VHS release is a highly-sought-after collectible (UPDATE: as of this writing, The Criterion Channel and other select streaming platforms have now had the film in their respective cycles).

I first encountered THE SHOUT the same way I first encountered many of my favorite films: alone, on late night television. This strange, dark and slowly paced film marked me the deepest and not a day went by that I did not think about it in some way shape or form. My fixation on it later amplified when I realized that basically no one I knew had ever seen it, let alone were aware of (or cared about) its existence and it felt as though it were mine, a secret slice of cinema whose fan club sported one member: me.

Imagine my delight one day, while sifting through the delete rack at Toronto's sadly now defunct Queen Video, I found that very same discontinued Columbia videocassette, lying there, faded, moldy and battered at the bottom of the shelf, being sold off for a lousy dollar. Money immediately changed hands and within seconds THE SHOUT was mine.

Alan Bates is larger-than-life in THE SHOUT.

Let me tell you a bit more about the film itself.

Church organist and erstwhile experimental music composer Anthony (the late, great John Hurt) and his comely wife Rachel (the also dearly departed Susannah York) live a quiet, idyllic yet sexually vacant life in the English countryside. Into their pleasant but unremarkable home comes a brooding, ruggedly handsome, hirsute wanderer named Crossley (the — sigh — *also* passed, still magnetic Alan Bates) seeking refuge and a hot meal, which the young couple skeptically oblige. It's not long before this belligerent, sneering animal of a man begins slowly, methodically manipulating and controlling Anthony and Rachel's lives, both physically and mentally. Turns out Crossley isn't just your run-of-the-mill raving psychotic narcissist, but rather is a kind of an aboriginal warlock, a dangerous outback -dwelling monster who claims to have murdered his children in order to learn the ancient art of psychic vampirism and the ever-useful skill of killing by shouting. Taking the disbelieving Anthony onto the moors one night, Crossley crassly proves his case by simply opening his mouth, drawing in air and letting loose a lethal primal shriek from Hell. Things get very nasty and, needless to say, do not end particularly well for anyone.

Told as an extended flashback to THE ROCKY HORROR PICTURE SHOW's Tim Curry, THE SHOUT is the kind of lyrical, intelligent, enigmatic and frustrating work of psychological horror that the Brits were once so very fond of producing in the 1970s and that are simply, and sadly, not being made at all anymore. Filled with deranged sex, haunting nightmare imagery and an aura of icy, inevitable doom, the picture plays like the bastard offspring of THE WICKER MAN, DON'T LOOK NOW and vintage Luis Buñuel, with perhaps a dash of THE CABINET OF DR. CALIGARI; a movie of surreal, shocking, confusing, terrifying and occasionally blackly humorous power and the kind of eyeball spinning head scratcher that stays with you for weeks (in my case, a lifetime), requires multiple viewings and asks far more questions than it provides answers to. Driven by a powerful score by Genesis alumni Mike Rutherford and Tony Banks, this is truly a living, breathing nightmare committed to celluloid. It's an essential horror movie that needs to be seen, discussed, and adored.

SHOWGIRLS (1995)

Starring Elizabeth Berkley, Kyle MacLachlan, Gina Gershon, Glenn Plummer
Written by Joe Eszterhas
Directed by Paul Verhoeven

Decades after 1967's VALLEY OF THE DOLLS and decades prior to 2016's THE NEON DEMON, Dutch director Paul Verhoeven's SHOWGIRLS, the over-the-top tale of ill-gotten fame, busted dreams and the skeezy, grimy underbelly of Las Vegas, dragged its garish arse across screens across the world. That the heavily hyped project (a reunion between Verhoeven and his BASIC INSTINCT writer Joe Eszterhas) fell flat on its busted back, much like Gina Gershon's Cristal does in the film, just made its myth all the more potent. And though SHOWGIRLS has been universally reviled and is now rather forcibly embraced as a cult film, the misleadingly marketed movie is really yet another in a long line of Hollywood horror films masquerading as something else entirely.

SHOWGIRLS casts SAVED BY THE BELL actress Elizabeth Berkley as Nomi, a scrappy young dancer who hitchhikes her way to Vegas with her heart full of hope and her head full of dreams. Those dreams are damaged almost right off the bat, when a cute young Elvis clone steals her suitcase and leaves her stranded in a casino parking lot. There she meets Molly (Gina Ravera), a friendly young seamstress working backstage at a big topless revue on the strip. For whatever reason, Molly takes Nomi under her wing and gives her a place to stay while she finds her footing. Nomi spends her nights peeling at a low-grade nudie bar, but after Molly takes her to work one night, she is dazzled by the lithe Cristal Connors (Gina Gershon), a superstar dancer who is the centerpiece of a garish show that makes STAYING ALIVE's "Satan's Alley" number look restrained. Once Nomi locks her eyes on this prize, there's no stopping her. Though she has admirers like the plucky blue-collar dancer James (Glenn Plummer) warning her not to crawl to deep into the belly of the beast, she refuses to listen and soon, she's in way over her head in a parasitic world where flesh is a commodity and femininity is distorted to fit the bleakest sort of fantasy.

Nomi (Elizabeth Berkley) works the pole.

SHOWGIRLS may have been made in 1995, but its soul is in the 1950s. The writing is arch, the tone of the film is pitched to 11, the drama is bubbling and boiling over. Really, it's as if Douglas Sirk directed SUSPIRIA. It's a cautionary tale masquerading as manic insanity and I don't think audiences understood what they were getting. SHOWGIRLS isn't an erotic thriller. In fact, it's not erotic at all, this despite the endless female (and male) nudity, spurting fluids and berserk sex (watching Berkley give lap dances and screw men in swimming pools is the stuff of legend). But the sleaze here is upsetting. Ugly. Forced. Empty. SHOWGIRLS is as tawdry and lurid as it is reputed to be, but and that's what gives it its feral soul; its grime is essential to the story.

But really what Verhoeven and Eszterhas are doing here is painting a sperm and blood-stained black velvet painting of a festering sore of a world; an empty, black hole that sucks in delusional, naive, men and women, turning them into meat-puppet mulch and excreting them back out, robbing them of their souls and leaving them to stagger around the blinking, flashing, electric-sex-soaked landscape as something less than human. In the case of Nomi, she's already damaged when we meet her. But she's crawled out of some sort of muck — which we find out about explicitly in the icky climax — and she's obviously convinced that life can't get any worse. She's seen the ugly. She knows the hideous. But she has no idea just how sickening a land this evil Oz really is.

I'm not sure what or who is viler in SHOWGIRLS. Is the monster Gershon's Cristal, a slinking star on the decline who sexually manipulates big time hustler/producer Zack (played with gross boyishness by Kyle MacLachlan) to get what she wants, toying with Nomi to suck her dry and destroy her? Or is it Zack himself, who womanizes, decimates, and then keeps the she-demon husks he helps make around as busted trophies to amuse him? Is the leering choreographer who jerks his desperate dancers around emotionally and degrades them physically? Is it the malevolent Andrew Carver (William Shockley) who uses his fame, privilege, and greasy charm to assault his admirers within inches of their lives? Is it Nomi, who really is such a narcissistic woman that we feel little pity for her pain during her claw to the top? Is it sex? The city itself? Or is it simply that poisonous side that pulses in all of us, the one that is desperate to be loved and admired and remembered; that ego that tricks us into thinking we're more than we are?

This is not a bad movie, despite the dipshits at those Golden Raspberry awards telling you otherwise and the cabal of sniggering cinema hipsters who howl like they're at a midnight screening of THE ROCKY HORROR PICTURE SHOW. No, SHOWGIRLS is really a very, very good exploitation picture about the very nature of exploitation and its dehumanizing effects.

It may not be an outright horror movie, but it's certainly a film of many horrors…

SOLE SURVIVOR (1984)

Starring Anita Skinner, Kurt Johnson, Caren Larkey, Brinke Stevens
Written by Thom Eberhardt
Directed by Thom Eberhardt

For years, no one talked about Thom (NIGHT OF THE COMET) Eberhardt's 1983 chiller SOLE SURVIVOR. It haunted video stores. It drifted across late night cable TV. That's where I saw it. But no one else I knew had seen it. I had no one to share my enthusiasm over the film with. I was God's lonely man. And before the internet, there were no communities to join. There was no way to find a copy of it to purchase, which is what I so wanted to do. But I did find a copy, eventually. And I watched it again. And I estimated that it just might be the scariest movie I'd ever seen. When I was writing for Canadian horror magazine *Rue Morgue* in my "Mad Musings of a Schizoid Cinephile" column, I wrote enthusiastically about the movie. Suddenly I was getting letters from people who had read that rave and had scoured eBay for that elusive Vestron VHS. A cult was swelling. And when Code Red licensed the film for DVD in 2008, they put my quote on the back of the box.

It was a moment of triumph!

These many years later, I'm not so sure it is the scariest movie I've ever seen anymore. But it's certainly one of them.

Anita Skinner's Denise suffers for being the SOLE SURVIVOR.

The film stars Chloë Sevigny-by-way-of-Gaylen Ross look-alike Anita Skinner as Denise Watson, the single living passenger found amidst the grim debris and broken bodies of a catastrophic plane crash. After the initial shellshock subsides (her blood-spattered, PTSD-fueled nightmares feature a wide-eyed, gut-leaking torso, an image that froze my veins as a kid), life slowly carries on, save for one rather distressing turn of events; it seems that everywhere that poor Denise goes, hollow-eyed, slack-jawed zombies follow. They stare at her through restaurant windows; they harass her in public parks; they block her way on country roads. They're everywhere, all the time and, alarmingly, their numbers are multiplying.

It doesn't take Denise long to realize the truth about her tormentors, that they are the recently risen angry dead whose mission it is to bring her briefly lucky ass back into the black where she belongs.

If this chilling narrative twist sounds familiar, it should. SOLE SURVIVOR echoes James Herbert's novel THE SURVIVOR (which was made into a film by DEEP RED actor David Hemmings in 1981) but takes its most distinct cues from Herk Harvey's immortal low budget 1962 mood-piece CARNIVAL OF SOULS, which in turn cribbed its DNA from the classic THE TWILIGHT ZONE episode "The Hitch Hiker", itself an adaptation of an Orson Welles-read radio play. The FINAL DESTINATION franchise (particularly the first film) seems to borrow much from SOLE SURVIVOR and so does David Robert Mitchell's contemporary horror hit, IT FOLLOWS.

What makes this understated shocker so memorable is Eberhardt's eye for atmosphere and use of music. Right from its first lonely frame, when the rumbles of

David Anthony's minimalist ambient score whispers across an empty, rain slicked city street in the middle of the night, we know that we're about to be plunged into the heart of celluloid darkness. And we are. And it's quietly horrifying.

SOLE SURVIVOR is a supremely slow, obscenely eerie exercise in dread, one that manages to reference Rod Serling, Ingmar Bergman and George Romero, sometimes within the same scene. It's an admittedly depressing picture, one in which we know our heroine is doomed and we can only watch, helpless, as every move she makes just slams another nail in her cosmically preordained coffin.

Why Eberhardt has all but disowned it is anyone's guess.

If you value skillfully orchestrated, low budget American death-dreams that seep under your skin and stay there, I advise you to seek SOLE SURVIVOR out. Before it finds you.

STRAIT-JACKET (1964)

Starring Joan Crawford, George Kennedy, Diane Baker, Leif Erickson
Written by Robert Bloch
Directed by William Castle

Anyone who saw the (somewhat fictionalized) FX series FEUD, knows the story of Hollywood legends and career-long "frenemies" Bette Davis and Joan Crawford. That remarkable and wildly entertaining show saw Susan Sarandon and Jessica Lange as Davis and Crawford, respectively, who lay down their never-ending professional rivalries long enough to co-star in director Robert Aldrich's hyper-melodramatic Gothic shocker WHATEVER HAPPENED TO BABY JANE? in 1962. As both glamorous leading ladies were well into middle-age at this point, with decent roles drying up (as they often did and sadly still do for women in cinema), the chance to essay such intelligently written and scenery chewing characters was a gift and with the critical and commercial success of the film, an unofficial subgenre of horror film often called *hagsploitation* was born. Both Davis and Crawford would lead the pack in these sorts of films (along with others like Shelley Winters, Olivia de Havilland et al), which always saw women past their youthful primes driven to madness and often committing murder or just so far gone into psychosis that they become easy marks for the plots of others. Watching "earth mothers" and noted aging screen beauties go bonkers translated into boffo box office...

But while Davis jumped into this new phase of her professional life with open arms, grateful for the work and success, Crawford did not go gently, feeling much of the post-BABY JANE material offered to her was beneath her, and was notoriously difficult to deal with. But master showman and horror producer/director

WARNING!
'STRAIT-JACKET'
VIVIDLY
DEPICTS
AX
MURDERS!
COLUMBIA
PICTURES
presents
STRAIT-JACKET
From the creator of 'Psycho,'
the director of 'Homicidal'
and the co-star of 'What Ever
Happened To Baby Jane?'
Starring
JOAN CRAWFORD
Co-starring
DIANE BAKER · LEIF ERICKSON · HOWARD ST. JOHN
with JOHN ANTHONY HAYES · ROCHELLE HUDSON · Written by ROBERT BLOCH · Produced and Directed by WILLIAM CASTLE A WILLIAM CASTLE PRODUCTION

extraordinaire William Castle (13 GHOSTS, HOUSE ON HAUNTED HILL) was up for the task and landed the actress for his 1964 shocker STRAIT-JACKET, a pulpified slab of post-PSYCHO slaughter that pushed — in typical Castle fashion — its mania and melodrama to fevered, dreamlike heights.

Like his 1961 murder mystery HOMICIDAL — a much more direct riff on Hitchcock's 1960 gender-bending game-changer — Castle laces STRAIT-JACKET with a heightened sense of reality and an (un) healthy undercurrent of sick sexuality. But while HOMICIDAL was penned by frequent collaborator Robb White (THE TINGLER), STRAIT-JACKET was actually written by PSYCHO source novel author Robert Bloch. And unlike HOMICIDAL — which stopped its story dead for the gimmicky Castle-approved "Fright Break" — STRAIT-JACKET employs no such audience-baiting shtick. Well, Castle DID arrange for exhibitors to hand out cardboard axes at the box office, but no similar carny tricks wind up on screen. Rather STRAIT-JACKET is and remains a potent dose of mania that has few peers and is propelled by Crawford's fully committed (in more ways than one) performance.

In the wild, surreal, and sensational opening, STRAIT-JACKET sets up the shenanigans to come, illustrating in tabloid-fashion how Crawford's boozy broad of a wife Lucy walks in on her philandering hubby having a tryst in their home with another woman. She goes bananas and grabs an ax, hacking the humping couple to pieces while her young daughter Carol watches in horror. It's a stunner of a first act and immediately jumps twenty years later to the present, with Crawford's traumatized little girl (played by Diane Baker) now all grown up and preparing for her murderous mom's release from the local loony bin.

Lucy, now cured but still obviously emotionally disturbed, is now a kinder, gentler woman who has paid for her crimes and had her illness eradicated after years of intensive — and grueling — treatment and only wants to be a good mother. Carol is on the cusp of getting married to a well-to-do lad (John Anthony Hayes) and all seems to be heading in the right, healing direction for the mother and daughter. That is until Lucy begins finding phantom severed heads in her bed and hearing strange sounds coming from locked rooms. And when a spate of gruesome ax murders grips the town, suspicion firmly — and unsurprisingly — falls on Lucy's trembling shoulders. Is she losing her mind again? Or is there someone else behind the gory killings?

Anyone who's seen a Castle film or read a Bloch shocker will likely figure out the serpentine mystery before the insane — and awesome — corker of a climax. But that's not why you watch STRAIT-JACKET. It's a film to savored for its over-the-top plotting, its leering characters (including a young George Kennedy as a sweaty and sinister handyman), its cauldron-bubbling oration and — for 1964 — its brutally graphic head-choppings. Hell, even the grand old Columbia Pictures dame gets her noggin lopped off in the film's final image. The entire thing is rapturously ridiculous and boiling-over brilliant.

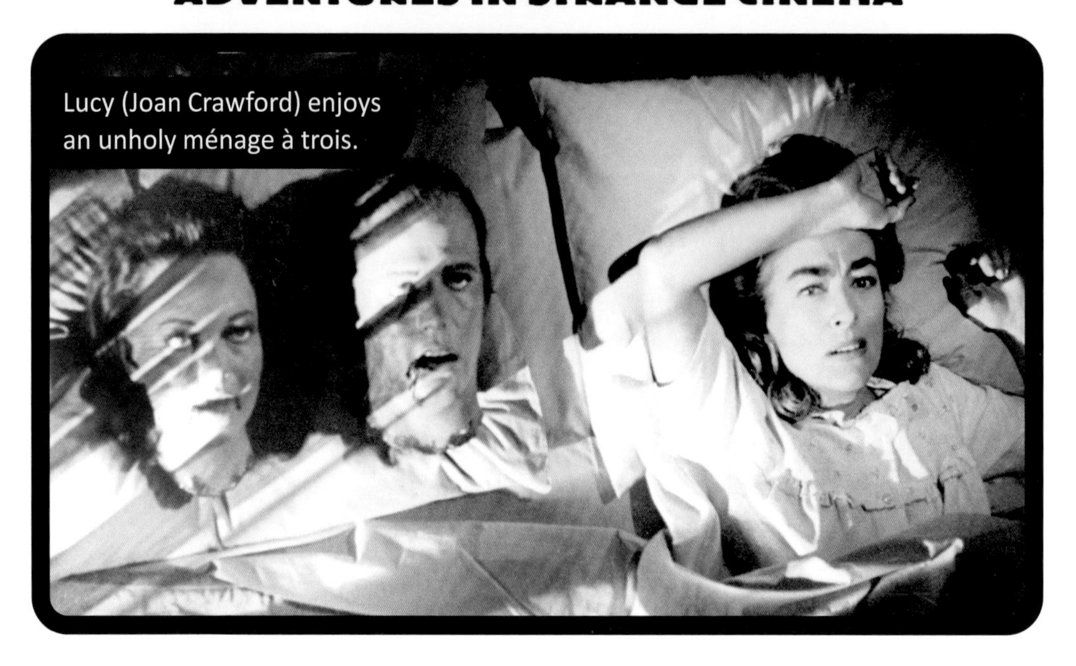
Lucy (Joan Crawford) enjoys an unholy ménage à trois.

But naturally, none of this hyperbolic cranium-removing mayhem would matter were it not for the presence of Crawford, who fearlessly dives into the part of Lucy, jerking the audience around from terror to pity to disgust to empathy and back again. In the film's most arresting encounter, Crawford goes up against her daughter's snooty future mother-in-law, standing her ground and defending her child's honor while defiantly admitting her crime and the pain she endured in its aftermath. It's a stunning, moving scene and certainly ranks right up there with the finest of Joan Crawford's turns.

I have great affection for this last leg of Crawford's career and life. In lesser films like Castle's own I SAW WHAT YOU DID and tawdry programmers like BERSERK and especially the unforgettably awful Freddie Francis romp TROG, Crawford refused to phone it in, dedicated to even the lowliest of roles. She may have been mourning her glory days and miserable that the bloom was off her rose, but she remained until the end a major artist and a consummate professional.

TALES FROM THE HOOD (1995)

Starring Clarence Williams III, Corbin Bernsen, Rosalind Cash, Wings Hauser
Written by Rusty Cundieff, Darin Scott
Directed by Rusty Cundieff

When one is critiquing a film, the thinking is that objectivity is key. A proper review must not reflect the writer's personal tastes but must evenly judge if the film is successful at its chosen level and respond accordingly. Well, fuck that. If you eat, sleep and breathe cinema, if you love it so much that it keeps you awake at night, if it makes your pulse pound faster and, in many respects, informs your view of the world, then objectivity is impossible. In fact, I think the very concept of a piece of film writing being removed from one's life experiences and leanings is an abstract one, even on an academic level. Art provokes response and every single human being who views that art will respond differently. That's the beauty of art.

So, with that verbose preamble, I'll say right here, right now that I am *crazymadinsane* in love with Rusty Cundieff's savage, smart and socially potent 1995 omnibus TALES FROM THE HOOD beyond all reason. Many say SCREAM saved and redeemed horror in the '90s. I hate SCREAM, that self-aware, sneering, smart-ass sitcom thing. And if the studio that released it had been savvier with their marketing campaign, they'd be saying that about TALES. It should have been "the one" that spawned the franchise, that kick-started the trends and Clarence Williams III's wild-eyed hell spawn mortician with his Satanic Don King hairdo should have been the guy people were dressing up as for Halloween.

But it was just too *black*. I mean, look at SCREAM, with its gaggle of pretty, porcelain white faces staring smugly at the pundits on that copied-to-death poster. A far easier sell to America than the ebony skull with the glowing gold tooth that grinned at you on the awesome TALES one-sheet. Savoy Pictures saddled the movie with a marketing campaign and tagline ("Chill... or be chilled...") that positioned the picture as a spoof, like a Wayans Brothers skewering of HBO's then-popular, campy series TALES FROM THE CRYPT. Ironically, those Wayans lads would find great success lampooning SCREAM a few years later.

No, TALES FROM THE HOOD is no spoof. It's not a send-up. It's funny, certainly, but often that humor — as it should always be in horror films — stems organically from the absurdity of the situations. What TALES really is, is a primal scream about black Americans in the urban '90s landscape, both marginalized and — even more potently — cannibalizing themselves; its power and relevance has not dulled an ounce.

The film sees a trio of macho, tough-talking and pistol-wielding gang-bangers descending upon the wildly Gothic funeral home owned by the aforementioned mortician Mr. Simms, so deftly essayed by THE MOD SQUAD's Clarence Williams III, who they think has a stash of cash and drugs. The punks demand that Mr. Simms cough up "the shit" to which the potentially insane embalmer retorts, "you want the shit? You'll be *knee deep* in the shit!"

Over the next several hours, Williams stalls his antagonists with the grim, supernatural stories of the young, black men who fill the coffins in his basement. We

Rosalind Cash has her own "Ludovico Technique" in TALES FROM THE HOOD.

get the story of the crooked, murderous cops (one played by the great Wings Hauser) who beat, frame, and murder a crusading black DA while a young rookie cop watches in horror… and ultimately turns a blind eye. Years later, the unjustly slain victim rises from the dead to exact revenge with the now homeless and substance-addicted ex-cop's help. Another story sees a teacher worried about a little boy who swears his bruises and broken bones are the result of a monster that hides in his home. Meanwhile, the kid's dad (comedian David Alan Grier in a very dark change of pace role) is getting plenty angry at the images his boy is drawing. The next story sees a sniggering former KKK-linked politico (Corbin Bernsen) defiantly moving into a former plantation slave house and running afoul of ghostly marionettes who demand bloody justice. And the final story, the corker, sees a lethal gang banger left for dead after a bloody street brawl and whisked away to a secret clinic where a majestic doctor (THE OMEGA MAN's Rosalind Cash) subjects him to a mind-bending, gut wrenching "Ludivico" -esque treatment to make him aware that the real enemy to "his people"… is him. And then there's that ending…

Oh, that ending. It's one for the books, baby. Wow.

In style, structure and tone, TALES FROM THE HOOD is more of a kissing cousin to Freddie Francis' still chilling 1972 Amicus adaptation of EC's *Tales from the Crypt* comics, with its somber tone, intense morality plays, Grand Guignol gore, black (in every sense) humor and supernatural punishments. But it's something else. Something angry and upsetting. Something sad. If Jordan Peele's breakthrough hit GET OUT is about the way racism now hides behind America's current grinning, faux liberal facade, TALES is about the pulse on the street, of how poverty and ignorance are causing young black men and women to fall into a chasm, one in which they rage war against themselves.

Cundieff and co-writer/producer Darin (FROM A WHISPER TO A SCREAM) Scott's film is a masterpiece. It's a perfect horror film and its messages aren't so heavy handed that they overtake the pleasures of the genre elements, rather the social spine enhances the film's fright factor.

TALES THAT WITNESS MADNESS (1973)

Starring Donald Pleasence, Joan Collins, Kim Novak, Jack Hawkins
Written by Jennifer Jayne
Directed by Freddie Francis

Often mistaken for one of Amicus Pictures' horror anthologies, Oscar winning cinematographer and veteran genre director (my, does he show up plenty in these pages!) Freddie Francis' 1973 omnibus TALES THAT WITNESS MADNESS is a superior British horror film and one of the finest examples of the multi-story shocker. Amicus of course cornered the market on these sorts of films throughout the 1960s and '70s and while they were all entertaining and skillfully produced, only 1972's EC comics riff TALES FROM THE CRYPT truly felt like it was pushing boundaries, like it was *dangerous* in

Uncle Albert (Frank Forsythe) has seen better days in TALES THAT WITNESS MADNESS.

some way. And despite that film's domestic PG rating, it still stands as one of the scariest and most disturbing horror movies this writer has ever seen. And it was directed by Francis. And TALES THAT WITNESS MADNESS is directed by Francis. You see where I'm going with this...

TALES — whose title oddly foreshadows Charles Bukowski's celebrated short story collection *Tales of Ordinary Madness* — opens with a dynamic credit sequence, with green X-rays of human skulls and brains dissolving across the screen, a clear indication that this picture is concerned with the cornerstone of the greatest genre pictures: that of the shadowy, mysterious, and easily damaged corners of the human mind. Its setup echoes that of Amicus' ASYLUM (directed by Francis' fellow Hammer horror colleague Roy Ward Baker) but Francis — again, a trained DP — frames the film with weird angles and low camera set ups, making us feel like something is dreadfully wrong right from the start.

A doctor (Jack Hawkins, in what was his final film) visits an impossibly antiseptic, retro-futuristic insane asylum run by the kindly Dr. Tremayne, played by future HALLOWEEN legend Donald Pleasence, already at this point a stalwart of the European horror boom. Like in ASYLUM, Tremayne leads his visitor to four separate cells, where near-catatonic patients while away their days staring at walls. Each patient's troubled past serves as a segment of the picture.

The first tale 'Mr. Tiger', is the scariest, a graphic quote on the classic Ray Bradbury story 'The Veldt'. In it, a little boy named Paul (Russell Lewis) lives with his hideous parents in a lovely English manor. The couple fight endlessly. About everything. And Paul simply withdraws, focusing on his toy piano and his new "imaginary" friend Mr. Tiger, an invisible brute that has a hankering for raw meat and bones. When Paul begins stealing these foodstuffs from the fridge and when claw marks begin appearing on doors and walls, mom and dad find enough common ground to talk to their son only to discover that the lad's imagination might be a bit more fertile than they thought. I remember watching this film as a child with my mother on cable and recall how frightened and disturbed I was by this story's climax and, admittedly, although ludicrous now, it still makes for a shivery psychotronic wallop.

The next story, 'Penny Farthing' is a semi-goofy romp with its roots in the Victorian ghost story. In it, the owner of a London antiques shop (Peter McEnery) becomes fixated on the ever-changing portrait of his late Uncle Albert and the massive, vintage bicycle left to him by his aunt in her will. When the man sits upon the penny farthing, he is inexplicably whisked back to the Victorian era where he meets and falls in love with a young woman named Beatrice who is the ringer for his girlfriend (both characters played by THE BIRD WITH THE CRYSTAL PLUMAGE's Suzy Kendall). Turns out the longer he spends in this phantasmagorical alternate dimension, the stronger the spirit of his long dead Uncle gets. Despite some of the silliness in this installment, Francis'

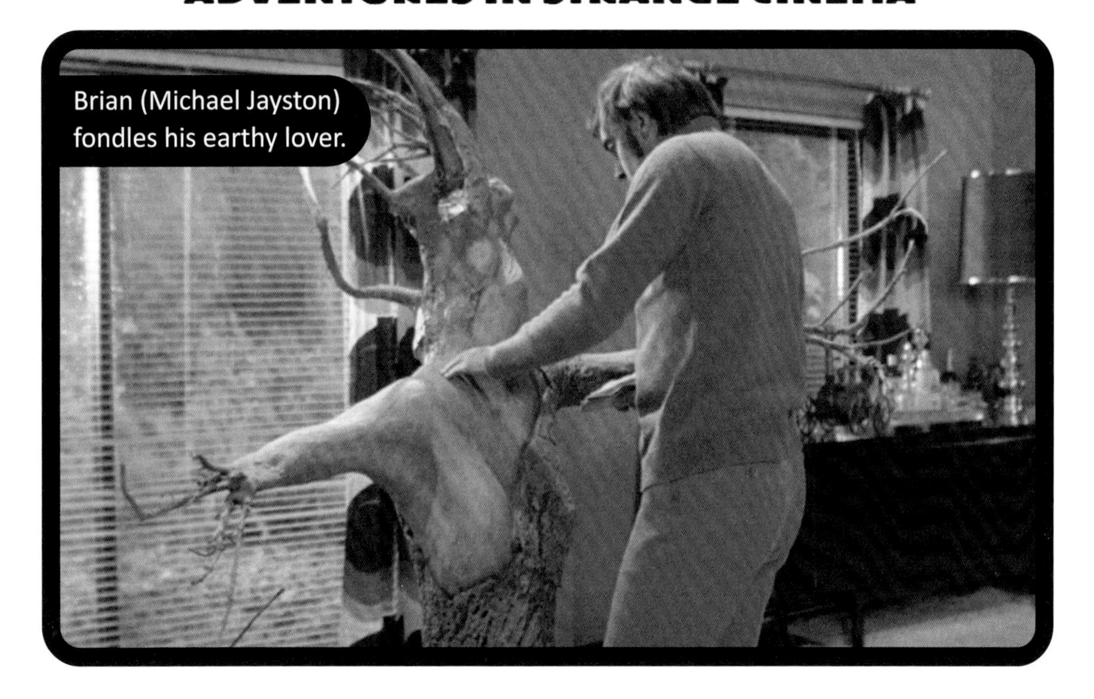

Brian (Michael Jayston) fondles his earthy lover.

directorial skill and eye for macabre detail prevail.

The most famous tale of the TALES comes next with 'Mel', a perverse romp that I wish could be extracted from the movie and fleshed out into a feature film. Francis' TALES FROM THE CRYPT star, sexpot Joan Collins, plays Bella, whose husband (Michael Jayston) brings home a desiccated tree trunk and proclaims it to be an art piece. The name "Mel" is carved into the tree and that's exactly what he calls it, becoming more and more connected and enamored by the thing. Soon Bella is genuinely threatened, the cuckold wife of a man who has taken a tree as his lover. She forces her deranged husband to make a choice. He does. You can probably guess the outcome. It ends rather happily... if you're a champion of man/bark love, that is.

The last story, 'Luau', is the weakest but still quality Grand Guignol and its essence likely served as the inspiration to the misleading and corny theatrical poster that was used to sell the movie and ensuing video release. VERTIGO's still gorgeous Kim Novak plays a book agent in love with her new client, a Hawaiian writer named Kimo (Michael Petrovich). But the writer seems far more interested in her comely daughter. When Kimo sets up a lavish celebratory Luau feast for mother and daughter, his designs on the younger woman become carnivorously clear...

Like in the oft mentioned ASYLUM, the framing narrative with the two doctors serves as the fifth story, with Nicholas believing Tremayne — who believes all these wild stories to be fact — to be himself insane. But is he? We won't spoil the stinger of an ending except to say that our pal Mr. Tiger makes a welcome re-appearance.

TALES THAT WITNESS MADNESS is a strong, potent horror film and its R rating is deserved. Although there isn't any graphic sex, the film is cruel, violent, and often alarmingly gory and even though I did watch it as kid... it's really not a good one for the tots. My own mother denies ever showing it to me. Funny how that works. Fascinatingly, it was one of two films written by veteran British actress Jennifer Jayne (from Amicus' DR. TERROR'S HOUSE OF HORRORS), the other being 1974's bizarre SON OF DRACULA, both written under her pen name Jay Fairbank. It's a shame she didn't write more as the script for TALES is literate and pulpy in equal measures and the dialogue believable throughout. And the score by Bernard Ebbinghouse is a blend of symphonic Gothic horror and lapses into a contemporary rock sound in key moments. Again, it serves the kinky, loose nature of the movie perfectly.

And while most modern horror anthologies serve as short film showcases, with different directors and styles and points of view bashed against each other, TALES — and its ilk — benefits from the consistency of a vision that a single director brings to a project. It feels wholly satisfying and is truly one of the weirdest and most undervalued portmanteau shockers ever made.

TANGO OF PERVERSION (1973)

Starring Lakis Komninos, Erika Raffael, Dorothy Moore, Vagelis Voulgaridis
Written by Lazaros Montanaris
Directed by Kostas Karagiannis

For serious cinephiles, there is nothing more joyous than the act of discovery, to stumble upon something secret, or to be exposed to a previously unknown strain of filmmaking that life has long denied you. And with the swell of high-quality home video over the past 20 years, its been a virtual renaissance for people like us. To unearth pictures we'd only read about and, in many cases had no idea even existed.

For this writer, so in love with the bizarre, stylish and exotic, discovering the existence of *Greeksploitation* was a revelation. As mentioned elsewhere in this book, I have long been a huge fan of the less-loved British-Greek horror film starring Peter Cushing and Donald Pleasence called LAND OF THE MINOTAUR (aka THE DEVIL'S MEN). That film (an ambient doom-horror movie with a pulsing Brian Eno score) was directed by Kostas Karagiannis under the name Costa Carayiannis and, though a glance at his credits reveal dozens of pictures, almost all of them were made exclusively for the Greek market. The thought of taking time to track down some of these pictures never even crossed my skull. Life is brief, after all.

TANGO
of PERVERSION
EASTMANCOLOR
A CARAR FILM
PRODUCTION

But, as it turns out, I was a rather ignorant person. Because, as it turns out, Karagiannis was an exploitation movie machine; a veteran slinger of cinema who, under various *nom de plumes* cranked out well over one hundred films for his "people" and has been on occasion compared to his Spanish contemporary Jess Franco. Not a fair example as Franco's works were, no matter the genre he was toiling in, almost always laced with elements of his own persona, his obsessions always struggling to push through and, as such, many of his pictures were difficult to enjoy on their own terms. But Karagiannis is interesting in that he very early on tapped on to homegrown commercial success, creating pure product to be mass consumed. Greek audiences were at odds with international cinema as they by and large were not interested in subtitles and rejected dubbed films outright. So, Karagiannis started making endless features of every sort: comedies, musicals, thrillers and yes, horror films. And he made a mint doing so.

Which is not to suggest his movies "behaved"! Two of those films that, outside of MINOTAUR are probably his best-known international pictures, crossed my desk a few years back from UK label Mondo Macabro, and my God are they spectacular works of cinematic delirium. Echoing US and European thrillers and piling on the sex and blood and unique Greek culture, this pair of Karagiannis capers are a kinetic blast of delirious weirdness that knocked this writer's socks off and one of them, 1974's TANGO OF PERVERSION, might just be one of my favorite trash films of all time.

Also known as TANGO 2001, this breathless, kinky and thoroughly entertaining romp is indeed perverted, ripe as it is with murder, deviant sex, voyeurism, necrophilia and worse. And yet, it's an oddly charming, cheerful picture, recalling early 1970s Spanish exploitation, gaudy fashions and eccentricities intact. In it, Karagiannis regular Larry Daniels plays a nickel-and-dime pimp/drug dealer whose girlfriend is having a hot and heavy lesbian affair with another stacked grafter who, like everyone in the picture, hangs out at the grotty Tango Club. In the middle of the melodrama, nibbling his nails and twitching, is social outcast Joachim (Vagelis Voulgaridis), a well-coiffed nebbish who is used by all and lets these miscreants regularly use his house for all manner of fucking. Unbeknownst to the *fuckees*, Joachim is a pervert who hides behind a two-way mirror and films their frolics. This footage comes in handy when Daniels finds his girl shagging her lady-friend in Joachim's pad and promptly kills the lover. Joachim opts to dispose of the corpse, but not before he has sex with it!

Soon, more murder, more corpse-shagging and ample blackmail spring up to stress out the characters and give the audience ample pleasures.

What a film! TANGO OF PERVERSION is an outrageous pig-out of upbeat sleaze and is even more fun in the badly English dubbed version. The music is fantastic, blending kitschy lounge rock laced with a traditional Greek folk music sound. The men's ties are huge, and the ladies' breasts are even huger. Best of all is Karagiannis' direction. Lively and leering, he always remembers to do the job he set out to do: entertain.

Daniels returned for another Karagiannis' joint, 1976's THE WIFE KILLER, which has often been compared to a traditional Italian *giallo* but is still very much a product of its country and director. Daniels, who with his spray on beard looks like a more handsome Chuck Norris, plays a broke playboy who pretends to love his comely and ultra-rich wife (Dorothy Moore, who was also in TANGO OF PERVERSION) while sleeping with his feral mistress (Leslie Bowman). Luckily, Daniels is good chums with a psychotic rapist/murderer who he struck a partnership with years ago, the result of blackmail and a need for a friend in his drug trafficking operation. He hires the killer to take out his wife and make it look like just another one of the psycho's victims. But, of course, complications arise, and crosses are doubled, sex is had, slaughter is plentiful and we, the viewers, clap our hands in infantile glee.

Not as joyously depraved as TANGO OF PERVERSION, THE WIFE KILLER (which is also known as THE RAPE KILLER!) is still a bang-up, greaseball thriller, with lush Greek locations, ladies and matter-of-fact cruelty. A big, brightly lit noir that, like TANGO, is so much fun, it just cannot really be offensive, no matter how hard it tries.

If you have yet to discover these movies and this skeezy subgenre, I suggest you do so. I sure would like some company in my obsession.

TATTOO (1981)

Starring Bruce Dern, Maud Adams, John Getz, Leonard Frey
Written by Joyce Bunuel
Directed by Bob Brooks

Recently, while rewatching Quentin Tarantino's magnum 65mm, locked-door mystery/giallo/western/morality tale THE HATEFUL EIGHT, I was once more struck by how damn good actor Bruce Dern is in that film. It's a deceivingly simple performance, mainly because the then 78-year-old performer never leaves the chair in which he sits, from the first time we see him to the point in which he loses his miserable life at the barrel of Sam Jackson's vengeful Smith & Wesson. But it's perhaps the most layered turn in the picture; subtle and oddly dignified even though his character is a coward hiding behind racist, "patriotic" bravado and by the end, even somewhat sympathetic.

But that's Dern. He's one of Hollywood's finest character actors and an artist who rarely gets the credit he's due. Not a traditionally "good looking" man, Dern has his own thing going on; a pointed look, almost rat-like, and when he opts to play an unsavory character (as in H8, HBO's BIG LOVE, THE COWBOYS et al) he is a fiend without

Kinsky (Bruce Dern) leaves his mark on Maddy (Maud Adams).

peer. And when he's given the task to carry a film himself, the results are startling.

Take, for example, director Bob Brooks' controversial 1981 psychosexual character piece TATTOO, a film that belongs to the experimentation of the 1970s, like most of the other great, misunderstood American thrillers of the early '80s (CRUISING and WOLFEN, I'm looking fondly at you). When the movie was released, it was almost universally reviled, condemned for being vulgar, trashy, pointless and criminally misogynistic, the latter claim being an odd one as it was written by a woman, filmmaker Joyce Buñuel, the daughter-in-law of the father of cinematic surrealism, Luis Buñuel. Sure, on the surface, the concept of a man keeping a woman prisoner to be his "thing" might be seen as being politically incorrect, but it's meant to be. It's not a film in favor of its antagonist so much as it is an allegory about the extremity of love, using the ancient art of inking skin as its fetishized hook. I'd call it a masterpiece, but I'm not sure it is. All I know is that it's just as incredibly powerful, strange, sensual and bizarre as it was meant to be. And I know that Dern, who is virtually ever scene, is mesmerizing in it; it's the ultimate Bruce Dern experience.

In it, Dern plays Karl Kinsky (an obvious nod to dangerously eccentric German actor and performance artist Klaus Kinksi), a brilliant, humorless Hoboken-based tattoo artist who lives by an odd, dichotomous moral code. He is obsessed with Japanese culture and iconography and has latched onto a kind of Samurai-steeped sense of honor and chivalry. He also loves porn and frequently combs the underbelly of New York to find the greasiest jerk-off joints he can. And yet, don't dare utter the F-word in his presence, or you'll stir his mania. Because, though it takes some screen time to totally figure out, Kinski is hopelessly insane. His mostly dormant madness wakes up fully when he's hired by a glossy Hollywood agency in love with his work to paint nude models with his patented bizarre and beautiful dragons and Asian imagery. One of the models, the gorgeous Maddy (played by the immaculate Bond girl Maud Adams) strikes his fancy and he launches a quest to court the woman, who is obviously far out of his league. But this class divide is exactly what intrigues the high-rolling Maddy. She's fascinated by this strange, troubled artist, by his rough edges and intensity and is flattered by his would-be "knight-in-shinning-Indian-ink" treatment of her. They begin a sort of uneasy friendship and quasi-courtship.

But when, after a night of sushi and conversation, Maddy dares utter progressive feminist views and worse, starts to cuss, Kinsky loses his mind and asks the shocked woman to leave. She does. And then Kinsky totally loses it. The ensuing stalker dynamic echoes that of TATTOO's closest sociopathic anti-hero cousin, Martin Scorsese's TAXI DRIVER, a close shadow of the relationship De Niro has with pretty political groupie Cybill Shepherd. That same pretty, progressive girl relationship was also exemplified in William Lustig's MANIAC, released the previous year and I'm not sure if its a coincidence that TATTOO shares that film's same fashion-centric device to hook that relationship. Could Buñuel have seen MANIAC? It's unlikely, but possible. The captive connection is also, of course kin to the Terrence Stamp/Samantha Eggar relationship in the classic thriller THE COLLECTOR. And later, Jennifer Lynch's BOXING HELENA, which is another film made by a disciple of a great surrealist filmmaker.

Anyway, Kinsky begins phoning Maddy, begging to see her and generally scaring the wits out of her. He goes to his family's coastal home and retrofits the abode as a prison/ studio and kidnaps the model. His intent? To mark her. To make her taught skin the canvas to etch his masterpiece on. And he'll do this. And she has no say in the matter.

It's here where most audiences tune out of TATTOO and yet I think this is the very point in which the movie comes to life. Instead of raping the woman with his body, he assaults her with his needle. The sequence where he slowly prepares his gear to do this and the immediate moment he begins to draw on her flesh while she is in a drugged-stupor is disturbing and Brooks blasts histrionic violin string scrapes across the soundtrack to mirror PSYCHO's shower scene. And when Maddy wakes to find the first illustrations permanently on her skin, her outrage and terror and misery is deeply affecting. No, this is indeed a rape scene, the images left on the woman's body akin to the psychological damage such an act irrevocably leaves on a victim.

But what got TATTOO into such hot water with disgusted audiences and critics was the fact that a semblance of a sensitive relationship continues in captivity, that Dern's "Norman Bates with a Needle" fiend treats Maddy like an object of affection and worship despite her protests, that she eventually plays along with the scheme, that she becomes aroused by his perversions and even begs him at one point to stop his kink and just make love to her like a man.

What is this daft film trying to say, exactly? Does it matter?

I do read TATTOO as a very dark, very ugly love story on one level, with the broken-minded Dern finding salvation of a sort through Maddy, who he imagines "needs" him. But the fascinating thing is that maybe she does need him. I don't read TATTOO as a film that takes place in reality. It's an art film, a dream, masquerading as mainstream studio film (in this case, a very brave 20th Century Fox). Maddy is somewhat lost herself. In a loveless relationship, at odds with the world she is enmeshed in. In giving the monstrous Kinksi her time and attention, she wakes something up, something dangerous, maybe in both of them. The last 10 minutes of the picture, dissolve into the abstract, with a strange sex scene and a death and the final shot, with Maddy standing nude and inked like a warrior, is one of the most powerful and metaphorically potent shots I've ever seen. Like the model has been oddly empowered, transformed. Like this horror needed to happen to her for her to find out who and what she really is.

That's socially irresponsible thinking of course. But who on earth said movies need to be socially responsible?

As Kinsky, Dern offers the best of what he can do, giving us a character who is in some respects, neither man nor monster, but a different species entirely. It's an unforgettable performance matched by a strong, fearless turn by Adams who should have had a much healthier career as an actress. She's remarkable. So is the movie.

TOMBS OF THE BLIND DEAD (1972)

Starring Lone Fleming, Cesar Burner, Maria Elena Arpon, Jose Thelman
Written by Amando de Ossorio
Directed by Amando de Ossorio

There was a period, a golden age for European horror, one that coincided with a demand in the US for grittier, sexier material, a wave launched post BONNIE AND CLYDE and one that evolved right in the middle of the visceral media coverage of the Vietnam war. With the MPAA loosening their belt, a wave of "new guard" young filmmakers emerging and the movies at the drive-in mirroring the real sex and shenanigans that went on in teenagers back-seats, European distributors saw an opportunity to make some money by injecting their fantasy films with grand dollops of suddenly commercial and permitted sex and violence, while never sacrificing that

JANO
LA NOCHE DEL TERROR CIEGO
CESAR BURNER · LONE FLEMING · HELEN HARP · JOSEPH THELMAN
DIRECTOR AMANDO DE OSSORIO
TECHNICOLOR
70 m/m
UNA COPRODUCCION PLATA FILMS (MADRID) INTERFILME P.C. (LISBOA)

Another unlucky lass falls prey to the Templars' savage swords.

patented atmosphere, eccentric narrative arcs and textural sensuality.

During that wild post BONNIE AND CLYDE wave of more "mature" genre films made in America in the late 1960s, European filmmakers and distributors saw an opportunity to inject their own fantasy films with grand dollops of suddenly commercial and permitted sex and violence. That they rarely sacrificed any of their patented atmospherics, eccentric narrative arcs and textural sensuality in the process, is exactly why those movies continue to fascinate.

In the earliest days of this boom came Spanish director Amando de Ossorio's terrifying and surreal 1971 chiller LA NOCHE DEL TERROR CIEGO or as it was known in the US and other English language territories, TOMBS OF THE BLIND DEAD (or in the truncated AIP version, simply THE BLIND DEAD). Often dismissed as a Latin redux of George A. Romero's NIGHT OF THE LIVING DEAD, TOMBS is something richer, darker and ripe with mythology. In it, three friends — macho Roger, his girlfriend Virginia and her college friend Betty — go for a pleasant train ride into the Portuguese countryside. However, as their journey progresses, we learn in flashback that Virginia and Betty had a secret lesbian relationship in school and when Roger and Betty appear to be getting a little chummier that she'd like, Virginia has a momentary breakdown, jumps from the moving train and wanders to the ruined nearby church nestled at the foot of the hill.

And that's when the terror begins.

Virginia's comely presence rouses a mummified sect of blood-drinking, centuries dead Templar Knights, their skeletal, eyeless, and hooded visages shambling out of their graves in a mass of fog, wielding swords, riding equally desiccated horses, and looking for victims. Shot in gauzy slow-motion, the Templar attack sequences are the stuff nightmares are made of and the horror film that supports their appearance is equally eerie, with composer Anton Garcia Abril's droning, chanting doom-symphony pulses in the background and sealing the harrowing deal.

Ossorio's signature magnum macabre opus would spawn three more Templar companion films 1973's ATTACK OF THE BLIND DEAD (aka RETURN OF THE EVIL DEAD), 1974's THE GHOST GALLEON (aka HORROR OF THE ZOMBIES) and 1975's NIGHT OF THE SEAGULLS, but none would reach the heights of fright that TOMBS offers in its finest hour. I even made my own little BLIND DEAD picture in 2021, an attempt to capture my memory of watching the first half-hour of TOMBS on big box Paragaon Video VHS in the 1980s, late at night, when I was 12. Incidentally, that Paragon release (distributed by Montevideo Video in Canada) was a rare uncut English dub, with the TOMBS OF THE BLIND DEAD title card and the flashback sequence of the living Templar's hacking away at a screaming victim's breasts and sucking her blood. All the rest of the nudity and gore was intact too, and yet inexplicably the brutal train-slaughter climax was cut out. Later, when Elvira showed the film on her Movie Macabre series, it was the same English dub print from Paragon with the sex removed *but* the train sequence was *intact*! That uncut English dub has never appeared on home video again to my knowledge, with the only English dub available being the censored-to-death American edit under the title THE BLIND DEAD title. Strange.

But I digress.

The undead blind knights rise from their graves.

At the center of TOMBS OF THE BLIND DEAD is a sort of humanity that grounds the picture. Said emotional core is anchored in a compelling turn by Spanish actress Lone Fleming as Betty, a strong woman whose love for her murdered friend spurs her on to solve the mystery of the blind monsters almost single-handedly. Along with TOMBS, she would also star in de Ossorio's ATTACK OF THE BLIND DEAD and his 1975 EXORCIST clone, DEMON WITCH CHILD as well as others like Mario Sicilano's BLACK CANDLES and 1973's IT HAPPENED AT NIGHTMARE INN directed by her husband of many years, the late, great, HORROR EXPRESS legend Eugenio Martin.

With her blue eyes, strong features and earthy sensuality, Fleming's presence always added a kind of intelligent beauty to whatever picture she graced and it's that intellect that makes her one of the most interesting survivors of the Spanish horror boom.

INTERVIEW: LONE FLEMING

CHRIS ALEXANDER: Let's go back to your early days in cinema. What was the climate in Spain like at the time, creatively speaking? Was it hard to find roles? Did you have to audition a lot?

LONE FLEMING: You know there were a lot of films going on when I came to Spain. Really, it was almost an industry because we had a lot of comedies, a lot of terror or horror films. Everybody was really working, and we didn't get a lot of money. You know I started from the bottom but I'm very professional and that is one of the most important things for you to get the role. If you're good, if they like you and you're professional then it's much easier.

ALEXANDER: At what point did you meet your husband? Was it during a film?

FLEMING: We met on the film, as you call it in United States, DEATH AT THE DEEP END OF THE SWIMMING POOL [aka THE FOURTH VICTIM] with Carroll Baker and Michael Craig.

ALEXANDER: Ah, so you met on set. That's fantastic. What was that initial connection? Was it love at first sight?

FLEMING: Yeah, it was. And then we went out and it went on and off and I went to Denmark, and I came back, and it went on and off again for many years and of course it was a secret.

ALEXANDER: Do you ever go back and watch any of your older films?

FLEMING: Sometimes if I have to go to a festival and I know they want to ask me about something then I go in and have a look at it. I never like myself in films.

ALEXANDER: Why is that?

FLEMING: I don't know [*laughs*]. When you do a role, you sink yourself so much into it that you don't know how you're going to come off on the screen. I never think

Lone Fleming's Betty smiles before the horror begins.

about if the light is correct on my face, if I look better this way, I just jump into the role, and I couldn't care less if I'm not pretty from that side or the other.

ALEXANDER: The late Jess Franco spoke often about how hard it was to make these kinds of films in Spain initially because of General Franco's pious rule. Did you feel any effect of that? Did it adversely affect the arts in your opinion?

FLEMING: I suppose it mostly affected the political side for writers, and for directors if it was a horror film and they wanted nude scenes they had to shoot it twice so the other European countries could buy it so sometimes they had to cut scenes but really, I hadn't been in a lot of scenes like that and I never made a completely nude scene.

ALEXANDER: Why was that? Why did you make that decision when so many of your colleagues were doing nude scenes?

FLEMING: I think it must have been because of my character and because I started living alone when I was 15 and I started working alone. I think I have so much luck in my life, and it must be something in my character that is serious that I want to do my work and that's it. I'm very open though so I don't really understand it.

ALEXANDER: What was your take on a lot of the horror films at the time when nudity and sexuality was so much in the forefront?

FLEMING: For example, Jess Franco's films? I knew him...

ALEXANDER: I knew you were friendly with Jess and his partner Lina Romay at some point. At what point did you know them?

FLEMING: Years ago, I went to a festival and Jess Franco was there and I had known Lina for years before that. I never met Jess before and it's funny because later, I

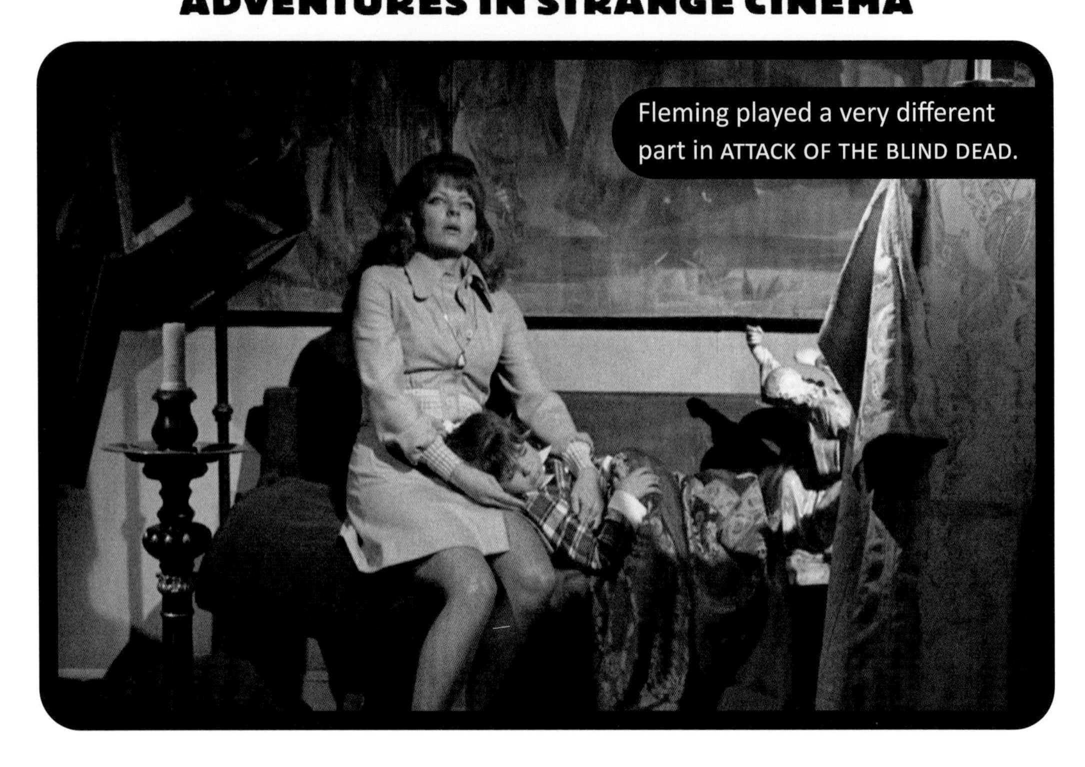
Fleming played a very different part in ATTACK OF THE BLIND DEAD.

met him again in Malaga, a year before he died, and he looked at me and said "Oh Lone! You must make a film with me!" I said yes and he looked at me and said, "no, you won't" and I said, "you're right!" [*laughs*]. He knew it! He was so sharp in his mind! He could just see in my eyes I would never make a film with him! [*laughs*]. He was really a funny guy. He could make everybody laugh. I only saw him twice in my life, but a man like that... you know immediately how he is.

ALEXANDER: Let's talk about Amando who obviously is a very different character, personally and creatively, than Franco. Can you talk about him both as a man and as a filmmaker?

FLEMING: As a man, well we worked three weeks together on the first BLIND DEAD. Amando and I got very friendly, and he was a close friend long after the movie wrapped and for some time, until I started up with Eugenio. We used to have coffee where he worked, and we talked about art. He was a very kind man but what I loved about him was that he lived in his fantasy world. He just loved the Templars. He never had children so those were his children and he lived it so much, you cannot believe it. He used to come down in the morning in Portugal where we were shooting, and he'd have these drawings and say, "Lone this is a scene — I know you understand me — and this is what I want you to do today." Really, he was directing through his drawings and I don't think many people know that and I don't think he did it in other films but he did it on that film.

ALEXANDER: What was it like shooting with the blind dead themselves? Was it at all a creepy experience or was it kind of goofy? Can you remember the climate on set when you were doing those scenes?

FLEMING: You know, it was creepy but fascinating because it was such hard work for Amando. You could say in this film he didn't direct us, his actors, too much because he knew he could rely on us so he was all the time working with the Templars. The costumes were so heavy, and it was hot and to make the men function in the costume — they were sweating, they couldn't talk. And to make the horses function it was incredible. I used to stand there when I wasn't shooting just watching him. He never tired. You could see how he loved it.

ALEXANDER: He was creating a new mythology with that film, whether he knew it at the time or not. Was TOMBS OF THE BLIND DEAD a big hit in Spain when it came out?

FLEMING: In Spain it went alright but in all other European countries it did very well. I know in Germany it was a number one hit and all in South America and all other countries. But you know Spain is different, what can you do about it? [*laughs*]

ALEXANDER: Do you think Amando ever felt marginalized in his own country to some degree about his work?

FLEMING: Yeah, maybe a little. He could have had better respect here, but it doesn't matter because he knows now how important his films are... really, he does, wherever he is.

ALEXANDER: So, you were in the second BLIND DEAD film — ATTACK OF THE BLIND DEAD — which is not as good as the first, but still an interesting, fun film and a great Templar picture.

FLEMING: I liked that role. I liked very much the scene where I save my daughter. I loved that. You know I don't think many people really look at that scene, but I think it's great.

ALEXANDER: It's the humanity of the film, in many respects.

FLEMING: Exactly. I loved that. Amando said to me, Lone I would very much like you to do this but of course it's not as big a role as TOMBS OF THE BLIND DEAD. I said don't worry, I would love to do it.

ALEXANDER: Let's flash back to TOMBS OF THE BLIND DEAD, to that scene, the flashback love scene between you and Virginia (played by actress Maria Elena Arpon). It's not an explicit scene at all, it's very romantic and gentle, but it's still a very early lesbian scene in a horror film. Can you talk about that?

FLEMING: [*laughs*] When we were going to make the scene, Amando came to me and he said "Lone, I don't know how to make this scene because I've never known a lesbian." I said "Amando, I haven't either! So, what are we going to do to?". He said, "Lone you must do it — you and Elena". I said OK. Go and buy a bottle of wine and a rose. I don't know why I asked for the rose. We drank half a bottle each and you know, we just did it so beautifully, I think. I really loved that scene.

TOYS ARE NOT FOR CHILDREN (1972)

Starring Marica Forbes, Harlan Cary Poe, Evelyn Kingsley, Luis Arroyo
Written by Macs McAree, Stanley H. Brassloff
Directed by Stanley H. Brassloff

It's arguable that the greatest sorts of exploration films dial back their visually explicit shocks in favor of the power of suggestion. The most obvious example might be PSYCHO, with its skillfully edited shower scene making us think we see more than we do. But that's not particularly fair, as PSYCHO was made by a major filmmaker and studio and released during a period where nudity, sex and extreme bloodshed were simply not on the mainstream menu. But later, the same Ed Gein-centric source material was mined for THE TEXAS CHAIN SAW MASSACRE, a 1973 release that was produced at a time when all manner of gushy thing was allowed and accepted on screen. And yet, CHAIN SAW, one of the most brutal and notorious pictures of its kind, refused to show too much either, using sound and suggestion and style to turn stomachs and smack its audience senseless. Other films, like 1971's BLOOD AND LACE, 1973's THE BABY et al also proved ample sleazy and upsetting while teetering between PG and R and using theme and tone to their advantage.

Which brings us to 1972's harrowing and hideous and unforgettable trash sorta-classic TOYS ARE NOT FOR CHILDREN. The film is as perverse and seedy as they come, telling the tale of the emotionally disturbed young woman Jamie (a fascinating one-shot turn from Marcia Forbes), who we first meet masturbating in bed to one of her many stuffed animals as she breathlessly chants "daddy, daddy", a sweaty session interrupted by her braying mother, who chastises her and accuses her of being "just like her father". Seems Jamie's dad was a cad who tom-catted around and eventually bailed on the family, leaving the vulgar mother to emotionally smother her only child. Though MIA, Jamie's pop has continued to send her toys, which she keeps littered around her room and whose presence have contributed to her bizarre, sexually stunted, childlike state of mind, where she pines for daddy's love while yearning for other more carnal pleasures.

While working in a toy store, Jamie meets the gentle Charlie (Harlan Cary Poe), who falls in love with her innocence and shared love of children's playthings. The pair soon marry, but Jamie is unable to consummate their union, bringing her stuffed bears and soldiers into their bed and leaving poor Charlie with a crushing set of blue balls. After a chance meeting with a cheery prostitute and her lecherous pimp, Jamie soon finds herself gravitating towards the world of sex work, creating a persona that caters to perverted men who want to screw their daughters. All of this bubbling, lurid melodrama soon leads to a climax that is both inevitable, pleasurably revolting and unforgettable.

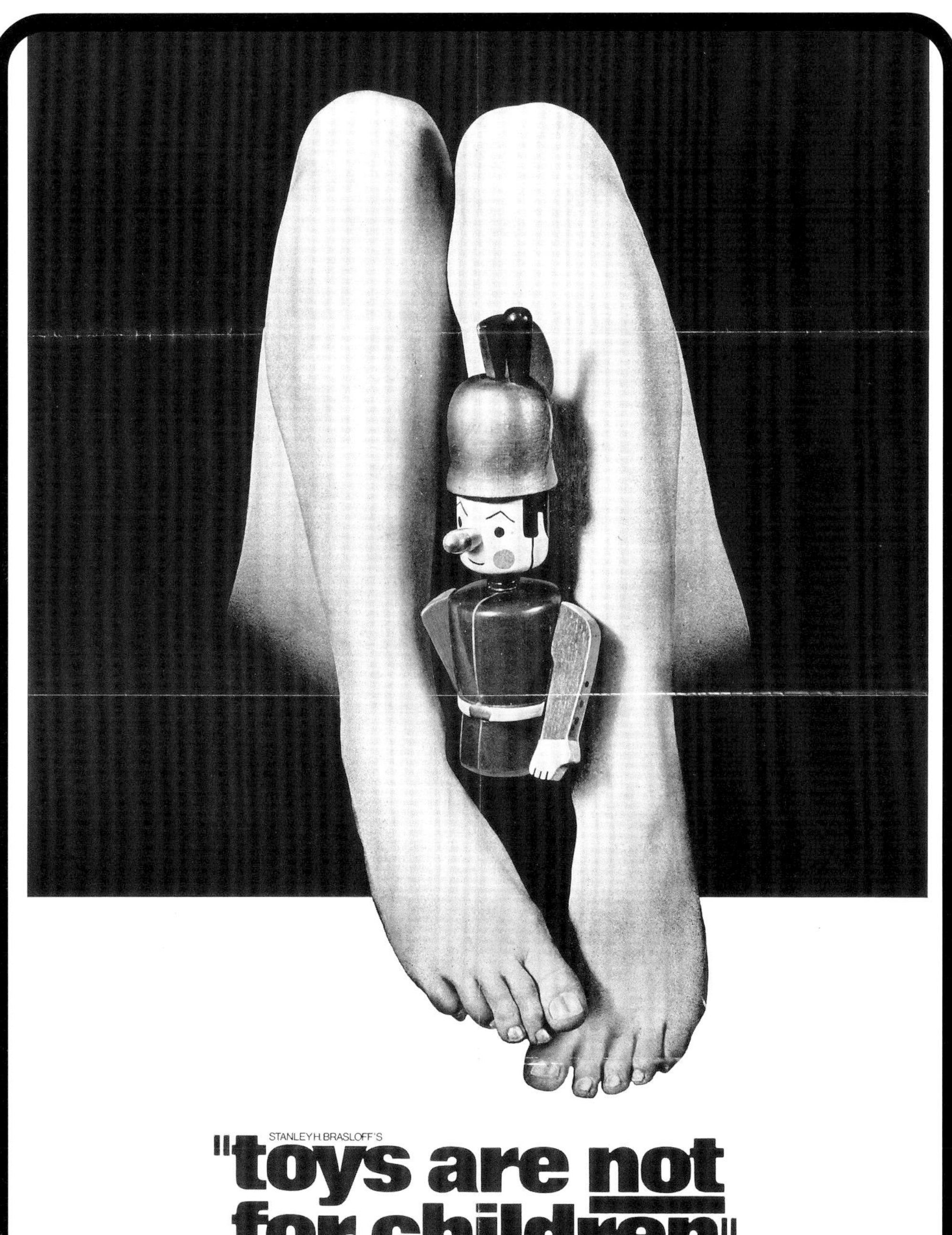
STANLEY H. BRASLOFF'S
"toys are not for children"
Starring MARCIA FORBES · HARLAN CARY POE · EVELYN KINGSLEY · FRAN WARREN · LUIS ARROYO Screenplay by MAC S McAREE · Original Story and Directed by STANLEY H. BRASLOFF · Music and Lyrics by CATHY LYNN · Scored and Conducted by JACQUES URBONT · Theme Song "LONELY AM I" Sung by T.L. DAVIS · Editing by JERRY SIEGEL · Post Production FIMA NOVEC · Electronic Sounds VARDI & HAMBRO · EASTMANCOLOR by MOVIELAB · Produced by STANLEY H. BRASLOFF and SAMUEL M. CHARTOCK · An SHB PRODUCTION Released by HEADWAY FILMS, INC. Distributed by MARON FILMS LIMITED
SINGLE & SOUNDTRACK ALBUM AVAILABLE ON HEART & SOUL RECORDS
R RESTRICTED
Under 17 requires accompanying Parent or Adult Guardian
nted In U.S.A.

And yet, despite its sickening concepts and character arcs, TOYS ARE NOT FOR CHILDREN rarely pushes the envelope of explicitness. There's some nudity, but not much. An attempted rape. Endless bad behavior and a central story that is as greasy and tawdry and taboo as they come. But director Stanley H. Brassloff chooses to focus his grindhouse opus on character first. Jamie is a tragic figure, a little girl whose perverse parents have battered her beyond repair. He also ensures that Charlie is equally as complex, a young man who loves his wife and is at a loss on how to fix her and make her love him just as much. Even when the unthinkable happens in the grim finale, we feel for the players involved. This is as much a titillating piece of trash as it is a Tennessee Williams tragedy.

TOYS ARE NOT FOR CHILDREN is a kind of masterpiece, I'm just not sure what kind. Its intelligence and restraint anchor its twisted story in reality. It would make an ideal double bill feature with THE WITCH WHO CAME FROM THE SEA, a far more visceral but thematically similar damaged female-driven exploitation gem.

THE TURNING (2020)

Starring Mackenzie Davis, Finn Wolfhard, Brooklynn Prince, Joely Richardson
Written by Carey W. Hayes, Chad Hayes
Directed by Floria Sigismondi

Somebody somewhere screwed up the story and spread the belief that all horror movies had to tear you to pieces, saturating the screen with sadism and nihilism and other sorts of negative isms. They forgot that once upon a time, people turned to darker filmed fantasies to immerse themselves in beauty, to experience a sort of sinister, out-of-body, sensorial trip; to lose oneself in a work of macabre imagination, of somber moods and grandiose imagery. I can't be sure exactly when jolts and jumps and spoon-fed, mundane logic superseded aesthetics in horror, but I know how lousy I feel when the world shrugs its shoulders in the wake of the release of a film — and a filmmaker — who has *not* forgotten what the essence of the genre is.

Such a picture is THE TURNING, and such a director is Floria Sigismondi, the artist whose landmark work making videos for David Bowie and Marilyn Manson (and many, many others) defined the look and feel of darker rock'n'roll in the 1990s. Her 2010 feature film debut THE RUNAWAYS was a logical extension of her love of sound and image, telling the true story of a young Cherie Currie (Dakota Fanning) and the titular band in a visually flashy fashion. But that movie's greatest power was when it dialed things down, when it focused on faces, inner voices and emotion. The brief sequence

Kate (Mackenzie Davis) feels the wrath of the spectral help.

where a tired, homesick Currie hears Don McLean's Vincent on the radio during a drive between gigs is itself a small, moving piece of cinema as poetry and secretly encapsulates everything the movie is about. Her second film, the recently released THE TURNING is indeed a horror picture, yet another dive into the well-worn weird world painted in Henry James' novel *The Turn of the Screw*. And while the trailer for this one spoke to appeal to the Friday night Blumhouse crowd, its PG-13 rating inviting almost all audiences in to see it, the actual film itself is something else, or rather it slowly, surely, *becomes* something else. In fact, THE TURNING has the ultimate effect of actually turning, of rotating, sensually, seriously. It's a movie that begins as a whole and then sort of melts into a swirling death-pool of subconscious imagery and primordial terror. In other words, it's the work of a great artist trying to remind the world of the real deal power of horror cinema and what it can do to its audience.

THE TURNING stars Mackenzie Davis as Kate, a fetching young woman who takes on the position of governess at the looming Fairchild Estate, her charge being seven-year-old Flora Fairchild (Brooklyn Prince), an orphan who lives in the mansion with her older brother Miles (Finn Wolfhard). The child of a mother deep in the thralls of mental illness, Kate immediately connects with the sweet but troubled Flora, while doing her best to navigate the increasingly strange, intrusive behaviours of the possibly disturbed Miles. After learning that the live-in horse trainer Quint had mysteriously died and that the previous governess had vanished without a trace, Kate begins to suspect something isn't quite right in the house, especially when the creepy caretaker (Barbara Marten) refuses to let Flora leave the grounds, the belief that she may in fact die if she does. Naturally, the estate is haunted and soon, Kate is falling deep, then deeper into supernatural psychosis, trying to uncover the central mystery, protect her charges and stop herself from unraveling completely.

You've been down this road before, whether it be in Jack Clayton's relatively faithful adaptation of the James novel THE INNOCENTS, or in similarly themed films like Dan Curtis' BURNT OFFERINGS or Alejandro Amenabar's THE OTHERS, so the mechanics of the plot in THE TURNING are simply there to propel it forward in a familiar way. But it's the singer, not the song and here, Sigismondi proves herself a virtuoso master of atmosphere, using Kate as her avatar to explore a pulsating netherworld of gently bent sex and spectral shenanigans. She knows how to push a shock sequence into high art, like in the latter scene where Kate is attacked — or imagines she is being attacked — by a severed hand. In most films of this kind, the scene would be a quick blast but here, Sigismondi lets it go on and on, turning it into an uncomfortable, endless assault on her central character and, in turn, us. And Davis sells it all, working with her director to etch a portrait of a woman whose vulnerable mental state might be either welcoming the ghastly phenomena she endures... or actually the very source of it. By the time the picture dissolves into free-form, gothic psychedelia until in breaks at its brilliantly ambiguous final shot, we have no idea how to read any of it. We just fall into it with Kate. And wait.

Outside of a flabby, expositional device with Kate connecting to her sassy friend in the "outside" world, almost every single thing about THE TURNING works; from its arresting costume design (all bright reds, oranges and knitted Irish sweaters) that is mated seamlessly with its muted production design, to the flawless performances (Davis is mesmerizing and the kids are charismatic without being obnoxious), to the jaw-dropping house itself, to its snake-eating-its-own-tail anti-ending, to its hypnotic end credits sequence, this is a sophisticated work of dread, decay, brooding mood and abstract storytelling coated in the sheen of a simplistic spook show.

THE TWILIGHT ZONE: NINE UNFORGETTABLE EPISODES (1959–64)

If you're a serious fan of THE TWILIGHT ZONE (and I most certainly am), it's vital to not only remember Rod Serling's classic, influential dark fantasy television series and each key episode's unforgettable and forever-discussed third act twist, but to muse on Serling's morality and humanity, the likes of which propelled almost every aspect of the show.

Serling was, in effect, dark fantasy television's premiere auteur and THE TWILIGHT ZONE (which ran for five seasons, 1959-1964) was first and foremost a vehicle for Serling to deliver provocative parables. He was writer with something urgent to say, someone who deeply cared about the plight of his fellow man. After earning awards and accolades for his pioneering dramatic teleplays in TV's formative years, Serling's attempts at deeper comment on subjects ranging from war atrocity to America's blatant racism were met with censorship. The answer to this nervous sponsor-induced silencing and word-butchering was indeed THE TWILIGHT ZONE, which Serling saw as a way to tell the tales he wanted to tell but cloak them in sugar-coated fantasy pills.

And while some of TZ's greatest episodes are beloved for their overt horror and science fiction sheen and exploitable elements, several of the series' finest installments were portals directly into Serling's soul, haunting stories about loss, alienation, death, regret and a yearning for simpler times.

Here then, are nine of TZ and Serling's most haunting, personal episodes.

WALKING DISTANCE (SEASON ONE)

The most affecting and personal of Serling's first season efforts, this one stars Gig Young as a middle-aged man who inexplicably wanders back in time into his home town, 30 years earlier. There, he meets his parents and the youthful incarnation of himself. Melancholy, profound and expressionist in its presentation, this is Serling weeping for the sweet days of his childhood long lost and then ultimately, making peace with and embracing the present. Gorgeous Bernard Herrmann score too...

THE LONELY (SEASON ONE)

Jack Warden stars as James Corry, as an unjustly convicted man in the near future, imprisoned alone on a desolate planet. While he sweats away his days and battles back his own endless loneliness, an empathetic supply ship captain stopping by on his quarterly run, drops off a crate containing a fully realized android female to keep him company. Initially, Corry balks at this mockery of femininity but, when the robot proves itself sentient and sensitive, he falls deeply in love with "her". A moody, dreamy, poetic episode about the penal system and the illusion of love, armed with a sad, unforgettable finale.

JUDGEMENT NIGHT (SEASON ONE)

Serling was disgusted by war, having endured the horrors of it firsthand, an experience that effectively broke his heart, and his body (the writer never properly healed from a severe leg wound in WWII). 'Judgement Night' is an unnerving tale of a German sailor drifting aboard a British passenger ship in the fog, haunted by a feeling of impending doom. A serious-minded comment on how war creates monsters and how those monsters eventually get crushed by karma, supernatural or otherwise. This one is hard to shake.

LONG LIVE WALTER JAMESON (SEASON ONE)

Beloved cult actor Kevin McCarthy (INVASION OF THE BODY SNATCHERS, tons of Joe Dante movies) stars as the titular gentleman, a learned professor dating a young woman and planning marriage. But when the lady's elderly father finds a century old photograph of Jameson, he begins questioning his future son-in-law about his true nature. Serling wrote most of the first season of TZ, but occasionally let writers he felt he identified with and whose material were in step with his sensibilities contribute. 'Walter Jameson' was penned by the great Charles Beaumont. It's a melancholy treatise on man's vain lust for immortality and how such pursuits don't always yield what we think they will, a theme that Serling himself would explore time and time again. The final moments of this episode are pure visual poetry.

THE AFTER HOURS (SEASON ONE)

This revered episode is most famous as the "living mannequin" one, loved for its final twist in which doe-eyed Anne Francis gets lost in a department store and discovers she's actually a dummy on "shore leave". But at its heart, this is a disturbing, profound and wrenching comment on identity, on stumbling through a consumer world and not connecting with anything or anyone. Years later, George A. Romero would quote the central theme mined here in DAWN OF THE DEAD, but add flesh-eating zombies.

THE HITCH-HIKER (SEASON ONE)

Three years before CARNIVAL OF SOULS, four years before Serling would incorporate the French film AN OCCURRENCE AT OWL CREEK BRIDGE into the series' fifth season and decades before SOLE SURVIVOR or the FINAL DESTINATION films, Serling's 'The Hitch-Hiker' had the power to disturb viewers. In it, a young woman drives the night highways, constantly met by a smiling, spectral hitchhiker who no one else can see. Disconnected from the world, the woman eventually discovers that she might not have actually survived that recent roadside accident after all. A ghost story of sorts that muses on the same concepts of alienation mined in The After Hours' and also the inevitability of death, of resigning oneself to the fates. A Serling-penned adaptation of an existing radio play, but one whose central themes hooked the writer and would show up in much of his writing, including the melancholy war time treatise episode 'The Purple Testament'.

DUST (SEASON TWO)

In a worn down, frontier New Mexico town, a poor farmer is sentenced to hang for accidentally killing a girl, much to the misery of his suffering family. While the town cries for blood, a repugnant, racist man dupes the man's elderly father into using whatever money the family has left to buy his "magic dust", which he claims will cause the town to forgive and to find the love needed to save his son. Of course, it's just sand. Or is it? A beautiful, tear-inducing episode that is really Serling rallying against the craven, casual racism and classism of capitalism and criticizing the futile, regressive act of answering bloodshed with more bloodshed. Lovely Jerry Goldsmith score too...

DEATHS-HEAD REVISITED (SEASON THREE)

Serling at his angriest. The writer addresses his Jewish ancestry and his oft-visited interest in the Holocaust for this visceral, horrifying tale; a kind of "Tell-Tale Heart" with Nazis and a kissing cousin to season one's 'Judgement Night'. In it, a war criminal returns under an alias to Auschwitz, years after the war, to sniggeringly reflect on his glorious, murderous past executing and torturing Jewish prisoners. He soon finds that the dead don't rest easy and that no matter how hard one tries to ignore it and evade it, the past always has a way of finding you. Horrific, intelligent and deeply affecting storytelling.

IN PRAISE OF PIP (SEASON FIVE)
The great Jack Klugman (a TZ regular) appears as a nickel-and-dime grifter who learns that his adult son, fighting in Vietnam, is teetering between life and death. In his grief, he drifts into an abandoned carnival where he meets a version of his son as a little boy. Reflecting on his failures as a father he also reevaluates the beauty of their early years together and begs the fates for one last chance to do the right thing and save his long-suffering boy. If you have children, this one will level you. Serling himself channeled the relationship he had with his youngest daughter Anne for this unforgettable, haunting episode about redemption, one of Serling's favorite themes.

THE TWILIGHT ZONE: THE SHADOW MAN (1985)

Starring Jonathan Ward, Heather Haase, Jeff Calhoun, Jason Presson
Written by Rockne S. O'Bannon
Directed by Joe Dante

Even considering how poorly Warner's 1983 theatrical attempt to revitalize the house that Rod Serling built fared at the box office (not to mention the tragedy that unfolded behind the scenes), CBS nevertheless dipped back into THE TWILIGHT ZONE well and green-lit a prime-time return of the series, this time to be filmed in full color and to be creatively propelled by some of the biggest names in dark fantasy entertainment.

The first season of the revamped THE TWILIGHT ZONE premiered on September 27th, 1985, and, from the opening credits on in, it was clear that this TZ was going to be a serious immersion into thoughtful — and terrifying — science fiction and horror. The theme music was an experimental wash of dread, only gently referencing the classic

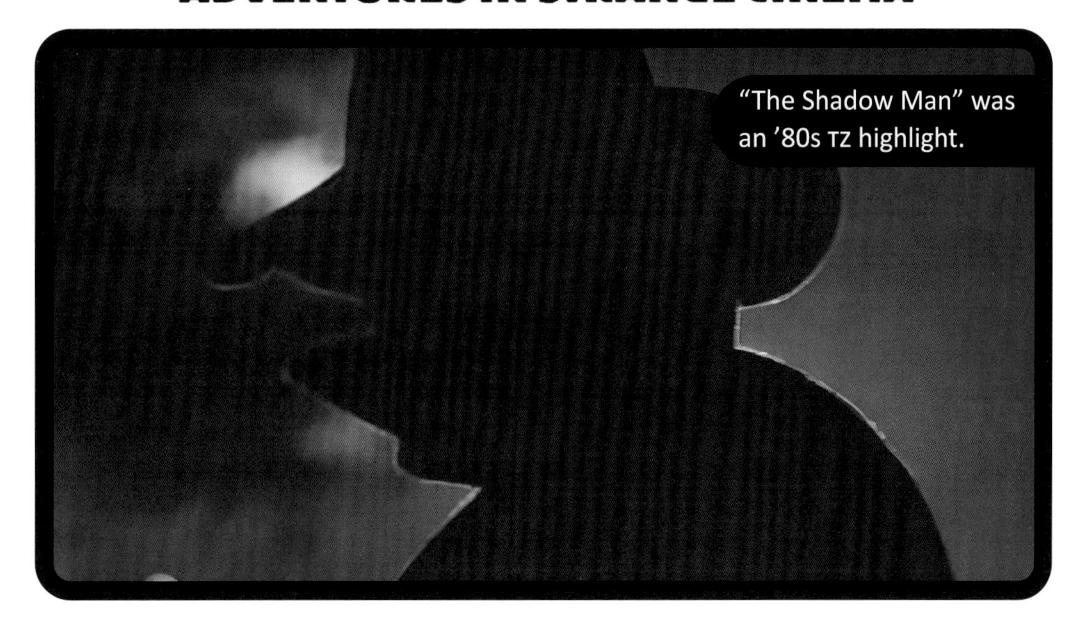
"The Shadow Man" was an '80s TZ highlight.

theme by Marius Constant, that was composed and performed by '60s cult band The Grateful Dead; key episodes were written by heavy-hitters like Harlan Ellison ('Shatterday') and Stephen King ('Gramma') and were directed by genre icons like Wes Craven ('A Little Peace and Quiet', 'Wordplay'), William Friedkin ('Nightcrawlers') and, of course, Joe Dante.

Dante's sole contribution to the 1985 TZ came in the shape of 'The Shadow Man', a tender tale of preteen angst and supernatural revenge. In it, a kid (Jonathan Ward) who is bullied and put-upon, discovers one night that an inky, humanoid phantom lives under his bed; a faceless, fedora wearing boogeyman who drifts into the room and, in a deep, sinister voice says, *"I am the Shadow Man and I will never harm the person under whose bed I live."*

More fascinated than terrified, the boy watches the spectral intruder slink out his window and into the night, only to learn the next day that a fiend matching The Shadow Man's description had assaulted some of his classmates after dark. Night after night, the ghoul returns and the attacks continue, but our hero is nonplussed. In fact, as he is the lone child in the school unafraid of the nocturnal spook, he becomes empowered, is seen as brave and, in turn, goes from zero to hero.

But, this being THE TWILIGHT ZONE, all does not end well; there is a dynamite twist in the tail end of Rockne S. O'Bannon's script that is beyond chilling and one that many now-grown children of my generation still shudder over.

Dante's installment of the aforementioned TWILIGHT ZONE: THE MOVIE, a riff on the classic TZ episode 'It's a Good Life' called 'Anthony', was one of the highlights of a middling film, though in it, the director seemed more interested in indulging his ever-present obsession with vintage Warner Bros. cartoons than in going after anything resembling stark terror. Here, however, Dante does indeed get dark; less Serling and more EC comics. 'The Shadow Man' has a dose or two of typical Dante mirth, but by and large, the episode is the stuff of nightmares, with the central villain being, in essence, an omnipresent predator, one whose focus on children is singular and sinister.

INTERVIEW: JOE DANTE

CHRIS ALEXANDER: Was 'The Shadow Man' shot before or after EXPLORERS?

JOE DANTE: After. That's why EXPLORERS' wrong-side-of-the-tracks kid, Jason Presson, plays the bully.

ALEXANDER: You were riding a commercial high after GREMLINS so was there any trepidation about diving into TV, however briefly?

DANTE: None, because I'd already done two episodes of POLICE SQUAD!, which was my first DGA (Directors Guild of America) job. And I'd already done an episode of AMAZING STORIES too, which made the new THE TWILIGHT ZONE look like poverty row.

ALEXANDER: You're obviously a fan of THE TWILIGHT ZONE. But unlike in TWILIGHT ZONE: THE MOVIE, you weren't shackled by the expectations of remaking any existing episode. Was there any conscious attempt to lock the spirit of Serling or were you simply making a Joe Dante short film?

DANTE: The '80s ZONE revamp was a different animal entirely from the Serling original, which was economically produced but benefited from the availability of the MGM backlot and studio gloss. The new series was shot very quickly at the former Republic Studios lot in Studio City, which only had a tiny backlot. Producer Phil DeGuerre was notorious for postproduction tampering, and this was one of the first TV series edited on videotape. This allowed for much editorial mischief, as evidenced by director Gil Cates' complaint that his 'Paladin of the Lost Hour' episode was botched by DeGuerre in cocaine-fueled editing and when televised, was officially credited to the fictitious DGA nom de plum Allen Smithee.

ALEXANDER: The Shadow Man himself is terrifying and obviously a visual nod to the character of The Shadow, yes?

DANTE: Certainly, in his costume, which was quite difficult to photograph by the way, as a black shadow against the sets.

ALEXANDER: There is mention in the story of The Shadow Man harming the children, but never killing. The ending of episode sees Jonathan Ward dangling in a chokehold... do you think the boy dies?

DANTE: You bet he does!

Dante considers his iconic status.

ALEXANDER: Did you have your pick of scripts when you came on board or were you assigned 'The Shadow Man'?

DANTE: As I recall, Rockne's existing script was pretty much a take it or leave it proposition. I don't recall much effort to enlist the directors in choosing material, although I can't believe that Friedkin just happened to end up with 'Nightcrawlers', which may be the best episode of the series.

ALEXANDER: Your Director of Photography on 'The Shadow Man' was Bradford May, a TV guy through and through. The short is very atmospheric and cinematic. Do you have any memories of the man?

DANTE: This episode was made in record time, just a few days and I do remember Brad as accomplished and confident. He ended up directing, which I think is where his heart was.

ALEXANDER: The music for 'The Shadow Man' is effective. It was composed by Merl Saunders, who played with Jerry Garcia (of The Grateful Dead) often. Did you work with Saunders closely?

DANTE: No. Once you hand in a TV episode, your involvement is pretty much over. I never met any of the music guys, who were hired long before I was.

ALEXANDER: The series really holds up... I had forgotten how many incredibly strong episodes there were in that first season.

DANTE: There were some very nice episodes. I only regret that because they were shot on film but edited on tape, no film record exists. Don't look for any HD or Blu-ray releases, because this technology only degrades when copied. It's quite likely that eventually, the '80s series will not exist in 20 years since it can't be upgraded. Luckily, the Serling series exists on film and can be preserved pretty much forever.

ALEXANDER: Speaking of that, which is your favorite classic Serling episode?

DANTE: 'Walking Distance'. 1959. Season one. Pure Serling. Pure sentiment. Pure Bernard Herrmann.

ALEXANDER: Mine too.

THE ULTIMATE THRILL (1974)

Starring Eric Braeden, Barry Brown, Britt Ekland, Michael Blodgett
Written by John Rester Zodrow
Directed by Robert Butler

In the pantheon of stories distressingly over adapted and ripped-off for cinema, Richard Connell's THE MOST DANGEROUS GAME sits high on the list. The story tells the tale of a wealthy hunt-happy lunatic who shifts his interests into stalking humans to be his next trophies, setting his "guests" loose on his remote property to give them a sporting head start. It's a great premise that has both an allegorical sting, a haunting anti-hunting soul and both hardcore action and blood-chilling horror.

And while there have been a handful of "legitimate" versions of the tome made (most impressively, the 1932 same-named Fay Wray riff), it's the rip-offs that are the most fun, everything from 1982's TURKEY SHOOT to 1993's HARD TARGET to 1994's SURVIVING THE GAME, movies that freely steal the premise and pervert it to their own ends. Lost amidst this slew of awesomely low-grade films is the totally bonkers 1974 sleaze-fest THE ULTIMATE THRILL (aka THE ULTIMATE CHASE). The movie is directed by the late Robert Butler, a veteran TV hack (and we're not saying that to be derogatory) who steered episodes of everything from the '60s BATMAN show to KUNG-FU to THE WALTONS to the small screen. But THE ULTIMATE THRILL is one of his few feature film undertakings and I'll be damned if it doesn't feel like a TV movie, albeit one armed with a bigger budget that presumably paid for the hospital bills for the myriad hot dogging skiing stuntman who fly off mountaintops like clockwork.

THE ULTIMATE THRILL stars soap opera legend Eric Braeden (Victor on THE YOUNG AND THE RESTLESS and who appeared as the villain — *sans* mustache — in 1971's ESCAPE FROM THE PLANET OF THE APES as Roland Parlay, a power-mad businessman with a

THE
ULTIMATE
CHASE
...FOR THE
ULTIMATE
THRILL
IS SHE WORTH
THE ULTIMATE THRILL
JOHN SOLIE

Michael Blodgett and Britt Ekland in THE ULTIMATE THRILL.

gorgeous trophy wife (played by the stunning Britt Ekland, from the previous years' cult masterpiece THE WICKER MAN) who combines business and pleasure at a Colorado ski resort. Initially charming, it soon becomes clear that Parlay is in fact a sadistic sociopath, a privileged maniac who treats his wife Michelle like another piece of his property and who is so soul dead that he becomes addicted to destructive behaviors. One of these transgressions is setting up scenarios in which his gorgeous missus is left as bait for horny men. Though Michelle rebuffs any passes made by anyone other than her husband, Parlay perverts these scenarios to make the clumsy suitors his prey. First, he obliterates hapless ski bum Michael Blodget, chasing him around the mountain in his helicopter before bashing him up and murdering him in cold blood. Then he tries the same thing on the savvier Barry Brown, who gives the tycoon a real run for his money.

In between Parlay playing these "dangerous games," he — and several other unnamed members of the supporting cast — ski. They ski a lot, in fact. If you've seen Bruno Mattei's HELL OF THE LIVING DEAD, you might remember all the damned stock footage of wild animals mincing around the brush. It's kind of like that here, but with skiers flailing around in slow-motion. The scenery is lovely (the movie was shot on location in Vail) and the ski scenes become almost hypnotic, meditative even, all set to the strains of Ed Townsend's delirious and amazing lounge music score.

But what makes THE ULTIMATE THRILL so mesmerizing is its leads. As Mr. and Mrs. Parlay, Braeden and Ekland offer complex performances that are unsettling in their suggestiveness. For example, after Parlay kills his first victim (that we see, anyway), he returns to his chalet to punish his wife for her imaginary indiscretions. His cultured veneer drops, he slut-shames her, beats her and then rapes her. And, like with Susan George in STRAW DOGS, it appears Ekland is liking the rape. Or at least has made peace with this being her "new normal", the price to pay for living a life of luxury. Is Michelle in on her husband's sick, murderous games? Does she get off on it? The movie never spells it out and it's all the more unsettling for it.

I don't think THE ULTIMATE THRILL has ever been officially on DVD. I bought it at a junk store on VHS for $5 when I was a teenager. A release via the long-defunct budget label Star Classics, with a hand painted box (that I used to think was ugly, but I now think is really cool). Video Gems also released the film on "Big Box" VHS, in a much sexier edition. But so far, outside of the odd bootleg, it's a damned hard film to find. Shame, that. THE ULTIMATE THRILL is a flawed, weird, exciting and morally confusing thriller with great performances and a stunning location. What more do you need from your art/trash cinema?

THE VAMPIRE'S NIGHT ORGY (1972)

Starring Jack Taylor, Dyanik Zurakowska, Jose Guardiola, Charo Soriano
Written by Gabriel Moreno Burgos, Antonio Fos
Directed by Leon Klimovsky

Among the endless spate of Hammer-esque Gothic horror and exploitation product pumping out of Italy and Spain in the early 1970s, there's one picture that I've always been oddly attracted to. It's a fascinating film really, a movie that has enough of a rudimentary, linear narrative drive to hook its audience and keep us engaged in the peculiar plight of its characters and immersed in its central mystery, but it also comes armed with a delightfully confusing, unknowable mythology and shifts gears freely between grisly horror, ghost story, sex romp, black comedy and palpable tragedy. The film I'm speaking of is director Leon (Paul Naschy's landmark Spanish shocker THE WEREWOLF VS. THE VAMPIRE WOMAN) Klimovsky's bizarre and haunting 1973 opus THE VAMPIRE'S NIGHT ORGY, a vampire picture like no other and a movie whose sensational, tawdry elements are tamed by kind of laid-back earthiness that rarely appears in fever-pitched films of this sort.

Following a similar setup to Jean Brismee's Belgian chiller THE DEVIL'S NIGHTMARE (aka THE DEVIL WALKS AT MIDNIGHT, another personal favorite), THE VAMPIRE'S NIGHT ORGY sees a gaggle of tourists (whose ranks include the great Jack Taylor (FEMALE

When the moon is up the fun begins.
INTERNATIONAL AMUSEMENT CORPORATION presents
the
VAMPIRES
NIGHT ORGY
JACK
TAYLOR
CHARO
SORIANO
DIANIK
ZURAKOWSKA
JOHN
RICHARD
DIRECTED BY
LEON KLIMOVSKY
TECHNICOLOR®

VAMPIRE and dozens of other Jess Franco favorites, here in a rare, genuinely heroic role) traveling by bus through the Eastern European countryside, a trip derailed when the driver suffers a heart attack at the wheel. Low on fuel and seeking medical assistance, the troupe winds up in the uncharted village of Tonia, a rustic, run-down but seemingly welcome place that indeed seems stuck in some sort of time warp. As the villagers accommodate our weary protagonists, they introduce the troupe to The Countess (the great Helga Line from HORROR EXPRESS and HORROR RISES FROM THE TOMB), the big *provolone* of Tonia whose grace masks a streak of entitled, supernatural evil. See, as the title suggests, this Hamlet is simply crawling with the living dead and The Countess is their Queen, lording over their antics and demanding sacrifice.

My point of entry with this fascinating bit of continental fangwork came in the form of legendary VHS horror and cult film mail order company Sinister Cinema. In the mid '80s Sinister Cinema was successful enough that they followed in the footsteps of Something Weird Video and had a domestic retail video release line which, I think, had its offices in Canada. In the now sadly long dead Sam the Record Man on Yonge Street in Toronto, they had a room upstairs that was piled high with VHS and laserdiscs (the section was dubbed Sam the Video Man, if I recall). There, I purchased a wave of movies from Sinister Cinema (as many as my 12-year-old self could afford) and among them was THE VAMPIRE'S NIGHT ORGY, here released under the title ORGY OF THE VAMPIRES (and employing the Italian poster art from Hammer's LUST FOR A VAMPIRE on the cover). It was a cut version of the film but to be honest, save for a few shots of the Countess's bare breasts, the movie is fairly non-explicit in any cut, this despite a title that promises a blood-spattered bacchanal.

No, THE VAMPIRE'S NIGHT ORGY doesn't rely on sex or cheapjack gore to get under its audience's skin. Instead, it simply trades in wanton weirdness. Dreamy, inexplicable abstractions that thankfully refuses to fully explain themselves. For example, the village sort of appears and vanishes at will (shades of H.G. Lewis' 2000 MANIACS). The villagers aren't just a gaggle of predators luring their prey either, they have a sort of hierarchy, with The Countess at the top and an array of henchmen and tradesmen under her. There's a tavern. A chef. A blacksmith. All manner of folks who work hard at keeping the facade of a micro-society going. In an oft repeated gag, The Countess' personal drone keeps hacking off some of the horrified working-class undead stiffs' limbs so they can use the meat to feed their mortal guests. It's just all so bizarre and arch and wonderfully daft.

But there's also a dose of eerie poetry coursing through the film. In the opening sequence, we see a funeral procession of vampires dropping a coffin and running scared while Klimovsky zooms into the face of a maggoty corpse. Why are the ghouls alarmed by this? Do they fear death? Who knows. Or how about the nighttime attack on the bus, where a pair of do-gooders are done in by a sect of elderly vampires who

The Countess (Helga Line) beds down with her latest victim.

don't have fangs but are simply missing teeth? In another bit, a little boy vamp simply wants to play with a little human girl and accidentally suffocates her while hiding her from yet another funeral gathering and then buries her and her doll crudely. And the ending is mysterious and gently disturbing and without resolution of any kind.

Paul Naschy worked under Klimovsky plenty and has noted that the director tended to rush through his work. You admittedly feel that here. But that "first draft" feeling is precisely why THE VAMPIRE'S NIGHT ORGY is so affecting. It feels sort-of made up as it goes along, like some sort of satanic jazz riff. Much like the histrionic lounge score that blares all over the movie, causing extreme disorientation, an element that has won some scorn from select corners of Eurohorror fandom. But the movie is charmingly all over the place and it's certainly got an energy all its own.

VENOM (1981)

Starring Oliver Reed, Klaus Kinski, Nicol Williamson, Sterling Hayden
Written by Robert Carrington
Directed by Piers Haggard

There are many pleasures to be had watching British Director Piers (BLOOD ON SATAN'S CLAW) Haggard's 1981 snakes vs. crooks thriller VENOM, but none as palpable as seeing diminutive madman Klaus Kinski browbeat and dominate the barrel chested man-ape

Oliver Reed sees the effect of the snake on poor Susan George.

Oliver Reed. The fact that both storied, iconic and notoriously volatile thesps appear in the same film is enough to send lovers of cult cinema into a state of rapture, but to witness them cast as a pair of hot-headed thugs, in a sort of Lenny and George, *Of Mice and Men* dynamic, is the sweetest and strangest of icing on a scaly cake.

This surreal bit of casting propels VENOM into a higher tax-bracket of awesome but the movie surrounding their onscreen scrapping (reportedly, they hated each other even more off screen) is pretty good too, though perhaps a bit more pedestrian than it should have been. Shame that. Because the maniacal novel on which the film is based on (by Alan Scholerfield) begs for a less-restrained approach, which is exactly what it would have received had VENOM's original director, Tobe Hooper, stayed on board. Hooper bailed 10 days into the shoot, forcing producer Martin Bregman (DOG DAY AFTERNOON) to drag Haggard (who was working almost exclusively on small-screen fare at the time) into the fold. Haggard's more somber, tasteful approach de-fangs some of the eccentricities of the source and the original character concepts (Kinski's look was originally a sort of Nazi-fetishist in black leather and jack boots) but also makes the movie both comfortably watchable and, surprisingly, endlessly *re*-watchable.

VENOM stars veteran actor Sterling Hayden (THE GODFATHER) as a legendary Hollywood animal wrangler living in London with his wealthy daughter and young grandson. The family's chauffeur is played by Reed and their maid is the lovely, crooked-teethed Susan George (STRAW DOGS, DIE SCREAMING MARIANNE), two domestics who have conspired with an international terrorist (Kinski) to take over the home and kidnap the kid for a lofty ransom request. Problems arise when the boy, an avid animal enthusiast himself, orders his surly chauffeur to accompany him to the local pet store where he intends to pick up a harmless snake to add to his menagerie. But the dotty storekeeper accidentally mixes up the benevolent reptile with the far deadlier cargo of a Black Mamba, intended to be sent to a lab but taken home by the unlucky lad in error. When the kidnapping drama thrusts into overdrive, that deadly nope-rope escapes, kills George and high-tails it into the guts of the house. As Kinski's plot begins to unravel, both the criminals and family run afoul of the Mamba, who pops up occasionally to sink his poisonous fangs into whatever warm body is nearby. Meanwhile EXCALIBUR's Nicol Willamson tries to negotiate with the terrorists and figure out a point of entry into the home before it's too late.

VENOM didn't make much of an impact upon release and critics were not particularly kind to it, but its cult following was inevitable. First there's that once in a lifetime assemblage of performers, all of them cast against type and chewing more scenery than the snake could ever hope to. Then there's the house itself, an opulent estate with a myriad sneaky little place for that horrible hisser to hide. The music is composed by the late, great Michael Kamen and it's an urgent, complexly orchestrated work that elevates the production values (which were already handsome for such a relatively modest picture). But those expecting a tawdrier exploitation film like the also-Reed starring snaker SPASMS or the berserk THE JAWS OF SATAN might be disappointed by how classy and restrained it is. And yet, no matter if VENOM pounds your pulse or just passes the time, there's something so charming about it; a quality that has made me revisit it over and over. In fact, I kind of want to watch it right now...

WHO CAN KILL A CHILD (1976)

Starring Lewis Fiander, Prunella Ransome, Antonio Iranzo, Luis Ciges
Written by Luis Penafiel
Directed by Narciso Ibenez Serrador

I first watched the 1984 Stephen King-penned horror film CHILDREN OF THE CORN with my parents on cable when I was ten and even at that relatively easy-to-please age, its punch-pulling pedigree was obvious. Here was a film with a shocking enough opening sequence (I especially winced at the bit where the creepy kids pushed the beefy chap's knuckles into the blender) and with a pair of solid enough lead actors in Peter Horton and Linda Hamilton and propelled by the grim concept of small-town kids locked on murdering everyone over 18. But the film was utterly undone by juxtaposing the eeriness of the killer tots with an inner look at their religion and societal structure and was totally torpedoed by an FX heavy ending complete with a silly corn-creeping demon.

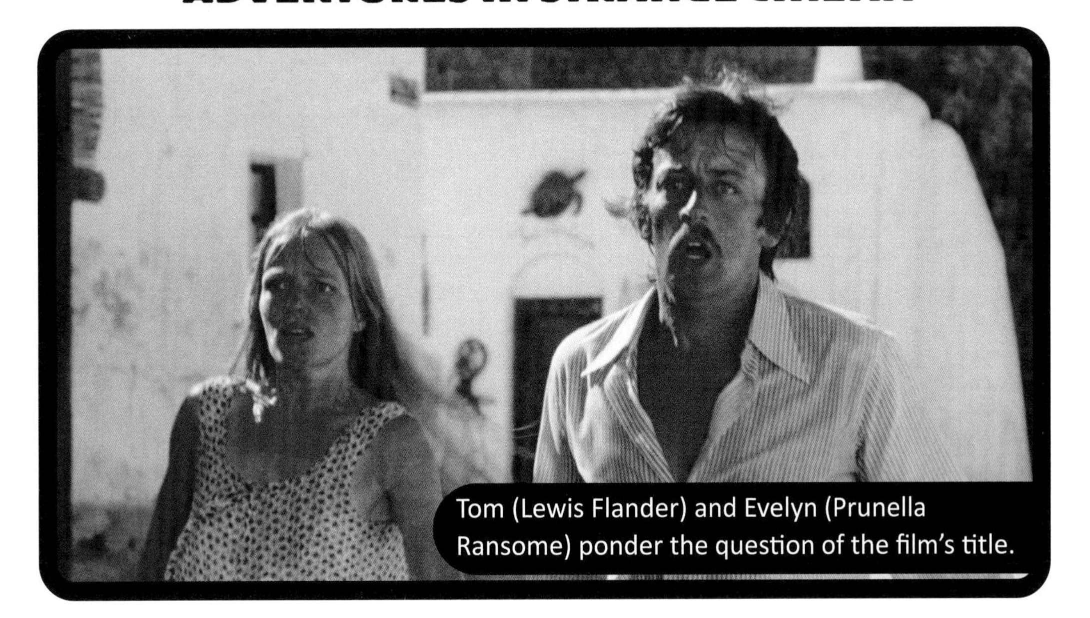
Tom (Lewis Flander) and Evelyn (Prunella Ransome) ponder the question of the film's title.

It's understandable that CHILDREN OF THE CORN shrugged and sunk its inherent horror deep into the weeds because, well, that's kinda what American horror movies did in the 1980s. This is not to necessarily dismiss '80s American horror films outright, because I generally like them for what they are — lighter in tone, conventional, accessible, and slick. But a movie about kids killing their parents and all adults within their sightline needs to cut deeper to the bone. It needs to have the courage of its convictions. King's own original short story played with suggestion and shadow to unnerve effectively. The film adaptation aimed to wrap the terror up with a tidy bow to please the multiplex set. The result is a picture that is neither fish nor fowl.

But nearly a decade prior, Spanish director Narcisco Ibanez Serrador tapped into the visceral, primordial horror of those who nature has designed us to protect rebelling against us instead (and cutting our throats) with his 1976 Spanish masterpiece WHO CAN KILL A CHILD? And where the King film's mission to freak-us-out flopped, Serrador's nihilistic shocker succeeds. This movie — even in its shorter, more direct US cut ISLAND OF THE DAMNED — is truly one of the most savage and upsetting movies that the genre has ever offered and yet — despite its sensational subject matter — it's anything but an exploitation film. WHO CAN KILL A CHILD? is a grim dose of mature, unsparing horror that demands as much attention as possible.

The film stars Lewis Fiander and Prunella Ransome star as Tom and Evelyn, a British couple who are celebrating the impending birth of their third child by leaving their other two kids at home and whisking themselves off to the Spanish coast for a sun-soaked holiday. Escaping the mainland, the pair rent a small boat and drive off to the tiny, remote island Almanzora and soon discover that, while beautiful, the isle is virtually

WHO CAN KILL A CHILD? offers up an entire island of "bad seeds".

abandoned... that is, save for a horde of children. These wide-eyed moppets unnerve our heroes instantly, staring and them wordlessly and often breaking into manic giggling. When Tom witnesses one little girl bludgeon an old man to death and later sees a dozen of them using his corpse as a gory pinata, he breathes past his nausea and begins to conclude that something is dreadfully wrong. Wrong with island and wrong with these fresh-faced little boys and girls, all of whom seem to be on a perverse crusade to sadistically torture and violently butcher every adult they encounter. As Tom and Evelyn try to leave the island, the blood-lusting brood block them and every turn leading to a shattering, disturbing climax that you won't soon forget.

On the surface, making children into monsters and forcing adult heroes to defensively slaughter them seems an easy mark. Horror movies are bought and sold on shattering societal taboos, after all. But Serrador is operating on an entirely different level. In the original Spanish and English cuts present on this release (the US cut is also here), Serrador treats us to a stomach-churning "mondo" style documentary that plays over the slowly unspooling opening credits. In it, the director employs a sickening wave of real 16mm footage of children being experimented on and murdered and dumped into mass graves by their Nazi tormentors, shots of juvenile Korean war survivors shambling through wreckage and the effects of nerve gas on kids during Vietnam. While damn near impossible to watch, this opening is Serrador's way of offering an allegorical explanation of the horrors to come. Here, he suggests that although we pride ourselves on being a species that protects and nurtures our children, we have a long, ignoble history of betraying trust and inflicting legacies of pain upon our offspring, of playing our "games without frontiers" and crushing our innocent successors in the process. And naturally, as pain begets pain, the cycle inevitably will continue.

Except here, whatever madness or virus has these children in its grip (refreshingly, nothing is explained, though it's clear the impulse to murder is spread through the children by eye-contact or touch) is a break in the cycle of pain. These kids do not kill each other. They mourn when one of their brethren falls. They are a kind of hive-minded *new* species that is driven to enact a kind of rough justice on the generations that came before them. In the 1975 sci-fi/horror classic SHIVERS, director David Cronenberg has said of the phallic sex-parasites that tear through their hosts, turning them into Freudian ID-fueled maniacs, that they are in fact the "heroes", wiping out the "old" to make way for the "new". I think that same philosophy can be applied to WHO CAN KILL A CHILD? The killer kids have but one purpose and that is to completely wipe the slate clean of the human beings that bore them, thus inheriting the earth and breeding a new master race, one that sticks together. On that tip there's just as much social parable here than there is in George A. Romero's zombie films. In fact, Serrador's film pre-dates Romero's DAWN OF THE DEAD, the film that first hammered home the idea of the dead as a new race inheriting the earth, by two years.

In lesser hands, WHO CAN KILL A CHILD? would be cold, cruel, and pointless. But it's not. There's a real poetry here and it's anchored by the lead actors' deft performances. Serrador takes enough time with the first half of the film to allow us to get to know them, to care about them, to emotionally invest in their doomed plight. And as the picture down spirals hard and fast into the unthinkable, we feel — along with revulsion, shock and terror — deeply, profoundly sad, a response that is accentuated by Serrador's THE HOUSE THAT SCREAMED composer Waldo de los Rios' dark, dissonant, delicate and moody score.

WHO CAN KILL A CHILD? is an exceptional and essential genre film. Once you see it, you will never forget it.

THE WITCH WHO CAME FROM THE SEA (1976)

Starring Millie Perkins, Lonny Chapman, Vanessa Brown, George Buck Flower
Written by Robert Thom
Directed by Matt Cimber

The job of every good horror film is to exploit, degrade and pervert that which society deems sacred, to suck us out of our comfort zone and shake our foundations. Ultimately, I've found — as have many other admirers of the genre — horror to be the

Molly REALLY KNOWS HOW TO Cut MEN DOWN TO SIZE!!
MOONSTONE PRESENTS:
The Witch Who Came From The Sea
A MATT CIMBER PRODUCTION
STARRING MILLIE PERKINS · LONNY CHAPMAN
CO-STARRING VANESSA BROWN · PEGGY FEURY
ALSO STARRING RICK JASON as "BILLY BATT"
INTRODUCING JEAN PIERRE CAMPS and MARK LIVINGSTON as "TADD" and "TRIPOLI"
MUSIC COMPOSED and DIRECTED by: HERSCHEL BURKE GILBERT
WRITTEN by: ROBERT THOM
DIRECTED by: MATT CIMBER

Molly (Millie Perkins) promises sex and delivers death.

most successful form of cinema to not-so-subtly remind us that life is *not* all strawberries and orgasms. That life is short, often painful. That the illusions we as a society work so hard to construct to make that short, painful life slip down our throats like sugar pills, are easily undone and that perhaps our only true defense against that which is inevitable is to accept and soldier on.

I find horror films — when they are on point — to be life-affirming, even when they come draped in extreme images of gruesome death, misery, and general malevolent mischief.

This may seem an odd statement to make when one is about to discuss Matt Cimber's leveling 1976 psychodrama THE WITCH WHO CAME FROM THE SEA, a harrowing work that has slowly, surely amassed a devoted cult following. But despite the film's jet-black subject matter and its wrenching portrait of a woman pushed into the deep end of psychosis, THE WITCH WHO CAME FROM THE SEA has a primal power that speaks loudly to the horrors of childhood abuse, and how — when left untreated — that trauma can decimate its victims and the many unfortunate people that surround them. It offers no trite solutions to its internal terrors, it offers no comforting *denouement* for the grisly journey of the "witch" of the title. Rather it serves as a stark warning, a barb-wired buoy bobbing in the seaside where most of its lyrical, lurid action unfolds. And while its oft-tread subject matter has been explored in horror cinema many times prior and since, there is simply no other film quite like it.

Working from a thoughtful, mature script by DEATH RACE 2000 scribe Robert Thom, Cimber's expressionist shocker expertly frames his canvas from the film's

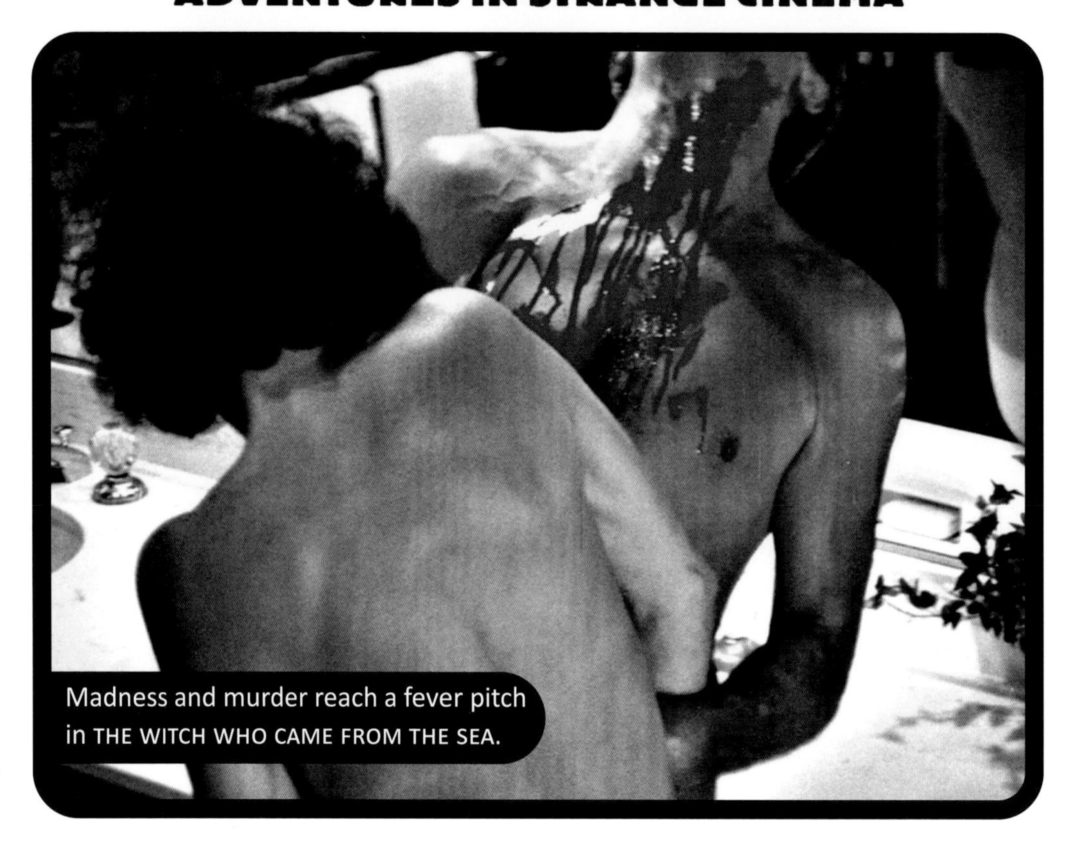
Madness and murder reach a fever pitch in THE WITCH WHO CAME FROM THE SEA.

opening sequence: a long, almost abandoned beach on an overcast day, waves crashing into the sand and over the lens of cinematographer Dean (HALLOWEEN, THE THING) Cundey's camera. This meditative, lonely visage is rendered even more melancholy by Herschel Burke Gilbert's beautiful, lilting flute and guitar score, music that speaks of the sea, and more importantly things "lost" at sea. Specifically, a woman lost at sea, hopelessly. That woman is the deeply disturbed Molly (a shattering, dissonant performance by Millie Perkins), a seemingly sweet, childlike lady who we first see embracing her beloved nephews, telling tales of their grandfather, a sailor who himself was lost at sea. The children obviously adore their seemingly eccentric aunt and she them. And it is at this level that Molly is happiest, in the company of children, safe and needed. Because in the real world, the one populated with peers and with expectations, Molly is barely hanging on.

Almost immediately, Cimber illustrates Molly's psychosis when she spots a pair of Charles Atlas comic-strip-esque bodybuilders on the shore, her eyes fixating on their muscles, their sweaty bodies, their bulging swimsuits. Cimber expertly crosscuts Molly's lust-locked face with flashes of these "parts" and eventually climaxes with bursts of cartoonish blood and the men hanging dead from ropes.

At this point we are barely five minutes into THE WITCH WHO CAME FROM THE SEA, and we are painfully aware that our protagonist equates sex and desire with death and is only calmed by the elemental nature of the sea and the "pure" love of children. Through direction, photography, sound and Perkins' wide-eyed, carefully controlled performance, we are completely committed to Molly's plight, wherever it may take us.

And naturally, nothing ends well for her.

Protected by her welfare-chained older sister and endlessly rhapsodizing on her long dead father — whom her sibling dismisses as a monster — Molly is a raging alcoholic and ritualistic drug abuser, a woman whose only protection from whatever demons have hold of her is to numb herself with substances and sex, something she seeks out like an innocent. She is loved by her salty dog boss Long John (Lonny Chapman), who owns the bar in which Molly works at and who lives for the moments he can get her in his bed. He also — like everyone close to her — enables her and turns a blind eye to her increasingly distressing psychological state. There are passages in THE WITCH WHO CAME FROM THE SEA where it seems that Long John's blind adoration might just "save" Molly, ground her, and serve as a lantern to help her find her way out of her fog-drenched, self-destructing state of mind.

But naturally, it can't. And it doesn't.

In protracted, slowed-down, and hallucinatory sequences that illustrate both Molly's intoxication and lapses into out-of-body darkness, we see Molly immersed in kinky sexual liaisons that end in torture and murder. First, with a pair of drug-juiced Football heroes who tag-team the beautiful woman, only to awaken the "witch", who ties them up and slowly, sadistically carves them to pieces. As the police investigate the crime, Molly declines further, ferally attacking a Hollywood hotshot, sexually fixating on the star of a shaving commercial and worse. And while Molly's lethal libido ramps up, we are treated to gut-punching flashbacks of Molly as a little girl, brutalized by her vile father. It all climaxes in one of the most affecting, tragic and strangely beautiful final acts I've ever seen a horror movie. If you can even call THE WITCH FROM THE SEA simply a horror movie. It is one, but it's so much more. It's a work of art and it's what all filmmakers who toil in dark cinema should aspire to be.

In some ways, THE WITCH WHO CAME FROM THE SEA reminds me of an adult version of the classic Swedish/German PIPPI LONGSTOCKING movies from the early 1970s. Astrid Lindgren's beloved child-waif Pippi is realized in those movies as a free-spirit, living alone in a candy colored world, blessed with unlimited wealth and super-human powers, the hero to all children and the scourge of responsible adults. Like Molly, Pippi pines for her long-lost sea Captain "Papa", of which she has a close but rather irresponsible relationship with. If you've seen those pictures, you'll know that they are adored mostly for their almost experimental nature and the way they are completely free of the crushing, pedestrian confines of conventional narrative. They move like a child's life moves, from adventure to adventure, from moment to moment. Undercurrents of serious social issues like child abuse are ignored, but there is most assuredly a darker side to the pictures that scratches just under their day-glow surfaces.

I see Molly as Pippi, all grown up. The world has moved on. The circus has left town. The magic has long since evaporated. She's alone at the Villa Villekulla, left to stare at her aging reflection and forced to confront the truth of her childhood. Unlike so many movies with a central character who is broken and psychotic, Molly is never painted as a villain. She is always, from the first frame to the final sequence, a victim. We cry for not only the broken woman she is, but the ruined child she was. She is OUR child, left alone, unguided, and unprotected.

INDEX OF NAMES

INDEX OF TITLES